# The Social Gospel in
# Black and White

# The Social Gospel in

# Black and White

## American Racial Reform, 1885–1912

## Ralph E. Luker

The University of North Carolina Press • Chapel Hill and London

Manufactured in the United States of America

The paper in this book meets the guidelines for permanence and durability of the Committee on Production
Guidelines for Book Longevity of the Council on Library Resources.

95  94  93  92  91     5  4  3  2  1

Library of Congress Cataloging-in-Publication Data
Luker, Ralph.
    The social gospel in black and white : American racial
reform. 1885–1912 / by Ralph E. Luker.
        p.   cm.—(Studies in religion)
    Includes bibliographical references and index.
    ISBN 0-8078-1978-6 (cloth : alk. paper)
    1. United States—Race relations.   2. Race relations—
Religious aspects—Christianity.   3. Social gospel.
    4. United States—Social conditions—1865–1918.
    5. Civil rights movements—United States—History.
    6. Radicalism—United States—History.   I. Title.
    II. Series: Studies in religion (Chapel Hill, N.C.)
E185.61.L85   1991
305.8′00973—dc20                                    91-50257
                                                        CIP

Portions of this work appeared earlier, in somewhat different form, in "The Social Gospel and the Failure of Racial
Reform, 1877–1898," Church History 46 (1977): 80–99, and
"Missions, Institutional Churches, and Settlement Houses:
The Black Experience, 1885–1910," Journal of Negro History 69
(1984): 101–13, and are reprinted here with permission of
the journals in which they appeared.

For Jean, Anne, and Amanda

# Contents

# Illustrations

# Preface

This book must have begun one day in the summer of 1962, when I stood at the corner of Auburn Avenue and Jackson Street in Atlanta and asked a pedestrian about Martin Luther King, Jr.'s, Ebenezer Baptist Church. It was an institutional church, he said, though I did not then know what that meant, and, yes, the famous leader of the civil rights movement often preached there on Sunday mornings. I was one of the Southern white college students who joined the movement in its early years and had come to Georgia after graduating from Duke University. At the time, I was out of jail on bond, as a result of charges stemming from my work with Floyd McKissick and Arthur C. Thomas in the movement in Durham, North Carolina. My admission to Duke's Divinity School had been revoked by a high-handed dean who feared that I wanted to go to seminary only to continue the civil rights agitation.

Deciding not to become a field worker with the Student Nonviolent Coordinating Committee, I came to Georgia in a program sponsored by the National Council of Churches. It placed white seminary students as assistant pastors in black congregations and black seminary students in white congregations for the summer. My assignment was to Macon's First Baptist Church, Colored, as it was then called. After allowing me to spend my first night at Macon's YMCA, its director discovered my reason for being there, advised me to get out of town, and said that in any case I could not spend another night at the Y. But I found a place to live and despite an attorney's warning to stay out of trouble because of my case pending in North Carolina courts, I became more deeply involved than ever. First Baptist's pastor, Van J. Malone, was a leader of the movement in Macon and I worked with him and William P. Randall, Sr., in the cause. I traveled to Savannah, Liberty County, and Albany with a Southern Christian Leadership Conference staff member, John H. Calhoun. At Savannah, we talked with Hosea Williams, the brash young leader of the Chatham County Crusade for Voters. In Liberty County, we visited SCLC's citizenship education project at Dorchester Academy, once operated by the American Missionary Association, and now directed by Andrew Young and Septima Clark. National attention that summer focused on Albany, where we met Martin Luther King, Jr., in Dr. William Anderson's living room, and participated in mass meetings and demonstrations.

My roommate and I visited Koinonia Farm near Americus, Georgia. We heard Clarence Jordan argue that the economic boycotts both by local white merchants against his integrated farm commune and by black Albany against its white merchants were coercive and, therefore, a form of violence. When the state's black Baptists convened in Macon, there were conversations with King's Morehouse friends, including Melvin Watson and the iconoclastic Sam Williams. Later, we went with delegates of the Macon branch to an NAACP convention in Atlanta, where we met such leaders of the movement as Daisy Bates, Ruby Hurley, Dr. Benjamin Mays, and Roy Wilkins. On the trip to Atlanta, I visited Ebenezer Baptist Church, where my friend, Hank Elkins, served as assistant pastor to Martin Luther King, Sr. and Jr., in the National Council program.

At the end of the summer, I left the South to study theology at Drew University in Madison, N.J. The Northern sojourn took me away from the movement, but it was an extraordinary academic experience. Drew's faculty included Bernard W. Anderson and Howard C. Kee in Biblical studies; Bard Thompson and Franz Hilderbrandt in historical studies; and Carl Michaelson and John Godsey in theological studies. Anderson and Michaelson later joined me near the end of the march from Selma to Montgomery. Easily as important to me were four others: Gordon Harland, Will Herberg, George D. Kelsey, and Nelle Morton. A Canadian by birth, Harland was an important interpreter of Reinhold Niebuhr and American religious thought, who taught me to think historically about the significance of the movement from which I had come. Once a leading Marxist theoretician, Herberg had reaffirmed his Judaism and become very conservative politically. I was awestruck by his encyclopedic knowledge, but he forced me to think by running roughshod over superficial liberal formulations and had little regard for the sanctity of my tender roots in the civil rights cause. Kelsey, on the other hand, grew up in that special division of the Kingdom: black Georgia Baptists. A dignified Southern gentleman, who had been King's teacher at Morehouse, he was our strongest link to the movement. But there was also Nelle Morton, a radical Southern white gentlewoman, who had played an important role in the movement in the South in the difficult years before there was a movement in the South.

Somehow, Kelsey and Morton still teach me about the best in Southern traditions and values. Before leaving Drew, I married a Yankee, Jean Crawford, whose father and grandfathers were steeped in Northern Methodism's social gospel. Besides being the mother of our two children, Jean's own career follows in that earnest tradition.

Writing this book did not actually begin until we went to Chapel Hill. Given my background, Robert Moats Miller suggested my topic and looked favorably on a seminar paper on the social gospel and race relations. He was gracious enough to allow me to disagree with him and taught me to honor American social Christianity with a critical eye. George B. Tindall taught me a fraction of what he knows about the South; and Joel Williamson encouraged me to learn more about race relations in the post–Civil War South. Under their guidance, the term paper stretched to a passable master's thesis and, finally, an improved dissertation. Yet, it was not the book I had in mind. There was much more work to be done. Appropriately, I came full circle years later, finally sending the manuscript to a publisher when I returned to Atlanta's "Sweet Auburn," Ebenezer Baptist Church, and the King Center as associate editor of the Martin Luther King Papers.

The writing stretched over more years than it should have. I published many other things in the meantime, but always returned to the big project. In those years, I incurred many debts. The financial assistance of the Ford Foundation and the National Endowment for the Humanities made the book possible. It would have been impossible without the aid of archivists and librarians at Allegheny College, the American Baptist Historical Society, the Amistad Research Center, Atlanta's First Congregational Church and the Herndon Home, Atlanta–Fulton County Public Library, the Atlanta University Center, the Chautauqua County Historical Society, Colgate-Rochester Divinity School, Cornell University, Duke University, Emory University, General Theological Seminary, Harvard University, Howard University, the Library of Congress, Lincoln University of Pennsylvania, the Martin Luther King, Jr., Center for Nonviolent Social Change, Inc., the New York Public Library, Oberlin College, the Ohio Historical Society, Princeton University, Swarthmore College, Tulane University, Tuskegee University, Union Theological Seminary of New York, the University of Chicago, the University of Delaware, the University of Massachusetts, the University of North Carolina, the University of Rochester, Virginia Polytechnic Institute, and Wilberforce University.

I am appreciative of the critical encouragement of readers and editors at *Church History* and the *Journal of Negro History*, critics at conventions of the

American Historical Association and the Organization of American Historians, and members of the Conference on Faith and History. The encouragement of Clayborne Carson of Stanford University, Will Gravely of the University of Denver, David E. Harrell of Auburn University, Samuel Hill and Bertram Wyatt-Brown of the University of Florida, William R. Hutchison of Harvard University, Victor J. Jackson, formerly of Oxford College, Maurice Luker of Emory and Henry College, and Paul Spickard of Brigham Young University, Hawaii, kept me at the manuscript. Finally, David Wills of Amherst College and Lewis Bateman, Ron Maner, and an anonymous critic for the University of North Carolina Press helped me turn an undisciplined manuscript into a book. Like the fine teacher that he is, Wills taught me much about the book that I had not understood. He suggested some of its best sentences. These friends bear much of the credit for the strengths of the book; any flaws that remain are my own.

# The Social Gospel in
# Black and White

# 1

# Introduction

"The fathers ate of sour grapes," says the preacher, "and the children's teeth are set on edge." His graphic words suggest that no generation is left untouched by the legacy of its predecessors. Normally, we adjust to that reality—their world was what we first knew—and find much in the past to cherish. On occasion, we try to shake free of our bondage to history and, by repudiation if possible, by confession if necessary, seek to reclaim our innocence. Nowhere in the American experience is the burden of history more evident than in the painful course of its race relations. Therein is much that needs repudiation, much to be confessed, and indeed much to be cherished.

In April 1906, the Congregational pastor at Springfield, Missouri, witnessed one of the decade's most brutal race riots. A mob of white men seized three black men, hung their bodies from an electric light post, which was surmounted by a replica of the Statue of Liberty, and burned them. Horrified by the mob action, the venality and weakness of local authorities, and his own inability to improve race relations substantially as a pastor, Harlan Paul Douglass gave up his church and devoted the next fifteen years of his life to the American Missionary Association's work for the education of black people. His book, *Christian Reconstruction in the South*, was the decade's most powerful statement of an evangelical neoabolitionism that helped to revive racial reform in the twentieth century. Douglass's interest in race relations is noteworthy because a decade earlier, while serving as a pastor in bucolic Ames, Iowa, he was among the first to use the term *the social gospel*.[1] It was given currency as the title of a journal published by white Christian communitarians in rural Georgia who hoped to build a school modeled on Booker T. Washington's Tuskegee Institute.[2] Referring generally to a fresh application of the insights of the Christian faith to pressing problems of the social order, it gained widespread circulation among contemporary religious reformers. In retrospect, historians have used it to describe late nineteenth- and early twentieth-century Christian efforts to address the social problems of the age, which they see as functions of urban and industrial growth.[3]

But if Harlan Paul Douglass's phrase lived on, awareness of his effort to apply the "social gospel" in race relations has not. Indeed, most historians do not see the prophets of American social Christianity as having much interest in race relations. The account most widely accepted was neatly captured in Rayford Logan's phrase, "the astigmatism of the social gospel." It suggests that, preoccupied with the ills of the new industrial order, the prophets of social Christianity either ignored or betrayed the freedmen and left their fortunes in the hands of a hostile white South. The indictment of the social gospel on this count hinges upon the racism of Josiah Strong, the faithlessness of Lyman Abbott, and the complicity in silence of Washington Gladden, Walter Rauschenbusch, and others.[4] If this is an accurate assessment, Abbott wrote his own indictment. "The selfish prejudice of indifference," said the *Christian Union*'s editor, "is not one whit more holy than the selfish prejudice of open aggression."[5]

This criticism of the social gospel prophets is widely shared, but there have been scattered voices of dissent. William A. Clebsch, for example, asserted that "it was the social gospelers, notably Abbott and Strong, whose theological thrusts first effectively challenged racial superiority in American Protestantism." By focusing on the interests of particular individuals or groups, however, Clebsch and other dissenters produced no reinterpretation of the movement as a whole.[6] More important, neither point of view quite comprehends both the high lights and deep shadows of American social Christianity's record in race relations.

The many historians who emphasize the social gospel's racial failures commonly assume the discontinuity of nineteenth-century religious reform and accept uncritically Arthur Schlesinger's treatment of the social gospel as the response of reform-minded churchmen to the urban-industrial crises of the late nineteenth century. A skillfully crafted work of historical synthesis, Schlesinger's study powerfully influenced more extended accounts by a generation of scholars.[7] Yet, if one thinks that slavery and the consequences of emancipation were the central issues of nineteenth-century American history, or if one believes, with W. E. B. Du Bois, that "the problem of the twentieth century is the problem of the color line," there is reason to question Schlesinger's thesis. Substantial as his contribution was, it has been justly criticized as construing late nineteenth-century religious history too largely in terms of stimulus and response. Thus, say its critics, it neither sufficiently appreciated the continuities of nineteenth-century reform nor gave sufficient attention to the theological positions from which the social gospel was articulated. Writing within Schlesinger's framework, Ralph Morrow treated Northern Methodist missions in the post–Civil War South as the finale to sectional crisis and Civil War. He documented at length the social mission of the Yankee Wesleyans among black people in Southern Reconstruction, but charged the missionary-minded Methodists with failing to be alert to the urban-industrial crisis on their home front.[8] Assuming the blinders of the Schlesinger thesis, historians may inevitably find their subject guilty of failing to see something or other. In race relations, it produced what might be called "the astigmatism of the historians."

The assumption of discontinuity and the a priori definition of the social gospel in terms of stimulus and response led historians to ignore its manifestations in black and Southern white churches alike.[9] Thus, studies of the social gospel written under the influence of the Schlesinger thesis did not treat race relations. Finding nothing of consequence in these studies, the historians of race relations concluded that the social gospel prophets were unconcerned. To complete the cycle, the authors of the former read the works of the latter and wrote introductions to new editions of their own books in which they confirmed the lack of interest.[10] The astigmatic historians sought to pluck the log from the prophets' eye!

But there is a way to interpret that part of our past more comprehensively. Sidney Mead suggested that there is a continuing theme in nineteenth-century religious reform. The disestablishment of religion in America withheld the state's coercive power from the church, he argued, but it did not mean the surrender of the age-old notion that "the existence and well-being of any society depends upon a body of commonly shared religious beliefs."[11] Under the conditions of disestablishment and by methods of persuasion, denominations and voluntary associations, especially home missionary societies, assumed the responsibility of inculcating those religious beliefs and values that could serve to hold the society together. Until home missions could accomplish their task of sustaining and redeeming the whole society, other voluntary associations were organized to alleviate particular social problems. Thus, while they sought to organize society by the extension of common beliefs and values, the voluntary associations promoted social reform on a wide range of public issues, including slavery and race relations.[12] By 1835, however, perfectionist influences were at work to sunder the very organizations that were charged with the task of binding the nation together. Only the shedding of blood eroded the influence of perfectionism.[13]

This conception of the organic structure of antebellum religious reform suggests a reinterpretation of both the origins and the nature of the social gospel. Its origins are found not in the response to urban-industrial problems but in the antebellum voluntary societies whose heart was the home missions movement, and the social gospel itself was less an abstract quest for social justice than it was the proclamation of those religious beliefs and values that could serve to hold the society together. Mission stations established first at the western and then on the southern frontiers of American society developed the techniques necessary to weave a social fabric similar to that of the urban East and North.[14] What Schlesinger and others have seen as an increasingly radical critique of industrial capitalism was, rather, a growing conservative awareness that industrial capitalism has been the radical force in American society, generating social change of unforeseen consequence, heedlessly disruptive of human community. Apart from this general sense of what the social gospel was, it is difficult to demonstrate that there was a cohesive "social gospel movement." Those who imagine otherwise can do so only by taking a part of it as equivalent to the whole, and the part they make primary has never been one that includes race relations.[15]

Conceiving the origin and nature of the social gospel as an extension of antebellum home missions and social reform movements offers a new approach to the social gospel and race relations. Given its basis in a conservative apprehension of social values, the social gospel's generally conservative biases in race relations come as no surprise. But to say that the social gospel prophets were largely conservative in their social views is not to say that they were indifferent to race relations. Rather, just as it moved toward its own fulfillment at the end of the nineteenth century, the social gospel movement's conservative racial strategies were in crisis because its three surviving traditions in racial reform were in sharp decline.[16]

First, the social gospel prophets could no longer rely heavily upon the home missions movement. It had played a crucial role in establishing missionary institutions in black communities throughout the South and had powerful support from the social gospel prophets in doing so. But that effort was severely handicapped by the financial crisis of the 1890s and lost its initiative to a new, more secular "benevolent empire" in education after 1900.

Second, the social gospel prophets no longer considered African colonization a means of alleviating racial problems in the United States. They rejected massive migration to Africa as a cruel hoax upon black Americans in the 1890s. The social gospel prophets did see an important missionary role for a select few in the redemption of Africa, but social Christianity's negative portrait of the "dark continent" was a taproot of both America's racism and its cultural imperialism.

Third, American social Christianity was divided over whether the franchise was a natural right, whether education or the franchise ought to have priority, and whether federal or state action was better suited to purify Southern politics. But the postemancipation tradition of civil equity among black and white leaders in racial reform collapsed in the mid-1890s as Southern states seized the initiative to disfranchise black citizens.

By the mid-1890s, lynching became the primary issue in American race relations. Forced to confront it as an issue of life itself, American social Christianity began to focus upon the elemental insights that black people were persons, that the right to life was natural, and that the right to a trial by one's peers was essential to American democracy. Yet, with the forces of racial reform in disarray, time seemed to be of the essence.

At the turn of the century, conservative Northern white philanthropists and Southern educators formed an alliance with Booker T. Washington to promote public education in the South. Black migration to cities built a constituency for black urban reformers with institutional bases in missions, institutional churches, and settlement houses within the black community. But disfranchisement, lynching, peonage, and urban riots created a new sense of racial crisis.

Aroused by the new sense of crisis, black and white racial reformers, many of them spokesmen for American social Christianity, explored a variety of uniracial and biracial means of addressing the situation. While the denominations organized the forerunner of the National Council of Churches in 1909, the racial reformers recovered abolitionist and home missionary strategies in reorganizing as the National Association for the Advancement of Colored People in 1910 and the National Urban League in 1911. A half century later, these and allied organizations formed the institutional core of America's civil rights movement.

Finally, the prophets of American social Christianity at the turn of the century were spread across wide spectra of thought in race relations. They often worked more at cross-purposes than toward a single end. But, at its best, mainstream American social Christianity developed a critique of both racism and cultural imperialism that built upon the rather elemental notion that black people were, after all, "persons." Acceptance of that notion, thought young Martin Luther King, would help to create the "beloved community." As with many of the earlier social gospel prophets, it was that conservative social value that was the capstone of his social thought.

# 1

## The Decline of

## Nineteenth-Century

## Racial Reform

# 2

## Christianizing the South

On 7 March 1894, two white teachers at the black college in Talladega, Alabama, set out in a horse-drawn carriage for an afternoon drive. Nearing the railroad tracks, their horse was startled by the approach of a train. Unable to hold him back, the women were horrified as the animal plunged to his death and their carriage was thrown against the engine. Hurled forty feet across a gully by the impact, both women were seriously injured. The younger teacher, Mary Strong, who had been at Talladega only six months, was taken to the home of the college president and lingered toward death for eleven days. "As she grew weaker, her mind wandered," a brother reported, "she spoke of flowers and of her pupils, both of which she loved." In the shared sorrow of her death, he wrote, "every man was a brother, every woman a sister. We are thankful for her unselfish, Christian life, and that she knew how to give herself to the service of her fellow men." At a memorial service on 20 March in the college chapel, townspeople, faculty, students, and family paid final tribute to Mary Strong. "The several pastors of Talladega participated in the service with tender words, fitly spoken," recalled her brother, Josiah. "One said that the thought impressed on him was that of the brotherhood of man. Here were different races, here were representatives of different sections of the country once at strife, here were different denominations all melted into one by a common sorrow."[1]

A teacher in the small black college in Alabama, Mary Strong was employed by the American Missionary Association in the home missionary army that labored in the nineteenth-century American hinterlands. Prior to the Civil War, home missions were aimed at areas of American society where Protestant influence was weakest, at those living on the frontier, and at old and new minorities, Indians, black slaves, the urban poor, and immigrants. The movement of Northern missionaries into the South after the war was not unprecedented, but the war made the South a new frontier and the missionaries responded to the unprecedented scale of its challenge. A mission executive later recalled that other work was set temporarily aside in order to give attention to "the great problem providentially opening among these freedmen of the South."[2]

When Union forces occupied Southern territory at Hampton, Virginia, and Port Royal, South Carolina, in 1861 and 1862, home missionaries moved in as teachers of the freedmen. Supported by Northern benefactors like William Furness, Edward Everett Hale, and Stephen Colwell, Port Royal's Gideon's Band of missionaries enlisted young ministers of social Christianity such as William Channing Gannett. Hampton and the Sea Islands became the setting for the final act of antislavery's crusade and the first act of the social gospel's redemptive enterprise. In the crucible of that experiment, the immediacy of abolition's demand was transmuted into the evolutionary vision of the social gospel's kingdom building.[3]

Two types of voluntary agencies for Southern relief and education developed as the war drew to an end: one organized on a local, nonsectarian basis and another structured on denominational lines. Denominational and personal interests heightened their benevolent competition, but they had differences of strategy. The nonsectarian agency was organized in May 1866. The American Freedmen's Union Commission was a merger of ten local freedmen's aid societies in Northern and Western cities with the American Union Commission, a society formed to aid loyal Southern white refugees. A young Congregational minister, Lyman Abbott, became executive secretary of and spokesman for the American Freedmen's Union Commission's vision of a South redeemed from its sins of ignorance and vice. He thought the position was "a rare opportunity to take some part in an individual and a social gospel."[4]

On a trip through the South in 1856, Abbott had been offended by slavery's brutal separation of families. After returning to the North, he considered joining the migration to Kansas, which Edward Everett Hale promoted, to fight the extension of slavery. But his father persuaded him not to go and to reject the abolitionists' "impracticable methods and uncharitable spirit." The nation had no right to interfere with slavery where it existed, he thought, but it was obliged to exclude it from the territories. If it did so, slavery would die out in the South as it had elsewhere. This mediating posture characterized Abbott's entire career. "My sympathies have been for the most part neither with the radicals nor with the reactionaries, but with the progressives in every reform," he later said. "I have been an evolutionist, but not a Darwinian; a Liberal [in theology], but not an agnostic; an Anti-slavery man, but not an Abolitionist; a temperance man, but not a Prohibitionist; an Industrial Democrat, but not a Socialist." In 1863, Abbott told his Terre Haute, Indiana, congregation that he would restrict the franchise to "the moral and intelligent."[5]

Abbott learned to mediate through hard experience. His American Freedmen's Union Commission was a jerry-built house of evangelical abolitionists, Garrisonians, and colonizationists in common cause to redeem the South. Its president was the Methodist bishop Matthew Simpson, a long-time colonizationist, serving with William Lloyd Garrison as a vice-president. Phillips Brooks and Octavius Brooks Frothingham reinforced the social Christianity of its executive committee. Its supporters included Henry Ward Beecher, James Freeman Clarke, Robert Collyer, Stephen Colwell, William Channing Gannett, and Edward Everett Hale. The size of the task in the South required a united effort, they believed, bringing Congregationalists, Episcopalians, Methodists, Presbyterians, Quakers, and Unitarians into the cooperative venture. "We have not only to conquer the South,—we have also to convert it," Abbott argued. "We have not only to occupy it by bayonets and bullets,—but also by ideas and institutions. We have not only to destroy slavery,—we must also organize for freedom."[6]

Abbott's work was handicapped by racial antagonism in the South and sectarian infighting in the North. The commission early took the high road of racial nondiscrimination. Wise friends of the freedmen do not insist that "the African race is equal to the Anglo-Saxon," Abbott wrote; nor do they admit "race inferiority." But they insist that the races shall enjoy "the same rights, immunities and opportunities; and that the white man's claim to superiority rests upon a very shadowy foundation." Pledging the commission to a doctrine of equal rights, Abbott proclaimed its motto: "No distinction of race, caste, or color in the Republic." In establishing public school systems, it was necessary to abolish the distinctions, he said. The commission would sponsor no school that fostered prejudice by excluding any child because of "his birth, his complexion or his social class & status." But Abbott warned that compelling racial coeducation was likely to compound the problem. "In my judgment, we cannot conquer life long prejudices by one battle," he told an abolitionist. In larger communities, "negro children will choose negro companions, the white children white companions," and "any attempt to enforce a companionship mutually repulsive will only postpone the day of perfect harmony & good fellowship." When a survey by commission agents suggested that coeducation of the races was unacceptable to both races in the South, Abbott sought to accommodate the hard reality. Coeducation of the races, as of the sexes, was a matter of expediency, he said later. "Justice demands that equal—not necessarily identical—educational advantages be offered to both races. It does not demand that they be afforded under the same roof."[7]

The sectarian attack on the American Freedman's Union Commission as secular or antireligious was a greater threat to its work. Abbott admitted the importance of denominational evangelism, but he portrayed the commission's effort as more truly religious because it was nonsectarian. It owed allegiance to no denomination, but "alone to the great cause of Christ" as found among the needy. "We desire the more our schools may be truly Christian because they are unecclesiastical," he wrote. But sectarian criticism struck home. Bishop Simpson resigned from the commission in the fall of 1866 and its evangelical vice-presidents were soon working against its interests. Led by restive evangelicals, local units in Chicago, Cincinnati, and Cleveland withdrew from the commission between 1866 and 1868 to join its leading sectarian rival, the American Missionary Association. Concluding that between the steps taken by most Southern states to establish public elementary school systems and the results of the denominational bodies' efforts to establish private normal schools there was no further need for their work, in 1869 the commission's executive committee voted to disband the organization.[8]

The American Missionary Association was the most important home missionary society working among the freedmen. Organized in protest against cooperation with slaveholders in missions, the AMA later sought to unite all evangelical missions among the freedmen under its auspices. By 1865, the Congregational, Free-Will Baptist, Wesleyan Methodist, and Dutch Reformed churches had made it their agent in freedmen's relief. Other denominations—United Presbyterians and Quakers in 1862, Northern Baptists in 1863, Old School Presbyterians and United Brethren in 1864, and Episcopalians in 1865—had already organized their own home missions work among the freedmen. After temporizing between cooperating with the AMA and the American Freedmen's Union Commission, the powerful Methodist Episcopal Church organized its own Freedmen's Aid Society in 1866.[9]

The relative importance of the missionary societies in Southern relief and education is suggested by their expenditures. The federal government's Freedmen's Bureau expended about $5,262,500 between 1865 and 1871, when it was disbanded. The more important nonsectarian freedmen's aid societies, most of which cooperated in the AFUC between 1866 and 1869, expended about $2,000,000 between 1862 and 1874. Compare that with the funds expended by home missionary bodies:

| | | |
|---|---|---|
| American Missionary Association | 1861–89 | $6,770,387 |
| Freedmen's Aid Society of the Methodist Episcopal Church | 1866–89 | 2,500,000 |
| American Baptist Home Mission Society | 1864–89 | 2,100,000 |
| Presbyterians | 1865–89 | 1,500,000 |
| Friends | 1862–89 | 600,000 |
| Protestant Episcopal Freedmen's Commission | 1865–78 | 325,278 |
| African Methodist Episcopal Church Society | 1868 | 58,737 |
| Afro-American Presbyterians | 1865–66 | 3,174[10] |

Estimating the contribution of Northern benevolence for Southern relief and education from 1861 to 1889 at about $21,000,000, three-quarters of it came from voluntary philanthropy, two-thirds of it through home missions agencies, over half of it from the three most important denominational bodies, and nearly one-third from the American Missionary Association alone. The figures are not precisely comparable because of the different lengths of time covered, but that incomparability highlights the strength of the home missions bodies. By tying themselves to the self-interest and support of the denominations, their work in the South continued long after the collapse of both the American Freedmen's Union Commission and the federal government's Freedmen's Bureau.[11]

To emphasize the importance of Northern missionary effort in postwar freedmen's education is not to deny other important forces in that work. Black denominations and the freedmen themselves played a more important role in the effort than official reports or a financial calculus can suggest. They were particularly important in establishing Sunday schools in black churches, promoting literacy and Christian education throughout the South. Before his move to Atlanta, for example, the grandfather of Martin Luther King, Jr., Adam Daniel Williams, received his only formal education from a black preacher in the Sunday school of a black Baptist congregation in rural Greene County, Georgia. The importance of Northern missionary institutions lay in their dominance of normal school education, that is, in teaching the teachers.[12]

Between 1865 and 1910, so many of the Northern white social gospel prophets were officers and supporters of the American Missionary Association that it may have been the most important vehicle of the social gospel prior to the organization of the Federal Council of Churches in 1909.[13] The classmates and kin of the social gospel prophets carried social Christianity into the Southern missions. The sisters of John Bascom and Josiah Strong taught in missionary institutions in the South; Atlanta University President Horace Bumstead was a classmate of both Amory H. Bradford and Charles M. Sheldon; and the grandfather of Norman Thomas was the first president of Biddle College, now Johnson C. Smith University.[14] Typically, major spokesmen for social Christianity sat on the boards of trustees of the missionary institutions and endorsed fund drives on their behalf. Edward Everett Hale was a trustee of Wilberforce University; Charles Cuthbert Hall was an officer of Atlanta University's board of trustees; Newell Dwight Hillis and Charles E. Jefferson sat on Fisk University's board of trustees; Josiah Strong was a trustee of Talladega College and was nominated for the presidency of Atlanta University; and Francis Greenwood Peabody served on Hampton Institute's board for over forty years.[15]

Northern social Christianity saw a divine purpose in its mission work. Iowa College President George A. Gates told the American Missionary Association that it had "the most glorious opportunity God ever gave to any people." It was "to preach the gospel of the solidarity of the human race," to take "the next great step in the coming of the kingdom of God" by asserting "the unity of the human race." The American Missionary Association was "pouring itself out prodigally for the lowest and humblest following in the footsteps of the Master," Gates argued. "If the kingdom of God is coming anywhere on this planet at this hour, it is coming through the work of this glorious Association."[16]

Following the destruction of the old social order, thought the home missionaries, both races in the South threatened to lapse into semibarbaric conditions. "The ignorance and viciousness of the Southern populations, white and black, are the root of the evil," said Washington Gladden. Two-fifths of the voters were illiterate, tutored in adultery, lies, and theft. So long as that was the case, murder and corruption would be rampant. "A democratic government in which such citizens bear rule must be full of rapacity and brutality," he concluded. "The rights of property will not be respected; public faith will not be kept. Universal suffrage in a population of this sort means universal pillage and universal war." Home missions intended to lift the South up, to sustain its people from an abyss of ignorance, vice, and violence, which Amory Dwight Mayo called the "Giant Despair of the Republic." Many home missionaries participated in political reconstruction of the South, but they believed that political solutions alone were insufficient to meet religious, moral, and cultural problems. "The real difficulty lies so deep that it remains almost untouched," said AMA Secretary Michael E. Strieby; "it is the ignorance and degradation of the blacks and the prejudices and hatreds of the whites—in other words it is in the *minds and hearts* of men." Ignorance, illiteracy, and embittered prejudice could not be overcome by legislation or political victories, he argued. They could be overcome only "by light and love," by education and the Gospel.[17]

Lemuel Moss, a Baptist minister and president of Indiana University, offered a symbolic rationale for Northern Christian missions in the South. "You can build an orrery by taking wooden balls and piercing them with iron rods, regulating their distances and relations to each other, and call it a wooden symbol of your solar system," he told a home missions convention, "but you can never build a solar system itself in that way. God's universe is constructed by the energy of the forces lodged in the hearts of the suns and the planets; and a free people will never be held together by any iron band." They could be held together only by something "powerful enough to assimilate and purify and elevate and unify" the "discordant elements." His denomination labored among groups that were "national rays that enter into the prismatic glory of our national life," said Moss. The Gospel of Jesus Christ would "synthesize" them, "blend them together," and create "the white light of a perfect freedom." Similarly, the *American Missionary* held that religion was the only resource powerful enough to assimilate diverse groups into a cohesive social community. "Only as men are united in the stronger bond made by conscience, reverence for the law of God and the spirit of obedience to his supreme commands" would the masses be united, said its editors. In the South, divine power could transform white prejudice into recognition of human brotherhood and implant practical Christianity in the hearts of black people. The social significance of the Gospel was its power to sustain a people from chaos. "The sun of our Republic" would set forever if the Gospel of Jesus Christ did not have the power "to purify the hearts of men and hold them together in loving relationship," Moss told his fellow Baptists. "Here is the solvent and here is the hope of our Republic and our national life. The Cross of Jesus Christ is the conservative element in our literature and in our politics."[18]

In their denominational provinciality, Congregationalists hoped to "Congregationalize" the South. Their Northern rivals would "Methodize" or "Baptize" it, according to their tastes, for to have been a loyal Congregationalist, Methodist, or Baptist during the war had been a way of being a good and true American. So, to convert the South to Congregationalism, Methodism, or "Baptism" was to convert it to Americanism. Viewed in its largest perspective, as they saw it, the task of home missions was to make the South American by making it Christian.[19] Missionary bands went into the South intending to convert the region, to Christianize its people, both black and white. Like the abolition of slavery, a revivalist's conversions were an *event*, but Christianizing was a *process*. An individual soul might be brought instantaneously into right relationship with God, but that of a people was redeemed only by proper associations over time. By the extension of Northern Christian influence into the South, the Southern people would be nurtured into the redeemed community. In 1865, a freedmen's aid society announced that "New England can furnish teachers enough to make a New England of the whole South." As late as 1892, Northern Methodism's Freedmen's Aid Society reported that the "border line has steadily moved toward the Gulf of Mexico for twenty-seven years. Let it move on until all opposition shall cease and the song of a triumphant and unified Methodism shall along all shores blend with the murmuring waves of the gulf and the roar of the oceans." The society's corresponding secretary, Dr. J. W. Hamilton, was more graphic. "The North is literally absorbing the South," he said. "Ichabod is written over every gateway along 'the borders'—and this absorption must go on until the end shall be, not fraternity, but identity. There will be no more South, it will be all North and all Christian."[20]

The process of Christianizing the South required the building of institutions to extend relief, education, and Christian influence to a needy people. Mission stations planted throughout the region were to be reproductive units of the redeeming community, serving the multiple functions of church, school, and social settlement.[21] As such, they were both the vehicle of Northern social gospel influence in the South and a primary means for the black South's appropriation of the social message. The teaching and preaching missionaries were moved by a message of social redemption and imparted it to their students in an education for citizenship. When a newspaper editor at Charlottesville, Virginia, warned a Northern white missionary not to go beyond reading and religion to political and sociological lessons, which might "inculcate ideas of social equality with the whites," she replied: "I teach *in school and out* the fundamental principles of 'Politics' and 'sociology' viz:— 'Whatsoever ye would that men should do to you, do you even so unto them.' Yours in behalf of truth and justice . . ."[22]

The periodical reading fare in the schools for teachers and students alike included the missionary and social gospel press: Edward Everett Hale's *Lend-A-Hand*, Lyman Abbott's *Outlook*, and William Hayes Ward's *Independent*. At the Gregory Normal Institute in Wilmington, North Carolina, Lura Beam recalled that "the favorite corner was the reading table, stacked with Webster's *Dictionary*, the *National Geographic*, the *Outlook*, and the *Independent*." From Augusta, Georgia, a teacher wrote to Hale's *Lend-A-Hand*: "If the friend who has sent us the magazine could only see how eagerly these colored girls and teachers read it and how much we are dependent on it for guidance, there would be no regrets for having sent it or fear of want of appreciation." There was something almost pathetic in reports from the lean and isolated missions. "We are so on the outside of society," wrote a missionary in Atlanta, "that whatever we do is approached by us with special effort and with the full understanding that we work alone. Georgia recognizes no duty to the colored element as far as 'lending-a-hand' is concerned." Occasionally, a Northern social gospel prophet, such as Amory Bradford or Washington Gladden, protested the social ostracism of missionaries in the South. But the only complaint of an advisor to the Hampton Institute club was that the school offered so many similar activities that the group scarcely found time to meet.[23]

Nowhere outside New England were the King's Daughters, Lend-A-Hand Clubs, Look Up Legions, Social Purity, Ten-Times-One, White Cross, and Willing Workers societies featured so regularly as in the Southern missions. These young peoples' societies, promoted by Hale, combined voluntary discipline in personal morality with social service. *Lend-A-Hand* published the protest of an Alabama teacher against the convict lease system as "the abomination of desolation" and "slavery without its ameliorating features." But the journal's essential message was social service. Atlanta's two clubs, organized

when Hale spoke there, helped to support a destitute old man, contributed to
the new orphanage for black children, and raised money to build a new
parsonage. Groups in Mobile, Alabama, and Lexington, Kentucky, volun-
teered to teach younger children and read to the illiterate aged.[24] In fact, as
Washington Gladden recognized, home missionaries in the South had long
experience in settlement work before it began in the Northern cities. "The
work of the college girls in the slums of New York is precisely the kind of
work that has been done for a quarter of a century by hundreds of college girls
and other[s], in the schools and the slab meetinghouses and the rude cabins of
the South," he told the AMA. "To the poor and the darkened and the degraded they have been called to minister—to those whose poverty and
darkness and degradation was no fault of their own."[25]

A s Southern white churches recovered from the ravages of war,
Northern proselytizing concentrated on the South's black population and
some Southern white churchmen joined the crusade to uplift and Christianize the freedmen. The concentration of missionary zeal on the black South
affected the missionaries' analysis of the problem itself. Two decades earlier,
they had taken the degenerating tendencies of both races in the South as a
threat to the Republic and just cause for their effort. Now they focused on
those tendencies among black people. At an AMA convention in 1893, the
Reverend Frank T. Bayley acknowledged the biracial character of the problem. "The first duty of the hour," he intoned, "is to awake to the peril of
ignorance, idleness, impurity, hatred, selfishness, covered by skins black or
white; abounding under both; existing in the North and in the South, but
massing their fearful front especially in the South." But because the Southern
white field was now limited, his appeal focused on the black South and its
threat to the Republic. "The whole course of history points to America as its
goal—as God's last and best among nations. It is ours to save America for
national stewardship in the kingdom of Christ," said Bayley. "If we help to
save our black brother he will become an element of blessing in the republic.
But if we neglect him, he promises to be a power for evil in our midst, a
poison in the body politic, a constant menace to our institutions and an
element in the retributive justice of God." The aspect of black life in the South
that most offended the Northern social gospel prophets was the "separation
of worship from virtue, of religion from morals." This danger, which struck

close to the heart of the social gospel, was a product of historical conditioning, they thought, but it measured the depths of paganism in which masses of
Southern blacks lived.[26]

The task of missionary social Christianity was to make "a new Negro," said
AMA Secretary W. E. C. Wright. What was needed was "the transformation of a
vast population trained as slaves into a population with the character, habits
and virtues of free men." Rejecting African colonization, but endorsing Josiah
Strong's cultural imperialism, a Methodist argued that "God has in reservation
a great work for the Negro to do in this country. Under the refining influence of
Anglo-Saxon ideas, civilization and religion, he is being fitted, strengthened for
that work." An Episcopalian missionary in Halifax County, Virginia, held that
every black neighborhood needed "one or two good, solid, educated, Christianized leaders of their own race. Three or four such in a county would do an
enormous amount of good."[27] This "new Negro" would be imbued with a
zeal to uplift the race.

Missionary zeal was evident in Wilmington, North Carolina's, black
churches where the pastors took Charles M. Sheldon's social gospel novel, *In
His Steps*, as the text for their evening sermons. Their congregations were
exhorted to make choices based on "What Would Jesus Do?" Uplift was
faithfully practiced at Tuskegee Institute. "Wherever the graduates of this
institution go," *Lend-A-Hand* reported, "old school-houses are repaired, new
ones are built, and there are unmistakable signs of progress." Translated into
the South's racially defined communities, the missionary spirit of uplift became the gospel of self-help.[28] After a long tour of Southern black communities, Boston's Samuel June Barrows praised the progressive spirit of self-
help that animated a new generation of Afro-American leaders in 1891. Barrows found black Americans were "raising and following their own leaders.
They are rapidly copying the organic, industrial, and administrative features of
white society. They have discovered that industrial redemption is not to be
found in legislative and political measures." In spite of an oppressive tenantry
system, black people were "passing into the higher stages of social evolution"
by accumulating property, developing skills, and acquiring a formal education, said Barrows. An increasingly ethical religion, a growing cooperative
spirit in trade unions, building associations, and benevolent guilds, and an
increasing racial self-reliance and self-respect would "secure for him the
respect and fraternal feeling of his white neighbors."[29]

As Barrows penned these words, there was some evidence of increased
regard for black people among some white Southerners. The social Chris-

tianity of Northern home missions found allies among white Southerners who remembered the missions to slaves. Because they were men who could not be ignored and because their attitude was so reassuring, Northern social Christianity may have seen their concern as more significant than it was. "Immortal is the honor that belongs to the memory of the Christian men and women of the South who preached the Gospel to the slaves," said Emory College President Atticus Greene Haygood. "And immortal is the honor due to those who, taking up the good work where the men and women of the South were . . . compelled to lay it down for awhile, have carried it on." Guided by older men, Haygood had conducted missions to slaves. He saw a continuity of purpose between that work and the new effort among the freedmen and invoked the best spirit of his own Southern Methodist tradition in its behalf. Much of his book, Our Brother in Black, was an apology for Southern white Christianity and he was critical of some aspects of the Northern missionary effort. But Haygood warmly endorsed the new effort, challenging his fellow Southerners to join Northern social Christianity in the effort to uplift and Christianize the freedmen. "For myself," he said, after reviewing the home missionaries' achievement, "I have reached a conclusion about this educational work among the negroes of the South: it is God's work."[30]

Haygood's sentiment struck a sympathetic cord with Leonard W. Bacon, a Connecticut Congregationalist, and an old abolitionist, Moses Pierce, who used Our Brother in Black to persuade Bacon's wealthiest parishioner, John F. Slater, of the importance of the cause. In April 1882, Slater chartered a fund for "uplifting of the lately emancipated population of the Southern States, and their posterity, by conferring upon them the blessings of Christian education." Former president Rutherford B. Hayes chaired the Slater Fund's board of trustees and Haygood became its agent. "A few ideas seem to be agreed upon. Help none but those who help themselves. Educate only at schools which provide in some form for industrial education," Hayes noted. "Let the normal instruction be that men should earn their own living, and that by the labor of their hands as far as may be. This is the gospel of salvation for the colored man. Let the labor not be servile, but in manly occupations like those of the carpenter, the farmer, and the blacksmith."[31] Under the persuasive influence of Slater funding, a competitive model for black education was coming to the fore.

Heretofore, mission schools that had classes beyond the elementary and normal levels usually offered a classical curriculum. It was rigidly structured, with emphasis on classical languages, natural philosophy, mathematics, men-

Southern Methodist Bishop Atticus G. Haygood, author of *Our Brother in Black* (Special Collections Department, Robert W. Woodruff Library, Emory University)

tal and moral philosophy, natural theology, and Christian evidences. At its best the curriculum was similar to that of better New England colleges. Its teachers were the products of such institutions and it followed from the missionaries' assumption that the South needed a reproduction of their own tradition and culture. For both races in the South, assimilation to this cultural tradition was assumed to offer prospects of social redemption.[32] Yet, an alternative to this vision had grown up alongside it. Basically Pestalozzian in its perspective, it rejected the idea that cultural and literary traditions could be imposed on a people. Rather, if genuine, such traditions were the product of centuries of development, and the education of a people essentially outside those traditions had to begin where they were. It must grow organically from their experience and deal with the concrete situations in life that they could expect to face. The Slater Fund trustees favored the second model, that was exemplified by Hampton Institute. Ironically, the course that was then deemed more progressive has since come under fire, with the suggestion of conspiracy.[33]

Yet, there is solid evidence to the contrary. Industrial education was not conceived for the education of black people. It had respectable credentials in abolitionist centers at Oneida Institute, Oberlin, and Berea College. More important, when the Slater Fund was formed, industrial education represented the most advanced thinking in academic reform, with broad appeal among educational reformers and black spokesmen. As a member of Ohio State University's board of trustees, Hayes's first priority was constructing a building for industrial training; Haygood urged the program upon his beloved Emory; and Henry Demarest Lloyd sought to endow a school for industrial education modeled after Hampton and Tuskegee institutes at Harvard University. In an era when the classical curriculum was being modified by an elective system and the pressure for mass education was intensified, defenders of the classical curriculum for black higher education appeared to be recalcitrants.[34]

"I would not touch it, except in such position that I could *lay myself out on it,*" Haygood told Leonard Bacon regarding the Slater post. "What I can't put my soul in I do not touch." He sought a kind of unity with God in doing God's work. "I believe with all my soul," he said to Hayes, "that God's hand is on me for these poor people. It is to me a sacred work." Responsible for dispensing $20,000 to $40,000 annually to black schools, Haygood seeded the South with the good news of industrial education from 1882 to 1892. By 1887, he assured Hayes that all of the better black schools in the South had undertaken some work in industrial training. Yet, Haygood also resisted forces within the board of trustees to make industrial training the all-encompassing program for black education by concentrating funds on three or four large machine shops. By spreading the funds widely, he hoped to generate South-wide sentiment for black education. In spite of vicious opposition, Haygood prodded Southern Methodists into their first venture in educating freedmen. Paine Institute in Augusta, Georgia, was headed by his first deputy at Emory, Morgan Calloway, a former slaveholder. The Augusta school was to be Emory in ebony.[35]

Episcopal Bishop Thomas Underwood Dudley of Kentucky joined Haygood in urging black education. With slavery's apologists, he held that the peculiar institution had been an important civilizing influence, binding the races into a relationship in which the advantaged extended their religion and culture to the disadvantaged. So he viewed with alarm the signs of a growing separation of the races in the post–Civil War era. "The separation of the negro race from the white means for the negro continued and increasing degradation and decay," said Dudley. "His hope, his salvation, must come from association with that people among whom he dwells but from whose natural guidance and care he has been separated largely by the machinations of unscrupulous demagogues." Southern white men of goodwill could not stand idle in the face of such danger, Dudley insisted. "The time is come for honest, manly effort to teach them that in our union is the only hope of both races," he counseled; "that separated from us, their neighbors and friends, they must retrograde toward the barbarism whence they are sprung, and, that then, alas! we might be compelled to wage relentless war against them for our own preservation."[36]

Dudley recognized the essential unity of humanity. Black and white Americans were "the descendants of one father, the redeemed children of one God, the citizens of one nation, neighbors with common interests," said the bishop, and yet they were separated by centuries of mental and moral development, "separated by inherited traditions, by the spirit of caste, by the recollection of wrongs done and suffered." The essential question was how the rights of all might be protected and how the disadvantaged might be elevated to a level at which they would no longer be a threat to the advantaged. Colonization and amalgamation were unthinkable on practical and moral grounds, he argued. Only "centuries hence," when black people had been lifted to a higher cultural level, might amalgamation be possible. But acculturation of black people through proper associations over time offered the possibility of a solution to the problem, said the Kentucky bishop. He accepted the freedmen's rank as a citizen and a churchman. What remained to be seen was whether he would be equipped for the full exercise of these responsibilities. Dudley lay the burden of education upon his fellow Southern white Christians. "White men of the South," he asked, "what answer shall we, the intelligent, the cultured, the powerful, the inheritors of noble traditions and of splendid ideas,—what answer, I ask in the name of God, of freedom and of humanity, shall we make to these men?" Bishop Dudley sounded the same themes as the Northern missionaries with a distinctly Southern accent, because as one who remembered the missions to slaves, he chaired the Episcopalians' Commission on Home Missions to Colored People.[37]

African Methodist Episcopal editor and future bishop Benjamin Tucker Tanner appreciated Dudley's article. "That a fly appears here and there in the gracious ointment is sadly true, but of itself the ointment is so charming and healthful that we prefer not to mind the one or two flyspecks," said Tanner. "The idea of a Southern bishop predicting the day when miscegenation will be accepted! To be sure he puts it off centuries, but even that is only incidental to the tremendous fact . . ." Tanner thanked the Episcopal bishop for offering the personal influence of Southern white Christian gentlemen to keep black people "from falling 'lower still in the domain of morals.' " But "to suppose if it be withheld, A.D. 2000 will find us worshipping fetishes," said Tanner, "is the merest moonshine."[38]

**D**uring the 1880s, Thomas U. Dudley, Atticus G. Haygood, and George Washington Cable joined many Northern white social gospel prophets in urging federal aid to education. They believed that the high rate of illiteracy in the South compounded the region's other problems.[39] The missionary-educators organized the National Education Assembly to lobby for federal aid to education. While some educators and sectarian leaders withheld their support, few means of alleviating Southern racial problems so united the social gospel prophets as did federal aid to education.[40]

The social gospel prophets' struggle for common ground in race relations was most evident at the Mohonk Conferences on the Negro Question in 1890 and 1891. For seven years the Quaker proprietor of a hotel at Lake Mohonk, New York, had sponsored conferences on the Indian, when former president Rutherford B. Hayes suggested a similar series of conferences on the Negro.

According to Hayes, the most influential men in its formation were Lyman Abbott, AMA Secretary Michael E. Strieby, and Rutgers College President Merrill E. Gates. Hayes presided over its annual sessions, Gates chaired its executive committee, and Isabel C. Barrows edited its annual reports. The conference brought together a wide array of white guests interested in race relations. "Republican and Democrat, Northerner and Southerner, ex-abolitionist and ex-slaveholder, radical and conservative," said Abbott's *Christian Union*, "will compare their views, seek each to put himself in the other's place and see with the other's eyes, and so endeavor to come to some common, nonpartisan, and Christian conclusions."[41] Amiable conclusions were easier because all of the conferees were white. George Washington Cable, Joseph Cook, Albion Tourgée, and the *Independent's* William Hayes Ward sought in vain to have black leaders invited to the conference. "A patient is not invited to the consultation of the doctors on his case," Lyman Abbott replied, when asked why no black people were invited. "I do not think I can be called a sensitive man," Booker T. Washington confided to Cable, "but the disposition on the part of many of our friends to consult *about* the Negro instead of *with*— to work for him instead of *with* him is rather trying and perplexing at times." When Cable and Joseph Cook boycotted the Mohonk Conference because of its failure to include black spokesmen, New York *Age* editor T. Thomas Fortune said: "Let Dr. LYMAN ABBOTT bite upon that fact."[42]

Even so, Northern editors, educators, and pastors, including Barrows, Amory H. Bradford, James M. Buckley, Charles C. Hall, Amory Dwight Mayo, Charles Parkhurst, Albion W. Tourgée, and William Hayes Ward, joined a few Southern spokesmen in the First Mohonk Conference. The education theme permeated its deliberations as Hampton's Samuel Chapman Armstrong and Southern Presbyterian R. H. Allen promoted industrial training, U.S. Commissioner of Education William T. Harris discussed normal schooling, AMA Secretary Joseph E. Roy defended the higher education of Negroes, and John Jay pleaded for federal aid to education. Recognizing that in twenty-five years of freedom black people had made considerable progress in religion, education, and industry, the conference platform called for increased industrial training for black youth in trades, agriculture, and homemaking; development of the Negro home as a center for "wholesome, cleanly, intelligent Christian" nurture; increased availability of a common school education to all black children and higher education for those prepared for it; development of moral self-reliance and an end to the crop lien system; government establishment of a postal savings system to encourage "habits of thrift and produc-

Mohonk Mountain House, site of the Lake Mohonk Conferences on the Negro Question in 1890 and 1891 (Mohonk Archives, Lake Mohonk, N.Y.)

tive economy"; and unselfish service by all Christians to help the Negro "to help himself—in education, in morality, in religion, and thus in civilization and in fitness for citizenship."[43]

It was, said Albion Tourgée, a "complacently admonitory 'platform.'" He had a rather jaundiced view of the Mohonk Conference from the outset and provided the only serious dissent from its amiable discussions. "Yes, I am going to Smiley's Mohonk Conference—not with any expectation of doing any good or getting any, but simply for the fun. I never knew any good to come out of such split and straddle efforts to make extremes meet," he told a black correspondent. "I have an unutterable contempt for the whole matter of watering-place gushiness which seeks to bait the Devil a little way towards heaven by agreeing not to say anything about the 'airs of hell,' which cling to his clothes. I shall say nothing; do nothing except absorb whatever absurdity there may be in the air." Such things were "good for Mohonk and no doubt very agreeable to those who wish to hear themselves talk, but as for the Indian and the Negro,—well you might as well try to cure cancer by giving me treacle as expect any good from such gatherings," he wrote. "They bear the same relation to existing evils that the 'Colonization Society' did to the abolition movement. It is earnest men who are willing to fight and die for right and who simply *cannot* tolerate wrong who compel progress and remedy evils."[44]

In the absence of black leaders, Tourgée broke his pledge of silent scorn to give an impassioned presentation of "The Negro's View of the Race Problem." Striking the amiable conferees from a blind side, Tourgée distinguished his understanding of the person and work of Christ from that implied in their discussion. "I cannot look upon him as merely a weak, tender, pitying nature, who stood beside the seething tide of human life and tearfully dropped anesthetics on its woes," he said. "My Christ is he of the knotted whipcords, who pities human woefulness less than he hated the evil conditions from which it springs." Tourgée loved

> . . . to think of him as a man, and believe in his divinity because he neither shunned the woes of humanity nor excused its evils.
> . . . to think that he lived in a cabin not much better than those we have heard so much about at this Conference; that he probably sat upon the floor, ate his food with his fingers, found his friends among the poorest poor, and would not be patronized by the rich;
> . . . to think that he knew human woe and its causes.
> . . . to think that the seamless coat he wore was often in need of washing, and that, like the colored man when freed from bondage, he had not where on earth to lay his head.

Tourgée condemned the presumption of white men pondering the future of black people without consulting them. He charged that Allen had a callous disregard of the evil influence of slavery, that Harris ignored the necessity of racial justice, and that Lyman Abbott reduced the conference to an absurdity by denying that there was a racial problem.[45]

The conferees were headed in the wrong direction from the beginning, Tourgée argued, because they misjudged their subject. "He is a new type, a new MAN. He has sloughed off the African, and is first of all things an American,—American in instinct and aspiration as well as largely in blood." That was evident to anyone "who studies him *as a man*, not as a mere appanage of the white race." Tourgée admitted that he did not always understand black people; perhaps only those who had endured with them could. "I have never been so sure as many of our friends what was the very best thing *to be done* for the colored man; but I have never doubted that the most exact justice and the fullest recognition of his equality of right must be the prime elements of any successful policy" that aimed at individual and racial growth. But the sting of Tourgée's sharp dissent was lost in the general anesthesia he so abhorred.[46]

Tourgée spurned an invitation to return to the conference the next year, but most of the others reappeared, as did additional Southern white spokesmen. The conference still included men of diverse points of view, but none so contemptuous of its mediating approach as Tourgée. Tensions rose during the session when A. L. Phillips, Southern Presbyterian field secretary for work among Negroes, explained that Northern missionaries to the black South might win better reception from Southern whites by confining their contact with Negroes to formal relations and otherwise conforming to local white social attitudes. "Never! Never!" cried the conferees. But their platform moved little beyond that of the previous year, except to call for federal aid to education, especially to sections where illiteracy was most common, and removing all barriers to the Negro's advancement "by the sure force of education, thrift and religion." After its second meeting, the Mohonk Conference on the Negro Question was abandoned. Located at a New York resort, it neither invited black leaders to help shape racial attitudes to new realities nor attracted sufficient participation by Southern white leaders to affect state and local policy. The Mohonk Conferences marked the end of an era in which it was assumed that Southern race relations could be reshaped by Northern initiatives.[47]

The nineteenth-century origins of the social gospel are found in domestic missions, of which the missions first to slaves and then to freedmen were an important part. Northern missionaries to the South feared that the races might degenerate to barbaric conditions in the postwar years and sought to sustain, regenerate, and redeem them by replicating Northern social Christianity in the South. As Southern churches recovered their footing, some of their leaders, drawing on the memory of missions to slaves, joined in the missions to freedmen. They rejected Northern missionary assumptions of Yankee superiority, but they too defined the problem largely in moral terms and saw its solution in the extension of white social and cultural norms to their brothers in black. Samuel June Barrows spoke for them all in arguing that the solution lay "in that hackneyed, threadbare word, 'education.' Educate the colored man," he told the Mohonk conferees, "and the colored man

will educate the white. Educate the white, and you will educate his colored
neighbor. Then neither race will have to look through a microscope to find
that God hath made of one blood all the nations of the earth."[48]

When Josiah Strong's sister, Mary, met her fate at a railroad crossing at
Talladega, Alabama, in 1894, she was engaged in what Amory Dwight Mayo
called "radical mission work among the lower orders of the Southern people." Its vision was radical; its methods and priorities were conservative.
Radical improvement in the social and political status of black people depended upon education to improve their industrial, family, intellectual, and
moral life, Mayo argued. Such progress required "the whole American people 'working together for good' " toward "a Christianized, republican civilization."[49]

# 3

# The Redemption of Africa

The origins of the social gospel lie in the hub of antebellum religious reform, the home missions movement; and the freedmen's aid societies were the primary vehicle for late nineteenth-century religious interest in race relations. But a second tradition in racial reform, African colonization and missions, had challenged the priorities and vision of home missions since the second decade of the nineteenth century. In 1889, a Baltimore resident wrote to the American Colonization Society: "I believe the redemption of Africa, through the aid and efforts of the educated descendants of the African slaves of the United States, will prove the most efficient means to settle the race question in the United States."[1] His simple creed uncomfortably juxtaposed the dual rationale for the second tradition in nineteenth-century social Christianity's quest for salvation in race relations: colonization was good for Africa; emigration was good for America.

Founded in 1816 to send free blacks from the United States to Africa, the American Colonization Society established Liberia on west Africa's coast and remained its chief American patron through the nineteenth century. After 1830, the society came under attack from both pro- and antislavery forces, but it passed from the center of controversy as antagonists on either side directed their fire upon each other. Yet, by any obvious measure the society's period of greatest activity was between 1848 and 1873.[2] Its appeal as a "middle way" between extremes attracted such progenitors of the social gospel as Leonard W. Bacon, Lyman Beecher, Stephen Colwell, William E. Dodge, Ezra Stiles Gannett, Bishop William Meade, William A. Muhlenberg,

Ephraim Peabody, and Anson G. Phelps.[3] Emancipation presented problems for which colonization had no immediate solution, so these men joined the home missionaries in promoting freedmen's education. Ezra Stiles Gannett became a pillar of the New England Freedman's Aid Society. His son, William Channing Gannett, joined other missionaries at Port Royal, South Carolina. But for many this was only an expedient to meet momentary needs. They sounded old themes with renewed determination. "It is a great deal easier" for the Negro "to Christianize and nationalize Africa than it is to Africanize the United States," wrote John W. Phelps in 1869. "So long as he remains here he will be a negro and we shall be Saxons; he will hew our wood, draw our water and fight our battles for us, and not for himself." Phelps's classic argument for colonization rejected the home missionaries' plan to create a homogeneous biracial society in America. It hoped to resolve America's racial problem by redeeming Africa.[4]

"Africanization" connoted black political domination of the deep South in Reconstruction. Even after its demise, Africa at home disturbed most white Americans. "How real an Africa may we find beneath the very shadows of our own dear homes!" wrote a Roman Catholic home missionary. "Not the Africa of the Nile and the Congo, but that of the Potomac and the Mississippi." In 1883, a Baltimore physician, Edward W. Gilliam, gave "Africanization" a more ominous meaning. Based on census data from 1840 to 1880, he projected a growth rate of 2 percent per annum for Southern whites. The black population's astonishing increase since 1870 suggested a growth rate of 3.5 percent per annum. The reason for the difference was the "superior fecundity" of black people in favorable working and climatic conditions, said Gilliam. Projecting population growth into the future, he predicted that 192 million whites and 768 million blacks would live in the South by 2020 A.D. It would be Africanized by sheer weight of numbers. Assuming black people to be unassimilable, Gilliam held that under such conditions white people would try to inhibit black ambition. "Unless relief comes, woes await the land," he wrote. The "dark, swelling, muttering mass along the social horizon, gathering strength with education, and ambitious to rise," would grow "increasingly restless and sullen under repression," the doctor said. Finally, "conscious of superior power, it will assert that power destructively, and, bursting forth like an angry, furious cloud, avenge, in tumult and disorder, the social law broken against it." While the size of the problem was still manageable, he concluded, colonization was the answer.[5]

But only one of ten public figures in an 1884 symposium agreed with

Gilliam's answer. The others called for redoubled efforts to educate and uplift the freedmen. "What is to become of us in 2020 if these alarming statistics prove to be true," a Methodist asked a decade later. Noting recent accounts of attacks by black men on white women in the South, he asked: "Ought we not, if from no other motive than simple self-defense, to do everything to Christianize and educate these people?" The prospect of an Africanized South was sufficient reason for many people long sympathetic to colonization to support black education. Francis Greenwood Peabody, Ephraim Peabody's son, joined Hampton Institute's board of trustees in 1890. William E. Dodge, a Colonization Society vice-president for twenty-two years, thought Africa was the ideal home for black people, but he generously supported Hampton, Atlanta University, Biddle University, Lincoln University, and Livingstone College. Colonizationists such as Dodge, Leonard W. Bacon, and Henry Codman Potter joined Southern white racial moderates to shape the policies of the John F. Slater Fund for Negro education in the South.[6]

Many of the social gospel prophets thought the Colonization Society was an anachronism. Colonization was "the wildest of conceits," a "tail-end relic of slavery," or a "scheme which could find lodgment only in the brain of a belated fossil." The society was an "antiquated concern" supporting "a lot of old fossilized office-holders" who met annually to praise their own benevolence and beg government aid to ship poor, unhappy Negroes off to Africa. "We may anticipate the emigration of all the sons of Israel from America to Palestine much sooner than that of the sons of Ham to Africa," said the Northern Baptists' Thomas J. Morgan. Colonization as an idea was "unworthy of sensible beings," Amory Bradford told the American Missionary Association. "We might as well try to bail Lake Superior with a dipper as to send the rapidly increasing Southern race by the ship-load to Africa."[7] When the social gospel prophets listed issues that were resolved, emigration was among the foremost. "The Negro is here to stay," they chorused, until the words became a cliché.[8] For some, it was a conspiracy to deny black people the rights of American citizenship. "To give up the struggle for justice now is cowardly if not fatal," said the *Independent*. "The battle should be fought out here for equal schools, equal ballots, equal rights of every sort." Emigration was a "mess of pottage which a cunning Jacob proposes to tempt our black Esau," said Albion Tourgée. By contrast with their near unanimous support of federal aid to education, when Senator Matthew Butler of South Carolina proposed legislation to subsidize black migration to Africa, it won little support from the social gospel prophets, North or South, black or white. They either opposed or did not support massive black emigration to Africa.[9]

But the idea that a select few black Americans had a providential mission to redeem Africa still had a large following in American social Christianity. "If I were young and black, no steamer could revolve its wheels fast enough to convey me to the Dark Continent," said Frances E. Willard. "I should go where my color was the correct thing, and leave these pale faces to work out their own destiny." Joseph Cook, Michael E. Strieby, Richard Salter Storrs, Josiah Strong, and many others saw providence in the simultaneity of emancipation in America and the opening of Africa to Western civilization. Most black people would remain in the United States to fight for education and equal rights, Strieby told an AMA convention, but that struggle was not at odds with the African task. "The grand achievement of Negro enlightenment will be America's safety and Africa's redemption," he said. It would "promote the welfare of two continents—to save our beloved land from the peril of a race warfare and to help on a civilization in Africa that shall redeem it from barbarism." In an appeal for home missions, Storrs saw providential opportunity in the coincidence of the two events. "If we will Christianize the colored people on our own shores, we shall have thousands of the very men to reach most powerfully those kindred tribes who are still in a state of pagan barbarism," said the old abolitionist. "God has fitted the two events together. All the colored population released from bondage here! All Africa opened to them, on the other side of the sea." Echoing Josiah Strong's rhetoric, Storrs concluded: "Here is the stamp, and there is the yielding wax, that the seal of Christ, with cross and crown, may there be set!"[10]

The idea that black Americans had a providential role in the redemption of Africa also appealed to Southern white churchmen. Methodist Bishops Atticus G. Haygood and Charles B. Galloway endorsed it. "Let the Christian Negroes in America get ready to carry the light of God to their brethren beyond the sea, who 'sit in darkness and the shadow of death,'" said Haygood. "And let Christians of the white race get ready to help them do their work." His students at Emory took a lively interest in colonization and African missions. Southern Baptists, such as Thomas Dixon, Jr., and Samuel Chiles Mitchell, shared the Methodists' enthusiasm. As a student at Kentucky's Georgetown College, Mitchell considered going to Africa as a missionary, but the thought was crowded by the idea that black missionaries ought to be there. "The ultimate good of slavery, if there could have been any good to be derived from it," he said, "is undoubtedly the freedom and enlightenment of the entire dark continent." Southern Presbyterians resolved young Mitchell's dilemma by sending a biracial team, the Reverend S. N. Lapsley and the Reverend William H. Sheppard, to found a mission in the Congo.[11]

$\mathbf{A}$merican social Christianity feared Africanization of the South. More commonly it identified black Americans with their ancestral homeland and looked beyond the replication of Northern society in the South to the replication of American Christendom by black Americans in Africa. It is important to understand how white America then perceived sub-Saharan Africa.[12] James Shepard Dennis, Robert Elliott Speer, Arthur Tappan Pierson, Joseph Crane Hartzell, and Frederic Perry Noble were its leading advocates of African redemption. Dennis and Speer were Princeton graduates and leaders in Presbyterian foreign missions. Dennis returned to Princeton after twenty years as a missionary to lecture on missions. His three-volume *Christian Missions and Social Progress*, the most complete study of foreign missions in its time, translated the usual appeals for foreign missions into the language of the social gospel. As secretary of the Student Volunteer Movement for Foreign Missions and the Presbyterian Board of Foreign Missions, Speer was a prominent American spokesman for foreign missions from 1890 to 1935.[13]

The lives of Pierson, Hartzell, and Noble suggest a transfer of social gospel interest from American freedmen to their African kinsmen in the 1890s. Pierson's father, Stephen, had shared the evangelical abolitionism of his employer, Arthur Tappan, and armed himself to protect Tappan's Manhattan store from antiabolitionist mobs. In 1889, young Pierson became editor of the *Missionary Review of the World*, the nation's leading journal of missions.[14] From 1870 to 1896, Hartzell led northern Methodist missions in the South. Elected to the episcopacy in 1896, he supervised Methodist work in Africa and became its leading advocate of African redemption. Noble was the son of Frederick A. Noble, long an officer of the American Missionary Association and Congregational spokesman for the social gospel. In 1893, young Noble became secretary of Chicago's Congress on Africa at the World Columbian Exposition. His two-volume work, *The Redemption of Africa*, drew on papers from the congress and was for decades the most comprehensive study of African missions.[15]

When these men lived and wrote, the dramatic explorations and death of

David Livingstone in Africa still held the imagination of the Anglo-American public. Apart from a century of work in Sierra Leone and Liberia, missions in sub-Saharan Africa were relatively new. But European imperialism brought an expanded missionary effort with it. By 1888, twelve British, thirteen Continental, and ten American mission societies were established there. Europe had stolen Africans from the continent for four centuries, Frederic Noble observed; but in fourteen years, from 1876 to 1890, it stole Africa from the Africans. "There is a hungering for land, which will never be made use of, a desire for domination over barbarous tribes, whom the dominator knows not how to govern," said an Englishman, "there is a kind of itch for taking possession of everything, as if the Creator had only been thinking of Europe, when he made the world." Yet, God moved in mysterious ways, A. T. Pierson argued. Human greed itself would be turned to His glory. "God is disclosing by His providence the great mineral, metallic and vegetable resources of the interior," he wrote. "So, through the very avarice of men and the higher love of science, the great unknown continent is to be settled by adventurous and far-sighted traders; and planted with Christian missions." The social gospel prophets saw much to criticize in imperialist greed, but they also saw in it an opportunity to treat appalling social conditions among Africa's people.[16]

Africa became the mirror of all that the social gospel missionaries feared in human society. "The same blackness of moral degradation prevails with ever-deepening shades" throughout Africa, one wrote. "The few faint and scattered gleams of light only serve to deepen and intensify the dense darkness that covers like a pall this truly benighted land." Africa's burden was "the crushing weight of a bondage more cruel and relentless than that of the Arab slaver, more deadly and destructive than that of the white man's rum—the bondage of a thousand years of ever-deepening sin." Sin thus characterized was not the sin of all humanity. It was an acquired bondage to a social matrix of evil in all its parts. At its heart was a pagan religion. Paganism was sometimes described in terms of a vacuum. "The super-natural of a mid-African nigger" is only what he calls the "shifting point where his knowledge of the actual ends and his yearning to know is balked," said William Stephen Rainsford. "The poor savage in Africa, denied the knowledge of the history of mankind and the arts, useful and beautiful," wrote Newell Dwight Hillis, "sits in his soul dungeon and starves to death."[17]

More often, paganism was described as having negative content, a "perversion and abuse of man's religious nature, thereby bringing his whole nature into bondage to evil." Its "superstition and priest-craft," said J. C. Hartzell, "held multiplied millions in gloom and sorrow" for centuries. In its lowest forms of fetishism, pagan religion inspired fear of evil spirits and enslaved life to "superstitious rules, charms and witchcraft," wrote Robert E. Speer. "We who live in the freedom of enlightenment," said James Dennis, "can hardly imagine the dread alarms of a life supposed to be in active contact with demons, exposed to their whims and spites, their deadly anger, and their cruel malignity." Islam contended with Christianity for the soul of Africa. It was superior to native paganism, but Islam was unable "to regenerate the human heart." By fostering polygamy, war, and slavery, it had become a part of the evil social matrix. "Exponents of true Christianity" had to come as "liberators from the reign of Superstition that is often cruel, from customs which range from the abominable and devilish to the vexatious and tedious, and from the domination of lusts and indulgences which of themselves become a slavery."[18]

A perverted, abusive religion led to an indolent character and debased morality, said the social gospel missionaries. Idleness was the "fruit of pride" among "African savages," wrote James Dennis. The "lusty barbarians" had such "undisciplined, flabby, and shiftless" ways that the typical African was a "worthless drone," except as "a professional warrior and plunderer." His vanity and conceit varied in proportion to the "density of his ignorance," he continued. The pitiful condition of the "proud savages" was due to their "intense satisfaction with their own fancied superiority, . . . a telling lesson of the social perils of pride." Self-satisfied ignorance and indolence led to poverty and periodic famines in which thousands of tribesmen died. James Dennis found a morality "truly appalling in its bestiality" among the "barbarous and savage races" of Africa. Family life was not far above "mere animalism" and the inferior lot of women was "painful and brutal," he noted. "Many a burly savage thinks it unmanly to treat her with kindness and consideration." She is "bought and sold like chattel" for a price so small as scarcely to rank her "superior to the domestic animals." Often, she ate with the dogs and could be grateful "if when her husband dies she is not tossed with his dead body into the same grave." The children, Dennis reported, "run wild and grow up with untamed and grossly tainted natures."[19]

The result was a people nurtured in deceit and savagery. "Poor *Africa* may be said to be a continent of lies and a paradise of thievery," Dennis lamented. "The native savage is trained in the arts of plunder, and lives by crafty wiles. Here, . . . a lie seems to be loved for its own sake, and a man must be taken for a thief and a rogue until he is proved to be the contrary." A continent of such people, among whom honesty, restraint, and morality were the exception, exemplified the human condition apart from law and culture. Without effective government, Africa was in a "constant state of anarchy and bloody hostility," a continent where "lust, revenge and rapine were continually on the warpath." Apart from foreign control, "Africa is a favorite hunting-ground of the outlaw and plunderer," Dennis wrote. "Robbery is a profession; murder is a commonplace incident. From the 'tiger-men' of the West Coast through all the central stretches of the Continent warfare and plunder are the most characteristic features of the savage life." James Dennis's picture of African brutality was nearly unrelieved. Africa was "a carnival of cruelty and beastly savagery" under the "dark shadows of brutal warfare." The west coast was a "hotbed of abominations" where "rivers of blood have been poured out in human sacrifice." He cheered a British expedition to Kumassi in 1895 that ended "a carnival of crime" and destroyed the power of Prempeh, a "king of beastliness and cruelty."

His "Festival of the Yams," with its six hundred victims, is no longer celebrated with ghastly immolations. The fetich-trees are not now soaked to the roots with the life-blood of his victims. His horrid mandate of the sacrifice of one of his slaves for his entertainment each night before he slept, has ceased. He can no longer offer four hundred virgins, that their blood may be mixed with the mortar to form a richer red in the painted stucco of his palace.

Dennis estimated that along the tributaries of the Congo in central Africa 20 million cannibals feasted on their hapless victims. Some tribes ate their own dead; others consumed the aged, infirm, or useless. In east Africa, young boys brought from the interior were fattened in pens and cooked for the tribal repast.[20]

The social gospel missionaries attacked two influences that exploited and compounded the moral depravity they described. The American and European liquor trade with Africa was "the most cruel curse ever inflicted upon the lost and hopeless continent," Frederic Noble said. "Nature-peoples must be sober or die," he explained. Liquor made them "moral Frankensteins for whom and with whom nothing can be done." Their "natural cruelty and bloodthirstiness" were "kindled by 'crazy waters' into the madness of demons." Noble urged the U.S. Navy to enforce international agreements restricting the liquor trade, as it had enforced earlier restrictions on the slave trade.[21] The other factor compounding Africa's social depravity was its domestic slavery. "A thing of the past" elsewhere, its "terrible apparition" rose from African jungles to defy "the genial powers of civilization and Christianity," wrote James Claflin. The "monster" was so entrenched in Africa's interior as to be "the one insurmountable obstacle to its civilization," he concluded. "And it is not slavery modified and tempered by civilization as it was in our Southern States, but slavery intensified by Mohammedanism and barbarism."[22]

Africa's domestic slavery did not offend the social gospel missionaries so much as the continued international slave trade. Carried on by Arabs, Hindus, Portuguese, Sudanese, and east coast Africans, it perpetuated "crime and war, the heart disease of Central Africa, and the devil's business," said Frederic Noble. It invaded peaceful communities, terrorized men awakened from their sleep, kidnapped women and children, and gratified "every instinct of lust and cruelty." Calling for suppression of the slave trade, Noble urged the Western powers to enforce international antislavery agreements. The ports of east Africa should be blockaded, if necessary, to mount a modern crusade against the trade, expel Portugal from east Africa, and pressure the Moslem states to abolish slavery.[23] Lyman Abbott, Augustus F. Beard, James Dennis, William E. Dodge, Hollis B. Frissell, David H. Greer, Henry Codman Potter, Josiah Strong, and Booker T. Washington endorsed the antislavery plans of Heli Chatelain. A Swiss emigrant to the United States, Chatelain organized the Philafrican Liberators League in 1895 to publicize African slavery and the slave trade and to train and resettle liberated slaves on unoccupied African territory.[24]

Beyond these problems, the social gospel missionaries espoused the same patience and missionary methods for Africa's redemption that they advocated for Southern salvation. "Africa is suffering from her own sins and the wrongs other countries have done through centuries," one wrote. "Sin and Salvation reach these benighted shores locked hand in hand. Has not Christendom sufficient patience and charity to pity Africa's faults and wait for her salvation?" As in the South, the missionaries insisted against all naysayers that Africa's people could be uplifted. Like the South, Africa needed the leavening influence of reproductive units of the redeeming community. In the interest of "spreading the Redeemer's Kingdom," said A. T. Pierson, "we ought to crowd pagan peoples with colonies of Christian workers, being put down in the midst of heathendom to represent what a man can do in his calling." The caption under the picture of a community of "christianized Africans" in

White missionaries with African converts to Christianity. Indicative of attitudes that often accompanied missionary work was the caption that appeared beneath the published photo (" 'Fishers'—not Eaters—'of Men' "), including the identification by name of each white missionary but none of the black converts. (James Shepard Dennis, *Christian Missions and Social Progress: A Sociological Study of Foreign Missions*, 3 vols. [New York: Fleming H. Revell Co., 1897–1906], vol. 1, opposite p. 152)

Dennis's *Christian Missions and Social Progress* unhappily called them " 'Fishers'—not Eaters—'of Men.' "[25]

As in the South, missionaries looked to industrial education as Africa's best hope. Among the industrial schools, Frederic Noble saw Lovedale Missionary Institution as "a fair type, almost an ideal type, of the industrial mission." Located 650 miles northeast of Cape Town, South Africa, it was founded by British missionaries in 1841 to educate native Africans and the children of missionaries. Lovedale introduced industrial education in 1855, but primarily offered a classical curriculum until 1870. Then, except for a few theological students, natives were excluded from classes in classical languages and it became primarily an industrial school. In 1896, South African authorities forced the school to exclude all white students. Thereafter, it was to educate native preachers, prepare teachers for native schools, and train natives in skilled crafts. Its purpose was to "Christianize," said Frederic Noble. "To Christianize successfully, however, it has proved of great service to civilize at the same time." In order to achieve these goals, Lovedale avoided sectarian identity. It advocated a gospel of applied Christianity and self-help for the redemption of Africa.[26]

Social gospel missionaries colored non-Christian Africa in shades of moral depravity in the belief that the picture was accurate and that it would elicit the sympathetic aid of Christian philanthropy. But the picture lent terror to the visions of those who believed that black fecundity foretold an Africanized South in the twentieth century and that, apart from white cultural nurture, black Americans were reverting to type. In the racial climate of the 1890s, the unintended effects of an argument often outweighed the substance of the argument itself. In 1891, Francis Amasa Walker sought to mitigate the fear of an Africanized South by showing that the census figures of 1890 proved that black people were not increasing beyond the rate of their white neighbors. The unintended corollary was that black people were failing in the struggle for survival. Frederick L. Hoffman's influential *Race Traits and Tendencies of the American Negro* in 1896 seemed to prove that conclusion. By then, even so constant an ally as Washington Gladden acknowledged that the freedmen were apparently not enduring the stress of freedom. Racists joined that idea with the continuing fear of a reversion to type to confirm an image of black people as a degenerating breed whose presence threatened the welfare of the whole community. The fear of a degenerating breed helps to explain the increased discrimination, frequent lynchings, and hardening patterns of segregation that the black South experienced in these years.[27]

Given that experience, black Southerners flooded the American Colonization Society with petitions for help. They were encouraged by AME Bishop Henry M. Turner, long an advocate of emigration to Africa and a society vice-president since 1876. Petitioners from South Carolina to Arkansas reported the spread of "emigration fever." His people were "in the spirit of emigration," said a South Carolinian. "There have never been such spirit in the state of S. C. before, as now, exist." A Georgian reported: "We all are just doing tolable well, but we need colonizing hear veary veary bad and a great many would go." An ambitious Tennessean wrote: "I want to Keep the Ball Roleing untill I can Role 500000 Collard Famleys in to Africa We have the thing hot now & God sake Help ous to Keep it Hot Help is all that my people waunts help my People a way From the South & so help me God in less than tenn years there will not Be left in the South 6000 Collard People." An Arkansan summed up a simple message for most of them. "We the negroes is Wanting to go to liberia. But we are Poore and is not able to pay much money."[28] Many petitioners thought that they would be better off almost anywhere else. "I think we ought to go to Liberia are some other Beria," one said. "I think we ought to go out of the United States." Many conceded that it was a "white man's country" and wished to go where they could live under a government and laws of their own making. Living with white people, wrote a Georgian, "Wee Pore Colored People ar treated Worsted than Dum Beast in these lands with them and I do Want to go to my owne Contry of Colored People Where I Can have my own People to Rule and Govern our lands Wee ar in a Enamys land and Contry."[29]

The theme of white oppression was constant in the petitions. "There is no people in the world any more oppressed than the people of Gadsden County, Fla.," said one. Another from Arkansas read: "Our people are so oppressed that it will be utterly impossible for the most of them to get away from their extreme enemies." At times, the humble petitioners approached a Biblical eloquence.

> I am oppress and I flee to you for Refuch
>     and we cry untoo you for help.

Another man wrote:

> Our troubles are not momentary,
>     it seams to be a persuing enemy.
> thear is danger when we think not
>     & trouble whear thear is no occasions. . . .
> we cannot stay heare & enjoy our rights
>     nor can we serve our Redeemer in peace.[30]

Petitioners for colonization wrote of economic deprivation, low cotton prices, and the inequity of farm tenantry in graphic detail. "They is harder on the Black Race than ever I seen here Before," wrote a man from Friars Point, Mississippi. "Something to eat is a very hard thing to keep up with." Another Mississippian agreed: "I works hard and get But little I have Been farming for the longest and the harder i Work the lesser I get." Others complained of the denial of civil rights. "It is better to go to Africa than to stay hear and vote at the musle of a pistol," wrote a Texan. "Our trial of that effect will come off next tuesday and I expect that many will not get to vote and Some lose their lives."[31]

Fear of white violence stirred many to think of emigration. "The people are very near dead to get a way from here for the whit's are killing us for nothing & our Sisters & wives are out Raged in our sight by White people," wrote a Mississippian. "The White Peopels of Houston County are killing the Colored Peopels on the road sid By nigte & what for iss Nothing," reported a Texan. "O Please Kine Fririend help us to Get Out of Houston Co." Another asked: "How much longger are We to be left hear to suffer & dy?"[32] Race relations in the New South were worse than slavery itself, some said, for it maintained the violence of social control without the melioration of paternalistic interest. "I believe that we was better off when we was slaves than we is now," wrote an Atlanta minister. "Their was a wall of protection around us our master and our mistes." Black people in his state were "fairing very bad," said a minister in Samantha, Alabama; "in Some places they whites holds the Pistols on you with one Hand and whip with the other and the Negro have to take it or die. Oh yes they Run the Negroes with Hounds dogs now days and times. As did before 1865. Oh may God help us to get out from here to Liberia."[33]

But Africa's negative image and reports of returning emigrants handicapped the Colonization Society's effort to promote African emigration. One correspondent feared the repetition of his situation in Arkansas. "We Wood like to Know Weather We Wood be treaded as Bad in libery as We in the U. S.," he wrote. "Ar tha any White People over in libery if tha ar there or if tha ar going there We do not Want to go there Becose We hafter Work hard and feed cloth them here and we dont Want to go 10 or 15 thousand Miles and do the same thing." Reports of starvation and slavery in Liberia cured emigration fever among others.[34] But most of the applicants dismissed such reports. A Floridian was told "we all would get eat up if we went there But I knew better," he continued, "for we are Being eat up here every day rite here in these United States the Big fish are eating up the little minners and how can we thrive at that?" Many applicants foresaw a natural paradise for black people across the sea. "Africa is a great and unexplored continent," one wrote. "Her wonderful rivers, immense forests and fertile soil eclipse every thing in this Paradise of the three Americas. it is the design of Providence to establish in the now wilds of Africa a great, prosperous civilized and Christianized nation of the Negro Race."[35]

The applicants felt a providential identification with an Africa that once had been their home and was now a promised land. They wrote seeking a way "back to the home of our forfathers The Place where God made for the Negro Race of people." A man from Arkansas reported that "We are try to get reday lik men fixen to cross Jordan." The sense of providential direction was strong. "I thank God that hard times making the negro Look for Africa," said a Mississippian. A whole world of meaning hung on the colonists' success. "Should it happen that they fail to fulfill the divine providence of a glorious Maker," a supporter wondered, "what shall become of him or us."[36] The applicants shared both a sense of their providential relationship to Africa and a program of responsibility for the homeland. "We ar Liveing in a civilized World here but Africa is not Civilize," wrote a Kansan. "We Want to Go as Missionary So We Can Help to Civilize Africa." "I cant reast night nor day for studying about them pore souls out there want the gospel Preach to them," said a South Carolina pastor. A fellow minister from St. Louis wrote: "I wants to go to Affrica to Spend the Rest of my days in preaching & trying to convert My People."[37]

Until 1892, the American Colonization Society held that emigration would resolve America's race problem and colonization would redeem Africa from bondage. Yet, it was increasingly unable to meet either the pleas of black Southerners for help or its own claims to a work of such importance. With a declining constituency, it sent 40 to 125 emigrants a year by using income from legacies and endowments and slowly liquidating its capital. Elected to their positions before the Civil War, the society's president and secretary, John H. B. Latrobe and William Coppinger, had grown old in office; society auxiliaries in Massachusetts, New York, Pennsylvania, and New Jersey were nearly moribund. Only the undying enthusiasm of a faithful few, worsening race relations in the South, and new interest in Africa sustained the belief that the society could play an important role in racial reform. But it faced crises that forced a redirection of its policies in 1892. President Latrobe, who had led the organization since 1853, died in September 1891. Five months later, Secretary Coppinger followed his comrade to the grave. At the same time, the society was publicly embarrassed and criticized when two groups of poor black people, who expected to go to Africa at society expense, were left destitute in New York. Meanwhile, AME Bishop Henry McNeal Turner returned from an African tour with renewed enthusiasm for emigration.[38]

The society chose New York's Episcopal Bishop Henry Codman Potter to succeed Latrobe. The son of a Pennsylvania bishop, he was nurtured in the antebellum Colonization Society's mediating spirit. At Virginia Theological

Seminary, he was influenced by Bishop William Meade and the Reverend William A. Muhlenberg, two long-time colonizationists. There too he confronted slavery more directly, when two of his fellow Northern students were forced to leave school for holding services for slaves. Three years after he became rector of New York's Grace Episcopal Church in 1868, Potter was made a life director of the Colonization Society. A year after his election to the episcopacy in 1883, he became a vice-president of the organization. "I fear I can do little to serve the Society," he told Coppinger, "but my sympathies were never more warmly with it, and I shall always be glad to be associated with its good work." Potter paid tribute to Liberia's benefactors, but his office was an honorary one and he apparently attended no society meetings between 1884 and 1892.[39]

The bishop was abroad when he was elected to the presidency in January 1892 and did not know he was being considered for the position. At the time of his election, he was addressing the British Christian Social Union. Contrasting the homogeneity of English dioceses with New York's racial patchwork, Potter said that the city's heterogeneity would be reflected in its Cathedral of St. John the Divine, where seven chapels would each be "devoted to the use of a different race of people." Press reports of his election and the destitute black emigrants, an unwonted part of New York's patchwork, reached him in England. Thinking he had little choice but to accept, Potter determined not to have a repetition of the New York embarrassment. In October 1892, he told the society's executive committee that its old policy of "indiscriminate colonization" had been "outlawed by time." The society would no longer aim to solve America's race problem; it would seek to renovate the Liberian social order. It would not send masses of destitute farmers, but a few industrious, well-educated black people to help Liberia assume its role in the redemption of Africa. "The American Colonization Society is not now engaged in the work of soliciting or stimulating the emigration of Negroes from the United States to Liberia," the committee reported a month later. Its work "must continue to be essentially colonization, but with less reference to the pressing importunities of applicants, and more regard to the wants of . . . African civilization."[40]

Potter joined the home missionaries in supporting education and equal opportunity for the freedmen. "There can be little difference of opinion now as to what that race, freed and enfranchised, is entitled to, nor what it needs," he said shortly before being elected president of the society. "It is entitled to an equal opportunity, it needs an education. Race prejudice dies slowly and

Episcopal Bishop Henry Codman Potter, president of the American Colonization Society from 1892 to 1899 (General Theological Seminary, New York, N.Y.)

hard. But, though injustice disappears slowly, it is less universal than it was, and I think steadily diminishing." But developments in the 1890s made Potter less sanguine about the decline of race prejudice and he shared the colonizationists' pessimism about legislative attempts to meliorate conditions in America. "Legislation can change a legal *status*," he granted, but "it cannot destroy a prejudice or extinguish a race antagonism. That such antagonism ought to be outgrown may be true enough, but as a practical consideration it is wholly beside the mark if, as a matter of fact, they are not."[41]

In reorienting the society away from a policy of mass emigration, Potter did spotlight an underlying source of the white prejudice and black self-contempt in America. It was the negative image of Africa, the general impression "that Africa is nothing but a 'dark continent,' barbarous, barren, unhealthy, impassable." He shared much of the missionary perception of African character. "Read the travellers' tales about the African negro from Zanzibar to the great Nyanze," the bishop told an Ohio audience, "and a greater scoundrel, thief, liar, traitor, brute-beast, does not walk the earth." But he shared also their insistence that the native character could be improved. "Then read the life of David Livingstone and follow the dusky band who, with a tenderness and reverence that no funeral procession excelled, carried his dead body all the way . . . to the ship that bore his sacred ashes to their final resting place in Westminster Abbey," Potter continued; "and then take care how you generalize about men, or races, or classes, on the basis of insufficient facts!"[42]

The Colonization Society's new task was twofold, said Potter. First, it must challenge the popular image of Africa, "the product of the imagination built upon the fragmentary foundation of a very partial group of facts," by calling attention to historic Africa, "the home of great peoples, the scene of memorable acts in human history, and the theatre of achievements, not alone in arms, but in letters and art of a high degree." Second, it must undertake a missionary responsibility. Taking his cue from disciples of Leo Tolstoy, Potter envisioned the rejuvenation of Afro-American character and the fulfillment of a racial destiny by the work of black missionaries in the struggle to redeem Africa. The society's task was to enable that to happen. "It is the force of a finer manhood for which Africa most of all waits today," he said. In the face of imperial conquests, Potter urged the society to send men and women to Africa who were prepared "to lay foundations, to build a society, to win the ignorant, to open a path for the light and the truth, and so to make straight in the desert [a] highway for the King and Kingdom that are to be!"[43]

But Potter was already under fire for trying to rejuvenate the Colonization Society. "Nothing astonishes me more" than to see him accept its presidency, wrote Wendell Phillips Garrison. Shortly after assuming office, Potter appointed a fund-raising agent for the society. Within months, the nation was struck by the panic of 1893. A year later the agent had not raised a dollar. The bishop intervened with a personal effort to raise money and breathe life into moribund society auxiliaries. In Boston's first public meeting on behalf of colonization in twenty years, Potter addressed an audience of 125 at the Old South Meeting House on 7 February 1894. Despite his eloquence, the meeting attracted more opposition than support. At the end of his talk, several black spokesmen rose to denounce Liberia and the society. A week later, black leaders met at Boston's Charles Street AME Church and passed resolutions denouncing Potter's address.[44]

Potter did win unexpected support from a colleague, Thomas U. Dudley of Kentucky, who became a Colonization Society vice-president in 1894, and Howard University's president, J. E. Rankin. The society had long pursued a wrong-headed course, said Rankin, but assistance to a select few who aimed at the redemption of Africa was sound policy. "Now at any rate, the Colonization Society means nothing that deserves criticism," he wrote, "and, perhaps, it is time to forgive what we conceive the errors of its earlier days." But Joseph Cook, an old warrior who neither forgave nor forgot, had attended the Old South meeting. Convinced of Potter's "Christian earnestness," he was willing to see him raise money to send all the Negroes back to Africa who wanted to go. But Cook would not drink Potter's new wine from old society wineskins. He recalled Benjamin Butler's reply to Lincoln's inquiry about exporting black people. "I find if our warships were laden until the gunwales kissed the waves, if all our merchant marine were brought into service, if you were to take as many of the colored people as you can to Africa," Butler had said, "there would be more Africans here when the ships came back than there were before they left, so rapid is the natural increase." Potter had not grappled with the size of America's black population, said Cook; he ignored their political emasculation, lynching, and the Southern white immorality that produced so many mulattoes. The bishop was dwelling in a never-never land that reminded Cook of Erasmus Darwin's scheme to put sails on icebergs and send them to equatorial regions in order to make the tropics inhabitable. Four months after Potter's visit, the Massachusetts auxiliary was again inactive. He continued his efforts to raise money for the society in parlor meetings with Percy Stickney Grant and David W. Greer in New York, but they were no more fruitful than the Boston effort.[45]

**P**otter's critics erred in mistaking his new program for the Colonization Society's old effort to export black Americans, but they understood that it did not directly address domestic racial issues. The new program was only one sign of energies rechanneled from domestic racial reform to African redemption in the mid-1890s. The World Congress on Africa at Chicago's Columbian Exposition in 1893 and Atlanta's Congress on Africa during the Cotton States and International Exposition of 1895 was spectacular evidence of it. Chicago's Columbian Exposition took place amid charges of racial discrimination. Some exhibits by black Americans and foreigners eventually appeared at the fair and a Colored Jubilee Day was celebrated in August 1893. But the exposition sponsored a series of conferences including the Congress on Africa, which was its most important event for black and white racial reformers.[46]

The congress was chaired by American Missionary Association Secretary Joseph E. Roy, who called it a "Lake Mohonk Conference on a larger scale." Frederic P. Noble, secretary of the congress, directed the development of its program. His advisory council included people interested in Africa at home and abroad such as George Washington Cable, Joseph Cook, Atticus Haygood, and William Hayes Ward, editor of the *Independent*. Hampton Institute's Samuel Chapman Armstrong and Tougaloo University's Frank Goodrich Woodworth represented missionary educators in the South. Edward W. Blyden, a distinguished African statesman, represented the continent's interests on the council; Blanche K. Bruce, Frederick Douglass, and John Mercer Langston spoke for their fellows in America. They and 140 other experts suggested topics and nominated speakers for the program, but its plans were handicapped by noncooperation. Suspicious of its Protestant tone, Roman Catholics did not acknowledge invitations to participate. Some racial liberals, like Albion Tourgée, doubted the value of such "side shows." Others, like George Washington Cable, insisted that it must address the political status of black Americans. Southern white racial conservatives were notably absent and, among Southern racial liberals, only Lewis Harvey Blair attended the congress.[47]

When the week-long congress opened on 14 August 1893, 50 experts presented papers and as many more sent papers to be read for them. Alexander Crummell and bishops Benjamin W. Arnett, Henry M. Turner, and Alexander Walters were among the important black religious leaders who addressed the congress. The first day's debate on imperialism in Africa featured admirers and critics of the rush for African territory. Vei Prince Momolu Massaquoi and Frederic P. Noble depicted the effect of the liquor trade in Africa; Noble and others called for action against the slave trade. Papers by George Washington Cable, Henry M. Turner, and others treated black achievements in manufacturing, trade, education, and the arts. The dual focus of the congress was evident in discussions of the political status of black people in America. Since few Southern white conservatives were there, the field was left to Lewis Harvey Blair, Frederick Douglass, and Frederick A. Noble, father of the congress secretary, to demand full implementation of civil rights for black Americans. Noting the opposition's absence, William Hayes Ward observed that "apologists for the caste-system do not like to defend their position before the world." Yet, the very absence of spokesmen for a cause that was winning its way through the South gave an air of unreality to expressions of noble sentiment.[48]

Debate on colonization during the congress did reflect external racial tensions. It broke out on the second day, when Bishop Turner reviewed the injustices done to his people in the United States and called for removal from the American Egypt to Africa. His position was seconded by a South Carolina minister, but Bishop Arnett spoke for the majority in rejecting emigration. The colonization debate resurfaced on the fifth day, when black spokesmen divided among plans for mass emigration, selective emigration, and remaining in the United States to fight for equal rights. But, on balance, the Chicago Congress on Africa gave little comfort to advocates of emigration. Benjamin F. Lee, editor of the AME *Christian Recorder*, spoke for many Northern black people in shunning Turner's solution. "To take a half million of the best colored men and women of this country from us would be a crime and as a theory is scarcely worthy of a thought," he wrote. "If we Congoes must be left here, we want some of the 'higher type' to remain for reasons too plain to require stating."[49]

Yet, many black Southerners were more sympathetic to selective or massive emigration. Denominational schools had long promoted a missionary spirit among Southern black students. In 1877, a leading Baptist preacher counseled a teacher of Richmond Negroes to "*emphasize*, Emphasize, EMPHASIZE the matter of giving intelligence about *Africa* and praying for Africa and working for Africa." The schools produced volunteers for African missions and black denominations took an increased interest in African missions.[50] In 1890, Southern Presbyterians sent William Henry Sheppard to the Congo. A graduate of Hampton Institute and the Colored Theological Seminary at Tuscaloosa, Alabama, Sheppard served for the next twenty years as an example of the providential role black Americans could play in the redemption of Africa. He and other black missionaries, such as Samuel Coles, functioned much as Bishop Potter envisioned. Coles became a skilled blacksmith and brickmaker as a student at the American Missionary Association's Talladega College. Years later, after he went to Africa, he was visited by a friend from the United States. The sight of the mission station astonished his friend. "Surely the buildings in front of him were those of Talladega College, surely the very spacing was as he remembered it in Alabama," said a missionary executive. "Mr. Coles had borrowed the blue-prints, taught the natives brickmaking, and reproduced his Alma Mater."[51]

Methodist schools were as zealous for African missions as their Baptist, Presbyterian, or Congregational rivals. Led by R. W. Keeler, a life member of the American Colonization Society, Northern Methodism's Central Tennessee College at Nashville established a training school for missionaries to Africa in 1889. But Methodist enthusiasm for African missions found its fullest expression in the Stewart Missionary Foundation at Atlanta's Gammon Theological Seminary. As the center for Turner's emigration effort, black Atlanta was receptive to the interest in Africa. Students at the city's black colleges often heard guest lecturers on Africa in these years and, when members of Gammon Theological Seminary's Literary Society debated the question of emigration, it was usually resolved in the affirmative. Shortly after the Chicago Congress on Africa, a Methodist pastor in Chicago, William F. Stewart, endowed the Foundation with a six-hundred-acre farm in Illinois. In connection with it, mission bands were organized in all the Methodist schools in the South and leading congregations of the denomination. Annual essay and hymnology contests stimulated missionary interest among black Methodists and the foundation gathered one of the country's largest Africana libraries at Gammon.[52] As plans for Atlanta's Cotton States and International Exposition developed, trustees of the missionary foundation decided to hold a Congress on Africa in conjunction with the exposition as had been done in Chicago.

Addressing a Sunday afternoon session of the congress, the venerable former executive of the Freedmen's Aid Society, Richard S. Rust, said that its "elevated thought, patriotic sentiment, and holy inspiration" reminded him of abolitionist meetings he had attended as a child. Just as Birney, Douglass,

Garrison, Phillips, and Weld had inspired "heroic effort for the freedom of the enslaved millions in our land," Rust prayed that the congress might succeed in "awakening an interest that shall redeem Africa." Frederic Noble gave a paper on African missions and J. C. Hartzell offered a sympathetic interpretation of imperialist ventures on the continent. Led by "Protestant England and Germany, Republican France and rising Italy, the power of Mohammedanism will be broken, and the Crescent in North Africa will wane before the uplifted Cross," he predicted, "and slave-traders' highways of crime and agony will be the . . . pathways of peace and prosperity; and fetish heathenism among her millions will gradually give way to the worship of the true God." Africans were "a belated race," Hartzell admitted, but the biblical promise that the first shall be last and the last shall be first suggested that the descendants of Ham might yet rule the proud sons of Japeth.[53]

Black spokesmen at the congress represented the divisions that plagued black and white racial reformers in the 1890s. Alexander Crummell, a Cambridge-educated theologian, outlined the rationale for black Americans' social mission to Africa. Christianity was not exclusively individualistic or otherworldly, he said. It aimed to develop social institutions for serving human needs, but because of cultural barriers, the conversion of a society would ultimately depend upon an indigenous ministry, not missionaries from abroad, black or white. By contrast, Bishop Henry M. Turner again argued for emigration of millions of black people back to Africa. They had been rescued from a barbaric slavery in Africa to study in a "heaven-permitted if not a divine-sanctioned manual laboring school" in America, he argued. Once that tutelage ended, it was appropriate to return to Africa, for "the whites will not grant social equality to the Negroid race, nor am I sure that God wants them to do it."[54]

Divisions within the black community were clearer in the speeches of two newspaper editors, T. Thomas Fortune of the *New York Age* and John H. Smythe of the Richmond *Reformer*. Fortune, the Northern mulatto, anticipated the absorption and assimilation of black Americans into the larger white community. The security of the nation depended on the emergence of a unified racial type, he argued, to parallel its common language and religious assumptions. Smythe, the dark-skinned Southerner, rejected both Turner's notion of slavery as a benign manual training school and Fortune's optimism about racial absorption. He saw no providence "in bringing the Negro here, in making of him, at best, a moral and mental imitation" of white people. "Every step made by the Negro . . . has continued him slave, though the institution as such has perished," said Smythe. "The inherited taint of the institution has removed him further and further from the land of his fathers, from his tribal and racial traditions (valued heritages of a people), and has tended to make latent in him, if it has not wholly destroyed, his best racial peculiarities and characteristics." More than Crummell or Turner, Smythe voiced a consistent black nationalism.[55]

The address of Gammon Seminary President Wilbur P. Thirkield showed how close the congress leadership was to Bishop Potter's thinking. "The relation of the American Negro to the civilization and redemption of his Fatherland" was one of the foremost issues of the day, said Thirkield. "God's hand must be recognized in his presence in America. Here he will stay. But the forefinger of that Hand points the way to Africa for the thousands who shall be agents of God in the redemption of the Dark Continent." Africa did not call "the weak, the poor, the ignorant of the race. Such may only relapse into barbarism. But Africa now needs the best brain, and the best heart, the finest moral fiber, and the most skilled genius and power that the American Negro can furnish for her civilization and redemption." Potter could not have made a clearer statement of the Colonization Society's new program.[56]

Despite Northern criticism, Potter's program found sympathetic verification in the missionary tone of Chicago's and Atlanta's congresses on Africa. But criticism mounted from another side. Within months of the society's announcement of its change of policy, Bishop Turner wrote to demand: "What is the Colonization Society doing to meet the urgent wants of the colored people hankering for Africa?" By 1893, he sought to fill the void caused by its rejection of mass emigration by launching his own journal to promote emigration, seeking to get regular shipping routes to Africa, and taking a well-publicized tour of the continent to inspire greater interest in it. After his rebuff by black delegates at the Chicago congress, Turner called a more sympathetic national convention of black Americans in November 1893 to consider emigration. Believing that "thousands and tens of thousands" of black people saw their condition much as he did, Turner said that he called the convention only after years of waiting for other black leaders in "the anti-emigration party or anti-Negro nationalization party" to address the situation and in the belief that "further silence is not only a disgrace but a crime."[57]

Eight hundred delegates appeared at Turner's Cincinnati convention and cheered his opening address, which appealed for an exodus. But when the convention's committee on emigration reported out a resolution asking

African Methodist Episcopal Bishop Henry McNeal Turner, spokesman for African emigration (Henry McNeal Turner Papers, Moorland-Spingarn Research Center, Howard University)

black people to "turn their attention to the civilization of Africa as the only hope of the Negro race as a race," it was clear that it would not pass. Hoping to avoid defeat, Turner returned it to committee for revision. At the same time, his thunder was being stolen by Albion Tourgée. Unable to accept Turner's invitation to attend the convention, Tourgée sent his greetings, which the delegates met with a storm of applause. They voted to establish a National Equal Rights Council under Turner's leadership to work with Tourgée's National Citizens Rights Association. The bishop avoided defeat on emigration by winning unanimous approval of a compromise resolution asking the council to consider recommending migration to sections of the country less oppressive to black people. Turner's emigration plan was repulsed and the Equal Rights Council died aborning. The bishop returned to Atlanta to harvest his sour grapes. "What under heaven would [I] want with a national convention of over seven hundred delegates to endorse African emigration, when at least two million of colored people here in the South are ready to start for Africa at any moment," he asked. Thereafter, Turner pursued his African dream through an International Migration Society. But, as with earlier attempts, its mix of illusion, fiscal irresponsibility, and petty thievery mocked the longing of his people for relief.[58]

Into this picture stepped the young teacher from Tuskegee, Alabama, Booker T. Washington. He spoke in Turner's Atlanta. His speech said many things to many people, but against Bishop Turner's elusive African dream, Washington posed a more realistic Southern strategy. "To those of my race who depend on bettering their condition in a foreign land or who underestimate the importance of cultivating friendly relations with the Southern white man, who is their next-door neighbor," he argued, "I would say: 'Cast down your bucket where you are'—cast it down in making friends in every manly way of the people of all races by whom we are surrounded." At the same time, Turner's efforts were repudiated by two old allies in colonization, Edward W. Blyden and Alexander Crummell. Blyden cited Washington's work at Tuskegee as meeting the needs of the hour. "All agitation for the movement for large masses of negroes to Africa is at the present time unwise and premature," he wrote. "What I would inculcate upon the negro in the United States now is a modest temperateness of behavior—an unpretentiousness and unambitious deportment. Politics at present is not his field. All bitterness and darkness of spirit, all sour unreasonableness, should be laid aside." Crummell cheered Blyden's repudiation of Turner: "I am very glad of his thrust into t[he] ribs of that truculent screeching & screaming creature—Bishop Turner." A few years later, the *Independent* commented: "Bishop Turner talks more and says more foolish things than any other bishop of the African Methodist Church."[59]

Ten days after Booker T. Washington offered his criticism of Bishop Turner's African dream at the opening of the Cotton States Exposition, thousands of black Baptists gathered at Atlanta's Friendship Baptist Church. Afro-Baptists had long been the largest single black religious community in the United States. Now, the frustration of their efforts to cooperate with both Northern and Southern white Baptists had crystallized in a determination to organize as a separate racially united Baptist convention. Earlier efforts had commonly called themselves an "American" Baptist convention. But in 1895, without rejecting the hope that lay in the full rights of American citizenship, they organized the National Baptist Convention. It was and is the largest Afro-American organization in the nation, "the church with the soul of a nation," cradling the aspirations of black Americans for national recognition into the twentieth century.[60]

If Turner's effort to maintain the emigration side of the Colonization Society's tradition ended in bankruptcy, Bishop Potter's attempt to reshape it for a twentieth-century missionary task was no more fruitful. He failed to stimulate new interest in the society or raise funds in the depression years. In 1891, the society and its New York affiliate sent Orator Fuller Cook to study Liberia College and promote the development of industrial education there. His early reports confirmed suspicions of weakness and mismanagement at the institution. In 1895, the society agreed to support his plan for an agricultural settlement and school in the interior highlands. It paid to construct a road into the interior, lay out a farm, and begin a girls' school. Cook also became president of Liberia College, but he presided over the collapse of all these efforts in the continuing financial crisis.[61]

In 1898, the American consul general in Liberia, William H. Heard, charged that "Prof. Cook came to Liberia with the idea that the white man must rule under any and all circumstances, and that his agency for the Colonization Society and presidency of Liberia College made him President of Liberia and manager of the [American] Legation." Heard's charges went beyond mere pique at Cook's high-handed ways. He reported that the farm settlement was operated by slave labor, as were many farms run by Liberians descended from American slaves. There, as in the Old South, the slave system had its whip and driver, and was justified as "a blessing to the natives and a means of civilization." Cook spent only three months a year in Liberia looking after the college and farm, said Heard. A professor managed the college and an overseer controlled the farm and slaves during the rest of the year. "The Colonization Society has missed its high and holy calling and is now the seeker after gold and the enricher of an individual who has no interest in Liberia, only as it affords him comfort and puts dollars into his pocket," Heard concluded. "Even the color line has been tightly drawn by this learned professor." In 1899, Orator Cook resigned as the Colonization Society's agent and Henry Codman Potter resigned as its president.[62]

**D**espite negative reports by white missionaries, Africa had long been a source of self-identity for black Americans. Missionary executives and the American Colonization Society saw a providential role for a well-educated few missionaries in the redemption of Africa, but masses of black people in the South were interested in returning to Africa. Yet they had ceased to be Africans and long experience in the United States had made them at least African-Americans. Their yearning to reify what was now at most a symbolic reality is best explained by the nation's failure to grant them full civil equality.

# 4

## In Search of Civil Equity

American social Christianity's primary response to race relations in the post-war South was the home missions emphasis on education. It was challenged by the African colonization tradition until the end of the nineteenth century. A third tradition stemmed from radical abolitionism's concern for the civil rights of black Americans. It held that education and civil rights were concurrent, not sequential, requirements for a free people. The weakness of this tradition was foreshadowed by division within the American Anti-Slavery Society in 1865. Black and white leaders in racial reform carried it into the 1890s, but its organizations collapsed in defeat by the middle of the decade.

In April 1865, just as Northern victory in the Civil War was abolishing slavery in the South, leaders of the American Anti-Slavery Society were locked in bitter debate. William Lloyd Garrison, Samuel J. May, Jr., and others reasoned that the abolition of slavery should be celebrated by the end of the society itself. There was more work to be done, they said, but it ought to be carried on in cooperation with other people of goodwill in the freedmen's aid societies. But Wendell Phillips, Frederick Douglass, and others argued that freedmen's aid was an "old clothes movement," that the struggle for equal rights was not yet won, and that the American Anti-Slavery Society should turn to that struggle with renewed vigor. The roots of division ran deep in Garrisonian abolitionism and, in its moment of apparent triumph, there was an irrevocable split in its ranks.

The division arose from conflicting priorities. Garrison had shocked his followers by denying that the franchise was a natural right and suggesting that universal suffrage for the freedmen should not be expected immediately. Under attack, he recanted, but the equivocation was a matter of record. Those who followed him in urging an end to the Anti-Slavery Society and rechanneling their efforts into the freedmen's aid societies were suspected of being insufficiently committed to the civil and political rights of the freedmen. Wendell Phillips's argument carried the day in 1865 by a margin of two to one. Garrison was invited to continue as its president, but he and his followers resigned from the Anti-Slavery Society. For Garrison, slavery was more a moral than a political issue. His message was that "immediate emancipation meant gradual rehabilitation, not social revolution." By contrast, Phillips measured the health of the republic by the continuing political agitation for reform of its institutions. Elected to succeed Garrison, Phillips presided over the society until 1870, when passage of the Fifteenth Amendment seemed to secure the civil rights of the freedmen and the society was dissolved.[1]

Phillips's active identification with and Garrison's criticism of labor reform in the postwar era was indicative of their differences. Emancipation of the slaves and the development of radical Republicanism led Phillips's associate in labor reform, Jesse Henry Jones, to vest hope in the Republican party as "wholly for Jesus Christ and Humanity." By 1871 Jones was convinced that the Republicans were irredeemably corrupt and he outlined elaborate plans for "A NEW POLITICAL PARTY, TO BE CALLED JESUS CHRIST'S PARTY." It would work for absolute political and social equality and abolition of all discrimination based on race, class, or sex. A year later, he and George Edwin McNeill organized Boston's Christian Labor Union, which has been called "the earliest known American organization dedicated to the propagation of social gospel principles." While they agitated for labor reform, Jones and McNeill promoted the civil rights of the freedmen. Like Phillips, they defined America's race problem in political rather than simply in moral terms and would use the church and state as instruments for radical social change. Apart from two or three personal friends, however, the Christian Labor Union's only supporter was a black minister in Arkansas.[2]

While the Christian Labor Union struggled to survive, Wendell Phillips relived scenes from his younger days. In January 1875, President Ulysses Grant ordered federal troops to sustain Louisiana's Republican administration in a disputed election. When a meeting to protest Grant's action convened at Boston's Faneuil Hall, Phillips was not invited because he supported the president. But he appeared anyway and was called to the platform to state his position. Prodded by hecklers, he argued that Grant was morally bound to preserve life and public order in the South. To have done otherwise would mean abandoning the freedmen to their enemies. "What more contemptible object than a nation which summons four millions of Negroes to [freedom] and then leaves them defenseless," Phillips asked. "What more pitiable object than the President, vested with full power to protect these hunted men, if he leave them defenseless?" Wendell Phillips was engaged in a rear guard action, but Jesse Jones recalled it as "His Last Battle and One of His Greatest Victories."[3]

Even among his admirers, like Boston's Monday Lecturer, Joseph Cook, and the Irish-American writer, John Boyle O'Reilly, Phillips's argument had no immediate support. Cook's family was modestly antislavery, but he became a prominent supporter of the American Missionary Association's work for freedmen's education when he began lecturing in Boston in 1874. Yet Cook believed that the civil experiment in Reconstruction had failed badly. "The problem of rightly reconstructing the Southern States has not been equaled in complexity in history," he told an AMA convention. "We think we have finished the case, but the case has nearly finished us. Did the negro succeed in Mississippi, where he had a majority? I am his friend, but he tried to fleece the white man there; and if I had been in Mississippi, I never would have submitted to the rule of black rascals or white." Declaring Reconstruction in the deep South a failure, Cook argued that "the negro has made mistakes and he is going to the wall, even when he has a majority; and his inferiority in politics results from his lack of education."[4]

After fleeing from an abortive rebellion in Ireland, John Boyle O'Reilly settled in Boston to become editor of the Roman Catholic *Pilot*. When Wendell Phillips defended federal intervention in Louisiana, O'Reilly thought enfranchisement of the freedmen had been a mistake and lamented the work of radical Reconstruction in the South. "God help the South!" said the *Pilot*. "Wrong after wrong has been done to her since the war." But on the one hundredth anniversary of Daniel O'Connell's birth, Wendell Phillips delivered a eulogy to the Irish nationalist. O'Connell was an agitator who was eager to speak a word for justice, Phillips told his Irish audience, a creator of public opinion who rejected the support of American slaveholders for Ireland's cause. O'Reilly saw the virtues of his hero exemplified in Phillips himself and determined to promote empathy between Irish and black Americans. On a Southern tour in 1885, O'Reilly stopped in Nashville where he saw segregated facilities in a railway station. In the "Waiting Room," white people were "carefully attended and comfortable" in "separate rooms for white men and women, well ventilated and well kept." The "Colored People's Waiting Room" was "a wretched, poorly-furnished room" crowded with men and women, where mothers sat with their children on an unwashed floor. After two days in Nashville, O'Reilly sensed that "something was the matter either with God or humanity in the South" and swore: "If ever the colored question comes up again, I shall be counted in with the black man." He urged a black audience to use the franchise to end segregation. "Among those who love justice and liberty," there ought not be "any question of race, or creed, or color," he said; "every heart that beats for humanity beats with the oppressed. The sympathy of the world is with you, and the time is not distant when you will tear down that infamous inscription from the Nashville depot."[5]

If the franchise gave inadequate protection, O'Reilly favored the primal weapons of racial unity, pride, and self-defense. He affirmed the unity of the human race, but he also saw beauty in God's creation of racial differences. He spoke eloquently of the qualities of the Negro. His natural kindliness and piety fit him to be a good citizen, O'Reilly said. "The negro is a new man, a free man, a spiritual man, a hearty man," he wrote. "And he can be a great man if he will avoid modeling himself on the whites." Continued aggression against black people in the South would bring an enraged public conscience to their defense, but the freedmen might have to rely upon primal instincts. A proud, united black people must be "strong enough to make the whole republic quiver when a black man is mistreated," for their struggle with Southern Anglo-Saxons was a struggle for survival. "No race has ever obtained fair play from the Anglo-Saxon without being ready to fight," said O'Reilly. "The Southern blacks are fighting for the existence of their race. And they cannot fight the Anglo-Saxon by lying down under his feet." Given that reality, he argued, "the black race in the South must face the inevitable—DEFEND YOUR-SELF!" A flood of protest condemned him for preaching an un-Catholic and un-American "gospel of blood and strife." O'Reilly replied that he had appealed only to "the great Catholic and American principle of resisting wrong and outrage, of protecting life and home and the honor of families by all lawful means" when all else failed. "We shall preach this always, for black and white, North and South, please God."[6]

When John Boyle O'Reilly died in 1890, a black lawyer in Boston recalled that the Irish editor came to his people's defense at the time of Wendell Phillips's death. O'Reilly had penned a tribute to the eloquent abolitionist:

His life was a ceaseless protest, and his voice
    was a prophet's cry
To be true to the Truth and faithful, though the world
    were arrayed for the Lie.
Come, workers; here was a teacher, and the lesson
    he taught was good:
There are no classes or races, but one human
    brotherhood;
There are no creeds to be outlawed, no colors
    of skin debarred;
Mankind is one in its rights and wrongs—one right,
    one hope, one guard.
By his life he taught, by his death we learn
    the great reformer's creed:
The right to be free, and the hope to be just,
    and the guard against selfish greed.

When Wendell Phillips's death and race relations in the South gave reason to despair, said the attorney, O'Reilly spoke "words in our behalf that were Christian, and anathemas that were just." In "bold and defiant language he denounced the murderers of our people and advised us to strike the tyrants back."[7]

B y 1885, the leading exponents of Wendell Phillips's social creed were not his Boston associates, but two men who experienced the Civil War and Reconstruction from rival camps, Albion Winegar Tourgée and George Washington Cable. Edmund Wilson suggests that they emulated the character of their rival sectional prototype. Tourgée, the Ohio-born carpetbagger, became a Yankee Cavalier; Cable, the New Orleans Confederate, became the Puritan conscience of the New South. Their embodiment of rival sectional characteristics was evident in their different strategies for racial reform, but their differences should not obscure their common purposes. Prior to 1900, the social gospel produced no more determined advocates of civil equity for black people than this strangely matched pair.[8]

Albion Tourgée inherited an inquiring religious instinct and love of controversy from his father, an Ohio farmer. The Western Reserve's tradition of a local democracy of landowning yeomen shaped his conception of the good society. Entering the University of Rochester in 1859, he was uncommitted to abolitionism and teased his fiancée about "the immense responsibilities which are resting on the women of America as regards the crying sin of Negro slavery." Caught up in the Republican campaign of 1860, Tourgée joined the Union armies marching to the South within six months of Lincoln's election. His experience in battle and first contacts with slaves produced the elements of a religious fervor for racial justice that distinguished his later career. Captured by Confederate forces in Tennessee, he studied Spanish and read Cervantes's *Don Quixote* during his four months in prison. Mustered out of the army, Tourgée married and moved to Greensboro, North Carolina, to practice law and enter the politics of Reconstruction. As a leader of the state's radical Republicans and Methodist laymen, he shared the home missionaries' sense of the need to redeem the "poor, misguided, and mismanaged South" from its "slough of ignorance and prejudice" by recreating it along Northern lines. In North Carolina's constitutional convention of 1867, Tourgée advocated reform of the criminal and tax codes, extension of the franchise and eligibility for office to all citizens, and the popular election of all state officers. Despite tough opposition from Conservatives, the carpetbagger fulfilled all of his campaign pledges except repudiation of the old state debt. Subsequently, he was elected a judge of Superior Court and served on a commission to revise the state's civil code. In the opposition press, a "Tourgée" was a "jackass" or a cross between "an ass and a lion." He was a target of Ku Klux Klan activity and a vigorous critic of the "Khristian Knights."[9]

By contrast, George Washington Cable was born to a slaveowning merchant family in New Orleans. The cosmopolitan city gave a rich background to his later novels, but his approach to social issues was largely influenced by the egalitarianism of the Declaration of Independence and the Calvinism of the Reverend Benjamin Morgan Palmer at New Orleans' First Presbyterian Church. "Principles were everything to me," he recalled. Leaving school at fifteen when his father died in 1859, Cable worked to support his family. "At sixteen I was for Union, Slavery, and a White Man's Government," he remembered. "Secession, when it came, seemed a dreadful thing. Yet . . . I soon learned to hurrah with a devout fervor for Jeff. Davis and the 'Stars and Bars.' I could sign the right of secession, too, 'and nail 't wi' scripture.'" When Union forces occupied the city in April 1862, the Cables refused to take the oath of allegiance to the United States. The boy and his sisters took refuge behind Confederate lines, where he joined the Southern army in October 1863. Years of military service matured his critical capacity. "One of the first things I learned without being taught," he recalled, "was the proneness of public sentiment to be wrong in any case." Rumors that Georgia would secede from the Confederacy caused the logic of secession to crumble. "But if I saw the unwisdom of secession," he wrote, "I saw no unrighteousness in fighting for slavery."[10]

When he returned to New Orleans, Cable still found in the proslavery argument a rationale for his part in the war. "I saw the Freedmen in all his offensiveness, multitudinous, unclean, stupid, ugly, ignorant, and insolent," he wrote. "If the much feared 'war of races' should come, I was going to be in the ranks of the white race fighting for the subjugation of the blacks." So he protested the intermingling of the races on horsecars and at teachers' meetings in postwar New Orleans. But the intellectual monument of the Old South began to crumble upon careful scrutiny. As a churchman and critic of Louisiana's corrupt politics, Cable became a New South reformer. He was interested in Presbyterian missions, prison reform, and attacks on the Louisiana Lottery Company. Talk of a "black peasantry" offended his egalitarian temper. As a reporter for a New Orleans newspaper, Cable watched the operation of the city's unsegregated school system. "I saw, to my great and rapid edification," he recalled, "white ladies teaching Negro boys; colored women showing the graces and dignity of mental and moral refinement; children of both races standing in the same classes and giving each other peaceable, friendly, effective competition; and black classes, with black teachers, pushing intelligently up into the intricacies of high-school mathematics." Beyond that, said Cable, "I saw that the day must come when the Negro must share and enjoy in common with the white race the whole scale of *public* rights and advantages provided under American government." When a New Orleans mob drove nonwhite students from an integrated public school, he decried both the mob's aim and its method. Cable's early short stories probed the injustice of caste distinctions that figured prominently in his later novels and his protest against segregation in 1875 prefigured his later work in racial reform.[11]

While Cable had yet to make his defense of the freedmen's civil equity, Albion Tourgée made his reputation as an advocate of black civil rights. His most important novels, published between 1874 and 1883, were a social history of the Civil War and Reconstruction. They told the story of a nation made up of two essentially different societies: one embodying a democratic liberty more or less in tune with the will of God manifest in the progress of the modern world, the other bound to an anachronistic social order based on racial caste. Told with an unabashedly Northern antislavery bias, the tale still sought to do justice to the best in both communities and expose hypocrisy and inhumanity on all sides. At worst, the novels suffered from shortcomings common to late nineteenth-century romances. Contrived plots with unlikely resolutions too often served merely as a framework for moralizing speeches the author could not suppress. "We do not think him a novelist primarily," wrote a sympathetic black critic. "He does not create many men of many minds. All his offspring are little Tourgées—they preach his sermons and pray his prayers."[12]

Tourgée was at his best in telling that part of the story closest to his own experience. *A Fool's Errand* and *Bricks without Straw* told of the promise and failure of Reconstruction. The former is only faintly disguised autobiography. Its hero, Comfort Servosse, like Tourgée, was born in the Midwest of Huguenot descent. Inspired by a sense of mission to help reconstruct the South, Servosse moves his family to North Carolina at the close of the war. His democratic egalitarianism leads him to advocate the rights of freedmen and their allies among poor white Unionists. Despite the warnings of friend and foe, Servosse emerges as a leader of the Union League and the constitutional convention that attempts to implement democratic reforms. These efforts meet powerful opposition in the Ku Klux Klan and Servosse ultimately realizes that his work has been undone by the white South's continuing commitment to white supremacy.

"We tried to superimpose the civilization, the idea of the North, upon the South at a moment's warning," Servosse/Tourgée reflected. "We presumed that, by the suppression of rebellion, the Southern white man had become identical with the Caucasian of the North in thought and sentiment; and that the slave, by emancipation, had become a saint and a Solomon at once. So we tried to build up communities there which should be identical in thought, sentiment, growth, and development, with those of the North. It was a FOOL'S ERRAND." The self-acclaimed "fool" distinguished between two types of the class. One was buffoon, the trifling jester. The genuine "fool," who was moved by "the poetry of faith" was the other. "He may run after a will-o'-the-wisp, which the Wise deride, but to him it is the veritable star of hope," said the Fool. "He differs from his fellow mortals chiefly in this, that he sees or believes what they do not, and consequently undertakes what they never attempt." The self-acclaimed Fool spoke, not in bitter self-reproach, but in the ironic, biblical mood of the "fool for Christ." He is the man who lives by faith and not by sight. Sharing a "simple, undoubting faith" with Genius, Fool is distinguished from his fellow believer in the eyes of the worldly wise by his lack of success. "If he succeed in his endeavor, the world stops laughing, and calls him a Genius; if he fails, it laughs the more, and derides his undertaking as A FOOL'S ERRAND."[13]

Having told his own story, Tourgée turned to the other side of the problem in *Bricks without Straw*. It tells how the freedman, as represented by Nimbus Ware, an intelligent but illiterate freedman, and Eliab Hill, a crippled, mulatto preacher, try to take advantage of the opportunities of their emancipation. As he assumes his new identity as a man and citizen, Ware affronts the white community's spirit of racial caste, which frustrates his effort. "I'se a free man an' ef enny on 'em comes ter Ku Klux me I'll put a bullet t'rough dem!" he says. "I will, by God! Ef I breaks the law I'll take the consequences like a man, but I'll be damned ef ennybody shall Ku Kluck me without somebody's goin' 'long with me, when I drops outen dis world!" But when Eliab Hill is martyred by disguised assailants, Ware realizes that resistance to the organized opposition is useless and leaves the South. Tourgée suggested that the appropriate biblical analogue for the emancipation of the slaves was not the exodus, but the ordeal of the children of Israel under the harsh Egyptian pharaoh. The nation gave the freedmen the form of freedom but denied them a sustaining sympathy in the period of transition. "We will not aid you nor protect you. Though you are ignorant, from you will we demand the works of wisdom. Though you are weak, great things shall be required at your hands," it said. "Like the ancient taskmaster, the Nation said: '*There shall no straw be given you, yet shall ye deliver the tale of bricks.*' "[14]

Protesting the injustice of the demand for "bricks without straw" in 1870, Tourgée began to appeal for federal aid to education in proportion to illiteracy in local communities. The plea recurred in both *A Fool's Errand* and *Bricks without Straw*. In a work of nonfiction, *An Appeal to Caesar*, he appealed to the "Caesar" of a democracy, its citizenry, for federal aid as the nation's just share of responsibility for the problem. The equality of the Negro was a part of the egalitarian trend of modern life, said Tourgée, a constitutional commitment and moral necessity. Theories of black inferiority were unfounded and irrelevant. "Whether the colored man is the equal, the inferior, or the superior of the white race has not been specifically revealed to me," he said. "Some things are self-evident, and among these is the fact that every argument and demonstration by which the inherent inferiority of the African of the United States has been so frequently established has been shown by the irrefragable evidence of experience to be false." Education was not required for the civil equality of the freedmen; but it would help to shape equality and minimize

social disruption as they assumed their rightful place in society. Federal aid
was no panacea, said Tourgée. Without adequate safeguards, it could support
an education in prejudice. Under adequate control, federal support for common schools could help both races in the South. But when the Blair Bill for
federal aid seemed to have a chance of passage in 1890, he feared that it would
give too little support to black schools and helped to defeat it.[15]

When Tourgée offered his summary appeal to Caesar in 1884, George
Washington Cable had just begun to fight. He addressed New Orleans's Christian educators in 1881 on the parable of the Good Samaritan. "The Samaritans
were a mongrel, half-idolatrous race upon whom the Jews looked down as
emphatically their inferiors," said Cable. America's Samaritans were the Chinese, Indians, Irish, and Negroes. "Do we love this neighbor as ourselves? Do we
do altogether likewise to this Samaritan?" he asked. "Do we give him our seat in
God's house? Or do we tell him to go to the gallery? When he makes his peace
with God, does he take the blessed cup and bread with us or after us? Have we
a brotherly love for the Samaritans of our land and of our times?" Admitting
that he did not so love New Orleans's Samaritans, Cable thought it was his
duty to act as if he did. In September 1883, he was to address the National
Conference on Charities and Corrections in Louisville, Kentucky, on "one of
the Negro's grossest wrongs," the convict lease system. En route, Cable saw a
mother and her daughter segregated in a railroad car with a gang of convicts.
"The mother and child sat on in silence in that foul hole, the conductor
having . . . refused them admission elsewhere because they were of African
blood," Cable recalled. "Had the child been white, and the mother not its
natural but its hired guardian, she could have sat anywhere in the train, and no
one would have ventured to object, even had she been as black as the mouth
of the coalpit to which her loathsome fellow passengers were being carried in
chains." The incident confirmed his determination to tell the story "first to the
South, and then to the world" and "demand a trial of the Freedmen's case in
the world's court on its equities."[16]

Cable tried "the Freedmen's Case in Equity" before students at the University of Alabama in June and the American Social Science Association at Sara-
toga, New York, in September 1884. The race issue was "the greatest social
problem before the American people," said Cable. It arose from conceptions
of the Negro as an alien, naturally subordinate and incapable of elevation to
civil equality. After the emancipation and enfranchisement of the slaves and
the withdrawal of federal troops, the South developed a system of "vicious
evasions," which prompted his review of sentiments hostile to the freed-

men's civil rights. "One of the marvels of future history," Cable predicted, would be that it was thought "a small matter for six millions of people to be subjected to a system of oppression so rank that nothing could make it seem small except the fact that they had already been ground under it for a century and a half." The nation could not tolerate a large class of noncitizens, he argued. "Every interest in the land demands that the Freedmen be free to become the same sort of American citizen he would be if . . . he were white."[17]

Cable claimed to speak for a silent minority, "thousands of Southern-born white men and women who see the wrong and folly of these things, silently blush for them, and withhold their open protests" because they doubt "the power of a just cause." Critical reaction to his position equated civil rights with social equality, said Cable; but the right of individuals to choose their social relations was not at issue. "All the relations of life that go by *impersonal right* are Civil relations," he wrote. "All that go by *personal choice* are Social relations. For the one we make laws; for the other every one consults his own pleasure." Social distinctions were natural in human relations, but civil distinctions of privilege or deprivation were anathema. "We have a country large enough for all the *unsociability* anybody may want," he said, "but not for *incivility* either by or without the warrant of law." In claiming to speak for a thoughtful Southern white minority, Cable appealed to a more cautious group, which counseled patience to all sides. The steady development of common sympathies over decades, they argued, would slowly win recognition of the freedmen's rights. Cable rebuked these social evolutionists for compromising civil justice. Their "heartless" position measured progress in geological rather than logical terms. Southern white self-interest, he said, was with the transcendent principles of justice in demanding recognition of the freedmen's civil rights like those of their fellow citizens. "We ourselves" could not have made "a cleaner, clearer statement of our case," wrote *AME Church Review* editor Benjamin Tucker Tanner. He bemoaned such "dead flies" in Cable's "Silent South ointment" as the distinction between the civil and social realms, but agreed that it might be well to take up one battle at a time.[18]

Cable moved to New England in 1885, shifting his primary appeal from the white South to the black and white North. He urged black audiences to exercise their civil rights to the fullest and told Northern whites that discrimination practiced against the freedman was aimed at his best aspiration. "As long as he is content to travel and lodge as a ragamuffin, frequent the vilest places of amusement, laze about in the streets, shun the public library and the

George Washington Cable, Southern critic of the new order of race relations (Louisiana Collection, Tulane University Library)

best churches and colleges, and neglect every political duty of his citizenship, no white man could be freer," said Cable; "but the farther he rises above such life as this the more he is galled and tormented with ignominious discriminations made against him as a public citizen."[19]

In 1887, Cable toured the South from Virginia to Louisiana and Tennessee. At Vanderbilt University, he appealed to the best in Southern and American traditions for justice in race relations. The Civil War had not resolved the race problem, he said. The North had won a war to preserve the Union and the South had found a way to preserve its caste system apart from slavery. Civil inequities visited upon the freedmen were maintained by the refusal of a national majority to interfere in the affairs of the separate states. The entrenchment of white supremacists behind the wall of states rights was reinforced by a growing opinion that their racial elitism was not only a necessary evil but a positive good. But racial elitism was an alien, un-American import, said Cable. What was needed was the Americanization of the South's ruling class. "Bring the men of best blood and best brain in the South today, not to a new and strange doctrine, but back to the faith of their fathers," he pleaded. "Let but this be done, and there will be a peace and a union between the nation's two great sections such as they have not seen since Virginia's Washington laid down his sword, and her Jefferson his pen." Despite warnings of a hostile reception, Cable found Southern audiences willing to listen and engage in reasonable debate. That response reinforced his belief that he spoke for a silent minority of Southern white opinion and was not far from a larger, more cautious group of Southerners.[20]

Convinced that a solitary crusade was insufficient to mobilize public opinion, Cable sought a base for broader influence. He organized an "Open Letter Club" to generate essays on regional problems from its members, exchange them for criticism, and publish the revised drafts as symposia in journals. With the help of Vanderbilt professor William H. Baskervill, Cable won the support of distinguished Southern professionals, such as Atticus Haygood and Johns Hopkins University's economist, Richard T. Ely, and pledges of support from important New York editors, including the Christian Union's Lyman Abbott, the Independent's William Hayes Ward, and the Forum's Lorretus Metcalf.[21] Believing that an open forum was sure of good results, Cable hoped to include viewpoints other than his own. It would be a town meeting in the press. Its test came in October 1888, when Senator J. B. Eustis argued that racial hostility was divinely appointed, natural in human affairs. It frustrated the work of Northern racial egalitarians in the South and manifested itself in antagonism to blacks even in New England. The Southern senator concluded that the problem was better handled locally, without hypocritical interference from outside agitators who should attend to problems in their own region.[22]

The racial problem was a matter for national attention because a handicap to a part of the nation affected all of it, countered Atticus Haygood. Were the North to leave the South to deal with the problem without help, it "would be guilty of an immeasurable injustice, of an unpardonable sin against the whole

American nation" and "the Kingdom of Jesus Christ in the earth," he argued. "For, whoever brought the Negroes to this country, whoever held them in slavery for shorter or longer times, the Northern people, under God, made them free people and voters, and so made the Negro problem a matter of concern to the whole American people." Eustis's insistence that racial hostility was inherent in human relations ignored a factor that Haygood thought was at the heart of the matter. "There is no place in his philosophy of the subject for the Providence of God," said the bishop. "No view of the Negro problem that leaves God out—that leaves out the conservative and saving influences of the Christian religion—can add anything of value to the discussion." Haygood found little to approve in Eustis's proposals. "No question involving the rights and wrongs of men . . . was ever yet settled . . . by any system of mere repression," he said. "And to those who believe in Jesus Christ it is equally certain that nothing can be rightly settled that is not settled in harmony with the teachings of the Sermon on the Mount." Hoping to mobilize the "silent South," Cable made Haygood's reply to Eustis the Open Letter Club's first topic for discussion. In February 1889, Cable, Baskervill, and other prominent white Southerners endorsed Haygood's response to Eustis in a symposium and reprinted it as a pamphlet for distribution throughout the South. Shortly thereafter, Cable launched a second symposium on the race issue. Richard T. Ely was to develop a third one on "The Economics of the Southern Question." Cable also proposed that the Open Letter Club treat the crop lien system and methods used to manipulate Southern black voters. Before the second of these projects was finished, his club was a dead letter.[23]

In November 1889, Cable was in Nashville to speak at Fisk University and confer with Baskervill and a black attorney, J. C. Napier, about the Open Letter Club. He dined with the lawyer and his family at Napier's home. "The love of the apostles for their fellowmen is marvelous, breaking down prejudices of creed and race," wrote Richard T. Ely. Supported by religious conviction and philosophical thought, prejudice against Gentiles, sinners, and outcasts in their day must have been even greater than racial prejudice in the South, he said. "We know what hostility would be aroused in our South should prominent church leaders eat at the table with negroes and otherwise associate with them on terms of social equality." Christian love carried Peter and Paul through many struggles across greater barriers to victory, Ely said. But George Washington Cable's meal with the Napier family became a public scandal in Nashville. Its press attacked him bitterly, spelling the end of the Open Letter Club. His associates were pressured to withdraw from it to protect themselves and their institutions. "We broke bread together. Was I wrong in that," Cable asked defiantly. "To anyone who answers yes, I can only reply, Shame on you!" Within weeks, Baskervill was threatened with physical violence if he invited Cable to return. He packed up the files of the Open Letter Club and shipped them off to his friend's home in New England. Never, since the end of the Civil War, had Cable's "Silent South" been quite so silent.[24]

**W**hile the Open Letter Club was breaking up, black people were organizing for civil recognition. In 1887, the black journalist, T. Thomas Fortune, called for the organization of an Afro-American League. His proposal sought to improve on the convention tradition in black politics by asserting political independence, maintaining a continuing national organization, and establishing local units throughout the nation. But it languished until Fortune found support among the black churches. With endorsements from the AME Zion pastor Alexander Walters and John Wesley Cromwell, the new editor of the *AME Church Review*, the proposal won widespread support. White people were not invited to participate in the league, but some of them endorsed it. Cautioning against undue secrecy, the *Independent* observed that "*Insurrection* is a bad word to get started." But a public organization dedicated to maintaining black rights through legislative and judicial processes could make a significant contribution, said the journal. "It will get not a little help from white men," said the editors, "and will need it."[25]

Albion Tourgée applauded the new black militancy. Black people had waited for others to act on their behalf and been dependent on the caprice and inconstancy of such support for too long, he said. Organization of the Afro-American League was a first step to "self-assertive freedom." In the South, it might lead some to martyrdom, he thought, but it was time for black men to have a list of martyrs who died for freedom "to counterbalance the rather overcrowded one which testifies to their long-suffering endurance of oppression." Tourgée privately confessed his hopes for the Afro-American League to a black educator. "It should be for action—*not display*," he wrote. "It should hold no public meetings, make no speeches, issue no appeals; but should represent the effective power of the colored race. You have had promises enough and pretty nearly laws enough. Now you should begin to demand enforcement and show your ability to *compell* [sic] performance of pledges." An old foe of Southern white vigilantes, still Tourgée admired their determination and tactical skill. The Afro-American League might learn from them. "It must work with a club not a nosegay," he counseled. "To be effective, the League should be at least semi-secret. It should hold no meetings beyond a few members; should keep no records, except the names and addresses of the officers; should be organized by word of mouth alone; and be as flexible and intangible as the Ku Klux Klan. Indeed, this should be your model."[26]

By late 1889, there were forty local affiliates of the league, from Boston to San Francisco in the West and Albany, Georgia, in the South. Summoned by Alexander Walters, 143 delegates gathered in Chicago for the National Afro-American League's organizing convention in January 1890. Joseph C. Price, president of Livingstone College, was elected its president and Fortune became its secretary. Educated at mission schools in North Carolina and Pennsylvania, Price founded the AME Zion college at Salisbury, North Carolina. His success seemed to make him a living example of the racial self-help of the "new Negro" that the missionaries acclaimed.[27] Over the objection of those who opposed accepting advice from any white man, a letter of greetings and counsel was received from Tourgée. But his plan for a Klan-like organization apparently had no support. Instead, the league adopted Fortune's plan for a national bank and bureaus of cooperatives, industrial education, migration, legislation, and problems peculiar to the South. The league endorsed the Blair Education Bill. It condemned the widespread loss of the franchise in the South but did not resolve in favor of federal intervention in Southern elections. The theme was self-help for survival.[28]

Archbishop John Ireland was one of the prominent white social Christians who supported the Afro-American League. A chaplain in the first regiment to respond to Lincoln's call to arms in 1861, the Minnesota prelate was a favorite at Grand Army of the Republic encampments and the most prominent Republican in the Roman Catholic hierarchy. In April 1890, Ireland's address at St. Augustine's Church in Washington, D.C., attracted wide attention for its bold attack on race prejudice. "My solution of the Negro problem is to declare that there is no problem to be solved," he said, "since we are all equal, as brothers should be, and we will in consistency with our American and Christian principles treat alike black and white. I know no color line. I will acknowledge none." It was not possible to reconcile the ideals of American Christianity with racial bias, Ireland insisted. "I warn those who continue to hold hatred" in their hearts "that the day of their repentance will come, and a bitter day for them it will be." Other racial egalitarians admired the archbishop's message. "We wish he were Pope," cheered the editors of the Protestant *Independent*. In January 1891, the Minneapolis branch of the Afro-American League invited Ireland to address an Emancipation Day celebration. White men were divided by class and intelligence, he told the black audience; that might be natural and acceptable. "But let there be no barrier against mere color," Ireland insisted. "The notion that God by special interposition marked off the subdivisions of the human family, and set upon each one an indelible seal of permanence is the dream of ignorance or bigotry." Civil equality and social integration was the only practical solution. "It is not possible to keep up a wall of separation between whites and blacks, and the attempt to do this is a declaration of continuous war."[29]

The founding meeting of the Afro-American League generated enough interest to add many new local chapters. Organizing fever spread a month later, when 445 delegates met in Washington, D.C., to form the Citizens' Equal Rights Association, which made Price chairman by acclamation. Repeating Atticus Haygood's and George Washington Cable's conservative arguments, Price said that black Americans sought civil, not social, equality. He quoted Edmund Burke's answer to the question, "Who are the real disturbers of society?" Burke and Price replied: "Those who attempt by outrage and violence to deprive men of any advantage under the laws proclaim war against society." The Equal Rights Association's platform stressed good conduct, education, and the acquisition of wealth as the means to break down the barriers to full civil rights. The home missionaries had done their job well. The black leadership advocated a conservative means to a radical end. Tourgée had misjudged the signs of the times. The black leadership had more of the Protestant ethic and less of the stuff that makes martyrs than he had hoped.[30]

I n arguing for federal aid to education, Atticus Haygood resurrected the dilemma over which Garrisonian abolitionists had split in 1865. "If Universal Suffrage, Then Universal Education," Haygood argued in 1889. The social gospel prophets agreed on the wisdom of having an educated electorate.[31] But when the terms of Haygood's equation were reversed and negated, social Christianity was seriously divided. Since the body politic was not wholly literate, the wisdom of universal suffrage was uncertain. Divisions among the social gospel prophets were complicated by reactions to the fraudulent and violent means that already produced widespread de facto disfranchisement in the South. In 1890, the divisions were evident in a public debate over the Lodge Federal Elections Bill and disfranchisement amendments to Southern state constitutions.

The social gospel prophets valued a broad extension of the franchise. In 1869, William Channing Gannett argued that the burden of proof belongs to him who would deny the vote to another man. "Perhaps a certain class is rightly excluded—but the appeal sh'd always be, *not give me, please, the suffrage,—* but—*Why am I excluded?*" he said as the nation debated the Fifteenth Amendment. "Not—*it w'd be a favor to have it,*—but to whom w'd it be an injury that I cannot have it? And if an injury, w'd it be so great a one as it is to me to do without it?" Twenty-five years later, Gannett admitted that it was commonly believed that "the Negro has not as yet justified his suffrage." But even if that were true, it did not follow that extending the suffrage to the freedmen was an error or that education would not lead to acceptance of their political rights. Lyman Abbott warned of antidemocratic tendencies in the United States. Some Americans would take the franchise from "the people" and restrict it to "the Anglo-Saxons," he warned in 1888. "Ask the Chinaman, the Indian, and the Negro how this violation of the divine law works. Mankind is not fit for self-government. That is true. But mankind are better fitted to govern themselves than any portion of mankind, however selected, are fitted to govern any other portion of mankind."[32]

Yet, the social gospel prophets did not think the franchise was a natural, inalienable right. Even those who argued that it was, said Gannett, recognized a practical difference "betw. men & men, as in case of criminals, paupers, children." Washington Gladden put it more clearly. "Suffrage is not a natural right, our own laws and the laws of every free country being witness," he said. "Natural rights are not subject to restriction and limitation. The suffrage is always restricted, and many of these restrictions never raise a suggestion of injustice." The primary condition for extension of the franchise was the prospect of its intelligent use. "Every intelligent person knows the first condition of popular government is education," Gladden continued. The North understood the need to nurture its children in American history and traditions if they were to direct the nation's future. But largely illiterate freedmen, growing numbers of untutored immigrants, and native white illiterates seemed to threaten the health of the state. "Would not the unprejudiced political philosopher be compelled to say that the average American citizen of the year of grace 1888 is not properly qualified for citizenship," Gladden asked, and "that the ballot, in the hands of such a person, is a dangerous weapon, with which he is liable to do himself and the country a great deal of harm?" Wilbur Fisk Crafts took note of agitation to extend the franchise to women. At her home in the Florida orange groves, he said, Harriet Beecher Stowe asked an unlettered black servant, who had at least a legal right to vote: "Sambo, don't you think I ought to have a right to vote as well as you?" "La, missus," he replied, "does you think women has sense enough to vote?"[33]

Without a narrowing of the electorate, Washington Gladden believed, "the breaking strain upon our political system will come within half a century." The white South's use of coercion to prevent damage by an unqualified electorate was unacceptable. "If the whole illiterate vote, white as well as black, were thus suppressed, the excuse would be more plausible," he argued; "but even then the question would arise as to what must be the effect upon the ruling class at the South of the practice of these methods of coercion." Its "habitual resort to violence and fraud" was teaching it "to despise the first principles of free government." Gladden's criticism of the violence and fraud practiced against Southern black voters was widely shared. "That the negro voter is intimidated, that he is deceived, that his vote when allowed to be cast is subjected to every species of jugglery known to practical politics, and that his pretense of voting is little more than a wicked and humiliating farce," said Frederick A. Noble, "are facts freely admitted, and what is more and most amazing, openly justified."[34]

Noble's concerns prompted A. J. F. Behrends, George Washington Cable, Joseph Cook, the editors of the *Independent*, Albion Tourgée, and other social gospel prophets to favor the Lodge Bill for federal supervision of elections in the South. Sustaining an old commitment to civil equity in race relations, the *Independent* argued almost weekly for federal intervention. "The Lodge bill is an attempt to secure pure and honest elections," it argued. "No exercise of power that is constitutional, no expenditure of money that is necessary, should be spared in obtaining free and honest elections." To those who argued that an honest election would result in black supremacy, the *Independent* replied: "As between a government which is based on fraud and intimidation and a government in the hands of Negroes there should not be a moment's hesitation." Brooklyn's A. J. F. Behrends held that "it is political equality upon which we must insist—a free ballot and an honest count. The corruption of the franchise is the gravest danger of the hour. Intimidation at the South must be extirpated by the strong hand of the law," said Behrends. "When I am told that we are forcing a race conflict by preaching political equality, I answer that this is the only way of avoiding it." George Washington Cable put it bluntly. "It is only a 'Force Bill' to those who cannot be kept from fraud except by force," he said.[35]

Joseph Cook called for federal intervention in the South in *Our Day* and his *Boston Monday Lectures.* "Unless the shame be soon erased from our national escutcheon," he declared, "we shall be pointed at by our successors in history as having paused in the work of reconstruction before the fetters of the freedmen were wholly stricken off." Southern white ruffians had conspired with cowardly Northern merchants and politicians to nullify the Fourteenth and Fifteenth amendments. "We yet have gold dust in our eyes; we yet have cotton in our ears," said Cook; "and the cry of seven millions does not stir us to decisive action." No section had a right to nullify a part of the Constitution, he argued. Lawlessness must be ended and black people must be educated. Present conditions could only lead to insurrection by a people too long oppressed. "I believe the negro has considerable spirit," Cook wrote. "I wish he had more. But as you educate him, as you give him property, by and by he will assert his rights under the stimulation of his own ambition, and perhaps under white leadership."[36]

Among the social gospel prophets, Albion Tourgée was the boldest advocate of federal intervention. The franchise was not a natural right, he argued, but once conferred it was inalienable. Under the Fourteenth Amendment, if the South tried to disfranchise black people by racial exclusion, it would reduce the size of the Southern congressional delegation. A literacy qualification would disqualify too many whites without disqualifying all blacks. Only a "deterring violence or neutralizing fraud" could save the Negro as a constituent and neutralize him as a voter. The only obstacle to this course, said Tourgée, was the objection of black and Northern white people to the enhanced political weight of Southern white voters. "There cannot be any guarantee of our domestic peace," he argued, "so long as the question of depriving a majority of the qualified electors of any State of the rights which they are solemnly guaranteed by law through any unlawful means is coolly discussed." Can we afford to admit that "white minorities have the right to nullify and subvert the law of the land, boldly, defiantly, and persistently," Tourgée asked, "in order to bar a lawful majority from the exercise of political power, merely because the minority demand it?" He conferred with President Benjamin Harrison, House Speaker Thomas B. Reed, and Republican members of the House Committee on Elections on the proposed legislation.

Tourgée thought the Lodge Bill was too weak, but he endorsed it as being better than nothing.[37]

Yet the Lodge Bill was a poor test of social Christianity's devotion to the civil rights of black Americans. Only 70 percent of the surviving abolitionists are known to have favored it. Both W. E. B. Du Bois and Booker T. Washington opposed the Lodge Bill; and neither the Afro-American League nor the Citizens' Equal Rights Association endorsed it. Indeed, the burst of black organizing energy in early 1890 had suggested the development of strong national organizations for the maintenance of civil rights. But within months the energy seemed to be spent and Thomas Fortune was complaining of Joseph Price's inactivity. In 1891, only thirty-three delegates attended the Afro-American League convention at Knoxville, Tennessee, where Fortune replaced Price as president. The delegates' resolutions condemned the spread of segregation and thanked President Harrison for his support of the Blair Bill. Two years later, Fortune declared the league bankrupt and himself disillusioned by the lack of public support. The Citizens' Equal Rights Association continued, if at all, only in scattered local chapters. By 1893, organized national effort among black people to sustain their civil rights had collapsed.[38]

Not surprisingly, then, many white social gospel prophets argued against the wisdom of federal intervention and the Lodge Bill. Perhaps recalling the bitter memory of British occupation of his beloved Ireland, Boston's John Boyle O'Reilly opposed federal intervention in Southern elections. Disfranchisement was "a step backward" into the "darkest era" of the nineteenth century, said AMA Secretary Michael E. Strieby, but he was skeptical of the Lodge Bill. "Legally and logically, it is right, but as a law it will be inoperative and irritating," he thought. "It is doubtful whether additional legislation would bring about any desirable result," echoed the editors of the *Andover Review*. "A general law placing elections under national control might be a mischievous tool of the party in power in other sections of the country, and would not reach intimidation and other influences under which the negroes are afraid to offer their votes at all." Lyman Abbott's *Christian Union* lobbied almost as vigorously against the Lodge Bill as the *Independent* argued in its favor. Neither public sentiment as a whole nor the best judgment of men who knew the Southern situation, said Abbott, would support the legislation. There were lamentable instances of fraud and violence in the South, but the proposed bill would not get at the root of the matter. Supporters of the Lodge Bill exaggerated the extent of the problem, Abbott argued, and would dangerously concentrate power in federal hands. "The evils which it proposed to cure are local, sporadic, and gradually disappearing under the influence of education and enlightened public sentiment," said the *Christian Union;* "the evil which it threatens to produce is National, permanent, and likely to grow with the growth of the Nation."[39]

Racial moderates who opposed the Lodge Bill saw greater hope for progress in electoral reform within the Southern states. Their favorite proposal was a literacy test for the suffrage.[40] Wilbur Fisk Crafts held that "one so shiftless as to be unable to read, and therefore liable to be venal, must be helped by outsiders to pick out his candidates, unless, as ought to be the case, he is excluded by an educational qualification." The literacy test for the suffrage was one of "the most hopeful symptoms of recent politics," said Washington Gladden. "If that measure can be honestly carried into effect in the South, the worst political evils of that region will be corrected." Issues of state were complex, Edward Everett Hale argued. It was reasonable to expect voters to be able to read about them. "At all events he ought to be able to read the ballot by which he expresses his preferences, and it is not a great deal to ask that he shall be able to read the constitution of the state, which he is to direct." Editors of the *Andover Review* and the *Christian Union* agreed. No state could deny or abridge the right to vote on account of race, color, or previous condition of servitude, the Andover theologians reasoned, but any state could abridge the right to vote because of ignorance. "Let the states impose an educational qualification. Then, if the negroes are so densely ignorant, they would be lawfully denied the right of voting. But if they can sustain a moderate test of intelligence, they are as well fitted to vote as many whites."[41]

While the social gospel prophets debated federal supervision of elections and literacy qualifications for the franchise, Mississippi adopted a new constitution requiring literacy of its voters. The constitutional convention's only black member, Isaiah T. Montgomery, enthusiastically supported the proposal. "He has done his people more harm than any score of them can do good for it in this generation," Albion Tourgée told a black Arkansas legislator, "not so much by his fool desire to be spoken of by the Democracy as 'the best nigger in Mississippi,' as by giving the Northern conscience an excuse for lethargy."[42] The *Christian Union* approved Mississippi's action, but the *Independent* was critical. We trust in "the inherent difficulty of formulating injustice purposely in organic law," said the *Independent* before the constitution was adopted. But within a month, it paid indirect tribute to the skill of Mississippi's lawmakers. "Of course it is utterly unjust," wrote the editors. "Nevertheless, injustice cannot be expected to be permanently successful; and we have no fear but that a few years will straighten all this out."[43]

Assessing events in 1890, Atticus Haygood captured his fellow white Southerners' state of mind. "Before they would have paid ninety-five cents on every dollar" to support public schools and "submitted to the conditions imposed in [the Lodge] bill," he told a black audience, white Southerners "would have wrecked the whole public school system" for the children of both races. The *Independent* found it hard to believe the "extraordinary assertion" from so knowledgeable an observer. If true, Haygood's was "a most painful confession." Within a year, the New York journal recognized the new reality in Mississippi. Thousands of literate Negroes had been disfranchised; "and if, in order to prevent them from voting, it is necessary that they shall not learn how to read," said the editors, "the people of Mississippi will see to it that they do not gain the necessary education." The lesson was painfully obvious. "A provision that no one shall vote who cannot read is a provision to limit education and not to encourage it. Restricting the ballot always restricts education; extending the ballot extends education. The ballot educates."[44]

Surveying the situation, Albion Tourgée looked for strength to stem the racist tide. It was not to be found among Cable's Southern white moderates. "So far as any regard for equal rights is concerned, the New South is very little better than the old one," he told a black attorney. "Mr. Cable's Silent South is a silent humbug—and always will be silent." Old Northern centers of abolitionism had joined a chorus of national reconciliation. "The modern New England policy of remedying an evil is to refrain from intimating that the perpetrators of wrong have any but the noblest and holiest aspirations," he wrote. It is a simple "notion that the only really human and Christian way to kill a cat is to overfeed it with sweetened cream. It is a very nice method but thus far it has cured no evils though it has wasted a deal of good cream and debauched the moral sense of many good men."[45]

Black people's failure to make an uncompromising demand for justice on their own behalf was more distressing. "I am beginning to lose confidence in the manhood of the race," Tourgée said, "and I almost fear to see the time when by its own wish and choice it shall be deprived of all claim of right—just as the free Negroes of the South in 1838 voted to disfranchise themselves." Nor was the race's leadership any more assertive. "I cannot but be angry when

I see their leading men striving for the reputation of being 'good niggers,' " he wrote. J. C. Price's praise of the Mohonk Conference in his journal, the *Southland*, was particularly irritating. "In this magazine published by colored men and claiming to represent the interests of the colored people," Tourgée exclaimed, "I find highly commended the resolutions of the Mohonk Conference of 1890—a conference of white men held to concoct advice for colored men, the resolutions of which were based upon the assumption of inferiority, pauperism and immorality on the one side and superiority, wisdom and purity on the other." Tourgée thought it was demeaning for Price to "beg" for the admission of black leaders to "the charmed circle" at Lake Mohonk.[46]

In advising W. S. Scarborough of his hopes for the Afro-American League, Tourgée called for a "hard, tough-headed, silent man at the head of it." Addressing its founding convention, he urged the Afro-Americans to choose "a leader who has a heart of fire, a brain of ice, a hand of iron," and, above all, "the supreme power of holding his sense—a Cromwell or a Grant." Four months later, disappointed with Price's timidity, he reminded the league president of his historic position. "Once in three or four centuries, perhaps, there comes a man who sees his opportunity, forgets himself and rises to supreme renown by accomplishing unforgettable good," he wrote. "Such an opportunity was offered you and I trust you may yet comprehend it; but I regret to say that I see nothing to indicate a realizing sense of the need of your race for a great leader. . . . It is a pity that the present opportunity should be lost; but God sharpens his own tools and raises up His own instruments." Shortly thereafter, Tourgée confessed his frustration to one of Price's associates. "If they were my people, I would not rest day or night until their wrongs were righted," he said. But

> it is useless for a white man to attempt to fight your peoples [sic] battles for them. He simply awakens the contempt of his own race and the suspicion of yours. It was not in vain that I dubbed myself a "Fool" a dozen years ago. My own race regard me as a crank; yours very generally as an intruder. I often laugh and am sometimes half-inclined to weep over the situation. A strange impulse has forced me to do what I have done, but I have a curious notion that I shall not do very much more.

Yet, somehow, Tourgée's "strange impulse" overcame his "curious notion." The old crusader felt a honing edge at work on him.[47]

When a bill mandating segregation on railway passenger cars came before

Louisiana's legislature early in 1890, the New Orleans branch of the Citizens' Equal Rights Association protested that it was "unconstitutional, unamerican, unjust, dangerous and against sound public policy." But on 10 July 1890, the bill passed the Assembly and was signed by the governor. New Orleans *Crusader* editor L. A. Martinet and R. L. Desdunes, who were leaders of the local Equal Rights Association, condemned the sixteen black members of the legislature, who could have blocked the legislation, they said, by withholding support from measures desired by the Louisiana Lottery Company until the Jim Crow bill was dropped. Martinet, Desdunes, and others formed a "Citizens' Committee to Test the Constitutionality of the Separate Car Law" on 1 September 1891. Tourgée had just announced the formation of a National Citizens Rights Association when Martinet contacted him about the case. Unlike Cable's Open Letter Club, it was a mass membership organization to lobby for civil rights. By contrast with the Afro-American League and the Mohonk conferences, its membership was biracial and concerned with civil justice for all American citizens. "I heartily approve your suggestion for a national organization, without the color or race line, to speak for the oppressed & Defend their rights," Martinet told Tourgée. "The American Citizens' Equal Rights Association has about gone down,—the proper men were not at the head—its last national convention was turned into a purely political resolution machine; and the 'Afro-American' League will not take the best of our people here. We want no distinct association & no distinct appellation." Shortly thereafter, Tourgée became legal counsel in the New Orleans case. His National Citizens Rights Association was born with the test of Louisiana's Jim Crow car law.[48]

Tourgée hoped for a million members of the association, but he believed several hundred thousand would be enough for powerful influence. In order to attract black Southerners, membership was secret and cost only the price of return mail. By collecting and publicizing information about civil inequities, massing support for candidates committed to social justice, and pressing for judicial and legislative relief, the NCRA would lead a new crusade to complete abolitionism's work. Tourgée was encouraged by the response to his proposal from Northern missionaries in the South. Support from Northern social Christianity was limited, but the Reverend David Gregg of Boston's Park Street Church sent assurances. "You are not '*alone*' in the great humanitarian cause," said the Boston preacher. "The true state of the case is, you are Elijah speaking right out for God & man; and we, (the 7000) are keeping silent & allowing you to carry the cause. Elijah carried it all the same."[49] At least 1 of

Albion W. Tourgée, founder of the National Citizens Rights Association (Chautauqua County Historical Society, Westfield, N.Y.)

"the 7000," George Washington Cable, became a member of the NCRA's administrative council. Tourgée's neoabolitionism took on an element of its predecessor's international character with the cooperation of an English Quaker, Catherine Impey, who edited a bimonthly journal, *Anti-Caste*.[50] His call for a new emancipation effort won support from old abolitionists and Union army veterans in the Midwest. "i think you have strucken the keynote this time," wrote a Nebraskan. "The National Citizens Rights Association is the best thing that i have seen for a long time. My services helped to make the Darky free, and now with the help of GOD and the Loyal American Citizens, I hope to live to see the day When a Colord Man can go to the poles and put in his little vote, and have it counted." From Weatherford, Texas, a white Republican veteran sent his support. "I am *with you* in the 'campaign,'" he wrote, "and hope to live—and *help*—to see the day when—we *poor white trash*—as well as the colored folks—will-know—and have the manhood to assert—our freedom."[51]

In Midwestern colleges where evangelical abolitionism had given way to new strains of the social gospel, students organized local chapters of the National Citizens Rights Association. Oberlin students promised to round up five hundred members for the new organization.[52] At Grinnell College, President George A. Gates and professors George D. Herron and Jesse Macy taught a radical social Christianity. They saw racial superiority as a matter of historical conditioning and the abolitionists as part of a great cloud of witnesses from John the Baptist to Mazzini, each haunted and hated in his own day. Yet Herron thought that time's revision of public issues had dated their methods. Had they foreseen that only a generation later "the race question would be one of the most perilous and neglected problems of American statesmanship, and that some of the most piteous appeals on the part of the weak to the strong would then be made by the black man of the south to the white man of the north," they might have turned in their tracks. Yet the unforeseen outcome would be turned in God's providence to His glory, Herron believed, in the great unfulfilled mission of this despised and disinherited race. For the present, there was a bitter judgment in the experience of "a race turned into freedom almost worse than slavery because of the shameful irresponsibility of the nation enslaving it." Grinnell's students promised Tourgée to help overcome the effects of the nation's neglect.[53]

The support of black professionals across the urban North was more important for the future of the civil rights effort. In Philadelphia, Dr. Nathan F. Mossell, a physician, Florence A. Lewis, a journalist, Henry O. Tanner, the artist son of AME Bishop Benjamin Tucker Tanner, and Matthew Anderson, a black Presbyterian pastor, formed a corps of Tourgée's civil rights activists.[54] In Washington, Anderson's fellow Presbyterian, Francis J. Grimké, his wife, Charlotte Forten Grimké, Jesse Lawson, and others rallied to Tourgée's side. He "stirred our souls to their depths, and made us feel, more strongly than ever before, that we, the colored people, must bestir ourselves, instantly and insistently, in this matter," Charlotte Grimké wrote. "Do not think that the majority of the thoughtful members of the colored race do not feel their wrongs most keenly, and suffer more intensely than words can express," she told the white crusader. "But the best and most effective mode of action has not always been apparent."[55] In Chicago, the law partners, S. Laing Williams and Ferdinand L. Barnett, Barnett's wife, Ida B. Wells, and the pastor of Chicago's Quinn Chapel AME Church, J. T. Jennifer, organized a chapter of the NCRA. "Pleas Dont let us alone," wrote one of Jennifer's parishioners to Tourgée, "for god knows I think Ever Blackman in the Worl loves you. at quinn chapel this after Noon call your name Ever man and woman shoted and stamp thar Feet and clap thar hand your name was jest as the day when thay Was set Free."[56]

Words of encouragement and pleas for help came from the lettered and unlettered in the South. A black Arkansan told of an island plantation in Louisiana where three hundred black people had never been emancipated and were commonly flogged. The black postmistress at Barnwell, South Carolina, wrote of multiple lynchings and sought advice on the formation of a local chapter of the NCRA. A black minister in Leland, Mississippi, enrolled seven members. "theys 7 men and well gron from 25 up to 35 years of age. this States very crual for colard people," he told the old carpetbagger. "It is rather Strange to us to here of a negros getting Kill tho whit People rejoices in killin us. if the whit People new that we Colard men was Joinning the National Citizens Rights Association they would Club them Selfs together and kill us or run us away." Others thought it impossible to convey the situation to Northern readers. "The brutal, yea, ultra-brutal atrocities of this Sunny Southland will never be published," wrote a professor at Wiley University, "for they would read so like a romance no one so far away as you are would give them credence." Often there was a pathetic plea for direction. "I have such an intrust for my raace," one woman wrote. "I feel like runing to and frow for help when I read how they re being murdered."[57]

Within six months of his announcement, Tourgée claimed over one hundred thousand members for the NCRA and, by its second anniversary, he said membership had reached a quarter of a million. But the organization had much of the evanescent quality he had prescribed for the Afro-American League. He may have overstated his intention in calling for a Klan-like organization in 1889, but three years later Tourgée was accused of organizing a "Black Mafia" to murder and intimidate white Southerners. As racial tension mounted in Mississippi approaching the election of 1892, black people armed themselves and asked Tourgée for shipments of guns "marked hardware." He counseled against such tactics, but four black Mississippians died, several were wounded, and seven were reported missing after racial clashes in the latter part of the year. All were members of the NCRA.[58]

Thirteen years after he had accepted the name "Fool," the NCRA's leader took another title from his opponents. "I am a 'fanatic,'" he confessed, "because I believe in the equal rights of all men, and in a God who is not partial to some of His children and cruel as an Aztec to others. You think God is on the side of the white man," he told a critic; "I think the white man would best be careful that he is on the Lord's side." It was not easy to keep even the Lord's people on the Lord's side in race relations. But the NCRA had greater success in influencing religious bodies than any other groups. In 1892, it lobbied in Northern Methodism's General Conference for a strong resolution denouncing prejudice, segregation, and lynching. With association prodding, the Northern Presbyterians' General Assembly enacted a resolution denouncing outrages against Southern blacks and New York Quakers had Tourgée's advice in a similar vain. Two years later, he helped prepare resolutions for the Baptist Young People's Union of America and a congress of black Catholics. Otherwise, successes were few. With Tourgée's help, a civil rights clause was added to New York's state constitution and Ohio enacted strong antilynching legislation. The association backed a boycott of the Chicago World's Fair of 1893. It pressed the cause at Republican state and national conventions, but its support of Thomas B. Reed for the Republican presidential nomination in 1892 met a rebuff in the renomination of Benjamin Harrison and the acceptance of a weak civil rights platform. At the same time, the Knights of Labor, meeting in St. Louis, sidetracked a resolution on race prepared with Tourgée's advice.[59]

Tourgée's vigor in pursuing these ends undercut much of his influence. Between 1888 and 1893, his column in Chicago's *Inter-Ocean* reached a wide Midwestern audience. But his attack on Republican faithlessness in 1892 and the financial crisis of the following year led to its suspension. During the recession, Tourgée sought to launch his own journal. "I think we need more than anything else a great journal that shall give special consideration to matters of this sort—the rights of the citizen—the duties of the citizen—and the conscience of the nation," he told J. C. Hartzell. "Not without 'cakes and ale' of course, and a smart sprinkling of 'applied Christianity.' You know the other kind worries me. I believe that I would almost be willing that all mankind should go to the Devil hereafter if they would only do God's will and apply Christ's philosophy here on earth." Several social gospel publicists encouraged his interest in a new journal. Addressing Tourgée as an "esteemed teacher," Indiana's Julius A. Wayland, editor of *The Coming Nation*, told the NCRA executive that a journal promoting the "social philosophy you so well understand" would make him "one of the most prominent and honored men of the nation."[60]

More substantial word came from *Our Day*'s Joseph Cook. In 1890, Cook had sought Tourgée as an associate editor for *Our Day*. Disturbed by the disappearance of his "trumpet calls to national and local righteousness in our treatment of our Afro-American citizens," Cook now wanted him to take over *Our Day* as a vehicle for the National Citizens Rights Association. After pronouncing the Afro-American League dead, T. Thomas Fortune hoped for an alliance with the NCRA and suggested that it absorb his New York *Age*. But Tourgée thought that Cook's monthly was an unlikely financial proposition and absorption of Fortune's newspaper might prejudice an appeal across racial lines. In March 1895, Tourgée launched his own periodical, the *Basis*. It reached a circulation of twelve hundred and collapsed within thirteen months. With it went all hope for the survival of the National Citizens Rights Association.[61]

The failure of the *Basis* and the National Citizens Rights Association coincided with the climax of the association's most important battle, the case of *Plessy v. Ferguson*. When Tourgée accepted the case, he was widely praised in New Orleans's Afro-American community. "May God Ever Remember one like you," one man wrote,

> & may angles Hover over in you nightly slumbers and may the archangles guid through the gates of Rest there to commune with Negroes in whose defese you have so long stood and may god be a soft-dying Pillow when you called home Please excuse bad Penmanship as the whip was my Pen before the war. Oh god if you & Brother Haygood was in this corept land Good bue and again may god Hold his Hand on your Honest Head.

After preliminary arrangements with the railroad, the conditions of the test case were established on 7 June 1892, when Homer A. Plessy, an octoroon, purchased a ticket in New Orleans for Covington, Louisiana, and refused a request to move from a white car to the Jim Crow section of the train. He was arrested and found guilty in New Orleans's Criminal District Court. On appeal, the state Supreme Court upheld the law's constitutionality and the case went to the United States Supreme Court. Tourgée's brief to the Court held that segregation was incompatible with the Thirteenth and Fourteenth amendments. It perpetuated slavery's caste distinctions and sought their legal sanction apart from personal ownership. Tourgée found that interpretation confirmed in the exception allowed for nurses of children of the other race. "The exception of nurses shows that the real evil lies not in the color of the skin, but in the relation the colored person sustains to the white," he observed. "If he is a dependent it may be endured; if he is not, his presence is insufferable. This act is plainly and evidently intended to promote the happiness of one class by asserting its supremacy and the inferiority of another class. Justice is pictured blind and her daughter, the Law, ought at least to be color-blind."[62]

As C. Vann Woodward observed, the case was charged with irony. Tourgée had directed that a person "nearly white" be selected for the test case. Part of his brief argued that the defendant was deprived of property without due process of law. "Property" in this case was the material advantage of "the reputation of being white." That part of the argument was not a defense of black people, but of a "nearly white" person against the handicap of a degree of color. A second element of irony came with the decision rendered by the Court in May 1896. The majority decision, sustaining the Louisiana law, was delivered by Justice Henry B. Brown of Massachusetts, while the lone dissenter was Justice John Marshall Harlan, a Kentuckian and former slaveholder. But for Albion W. Tourgée and his band of racial egalitarians, surely the cruelest irony of all was that in the climax of their crusade, the Supreme Court approved the formula of "equal, but separate."[63]

T he social gospel's primary mode of interest in race relations between 1865 and 1900 was in missionary education. A second tradition looked to African colonization and redemption. A third tradition focused on the civil rights of the freedmen. When the war ended, however, even the most militant abolitionists were divided between the home missionaries' and the civil egalitarians' ways of defining and "solving" the problem. As though guided by the counsel of Wendell Phillips, the nation chose first to enfranchise and then to educate the freedmen. The Phillipsian tradition was carried on by George Washington Cable, Joseph Cook, T. Thomas Fortune, Archbishop John Ireland, Albion Tourgée, the *Independent*, and others, but its institutions of racial reform faced an awesome toll between 1888 and 1896. The Open Letter Club, the Afro-American League, the Citizens' Equal Rights Association, and the National Citizens Rights Association rose and collapsed, the victims of racial hostility, inadequate leadership, and economic dislocation. By 1896, Joseph Cook had turned *Our Day* over to new management, Tourgée was preparing to go abroad, and Cable turned to other matters. Given the failure of Reconstruction and continued strife in Southern politics, the nation chose to reverse its priorities. Now, it would educate and then enfranchise freedmen. So the social gospel prophets gave virtually unanimous support to federal aid to education and were seriously divided over the wisdom of federal supervision of Southern elections. But if the flaw in the nation's earlier effort seemed evident in electoral corruption and strife, that of the new approach was as real if less dramatic. Denied the claim of the ballot on funds for schools, black people would now, in effect, have neither the vote nor an education.[64]

# 5

## The Savage End of an Era:

### Barbarism and Time Unredeemed

Fearing that the South would lapse into barbarism after its defeat in the Civil War, Northern social Christianity hoped to replicate a social order that would sustain civilized ways of life and mitigate racial conflict. But, through Reconstruction and into the twentieth century, conflict etched dark shadows on the bright pictures painted by agents of the New South. Until the late 1880s, there were more white than black victims of lynching in America, so the lynching of black people in the South received little distinct notice. Lynching peaked about 1892 and generally declined thereafter, but the percentage of victims who were black grew rapidly. Public attention was drawn to the problem just as it became increasingly a racial and regional problem, the major racial issue of the decade. As an issue, lynching revealed the essentially conservative character of the American social gospel. Its Northern critics appealed to the conservative value of law and order to condemn it. Its Southern "apologists" appealed to the conservative value of honor to explain it. The effort to control it produced the last victories of nineteenth-century racial reform. But it was not the lynching of black people that first won public notice.[1]

In March 1891, eleven Italian workmen acquitted of complicity in the murder of New Orleans's police chief were seized by a mob and summarily put to death. The mass murder was censured by the national and international press. "No provocation can justify such a crime against public order, the sanctity of human life, and the good name of the country," said

Lyman Abbott's *Christian Union*. The "worst feature in the whole miserable business" was local public opinion's endorsement of this "outbreak of savagery" by "self-authorized executioners," said the New York journal. But a local grand jury returned a verdict of "death at the hands of an unknown party." When Italy demanded an indemnity for the murder of eleven of its citizens, the United States government paid $25,000 to the Italian government.[2]

In the months after the New Orleans murders, lynching became increasingly commonplace, supplying regular filler in editorial pages. "The other day a Negro in Texarkana was burned to death by a mob," said the *Independent*, "and the woman on whom he was accused of having made an assault was brought forward and required to light the kerosene." The Nashville *Christian Advocate* cried: "In the name of civilization, in the name of humanity, in the name of God, we protest such things." A year after the New Orleans murders, lynch mobs were killing twenty victims a month in the United States. Long noted for its concern for the plight of black Southerners, the *Independent* sought an optimistic note. "We believe outrages are gradually diminishing, and that public sentiment is slowly improving," it said; "in certain districts there has been a new outbreak of intolerance. But we believe it will be brief, and that it does not indicate anything more than eddying in the onward current in the stream of liberty."[3]

Black leaders saw the absurdity of such optimism. African Methodist Episcopal Bishop Benjamin Tucker Tanner pointed out that racial abuse was escalating. In May 1892, twelve hundred black people met at Columbus, Ohio, to protest the racial violence. They cited recent outrages in the South, set aside 31 May as a day of prayer and fasting, and resolved to fight the spreading terror. "We urge agitation; we urge the prosecution of every peaceful remedy," they said, "and especially do we urge the organization of all Afro-Americans for mutual protection" and to rally the support of white Americans "who feel compromised by the lawless elements in their midst." At the same time, Dr. Charles H. Payne shocked a general conference of Northern Methodists with the fact that in the last twelve months 150 Negroes had been lynched, 7 burned alive, 1 flayed alive, and 1 disjointed. Prodded by Payne and Albion Tourgée, the Methodists called upon the church, the press, and the government to use all "legitimate authority and influence to put an end to the injustice and wrong" committed against black Southerners, who were victims of "violence, mob law, lynching and other outrages against humanity." Congregationalists and Northern Presbyterians joined the Methodists in condemning lynching.[4]

A white Southern Methodist bishop, Oscar P. Fitzgerald, said that Northern critics showed too little sympathy for female victims of "unspeakable crime." Perpetrators of such crimes put themselves beyond the protection of the law, he argued. "No offense does, or ought to, outlaw its perpetrator in a civilized community," replied the Independent. "Bishop Fitzgerald is simply condoning murder when he excuses lynching on the ground that the crime with which the man is charged is an atrociously detestable one." The "unspeakable crime" against women was charged in only a third of the known cases of lynching. "The real fact is that the South is yet in a state of partial barbarism. It condones murder." The Independent lamented that Southern political leaders who condemned lynching had "spoken a truer Christian word than has a Bishop of a Christian Church." Fitzgerald countered that he exonerated most black Southerners of complicity in the outrageous crime and had no sympathy with mobs or lynching. "I made a plea for fairness and moderation," he noted, "saying that the perpetrator of a certain crime, whether black or white, was outlawed in every part of the country." That was exactly the point, his Northern critics replied. Insofar as he held them to be beyond the law's protection, Fitzgerald apologized for the lynching of persons charged with an atrocious crime. Frederick Douglass and the Independent held that even a person guilty of rape was entitled to a fair trial. No lawless mob of a dozen or a hundred men had a right to declare Fitzgerald or anyone else an outlaw, said Douglass. "We have courts, juries and governors to determine that question and it is a shame to the South that it holds in its bosom a Bishop of the Church of Christ who could thus apologize for the subversion of all law." Douglass pleaded for those "merciful maxims of law and order" which were necessary to protect "the liberty, the security of the citizen, and the maintenance of justice for the whole people."[5]

The decade's antilynching crusade was not sparked by Northern black leaders like Douglass, Tanner, and the Ohio protesters, by Northern white churchmen in Congregational, Presbyterian, and Methodist conventions, or by Northern white editors of the Christian Union and the Independent. The drive came from a black woman, Ida B. Wells, who was closer to the experience of lynching than any of the others. Born in 1862 at Holly Springs, Mississippi, she was the daughter of skilled slaves. Her father became a trustee of the Northern Methodists' Rust College in Holly Springs, where she was educated. Orphaned at fourteen, Wells became a country schoolteacher to provide for her family of five brothers and sisters. After moving to Memphis, Tennessee, she began her civil rights crusade in 1884 by filing suit against the Chesapeake,

Ohio & Southern Railroad for excluding her from a car reserved for white passengers. The suit was lost on appeal to the state supreme court, but it whetted an appetite for public advocacy and a career in journalism. In 1889, Ida Wells became editor of the Memphis *Free Speech and Headlight*.[6]

In March 1892, the new waves of racial violence lapped at Memphis's levees. Three black men, charged with wounding some white men, were taken from jail, carried outside the city, and shot to death by a white mob. A friend of one of the victims, Ida Wells took up the black community's cry for the killers to be brought to trial. When there was no serious investigation, she challenged the rationale usually offered for lynching. "Nobody in this section of the country believes the old thread-bare lie that Negro men rape white women," Wells argued. The truth was that white women were sexually attracted to black men. By the time her newspaper was in circulation, Ida Wells was on her way to Philadelphia for a church convention and missed the reaction. Inflamed by lurid editorials in the white press, white men seized the *Free Speech* office, drove off the staff, and sold its equipment to pay its creditors. Warned not to return to Memphis, Ida Wells went to New York, took a position with T. Thomas Fortune's New York *Age*, and published an attack on the usual defense of lynching. Fortune's paper circulated to many Northern white periodicals and, although she recalled stirring no comment among them, Wells began to make her influence felt. Her article inspired Frederick Douglass to his own attack on lynching and the *Independent* commended it to its readers. "If American conscience were only half alive, if the American church and clergy were only half christianized, if American moral sensibility were not hardened by persistent infliction of outrage and crime against colored people," Douglass told her, "a scream of horror, shame and indignation would rise to Heaven wherever your [words] shall be read."[7]

On 5 October 1892, prominent black women in New York, Boston, and Philadelphia held a mass meeting in New York to raise money to republish Ida Wells's attack on lynching. It retold her experience in Memphis and defended "Afro-American Sampsons" who were betrayed by "white Delilahs." The cry of rape had been raised so often to justify the lynchers' foul deed, she argued, that well-intentioned people of both races accepted its accuracy and inevitable result. But the white community was largely indifferent to the rape of black women. "The miscegenation laws of the South leave the white man free to seduce all the colored girls he can," Ida Wells wrote, "but it is death to the colored man who yields to the force and advances of a similar attraction in white women. White men lynch the offending Afro-American, not because he is a despoiler of virtue, but because he succumbs to the smiles of white women." Drawing her evidence largely from the white Southern press, Wells cited instances of white Delilah drawing black Sampson into illicit relationships. "The utterances of the leading white men show that it is not the crime but the *class*" that matters, she said. Bishop Fitzgerald and his ilk were apologists for those who lynch the rapists of white women only. There was ambiguity in Ida Wells's argument. At times she seemed to call for impartial administration of the law regardless of the race of the principals. Elsewhere, she seemed to want the white rapists of black women to meet the same illegal fate as their black counterparts. In either case, she saw her people as victims of the South's lawmakers and lawbreakers. Like George Washington Cable, she portrayed a South silent before racial injustice. But Cable's silent South was a muted reservoir of racial goodwill. Wells's silent South was a boiling cauldron of ignorance, indifference, and malicious intent. Southern men and women who disapproved of lynching and remain silent, she concluded, "are *particeps criminis*, accomplices, accessories before and after the fact, equally guilty with the actual law-breakers" who persisted only because forces of law and order were not used against them.[8]

From New York, Ida Wells joined the lecture circuit. She addressed an audience of veteran abolitionists in Philadelphia and met Catherine Impey, editor of the English journal, *Anti-Caste*, who was studying American race relations. Frederick Douglass, Mary Church Terrell, Anna J. Cooper, and others promoted a mass meeting in Washington, D.C., that packed Metropolitan AME Church in February 1893, for an evening of antilynching agitation. Ten days later, the black crusader appeared in Boston, where she contacted the heirs of abolitionism and women's suffrage leaders. There, she addressed her first white audience in a guest appearance for Joseph Cook at Tremont Temple. Ida Wells invoked the spirit of the city's old reformers in behalf of her cause. "I long . . . for the Garrison, Douglass, Sumner, Whittier and Phillips who shall rouse this nation to a demand that mob rule shall be put down," she cried, "and equal and exact justice be accorded to every citizen of the land of the free and the home of the brave." Her experience in Memphis was part of an increasing Southern violence, including the murder of the Italians in New Orleans two years earlier, she told the Bostonians. Despite public clamor and international embarrassment, the federal government had shown its impotence before Southern mobs. But the nation failed to see the pattern of Southern defiance of law and order. "In the past ten years over a thousand colored men, women and children have been butchered, murdered and burnt in all parts of the South," she said. "The details of these horrible outrages seldom reach beyond the narrow world in which they occur. Those who commit the murders write the reports. The victims were black, and the reports make it appear that the helpless creatures deserved the fate which overtook them."[9]

As she spoke, new evidence of Southern brutality had won public attention. On 1 February 1893, Henry Smith, a black man, was lynched in Paris, Texas. Six days earlier, he had reportedly abducted, raped, and murdered four-year-old Myrtle Vance. Then, said Atticus Haygood, Smith took the child by the heels and "in the wantonness of gorilla ferocity" tore her body asunder, covered the dismembered carcass with brush, and slept by it through the night. In the morning, he escaped to Arkansas. When he was captured, Henry Smith was returned to Paris, where a crowd of thousands had gathered. Bound to a chair on a large wagon, he was driven through the streets and into the countryside, where a platform was erected ten feet above the ground. While a tinner's furnace heated irons to a white intensity, Smith was tied to a stake that ran from the ground through the platform. The father, uncles, and fifteen-year-old brother of his supposed victim took up the irons. Beginning at Smith's feet, they "slowly branded his body, while the mob howled with delight at his shrieks," Ida Wells told her Boston audience. But she was discreet.

While the irons were drawn and redrawn up his legs, Henry Smith twisted. He writhed in pain as the flesh scarred, burned, and peeled away from his bones. When the red-hot irons were pressed into his groin, Henry Smith shrieked in agony. Still, the Vances traced their branding irons up and around his body. "Red hot irons were run down his throat and cooked his tongue," said Ida Wells; "his eyes were burned out, and when he was at last unconscious, cotton seed hulls were placed under him, coal oil poured all over him, and a torch applied to the mass." The ropes that bound Henry Smith burned through, he fell from the scaffold, and, though his body seemed to be cooked throughout, the mob coaxed him back to consciousness. Repeatedly, he tried to roll away from the fire, each time to be trampled by the mob and thrust back on the flames. Ten to twenty thousand people, both black and white, witnessed the death of Henry Smith. Children of both races taunted and jeered at him, said a black minister; their faces twisted into masks of hate copied from their impassioned elders. Photographers captured the scene; reports said that the cries of the victim were recorded by graphophone. In the following days, relic hunters picked through the ashes. The newspapers said that one man fashioned a watchcharm from a kneecap; a black man carried away a rib bone to hang over his door for good luck.[10]

Public reaction to the ghastly detail of Henry Smith's crime and punishment made lynching the foremost race issue of the decade. In the South, public men squared off in debate. Across the state from Paris, an Episcopal priest, Edgar Gardner Murphy, called a public meeting in Laredo, Texas, to protest the lynching. He understood the deep passions that led to it, Murphy later wrote, but "my whole heart cried out against the form of the Negro's punishment for I then foresaw that it would be taken as a precedent for many spectacles like it." He was supported by civic leaders in Laredo. The mayor chaired the gathering, the district attorney was its secretary, and Murphy introduced the resolutions. Denying any sympathy for the black criminal, they condemned the "orgy of torture and festival of agony" as an "unnaturally and incomparably barbarous" punishment "unequalled in the history of any land or time or people." It dishonored the community, elicited sympathy for the unworthy, and threatened to undermine legal processes. "The principle of satisfaction is thoroughly futile and inadequate in the punishment of such a crime," said the resolves. "The idea that there can be any satisfaction for a crime so unutterably despicable as that which the negro had committed is entirely false. The truth that vengeance is God's is not the rebuke but the only adequate assurance of justice." The meeting was called to condemn the lynching, but the resolutions met opposition. After passing, they were signed by only twenty-one men. Yet Murphy was proud of his work. "If our course had been taken throughout the South," he wrote, "there never would have been another negro 'burning' with all its imbruting consequences."[11]

Laredo's opposition to Murphy's resolutions was part of a larger Southern tendency to excuse mob action. "The spirit of apology for the crimes of the mob runs riot in all directions," said the Northern Methodists' *Christian Educator*. "The press, both secular and religious, joins the rabble, to approve and applaud the outlawry." Southern Methodism's Richmond *Christian Advocate* went beyond Fitzgerald's response to Northern criticism. "The Southern people live in the midst of a race but a short remove from barbarians of the lowest type," said its editor. "Only fear of their superior neighbors and the certainty of a swift retribution hold down the savage passions of these sons and grandsons of the Voodoo African," he wrote. "In certain sections the heathen practices have revived, and there is retrograde, showing how slight is the hold on civilization. Once in a while the demon masters the brute, and the black barbarian commits hideous crime too atrocious for imagination." Where legal processes are slow, the victim's kin retain a natural right to retribution, the editor argued. Northern critics lacked sympathy with white victims and portrayed the "black beast" as an "angel in ebony."[12]

Such rationalizations reacted to sharp Yankee criticism, like that of Benjamin Orange Flower, the editor of Boston's *Arena*. But the racial assumptions of his critique differed little from those of lynching's Southern apologists. Henry Smith was at best only a few degrees removed from the gorilla or the lion of his African fatherland, Flower said. "Some of his ancestors probably belonged to the most brutal and degraded tribes of the dark continent." Since emancipation white men had done little to educate him and had tempted him with rum which "dethrones sanity, silences reason, fires the blood, and inflames the brute passions." No thoughtful man would claim that "the uneducated, rum-crazed negro" should be treated worse than a white man guilty of a similar crime, Flower wrote. Lynchings call "the ancient wild beast in man" to the surface, kill the regard for law and order that holds "the fabric of society" together, and threaten to debase it to the criminal's level. If they were necessary to protect the sanctity of the home against the rapid increase in black criminality, the South was trembling on the brink of chaos. They would influence the imitative minds of the black child-race and the children of both races as examples to be copied. "Oh, fellow countrymen of the South, take heed! Do not imagine that rekindling the fires of the Middle Ages will protect your homes," Flower warned. "Pause; retrace your steps; assert the dignity of the law. Be just, inexorably just, to the black man from this day forth, that your homes and your loved ones may not fall victim to the hate you yourselves are kindling."[13]

**D**iscussion of lynching spread to Great Britain, where Isabelle Fyvie Mayo, a novelist, and Catherine Impey, editor of *Anti-Caste*, organized the Society for the Brotherhood of Man and invited Ida Wells to undertake a British lecture tour. Thinking she had made little impact on the North, Ida Wells went to Scotland in April 1893. Her tour drew large audiences at Aberdeen, Huntly, Glasgow, and Edinburgh, Scotland, and at Newcastle, Birmingham, and Manchester, England. As British public opinion had promoted the abolition of slavery in America, Wells said at Birmingham, aroused British sentiment against lynching would strengthen the hand of those Americans who were fighting it.[14]

Ida Wells's British tour was sponsored by a varied lot of Victorian reformers whose interests ranged from vegetarianism to temperance. At Edinburgh, she met an old supporter of Frederick Douglass's antislavery campaign. At Southampton, Canon Wilberforce, dean of the cathedral and grandson of William Wilberforce, received her. Mayo had taken some East Indian men into her home while they studied in Scotland, including Dr. George Ferdinands, who helped to promote the lecture tour. During the campaign, Miss Impey wrote to him that she returned the love she thought he hesitated to express because of his color. She had told her family that she would shortly prove her commitment to brotherhood by taking his hand in marriage. Confused and unwilling to play black Sampson to Impey's Delilah, Ferdinands showed the letter to Mayo. Mayo's indignation swelled to outrage when Impey refused to withdraw from the antilynching campaign because of her indiscretion. Certain that the love-smitten Quaker would embarrass the work, Mayo asked Ida Wells to repudiate her. Impey was "a nymphomaniac," she explained, "the type of maiden lady who used such work to meet and make advances to men," and "was likely to write such letters to others who might strike her fancy and throw suspicion on our cause." Ida Wells refused to repudiate Impey, Mayo withdrew her support from the lecture tour, and Wells returned to the United States. The Scottish novelist wrote full explanations of Miss Impey's indiscretion to allies in America, including Frederick Douglass, T. Thomas Fortune, and Albion Tourgée. "For a 'secret' it seems very badly kept," Tourgée said, "considering the number that are engaged in holding it down." By July 1893, said Fortune, the incident had "placed the Scottish and English branches of the work by the ears."[15]

Ida Wells's British antilynching lectures did win attention in the American press. The *Independent* thought she was within her rights to take her message overseas but warned that foreigners could easily get the wrong idea. "There are such terrible incidents as she has narrated, but they are not usual," said the editors; "and we have no question that, taking the South as a whole, things are better, and that the Negro is more secure in his rights and is making better progress than ever before. Things are bad enough, but they are not wholly black by any means." But an Afro-American clergyman challenged the *Independent*'s optimism again.[16]

In June 1893, Francis J. Grimké attacked the Anglo-American pulpit's record on lynching as "one of the most discouraging features of the so-called Negro problem." The pulpit's task was to declare God's Word, "to cry aloud and spare not, to lift up a standard for the people," he said. It issued reams of sermons against gambling, liquor, polygamy, and Sabbath desecration, but rarely said a word against lynching. How could one explain the silence? "The pulpit is not ignorant of the actual condition of things," said Grimké; ministers are generally well informed. Denominational conventions had condemned lynching, but the black Presbyterian doubted that their influence reached lay people in the pew. The preachers were more likely to speak in the spirit of Fitzgerald's "palliation or justification" than in condemnation. Southern lawlessness showed that its pulpit was "recreant to duty and false to the God whom it professes to represent." The Northern pulpit's silence implied acquiescence in the Southern outrages. "The Anglo-American pulpit is very largely responsible for much of the suffering and indignity" imposed upon black people, Grimké argued. "Its silence is a tacit admission" by the ministers that "these outbreaks of lawlessness, these invidious distinctions, and the insults that are heaped upon us, are right; that they see nothing inconsistent with the religion which they profess; or . . . that altho they see these things to be wrong, they are afraid to lift up their voices against them," he wrote. Grimké ended with a prayer that God would put "a little more backbone and strength of character and conscientiousness" in the pulpits of the land, filling them with "men who love righteousness and hate iniquity, who are not afraid to do their duty, or afraid of suffering, if need be, in the cause of truth and justice."[17]

While Grimké indicted the Anglo-American pulpit, the debate between Northern critics and Southern apologists moved toward a consensus. Many white Southerners premised their argument on the inalienable right of the individual to protect his home and family from outrage by a black minority that was slipping steadily toward barbarism. Northern critics insisted that, however despicable the provocation, an extralegal response by a "civilized majority" was inappropriate and dangerous. But articulate Southerners with an organic view of society were abandoning a stimulus-response analysis of the problem. An inhumane reaction to an inhumane act could portend the declension of both races into barbarism. After the Paris, Texas, lynching, Nashville *Christian Advocate* editor E. E. Hoss contemplated the horrible thought. "That a Christian community in the closing years of the nineteenth century should have deliberately burned the author of the fiendish crime seems incredible," he wrote. "We turn our eyes away from it. It is awful, awful!

The original offense, and the swift penalty, reveal a demonical side in human nature that startles us. Are we savages? Is our civilization only skin deep? Does our religion count for nothing?"[18]

Other factors mitigated Northern self-righteousness. Southern churchmen were trying to prevent evil and build institutions of social redemption, Amory Dwight Mayo told Northern churchmen. "Every barbarous act of a drunken Southern mob is heard of the next morning from Maine to California," he wrote. With it should go the record of "temperance reformation in the same county, the progress of the public schools, the devoted labors of the clergy and the splendid service of multitudes of young women in 'every good word and work.'" Lynchings in the North and West reminded critics there that the problem was not simply regional. "Are we a nation of barbarians?" asked the *Independent*. "A mob in Louisiana encourages a mob in Virginia, and a mob in Virginia encourages one in Indiana, and one in Michigan may incite one in New Jersey or Massachusetts. It is not safe for the country to have such horrible scenes enacted anywhere in it." Members of the mobs were not civilized, the editors concluded. "They were savages, barbarians. We talk of Kurdish atrocities, of African cannibalism, of Indian tortures, but nothing more atrocious or horrible is enacted anywhere on the face of the earth. Are we a nation of barbarians?" Albion Tourgée seemed to say "yes" to the rhetorical question. "The mere matter of lynching is a bad thing," he wrote, "but in itself it is no very serious matter. The lynching of four or five hundred or even a thousand people in a year, in the United States is no great loss. We could spare that many more and be improved and there are probably three times that number who ought to be hanged." Lynching was a symptom; the disease was anarchy, "defiance of law *with public approval and endorsement*," and its symptoms were national.[19]

Interracial violence was only one dimension of late nineteenth-century social conflict. In the South and West, agrarian discontent was diffused and channeled through political action. In the urban East and Midwest, "new immigration" brought unprecedented numbers of southern and eastern European immigrants with political and religious commitments that seemed alien to those of older Americans. The related struggle of organized labor with the lords of industry was more dramatic. Violence punctuated the struggle between workers in and owners of American industry from the general railway strike of 1876 to the explosion of a bomb in Chicago's Haymarket Square a decade later and the Homestead and Coeur d'Alene strikes of 1892. In June 1893, Illinois Governor John Peter Altgeld released from prison three men who were implicated in the explosion at Haymarket Square. Their parole was a "direct provocation to anarchist outrages," said Atticus Haygood. "Blood will cry from the ground to just Heaven" against Altgeld. "He is an incarnate menace to all our institutions." Worse than loosing "anarchist-murderers" on society, said Haygood, Altgeld's action encouraged "the whole Anarchist population of the country," discouraged law enforcement officers, and undermined public faith in orderly processes of government. Public faith in government's ability to maintain order was central to the emerging consensus among the social gospel prophets on the issue of lynching. "Whatever tends to destroy the confidence of sober-minded people in the civil authority," said the bishop, "adds more than words can tell to intensify that state of mind that empties jails by the prompt hanging and shooting of its inmates, or that makes an end of them before they are imprisoned." Haygood called for "Law and Order Leagues" to support legal processes; their failure was too fearful to contemplate. "A country given over to Lynch law is damned," he concluded. "A government that is indifferent to Lynch law is foolish and criminal. A government that can put Lynch law down and will not try to do it, is itself a traitor to government. A government that cannot, is weak and contemptible."[20]

Two months later, Haygood tried to nail together a common platform for people North and South against lynching. He argued that in an unorganized society individuals had a duty to punish violations of the natural law, but that in an organized society execution at individual discretion was a crime against society. Beyond that, "lynching is a crime against God and man," he said. "Punishment by government, according to law, represents the judgment of God; punishment by lynching is vengeance. Legal punishment educates men into respect for law; lynching educates them into contempt for law." More than any criminal whom it punishes, lynching undermines the law, Haygood wrote, for "lynching is anarchy. If government is so weak or bad that it cannot, or will not, enforce the law, the remedy is not lynching; it is revolution." The bishop condemned lynching, but he also explained that it resulted from no cruelty, superstition, ignorance, or primitive condition peculiar to the South or the nation. It grew from a determination to protect the honor of women. That was an elemental force, universal in human nature, which had an especially strong hold on Southern white men, said Haygood. Referring to the testimony of E. E. Hoss of the Nashville *Christian Advocate* that three hundred Southern white women had been raped by black men in the past three months, he said that the figure was a conservative one. Given the undermining of the white community's confidence in government during Reconstruction, the increase in interracial outrage provoked a temporary insanity that resulted in extralegal execution of the universal impulse. Haygood appealed to black leaders and their Northern white friends to appreciate the necessity to end the rape of white women, for it was rape, not lynching, that threatened society with a barbaric anarchy.[21]

Rather than nailing together a platform on which people of goodwill could stand, Atticus Haygood breathed new life into the old public debate. The *Forum's* Walter Hines Page, a Southerner in exile, plumbed the shallow depths of his argument. Haygood had worked tirelessly to alleviate the race problem, had condemned lynching, and had no apologetic intent, said Page, but the plea of "emotional insanity" was insufficient. "Pray, what ails any mob?" he asked. "The question lies far back of this: for the community accepted and acquiesced in the mob's work." The greatest danger was not the insanity of the mob, said Page, but "the permanence of the insanity and imbecility of the public sentiment that accepts the mob instead of law." J. R. Slattery, rector of St. Joseph's Roman Catholic Seminary in Baltimore, joined the criticism of Haygood. The plea of temporary insanity undercut his condemnation of lynching, said Slattery, for the plea cut two ways. A rapist could offer the same excuse as an evasion of criminal responsibility. More important, Haygood assumed that every Negro lynched was guilty of rape, when only a third of them were even charged with rape. As for Hoss's figure of a hundred rapes a month, Slattery asked for substantiating evidence. It was "almost unpardonable" for "professed teachers of Christ's charity" to "exaggerate anyone's shortcomings," said the Roman Catholic missionary, especially those of "the unfortunate Black Ishmaelites of our Southland. Love cares not to see failings, sin and the like, save to amend and correct them, surely not to parade them openly."[22]

While the *Independent* carried the debate into 1894 with a symposium on lynching, Joseph Cook invited Baptist missionary executive Thomas J. Morgan and the African prince, Momolu Massaquoi, to discuss it at Boston's Tremont Temple. Recalling a Nashville lynching two years earlier, Massaquoi turned missionary rhetoric on his host country. "You speak about the savage in Africa," said the prince. "But right here in this country I have seen more savagery than I have seen all my days in Africa. I consider no country 'The home of the free, the land of the brave,' where the weak are oppressed and where the heel of the strong is always upon the neck of the weak." Next at the podium, Morgan cried: "Oh, my ears tingled when we were charged here as being more savage than the Africans in the jungles of Africa, and I tell you it is true." The savagery was caused not by black crime, said the Baptist missionary, but by the "color prejudice" deeply ingrained in white people.[23]

While Americans renewed their debate on lynching, the anti-lynching work of the British Society for the Brotherhood of Man languished for six months because of the estrangement between its two founders. Eventually, they agreed on a compromise candidate to direct the society and that Ida Wells should return for another tour to renew the British antilynching movement. Wells began her second tour in Liverpool, where she won the support of the pastor of England's largest dissenting congregation outside London, Charles F. Aked. He had refused her a platform on the earlier tour, because he doubted the truth of her message. But since then Aked had visited the United States to preach at Lyman Abbott's Plymouth Church in Brooklyn and attend the World's Fair. There he read news accounts that anticipated a Kentucky lynching. Shocked by the authorities' failure to intervene, he returned to England convinced of the need for an antilynching crusade. With Aked's support, Ida Wells lectured to large audiences in Liverpool and Manchester, where her message won the endorsement of influential religious, political, and editorial spokesmen. On 22 March 1894, a large gathering at Liverpool's Hope Hall heard her lecture and approved Aked's resolution that the conditions she described were a reflection on "the administration of justice in the United States, and upon the honor of its people." Unitarian preacher Richard A. Armstrong of Hope Street Church was critical of his New England brethren. "Are you so busy laying wreaths on the tombs of Channing and of Parker, of brave John Brown and your immortal Garrison," he asked American Unitarians, "that you have no time to heed the seizure of untried men and women, their execution with every device and torture, and acquiescence of all the guardians of law?" In the spring of 1894, Ida Wells won support from the bishop of Manchester and gatherings of English Baptists, Congregationalists, Methodists, and Unitarians.[24]

In June, the antilynching crusade moved to London, where Moncure D. Conway, an old Southern abolitionist, welcomed Ida B. Wells to his South Place Ethical Culture Institute. The Southern Methodists, Fitzgerald, Haygood, and Hoss, had been regular targets of her attack on "apologists" for lynching. Now she added two Northerners better known in England, evangelist Dwight L. Moody and temperance crusader Frances E. Willard. Moody had conducted many evangelistic tours of England and Willard was a guest of the British Temperance Union president, Lady Henry Somerset, from 1892 to 1894. On her first tour, Wells was asked if Moody and Willard opposed racial discrimination. She recalled that Moody condoned it by appearing before groups that enforced racial segregation and was not known to have spoken against lynching. Frances Willard won respect for the temperance movement in the South, she said, by not criticizing the region's racial practices and "practically condoning lynching."[25]

Challenged on her first tour to substantiate the charges, Ida Wells returned to England with her evidence in 1894. After a Southern tour in October 1890, Frances Willard had been asked about the race problem and the "Force Bill." Northerners should not inflame the desperate Southern situation, she said. There, "great dark-faced mobs," rallied by the promise of whiskey, multiplied like the locusts of Egypt and constituted a fearful threat to the sanctity of the Southern home. They were a stolid mass of ignorant voters on whom anti-temperance forces could rely. "Would-be demagogues lead the colored people to destruction," said Willard. "Half-drunken white roughs murder them at the polls, or intimidate them so that they do not vote. The fact is that illiterate colored men will not vote at the South until the white population chooses to have them do so." Willard's interview was not quite the full justification of "fraud, violence, murder, at the ballot box; rapine, shooting, hanging and burning" that Ida Wells claimed it was. But Lady Henry Somerset threatened to see that Wells would never again lecture in England if it were published in *Fraternity*, the organ of the British Anti-Lynching League.[26]

After the article appeared, the *Westminster Gazette* published an interview between Lady Henry and Frances Willard. The British temperance leader referred to charges that white Christians, including Moody and Willard, had done nothing to oppose lynching. Willard cited the Northern Methodists' condemnation of lynching two years earlier and said that "the concurrent opinion of all good people North and South, white and black, is practically united against the taking of any human life without due process of law." American outrages took place on the edge of civilization where orderly legal processes were not yet secure. Indicting the whole society for such peripheral violence, she said, was as justified as holding London responsible for similar outrages in Bulgaria. She did not condone lynching or any injustice to colored people, but the enfranchisement of illiterate voters, North or South, was a mistake that had done irreparable damage. The security of the home in the rural South was threatened, presumably by drunken roaming freedmen, but "no crime however heinous can excuse the commission of any act of cruelty or the taking of any human life without due course of law." Ida Wells pointed to the incongruity between Willard's disdainful remarks about drunken Southern Negroes and her tolerance of the color line in Southern temperance societies. But "Miss Willard is no better or worse than the great bulk of white Americans on the Negro question," she said. "They are afraid to speak out, and it is only British public opinion which will move them, as I am thankful to see it has already begun to move Miss Willard."[27]

The controversy drew attention to Ida Wells's antilynching crusade. The *Christian World*, the *Contemporary Review*, the *Economist*, the *Labor Leader*, the *Methodist Times*, the *Review of the Churches*, the *Review of Reviews*, the *Spectator*, the *Westminster Budget*, and the London daily press took up the issue. Aked and Conway organized the British Anti-Lynching League to bring moral pressure on the United States to suppress lynching. When the names of its supporters were released, Lady Henry Somerset and Frances Willard were among them. The list was long and prestigious, headed by the duke of Argyle and Mrs. Humphrey Ward. The archbishop of York signed on with other prominent churchmen, including Aked, Armstrong, Conway, Newman Hall, and W. F. Moulton. The editors of the *Contemporary Review*, the *Manchester Guardian*, and important London dailies joined more than a dozen members of the House of Commons in support of the league. By July 1894, when Ida Wells left England for America, the British Anti-Lynching League was ready to carry on. Her second antilynching tour of England won considerable notice in the American press. "A masterly flank attack," said the *Independent*, which wondered whether "those who were callous to Northern criticism may feel somewhat sorer when they hear what is said in other countries."[28]

Amory Bradford, the Congregational pastor at Montclair, New Jersey, agreed with the *Independent*. Americans seemed to claim a monopoly on altruism when they decried injustice in South Africa, Turkey, Russia, and elsewhere, he wrote. But Christian England's criticism of American lynchings brought a rude awakening. "Their protest is a just one," Bradford said. "No excuses or explanations can mitigate the force of the indictment; the facts are too evident to be explained away." Whether black people were inferior or superior, enfranchised or disfranchised, he argued, they had not been treated justly by church or state in America. When a Northern Methodist bishop argues in favor of segregating black Methodists, when prominent Episcopalians refuse to associate with their black brethren and threaten to drive a bishop from his diocese for treating a black priest like a Christian gentleman, and when the main obstacle to the reunion of Northern and Southern Presbyterians is that Southern churchmen will not associate with black Presbyterians, said Bradford, "it is high time for those who believe in practical Christianity to ask if the Master is being crucified afresh." Bradford distinguished between appropriate roles for white and black leadership in race relations. "We are often told that it is best to let the Negro work out his own salvation, that he will get better treatment as he can command it; that the rise of the colored race will be an evolution; that it cannot be forced," he noted. That did not "lessen the awful scandal and shame" of American Christianity in accepting current conditions. "Such talk is wise and right for the colored people themselves," said Bradford; "it is magnificent when coming from Booker T. Washington, but mere evasion of an evident duty when coming from a white man." The New Jersey clergyman returned to the criticism from abroad. "The saddest part of the whole matter is that so many are willing to be quiet and try to find excuses for things which in themselves are awfully and inexcusably wicked," he lamented. "With shame and humiliation we are compelled to answer our brethren beyond the sea that there is reason for their kind but severe arraignment of our conduct."[29]

In an *Our Day* symposium on lynching in the summer of 1894, Joseph Cook noted that the previous decade had seen a threefold annual increase in the lynching of Negroes. He chided Episcopal Bishop Henry Codman Potter for not addressing the issue and challenged Haygood's claim that lynching was due to black men raping white women. Northern men should not be hoodwinked by the outcry against "Negro crime," Cook wrote. Lynching's cause was a "Philistinish provincialism," the fiendish spirit of caste. "It is pitiable, it is to the last degree loathsome, it is ghastly in the degree to which it is benighted, belated and barbaric!" exploded the Boston preacher. If the federal government had no authority to end the Southern atrocities, he concluded, the Constitution should be amended to authorize it. To his critique of Haygood and Potter, Joseph Cook added those of Frederick Douglass and Lewis Harvie Blair, who claimed that bishops were soft on lynching. The picture drawn by Atticus Haygood and Frances Willard of the Negro as "a moral monster, ferociously invading the sacred rights of woman and endangering the homes of the whites" came not from avowed enemies, Douglass admitted, but from "the fairest and most humane of the Negro's accusers." But he disputed it, noting that the moral character of black people was above reproach during the Civil War and Reconstruction when opportunity for sexual assault was greater. In any case, Douglass concluded, the lynch mob was an inappropriate judge of guilt or innocence.[30]

Blair had already boldly addressed the race issue, but his isolated Southern racial liberalism spoke of lynching in tones of bitter sarcasm.[31] Savage Africa, pagan China, and effete Europe had nothing like lynchings, he said. They were a "distinguishing feature of American Evangelical Christian civilization." Once a rare occurrence, they had become a popular pastime and, with the refinement of technique, an American fine art. Selecting a model of lynching as a fine art from dozens of examples, Blair pointed to the case of William Black, a young man recently released from prison for having stolen some clothes. When Black returned to his hometown, he was seized by David Ready and tied to a tree. Ready knelt in prayer for the salvation of Black's soul. After he pronounced the "Amen," David Ready rose and shot William Black. The bystanders did not object and no arrest was made. "Henceforth the Readys should be distinguished and honored as related to David Ready," Blair wrote. "The scene is highly Druidic and therefore dramatic; twilight; gloomy forest; long sepulchral moss swaying solemnly to the evening breeze; a youth returning home, caroling perhaps a song of deliverance; David Ready as envious Fate, surrounded by approving neighbors, in solemn enclave; the joyous and unsuspecting youth suddenly seized by David Ready as Fate, and bound to a tree; David Ready as priest wrestling in prayer for deliverance of the youth; the fatal shot and death of innocent youth." But Ready could refine his skill at the fine art, said Blair. The subject should be loosely tied to a stake and branded with hot irons. That would allow for as much squirming as possible and not hurt a tree. Fire was more dramatic than a gun, he thought, and pine splinters spaced at random on the body could be lit one at a time like a Christmas tree. "This will not kill," wrote the bitter Southerner, "but the wriggling and writhing will entertain and the shrieks and screams that will awaken the echoes of the dark forest will edify. By the light of the splinters Mr. David Ready could line out a penitential hymn. He could appropriately request the youth to groan." Ready had not used every opportunity for drama, said Blair, but he could improve with practice, since his first performance had the community's approval.

Indeed, critics of the art were scarce anywhere in America, said Blair. "Preachers are too busy saving souls and everybody else too busy making money to give a thought to these things; or if we think, we think about this," he wrote:

If we did not lynch we would be like benighted Africa, or stereotyped China, or revolutionary South America, or effete Europe, where lynching is unknown. The United States is the native heath of lynching and we have the biggest lakes, longest rivers, broadest prairies, highest mountains, the smartest men, brightest women, prettiest children, finest babies; the most lawyers, doctors, preachers and idiots; the most lunatics, paupers, masons and church-members; in a word, the most, best, greatest of everything, and we lynch, as the church members pray, without ceasing, and if lynching be not the cause of it all then logic is not logic.

But a well-known bishop said there were fewer lynchings than the press reported, Blair concluded. "On this subject there is but one opinion," the churchman had said. "The people lynch for one thing and one thing only. In all the years I have lived, I have never known a doubtful lynching." Since none of the lynchings Blair had cited were for that "one thing," since the word of a bishop was undoubtedly true, and since all the cases cited were said to have occurred in the bishop's neighborhood, Blair suggested, one could conclude that they had never happened. Indeed, the bishop erred in admitting the occurrence of lynching. "I have lived in the same region quite as long as he," wrote the Virginia Presbyterian, "yet I never saw a lynching, or ever saw a man that had ever seen a lynching, or ever saw a man that had ever seen a lynching up to the fourth or fifth generation." If the bishop was justified in denying that lynching occurred except in cases of rape, he wrote, "I am justified in denying lynchings altogether."[32] As a critic, Lewis Harvie Blair proposed refinements of the High Art of Lynching and theologies of the absurd.

**W**hen Ida Wells returned from England, prominent American reformers joined the antilynching cause. Noting the organization of the British and an American Anti-Lynching League, with its headquarters at Providence, Rhode Island, Lyman Abbott's *Outlook* invited "all Christendom" to arouse American authorities to "the duty of preventing and punishing mob violence, however led, sanctioned or applauded." The American Anti-Lynching League won support from politicians like Carl Schurz and W. Bourke Cochran, American labor's Samuel Gompers, and Richard Watson Gilder, editor of the *Century Magazine*. Such prominent churchmen as Roman Catholic archbishops John Ireland of St. Paul and Francis Janssens of New

Orleans, New York's Presbyterian pastor John Hall, and Protestant Episcopal bishops David Sessums of Louisiana and Hugh Miller Thompson of Mississippi endorsed it. But there were strong forces diffusing the antilynching sentiment. Just as English criticism and Ida Wells's return renewed America's antilynching movement, violence in the massive Midwestern Pullman strike put lynching into a broader framework of threats to public order again. Calling the strike a "civil war," Atticus Haygood said that the South was free of its shame, but the Northern center of "reverence for law and the sacred rights of man" was reduced to helplessness by the striking mobs. Haygood happily condemned their violence as "lynching by wholesale." More sympathetic to black people than to organized labor, the *Independent* praised Haygood's condemnation of the strike, but doubted the worthiness of its sectional apologetic.[33]

Ida Wells found distressingly little support even from those who took a public stand against lynching. As pastor of Brooklyn's Plymouth Church, Lyman Abbott held her antilynching crusade at a distance. She addressed an enthusiastic crowd at Brooklyn's Academy of Music in behalf of the cause but spent two weeks trying to get a hearing with Abbott's influential congregation. She had letters of endorsement from England's leading clergymen, but Abbott put her off until a deacon intervened to get her a fifteen minute spot at the end of a morning service. Weeks later, Wells had a similar experience in Chicago. Associates in England encouraged her to contact the Reverend Frank Gunsaulus, pastor of the Windy City's Plymouth Congregational Church. Initially, he agreed to devote a Sunday evening service to an antilynching appeal. But at the appointed hour, the church was dimly lit and the pastor was absent. Gunsaulus finally appeared when Wells refused to conduct a service without him. He made no excuse, she recalled, "but his introduction was hearty enough and his denunciation of lynching was all that could be expected."[34]

From Chicago, Ida Wells went to St. Louis, where the initial success of her antilynching meeting was lost in a tide of Southern sentiment. In Kansas City, her meeting was successful and she met with the city's ministerial alliance. But when a resolution endorsing her antilynching crusade was introduced, the preachers fell into rancorous debate. Disturbed by hostile feelings, one of the ministers restored order by singing out a carelessly chosen hymn, "Blest Be the Tie That Binds." Weeks later, in San Francisco, Christian love failed again to bind the city's preachers together under an antilynching banner. Charles O. Brown, the city's leading social gospel minister, led the fight to approve

Ida B. Wells, lynching's most outspoken critic in the 1890s (Special Collections, Joseph Regenstein Library, University of Chicago)

antilynching resolutions, but reports of the effort focused attention on the dispute and away from the problem of lynching.[35]

If white ministers across the North did not embrace her antilynching crusade with enthusiasm, Ida Wells got no strong support from black people. When she returned from England, T. Thomas Fortune, president of the moribund Afro-American League, circulated an appeal to hold fund-raising mass meetings for the antilynching effort. Wells waited a month in New York with no response. When it became known that she would be interviewed by the *New York Sun* in August 1894, a committee of black men asked to her to tone down her charges about the attraction of white women to black men. The request was denied. Weeks later, Wells was in Philadelphia, where her mass meeting was followed by conferences with white Baptist, Congregational, and Methodist clergymen. But she met strong opposition among pastors of the African Methodist Episcopal Church. Although she belonged to the denomination, the editor of the AME *Christian Recorder*, J. C. Embry, and others doubted the wisdom of endorsing the work of a woman unknown to them. Wells stormed out of the African Methodists' meeting. "That was the beginning of a great deal of the same sort that I received at the hands of my own people in the effort to follow up the splendid work which the English people had begun for us," she recalled. In July, the Colored Teachers Association of Georgia tabled a resolution endorsing her work and black Democrats kept the antilynching crusade under heavy fire in the election years of 1894 and 1896.[36]

Finally, the public feud between Ida Wells and Frances Willard was renewed in the fall of 1894. Even among Wells's closest associates, few people took so strong a stand as hers. At Rochester, New York, where her hosts were the Unitarian pastor, William Channing Gannett, and Susan B. Anthony, the black crusader discussed Willard's position with the elderly suffragette. Anthony had repudiated an attack on Wells and fired her own secretary for refusing to take dictation from her. But the Rochester feminist confessed that she understood Willard's position. Frederick Douglass was the first man to stand by the feminists in 1848 and was an honorary member of the National Women's Suffrage Association from its inception, she recalled. But when the NWSA met in Atlanta many years later, Anthony avoided offending Southern white women by asking him not to attend its convention. When Southern black women asked her to help form a branch of the NWSA, she refused on similar grounds. Ida Wells assured Anthony that she had erred and challenged her hostess's belief that women's suffrage alone would solve society's ills. The two reformers endorsed each other's causes, but different priorities led each to reject the other's as absolute.[37]

When the Woman's Christian Temperance Union met in Cleveland, Ohio, Frances Willard condemned lynching and denied that she or the WCTU had ever condoned it. But Southern delegates blocked a resolution condemning the atrocities. In her annual address, Willard said that Ida Wells's "false and unnecessarily inflammatory" rhetoric was harmful to a cause they both supported. "The zeal for her race has clouded her perception as to who were her friends and well-wishers in all high-minded and legitimate efforts to banish the abomination of lynching and torture," said Willard. "The statements made by Miss Wells concerning white women having taken the initiative in nameless acts between the races . . . has put an imputation upon half of the white race in this country wholly without foundation." Ida Wells denied the

charges. "Miss W has never forgiven me for telling what she said in condona-
tion of lynching and she could not resist the opportunity to strike back at me
thro her association," she told Albion Tourgée. "The entire organization
believes I 'misrepresented the W.C.T.U.' while in England." Tourgée defended
the black crusader, but Willard claimed that she had been treated unjustly by
"good Frederick Douglass, by percussive Miss Wells and some others." It was
"particularly painful to me to be counted on the wrong side in this controversy," she said, "because I am a dyed-in-the-wool Abolitionist; my father's
house was a station on the underground railway (in Oberlin); I learned to
read out of the 'Slave's Friend,' and I have always treated colored people as I
treated white in every respect." Recently, she had threatened to walk out of
the prestigious Chicago Women's Club if it rejected a black applicant for
membership. The temperance crusader repeated her objection to Ida Wells's
claim that lynchings occurred because white women enticed innocent black
men into illicit relationships and salvaged their reputations by abandoning
their dark lovers to howling mobs of white men. Ida B. Wells "is a bright
woman," Willard concluded, "and I have nothing against her except that
she has not the balance and steadiness that are requisite in a successful
reformer."[38]

There was additional criticism of Willard's position from the National
Association of Colored Women, but a public letter issued from Boston in
February 1895 was the final blow of the tempest in a temperance teapot. It
repudiated "wrong impressions concerning the attitude of Miss Willard toward the colored people in America" that had been given "in certain quarters." The WCTU let each state unit regulate its internal affairs, said the letter,
but Willard had always opposed the color line and black women were
welcomed as officers of the national organization and delegates to its convention. "We feel that for any person or persons to give currency to statements
harmful to Miss Willard as a reformer is most misleading and unjust," said the
letter. "Through her influence many of the State Unions have adopted resolutions against lynching, and the National Union has put itself on record in the
same way, while the Annual Addresses of the President have plainly indicated
her disapproval of such lawless and barbarous proceedings." Frederick Douglass, William Lloyd Garrison, Jr., Francis Jackson Garrison, Lyman Abbott,
Joseph Cook, Thomas Wentworth Higginson, and Julia Ward Howe joined
others in signing the letter.[39]

The public rebuke from leading racial reformers appeared even as Ida
Wells's effort at other points came to a disappointing end. When the British

Anti-Lynching League proposed to conduct an investigation of lynching in August 1894, Southern spokesmen objected. "We challenge investigation by all persons who have the right to investigate these charges," said Georgia Governor William J. Northen, "but any attempt on the part of Englishmen, tainted by their own national crimes, to arraign us for trial must be considered a gross impertinence." The Nashville Christian Advocate suggested an alternative. "Let the Englishmen protest, let our Northern brethren protest, let Ida Wells protest—that is all right, we join them all in protesting against lynching, and will go as far as any to put a stop to it, but to go that far and cease is to stop far short of duty," said the Southern Methodists. "What is needed is a few Englishmen, and a few Northern men, and a few Ida Wellses to come south . . . as missionaries among the colored people, and teach them better morals." Such Northern journals as the Independent, Our Day, and the Outlook favored the inquiry, but the British Anti-Lynching League abandoned its plan altogether. Lacking support from Northern white religious bodies or the black community, abandoned by her British allies, and repudiated by some of the nation's leading racial reformers, Ida B. Wells closed her antilynching campaign in June 1895.[40]

Yet there was still widespread antilynching sentiment. The national religious press kept the issue before the public. Lyman Abbott's Outlook sought a congressional investigation of lynching; the New York Independent editorialized repeatedly on the subject; and the Southern Methodists' Christian Advocates mustered regional opinion against it.[41] Individual Southern ministers occasionally witnessed against lynching. In 1895, a mob gathered outside and rushed into the jail at Frederick, Maryland, to seize Jim Bowens, a black man accused of assaulting a white woman. Two white officers of the local Salvation Army, Captain Eugene Mott and Lieutenant William Antrim, pushed their way to the front and pleaded for Jim Bowens's life. Shoved away, they followed the crowd to the site of the lynching. Moving to the condemned man's side, they asked to pray with him. The lynchers uncovered their heads as the black man repeated the Lord's Prayer after the army officers: ". . . Thy Kingdom come, Thy will be done . . ." Some members of the lynch mob solemnly joined in the prayer. Jim Bowens vowed his innocence until the rope choked the words in his throat. Mott and Antrim returned to their barracks to pray for the lynchers and their victim. "Salvation Army, be quick!" screamed The War Cry, the "lynching craze" must stop. The victims of black crime were to be pitied, but black men were "also victims of terrible cruelties and assaults." Lynching, said The War Cry, was "horrible . . . atrocious."[42]

Other Southern ministers and missionaries joined the antilynching effort. In the summer of 1894, Professor George W. Henderson of the American Missionary Association's Straight University persuaded Benjamin Morgan Palmer, pastor of New Orleans's First Presbyterian Church, and William Preston Johnson, president of Tulane University, as well as leading black citizens of New Orleans and Louisiana's Roman Catholic hierarchy, to petition the state legislature against lynching. Southern ministers, like the Reverend S. Reece Murray of Baltimore, lectured their congregations on the Christian basis for the rule of law in society and the sacredness of human life. The Louisiana legislature adjourned without action on Henderson's petition, but the governors of Georgia, Maryland, Texas, and Virginia pressed for legislative action. Georgia and North Carolina passed antilynching legislation in 1893. Two years later, South Carolina moved against lynch law and Georgia strengthened its measures. In 1897, Kentucky, Tennessee, and Texas passed antilynching legislation.[43]

Lynching became increasingly a racial and a regional problem in the 1890s, but Northern social gospel prophets were not silent. The Reverend Wilbur Fisk Crafts held that "sexual impurity" among Negroes was partly a legacy of slavery. Part of the blame lay upon their religion, which, with noble exceptions, was unduly emotional and offered too little ethical instruction and discipline. White denominations had made no adequate effort to make the religion of black people more ethical, Crafts said. But lynching was no remedy. "It is but the outburst of the same savagery that seeks to punish," he argued. Even the death penalty for rapists did not prevent white mobs from seizing black men already sentenced to die and summarily lynching them. "Lynching calls for our severest condemnation, as a strange outburst of savagery, increasingly common in the North, yet more frequent in the South," said Crafts.[44]

A lynching in North Liberty, Ohio, stirred the Presbyterian pastor, J. A. C. McQuiston, to challenge the community's social conscience from the pulpit. Compelled by "a stern sense of duty" and "righteous indignation," he appealed to "those who have it in their power to determine what the moral character of this community shall be." The biblical concept of the sacredness of human life was at stake, said McQuiston. Citing the Sixth Commandment, he argued that "unless God has given other directions concerning life supplementary to that prohibition, no man can take the life of another under any condition whatever without incurring the wrath of God and resting the stain of murder upon his soul." Only the authority of God standing behind civil government could sanction the taking of human life; apart from that, it is murder. Thriving on the collapse of civil law, malicious design, and the fears of an overwrought people, said McQuiston, lynch mobs set an example of disregard for law, encourage further violence, and diminish regard for the value of human life.[45]

In nearby Columbus, Washington Gladden, the leading advocate of social Christianity in his day, chaired the American Missionary Association's committee on lynching. Aware of black complaints that white clergymen had not addressed the issue, Gladden noted the association's long record of opposition to the outrages and called for "further testimony against that form of lawlessness." Gladden spoke with embarrassment of lynching in the North and pleaded for the creation of sound public opinion on the matter. "Such outrages are a disgrace to our civilization," his resolutions said. "They indicate not only a lack of self-control on the part of the perpetrators, which proves them to be unfit for citizenship in a republic, but also a shameful moral cowardice and indifference on the part of the citizens who look on and have no effective word of protest to utter." Gladden asked the citizens of every state to unite for law and order against the anarchy of lynching. "Law is not vindicated by a relapse into barbarism."[46] Like Edgar Gardner Murphy, Reece Murray, and Benjamin Morgan Palmer in the South, Wilbur Fiske Crafts, J. A. C. McQuiston, and Washington Gladden appealed to the sacredness of human life and the necessity of law and order to shape attitudes hostile to lynching in the North. In 1896 and 1898, Ohio passed stringent antilynching legislation; in 1899, Indiana and Michigan followed suit. These were the last victories of nineteenth-century racial reform.[47]

**N**ineteenth- and twentieth-century traditions of religious and racial reform seemed to live in antagonistic symbiosis. Two decades before the Civil War, denominations and voluntary societies that nurtured the religious basis for national unity were themselves rent by sectional division over slavery. A half century later, as their philanthropic and social gospel heirs moved toward a new benevolent empire and conformation in the Federal Council of Churches, the traditions of racial reform were in disarray.[48] But the social gospel prophets were not indifferent to race issues. They may be faulted not so much for complicity and indifference as for division, failure, and the despair that comes from defeat.

The social gospel prophets were divided in race relations. Black spokesmen often looked to them for precept and example. George W. Cable, Bishop Thomas U. Dudley, Archbishop John Ireland, and Bishop Henry Codman Potter were exemplary in racial relations, said Richard T. Greener. But Charles W. Chesnutt saw that their divided counsel was one of the problems. "Mr. George W. Cable advises the colored people to unite and by every peaceable means to forward their own cause," he wrote. Some advise emigration; others say black people should remain here to demand their rights as American citizens. Some suggest massive migration from the South; others advise remaining there. Some advise avoiding racial unity and bloc voting, while others insist that it is the path of salvation. "Judge Tourgée openly predicts a guerilla warfare of races, and can only advise the colored people to defend themselves in an uneven and hopeless conflict," Chesnutt wrote. "When the colored man has read . . . the conflicting advice which his friends have given him, he is apt to reach the conclusion that his counselors are as much in the dark as he himself is." In the babble of voices, black people and Northern white social gospel prophets were inclined to hear the most congenial Southern white voices. Citing evidence of racial goodwill in the New South, black attorney D. Augustus Straker said: "Judge Tourgée prepared the ground in his 'Fool's Errand' and 'Bricks Without Straw'; Mr. Geo. W. Cable and Dr. Atticus Haygood planted the first seed." But Straker also saw danger in the drive for reconciliation between North and South. "We must not be left in the bloody chasm while others shake hands" over it, he warned. "We alone did not dig the chasm, and ought not to be left unthought of in bridging it."[49]

The social gospel prophets defined the racial problem and sought its resolution in a variety of ways. For most of them it was a problem of culture, whose solution lay in a common culture of education and religious values. Given this development over time, other differences would recede. A second tradition despaired of a just solution in America and sought it abroad. America's race problem might be alleviated spatially, either by returning black people to Africa or redeeming Africa with select missionaries. A third tradition in racial reform defined the problem in terms of social justice. It foresaw continued racial strife and held that black people must be prepared to defend their own interests. All of these solutions were frustrated in the mid-1890s.

All of the organizations of racial reform faced the effects of the depression. In 1893, it cut deeply into the receipts of all the benevolence agencies and compelled drastic retrenchment. Within a year, the effect was staggering. "The present unexampled financial straitness has crippled philanthropic enterprises beyond anything I have ever known," wrote Henry Codman Potter, "and even Church work, everywhere, is struggling to keep its head above water." Conventional economic wisdom guided the American Missionary Association and made operating in the black an article of faith. Despite retrenchment, its debt grew to $83,000 in November 1894. Further retrenchment gave little relief; the debt rose to $98,000 the next year. The problem was so serious that the reserved *American Missionary* summarized it in a headline: "Our Present Condition. Help!" The AMA differed from other missionary societies only in being newly poor. Over a twenty-year period, the Freedmen's Aid Society of the Methodist Episcopal Church had accumulated a debt of $175,000 by November 1893. In nine months, it leaped toward $200,000. The panic of 1893 found the American Baptist Home Missionary Society with a debt of $100,000. After three years of struggle, it had grown by $30,000. The Domestic and Foreign Missionary Society of the Protestant Episcopal Church carried a $100,000 debt by July 1895.[50]

In the field, retrenchment meant local "self-help" for those least able to help themselves. In 1893–94, Northern Methodists offered teachers in its Southern schools contracts calling for a 12.5 percent reduction in salary, with provision for another similar reduction if necessary. The following year, subsidies were withdrawn from marginal schools and severely cut in stronger institutions. The Methodists' Haven Academy at Waynesboro, Georgia, for example, was the only school for black children within thirty miles in the black belt. When it became completely dependent upon meager local private sources, the school was closed. The American Missionary Association was prepared to curtail its work further if necessary, but the directors warned that the reduction would come at great human loss. "Must the life-blood of these missions to the poorest, the most needy of all the peoples in America be shed?" asked the *American Missionary*. "Does not the condition of these lowly and helpless millions cry out to God against it?"[51] An ominous sign in the financial crisis was the decline in legacies. "To retrench as suddenly and severely as the receipts—especially from legacies—decreased, would have been most disastrous to the work at every point," said the *American Missionary*. It was as if a generation of the committed had passed on, leaving its largess behind, but that there were none to follow after them. In any case, recovery from the recession came slowly. The American Missionary Association's income dropped from $482,500 in 1891–92 to $357,500 in 1894–95. Meanwhile, the debt had to be paid. By economizing measures, the AMA cleared itself of debt by 1900, but it did not regain its previous level of income until 1903–4.[52]

Beyond their division and partially as a result of the depression, the three traditions in Christian racial reform faced institutional crises in the mid-1890s. Northern social Christianity reached across the sectional chasm in the Mohonk conferences of 1890 and 1891 to form an educational alliance with the Cables, Dudleys, and Haygoods of the South. After two annual sessions, the Mohonk conferences were discontinued, victim of the very divisions they sought to bridge. When Northern social Christianity renewed the gesture in 1898, it embraced Southerners with a larger constituency and more conservative racial views. The decade also saw the demise of both Bishop Potter's and Bishop Turner's versions of the "African dream." Turner's continued plea for massive emigration aroused hopes it could not satisfy and lent them to the cruel exploitation of charlatans. Bishop Potter's plan to turn the American Colonization Society into a nondenominational missionary agency sending selected black American missionaries to redeem Africa ended in the society's sponsorship of slavery on African shores. The 1890s saw, finally, the collapse of the racial reformers' work for civil equity. In 1890, Cable's effort to rally the "silent South" with his Open Letter Club came to a disappointing end. Black efforts in the Afro-American League and the Citizens' Equal Rights Association largely collapsed by 1893. Death and discouragement took its toll among the black leaders, as well. Joseph C. Price died in 1893; two years later, he was followed by Frederick Douglass. T. Thomas Fortune turned from the Afro-American League to try to salvage his newspaper and Ida B. Wells abandoned her antilynching efforts in 1895. Albion Tourgée's National Citizens Rights Association sputtered to a quiet death in 1896 and the judge left the country on another errand.

Division, depression, defeat, and death, financial distress and institutional collapse were fertile grounds for despair in the mid-1890s. If the social gospel prophets despaired of success in race relations, they had reason. The federal government refused to act. They asked for federal aid to education. They divided between the Lodge Bill to provide federal supervision of elections in the South and state action to disfranchise illiterates. They opposed the Butler Bill to colonize black people in Africa. The federal government failed to approve any action. Their own voluntary associations were in disarray. Defeat could lead to despair.

The only hope seemed to lie in an appeal to time. For the Northern social gospel prophets, the death of Frederick Douglass in 1895 was a time to reflect on how far the nation had come in race relations since his birth and how far it yet had to go. William Channing Gannett preached the funeral oration at

Douglass's adopted home at Rochester, New York. "For forty years before the war the streams of national life were really running into one,—the great dark stream of slavery," he said. With emancipation, "for Frederick Douglass, also, America became the land of opportunity." Too often, it was opportunity to be insulted, Gannett lamented, and forgiveness was expected in return. "Douglass has met Phillips and Garrison and Lincoln and Toussaint L'Ouverture," said Joseph Cook in a Boston benediction. "And may we so live as to be worthy of being received at last into that company where all prejudice of race is forgotten."[53]

Chicago's Unitarian pastor, Jenkin Lloyd Jones, who had fought in the Civil War, argued that the North had won the freedom of Frederick Douglass and his people but had not paid for it. "The awful story of years of war, the million graves, the burdened pension rolls, the sad dreariness still at the heart of life in so many homes" were "too slight an amends for the wrongs of slavery, too cheap a price to pay for real manumission," said Jones. "They began a payment which is still uncompleted." Freedom lovers would continue to pay for it by fighting the cancer of race prejudice growing in the North. "Let the brave life of Frederick Douglass show us how large [the] task was, how little of it has yet been accomplished, how much there is yet to do," he pleaded. "We will not be discouraged, but bear on, work on, fight on, love on, and love ever." As for the South, Jones's realism seemed to belie his brave commitment. In his last public address, Frederick Douglass had decried its violence against his people. "This arraignment is too sadly true," said the Unitarian pastor. "Our Southern fellow-citizens had dire provocations and we must be patient with these outcroppings of violence. The patient army which sleeps in the unmarked graves of Southern battlefields expected this. In their name we can wait for the educational renovation of time."[54]

The appeal to time was not new. The missionary enterprise in the South assumed that it would take time. "Human nature is constructed of such flexible materials that it adjusts itself to existing facts, if not suddenly, yet surely by the gradual process of change," said the *Independent*. "The *patient waiting* for moral and natural forces to accomplish results is one of the ordinances of providence. Time is a great element in relation to events." A Methodist missionary wrote that "the Race problem will find its solution in God's good time. Under God's providential hand the now discordant elements will gradually assimilate." Amory Bradford counseled supporters of the American Missionary Association that "in all plans we must remember the time-factor. Great objects require long periods for accomplishment. There are a thousand difficulties to overcome." When new reports of racial conflict filtered north in 1890, the *Independent* condemned the "sickening" violence, but added: "Time and Christianity will settle the relation of the races aright." That did not mean the solution would come without strife. "The time will come when the Negro will be shot and when a race war will be threatened," said the editors. "We expect the murders in a hundred places; we do not expect the race war. Justice will in the end prevail. But the process of settlement will be long, difficult and bloody." A year later, the *Independent* returned to its theme of confidence in the processes of time to remove the burdens under which black Southerners labored. "If they are not wholly removed, we can leave them to the sure influences of those slow and silent forces of education, religious, scholastic and industrial, which are strong enough, in time, to right all wrongs," said the editors. "Our chief trust must be in those silent beneficent forces, embodied in the Church and the school, which are able to conquer every evil and to solve every problem."[55]

Shortly after the death of Frederick Douglass and just before his own, Atticus Haygood raised the appeal to time to the level of sacred wisdom. He had devoted his best years to the alleviation of the race problem, but he denied knowing its solution. "He who claims to have solved this 'negro problem' is an ignorant person," said Haygood. "It is an equation—in every way most complicated—with many unknown and some unascertainable quantities." It constantly frustrated those who were in a hurry to solve it. "We are in a hurry about everything," said the bishop. "But God is not in haste about anything." Save that He would do right by both black and white people, said Haygood, the chief unknown quantity in the racial equation was what God was doing about it. "He who truly knows that God is fair in all His dealings with the human race can never be without hope of any problem, present or to come," he argued. The providence of God guaranteed that the sheer passage of time was redemptive in its effect. "It will be clear gain to Christian America to keep in mind that the negro problem calls for faith in time and the God over all who determines all times and seasons, and who is surprised by nothing that this great universe can evolve," wrote the bishop. "He who believes that God has done less than his best for his children does not truly believe in God at all."

Haygood's disavowal of any solution to the race problem was misleading, for he merely reversed the major and minor themes of the home missionaries. They had trumpeted "EDUCATION" and hummed "over time." Haygood shouted "TIME" and whispered "with education." Any solution of the race problem, said the bishop, depended upon the success of the missionary educators. There was widespread disappointment among their supporters with their achievement. "We must work harder at all our problems; if we are to really succeed, we must remember the time element. God's work cannot be hurried," Haygood concluded. Even in the face of discouragement, Christians could be confident that "Christian education and the preaching of the gospel do elevate and save men." They could be sure that "He who is the Father of men is also Ruler of the universe. And our God and Father is doing all he can to save every soul of man. The humblest and feeblest worker for God and man, sincerely trying to do good, will not, cannot, fail of doing good."[56]

Haygood's counsel of patience with time struck a sympathetic beat in the tiring hearts of nineteenth-century racial reformers, but they remained divided over what would or should happen in time. Josiah Strong and a small army of Northern missionaries in the South would nurture the seed of a common national culture, but racial and geographical determinisms led others to be skeptical of cultural imperialism. New Haven's pastor-theologian, Theodore Thornton Munger, thought that a racial determinant guaranteed the deterioration of some ethnic groups. "Christianity allies itself most readily to the strongest races, entering into them as quicksilver mingles with gold," said Munger. "The strong race opposes it at first with the stoutest will, but at length accepts it because, at bottom, they sympathize. A weak race debases Christianity when it receives it; it cannot stand up under its stout duties, but the strong race takes it at its full measure." Munger thought that his own "Anglo-Saxon blood" was the "best in the world," retaining virtue as an inheritance and shunning vice as alien. Lesser races were inherently lazy, listless, and forceless, but those qualities contradicted the nature of an Anglo-Saxon. Josiah Strong was nearly as extreme in his praise of the Anglo-Saxon. But Munger located a race's capacity to survive in a biological inheritance; Strong believed that Christianity equipped a race for survival.[57]

Sociologists Charles R. Henderson, Albion Small, George Vincent, and F. H. Wines said that geography precluded the imposition of Northern cultural patterns on the South. Wines spoke of "christianizing" or "Americanizing" immigrants in the North and Negroes in the South, but he denied the possibility of importing Northern civilization and customs into the region. Henderson hoped to identify regions "better adapted to some races than to others, so that the population may be varied and yet each people enjoy the home best adapted to its physical peculiarities." Otherwise, Henderson,

Small, and Vincent speculated that some weaker races such as the American Indian might be destroyed in the struggle for survival, some like the Negro reduced to servility, and others like the Chinese elevated from inferiority to equality in society. But even in the 1890s some of the social gospel prophets, such as Amory Bradford, rejected racial and environmental determinisms to reaffirm human freedom. People frequently make choices contrary to what might be expected from their biological and environmental influences, he argued.[58]

But for most of the social gospel prophets America's experiment in racial pluralism was a providential challenge whose end was yet unforeseen. "Into this continent God has thrown this heterogeneous people, in this effervescent and seething mass, that in the struggle they may learn the laws of social life," said Lyman Abbott. "African, Malay, Anglo-Saxon, and Celt, ignorant and cultivated, rich and poor, God flings us together under institutions which inexorably intermix us, that he may teach us by experience the meaning of the brotherhood of man." For some, like Charles M. Sheldon, the end was simply stated. "In the largest and truest sense there is no 'negro problem' any more than there is an 'Anglo-Saxon problem,'" said Sheldon. "The only problem is the 'human problem.' And it is all capable of being resolved in simple terms which apply equally to every race and condition."[59]

Thus, many of the social gospel prophets thought that time would offer benevolent influences upon American race relations. Given the growth of communications and the breakdown of cultural barriers, said Massachusetts Unitarian George Batchelor, the intellectual and ethical evolution of a race that had once taken five thousand years might be shortened to fifty years. "Changing all the conditions, except the fixed environment and physical heredity," he wrote, "there is nothing to prevent the African race gathering up in a generation all the good of the past which it has the capacity to assimilate." Time would reveal not only that the Negro was assimilating but that race prejudice was declining. Just as slavery is a thing of the past, said Jenkin Lloyd Jones, race prejudice would also disappear. "The time is coming," he argued, "when inward worth, merit of soul, heart-life, thought-life, God-life will be respected, coveted, fellow-shipped, wherever found." Deeply rooted as it is in human nature, echoed Maurice Bloomfield, prejudice lacked support from any ethical system that was not an ethic of selfishness. "We must hope for the day," said the Johns Hopkins professor, "when the instincts and traditions of race-prejudice will be so completely surrounded, so strongly pressed upon, by growing culture that they will be forced to join the numberless shades of defunct atrocities of the past." In time, race prejudice must disappear, said Washington Gladden, for "if anything is central in Christianity, it is the obliteration of the lines of division between races and nationalities, and the inclusion of the world in one brotherhood."[60]

**A**fter 1895, Atticus Haygood's appeal to time as redemptive was a word of sacred wisdom in race relations. There were few who anticipated what Martin Luther King, writing from the Birmingham jail, would call "the myth of time." There were few to recall the warning of AMA Secretary C. J. Ryder. "It is sometimes said that time will settle these monstrous inequalities that prevail in the South," he said; "but time never settles anything. Mischievous forces only increase in power, the longer they are permitted to operate. There must be set in operation beneficent forces, in order to make the element of time useful. Agitation is needed, patriotic, prayerful agitation."[61] King and Ryder knew what Atticus Haygood obscured: that the hand of God is not always immediately apparent in human history. Time had witnessed growing racial hostility in the South and the crises of racial reform in the North. Time had seen the Supreme Court accept racial segregation and the Congress refuse to act. In the long run, it would witness reversals on all those fronts. But the wisdom of King and the AMA secretary is superior to that of the Southern Methodist bishop, for the reversals came only after a long struggle by the new organizations of racial reform in the twentieth century. In the ebb and flow of history, there is no redemption in the sheer passage of time.

# 2

## The Racial Mission Renewed

# 6

## Education for Service

In March 1866, the Freedmen's Bureau placed a young Union army general, Samuel Chapman Armstrong, in charge of ten thousand freedmen at Hampton, Virginia. His plans for their future drew on the experience of his father, a Presbyterian missionary to Hawaii, who became the island kingdom's minister of public instruction, and his mother, who taught in a Pestalozzian infant school in Brooklyn, New York, before her marriage. They also drew on his memory of the Hilo Manual Labor School for native Hawaiians, where students paid their tuition by manual labor, and on his own studies at Williams College, where he met Robert Curtis Ogden, a young New York merchant. Their lifelong friendship would have an important effect on the South, both black and white.[1]

**W**hen he took up the Freedmen's Bureau work at Hampton, Samuel Chapman Armstrong appealed to the American Missionary Association and Ogden's associates in philanthropy for money to purchase 159 acres, which became the grounds of Hampton Institute. It grew into the lengthened shadow of the young missionary general. It is impossible "to speak of the work at Hampton without thinking at once of Gen. Armstrong," said Boston's Samuel B. Capen. "One is the body and the other the soul working through that body." Hampton's program interlaced the military discipline of drill and inspection with the pious nurture of morning and evening prayers. Elementary studies in grammar and arithmetic led to more advanced work in natural philosophy and moral science. They were paralleled by training in agriculture, home economy, carpentry, printing, sewing, and shoemaking. If his compatriots at church-affiliated schools in the South sought to transplant Northern Christian culture via a classical curriculum, Samuel Chapman Armstrong's Christian athleticism stressed the discipline of the Protestant work ethic.[2]

In 1874, Robert C. Ogden joined the board of trustees as a colaborer with Armstrong in Hampton's redemptive work. They thought it was resolving the problem of race relations in terms of a practical Christian sociology. "Sociology is the great practical science of the day & leads all others," Armstrong told Ogden. "The Kingdom of Heaven will come through sociology well studied and applied wisely in a level headed way." He believed that Ogden's business career prepared him to speak of the redeeming influence of work as exemplified at Hampton. "I have no fear of the race question so long as Hampton is strong & sound," said Armstrong. "I am satisfied that Hampton has facts & results that mean peaceful solution of race problems." By 1890, Hampton's industrial education was widely admired by Northern social Christianity. Richard Heber Newton called it "the finest example of industrial education that the nation possesses." Edward Everett Hale's *Lend-A-Hand* praised the school in martial terms. "All honor is due the founders and faithful teachers, who have resolved that with God's help this work should be done," pealed the helpful journal. "They have been armed for the war, and every year sees the victory coming nearer." Lyman Abbott lauded Hampton's rigorous methods. "This is just the discipline the Negro race needs to fit it for manhood," he said. "The discipline is not for punishment; it is for development, and out of it there grow nobility of nature and nobility of service."[3]

When he was stricken with a partial paralysis in late 1891, Armstrong's Boston friends gathered at Old South Meeting House to pay tribute. Edward Everett Hale and Phillips Brooks honored him as one who saw emancipation through to fruition. "I think that Gen. Armstrong has done more in the problem of reconstruction than any man before the country," said Hale. Samuel J. Barrows, Samuel Eliot, George A. Gordon, Edwin Doak Mead, and Booker T. Washington, the principal of Tuskegee Institute, joined in an appeal to sustain Armstrong's work in his hour of affliction. "What a creator of manhood General Armstrong has been!" Gordon cried. He has "put soul where there was no soul, life where there was no life, power where there was no power." Life and power slowly ebbed from the body of Samuel Chapman Armstrong. In the spring of 1893, American social Christianity mourned his passing. The theme of self-sacrifice reverberated in tributes to his memory. "One of the wonderful lessons I learned from him was his utter indifference to self," Charles Parkhurst recalled. "His heart was not a vortex drawing everything to itself, but a fountain continually flowing out in blessing without thought of self." Lyman Abbott's *Christian Union* testified that "a more heroic, self-sacrificing, self-devoted apostle and soldier of God never lived than General Armstrong." He had never thought of himself as an American citizen, but George A. Gordon called Armstrong "the first citizen of the nation." Mourning his death and that of Phillips Brooks, Lyman Abbott's *Christian Union* compared their careers. "Few had any conception of the grasp General Armstrong had on the Christian people of the North," said the journal. "He was the true nineteenth century hero, our most chivalrous American, the knightliest citizen of the Republic. If Phillips Brooks was the pre-eminent preacher of this decade, surely General Armstrong was the pre-eminent servant of mankind."[4]

The spirit of Samuel Chapman Armstrong enlivened and haunted Hampton Institute. Six months after his death, students celebrated his birthday with a parade. Led by the boys battalion, they marched from his grave to Armstrong Memorial Chapel, where Robert C. Ogden took Joshua's parting charge to the children of Israel as his text. "As Lincoln was the Moses of the Freedmen, leading them out of captivity," said Ogden, "so was Armstrong their Joshua, leading them into that knowledge of the Lord that should teach them to occupy in righteousness and peace that freedom into which they had been brought." Freedom should be exercised after Armstrong's example in sacrificial service to others, Charles Parkhurst told the students. "He burnt himself out in the great work for God and the world—burnt himself out for you—into you," said the New York preacher. "You on whose lives have been put this fine stamp of sweet, strong, Kingly personality lay [yourselves] down for others, body, soul and spirit, as he did." The theme of self-giving so pervaded Hampton that John Greenleaf Whittier called it "the Christlike school."[5]

Self-sacrifice could not mean giving up the school, however. In the depression years of 1893 and 1894, trustees and faculty of Hampton Institute reorganized for the future. Robert Ogden became chairman of its board of trustees. Hollis B. Frissell, the institute's chaplain, was Armstrong's successor. Ogden and Frissell were committed to the nonsectarian Christian athleticism and work ethic that drove Samuel Armstrong. During the difficult depression years, Ogden advised Frissell on the latest methods of charitable fund-raising to sustain Hampton's work.[6] They counted on the support of other trustees, such as George Foster Peabody and Francis Greenwood Peabody. They were two types of the men Ogden called on to promote Southern education. George Foster Peabody was a Southern-born New York financier and Episcopal layman. Charmed by Armstrong, he joined Hampton's board of trustees in 1884. Francis Greenwood Peabody became a member of the board six years later. The son of a New England Unitarian pastor, Francis Greenwood Peabody studied theology at Harvard and in Germany. In 1880, he joined the faculty at Harvard, where irreverent undergraduates called his popular course in practical Christian social ethics "Peabo's drainage, drunkenness, and divorce." George Foster Peabody brought to Hampton the power and influence of nouveau riche lay benevolence; Francis Greenwood Peabody blessed it with the sanction of an old New England clerical-academic benediction.[7]

From 1890 until his death in 1936, Francis Greenwood Peabody was Hampton's leading advocate in Northern social Christianity. His father, Ephraim Peabody, believed that slavery was wrong and had assisted fugitive slaves, including Frederick Douglass and Josiah Henson. The younger Peabody recalled hearing Father Henson tell of his escape from slavery, his struggle for an education, and the trials of fugitive slaves seeking refuge in Canada. During a communion service one Sunday, he remembered seeing "a runaway slave, who was a familiar visitor in my home, coming slowly up the side aisle, after the 'white folks' had partaken of the Lord's Supper, and kneeling at the chancel rail to receive the bread and wine, as though he had heard the great words, 'Where the Spirit of the Lord is, there is liberty.'" But Ephraim Peabody was a cautious critic of slavery. "Slavery is bad, but there are many things worse," he said. "It is better that men should remain slaves, than be converted by touch of freedom into idle and sensual savages." Freedom could lead to amalgamation, the creation of a degenerate mulatto race. Free black people would continue to serve as "hewers of wood and drawers of water" for white people. Ephraim Peabody thought African colonization was the only charitable solution, acceptable to Southerners and supportive of the Union and the rule of law. Years later, his son said the Civil War proved both conservatives and radicals were mistaken, as God worked His mysterious will both to free the slaves and preserve the Union.[8]

Francis Greenwood Peabody was a conservative idealist who believed that behind the egocentric motivations of mankind and painful human conflict was a will shaping the good from evil appearances. He rejected the excesses of liberal individualism. "The religion of the twentieth century must contemplate the world, not as a chaos of competing atoms, but as an organic and indivisible whole," said Peabody. "It must socialize its hopes and save people, not singly but together, the poor with the prosperous, the employed with the employer, the Oriental with the Occidental, the Black with the White." Jesus' significance for social questions lay not in his definition of a social program but in the moral energy with which he directed conflicting purposes toward higher ends. The historical circumstances of his life were such that he offered no particular instruction in race relations, Peabody argued. Jesus' significance for current social problems was "not one of social organization or method, but of a point of view, a way of approach and an end to attain," said the Harvard ethicist. "His social gospel is not one of fact or doctrine, but one of spirit and aim." Jesus was primarily "not a reformer, but a revealer; he was not primarily an agitator with a plan but an idealist with a vision."[9]

Conditioning as slaves discouraged self-reliance, initiative, and persistence, Peabody thought, making black people little more than "patient and docile animals." The traits were evident in their loyalty to former masters and false friends. But as soldiers and freedmen, black people had been brave, grateful, teachable, and unresentful. They had a rare gift of humor and a genuine religious capacity. "A race which had remained loyal even to slaveholders might be trusted to exhibit similar loyalty to teachers and friends," Peabody argued; "a race which had been brave enough to make good soldiers might be willing to wrestle with the rudiments of education; a race which was essentially religious might be led to develop an unstable and intermittent piety into a rational and ethical faith." Unhampered by "tradition and self-esteem," black people were "impressionable and imitative." The key to their development lay in external influences upon them. Peabody thought that interracial contact between white and nonwhite had often sapped the cultural strengths of the latter and left them defenseless against the vices of the former.[10]

The task of race relations in an "age of problems" was to remove black people from the "problem" category, said Peabody. He asked Hampton Institute students to consider: "Am I a problem? Have people got me on their minds, on their nerves? When a man pays his bills, loves his wife, lives in industry and thrift, he is nobody's problem," said Peabody. "The reform agent and the walking delegate are not thinking about him; he is a forgotten man; he has escaped being a problem." Other problems might be difficult to solve, but the answer to "the Negro problem" in America was clear. Reasonable people, North and South, black and white, agreed on *education*. He was aware of the claims of social justice, but Peabody thought that education for industrial employment was the strongest basis of a social policy for Southern race relations. The essential conservatism of his social critique was evident in his

Francis Greenwood Peabody, Northern social Christianity's foremost academic spokesman for the Southern education movement (Andover-Harvard Theological Library, Harvard University)

remark that, by inculcating the integrity of labor, black people might become "one of the great conservative forces of the nation, holding us to private ownership, sound finance, honest politics, and public security!"[11]

Peabody saw Hampton as embodying the best hope for black America. It joined manual training to mental discipline and moral nurture to deal with the whole man. "The mind shall be made intelligent for the service of the race, the hand shall be trained to bear a part in the progressive movement of the trades, the heart shall be quickened and inspired," he wrote. "So Hampton's gift to the world is that gift of wholeness . . . —heart, head, and hand—all sanctified for others' sake." Repeatedly, the Harvard Unitarian couched Hampton's doctrine in trinitarian terms. Hampton "is a school of labor, and of love, and of life," he wrote. "Its religion is first a gospel of work, and then a gospel of service, and finally a gospel of consecration. Its education is first of all the will to labor, then of the heart to love, and then of the soul to live. Its salvation is first from idleness, and then from selfishness, and then from lifelessness." It was a laboratory where progressive education was tested. "One of the most dramatic ironies of the history of education," Peabody argued, was that the idea of teaching the pupil as a whole person was "an original discovery" of Hampton's founder. This philosophy of education, treating the whole person and honoring the integrity of work, should inform the education of white and black people, he thought. Peabody dismissed charges that Hampton's industrial education was inadequate. Black people should aspire to the highest position they could fulfill, he said; and there were too few strictly academic black institutions. But Hampton's education was what the vast majority of black students needed. Peabody was so certain that it offered a divine plan for black Southerners that he endowed Hampton's directors with a hallowed visage. He compared Armstrong, Frissell, and Ogden with Jesus Christ. Armstrong was the subject of a nineteenth-century transfiguration event and the bringer of the abundant life. Ogden's Wall Street office was transformed into a latter-day "upper room."[12]

Francis Greenwood Peabody was social Christianity's most important spokesman for Hampton Institute, but others supported it. New York's Episcopal Bishop David H. Greer and Presbyterian pastor Charles H. Parkhurst also served on Hampton's board of trustees. When the very educability of black people was under attack, many social gospel prophets stood by its promise. Its education was "exactly fitted to meet the present needs of society and to fit the nobler nature of man," said Charles Fletcher Dole in 1897. Three years later, Theodore Thornton Munger was vacationing at Hampton when

Charles F. Thwing of Western Reserve University reported "significant ignorance about the Bible among college students." He called Thwing's article to the attention of a Hampton faculty member, who gave a similar test to her students. They scored significantly higher in biblical literacy than did the Northern white college students. Munger found "the prevalence of the student habit of mind" at Hampton. "Those who are seriously laboring to educate the 'tinted races,'" he said, "are not dealing in uncertainties. They not only know that in a real sense the negro can be educated, but that such education as that given in their institutions is the most hopeful ray yet cast upon a problem of enormous difficulty—a problem that belongs to time and to Providence, too great and complex for man except as he labors and trusts and waits." In humble confidence, Munger concluded, "they are giving themselves to a task of incomparable difficulty with a heroism that is itself the surest pledge of ultimate success."[13]

**H**ampton's most prominent graduate, Booker T. Washington, was prime evidence of the missionaries' success. His style was more secular than theirs. But for many of the social gospel prophets his gospel of practical Christianity, the work ethic, self-help, and education for service was American social Christianity's message in race relations. Born a slave in southwest Virginia in 1856, young Washington moved with his family to Malden, West Virginia, at the end of the Civil War. He got the rudiments of an education at the African Zion Baptist Church in the black community of Tinkersville. Taken into the home of a local white couple as a houseboy, Washington learned lessons in cleanliness, thrift, and hard work from his mistress. In 1872, he entered Hampton Institute and met Samuel Chapman Armstrong. "He made the impression on me of being a perfect man," said Washington; "I was made to feel that there was something about him that was superhuman." Booker T. Washington modeled "his career, his school, his social outlook, and the very cut of his clothes after Armstrong's example," said his biographer.[14]

At Hampton, Washington received the industrial education that became his life's work when he adopted it, almost unchanged, at his own school. Allowing impoverished students to work their way through school by apprenticeship in a trade, industrial education was a technique for teaching manual skills and mental discipline through practical object lessons. Inculcating the values of thrift and industry, it could be seen as providing skilled labor to a modern technological society, opportunity for working people to rise in the world, or a means to make them content with their lot. At Hampton, Washington also studied the Bible under the reserved liberal piety of a New England school marm. After graduation from Hampton and teaching in West Virginia, Washington studied theology at the Northern Baptist's Wayland Seminary in Washington, D.C., for six or eight months. He claimed to have "derived great benefit" from it, but the experience reinforced his doubts about classical education and urban life. Called to Hampton Institute by General Armstrong to teach night school and work with Indian students newly admitted to Hampton, Booker Washington earned Armstrong's growing respect. When he was asked to nominate a candidate to lead a new state institution for black students at Tuskegee, Alabama, Armstrong recommended Washington.[15]

The school opened in temporary facilities on 4 July 1881. Within months, the young principal purchased land for Tuskegee Institute. Within a year, Booker Washington made the first of many trips to the North to raise money for his new school. He called on Washington Gladden in Springfield, Massachusetts, on 5 May 1882. Gladden gave him a cordial reception, but neighboring pastors were more generous. As Washington developed a maturing taste in reading and experience in public speaking, he learned to say what his audiences longed to hear by paraphrasing those who were popular among them. His speech to Alabama's State Teachers' Association on 11 April 1888 abstracted remarks from Josiah Strong's *Our Country* on "social progress." When the Reverend Caleb Davis Bradlee sent Washington a copy of his *Sermons for All Sects*, which admonished "the poor and down cast to accept their lot and fulfill their mission by hard work," he expressed appreciation for the book's "practical religion." By the late 1880s, Washington's Northern contacts were strong enough for Chicago's Jenkin Lloyd Jones to say that he "is well known to the Unitarian workers of the country, and enjoys their confidence." Jones hoped his appeal for fifty-dollar scholarships would "not fall on deaf ears." The Tuskegee principal won such confidence by telling his audiences what they wanted to hear and by quiet public accommodation to legal discrimination. As a black leader in the rural South, his private opposition to discrimination led to a split between his public and his private self, which became more prominent as the years passed.[16]

Like Armstrong, Booker T. Washington believed that the key to improving black life in the South was to develop his institution as a model. In 1890, he published an attack on black clergymen as unfit to lead the race. The few well-trained Congregational, Episcopal, and Presbyterian ministers were out of touch with the black masses, he argued; three-fourths of the black Baptist and two-thirds of the Methodist ministers were "unfit, either mentally or morally, or both, to preach the Gospel to anyone or attempt to lead anyone." Too many black clergymen were like the one who lay down his hoe on a hot July day, saying: "O Lord, de work is so hard, de cotton is so grassy, and de sun am so hot, I bleave dis darkey am called to preach." Despite widespread angry reaction, some black leaders, including AME Bishop Daniel A. Payne and Ida B. Wells, came to Washington's defense. But, in response to the problem he described, Tuskegee received $10,000 to establish Phelps Hall Bible School. There, pastors trained in a "simple, direct and helpful" nondenominational curriculum were prepared for a rural ministry of practical Christianity. Lyman Abbott gave the dedicatory address.[17]

The pastor's school was part of Tuskegee's mission to the rural black South. Tuskegee was, "by no means, a local institution," said its Northern agent. It was "the real industrial center for the Black Belt region, not only of Alabama, but of all the southern states." Around this hub of agencies for social betterment in the rural South, said its promoters, spun mothers' meetings, YMCA work, a Young Women's Missionary Society, and a Temperance Legion. Sociologist Edward A. Ross voiced the theory behind the activity. "It is now recognized that not churches alone will lift the black race; not schools; not contact with the whites; not even industry," said Ross. "But all of these cooperating can do it. The growth of new and higher wants, coupled with the training to new skill, is the best lever for raising the idle, quarreling, sensual Afro-American. Certainly the infecting of the backward portion of the race with a high estimate of cleanliness, neatness, family privacy, domestic comfort, and literacy is quite as truly a moralizing agency as dread of future punishments or love for an ethical God." Tuskegee was the rural equivalent of the contemporary Christian urban mission.[18]

The Tuskegee Summer Assembly and the Tuskegee Negro Conference were two of its more important activities. Promoted as "the first attempt at a Chautauqua ever made by Negroes for Negroes," the Summer Assembly was held during two weeks of August at Phelps Hall. Eighty to a hundred pastors, teachers, businessmen, and parents attended its lectures in theology, domestic economy, and pedagogy by Booker T. Washington and others. It offered orchestral music, "innocent games" like croquet and tennis, and "drives in the country." The Tuskegee Negro Conference drew eight hundred to a thousand black farm workers each year. It combined the spiritual fervor of an evangelical camp meeting with the moral earnestness of a settlement-house mothers' club. In its morning sessions, Washington sought testimony about farm ownership, rentals, housing, and crop mortgages from the delegates. He asked about schools, length of terms, quality of teachers, and support from public taxes. Conferees discussed religious conditions and the quality of the clergy. Afternoon sessions at the Negro conference offered counsel about conditions outlined in the morning. Its resolutions called for hard work, rural self-help, farm ownership, improved churches and schools, crop diversification and rotation, and ending the crop lien system.[19]

The links from Hampton through Tuskegee to other schools exemplified the missionaries' hope for reproductive units of the redeeming community. Washington's work centered at Tuskegee, but in the late 1880s he also superintended Congregational schools at Society Hill, Cotton Valley, and East Tallassee, Alabama. Kowaliga Industrial School, thirty-five miles from Tuskegee, and Snow Hill Normal and Industrial Institute, ninety miles from Tuskegee, were inspired by Washington's school. Alabama's Mt. Meig's Institute, founded by a Tuskegee graduate, was called "Tuskegee's Child and Hampton's Grandchild." When white missionaries founded Calhoun Colored School at Calhoun, Alabama, in 1892, they modeled it on Hampton and Tuskegee. "Away with any so-called education which cannot regenerate the souls of men and women and redeem the social life and the economic life of [the] community," said the Reverend Pitt Dillingham. "Calhoun has a very practical idea of what the kingdom is, and it joins heartily in the new prayer going up all over Christendom, Thy kingdom come on earth as in heaven." By the mid-1890s, Washington's example was well known to social gospel prophets across the North. At Chicago's Plymouth Congregational Church on 27 January 1895, the Reverend Frank Gunsaulus, Bishop Samuel Fallows of the Reformed Episcopal Church, Jenkin Lloyd Jones, Graham Taylor of the Chicago Commons, and Edward W. Bemis of the University of Chicago heard him explain Tuskegee's industrial training in carpentry, milling, and brickmaking and bricklaying for boys, in dressmaking, housework, nursing, and sewing for girls.[20]

Washington's most important public address came at the Atlanta Cotton States Exposition on 18 September 1895. Before an audience of thousands, he spoke of the two races' common economic interests in the South. "Cast down your bucket where you are," he told black people; "cast it down in making friends in every manly way of the people of all races by whom we are surrounded. Cast it down in agriculture, mechanics, in commerce, in domestic service, and in the professions." He urged his white listeners to cast down their bucket among the black work force for employees. "In all things that are purely social we can be as separate as the fingers," Washington allowed, "yet one as the hand in all things essential to mutual progress." His meaning seemed clear and the audience roared its approval. In appealing to economic solidarity, the Tuskegeean suggested that divisive issues be set aside. "The wisest among my race understand that the agitation of questions of social equality is the extremist folly and that progress in the enjoyment of all the privileges that will come to us must be the result of severe and constant struggle rather than of artificial forcing," he said. "No race that has anything to contribute to the markets of the world is long in any degree ostracized." With cooperation between the races and the decline of sectional animosity, an infusion of Northern capital would bring material prosperity, "a new heaven and a new earth," to the South.[21]

The Atlanta address was widely praised. J. W. E. Bowen and W. E. B. Du Bois sent word of their enthusiasm. The freedmen must be taught to "love work," said Bowen. If white people offered economic opportunity to blacks and black people cooperated politically with whites, Du Bois said in the New York *Age*, "here might be the basis of a real settlement between whites and blacks in the South." Despite some black criticism of the Atlanta address, Northern heirs to abolitionism were supportive. The *Independent* declared Washington "fit to be the prophet and leader of his race. He preaches to his own people the gospel they most need." His objection to the Supreme Court's decision in *Plessy v. Ferguson*, which accepted the "separate but equal" doctrine in 1896, appeared in Joseph Cook's *Our Day*. "This separation may be good *law*," he admitted, "but it is not good common sense." Nature is responsible for racial distinctions, as for differences in hair color, he noted, and segregation according to the one makes no more sense than according to the other. "An unjust law injures the white man, and inconveniences the negro," he argued. "No race can wrong another race simply because it has the power to do so, without being permanently injured in morals, and its ideas of justice."[22]

After 1895, Booker T. Washington was the black man for all seasons in American social Christianity. Boston's Charles Fletcher Dole and George A. Gordon joined Tuskegee's board of trustees. Samuel June Barrows, editor of the *Christian Register*, sought his endorsement in a race for Congress in 1896. Four years later, Barrows's wife, Isabel, persuaded a Southern white woman to donate 800 acres of land near Anniston, Alabama, for a black school. Rochester's William Channing Gannett became a contributor to Tuskegee from 1898 to 1914. Ohio's Washington Gladden praised the Tuskegeean's rousing black people to self-help as "the very voice of God to them. Few prophets have answers in any generation with a clearer commission or a weightier message than God has given this noble black man," said Gladden. In Chicago, Henry Demarest Lloyd declared "Hampton and Tuskegee are the best schools in the United States." In 1899, Jane Addams hosted Margaret Murray Washington and the National Association of Colored Women; and Shailer Mathews sponsored her husband's visit at Chicago's Baptist Social Union.[23]

The social gospel press carried countless articles with a positive image of Washington, often in contrast with a stereotype of the "colored man." The familiar story of a man born in slavery and struggling upward to a position of racial leadership began to resonate with mythic themes in American literature from Benjamin Franklin to Horatio Alger. This man of humble origin was "the Moses who is leading the Southern negro out of the Egyptian bondage of ignorance" or the Joshua of his race. The "colored man" might be Christ-like, long-suffering, unresentful, and docile, a naturally religious person. But he was also a "natural politician," venally lining up for a political appointment. By contrast, said evangelist Thomas DeWitt Talmadge, the wisdom, good humor, and noble purpose of Booker T. Washington were the marks of a noble man. He sought no office. He created a position for himself and wanted nothing except to educate the young people of his race for life. By its disciplining influence, Tuskegee would correct ethical weakness. "There are no idlers in Tuskegee," said A. T. Pierson; its religious emphasis was not theoretical or emotional but practical. "Of all the lessons that need to be emphasized in the South, none is more needed than this, of *practical* Christianity."[24]

The white social gospel prophets were offended by the weak ethical dimension of the "colored man's religion." It is "emotional rather than ethical," said Washington Gladden; "it makes raptures the *essential* thing and cares nothing for righteousness." The "colored man's chickens and watermelons," as Booker T. Washington said, were "gathered from various sources." Washington told the story of a black man who testified to a weekly class meeting: "I'se had a ha'd time since our las' meetin'; I's been sometimes up and sometimes down. 'spect I's broken eb'ry one ob de ten comman'ments since our las' meetin', but I tanks God, I's not los' my 'ligion yet." Francis Greenwood Peabody gave the story broader application. "It seems a grotesque separation of faith from morals," he said, "but it is not more ludicrous and much less shameless, than the practices which to many cultivated people appear consistent with Christian discipleship and Christian worship." Few challenged the application of the story to black religion. The number of lynchings for "beastly crimes," the character of their dance, worship, and

Booker T. Washington, founder of Tuskegee Institute (First Congregational Church, Atlanta, Ga.)

religious leaders testified to its ethical weakness. "Without ambition in material things," wrote A. T. Pierson, "they live without self-restraint in moral things, their careless natures joined to their state of poverty and ignorance tend to divorce morality from their religion."[25]

But by 1898 New York's two journals of social Christianity, the *Independent* and the *Outlook*, differed considerably in their attitude to Booker T. Washington. The educator saw William Hayes Ward's *Independent* and the American Missionary Association as centers of Northern reform that had not fallen to his spell. "Personally, Dr. Ward is all right," Washington wrote, "but the paper is very much under the influence of the American Missionary Association, whose officers do everything in a sly way to hinder the work at Tuskegee." Six months later, the *Independent* condemned "The Worship of Booker T. Washington." It is wrong to "set him up as a sort of idol on a solitary African pinnacle and worship him," said the journal. "While we give all honor to Booker T. Washington, and while we highly value his work, we do not give it the primacy which some others do." He was merely a "sensible, prudent man, somewhat hampered in his utterances by his dependence on the Alabama legislature for his appropriation."[26]

By contrast, the *Outlook's* Lyman Abbott was the social gospel's most important publicist for Booker T. Washington. With thirty-five years of experience in race relations, he thought himself a moderate. He favored federal aid to education in 1890, opposed the Lodge Bill for federal inspectors of elections in the South, and preferred state restrictions of the ballot to literate men. In the decade of American imperialism, Abbott praised the Anglo-Saxon. America was not "officially Anglo-Saxon," but it was practically so, he said. Its ruling force in education, politics, and commerce "is not Celtic, nor Slavic, nor Semitic, nor African, nor Mongolian, but Anglo-Saxon." Abbott was proud to be an American, but said "in some sense it is a greater thing to be an Anglo-Saxon—I am proud that I belong to that race which dominates the world, whose branches stand together shoulder to shoulder, hand to hand, promoting intelligence, liberty, culture and civilization." His confidence in the national destiny rested on that assumption. "What does all this mean," he asked, "but that the Anglo-Saxon race is to act as a leader, and in the United States is to take no inferior place in leadership toward that brotherhood of man founded on justice and liberty which is the kingdom of God?"[27] His assumption seemed to contradict his objective.

Abbott insisted that Christian missions should serve all humanity. "No longer can we draw a line and put on one side men like the negro slaves, and say, they are not worth it, and on the other side an Anglo-Saxon race and say, they are worth it," he wrote. "All men are men; all men are God's children." But missions should not be ethnic transmuting pots. An Englishman had dismissed English missions as an effort to convert Hindus into second-hand Englishmen. If American missions were "an attempt to make Malays and Hindus and Negroes and Indians into second-hand Puritans," said Abbott, "the less we have of such missions the better." He rejected both missionary cultural imperialism and the idea that Latin, Malay, or Negro races were prepared for universal suffrage or self-government. Booker T. Washington, the model of what American missions could do among black people, summarized their attitude: "We believe in manhood suffrage, but manhood must come first, and suffrage afterward; not suffrage first and manhood" afterward. They would accept a restricted franchise, so long as the restriction was not racial. "An educated and cultivated Booker T. Washington shall not be turned away from the polls because his face is black," Abbott said, "while an ignorant, incompetent, drunken white man is permitted to cast his vote because his face is white."[28]

In December 1899, Lyman Abbott invited Washington to submit an autobiography to the *Outlook*. Washington hired a ghostwriter, Max Bennett Thrasher, to help draft the chapters of his story. Abbott advised the Tuskegee principal on organizing and presenting the story. "The pictorial side of your life, the experiences through which you have passed, the incidents which you have seen, out of which your generalizations have grown, will be of the first interest and the first value to your readers," said the New York editor. The joint effort of Booker T. Washington, Max Thrasher, and Lyman Abbott produced a minor classic in American literature, *Up from Slavery*. Serialized to the *Outlook*'s 100,000 subscribers, it was an immediate success. It "proved conclusively," said Ernest Howard Crosby, "that its author was one of the best and ablest men in the country, black or white." *Up from Slavery* was "a marvelously human book," said George A. Gordon. It showed "the desperate endeavor of a poor, starved life to get into fellowship with the great, resourceful and powerful race of man." Washington Gladden predicted that *Up from Slavery* would "rank among the world's great autobiographies." Its simple prose reflected the manliness, modesty, and good sense of the man. It emphasized economic development and insisted that fitness for the franchise must precede its exercise. "I believe that this principle is sound and solid," said Gladden, "that it applies to white people as well as to black people; and that it would be well if our entire political fabric could be rebuilt on this foundation." Few men of any color were more entitled to the nation's gratitude and honor than Booker T. Washington, for he embodied the American idea. "He believes in manhood more than in money or in office; he believes in service more than in self-aggrandizement." Despite his honors, Gladden concluded, Washington thought "less of praise to be gained than of work to be done" and was "ready to do what he can and to take such reward as Heaven shall send. May God give him forty more years of service for his race and his country with the increasing confidence of his fellow countrymen."[29]

*Up from Slavery* fixed Booker T. Washington's stature as the model black leader in the mind of American social Christianity. When President Theodore Roosevelt's lunching with him provoked bitter protest from the white South, Northern social gospel prophets rose to defend both men. Washington was "a good man, a Christian man, a scholar, a gentleman," said Topeka's Charles M. Sheldon. "Any man who is privileged to have Booker Washington to eat with him at his table should feel himself honored." George A. Gordon spoke for Paul Revere Frothingham, Thomas Wentworth Higginson, Bishop Henry Codman Potter, William Jewett Tucker, and others. "Every good citizen of the country admires President Roosevelt," said Gordon, "and every good citizen admires his guest." But Washington's social relations with Northern white friends were always a delicate matter. When Massachusetts's Episcopal Bishop William Lawrence visited Tuskegee, the principal unexpectedly asked him to greet an audience. "When Dr. Washington comes to Boston, my children always want to have him come to lunch or dinner," Lawrence began; "it is a pleasure, therefore, to me to be entertained by him here." The crowd's reaction showed that something was amiss, so he quickly ended his greeting and sat down. Only the pleas of influential persons kept reporters from sending news across the South that the Tuskegeean was teaching social equality between the races. The bishop asked a knowledgeable friend what would happen if a white Southerner entertained Booker T. Washington. The friend replied: "He would never do anything else."[30]

The "Would You Take Booker T. Washington to Lunch?" debate stretched from the sublime to the ridiculous. Amory H. Bradford envisioned a dinner party hosted by the president at which a Jewish philanthropist, an Indian physician, a Chinese Christian pastor, and a black leader planned the inauguration of the Kingdom of God in pluralistic America. "Such a dinner-party all lovers of humanity would approve," Bradford vowed, "and some such scene I firmly believe all loyal citizens of the republic will sometime demand." The debate reached a low in 1903, when an Indianapolis chambermaid refused to make up a bed in which the Tuskegeean had slept. In response, the pastor of Brooklyn's Plymouth Church, Newell Dwight Hillis, invited the black educator to address his congregation. If Washington spent the night at the parsonage and anyone refused to make up his bed, said the pastor, "I will gladly make it up myself, and consider it an honor to do so." If Hillis wished to make up Washington's bed, replied the *Atlanta News,* no one would object. "If he wants to sleep in the bed after Booker Washington has slept in it, let him do so," said the *News.* "Or, if he wants to sleep in the bed with the Tuskegee educator, by all means let no obstruction be placed in the way of the clerical negrophilist."[31]

Nonetheless, the translation of *Up from Slavery* into French, Spanish, German, Norwegian, Swedish, Danish, Finnish, Russian, Arabic, Zulu, Hindi, Chinese, Japanese, and Malayan gave Washington international renown. By 1902, Robert E. Speer wrote of his influence abroad. The missionary executive of a boys school in Nanking, China, said that "the practical wisdom and sagacity which Booker Washington has brought to bear upon the education of the Negroes is the same that is largely needed in dealing with the poorer classes in China." Recently three men of "the better class of the Chinese" had called for establishing an industrial mission at the Nanking boys school. After reading Washington's autobiography, a missionary wrote from Kobe, Japan: "Truly he is an exceptional man. It is like a fairy tale to think of a man who does not know when he was born, or who his father was, and to read how he finally came to take afternoon tea with the Queen of England and dinner with the President of the United States." Admitting himself to be "a Southerner of the Southerners," the missionary yet concluded that he felt a "justifiable pride in recalling that I am a fellow-statesman of Booker T. Washington."[32]

Georgia's Christian Commonwealth Colony illustrates Booker T. Washington's hold on American social Christianity. Founded in 1896 by white Christian socialists from Florida, North Carolina, and Nebraska, it included several hundred people on a thousand-acre cotton plantation, thirteen miles east of Columbus, Georgia. The colonists withdrew from society to celebrate the spirit of brotherhood, which "does away with artificial barriers and gives one natural connection with all one's kind." By common ownership of property and industrial cooperation, they hoped to establish a local unit of the Kingdom of God. As socialists, they sought an equality of effort and respect that also maintained individual differences. As idealists, who thought that no evil plant was devoid of good fruit, they believed the Spanish-American War was providentially uniting the nation, which had been divided for forty years. But their critique of imperialism played upon racial fears. "An inferior race in our own land is problem enough," said their journal, the Social Gospel. "How, then, can we rightly govern a far-away dependency of eleven millions of ignorant, superstitious, half-civilized and degraded people?" Rudyard Kipling's "The White Man's Burden" was a divine ideal by which no nation could live. They feared its words of moral obligation would serve as "a cloak for the ambition and greed of those who are in power." Yet, the colonists' sense of providence was strong. The evil of imperialism might be inevitable, but more certain was the final triumph of good, even if it was the overthrow of a corrupt American regime.[33]

Membership in the colony was open to all who would submit to its covenant and contract, surrender all goods to the community, and work for the common good. Visiting there in the late 1890s, Jane Addams found that bitter poverty kept it from being flooded with pauper applicants for membership. Black people apparently did not seek to join the colony. Its relationship with black neighbors differed little from that of other white landowners. When a pine section of the plantation was cut and burned over for planting in 1900, a crippled black widower and his three daughters agreed to sharecrop the land. "We furnish him with a mule and with all his provisions at cost to us and he is to return the amount to us in cotton next fall." The community's desire for moral betterment was expressed even here. "The girls are good workers and will help their father 'make a crop,'" said the Social Gospel. "No person can really know these colored people and their problems without seeing that together and co-ordinate with their need of better economic conditions is their need of ideals and a love of the beautiful."[34]

The Christian Commonwealth colonists found ideal moral nurture and practical economic improvement embodied in Booker T. Washington's Tuskegee Institute. In 1898, three of them went there to find the "true archimedean lever for the elevation of a race," said the Social Gospel. "Here was taught the trinity of skilled industry, education of mental powers, and an inspiring Christianity; and the effect is to implant a self-reliant and self-respecting character that marks a high order of useful citizenship." Critical of liberal arts institutions as slighting the pursuit of "serviceable knowledge," the colonists hoped to build a school to "remedy the ill effects of our factory system on the white race" and prepare young people for "the altruistic life of cooperative brotherhood." But just as they made plans to build the school, an epidemic, financial strain, and internal division struck the Christian Commonwealth Colony. It collapsed in June 1900.[35]

**A**nother force gathering in the late 1890s made a larger impression on the South than the Christian Commonwealth. In 1897, the Reverend Edward Abbott, editor of the *Literary World* and brother of Lyman Abbott, visited a resort at Capon Springs, West Virginia. Referring to the Mohonk conferences on Arbitration, the Indian, and the Negro, he suggested a similar conference on Southern education to his host, Captain W. H. Sale. Bishop Thomas U. Dudley of Kentucky convened the First Capon Springs Conference for Christian Education in the South on 29 June 1898. Its leaders included Amory Dwight Mayo, Jabez Lamar Monroe Curry of the Peabody and Slater funds, and Hollis B. Frissell of Hampton Institute. Black people were not invited, but white officers of black institutions attended the conference. The conferees heard papers on and commended support of elementary, industrial, and Christian higher education in the South.[36]

The conference dropped "Christian" from its name at its second meeting. Attendance was doubled by a contingent of Northern white philanthropists, including Robert Curtis Ogden, George Foster Peabody, and William H. Baldwin. It was chaired by J. L. M. Curry, seconded by Ogden, who was impressed by the critical state of American race relations. "I am growing very intense upon the Negro question," he told Peabody. Ten years would decide if "as a mass his race is to rise or fall in this country. I very much fear the fall. The main hope is in Hampton and Hampton ideas. Our first problem is to support the School; our second is to make the School ideas national." The Second Conference made ominous decisions about its direction, resolving that education of white people was the South's most pressing need, secondary and industrial education should be encouraged, and more reformatories, especially for black incorrigibles, should be established. The conference chose as its agent the Reverend George S. Dickerman, a Congregational pastor who became field superintendent of the American Missionary Association in 1893. Two years later, he accused AMA officers of fiscal irresponsibility. In 1898, Dickerman joined Hampton Institute's staff and took his charges to an AMA convention, where they were rejected. So the conference's agent was "a persistent and discredited critic of much of the best work in the South," said the

*Independent.* But it was just one more conference on Negro education at which none of those most concerned was invited to attend. "Several years ago Mr. Smiley called such a June conference at Lake Mohonk to parallel his October Indian Conference," the *Independent* recalled. "They could stand Indian guests, but not negro. This same cause will make the Capon Springs Conference the organ of the Southern, not the Northern, workers in the cause." Both black people and the most important denominational agency in the field were unrepresented at the Capon Springs Conferences on Education in the South.[37]

In January 1900, William H. Baldwin, president of the Long Island Railroad, led a party of white visitors, including Ogden, Curry, Frissell, George Foster Peabody, J. G. Phelps Stokes, the Reverend Charles F. Dole, and Isabel C. Barrows, to Tuskegee. There, they met a white Episcopal priest, Edgar Gardner Murphy of Montgomery, who addressed the faculty, students, and visiting philanthropists. Invited to meet with Tuskegee trustees, Murphy explained his plan for a conference on race relations in the South and won support from Baldwin, Ogden, and Peabody. Murphy's plan to include Washington and other black spokesmen in his conference was rejected by its Southern white sponsors, but he consulted with Washington about it. The Montgomery Conference on Race Problems of the South won critical interest in the North. Lyman Abbott's *Outlook* said that it was time to recognize that Southern race problems were in the hands of Southern white men. But pointing to the precedent of the Mohonk conferences, William Hayes Ward's *Independent* said that it would be "a meeting of white people to talk about the negro. That was a condition which killed a negro conference which Mr. Smiley tried for two years to carry on."[38]

The Conference of the Southern Society for the Promotion of the Study of Race Conditions and Problems in the South drew the largest audience in the city's history to Montgomery's auditorium on 8 May 1900. Excluded from the program, black observers were restricted to the arena's segregated galleries. Former secretary of the navy Hilary Herbert opened the meeting with praise for the removal of the Negro from Southern politics, pointed to signs of the race's deterioration, and called for education to prevent its decline. In a concluding address, New York Congressman W. Burke Cochran argued for repeal of the Fifteenth Amendment, but tried to refute racial pessimism with a sweeping gesture to the well-dressed audience in the segregated galleries as living evidence to confute theories of degeneracy. The Northern and black press criticized the Montgomery conference. Its "predominate sentiment" was "against the conclusions of justice," said the *Independent*. "The only solution is equal conditions, equal opportunities, equal rights, and every Southern conference will help it along." Bruce Grit dismissed Murphy's conference in the *Colored American* as "a gathering of Pharisees who continually thanked God that they were not as other men." But it exceeded Murphy's "most sanguine expectations," proving that intelligent men could deal with critical issues "without going into hysterics." Since it would promote first-hand investigation of conditions, Booker T. Washington said that "on the whole, I cannot but feel convinced that this Conference is going to serve a good purpose." Nothing came of Murphy's plan to establish a journal to deal with race relations on a worldwide scale and hold a second annual session of the Southern Society, but he was launched on an important career in racial reform.[39]

Attention fixed upon the Montgomery conference temporarily drew interest from the Capon Springs Conference. Its attendance declined in 1900 and the important lay trinity of Baldwin, Ogden, and Peabody was absent. But Ogden was elected president of the Capon Springs Conference in his absence. The new president of the Conference on Education in the South was a large man, with a fine white beard and pince-nez glasses. With a Yankee merchant's shrewdness and flair for public relations, he brought to the Southern education movement the mentality of a Presbyterian businessman who made charity and good works synonymous with his vocation. Determined to make the Conference on Education in the South more effective, Ogden moved its next meeting from the West Virginia resort to Winston-Salem, North Carolina. "Throughout the South a class of people is arising with a larger understanding of the intellectual conditions and educational needs of their section," he said. "At present they are somewhat lonely, and it would be a very great advantage to bring Northern sympathy into touch with a number of these people." Engaging the Pennsylvania Railroad's finest private train, with two dining cars and fresh flowers daily in each compartment, he launched a series of annual excursions from the North in the interest of Southern education at a cost of $8,000 to $25,000 per year. "My own relation to the whole affair is much like that of a conductor to a street car," Ogden said; "my duty being to ring the bell for the starting and stopping and so much intent upon the progress of which that I cannot take in very clearly what the passengers are talking about." But he was gathering around him a network of contacts and forces that became the "Ogden movement."[40]

In its first year, when a New York paper carried the story headline "MEN OF MILLIONS TO REDEEM THE SOUTH," Ogden's party took John D. Rockefeller, Jr., George Foster Peabody, William H. Baldwin, Lyman Abbott, Bishop W. N. McVickar, Francis Greenwood Peabody, and Charles H. Parkhurst to Hampton Institute, Winston-Salem, North Carolina, and Tuskegee Institute. "I shall have to get instruction from others," said Parkhurst, "to acquaint myself with the colored problem." For others, the object was "talk, laughter, argument, observation, comradeship." Amid the uproar, an observer recalled, "Professor Peabody would tell of a man who inscribed on the tombstone of his wife: 'Tears cannot bring her back, therefore I weep.'" Bishop McVickar told of a Kentuckian "who, drinking his first glass of milk punch, exclaimed: 'Heavens, what a cow!' And someone told Booker T. Washington's favorite little tale of a Negro seen lying in the shade of a tree early one afternoon. Asked what he was doing there, he said: 'Oh, I'se waiting 'till it's time to quit work.'" Suspicious Southerners referred to Ogden's touring guests as "picturesque junketers," "Pullman car philanthropists," and "the swell-belly parade."[41]

Besides the Northern guests, North Carolina Governor Charles B. Aycock, Charles D. McIver, Charles W. Dabney, and other leaders of the Southern education movement joined the seventy persons who gathered in Winston-Salem for the fourth annual conference. Lyman Abbott, Charles Parkhurst, and Francis Greenwood Peabody spoke there. Abbott restated Atticus Haygood's theme. "There can be no universal suffrage without universal education," said the New York editor. "Some would put suffrage first and education afterwards. I would put education first and suffrage afterwards." The conference's most important act was to establish an executive committee to raise and direct funds for a campaign for a stronger public school system in the South. In Atlanta, Francis Greenwood Peabody took half of the Ogden party to Atlanta University where he gave an address. The remainder joined a black congregation at the Reverend Henry Hugh Proctor's First Congregational Church, where Charles Parkhurst spoke. "When it comes to the resurrection, I presume we shall all be of the same color," he said. "I don't know whether we shall be black or white, and I don't know that it shall make any difference what color we are. We may be red, or black, or blue, or green. After all, it is the soul that counts." The remarks provoked Georgia's Governor Allen D. Candler. "This man Parkhurst is an old crank, as everybody knows," said the governor, who criticized the New York preacher for stirring his audience to a pitch of color conceit, making them impudent to their white neighbors. "Really," said the *Independent* of Parkhurst's comments, "this is not seditious."[42]

But when the Ogden party returned to the North, Parkhurst and Abbott had capitulated to white racism. "We learned to look upon matters more in the way in which the Southern mind regards them," Parkhurst told his Madison Square Presbyterian congregation. "The less the negro talks about his civic rights under the Constitution, particularly the right of suffrage," he said, "the better it will be for him. The undiscriminating act by which the negroes obtained the right to vote was a blunder." The *Independent* rejected his claim. Enfranchising the freedmen, said its editors, was an act of "magnificent courage and justice." Noting Parkhurst's advice that black Americans "learn to work," the New York journal exclaimed: "As if they never worked! Negroes are individual human beings having just the same human rights that everybody else has and to be treated no differently." For his part, Lyman Abbott announced that "we have got to get rid of the more or less vague idea that all men are created free and equal." The "attempt to force either political or social equality" inflicts "incalculable injury on the negro and the Nation." Fisk University President James G. Merrill was closer to the mark. "The trouble is that, both North and South, men are forgetting negroes are Americans," said Merrill.[43]

In November 1901, Ogden announced the organization of the Southern Education Board. It was chaired by Ogden, with Edgar Gardner Murphy as executive secretary and Booker T. Washington and George S. Dickerman as field agents. The Southern Education Board organized a propaganda campaign to win increased state and local support of public schools throughout the South. The campaign had a budget of about $40,000 per year for ten years, underwritten by contributions from Andrew Carnegie, George Foster Peabody, John D. Rockefeller, Robert C. Ogden, and the Russell Sage Foundation. Its task was enormous. The South's illiteracy rate in 1900 was as high as it had been in 1850. Of 217 counties in the United States in which 20 percent of voting-age males were illiterate in 1900, 212 were in the South. The average school term in the Southern seaboard states was a hundred days, about half that of New England. Only three-fifths of the school-age children were enrolled in school. Less than three-fifths of them were in school on an average day. So only a third of the South's school-age children were ordinarily in a classroom. Southern school systems were impoverished. Per pupil expenditures, teacher salaries, the value of school property, and the number of library books lagged far behind national averages. Finally, the half-loaf with which the

South supported its public schools was inequitably divided by the dual system of racial schools.[44]

The Southern Education Board joined a network of philanthropic boards active in Southern education. It established a community of interest with the Peabody and Slater funds at its first meeting. When the General Education Board was founded six months later as an instrument of John D. Rockefeller's benevolence, it became "a permanent 'steering committee' for Northern sentiment" in Southern education. Membership on the Southern and the General Education Boards was interlocking, with Baldwin and Ogden serving successively as presidents of the latter and Peabody as treasurer of both. Rockefeller's first gift of $1 million to the General Education Board grew to $53 million by 1909. Members of the Southern Education Board served as agents of the Peabody, Slater, and General Education boards and when the Anna T. Jeanes Foundation for black elementary education in the South was established in 1907, a majority of its trustees were members of the Southern Education Board. Ogden was at once president of the Southern and General Education boards, trustee of the Jeanes Fund, president of Hampton Institute's trustees, and a trustee of Tuskegee. This philanthropic network was a new "benevolent empire," unmatched in the United States since the Civil War. "Virtual monopolistic control of educational philanthropy for the South and the Negro" placed "a special responsibility for wise judgment and action" on these boards, wrote Louis Harlan. "In their early years their work seems to have suffered more from excessive caution than from any abuse of power."[45]

The cadre of Southern Episcopalians and Northern Baptists atop the administrative hierarchy of the new "benevolent empire" espoused the social gospel. The new philanthropic elite included Edgar Gardner Murphy, executive secretary of the Southern Education Board; Wallace Buttrick, executive director of the General Education Board; Frederick T. Gates, president of the General Education Board; and James Hardy Dillard, president of the Jeanes Fund. Born in Arkansas and raised in Texas, Murphy studied philosophical theology at the University of the South and at New York's General Theological Seminary. In parishes at Laredo, Texas, Chillicothe, Ohio, Kingston, New York, and Montgomery, Alabama, his ministry combined a broad church theological liberalism and a thoughtful conservative's approach to child-labor reform, public education, and race relations. The only layman in the new elite, Dillard was a Virginia Episcopalian who studied at Washington and Lee. After teaching school in Norfolk, New York, and St. Louis, he went to Tulane University in 1891 as professor of Latin. There, he became a public citizen, active in the Child Welfare Association, the Free Kindergarten Association, and the state board of education. His interests included Henry George's Single Tax and the Episcopalians' Christian Social Union. A trustee of several black colleges, he secured a branch for Negroes when he was president of the New Orleans public library. In 1907, Dillard became president and director of the Negro Rural School Fund, endowed by the Philadelphia Quaker, Anna T. Jeanes.[46]

Wallace Buttrick and Frederick Gates, both New York Baptists, were born in 1853, graduated from Rochester Theological Seminary, ordained in the Baptist ministry, and served congregations in Minnesota and New York. In 1888, Gates became corresponding secretary of the American Baptist Education Society. Impressed with his ability, John D. Rockefeller made him an advisor on financial affairs. As a pastor interested in social issues, Buttrick joined Samuel Zane Batten, William Newton Clarke, and Walter Rauschenbusch for meetings of the Marlboro Brotherhood of the Kingdom Conference. In 1900, Gates asked him to study American Baptist Home Missionary Society schools for Negroes in the South. After he toured the schools, Buttrick's report led to his selection as executive director of the General Education Board. "I am more and more impressed with the idea that the teaching of Jesus has never had a fair show," Buttrick told Robert Ogden. "Lately I have come to see that the teachings of Jesus abound in helpful social teachings not only for his day but for all times and for all peoples."[47]

The Southern Education Board met for a week each winter in Robert Ogden's New York offices; its Southern campaigners rested each summer at Peabody's estate on Lake George, New York. Booker T. Washington served as an agent for the Southern Board, met often with its Northern members, and spoke from the same platform with its Southern members. But he did not attend board meetings, Ogden failed to get him on the program of the Conference on Education in the South, and black people were never invited to its meetings. From the beginning, the work of the Southern Education Board was viewed with skepticism in some Northern circles. The *Independent* quoted an early broadside: "If the negro question is to be settled aright, it must be settled by educated, intelligent white men, and not by ignorant ones [why not by negroes?]. This being the case, the highest welfare of the negro lies in the better education of the whites [why not of negroes?]. The solution of this problem is to be found in teaching the negro to work, and so to be a self-respecting citizen." The statement apparently meant, said the *Independent*, that "we must educate the whites, to teach the negroes to work, who already do most of the work, and this will 'solve the problem'!" Northern egalitarians would not be deceived by such "muddled non-sense," said the editors.[48]

When the Ogden train left for Hampton and Tuskegee in April 1902, it carried Felix Adler of the Ethical Culture Society, William Adams Brown of Union Theological Seminary, Wallace Buttrick, Paul Revere Frothingham of Boston, Percy Stickney Grant of New York, the *Outlook's* Hamilton Wright Mabie, Oswald Garrison Villard of the New York *Evening Post*, and Lillian Wald of the Nurses Settlement. Addressing the conference, Adler held that a "true democracy" must fulfill two conditions: everyone should do the work for which he is best fitted; and an aristocracy of merit should rule, "a house of aristocracy, the gates of which shall ever be open, both those that lead into and those that lead out of it." Like a knight errant, he said, the Ogden party treaded stony paths, penetrated thorny hedges, slew Monsters of Prejudice on the way to the South's enchanted palace to awaken her Sleeping Beauty and win her for a perpetual union.[49]

By 1903, the "Ogden movement" was a powerful coalition. But it sought to avoid public controversy and threats from either side of its consensus. It hoped "to find the right line of action so far as we can discover it," Ogden wrote, in "the simple faith that ultimate good is sure to result from sincere and earnest effort to keep on our way without discouragement" and that "a broader intelligence and purer conscience may ultimately bring public opinion, public journals and public authorities in harmony with the causes that make for a better Christian civilization." Lyman Abbott outlined its platform in race relations: (1) the Negro is here to stay; (2) the Negro would remain a separate race; (3) the races serve the common good by living together in peace; (4) Negroes must be given primary and industrial education; (5) black leadership must be offered higher education; (6) states may determine voter qualifications; and (7) education and property qualifications enforced equally on both races are acceptable.[50]

Denominational missionary agencies, particularly the American Missionary Association, were a threat to the education coalition. The Southern Education Board executives, Edgar Gardner Murphy and George S. Dickerman, were at the heart of suspicion between the new benevolent empire and the old missionary agency. When he became field agent of the Southern Education Board, Dickerman continued to circulate his charges of fiscal irresponsibility

Robert C. Ogden, William Howard Taft, Booker T. Washington, and Andrew Carnegie (left to right) at the celebration of Tuskegee Institute's twenty-fifth anniversary in 1906 (Tuskegee University Archives)

against AMA officers. When AMA President Washington Gladden asked its staff about them, they dismissed the charges as "captious and unworthy of serious attention." During the recession years, 1892 and 1893, money from the Daniel Hand Fund was used to prevent the closing of some schools in the South, the staff said, but "the income from the fund has been sacredly devoted to the purposes named in the will, and nothing in the nature of misappropriation has ever taken place."[51]

The AMA and the education coalition differed over more than this. Murphy alluded to it in planning the Conference on Education in the South in 1903. "Under contemporary conditions the discussion of any phases of the negro is a rather difficult undertaking," he told a Southern clergyman. "If it is to be done at all, it is to be done by a Southern man. I have turned from such men as [AMA President] Washington Gladden and others." Murphy invited the Southern clergyman to speak, encouraging him to reject all thought of social equality. Since public opinion held that Negroes should be educated, said Murphy, it was in the white South's interest to control it. The difference was more explicit in an exchange between Dickerman and Chaplain Edward T.

Ware of the AMA's Atlanta University. Dickerman charged that Northern missionaries had made "educational mistakes" after the Civil War and that the missionary institutions taught social equality. "I say we do not teach social equality—it cannot be forced upon people," Ware replied. "It does not make the student the social equal of the teacher if they sit at the same table in the school dining room." But Northern missionaries "who came South directly after the war believed that the Negro was a *man*" with "capabilities and ought to have opportunities for the development of the highest that was in him," said Ware. "They believed that God was no respecter of persons and that man had no right to be. They believed in universal brotherhood. The world in which they lived was against them, but they believed these things and were undaunted because they were sure that they were working the work of God." There were many still in Southern schools "who will not burn incense to the god of prejudice," Ware wrote, "but there are those who would like to see every one interested in education also interested in making the Negro learn to keep his place—his man-appointed place."[52]

Officers of the American Missionary Association occasionally participated in Ogden's Southern education tours, but they did so as guests, not as insiders. When Ogden's train pulled out of the North in April 1903, it carried social Christianity's foremost apologists for the education coalition, Lyman Abbott and Francis Greenwood Peabody. At Hampton, Abbott argued that black Southerners should have an equal opportunity in life, equal opportunity in industrial and higher education, and the opportunity to participate in government when they showed the capacity for it. At the Conference on Education in the South at Richmond, Peabody assured conferees that they had achieved a rare and wise consensus. The Philippines, labor unions, and socialism were divisive issues whose solution was uncertain. But reasonable men no longer debated "what should be done for the South, and by the South and with the South," said the Harvard ethicist. "Illiteracy is inconsistent with democracy." Education "begins at the bottom and not at the top" and "does not mean political service or racial antagonism." North and South have a common stake in it as the "key" to social order and security. The North should accept the "sacrifice" made by Southern states for education as "the most honorable achievement of modern American statesmanship," said Peabody; "all this is conclusively determined, and this is the common faith in which we meet."[53]

The influence of the coalition's consensus was carried to the National Conference on Charities and Corrections in Atlanta by its president, Robert

W. DeForest, and to the People's Institute at New York's Cooper Union by Percy Stickney Grant. In his address, DeForest elevated the coalition's claim that "the negro problem is essentially a southern problem and must be solved by southern people" from the level of pragmatic compromise to a sociological principle. The Negro was the white South's "problem," just as European immigrants were New York's and the Chinese were California's problem. At Cooper Union, the pastor of New York's Church of the Ascension attacked the theory of racial equality that led to enfranchisement of the freedmen. Grant said that evolution had demonstrated the inequality of the races, the intractability of racial differences, and the folly of impatience with natural forces and insistence on "forcing the lower into the higher." When education and the natural processes of competition made black people fit for the franchise, he concluded, it could be given to them.[54]

By 1904, when Booker T. Washington privately complained that leaders of the education coalition were not consulting black leaders, Ogden voiced his paternalistic defense. "My first and principal motive is the good of the colored people in the South and the encouragement of forces in the Southern States that will accomplish much good for both races," he said. "There is a great deal of the seed of the Kingdom of Heaven growing secretly. The world does not see it, but yet it exists." But the tenuous character of his consensus deepened Ogden's caution. "I am more deeply impressed every day with the complications of the Southern situation," he told Baldwin. Not one man in a hundred understood it. "The South is insane on the Negro question," he wrote. "Not one Southern man in ten thousand approaches correct views. White illiteracy is a body of death. The relation of the races has involved real complications quite aside from prevailing injustice. We are doing good but can destroy it in five minutes." But black leaders had reason to despair of the coalition. By 1904, Lyman Abbott had endorsed constitutional amendments in Alabama, Louisiana, Mississippi, South Carolina, and Virginia that combined literacy and property requirements with a poll tax to disfranchise black voters in massive numbers. "Any man is entitled to vote, black or white, if he can read the English language, owns $300 worth of property and pays his poll tax," he said. "And men call that disfranchising the negro. I believe in this honest endeavor" to limit the suffrage to men of sufficient intelligence, prudence, economy, and patriotism, said Abbott. It should have, "not our grudging acquiescence, but our cordial and hearty cooperation."[55]

In April 1904, Ogden's Southern tour included Edward Cummings of Harvard, Thomas Wentworth Higginson, Massachusetts's Episcopal Bishop Wil-

liam Lawrence, and Anson Phelps Stokes. At Hampton, Higginson recalled a
fine meeting of speeches, jovial storytelling, and rousing spirituals. As the
train passed through North Carolina, he saw deserted cotton fields, solitary
Negro cabins "swarming with women and children," and a new cotton mill
region of "absolutely ignorant" white people from the mountains. Bishop
Lawrence recalled waking up on the train one Sunday morning near the
Calhoun School in Alabama and catching an unforgettable glimpse of the
South: "A great company of negro men, women and children in wagons, on
horse and muleback, many barefoot and walking, yellow bandannas and red
flannel petticoats flashing in the sunlight." Here, where eleven out of twelve
people were black, Northern missionaries had been working for ten years at
the Calhoun School. "One smart Yankee girl, a physician," said the bishop,
walked or rode "in black and lonely country unattended day or night." As the
Ogden party left its train for the School, he recalled, "a massive black woman,
with brilliant bandanna and skirt, slipped off her mule and gave me a 'leg up'
onto her saddle."[56]

At Birmingham, Southern Methodist Bishop Charles B. Galloway of Mississippi addressed the Conference on Education in the South. He did not
know what the Negro might become, but the bishop said that he should be
treated in accord with the ethic and spirit of Jesus and have equal opportunity
to fulfill his destiny. Noting racial hostility in Mississippi, Galloway denounced
the cry of "white supremacy" as "the emptiest cant." Racial segregation and
disfranchisement were settled issues, he said, but black people should be
guaranteed educational opportunity and equal protection of the law. His
message was sharply criticized in Mississippi, but Ogden thought it was
"epoch-making," sure to influence the region profoundly. Higginson had
abandoned advocacy of black people's civil rights two decades earlier and
avoided controversial issues in public appearances on the trip through the
South. But he and Cummings were so impressed by their experience in the
Ogden party that they appeared before a group of Boston's black radicals to
declare their solidarity with Booker T. Washington and the Southern education movement. In an article emphasizing the common humanity of the races,
Higginson speculated about miscegenation in the future. The Southern white
press bitterly attacked him for advocating race mixing and Ogden for bringing
the old miscegenator into the region.[57]

In 1904, William DeWitt Hyde joined the education coalition's common
ground in race relations with "A National Platform on the Race Question."
Frankly recognizing its compromises, the Bowdoin College president offered

planks that acknowledged significant racial differences, affirmed a deeper unity between the races, and recognized that racial policies would vary among the regions depending upon the concentration of the black minority within them. He proposed to accept racial segregation and restrict liquor sales where large numbers of black people lived. Illicit interracial sex should be condemned and punishment for brutal assaults by members of one race upon those of another should be swift, certain, and severe. But standing before the law and qualification for the franchise should be exactly the same for both races. Hyde proposed primary and industrial education for the masses and higher education to talented black people for racial leadership. He favored support of Southern education, the pragmatic direction of the General Education Board, and federal aid to education if the South asked for it. The *Independent* rejected his platform. The "tint and taint" of Hyde's premise that "differences between the races are deeper than the skin" and must be expressed in race relations "discolors and distempers the whole platform," said its editors, "for it accepts race differentiations as a principle to control the treatment of the races."[58]

When the Ogden party departed for Hampton, Columbia, South Carolina, and Tuskegee in April 1905, it included Ernest Hamlin Abbott of the *Outlook*, Edward T. Devine of New York's Charity Organization Society, Arthur W. Kinsolving of Brooklyn, Samuel Chiles Mitchell of Richmond College, and Boston's Robert Treat Paine. Following a conference at Columbia, which did not arouse much enthusiasm for popular education in South Carolina, Ogden's train had a disastrous wreck at Greenville. Some railroad employees were killed and members of Ogden's party were seriously injured. The wreck triggered criticism of the propriety of the annual Southern trips. Hired by Charleston's *News and Courier* to do a series of articles, Thomas Dixon, Jr., launched a virulent attack on Ogden as "a fanatic of dangerous and far-reaching power" in race relations. With "his crazy notions about the negro," Dixon charged, Ogden had engaged in "a loathsome and disgusting performance" by introducing Booker T. Washington to a Cooper Union audience in New York. He had even given the Tuskegee educator a familiar tour of his Wanamaker's department store.[59]

Dixon's articles led to a whispering campaign against the education reformers. Ogden's black friends, T. Thomas Fortune, Booker T. Washington, and Philadelphia's Presbyterian pastor, Matthew Anderson, agreed that Dixon's racial attack was "too contemptible for notice" and "so absolutely absurd as to make a denial or explanation purely ridiculous." But soon after the wreck Robert Ogden vowed to discontinue the annual Southern tours. Other friends urged him to be steadfast in the educational awakening. Josiah Strong wrote of his "joy in the educational revival which is taking place in the South, and to which you have doubtless contributed more than any other man." Ogden rendered a valuable service to the country, Strong wrote, "in helping to remove some of the old prejudices between North and South, and making these two sections one sympathetically as they are one politically."[60] Persuaded to relent, Ogden continued his excursions for a few more years. But the wreck and continuing criticism weakened his movement's effectiveness.

Partly because of the "Ogden movement," the annual excursions, the Conferences on Education in the South, and the propaganda campaign of the Southern Education Board, Southern public education expanded remarkably after 1900. Expenditures on education increased by 180 percent in Virginia, North and South Carolina, and Georgia between 1900 and 1912. By 1915, the average school term increased by a month in each of those states, except North Carolina, where it was extended by two months. Enrollment also increased, so that almost half of the South's school-age children attended school daily. The average North Carolina child attended twenty-two days of school in 1900, but that increased to sixty-six days by 1915. Per pupil expenditures doubled in the four south Atlantic states, again except for North Carolina, where they tripled. The value of public school property increased fourfold in Virginia and Georgia and eightfold in North and South Carolina. The average teacher's salary tripled in North Carolina and doubled in the other three states. Impressive as the gains were, the South was still handicapped by poverty, still lagged far behind the rest of the United States in public education, and increased support yielded only a small gain on national averages.[61]

The Southern Education Board played a major role in expanding educational opportunity for white children, but it failed to improve public education measurably for black children. As early as 1906, Booker Washington told Ogden that "a great deal is being done in the way of improving the white public schools." He did not complain about black public education in larger communities. But "in the country districts I am quite sure that matters are going backward," said Washington, "and I am afraid that the Southern members of the various boards do not put themselves on record in a straight and frank manner as much as they should." Additional taxes to extend school terms meant little so far as black schools were concerned. "In many cases in Alabama teachers are being paid as little as Ten dollars per month. This of course means no school. I actually saw a contract made between a Negro teacher and a school official, to the effect that he was to teach school at the rate of $1.60 per month." The justice of his complaint was common knowledge to leaders of the Southern education movement. "Passionate and rapidly developing enthusiasm for white education is bearing sharply and adversely upon the opportunities of the negro," Murphy told Wallace Buttrick. "There is not only no chance to help the situation of the negro educationally, but it is steadily growing worse and their schools are being hampered and impoverished where they are not actually abandoned."[62]

A Northern teacher in the South illustrated the problem by an example at Athens, Georgia. When the town fathers established a public school system in the late nineteenth century, they bargained with black voters. If they supported the measure, schools of equal size and similar structure would be built for each race. When the teacher visited Athens several years later, the town's black and white students each had a fine brick building. As white enrollment grew and the community's black voters were disfranchised, the board of education found it cheaper to move black students from their school and make it a second facility for white students instead of building another brick school. The black students were sent to a less satisfactory frame building on the edge of town.[63] That reality made the theme of Atticus Haygood, Lyman Abbott, and Booker T. Washington—education, first; then, the franchise—tragically superficial.

**R**ealization that the education campaigns were widening the gap in the quality of education for black and white students in the South may have been a factor in the decline of the Southern Education Board after 1907. Robert C. Ogden died in 1913, the Southern Education Board merged with the General Education Board a year later, the education campaigns ended in 1915, and the last Conference on Education in the South was held in 1917. They had led an educational awakening in the South. Tax funds for Southern public education continued to grow through the next decade. But the reformers' compromise with racial discrimination meant that the segregated schools grew increasingly "separate and unequal."[64]

# 7

# Urban Mission

America's black urban ghettos were already in embryo by 1900, when seventy-two American cities had black populations of over 5,000. Seventy percent of black people in the North lived in cities. Washington, D.C., had the world's largest black community, numbering over 86,000. By 1910, New York and Washington both had more than 90,000 Negroes; Baltimore and Philadelphia had black communities of more than 80,000. Within the Northern metropolis, these communities were still relatively small. "Chicago is out of the negro belt," James Clark Ridpath wrote in 1890. "You will walk several squares through the heart of the metropolis without seeing a single dusky face in the throngs that surge along the streets." But between 1890 and 1910, New York's black community grew from 1.4 to 2.0 percent of the city's population. Chicago's black population increased from 1.3 to 2.0 percent of its total; and black Philadelphia grew from 3.8 to 5.5 percent. In cities along the border, black communities were a more substantial factor in 1910, with 9.3 percent of the population in Indianapolis, 10.4 percent in Wilmington, 15.2 percent in Baltimore, and 28.5 percent in Washington. "In every important Northern city," said Ray Stannard Baker in 1908, "a distinct race-problem already exists, which must, in a few years, assume serious proportions."[1]

In 1900, 90 percent of black Americans still lived in the South, where only 18 percent of them lived in cities. But Baton Rouge, Charleston, Jacksonville, Montgomery, Savannah, Shreveport, and Vicksburg were more than 50 percent black. New Orleans's black community exceeded 77,000; and Memphis had more than 50,000 Negroes. There and in Atlanta, Chattanooga, and Louisville, the black population was growing rapidly. Memphis's black community tripled in twenty years; Chattanooga's grew by 600 percent.[2] Black urbanization would transform the nature of American race relations. Normative rural patterns of racial paternalism and deference did not readily translate to the city. There, strangers with no accepted pattern of relations felt crowded by physical proximity, making social distance seem all the more necessary. Even as the ghetto grew, the walls around it were strengthened. Many blacks fought their exclusion by the city's white residents. Others turned to building separate institutions for the life of the community. Even as they were excluded from the franchise in the South, blacks in Northern cities were forming a base for new political influence in decades to come. Finally, the city reshaped the typical form of racial violence from lynching to the race riot.

**A**ll that imperiled American civilization, Josiah Strong argued in 1885, was enhanced and concentrated in the city. Twenty-five years later, Frank Mason North warned that "the negro will not be a successful factor in our modern civilization unless he can survive the test of the city." Shunned by organized labor and forced to live under conditions that could degrade anyone, black people faced severe obstacles in the city. "Through sea and desert he may be led," said North, "but he comes to the Kingdom only through the conquest of the high-walled cities." Early studies by social reformers showed that the perils of life in black urban communities were real enough. Black Americans had higher mortality rates than other urban groups, particularly high infant mortality. The death rate from tuberculosis among black adults was staggering. They paid higher rents for inferior housing, received lower wages at more menial jobs, and had higher crime rates than other urban groups. Finally, black urban communities had a high percentage of unmarried young people and women outnumbered men by a ratio of six to five. But black Americans moved to the city despite the social gospel prophets' warning about the perils of crime and pauperism, intemperance and vice, industrial and class conflict. "First, there is in the great cities an in-draught, like that of a whirlpool, drawing in all floating elements about them," Francis Greenwood Peabody told Hampton's alumni, "then there is a down-draught, and these elements go to the bottom and become a solid residuum." Like a great dragon, said Peabody switching metaphors, the city first invites and then consumes them.[3]

Other social gospel prophets spoke more graphically of the peril of urban life to black Americans. Benjamin Orange Flower took readers of *Civilization's Inferno* to Boston tenements where "creaking stairways are worn and carpeted with filth; the walls and ceilings blistered with the foul accretions of months and perhaps years." The air was "heavy with odors of spoiled fish, decaying vegetables, smoke from old pipes, and stale beer," he wrote; the noise mixed "snatches of low songs, oaths, coarse jests, and the savage voices of poor wretches whose brains are inflamed and tongues made thick with rum." In a filthy den, he found a lovely young Creole woman, whose companion was "a low-browed, thick-necked negro." The "sunshine of girlishness" blended with the "shadow of vice" in the young woman, Flower said. She did not yet bear the signs of debauchery, "save in a certain expression of the eyes and a brazen smile, which speak volumes against the probability of restoration."[4]

A New York City missionary described similar scenes, but insisted on the possibility of restoration. Nightly, she visited saloons in the Bowery to seek an audience for her meetings. "Bare-headed colored women, in soiled calico dresses, with sleeves rolled up, stopped before entering the brothels to join with rough-looking sailors in a 'break-down,'" she recalled. Pushing past the painted women outside the Black and Tan Saloon, the missionary entered its dingy, narrow bar room. Its stale air smelled of tobacco and cheap rum. The proprietor kept a club within reach to break up knife and razor fights that sometimes broke out among his patrons. Women of all shades, from coal black to light tan, in flashy dress and cheap jewelry, entertained white, black, and yellow men. "Dusky negroes" sat at card games in a back room. Downstairs a small band played wheezy music in a room crowded with dancers of mixed races. The city missionary did not think the indiscriminate interracial mixing at the Black and Tan Saloon was a paradigm for the Kingdom of God, but she invited a young mulatto woman to her meeting.

"Me go to meetin'; wal I guess you dunno who you's invitin'," said the woman. "Why I'se a sinner, I is; you don' want no such as I is; I ain't good 'nuf to go to no meetin'."

"Oh yes, you are," the missionary replied; "Christ came to save lost sinners, however bad. He came for the lost."

Leaving the Hell Gate Saloon one night, the city missionary found a "burly negro" standing near a drunken woman clinging to a lamp post. The thin, consumptive woman wore only a dirty calico dress which barely covered her nakedness. Her hair was matted and tangled, her face bruised and swollen. She was a slave of the huge Negro who had blackened her eyes when she had not brought him enough money. The city missionary invited the beaten woman to her meeting. She appeared at its close, asked for prayers, and showed a desire to lead a better life. The twenty-seven-year-old woman had lived for nine years on Baxter Street and had no home but the den of infamy from which she came. So the city missionary decided to take her to a Christian mission home. As they left for the horsecars, the women were confronted by the burly Negro:

"Whar you folks taken' dat gal to?" Alone, near midnight, on a dark street, the city missionary sent the woman ahead and grabbed the black man by the coat, crying:

"I am taking her to a Christian home—to a better life. If ever you prayed for any one, pray for her; I know you are a bad man, but you ought to be glad to help any girl away from this place. So pray for her as you have never prayed before." She spoke so rapidly that the black man was speechless, and she ran on before he recovered from his astonishment. The woman who was saved from life on Baxter Street that night gave her testimony to thousands of New Yorkers before she died two years later.[5]

The black family in post-Reconstruction America was more cohesive than these sketches of the Boston Creole and the painted women at New York's Black and Tan Saloon suggest. It largely survived the move to the city, but the move was into crowded quarters. The nuclear family was often replaced by an extended family or an extended family with live-in boarders. Crowded conditions were an effect of being charged the highest rates for the poorest quality housing. "Some of the buildings in which negroes live are of course the most expensive of all proportionately to the accommodations provided," Edward Devine said in a study of Albany, Syracuse, and Troy, New York. "In each of the several districts the colored people are relegated to the least healthful buildings which are unoccupied." Crowded living conditions were full of moral significance for the social gospel prophets. "The family home is the basis of our modern civilization," Jacob Riis argued, and A. J. F. Behrends held that "overcrowding is first lieutenant in the army of paupers and criminals, whose captaincy belongs to intemperance." The plantation Negroes' one-room cabin was "one of the most serious difficulties in improving the morals of the negroes," said Wilbur Fisk Crafts. But the Southern white social worker Julia Tutwiler looked at urban tenement houses and countered that black people were better off in a one-room cabin "with God's light and air all around it." William Howe Tolman held that "one room, whether a tenement or a cabin, does not make an ideal home, and boys naturally seek pleasure and recreation outside of it." He called for "public places of recreation, reading rooms, libraries, coffee houses, gymnasiums, and public baths" as rivals to the saloon. They all agreed with Craft's claim that "Christian training and crowded tenements are contradictions. For the best moral culture there should be one room for each, not one room for *all*, the members of a family." If all that imperiled American civilization was concentrated in the city, as Josiah Strong said, the concentrated Negro was both peril and imperiled.[6]

Among urban Christianity's agencies for constructive relief of crowded tenement conditions, the Young Men's and Young Women's Christian Associations were largely segregated. The first "Y's" in America were organized in the 1850s. In 1853, the first black YMCA was founded in Washington, D.C. After emancipation, four more black urban Y's were founded and the first black student YMCA was founded at Howard University in 1869. The movement flourished in the next decade. South Carolina alone reported seventeen black Y's in the mid-1870s. In 1879, the Reverend Henry Edwards Brown, a black alumnus of Oberlin, the founder of Talladega College, and for three years its president, was hired to promote the YMCA among black people. His success with city associations was limited, but his work in black colleges progressed rapidly.[7]

In 1890, Charles M. Sheldon of Topeka's Central Congregational Church announced that he would work part-time among segments of the city's population. His plan to spend a week in black Topeka stretched to three weeks of study. Hearing that black people were barred from some hotels and restaurants in the city, Sheldon asked a young black professional man to visit such places with him. They ate together at one restaurant and found no difference in the service when they went separately to another. At a third, where racial discrimination was reported, the black man ate his meal with no disturbance, "except possibly to his digestive apparatus." But, when they went to Topeka's YMCA and the black man applied for membership, he was "politely refused admission on the ground of color." Sheldon's experience "throws a curious side light upon some forms of the so-called Christianity of our time," said *The Unitarian.* "If Jesus taught anything, he taught human brotherhood—that before God there is no rich or poor, no black or white."[8]

But Sheldon's discovery at Topeka's YMCA was commonplace. By 1890, as black urban growth had increased the need for such agencies, central Y's increasingly resisted black applicants for membership and some black branches of city associations were growing. AME pastor Reverdy Ransom called for an "international, undenominational Christian organization" to show young black men how to use their time profitably and face "the perils of the city." In a swipe at secret fraternal orders popular among black men, he asked: "Which is more profitable, parading in regalia, grips, passwords and feathers or a comfortable room with books, papers, innocent amusements and religious culture?" Ransom feared that the YMCA would never meet the needs of black youth. W. E. B. Du Bois saw "a grave and dangerous lack of proper places of amusement and recreation for young men." He called for a YMCA with "books and newspapers, baths, bowling alleys and billiard tables, conversation rooms and short interesting religious services" rather than "endless prayer meetings and loud gospel hymns in dingy and uninviting quarters."[9]

Black Chicago, Cleveland, and New York were divided by moves to establish separate YMCAs, but black Y's were growing in the South. The Norfolk, Virginia, association hired the first black YMCA secretary, William A. Hunton, in 1888. In 1889, Richmond's Y hired the Reverend J. Milton Waldron as its secretary and became the first local black association to own its building. When Hunton's work at Norfolk prospered, the Y's international committee hired him as secretary for Negro Work. Like Brown, Hunton gave his time increasingly to students. By 1896, forty-one of sixty black associations were in colleges. Seven city associations, in New Haven, Philadelphia, Baltimore, Washington, Richmond, Norfolk, and Louisville, had secretaries. In 1898, when Hunton attended to black troops in the Spanish-American War, Jesse Edward Moorland joined the YMCA staff to focus on its city work. Moorland and Hunton began conducting summer conferences for black YMCA secretaries in 1900 and their work among black men expanded rapidly. In 1905, Fisk University alumnus George Edmund Haynes joined the national staff. Three years later, President Taft noted that half of the ten thousand men in black colleges were active in the YMCA.[10] By contrast, the YWCA had only a few weak black centers, in Washington, New York, and other Northern cities. In 1907, Grace Dodge called a conference of Southern white women at Asheville, North Carolina, to discuss YWCA work among black women. At first refusing to discuss it, the Southern women finally agreed reluctantly, so long as the work was done entirely from the New York headquarters. Thereafter, more black student and city YWCAs were established and others were strengthened.[11]

There were nineteen black YMCA buildings across the country in 1910, when Sears-Roebuck magnate Julius Rosenwald offered to give $25,000 toward black Y buildings, if it were matched by $75,000 from other sources. Forces in black Chicago that vigorously opposed a separate YMCA twenty years earlier were nearly silent in 1910. In Cleveland, the black community was still divided on the issue, but Rosenwald's offer brought the division into the open and delayed the establishment of a black YMCA in Cleveland for years. But by 1920 the Rosenwald offer led to the building or completion of black YMCAs in Atlanta, Baltimore, Brooklyn, Chicago, Cincinnati, Columbus, Indianapolis, Kansas City, New York, Philadelphia, St. Louis, and Washington. Rosenwald's benefaction was a significant response to growing needs in black urban communities, providing major social centers. But it institutionalized segregation of the YMCA. "Negroes have been gradually excluded from Young Men's Christian Association buildings in large cities and segregated in separate bodies, while from the first they were in nearly all cases refused admittance to Young Women's Christian Associations," said W. E. B. Du Bois. The segregated Y was "flourishing" and doing great things because of earnest, self-sacrificing secretaries who "counseled them to ignore the stigma." But "compulsory and humiliating" segregation in the Y's made them "monuments to a miserable unchristian and unmanly prejudice," Du Bois argued. "The good accomplished is no excuse for the insult offered."[12]

**D**espite segregation, mainstream social Christianity still thought in terms of a mission to black America. A mission is a seed with mutant potential, capable of becoming something else, several other things, or nothing. The nineteenth-century missionary movement was inclined to a process of replication, of Eastern society and institutions in the West, of American society and institutions abroad. When the Civil War created an opportunity to build Southern society on foundations other than slavery, Northern evangels saw the missionary task of Reconstruction as replicating Northern society on Southern soil. The task was to make the South American by making it Christian. So it sought to plant the South with centers of civilizing influence, reproductive units of the redeeming community, serving the multiple functions of church, school, and social settlement. Among the remarkable successes and failures of this missionary vision, none are so well known as Hampton Institute and its progeny. Founded in 1869, Hampton begat Tuskegee fifteen years later and Tuskegee begat many replicas.[13] Neither their rural Southern locations nor, in the cases of Hampton and Tuskegee, their partial state support should obscure the multifunction mission of these institutions as church, school, and social settlement. In a variety of related activities—the Tuskegee Negro Conferences, a summer Chautauqua, the Phelps Hall Bible School, mothers' meetings, YMCA work, a young women's missionary society, and a Temperance Legion—Tuskegee was a rural social settlement.[14]

As Hampton and Tuskegee matured, the social settlement became distinguished from the primary institution. A Hampton graduate, Janie Porter Barrett founded its Locust Street Settlement in 1890 by inviting girls to meet once a week as a homemaking club. In 1902, she built a clubhouse on Locust Street. Its activities included clubs for women, young people, and children, a playground, and classes in cooking, sewing, quilting, embroidery, stenciling, and gardening. In 1897, Margaret Murray Washington founded the Elizabeth Russell Settlement at Tuskegee. It had a day school and gardening space for children, a Sunday school, and classes in sewing, cooking, and agriculture. Its purpose, said Washington, was "to better family conditions of the colored people on the plantation in the matter of cleanliness, education, uprightness—to teach them how to live." When Robert A. Woods and Albert J. Kennedy issued their *Handbook of Settlements* in 1911, however, they saw the Calhoun School and Settlement at Calhoun, Alabama, as an example of the earlier type of institution. It was a graded school; a church that held Sunday and mission services, engaged in church visiting, and celebrated the Christian holidays; and a rural settlement, doing sociological studies of the area and offering farmers' conferences, mothers' meetings, teachers' institutes, agricultural fairs, and a medical mission.[15]

The literature on settlement houses invariably says they were inspired by an English example and adapted to American urban immigrant communities. But contemporary observers such as Jane Addams, W. E. B. Du Bois, and Washington Gladden saw missions as precursors to settlement houses.[16] There was considerable continuity of method and purpose and some suggestive evidence of continuity of personnel between Northern missions in the South and urban social settlements.[17] Clearly, the black experience with settlements points to an American root, planted even in the rural South, for the settlement house movement in these multifunction missions. If missionary methods were pioneered on the Southern frontier in Reconstruction, they were implemented in Northern and Midwestern cities to reweave a social fabric badly frayed by the stress of industrialization, immigration, migration, and social conflict. There, missions as proto–settlement houses were an important part of the black urban experience. There were settlement houses in black New York, Philadelphia, Indianapolis, Louisville, and Topeka by 1900. The origins of these settlement houses underscore their close relation to religious missions.[18]

Founded in 1865 as the African Sabbath School Association, the New York Colored Mission was an expression of Quaker city mission philanthropy. When it purchased a building in "the Tenderloin" as a school for black children, the Society of Friends and black ministers held services and religious classes there. Through the 1870s and 1880s, the mission expanded its social services to a nursery, a medical mission, home visitors, an employment bureau, temporary housing, and inexpensive meals. In the depression winter of 1893–94, the mission tried to meet desperate needs in the black community with tons of coal and barrels of food. Thereafter, a boys' club, Friday night socials, and classes in homemaking made the New York Colored Mission the city's most important settlement house for the black community prior to the twentieth century.[19]

Philadelphia's Starr Center began in the library and industrial school philanthropy of Quaker women on St. Mary Street, "a narrow, dirty street, a crowded alley filled with children and adults, with dogs and cats, with garbage and refuse, the air with cries and rough language." There, Mom Hewitt peddled food from her counter of cold victuals, blind Susan preached her daily sermons, and black women swallowed their policy tickets when cornered by the police. In 1892, the College Settlement Association joined the Quakers to form the Philadelphia College Settlement. Six weeks in Philadelphia was "a startling experience, for the House was in a rough negro quarter and what we young women had to offer was not quite what was needed there," said Vida Scudder. But "I gained a vivid feeling of life in the social depths." Philadelphia had two other settlement houses in black areas by 1898, Neighborhood House on Addison Street and the Eighth Ward Settlement House on Locust Street, and the College Settlement Association withdrew from the center on Lombard Street, which was reorganized as the Starr Center. It occupied a full square block including the Starr Garden, a gymnasium, and a playground. Stuart Memorial Church housed its library and classes in cleaning, cooking, and carpentry. The center offered cooperative buying programs, inexpensive lunches and milk for school children, university extension courses, a sick-benefit society, a savings system, a medical dispensary, and a visiting nurse.[20]

An important service of settlement houses was to conduct systematic sociological studies of their neighborhoods. In 1896, the Philadelphia College Settlement and the University of Pennsylvania supported W. E. B. Du Bois's pioneering study, *The Philadelphia Negro*. Believing racial problems were rooted in ignorance and using Charles Booth's *Life and Labor of the People of London* as a model, he hoped to present an "objective" picture of black Philadelphia. Du Bois found that discrimination in housing and employment by the city's landlords, employers, and trade unions caused serious problems for the black community. As a critic of his own people, he found their morals lax, their households poorly managed, their money foolishly squandered, and their social agencies inefficient. But Du Bois urged the black elite to give leadership to alleviate the problems. He urged the white people to support black leadership and enlarge opportunities for Negroes. The social gospel press praised his presentation of both the redeeming and the damning sides of black urban life. Persuaded by Du Bois's argument that discrimination gave Philadelphia "its idle and vicious negro class, so that the city's wrong-doing reacts upon itself," the *Homiletic Review* said that "the negro needs Christian sympathy and help."[21]

In the Midwest, three examples of urban missions as proto–settlement houses in the black community suggest that missions and settlement houses were generically related, essentially conservative institutions to reweave a deteriorating social fabric. In 1890, Charles M. Sheldon's three weeks in black Topeka focused on "Tennesseetown," a black section near his Central Congregational Church. A decade earlier, hundreds of Tennessee "exodusters" led by Benjamin "Pap" Singleton had settled there. Moved by his discovery of the effects of prejudice, poverty, and vice, Sheldon encouraged his church's Christian Endeavor Society to rent a building in the neighborhood. Soon, the Congregational pastor and his youth had created a library, a kindergarten, a mothers' auxiliary, and a Village Improvement Society. But for Sheldon the mission's finest hour was Sunday evening when the white young people worshiped with black residents of Tennesseetown. "I have often thought that in the singing of those songs where the black and white unison rose together in the heart of that American Africa," he recalled, "my young people came to feel the oneness of the human family more deeply than in all the work they did for the welfare of those brothers and sisters of ours."[22]

Louisville, Kentucky's, John Little Mission began in the winter of 1897–98, when the needs of impoverished black people in the eastern section of the city caught the attention of students at the Presbyterian Theological Seminary.

To Sunday school and worship services, the students added classes in domestic arts for young women and manual training for young men. In 1904, a white native of Alabama who was one of the founding seminarians, John Little, assumed supervision of the Presbyterian mission. It expanded to two sites, offering worship and religious education, vocational training, sports, recreation, and public health programs to the city's black community.[23]

Inspired by Oscar Carleton McCulloch's preaching of the social gospel at Plymouth Congregational Church, the Charity Organization Society began neighborhood work among the poor in northwestern Indianapolis in the late 1880s. Subsequently, it became "inexpedient" to operate on a biracial basis. In 1898 or 1899 the Flanner Guild, a settlement house for black children, opened in a neighborhood of tenements and small cottages on Colton Street. After early financial troubles, the Flanner Guild was put on a stable foundation about 1903 by a combination of public money, private subscriptions and fees, and volunteers who offered the city's black community a day nursery, a home for unwed mothers, boys' and girls' clubs, classes in domestic arts, an employment bureau, athletic and gardening programs, and a choral society and orchestra for adults.[24]

The Flanner Guild is instructive in several ways. Its name, following Stanton Coit's adoption of a Ruskinian medieval ideal, indicates its early place among American settlement houses and is the only instance of it among black settlement houses. More important, its sponsorship by Indianapolis's Charity Organization Society suggests that the settlement house movement was closer to traditional charity organization than is usually thought. But both its eventual sponsorship by a denomination, the Disciples of Christ, and its inclusion of religious services as a part of its program were common in black settlement houses, suggesting that the movement was even more closely tied to religious missions. The settlement house movement was a religious movement from the beginning and the religious motive remained at its heart. As Charles R. Henderson said, settlement house workers eschewed the provincial, sectarian, and divisive elements of religion, but they celebrated the "central, vital, common elements" of religious faith. They were less interested in correct doctrine than in right living.[25] In the North, black settlement houses grew rapidly in the first decade of the twentieth century. By 1910, settlement houses served black communities in Baltimore, Boston, Brooklyn, Buffalo, Chicago, Cleveland, Columbus, Indianapolis, Milwaukee, New York, Philadelphia, Topeka, and Washington, D.C. Even such small cities as Enᵍᵣᵉwood, New Jersey, and East Greenwich, Rhode Island, had settlement work among black people.[26]

**U**rban missions were the prototype both for settlement houses in black communities and for "institutional churches," an important way the church met the urban challenge. An institutional church was "an organized body of Christian believers who find themselves in a hard and uncongenial social environment," said the Reverend S. Timothy Tice. He urged a black audience to "supplement the ordinary methods of the gospel, such as preaching, prayer meeting, Sunday School and pastoral visitation, by a system of organized kindness, a congress of industries which, by touching people on physical, social, and intellectual sides, will conciliate them and draw them within reach of the gospel." But America itself, rural and urban, North and South, was always "a hard and uncongenial social environment" for black people. Perhaps for that reason, the church had long been the central social institution in the black community, with a variety of functions apart from worship and religious education.[27]

In Philadelphia, Russell Conwell's Grace Baptist Temple, Temple College, and Samaritan Hospital, built between 1884 and 1892, provided a wide range of services to the city. But the College served few black Philadelphians. The scholarships it offered through churches were unavailable to black churches. A black woman who applied for admission in 1893 was advised to go elsewhere. Two years later, she was admitted despite student body objections. In 1910, Conwell said he was disappointed that so few black students had graduated from Temple. "In the primary grades, and in parrot learning by rote," he said, Negroes "did fairly well; but in the higher intellectual levels demanding original powers of thought, the race as a race seemed largely incompetent." In New York, William Stephen Rainsford prodded fashionable St. George's Episcopal Church into becoming an institutional church, with club work and industrial education. Rainsford's forceful methods drove some parishioners from the congregation, but drew others to it. In 1894, he announced the addition of a new baritone soloist to the choir, a black man, Harry Burleigh. "Division, consternation, confusion, and protest reigned for a time," Rainsford recalled. "Well, my choir held together! I don't think I lost a member of it even if I forced into it a black brother. And Harry Burleigh's sweet baritone voice still leads the choir which he entered against much protest then; and St. George's is proud of him and loves and honors him as a Christian man." A businessman later said: "I came as a stranger and the usher put a poor coloured woman alongside me. That is the church for me, I said to myself."[28]

But few black Americans experienced institutional churches from a seat in its college classrooms, in St. George's choir, or beside a white businessman. Indeed, black people living in Northern cities were "far less romantic to us than are their brethren, the freedmen, living in the South," said New York's John B. Devins. "I have never heard of a freedmen's board carrying the gospel to the negroes of our city." At the same time, the black Episcopal priest, Alexander Crummell, found black churches woefully lacking in the zeal for good works and institutional efforts to meet the needs of the urban community. Devins and Crummell might have seen George W. Moore's Lincoln Memorial Congregational Church in Washington, D.C., as a case of small beginnings. Starting with 11 members in "Hell's Bottom," Moore's congregation grew to 270 members by 1892, when the last of the saloons in its neighborhood closed and the YMCA branch, which its members organized, bought the largest of the saloon buildings. With a Sunday school of 200 students, a Christian Endeavor Society, a Woman's Christian Temperance Union, a Loyal Legion, a Women's Missionary Society, and an organization for young men, Lincoln Memorial offered the club work common to institutional churches. Beyond that, it had a sewing school for girls, a free kindergarten for children, and classes for volunteers in cottage meetings and hospital and charitable visitation.[29]

The earliest black institutional churches were in denominations outside the black mainstream: New York's St. Phillips Episcopal Church, the Episcopal Church of the Crucifixion and the Berean Presbyterian Church in Philadelphia, and Atlanta's First Congregational Church. In New York, St. Phillips was founded as a mission by black members of Trinity Episcopal Church and was long said to be the city's most exclusive black congregation. In 1875, St. Phillips established a home for elderly women. Hutchens C. Bishop became St. Phillips's rector in 1886. Six years later, the Reverend Algernon Sidney Crapsey, a white priest from Rochester, conducted an evangelistic mission at St. Phillips. Mr. White, a tall West Indian who was the senior warden, met Crapsey at the church. "Instinctively and without a moment's hesitation, I stepped forward and laid my hand on the arm of Mr. White," Crapsey said. "Mr. White, with your permission, I will walk with you; we can talk together as we go along." When the Rochester priest met with the vestry at the close of his mission, White said: "Mr. Crapsey, no white man in America ever acted in such a manner toward me as you did on the morning of your arrival." Crapsey thought that his treatment of the senior warden as a gentleman accounted for much of the success of his mission. We will "have the Negro Question with us," he said, "until the white man recognizes the fact that he is nothing but a man and every other man is his equal and that the color of his skin is an indifferent matter."[30]

St. Phillips built a parish house and rectory in 1895 and Hutchens Bishop organized a St. Christopher's Guild for young men. When he told a Hampton Institute Conference that they were allowed to play cards and billiards and smoke cigarettes in the parish house, a conservative black woman thought: "It's a good thing he's a'Pisc'palian. Ef he was a real preacher, a Baptis' I mean, he'd be carried out yonder in Hampton Roads. Yo' hear me." But the St. Christopher's Guild offered the young men a glee club, amateur dramatics, and a strong athletic program, with track teams, amateur boxing, and the country's first black basketball team in 1908. Hutchens C. Bishop was also a shrewd businessman. As the city's black population began moving north in the early twentieth century, he traded on rising real estate prices in mid-Manhattan and his own light skin color to buy property from white people who sought to keep black people out of Harlem. St. Phillips sold its property on 30th Street and bought ten apartment houses on West 135th Street, which had previously excluded black tenants. It built a large new stone English Gothic church and parish house, designed by the black architects, Tandy and Foster, on West 133rd and 134th streets. Its "well arranged rooms, its gymnasium, and its corps of enthusiastic workers," said Mary White Ovington, would make St. Phillips "a powerful force in the Harlem Negro's life."[31]

Both Philadelphia congregations began as religious missions and developed important social services under the leadership of able pastors. Founded in 1846 as a mission on poverty-stricken Bedford Street, the Church of the Crucifixion served a congregation of black people but was governed by white vestrymen. In the late 1870s, the vestry called a black priest, the Reverend Henry L. Phillips, to serve the mission. He was, said W. E. B. Du Bois, "a man of sincerity and culture, and of peculiar energy." Finding a small congregation and few resources to support its dilapidated building at Eighth and Bainbridge, Phillips spent twenty years building a church, a parish house, a summer home, and a $25,000 endowment. "The point is to have well-organized institutions for the immediate relief of all pressing wants," said Phillips, "while provision is being made by which these people will have an opportunity for

providing for themselves." By 1898, said Du Bois, the Church of the Crucifixion offered "the most effective church organization in the city for benevolent
and rescue work." It reached "a class of neglected poor whom the other
colored churches shun and forget and for whom there is little fellowship in
white churches" by supporting the Fresh Air Fund, two branch missions, a
vacation school for thirty-five children, an ice mission, a home for the home-
less, a parish visitor, a musical program, and university extension courses.[32]

In 1878, members of Philadelphia's Lombard Street Central Presbyterian
Church, a black congregation, established a Sunday school mission in north-
west Philadelphia. A year later, the Reverend Matthew Anderson became
pastor of the Glouchester Presbyterian Mission. A Pennsylvanian, he studied
at Ohio's Iberia College, Oberlin College, Princeton Theological Seminary,
and Yale Divinity School. In 1880, his mission was reorganized as the Berean
Presbyterian Church. By 1884, it had built a substantial blue-marble building
on South College Avenue. Twelve years later, Anderson noted that the church
had less than a hundred official members, but a constituency of three hundred, with one hundred and fifty persons in Sunday school. The Berean
Church had a Woman's Christian Temperance Union of sixty members, a
Christian Endeavor Society of forty, a kindergarten, a boys' cadet corps, two
literary societies, an employment bureau, and a medical dispensary. The
Berean Young Women's Parlor offered literary classes, a light supper, and
weekly socials for young women employed as domestics. The church owned
a summer cottage at Point Pleasant, New Jersey, where it held Bible conferences and lecture courses. The Berean Building and Loan Association,
established in 1888, enabled black families in its vicinity to buy 150 homes in
its first twenty years. In 1899, Anderson founded the Berean Manual Training
and Industrial School, which gave classes in carpentry, upholstery, millinery,
electricity, sewing, dressmaking, stenography, cooking, and tailoring to a
thousand students in its first ten years.[33]

Until 1900, when African Methodist Episcopal pastor Reverdy Ransom
founded Chicago's Institutional Church and Social Settlement, black institutional churches had appeared only in denominations marginal to the black
experience: Congregational, Episcopal, and Presbyterian. Reverdy Ransom
studied at Oberlin, where he heard the social gospel from Joseph Cook, John
B. Gough, and Thomas DeWitt Talmadge, and lost a scholarship after organizing a protest against segregating black women at a separate table in the Ladies
Dining Hall. He transferred to Wilberforce University, where he hid his
"heretical" views from conservative black professors. Ransom's theological

liberalism and prophetic social message eventually made him the foremost black spokesman for the social gospel in his generation.[34]

Ransom was ordained in 1886 and served congregations in Pennsylvania, Ohio, and Illinois. His "vision of the need of social service" came at Allegheny City, Pennsylvania, where he walked "through the alleys and climbed the dark stairways of the wretched tenements, or walked out on the planks to the shanty boats where our people lived on the river." At Chicago's Bethel AME Church in 1896, he organized a "Men's Sunday Club" of five hundred men who met weekly to discuss moral, social, and cultural issues, supported Ida B. Wells in establishing a kindergarten at Bethel Church, and opened the church to the Manassa Society, an organization of seven hundred men and women in biracial marriages. As Ransom worked with Jane Addams, Clarence Darrow, Bishop Samuel Fallows, the Reverend Frank Gunsaulus, Robert Ingersoll, Shailer Mathews, Mary McDowell, Graham Taylor, and other prominent re-formers in Chicago, he felt that traditional black churches did not meet the needs of black migrants to the city. With the encouragement of Bishop Benjamin W. Arnett, Ransom left Bethel Church in 1900 to found Chicago's Institutional Church and Social Settlement to serve both new migrants and middle-class black Chicagoans. It opened in a building with an auditorium seating twelve hundred, a dining room, a kitchen, a gymnasium, and eight other large rooms. Its activities included a Men's Forum, a Women's Club, a nursery, a kindergarten, clubs for boys and girls, a print shop, and an employment bureau. It offered concerts, classes in sewing, cooking, and music, and lectures by leading black and white speakers. Ransom hired two University of Chicago seminarians, Monroe N. Work and Richard R. Wright, Jr., to assist him with the boys' club.[35]

Reverdy Ransom mediated between angry white strikers and black strike-breakers in 1902. His attack on the policy rackets in Chicago led to the dynamiting of the Institutional Church and Social Settlement a year later. But the end of Ransom's experiment came at the hands of religious conservatives in his denomination. Fearing his influence in the pulpit, they won Bishop Abraham Grant's support for an edict forbidding him to preach on Sunday morning. When that was revoked, they barred members of their congregations from participating in Institutional Church programs. When rumors spread that Ransom would be removed from his position in 1904, he left Chicago for Boston and an appointment under Bishop Arnett. His conservative successor at Institutional Church had a mandate to "make it a regular AME Church, to cut out the social foolishness and bring religion back."[36] But

Reverdy Ransom, black social Christianity's foremost early spokesman (Wilberforce University Library, Wilberforce, Ohio)

Institutional Church and Social Settlement in Chicago was the first attempt to found either of those kinds of institutions in a denomination of the black mainstream. Owned by the African Methodist Episcopal Church, it ministered to a constituency more than a membership and worship was at the heart of its life. It may best be understood as an urban mission, pregnant with the potential of becoming either an institutional church or a settlement house.

Experience at the University of Chicago and at Institutional Church launched Monroe Work and R. R. Wright, Jr., on pioneering careers as sociologists and advocates of social Christianity. At Chicago, they were drawn to the social Christianity of Charles R. Henderson, Shailer Mathews, Albion Small, and Graham Taylor. Small and Taylor encouraged Monroe Work to pursue graduate study in sociology at the university, and he devoted his life to sociological inquiry as the basis for social reform in the South. He took Ransom's idea of a Men's Sunday Club to Savannah, Georgia, where, with the help of R. R. Wright, Sr., he organized one modeled on the one he had known in Chicago. It focused attention on important social issues, served as a forum for information and informed viewpoints, and mobilized public opinion for social improvement. Shailer Mathews knew little about black Americans, said R. R. Wright, but he took a special interest in the black seminarian, becoming his teacher, friend, and confidant. "I loved Mathews. My dealings with him convinced me that it was possible for some white people to be fair to Negro-Americans. He wrought a revolution in my thinking," said Wright. "Brought up with a theology which took but little account of social conditions and concerned itself chiefly with 'getting to heaven,' I found in the social gospel a more satisfying meaning and purpose for Christianity than ever before." Wright recognized the American origin of the idea when he organized Chicago's Trinity Mission and Culture Center in 1905. Two years later, he moved to Philadelphia for graduate work at the University of Pennsylvania, continued his social ministry at the city's Eighth Ward Settlement, and became editor of the AME *Christian Recorder*.[37]

Reverdy Ransom carried the idea of Institutional Church and Social Settlement to major AME congregations in Boston and New York. When he became editor of the *AME Church Review* in 1912, he adopted a version of the original concept at New York's Church of Simon of the Cyrene, which ministered to the city's black social outcasts. By then, with the concentration of black people in Harlem, other important black congregations—Abyssinian Baptist, Bethel AME, Mount Tabor Presbyterian, St. Cyprian's Episcopal Mission, and St. Mark's Methodist Episcopal—were following the example of St. Phillips Episcopal Church, whose ministry passed from Hutchens C. Bishop to his son, Shelton H. Bishop.[38] By then, black urban congregations across the North—African Methodists in Philadelphia, African Methodists and Episcopalians in Kansas City, Methodists and Roman Catholics in Cincinnati, African Methodists in Detroit, and Congregationalists in Springfield, Massachusetts—were adopting the institutional church model.[39]

Black institutional churches developed more slowly in the South. Perhaps because they did not have ready access to white philanthropy, black Baptist congregations were slower to adopt the ambitious social program of institutional churches. But Norfolk, Virginia's, First Baptist Church was the first example of it among black Baptists. In 1891, the Reverend Richard H. Bowling, a Hampton graduate, became its pastor. Sixteen years later, the congregation built a large building to house institutional church services. When Bowling died in 1914, he was succeeded by his son, Richard, Jr. By 1920, the church had a paid staff of seven persons, an employment agency, a nursery, a kindergarten, a library, a home for elderly persons and unwed mothers, an information service, a milk dispensary, a playground, a drum and bugle corps, a mothers' clinic, and gospel teams for evangelism at the city jail and in neglected corners of the city.[40]

The institutional church model was especially important for urban Baptist congregations in the twentieth century, as centers of religious life to be sure, but also as social service agencies and bases of political power. The latter aspect seems to be particularly the case in Baptist congregations passed from father to son as if they were a part of the patrimony: Alfred and Russell Conwell Barbour at Galveston's Macedonia Baptist Church; Washington and Gardner C. Taylor at Baton Rouge's Mt. Zion First Baptist Church; the Richard H. Bowlings, Senior and Junior, at Norfolk's First Baptist Church; the Benjamin Joseph Johnsons, Senior and Junior, at Atlanta's Mt. Calvary Baptist Church; the Junius Caesar Austins, Senior and Junior, at Chicago's Pilgrim Baptist Church; the Marshall Shepherds, Senior and Junior, at Philadelphia's Mt. Olivet Baptist Church; and the Adam Clayton Powells, Senior and Junior, at New York's Abyssinian Baptist Church. More remarkable is the passage of the pulpit through three generations of the William H. Grays, I, II, and III, at Philadelphia's Bright Hope Baptist Church; and the tragic instance of Martin Luther King, Sr., who succeeded his father-in-law, A. D. Williams, in the pulpit of Atlanta's Ebenezer Baptist Church and hoped to pass it on to his sons, Martin Luther King, Jr., and A. D. Williams King.[41] The intimate weave of church and family in these twentieth-century urban black Baptist congregations is a remarkable manifestation of the nineteenth-century missionary movement's challenge to urban and industrial dislocation.

The black experience with missions, institutional churches, and settlement houses suggests that they are generically related institutions—indeed, a family of institutions. The English social settlement fathered and gave the medieval surname, guild, to some of America's early settlement houses, but American missions mothered them and their stepsister, the institutional church. Two factors distinguished the three institutions from each other. First, an institutional church ministered primarily to a membership; a mission and a settlement house ministered primarily to a constituency. Second, worship often occurred at settlement houses, but it was a secondary activity among many such activities. At missions and institutional churches, worship was the central act of the community's life together. In the black community, the earliest institutional churches and settlement houses were founded as missions. Once they were established as model institutional churches or settlement houses, others, never known as missions, were established after the example of the model.

**B**ut the story of urban racial reform, social research, race riots, institutional churches, settlement houses, and interracial cooperation is a tale of two cities: New York and Atlanta. Settlement houses did pioneering sociological studies elsewhere, but New York's Federation of Churches and Christian Workers was organized in 1896 to conduct sociological surveys of the city for its churches, missionary societies, and charities. In 1897, the federation's Second Sociological Canvass studied conditions in the black community. Supported by such white New York pastors as Robert Collyer, W. H. P. Faunce, Walter Laidlaw, Richard Heber Newton, and Minot J. Savage, it led to the building of churches, libraries, a public park, a model tenement, and a kindergarten in black sections of New York.[42] Lillian Wald's Henry Street Settlement, founded in 1893, and Mary Kingsbury Simkovitch's Greenwich House, founded in 1902, were open to black people in lower Manhattan. But the city's second settlement serving black people primarily was Victoria Earle Matthews's White Rose Mission. Once described as "a Salvation Army field officer, a College Settlement worker, a missionary, a teacher, a preacher, a Sister of Mercy, all in one," Victoria Earle Matthews made an early study of the exploitation of black female migrants from the South by spurious employment agencies. She founded her mission in 1898 to provide lodging and meals for young women until they could find work. Two years later, when it moved into larger quarters, the mission became a settlement house, with a library, recreation facilities, a kindergarten, mothers' clubs, and classes in the domestic arts, religion, and race history.[43]

But New York witnessed a "city-disgracing injustice," said the Federation of Churches, in 1900. After midnight on 13 August, May Enoch summoned her common-law husband, Arthur Harris, from McBride's Saloon near Forty-first Street and Eighth Avenue in New York's "terrible Tenderloin." When she did, a white plainclothes policeman, Robert Thorpe, charged her with soliciting. Harris objected and was clubbed in an ensuing fight with Thorpe. The black man pulled a knife and cut the plainclothesman twice, so severely that he died the next day. Two nights later, a fight broke out near Thorpe's house between a black man and a white man, which triggered a riot. Men and women poured out of neighboring tenement houses as word spread that the "nigger chase" was on. A mob of up to ten thousand people ranged up and down Broadway, Seventh and Eighth avenues, attacking black people in streets and alleys, in hotels and saloons. They were pulled from the streetcars and beaten. Dozens of blacks, but few white people, were arrested. There are no reliable estimates of the numbers of black people who were injured. Witnesses testified that many were badly hurt and the police did little to stop it.[44]

On 16 August, it rained in New York, cooling tempers on both sides. There was sporadic racial violence in the city for another month, but the riot was over and the community was shocked at what had happened. "No negro was safe on the streets. Dogs would not have been treated with such indiscriminate cruelty," said a writer for the *Social Gospel*. "Man's inhumanity to man exceeds even his inhumanity to the dumb brutes." The *Independent* traced the New York riot to race hatred, "the fountain of the whole evil." Shortly after the riot, Charles H. Parkhurst, who had fought to clean up the Tenderloin between 1892 and 1895, asked Mary Church Terrell, the black clubwoman, to address his Madison Square Presbyterian congregation. "While I was talking one of the colored men who had been a victim of the interracial strife walked in with his head bandaged," she recalled. "It was a striking object lesson of the conditions which sometimes obtain in the North." In September, black leaders in New York met at St. Mark's Methodist Church to demand the law's protection and the prosecution of the guilty. With the aid of Frank Mason

North, a white Methodist missions executive, T. Thomas Fortune, William H. Brooks, Hutchens C. Bishop, P. Butler Thompkins, and Charles T. Walker organized a Citizens' Protective League, which fought unsuccessfully to bring rioters and complicit policemen to justice.[45]

The New York Colored Mission and Victoria Earle Matthews's White Rose Mission shared the burden of social service in the black community with branches of the YWCA and YMCA, founded by Charles T. Walker with the help of S. Parkes Cadman, Booker T. Washington, and bishops Charles H. Fowler, Henry Codman Potter, and Alexander Walters. In 1906, Lillian Wald's Henry Street Settlement opened its Stillman Branch for Negroes on Sixty-second Street as the first nonmissionary settlement house for New York's black community. Its nursing services, library, playground, clubs, and classes in history, folk dance, carpentry, domestic science, sewing, and drama lacked the religious emphasis of earlier missions. Two years later, Brooklyn's Lincoln Settlement opened on Fleet Street. Merging already existing nursing services, a nursery, and a kindergarten, Lincoln Settlement offered clubs and classes to a section of Brooklyn where black people had lived for a century. In 1911, Stillman House became a branch of the Lincoln Settlement.[46]

In connection with New York's settlement houses, three social workers, Frances Kellor, Mary White Ovington, and George Edmund Haynes, built on the investigations of the New York Federation of Churches and Victoria Earle Matthews to establish the National Urban League. The daughter of a financially secure white, middle-class family in Columbus, Ohio, Frances Kellor studied at the University of Chicago. Her work with Charles R. Henderson in sociology led to an important series of articles on "The Criminal Negro" in 1901. Disputing the idea of a "criminal type," Kellor challenged Henderson's location of the cause of black crime in racial inferiority and argued that an impoverished social environment was a sufficient explanation. As a fellow of the College Settlement Association, Kellor examined environmental effects on black people in *Out of Work*, a study of the criminal links between New York employment agencies and saloons, gambling houses, and brothels. She retraced Victoria Earle Matthews's steps to find agents of unscrupulous Northern employment agencies throughout the South. In 1905, Kellor and Henry L. Phillips formed local Associations for the Protection of Negro Women in New York and Philadelphia to improve urban working conditions for them. A year later, the local associations merged to form the National League for the Protection of Colored Women (NLPCW).[47]

The daughter of a wealthy white merchant, Mary White Ovington grew up near working-class districts of Brooklyn, but "no place was more remote than the section of the city in which persons of a different caste lived," she recalled. Ovington studied at private preparatory schools and Radcliffe College, but the most important early intellectual influence was her Unitarian pastor, the Reverend John White Chadwick. He tutored her in a gospel of evolutionary optimism, social reform, and women's rights. Drawn to settlement house work, in 1896 Ovington opened a settlement among white working-class people in Brooklyn's Greenpoint. In seven years, Greenpoint Settlement grew from a five-room house into a forty-room settlement. "That I should later work for the Negro never entered my mind," she recalled.[48]

But Mary White Ovington was a socialist and a Unitarian of abolitionist descent. Her grandmother had followed William Lloyd Garrison and Samuel J. May; her father had left Brooklyn's Plymouth Congregational Church when Henry Ward Beecher supported a missionary association that tolerated slave-holders. In 1903, Charles Spahr, an editor of the *Outlook*, reintroduced her to race relations by inviting Booker T. Washington to address the New York Social Reform Club. The program also featured a black physician who spoke of infant mortality, employment discrimination, and housing conditions in black New York. "To my amazement I learned that there was a Negro prob-lem in my city," she wrote. "I had honestly never thought of it before." Initially, she planned to found a settlement house among New York Negroes, but Mary Simkovitch of Greenwich House persuaded her that more informa-tion on black urban problems was needed. In 1904, as a fellow of Greenwich House, Ovington began a study that led to publication of *Half a Man: The Status of the Negro in New York*. Two years later, hoping to expand employment oppor-tunities for black New Yorkers, Ovington, *Charities* editor Paul U. Kellogg, William J. Schieffelin, president of the Armstrong Association, and William L. Bulkley, the first black principal of a New York City school, organized the Committee for Improving the Industrial Conditions of Negroes in New York (CIICN).[49]

A native of Pine Bluff, Arkansas, George Edmund Haynes completed his undergraduate work at Fisk University in 1903. At Yale University, he earned a master's degree in sociology with William Graham Sumner. Haynes entered Yale Divinity School, but soon left in order to support a widowed mother and sister. In 1905, he became a traveling student secretary for the YMCA, based in Atlanta with William A. Hunton, Jesse E. Moorland, and Willis Duke Weather-ford. In 1908, Haynes left the YMCA to earn a doctorate in sociology and social work with Edward T. Devine, Franklin M. Giddings, Samuel McCune

Lindsay, and E. R. A. Seligman at Columbia University and the New York School of Philanthropy. Urged by Devine to study black migration to cities, Haynes became convinced that it would create large black urban communities and called for a strategy to help black migrants adjust to urban life. He hoped to persuade black colleges and universities to prepare social workers for the task. Told by the YMCA that his idea was outside its areas of responsibility, Haynes turned to Ruth Standish Baldwin for help.[50]

The widow of William H. Baldwin, Jr., Booker T. Washington's advisor among Northern businessmen, Ruth Baldwin was chairman of the NLPCW and a member of the CIICN. She proposed to make Haynes executive director of the committee and expand its work as he suggested. Stunned when it rejected her proposal, Baldwin organized the Committee on Urban Conditions among Negroes (CUCAN) in May 1910. With Haynes as executive director and chaired by E. R. A. Seligman, the new committee's founders included Felix Adler, Samuel H. Bishop, William H. Brooks, William Adams Brown, Edward T. Devine, John Haynes Holmes, Adam Clayton Powell, Reverdy Ransom, and Alexander Walters. The committee gathered information on the work of twenty organizations dealing with black people, operated summer camps for New York's black children, and opened a playground in Harlem. It merged with the NLPCW and the CIICN to become the National League on Urban Conditions among Negroes in October 1911. Haynes served as director, with Adler, Baldwin, Bishop, Brooks, Bulkley, Kellor, Powell, Schieffelin, and Seligman on its executive and finance committees.[51]

In the meantime, Fisk University President George A. Gates invited Haynes to launch a department of sociology and social work at the university. The New York committee agreed to hire an assistant for local operations. Haynes would continue to be director of the National Urban League, serve as editor of the new Social Service Department of the *AME Church Review*, and establish a program in social work at Fisk. Developed with a parallel program for white students at George Peabody College and Vanderbilt University, the American Interchurch College for Religious and Social Workers was endorsed by the Federal Council of Churches. In the new program at Nashville, Gates and Haynes recovered the vision of three generations of the American social gospel: at Fisk, founded by AMA missionaries to the South in 1866, George A. Gates, who was George D. Herron's covisionary of the Gospel of the Kingdom at Grinnell in the 1890s, sought out George Edmund Haynes, a promising Fisk alumnus and Yale seminarian who was one of the first black professional social workers, to train a new generation of black social workers. They would receive practical experience at Bethlehem House, a home missionary project sponsored by Southern white Methodist churchwomen. The new black social workers learned a professional language different than that of their missionary parents and grandparents, but they still hoped to make "civilization's inferno" more like the city of God.[52]

**N**ew York's story of social research, race riots, settlement houses, institutional churches, and movements for interracial cooperation was closely paralleled in Atlanta. In 1901, Tulane University President Edwin A. Alderman claimed that no Southern college offered a program studying social problems. His point served a rhetorical purpose, but he was wrong. Jerome Dowd held a chair in sociology at North Carolina's Trinity College by 1895. Among Southern seminaries, Southern Baptist Theological Seminary, the Episcopalians' Virginia Theological Seminary, and the Methodists' seminary at Vanderbilt University offered courses in applied Christianity and sociology by 1900. Alderman also ignored the annual conferences sponsored by the region's black institutions and neglected W. E. B. Du Bois's pioneering sociology at Atlanta University. Du Bois put the development in a larger perspective. "The Mohonk conference undertook the subject for several years, and then abandoned it, but the subject was revived upon a substantially similar plan by the conferences at Capon Springs, out of which have grown the interesting annual meetings of the Southern Education Conference," he said. But those conferences excluded black people. "On the negro side arose, in the years 1890–1900, a series of regular conferences which have had large success," Du Bois wrote. "The idea of these conferences began at Talladega College and Tuskegee Institute, and was extended and developed at Atlanta University, Hampton Institute, and others."[53]

After consulting Harvard sociologist Edward Cummings, President Horace Bumstead launched the annual Atlanta University Conference on Urban Negroes in 1896. Proceedings of the first two conferences were already published when Bumstead hired Du Bois to direct the university's program in sociology and the conferences. Du Bois dropped the series' focus upon urban life. But he hoped that his program of empirical research on ten topics, one each year for ten years, might be repeated ten times over to produce a century of accumulated data as a guide to scholars and public policy. His ambition for the Atlanta University series exceeded his grasp because of inadequate methods and financial limitations. But his sociological studies offered data and a variety of perspectives on race relations to other writers for decades to come.[54]

Atlanta's First Congregational Church was closely related to Atlanta University and its conferences. Founded in 1867 by the missionary administrators and teachers of the university and the Storrs School, First Congregational was biracial and served by white pastors until 1894 when Henry Hugh Proctor became its pastor. Like Du Bois and George Edmund Haynes, he was an alumnus of Fisk and, like Haynes, of Yale. Proctor was "a magnificent specimen of a man, six feet two or three inches, and finely proportioned, with the dignity and self-command of the true orator; it is easy to understand the hold he maintains over this large congregation," said Washington Gladden. "At a glance, I should have thought him a Methodist," Lura Beam wrote. "He lacked entirely the Congregational austerity, the Emersonian residue. He came singing transcendentalism, and the vigor of his natural endowment gave him social acceptance from both races." In four years, Proctor's church membership doubled to over four hundred and it became self-supporting. Apart from worship services and Sunday school, the church sponsored a temperance society, a Christian Endeavor Society, a Working Men's Club, a Women's Aid Society, and a Young Men's League. By 1902, the *Atlanta Constitution* was taking note of Proctor's sermons at First Congregational Church. On a trip south, the *Outlook*'s Ernest Hamlin Abbott declared that "without exception, white or black," his "was the most progressive and best organized church I saw in the South," with an influence exceeding that of some congregations five or six times its size.[55]

In 1901, Proctor helped to defeat a move to disfranchise black Georgians. Noting "a carnival of crime among the lower element of the colored people of Atlanta" in 1902, he traced it to the city's "hot-bed of crime," its dance halls, and persuaded the city council to close them by refusing to renew their licenses. When Washington Gladden visited Atlanta in 1903, Proctor was preparing to preach on "The Redemption of Decatur Street," a disreputable section where "the most depraved and degraded portion of the colored population is found." The readiness of Southern whites to take Yankee visitors there to illustrate the character of black people offended the black pastor. "But we cannot help this injustice," said Proctor, "all we can do is to abolish the slum, if we can; let us lend our energies to that." The slum was composed of black and white, Jews and Gentiles, "a motley Mixture," Gladden noted. "The undertaking is sufficiently difficult; but the readiness to take it up showed a good spirit." When a new city administration favoring an "open town" took office in 1905, H. H. Proctor activated a coalition of religious leaders and the press to lobby the city not to reopen the dance halls. In September 1906, he appealed again to the council to close the "dives," which he thought threatened the city's peace.[56]

Despite Proctor's effort, Atlanta was a racial tinderbox by 1906. The atmosphere was largely shaped by a political campaign in which rival candidates exchanged vitriolic antiblack rhetoric and newspapers displayed lurid headlines about a wave of "negro crime." On Saturday, 22 September, crowds of white men and black men and women gathered as usual along Decatur Street's strip of gambling dens, saloons, diners, pawnshops, and brothels. By 9:00 P.M., stirred by rumors and fresh newspaper accounts of black assaults on white women, white gangs began to attack isolated Negroes. Mayor James Woodward and the police commissioner tried to quell the disorder, but they were shouted down. When the saloons, clubs, and theaters closed at 10:00 P.M., the mob of angry white men grew from five thousand to ten thousand and turned from the pleas for order to widespread attacks upon black people. In two major struggles, hundreds of blacks fought off thousands of whites. With little opposition from the police, the mobs moved toward Auburn Avenue, raiding and looting business establishments, derailing trolley cars, and beating and killing black people on the way. A smaller white gang attacked Alonzo Herndon's barbershop, where a lame bootblack tried pathetically to outrun the mob. He was caught and beaten to death. Two black barbers did not resist, but they were shot and beaten to death. Their mutilated bodies were dragged to the Henry Grady monument where souvenir hunters tore them apart. At the main entrance to the Piedmont Hotel, a black man was tortured to death as hundreds of white men shouted: "Burn him! Kill him!" When that was done, his fingers and toes were divided among the souvenir hunters. "Once permit the shackles of law and order to be cast off," said Ray Stannard Baker, "and men, white or black, Christian or pagan, revert to primordial savagery." As news of the riot reached black neighborhoods, President J. W. E. Bowen opened buildings at Clark University to black refugees, street lights were put out, and men and women prepared to defend their homes.[57]

Sunday morning's light broke over a quiet, but wounded city. "The Church bells tolled the next morning for Sunday service," said Walter White. "But no one in Atlanta believed for a moment that the hatred and lust for blood had been appeased. Like skulls on a cannibal's hut the hats and caps of victims of the mob of the night before had been hung on the iron hooks of the telegraph poles." At least twenty blacks were dead and scores were wounded. Georgia's governor ordered five companies of state militia to patrol the city. But through Sunday afternoon and evening rumors swept over the white and black communities that mobs of the opposite race were moving against them. White mobs killed two more black men on the Sabbath. On Monday evening, a squad of county police and white vigilantes converged on Brownsville, a section that included Clark University and Gammon Theological Seminary, and arrested black citizens for possessing weapons. Ambushed by blacks, the force lost its leader and three officers before fleeing. Brownsville was then sealed off. On Tuesday, police searched every house in the area, added four more black dead, and arrested three hundred black people, including J. W. E. Bowen. There were sporadic fights and gunfire on Wednesday. By Thursday a sullen peace returned to Atlanta. Official reports listed one white and twenty-five black deaths; six times that number of blacks were seriously wounded.[58]

The Atlanta riot's savagery shocked the nation. "Temporarily civilization was suspended," said Lyman Abbott's *Outlook*. "For brutality and wanton cruelty and fiendish rage and indiscriminate savagery one would have to turn to accounts of massacres in Russia or Turkey for a parallel." William Hayes Ward's *Independent* extended the comparison. "It was as bad as a massacre of Jews in Russia, as senseless and as barbarous," said the editors, "and we ask our President to protest to the Russian Government against Kishinief, Bialystok and Siedlee!"[59] The social gospel prophets did not unanimously condemn Atlanta's racial violence. Southern Presbyterian Alexander McKelway held the black "criminal class" responsible for the riot. "For the first time," he cheered, "the negroes have been impressed with the truth that the individual criminal who lays his hand upon a white woman is a menace to the mass."[60] But others feared that the Atlanta riot was merely a prelude to a race war that would spread across the South and called for racial self-restraint. "Let nobody suppose that the Atlanta riot was *sui generis* and therefore not subject to multiplication," said a Southern Methodist. "It was more than local—it was a symptom of a disease as widespread as the South itself."[61]

Leading white Atlantans, including the president of the Chamber of Commerce and attorney Charles D. Hopkins, had gathered to discuss the situation at the Piedmont Hotel on Sunday, 23 September. Since its colleges had not yet opened for the year, much of Atlanta's black leadership was away from the city when the riot began. W. E. B. Du Bois, H. H. Proctor, and Booker T. Washington rushed to Atlanta upon hearing of the violence. Intent on quelling the riot, Hopkins contacted Proctor and they gathered a group of twenty white men and twenty black men to meet two days later at the courthouse. "We have boasted of our superiority and we have now sunk to this level—we have shed the blood of our helpless wards," said Hopkins. "Christianity and humanity demand that we treat the Negro fairly. It is our Christian duty to protect him. I for one am willing to lay down life rather than have the scenes of the last few days repeated." The men formed a committee to restore order and continue discussions between leaders of both races in the city.[62]

Observers spoke with uncertainty of the Atlanta movement's direction in its early stages. Du Bois participated in the biracial meetings after the riot, but he later dismissed them as "gotten up primarily for advertizing purposes." Booker T. Washington's ghostwriter, Robert E. Park, wrote: "They are planning to form some organization here among the whites on the order of the Ku Klux—some organization at any rate to take counsel and measures to suppress assaults on women." But if the Atlanta movement was comparable to the Klan, it sought to put white robes on black men. "There has been an appeal to the leaders of the Negro race to assit [sic] them," said Park. "I think there is an opportunity here to turn this movement to some good, if it can be handled rightly." Washington told Edgar Gardner Murphy that the basis of this "sanest, wisest and most helpful undertaking that has been put on foot by Southern white people to change present conditions" was "justice to the Negro." Hopkins "is trying hard to keep faith with the Southern traditions," Park told Washington, "while he at the same time realizes that he is engaged in a revolutionary enterprize."[63]

Hopkins's "revolutionary enterprize" was the Atlanta Civic League, an organization of two thousand white members. Proctor secured fifteen hundred members for a parallel Coloured Cooperative Civic League. Executive committees of the two leagues met regularly for concerted action. "It is the purpose of the league to place very largely the responsibility for maintaining order among the blacks upon that race," said a reporter, "giving them a fair and reasonable opportunity to accomplish this end and then hold them responsible for the result. None of the gentlemen who have been prominently connected with the league have any fear of the result."[64] Prompted by a series of letters from ministers to the Atlanta *Constitution* and an editorial by its editor, Clark Howell, about the city's race relations, former Governor William J. Northen and Atlanta pastor John E. White took another approach. As president of the Business Men's Gospel Union, Northen began a speaking tour of the state. His condemnation of mob violence and call for the organization of "Christian Leagues" to promote interracial cooperation between the "best men" of both races was based on his understanding of the ethics of Jesus.[65]

Willis Duke Weatherford instigated a third manifestation of the Atlanta movement for interracial cooperation. A Texan, he studied literature at Vanderbilt University with William H. Baskervill, George Washington Cable's associate in the Open Letter Club. Weatherford subsequently published his dissertation, *Fundamental Religious Principles in Browning's Poetry*, which showed the influence of theological personalism on him. In 1902, he became a student secretary of the YMCA. Like Hopkins and Northen, Weatherford assumed that improvement in Southern race relations depended on regular consultations between the "best men" of both races. In April 1908, he met in Atlanta with William A. Hunton, Jesse E. Moorland, President John Hope of Atlanta Baptist College, Professor John Wesley Gilbert of Paine College, and Dr. Walter Russell Lambuth, missionary secretary for the Methodist Episcopal Church, South. These men, all related to the YMCA, agreed that Weatherford should write a book on race relations to be used in YMCA studies throughout the region. Weatherford's *Negro Life in the South* was notable, not for originality, but for its attempt to synthesize the most recent research and highest ethical values in race relations. Arguing from self-interest and altruism, Weatherford drew on the work of both Booker T. Washington and W. E. B. Du Bois and the diverse perspectives of Edgar Gardner Murphy, Harlan Paul Douglass, and Josiah Royce. He urged white collegians to study and involve themselves in efforts to improve the quality of life for black Americans. In the decade after its publication, thirty thousand Southern white college men and women read his argument that "It is not the negro that is on trial before the world, but it is we, the white men of the South."[66]

After the Atlanta riot, there were also significant efforts to build institutions of social redemption in the black community. Before the riot, the city had a few small religious missions and orphanages. In 1905, the daughter of Atlanta University's founder and sister of its third president, Gertrude Ware, founded the Gate City Kindergarten Association in response to needs identified by the Atlanta University conferences. Black Atlanta had no settlement houses. In 1908, Lugenia Hope, the wife of President John Hope, founded Atlanta's Neighborhood Union, whose motto was "And Thy Neighbor as Thyself." A patient, soft-spoken, yet forceful woman, she gathered a group of faculty wives and other college-educated black women. After surveying the city's west-end section around Atlanta University, the women established a health

Atlanta's First Congregational Church, with Henry Hugh Proctor in inset (Herndon Foundation, Atlanta, Ga.)

clinic and community center with Bible schools, classes, and clubs for boys and girls. As the work grew, the college women divided the city into sections, appointed a resident leader in each area, established a neighborhood center, and tried to rid their blocks of prostitution and gambling houses. When they found additional problems in inadequate public education, health, and safety conditions, the women lobbied the school board and the city council for improved city services.[67]

After the Atlanta riot, H. H. Proctor had a vision. "For ten years I had sat on my porch near the church and seen the people of my race go by the church down to the dive, into the prison, up to the gallows," he recalled. "While the dive was wide open, illuminated and attractive," his church was locked, barred, and dark. "God helping me," Proctor said, "I will open my church and make it as attractive as the dive." Taking advantage of the sense of crisis following the Atlanta riot, he mounted a campaign to build an institutional church for black Atlanta. President-elect William Howard Taft visited the new building before it opened in January 1908. Later, former president Theodore Roosevelt inspected its Sunday school rooms, library and reading room, model kitchen, gymnasium, showers, lavatories, auditorium, offices, ladies' parlor, and galleries. First Congregational Church offered an employment bureau, a home for working women, a prison mission, and a music festival. Proctor aimed to save the whole person. "Save the body alone, and you have a Jack Johnson," he said, "save the mind alone and you have a Robert Ingersoll; save the soul alone, and you have an Uncle Tom; but save body, mind, and soul, and you have an Apostle Paul—a Jesus Christ!" Thereafter, Northern social gospel prophets gave their approval to Atlanta's new institutional church. Proctor invited Washington Gladden to give the dedicatory address. "To have you speak to us in our attempt at applied Christianity would be a source of inspiration from one who has shown himself a real friend to our people we could never forget." After inspecting the building throughout, Proctor recalled, Philadelphia's Russell Conwell examined the doorstep to see how it was worn. It passed the test. On a visit to Atlanta to study the riot, Bruce Barton spent a Sunday at First Congregational Church and wrote of it as "The Church That Saved a City."[68]

# 3

# Civil Wrongs, Civil Rights, and Theological Equations

# 8

# A Prophetic Minority at the Nadir

The collapse of the civil rights organizations in the mid-1890s left the social gospel's advocates of the rights of black Americans with no rallying point. By 1900, the missionary agencies were recovering from the recession and Robert C. Ogden was gathering Northern philanthropists and Southern educators into his powerful coalition. Ten years later, the National Urban League was also addressing urban racial problems in terms congenial to the home missionaries. But in 1900, those who were concerned primarily with the civil rights of black Americans could look only to racial solidarity in the Afro-American Council.

In 1898, five years after T. Thomas Fortune gave up on the Afro-American League, Bishop Alexander Walters of the African Methodist Episcopal Church, Zion, persuaded him to convene a meeting to organize an Afro-American Council in Rochester, New York. Fortune presided at the meeting, but the conferees elected Bishop Walters as its president and Ida B. Wells-Barnett as its secretary. Its address to the nation cited the convict lease system and lynching as the most pressing grievances of black Americans. When the council reconvened in Washington, Wells-Barnett of Chicago and Dr. Nathan F. Mossell of Philadelphia led a radical Northern faction in attacking Booker T. Washington and the McKinley regime for not defending the rights of the race. Bishop Walters's mediating address insisted that there could be no peace until black people were accorded equal rights, but allowed that it might be a century before that happened. He endorsed industrial and higher education for his people and said literacy and property qualifications for the franchise were acceptable, if they were applied equally across racial lines. In short, said Walters: "Let us improve our morals, educate ourselves, work, agitate, and wait on the Lord." Under his mediation, the council's address to the nation called for political agitation in the North, reliance on education and economic development to lead to civil rights in the South, and support of industrial and higher education and federal aid to public schools. The address claimed all rights guaranteed by the Constitution and held that universal suffrage was the best safeguard of liberty, but it did not oppose literacy or property restrictions. It concluded with an attack on lynching, segregation, and the convict lease system.[1]

The social gospel press addressed the issues raised by the Afro-American Council in similar terms. England's William T. Stead could overlook a few lynchings between Anglo-American friends. "However painful these crimes of violence may be, they are comparatively few in number," he said; "100 lynchings among 9,000,000 negroes is a blot on the sun, no doubt, but it is not an eclipse." But *Bibliotheca Sacra*, the *Chautauquan*, *Homiletic Review*, the *Independent*, *Missionary Review of the World*, and the *Outlook* vigorously protested lynching. "Could anything be conceived more brutalizing than such a display of savagery?" asked the *Homiletic Review*. Apache Indians, African cannibals, Chinese Boxer rebels, Kurds, and Turks did nothing worse, said the editors. "Where else than in America can such an act of lawless barbarity be perpetuated?" asked the *Independent*. "Are these men, that do such things, and do they call themselves Christians, and go to churches, and hear the laws of Moses and the love of Christ?" When Georgia Governor Allen Candler condemned "perpetual intermeddling" by Yankee "fools and fanatics," the *Independent* admitted: "We have intermeddled and we propose to keep intermeddling wherever we find what appear to be wrongs that need to be righted." Other spokesmen for social Christianity sought the causes and means of preventing lynching. Faced with the "retrogressive development" and "social terror" of black people since emancipation, a Pittsburgh Methodist found, respectable white Christians in Alexandria, Virginia, were ready to forgo legal processes and resort to primitive instinct. A Southern Methodist clergyman called for stronger legislation to preserve legal processes, more courageous public officials, an enhanced regard for the law among citizens, newspaper campaigns against crime and prejudice, and education of black leaders and teachers of righteousness.[2]

In 1900, Ida B. Wells-Barnett returned to her crusade as chairman of the

Afro-American Council's Anti-Lynching Bureau. "Our country's national crime is lynching," she said. It was not the exceptional, irrational act of a crazed mob, but "the cool, calculating deliberation of intelligent people" who think "there is an 'unwritten law' that justifies them in putting human beings to death" without legal process. She called on the nation's sense of honor, economic well-being, and patriotism to stop lynching. Later, when a white man and a black man murdered two officials at Emporia, Virginia, a white mob lynched the black man. Urged on by Negroes demanding equity, they hung his white partner in crime, as well. The *Independent* pleaded with black leaders "to tell their people to defend their rights even to blood, but never, never take guilty participation in lynching white men or black." The advice was all right in theory, Wells-Barnett replied, but "it seems like giving a stone when we ask for bread." Black people had appealed in vain to "the Christian and moral forces of the country to create a sentiment against the lawlessness and unspeakable barbarism" for twenty years. Only when the nation's white leaders joined in the appeal for justice, she said, could there be any hope of success.[3]

Jane Addams's antilynching appeal acknowledged the right of citizens to protect themselves by legal processes. But the resort to cruel illegal revenge is a turn to a "savage state of dealing with criminality." Brutality begets brutality, she said; lynchings promote further lawlessness among both black and white people. Addams made a feminist's argument against lynching as an act of chivalry. Bloodshed and arson are the handmaid of lust, she said. Women know that they are secure only "where law and order and justice prevail; that the sight of human blood and the burning of human flesh has historically been the signal for lust; that an attempt to allay and control it" by lynching "is as ignorant as it is foolish and childish." A woman protected by such brutality was still a man's possession, she argued, secure only to the degree that her "lord and master" was strong or weak. Ida Wells-Barnett commended the essence of Jane Addams's plea, but challenged its assumption that lynching occurred largely in response to charges of rape. In the past five years, she said, it led to less than 20 percent of the lynchings of black Americans. Far more lynchings were due to mere suspicion of a misdemeanor. "The Christian and moral forces of the nation should insist that misrepresentation" had no place in the discussion of lynching, she concluded, "and that truth, swift-winged and courageous, summon this nation to do its duty to exalt justice and preserve inviolate the sacredness of human life."[4]

When Southern white clergymen joined the antilynching chorus, Mississippi Episcopalian Quincey Ewing's sermon was widely praised. The *Colored American Magazine* prefaced it with lines from Whittier:

Thank God for the token! ——
Thank God, that one man as a *freeman* has spoken!

The Sermon on the Mount and Mississippi's Constitution were his text. Ewing found it painful to speak of "one of the dismalest crimes of the ages" for it was "perpetrated in the southern land by southern men." But a lyncher is "a murderer in the eyes of Almighty God, unless God Almighty sits blind or asleep upon his throne while the lyncher does his devil's work," said the priest. "He is a murderer, because the law of the state of Mississippi has no other name for him." Mississippians could take no pride in their state if murderers feared no prosecution. "If that is a civilized state," he asked, "who will define for us a barbarous one?" White Mississippians condoned lynching black people not for fear of black domination or racial equality. "Why, white men of the sort that gather in mobs to 'lynch niggers' are doing more right here in this town to batter down" barriers to "social equality than has ever been done by the Negroes in all their history as American citizens!" Ewing charged. "I need not be more explicit; you know what I mean; and, if possibly you do not, keep your eyes open as you walk your street and you will know!" Black people were lynched in Mississippi because they were a subordinate race, without legal protection. Ewing called for laws to hold local officials responsible for enforcing legal processes. If they did not preserve order, the governor should be empowered to act. If that were not enough, said Ewing, the federal government should intervene and the state revert to territorial status. Meanwhile, he called for law-and-order leagues to prevent lynching and declared his willingness to face any mob. Ewing's antilynching sermon was "one of the most eloquent, most courageous, most Christian sermons we have ever read," said the *Independent*, "worthy of the greatest pulpit orators and prophets in our history."[5]

Some of the social gospel prophets thought that they could also speak for many Americans in defense of black civil rights. "Demonstrations of the fallacy and injustice of race and color distinctions" were solving the race problem, said Boston's Benjamin Orange Flower. "It can only be solved by leaving the question of color entirely out of account, and so according to the negro his rightful place as a man." Even late in the 1890s, some social gospel prophets saw no threat to America's experiment in democracy. Black men still had the franchise, said Baptist missionary Thomas J. Morgan, and there was "no marked public sentiment, either North or South, looking toward depriving them of it." Like members of the Afro-American Council, many social gospel prophets accepted literacy qualifications for the franchise, if they were equally enforced. So, when Louisiana disfranchised its illiterate voters, the *Independent* and the *Outlook* underscored the state's moral responsibility to educate those whom it had disfranchised.[6]

While Northern journalists spoke of moral responsibility, a white mob ended the vestiges of Reconstruction's "Negro domination" in a municipal revolution at Wilmington, North Carolina. A fusion of Republicans and Populists had won control of its city government in March 1898. But racial tensions were so high that Fusionists agreed not to contest other local offices in an election the following November. Two days after the election, an armed mob of red-shirted white Democrats led by Alfred M. Waddell seized control of the city, took resignations from Fusionist officeholders, and named Waddell mayor and others from their ranks to the remaining vacancies. When an overwhelmingly Democratic legislature convened in January 1899, it approved a constitutional amendment to guarantee "white supremacy" in the state by a literacy test and a poll tax. To avoid disfranchising white illiterates, it included a "grandfather clause" exempting potential voters from the test if their forefathers had been qualified to vote in 1867. The amendment was to be submitted to a statewide referendum in August 1900.[7]

A protest meeting of five thousand people at New York's Cooper Union cheered a letter from the Episcopal priest Richard Heber Newton condemning the Wilmington riot. The crowd "fairly went wild" over Presbyterian Charles H. Parkhurst's call for federal intervention in the South and heard black Methodist pastor W. H. Brooks advise that "If die we must, let us die fighting for our rights." Despite the outcry, little could be done to reverse the result. "The outbreak in North Carolina is a crime against the ballot pure and simple," said the *Independent*. "In Peru or Nicaragua or Paris we should call this revolution. We must not think of it as an ordinary outbreak of hot mob violence. It is a cool, determined, malicious attack on the free government of the State." Seeing no federal authority to intervene, the editors wondered about the Fusionists' abject surrender. "A majority that will not claim and hold its rights of freedom is not fit to be free," said the *Independent*. "They must suffer until they learn a little more manhood and courage." But the *Outlook* blamed the violence on Reconstruction's "unstatesmanlike" grant of unlimited suffrage, the "criminal folly" of both sides in stirring race hatred, and the weakness of Republican Governor Daniel J. Russell and his failure to preserve order. "Mere numbers cannot permanently confer political power. A subject race can become politically powerful only as it becomes virtuous, self-restrained, and intelligent," said the *Outlook*.[8]

White Southerners defended the Wilmington insurrection. How could the Yankee conscience condemn the Wilmington insurrection, asked Elijah Embree Hoss, while condoning a revolution of white settlers in Hawaii that ousted the native queen and enabled the United States to acquire the Pacific islands? North Carolina's Alexander J. McKelway was the Wilmington revolution's leading apologist. When the Fusionists took office, Wilmington was seized by a wave of crime and authorities failed to preserve order, he said. The result was anarchy: "a carnival of crime," "burglaries of nightly occurrence," "incendiary fires of frequent occurrence," and "insulting language and conduct to white women." The city's intelligence, power, and wealth stepped into the breach to bring order out of chaos. Condemning crime that grew in the face of impotence, McKelway justified crime enforced by power. "If ever a revolution was justified by the results, this one has been." Peace and prosperity had returned to the city, he argued. "All of which proves that the majority of numbers cannot always rule when there is weight also to be considered." Events in Wilmington would encourage North Carolina to restrict the ballot, he predicted, excluding the race "whose ignorance, venality and cowardice have been a standing temptation in politics to fraud, corruption and violence."[9]

As disfranchisement advanced in North Carolina, the *Outlook's* Charles B. Spahr toured the South to report on "The Negro as a Citizen." Born in an Ohio Methodist parsonage, Spahr founded New York's Social Reform Club and took seriously his egalitarian values. "I can't find it in my heart to have any one black my boots," he once said. "Somehow, it seems to me undemocratic." Encouraged by Populist appeals to black voters in the 1890s, Spahr now feared that the Populists' collapse into the white man's Democratic party would lead to black disfranchisement throughout the region. If North Carolina joined Louisiana, he thought, black suffrage was doomed for a generation. Spahr saw that the education of black people could not rest upon white people's sense of moral obligation, for many white Southerners objected to educating black people because it spoiled them as servants. That was its best feature, because it Americanized the sons and daughters of slaves, making them less servile and more self-assertive. "The treatment of the negro as a man is the very cornerstone for the elevation of his manhood," Spahr argued.

White Southerners did not believe democratic principles of equal rights or Christian principles of brotherhood applied to their relations with black people, Spahr said. But the situation could be rightly resolved only by "the simplest applications of the principles of Christianity and democracy." Loss of the suffrage would deny black people the political leverage to guarantee public support for black education. "Disfranchisement means injustice all along the line." He hoped that disfranchisement could be resisted until the white South again divided its vote along economic lines, when black and white workers might recognize their common interests.[10]

Georgia rejected disfranchisement in 1899, but North Carolina joined Louisiana, South Carolina, and Mississippi in disfranchising black voters in 1900. Alexander McKelway defended North Carolina's violation of democratic law and order. Fusion government was the last vestige of Reconstruction's inverted pyramid, said McKelway; its toppling was inevitable. Registration procedures may have been unjust; intimidation was certainly a factor. One could hardly speak of the Red Shirts "without a smile," he wrote. "They victimized the negroes with a huge practical joke, the point of which was the ridiculous timidity of the black advocates of manhood suffrage," said McKelway. "A dozen men would meet at a crossroad, on horseback, gallop through the country, and the negro would quietly make up his mind that his interest in political affairs was not a large one anyway." North Carolina's law would survive a test of its constitutionality, it was the right ethical alternative to black domination or continued intimidation, and its passage had pacified the state's racial turmoil, said McKelway. The "reverend apologist" might think it was a joke, answered the Independent. It may have been "hilarious sport to the prancing red-shirted young men who galloped over the country firing off their guns about the negro houses." But "was it funny when women were whipped for screaming in their fright?" asked the editors. "Is it funny when in a whole county with a large negro population, only two men dared cast their votes against the amendment? This was no fun or farce; it was dead earnest, and it meant death to those who would resist." Freedom of thought, speech, and the ballot were violently suppressed in North Carolina, the Independent said, but it could not go on forever.[11]

The North Carolina revolution disturbed the conscience of the Northern social gospel. The Independent and the Outlook criticized developments in North Carolina. "It is perfectly legitimate for a community to confine the suffrage to those who can read and write; it is not legitimate to give the suffrage to ignorant whites and deny it to educated blacks," said the Outlook. Threats and terror suppressed freedom of speech and the press and prevented black and white men from voting in the state. Under the Fourteenth Amendment, both journals said, suffrage restriction would lead to reducing Southern representation in Congress. Urging the American Missionary Association to "Educate, Evangelize, Enfranchise," Boston's Joseph Cook called disfranchisement "a national peril." AMA delegates demanded that franchise requirements "respect the manhood of the Negro, and shall apply to white and black, without regard to race, color or previous condition."[12]

*Homiletic Review* directed the preachers to Deuteronomy 15:7: "If there be among you a poor man of one of thy brethren, thou shalt not harden thine heart, nor shut thine hand from thy poor brother." The sermon notes questioned the cry of "negro domination." Black people were a majority only in Mississippi and South Carolina. The races were about equally represented in Louisiana. Elsewhere in the South the white population was in a clear majority. But disfranchisement swept through Alabama, Georgia, Maryland, and Virginia within two years. When Virginia's constitutional convention disfranchised the state's black citizens, without even submitting the matter to a plebiscite, the *Chautauquan* headline read: "The Virginia Constitution versus Democracy." Writers for the *Homiletic Review* and the *Social Gospel* questioned the wisdom of disfranchisement. "The colored man by the terms of the Constitution is a citizen of the United States," said John Smith. "Can the white man safely rob him by political trickery of his citizenship because his skin is black? To use the ballot wisely the negro must be educated. Can the South afford to leave him in ignorance, except so far as Northern benevolence shall rescue him? Are not far-reaching consequences of evil involved in the present 'white man's' policy, for both races?" Disfranchisement threatened American democracy, warned the *Independent* and the University of Wisconsin's John Bascom. There was danger of tyranny from above and from below, said Bascom, "but the first danger is far more urgent and prevalent than the second."[13]

In July 1901, as thoughtful Americans gazed on the light that lynching threw on distinctions between American civilization and primitive society and wondered at the meaning of disfranchisement for the experiment in democracy, American socialists gathered in Indianapolis to organize their party. Black Americans were still so largely tied to the land in the late nineteenth century that Henry George's Single Tax was more attractive than socialism. The Colored Farmers' Alliance and such black intellectuals as T. Thomas Fortune, T. McCants Stewart, and D. Augustus Straker supported the Single Tax. In turn, Single Taxers like Henry George and James O. S. Huntington were fairly enlightened in race relations.[14] But Richard T. Ely and Chicago's Alexander Clark warned that socialists hoped to win black recruits, and such black intellectuals as Cincinnati's Peter H. Clark and Chicago's Reverdy Ransom were drawn to socialism. AME pastors Ransom and J. T. Jennifer debated its merits in the mid-1890s. Ransom spoke for black working-class solidarity with the socialists and Jennifer espoused a reformed capitalism for black entrepreneurs.[15] At the turn of the century, white Christian socialists such as William Dwight Porter Bliss, Herbert N. Casson, George D. Herron, and Henry Demarest Lloyd were interested in racial reform. Casson's articles on "Slavery" and "The Negro and Present Social Reform in America" in Bliss's *Encyclopedia of Social Reform* asked friends of humanity to build "a public sentiment friendly to the negro as a citizen, as a laborer, and as a man, until the African race is merged at length into a composite American nationality."[16]

As Iowa's social gospel prophet, George D. Herron, began to argue that private ownership of material resources is a crime against God, man, and nature, he inflamed critics of his work at Grinnell College. A move in the board of trustees for his dismissal was defeated in June 1899, but four months later Herron resigned unexpectedly. The *AME Church Review* watched the struggle at Grinnell with interest. "There are still men of the old stuff who would dare to give up their life (if the age requires it), and who do give up their living (since the age requires it) rather than cease proclaiming the truth as God gives them to see it," said the journal. "When men have a mission which the world rejects, let them bravely sever the relation founded in the old order, and [launch] forth into the deep with abiding faith in God's power to take care of His own." One could not expect an unredeemed world to reward the prophet who attacks it, concluded the black editor, so "all honor to the manhood, the sweetness and the courage of Prof. Herron." After leaving Grinnell, Herron joined the campaign of the Social Democratic party's nominee for president, Eugene V. Debs. His platform called on wage earners of the United States "without distinction of color, race, or sex" to organize and "wage war upon the exploiting class until the system of wage slavery shall be abolished and the cooperative Commonwealth established." For Herron, Debs's defeat underscored the need for socialist unity.[17]

When American socialists met at Indianapolis to charter a united Socialist Party of America, they chose Herron as chairman. The convention included three black delegates: William Costley of California, and John H. Adams and Edward D. McKay of Indiana. They were "by no means the least intelligent and earnest of the delegates," said Morris Hillquit, attesting to "the fact that socialism had begun to take root among the colored race." But William Costley's resolution on the attitude of the party to the Negro set off acrimonious debate. Adams and McKay opposed the resolution because black people wanted no special favors, but Herron argued that "I would prefer that we lost every white vote in the South than to evade the question which is presented today in that resolution." Finally, he was asked to prepare a resolution. In deference to the wishes of Southern delegates, the convention deleted a clause from his resolves about "the persecution of innocent members of the race, their severe punishment for trivial offenses, their lynching, burning and disfranchisement." As approved, his resolution held that the Negroes' condition resulted from their former servitude, that it was maintained by capitalists who hoped to keep white and black workers divided to exploit them both, and that traditional institutions betrayed the Negro in his struggle against disfranchisement and violence in order to keep the economic favor of the capitalist class. It assured black people of the party's sympathy in the struggle against oppression and welcomed them to the fellowship of all who suffered from capitalist exploitation. Two years later, the party's convention dropped the resolution at the advice of Debs who argued that the Socialist party made no special appeal to any race. George D. Herron's appeal for black rights was the only such statement approved by a national socialist body from 1901 through 1912.[18]

While the American left addressed and avoided the race issue, a Southern and a Northern white churchman sought common ground in race relations. Andrew Sledd was a Virginian who studied at Randolph-Macon and Harvard. An ordained Southern Methodist minister, he went to Atticus Haygood's Emory College to teach Latin in 1898. When he married the daughter of a powerful Southern bishop, Warren A. Candler, his position seemed secure. But in 1902 Emory's Latin professor advocated a "via media" between radical Northern egalitarians and radical Southern racists. He thought it lay in recognizing that "the negro belongs to an inferior race, but the negro had inalienable rights." The white South often ignored them by relegating all black people, regardless of character, to the "lowest place in public esteem and treatment." Lynching was the most extreme example of the denial of inalienable rights to black people. "It is not necessary that the negro should be the social equal of the white man," said the professor. His "political privileges" could be curtailed "without injustice or offense," if the curtailment applied equally to both races. If the North did not impose an artificial racial equality upon the South and if the white South realized that black people had rights it was bound to respect, then black Americans could succeed or fail according to their merits. Within months of Andrew Sledd's modest appeal, white opinion in Georgia was whipped into a fury against him. He was burned in effigy, his powerful father-in-law was helpless to protect him, and Emory's board of trustees accepted Andrew Sledd's letter of resignation.[19]

In 1901, Washington Gladden was elected president of the American Missionary Association. A member of the AMA from the outset of his ministry, he was a trustee of Berea College and served as vice-president of the AMA from 1894 to 1901. In his presidential address, Gladden said that "the neediest, most ignorant, most helpless are nearest to Christ; it is to them, if we are upon his errands, that we go first." This "Christly compassion for the needy" had "sprinkled the cotton fields and the cane-breaks of the South with schools and mission stations, to bear light to them that sit in darkness." He warned the wealthy, powerful, and racially prideful: "Despise not these little ones." A day of judgment and deliverance was at hand; never was the race question more difficult than in the current crisis. "The disfranchisement of ignorance or of moral worthlessness is not to be deprecated," Gladden allowed; "but the drawing of the line of political privilege between the ignorant white man and the ignorant black man is a wrong that cannot endure." The South could not build a civilization on a permanent injustice, he concluded, because "this is a Christian age and a Christian nation, and He who counts the poor and the needy among His friends has come to reign, and will reign, until He has put all His enemies under His feet."[20]

**A**s Gladden and Sledd grappled with America's race problem, they faced a year of crisis in race relations. In 1903, terror stalked the Southern countryside; freedom of speech was threatened in the region's citadels of culture. White farmers in Georgia, Mississippi, and Texas drove off black farmers and seized their property. James K. Vardaman was elected governor of Mississippi in the most racist campaign in the state's history. The racist tide swept North into national centers of power. In Maryland, where black people were only 20 percent of the population, Democrats sought to disfranchise them. In New York, Thomas Dixon's dramatization of his racist novel, *The Leopard's Spots*, was popular on Broadway and the school board removed Harriet Beecher Stowe's *Uncle Tom's Cabin* from libraries because of its "distorted" view of slavery. President Theodore Roosevelt withdrew civil service appointments of black people in the South; and the Supreme Court accepted disfranchisement, encouraging demands for repeal of the Fifteenth Amendment.[21]

Two of New York's social gospel prophets came to the defense of black people early in 1903. Charles H. Parkhurst of Madison Square Presbyterian Church attacked America's record in race relations. "Although we claim to be a civilized people," he said, "there is a degree of barbarism in our treatment of the black race that is not exceeded in any part of the world. And although we send out missionaries to Christianize other lands, there are communities in the South as unchristian as any part of heathendom." Accosted by a white Arkansan after the service, Parkhurst cited lynching and disfranchisement as examples of Southern barbarism. "There is more sulphur in the air because of some remarks that Dr. Parkhurst exploded yesterday," Robert C. Ogden told Wallace Buttrick. "I wish that the best friends of the country could see that temper and violent language do immense harm, and that our only solution is through sane, conservative and patient consideration of the race issue." Through 1903, Ogden lamented racial agitation on all sides, fearful that in race relations the nation's center would not hold. Two weeks later, Lyman Abbott's successor at Brooklyn's Plymouth Congregational Church, Newell Dwight Hillis, prayed for protection from the racist tide. "We ask thee, O Lord, that Thou wilt raise up men who will save us from this new and damnable heresy that this is a white man's country, and that there is no place here for the black man," he prayed. The son of evangelical abolitionists called for a new abolitionism to save the nation from bondage to prejudice. "Save the black race from hatred; save the white man from supercilious contempt," he prayed; "save both from narrowness and selfishness, and lift them up until each learn to love his fellow-man made in God's own image."[22]

In Chicago, the race crisis alarmed Henry Demarest Lloyd and William Mackintire Salter. Lloyd admired Hampton, Tuskegee, and Booker T. Washington, but by 1903 he doubted the adequacy of their racial policy. At Hull House, he raised concern about the South's caste system and foresaw dire consequences if Americans allowed "the rights of the humblest to be invaded." In March, the author of *Wealth against Commonwealth* told W. E. B. Du Bois that race was the most critical issue before the American people, "equaling, if not surpassing, in immediate and remote influence the question of the trusts." As months passed, Lloyd became convinced that the race problem was "the most terrible of all those we face. I see in it at least two civil wars. In it are concentrated the intensest aspects of our labour question, of the imperial question, and of deeper problems still." He warned Northern white laborers: "Let there be one Samson, prisoner, holding to the pillars of our temple, and we are undone. We leave the blacks unprotected in the South only to see them brought North to take our places in the mines and mills." The socialist necessity was to establish justice where people were, lest they be driven abroad. Disfranchising Southern black voters was exactly the wrong move. "If we have the right to disfranchise the Negroes," Lloyd told a Southern socialist, "the plutocrats have a right to disfranchise us. The disfranchisement of the Negroes is a policy of ruin for the white people of the South." The problem could not be solved by returning to predemocratic practices. "Take away the vote, and we will attempt again what has always failed—to govern men without help from them," Lloyd wrote. Efforts to promote democratic labor organization would be defeated across the nation, "unless our 'scheme of things entire' is broad and deep and just enough to find out how the Negro can be taken into the brotherhood. *The last thing you white people of the South can afford is to have the Negro among you without a vote.*"[23]

On 31 March 1903, William Mackintire Salter asked "Is the Nation Going Backwards?" in race relations. The son of evangelical abolitionists, Salter strayed from theological orthodoxy to become an Ethical Culture Society lecturer in Chicago. America had imperfectly embodied the equality, fraternity, and unity of humanity since emancipation, he said. But that was threatened by those who would bar black people from education, voting, and public accommodations. The spirit of caste is wrong, undemocratic, and un-American, Salter argued: "wrong because it is against the ideal of human brotherhood, undemocratic because . . . there can be no castes in a democracy, unAmerican because it is against the letter and the spirit of our Constitution and law." Salter accepted limits of character or intelligence on the franchise, but cries of "Negro domination" and "social equality" raised false issues. Slavery's legacy to the twentieth century was the peculiarly American stigma of race and color. "Our contempt is thus in a way a confession and a reminiscence of our sin," said the preacher. Yet, he hoped that prejudice would be outgrown, allowing black people to demonstrate their capabilities. "If, while reasonable restrictions on the franchise are admitted, there is no yielding to those who would humiliate the black man as such," said Salter, the tide would turn "and the nation go on towards the destiny that befits a great, free and generous people."[24]

But Northern egalitarians, such as the leaders of the National Woman's Suffrage Association, often skirted the race issue when they went South.

Mississippi suffragette Belle Kearney held that property and literacy qualifications only temporarily restrained the threat of black political domination, because they would stimulate black men to buy property and become literate. Women's suffrage was needed to "insure immediate and durable white supremacy," she argued. Deferring to its Southern hosts, the association tried to avoid the issue at a New Orleans convention in 1903. But the Southern audience demanded that its president, Anna Howard Shaw, discuss women's suffrage and racial equality. "If by granting political equality you lay the foundation for social equality, you have already laid that claim," she said. "You did not wait for woman suffrage, but disfranchised both your black and your white women, thus making them politically equal. But you have done more than that. You have put the ballot into the hands of your black men, thus making them the political superiors of your white women. Never before in the history of the world have men made former slaves the political masters of their former mistresses!" In a nation of immigrants, Shaw continued, American women were governed by men of every color, nation, and race. "If American men are willing to leave their women in a position as degrading as this," she concluded, "they need not be surprised when American women resolve to lift themselves out of it." The feminist logic of her response was as clear as its racial implications were ambiguous. Everyone hearing what they wanted to hear, the audience roared its approval.[25]

As Anna Howard Shaw played on racial fears to win support for women's rights, New York Republicans debated disfranchisement. With Booker T. Washington's support, Robert C. Ogden defeated a Union League Club resolution asking Congress to reduce Southern representation in proportion to the disfranchisement of its voters. After the Union League debate, Ogden joined Lyman Abbott and Booker T. Washington in a Madison Square Garden rally for Hampton and Tuskegee. There, Abbott commended the record of North Carolina's recent legislature as "highly creditable to the experiment of restricted suffrage now on trial." Given white superiority and the massive numbers of black illiterates, he argued, the franchise for black people must await their education. A week later, Abbott repeated the theme at the Conference on Education in the South at Richmond, Virginia. "Education is for service," he said, "and that education is highest which best fits a man to render the service he can best render to the world." His rhetorical ambiguity appealed both to advocates of the Christian vocational ideal and to white Southerners who wanted obedient servants and field hands. Abbott won hearty rounds of applause from a largely white Southern audience by reiterating his belief that the suffrage is a privilege, not a right, and that manhood suffrage meant manhood first and suffrage afterward. The white Episcopal priest from Rochester, New York, Algernon Sydney Crapsey, was sitting near black people, "roped like so many beasts," in the segregated balcony of the theater where Abbott spoke. He watched "their sad, hopeless faces become sadder and more hopeless, while down below the white people cheered the speaker to the echo." Abbott's doctrine of "Manhood first and Suffrage afterwards" was "a mere truism if taken literally," he thought. If applied in the North, his definition of manhood as perfect self-control and high intelligence would reduce the electorate to a few college professors, railroad presidents, and newspaper editors, Crapsey thought, and "of these many would be found wanting." In the South, it was "a justification of that attitude of mind which of old enslaved and has now disfranchised the Negro and placed upon him the badge of social inferiority."[26]

Lyman Abbott's remarks touched off fireworks in the North. Boston's black radicals dismissed him as "an eternal sorehead." The *Outlook*'s Charles B. Spahr begged him and Booker T. Washington to assert the Negro's need of the franchise to protect his other rights. Francis Jackson Garrison and black novelist Charles Waddell Chesnutt asked Washington to distinguish between Abbott's position and his own. The "reactionary talk of men like Lyman Abbott is the worst possible obstacle" to Southern men who would build the South "on the only sure foundation—equality of rights & privileges," said Garrison. "I believe in manhood suffrage, and the speeches of the Northern men at Richmond, truckling away the fundamental rights of citizenship, have filled me with a very wholesome disgust," Chesnutt told Washington. "On this franchise proposition, I think you are training in the wrong." Chesnutt spoke for other black radicals, such as Richmond attorney James H. Hayes, president of the National Negro Suffrage Association, who toured the North to win support for black suffrage. In Rochester, New York, he joined Susan B. Anthony and Unitarian pastor William Channing Gannett in a rally at Central Church to protest discrimination and disfranchisement. Women and black men were "in the same boat," fighting for the right to vote, Anthony said. She argued for reducing Southern representation in Congress until franchise restrictions were removed. Hayes hoped the federal courts would reject disfranchisement.[27]

Hayes's hopes were destroyed in early May, when the Supreme Court ruled in a five to three decision against the black plaintiff in *Giles v. Hunter*. In a case secretly financed by Booker T. Washington and the Afro-American Council,

Cartoon in William Monroe Trotter's Boston *Guardian*, caricaturing Booker T. Washington as he salutes, in return for money, Northern white philanthropists Robert C. Ogden and William. H. Baldwin and social gospel preachers Lyman Abbott and Charles Parkhurst, over the graves of Negro votes, social rights, and higher education. The headline above the cartoon read "Group of Mourners in 'the New Burying Ground'" and the caption beneath read "Private Scene Just for the Professor and His 'Friends.'" (Boston *Guardian*, 30 May 1903)

Jackson Giles argued that provisions in Alabama's new constitution were a conspiracy to disfranchise black citizens and asked the Court to place his name on the registration lists. Speaking for the Court, Justice Oliver Wendell Holmes held that if Giles's contention were true the Court would become a party to the unconstitutional state action by granting the relief requested and that it lacked the power to enforce any other decision. The majority recommended that Giles seek redress from legislative or executive branches of the federal government. "This reasoning is deemed by many commentators exceedingly weak—'quibbling,' in fact, is the word used by some," said the *Chautauquan*. Recalling the Dred Scott decision, a black newspaper in Boston referred to Holmes as a "second Roger Taney." The Giles decision dimmed hopes that the Court would reject disfranchisement as unconstitutional and encouraged Southern extremists to seek repeal of the Fifteenth Amendment.[28]

Six weeks after his attack on lynching and disfranchisement in the barbarous South, New York's Charles H. Parkhurst seemed to turn on his own argument. Black Americans should be grateful for their apprenticeship in slavery, he said; black people who were not otherwise governed would be better off enslaved. The *Independent* urged the "frank-spoken" Parkhurst to compare the thrift and morality of Zulus under British freedom with the theft and immorality of American Negroes nurtured in slavery. The *AME Church Review* said tracing the course of his remarks would be "hard work for the casuists," but "it seems to be a case of a sandwich with white bread on top, brown bread underneath, and a much compressed piece of Ham in the center." Parkhurst returned to the race issue at the National Conference on Charities and Corrections in Atlanta. He echoed Booker Washington's plea that Negroes be judged by the best among them, not the worst, and urged patient rather than hasty effort at solving the race problem. But one of Reconstruction's errors, said Parkhurst, was its assumption that "altering the colored man's condition altered the colored man; that letting a wolf out of a cage domesticated the wolf; that substituting coat and trousers for swaddling clothes makes an infant a man; and that emancipation not only relieved the slave of his fetters, but qualified him as a citizen." Back in New York, Parkhurst faced charges that he had said he regretted the end of slavery. Trying to pull one foot out of his mouth, he plunged the other one down his throat, saying that he merely meant that "niggers" were unfit for citizenship. "I call them *niggers*," Parkhurst said, "because that is what they call themselves." They would never be assimilated by the nation. "They never, never, never will contribute, in any part, toward forming the national type of the Americans of the future," he argued. "They grow blacker and blacker every day. Their color forms a physical barrier, which even time, the great leveler, cannot sweep away." Astonished at his outburst, the *Independent* said that since intelligent black people never used the term "nigger," Parkhurst must only know "illiterate, ignorant negroes" who accepted it from white bigots. "Uncle Charlie" was fearful that "Parson Abbott and his gang" would pass him in the parade of "fools" who would disfranchise black people, said Boston's radical *Guardian*. His latest deliverance stooped "to saying cusswords and to braying laureate of the long-eared kind."[29]

Howard University's William A. Sinclair and Brooklyn's Newell Dwight

Hillis took Parkhurst's outburst seriously. Emancipation could no more transform slaves into responsible freedmen than could amnesty transmute traitorous Confederates into loyal citizens, Sinclair argued. But the North rightly believed that an ignorant but loyal black man was a better citizen than an educated but disloyal white man. Assimilation was a matter of culture, not of blood, he said. Thousands of black people had assimilated American values; and thousands of white people were as alien to them "as if they had not been born and raised in a land where the gospel of Christ is preached from every hill-top and in every valley" and where the people are dedicated to the principle of equality before the law. The American national type of the future was not a matter of race, he argued, but of intellect, heart, soul, patriotism, loyalty, and discipleship. Parkhurst might "dance his jig" on prostrate Negroes, Sinclair suggested, but his racial insults cast doubt on his standing as a preacher of Christian righteousness. Until he closeted himself in prayer, wrestled with his God, and assimilated the mind and spirit of Jesus Christ, his eloquent learning and "pure white skin" counted for nought. Newell Dwight Hillis saw Abbott's and Parkhurst's remarks as evidence that the country was "suffering from a reaction" in race relations. "The colored race have known a month of such depression and sorrow and heartache as they have not known in forty years," he said, and "there is reason for the depression." The preachers' remarks showed that the nation's leaders were losing faith in the equality and right of suffrage for all races. "If the Negro is to be disfranchised then the Declaration of Independence is wrong," said Hillis. "If universal suffrage is wrong, then the fifteenth amendment to the Constitution must be given up; then Abraham Lincoln was wrong in his speech at Gettysburg and the million soldiers who gave up their lives for liberty spilled their blood in the interests of folly and superstition."[30]

Lyman Abbott and Newell Dwight Hillis, Henry Ward Beecher's successors at Brooklyn's Plymouth Church, were now struggling with each other for Beecher's mantle on the suffrage. In May, the *Outlook* cited an 1865 sermon in which Beecher had said: "I am satisfied that while we ought to claim for the colored man the right to the elective franchise, you will never be able to secure it and maintain it for him, except by making him so intelligent that men cannot deny it to him." Beecher's words were prophetic, said Abbott; since universal suffrage was not matched by universal education, it failed. Now the nation must provide education first and the franchise would follow. Abbott misread Beecher's argument, Hillis contended. He had said "we must insist on suffrage for the negro; that races, like children, are trained by responsibility; that the poorest government of an ignorant man who governs himself is better than the best government that is imposed upon him from without." Beecher had said that given two centuries of slavery it might take a century to produce effective black educators and orators. But only forty years after emancipation black people had, in Booker T. Washington, an educator and orator whose reputation and fees surpassed those of most white educators and orators. Those who would disfranchise the Negro contend not just with black people and their white friends, said Hillis, but with God, as enemies of love, brotherhood, and righteousness.[31]

White liberals and black radicals rallied to Newell Dwight Hillis's side in the war for Beecher's mantle. Hillis was "in line with the traditions of Plymouth Church," said the *Independent*; while Abbott was one of "the most popular Northern men among the old leaders of the South." Hillis's message made him a fitting heir to Henry Ward Beecher, said Chicago's militant *Broad-Ax*. "We still have a few brave men who are not morally dead to the higher ideals of human society," said the *Broad-Ax*; "they cannot be bought or bribed with gold to spit upon the Declaration of Independence and to belittle the Negro by making it appear that he is nothing more than a wild animal and not entitled to participate in the affairs of this government." A black suffrage conference in New England condemned Abbott and Robert Ogden as "avowed enemies of the race." Yet Abbott would not lay down his arms. Two weeks after Hillis's attack, the *Outlook* published an 1885 letter by Henry Ward Beecher purporting to show that Beecher had not believed in universal suffrage and that his rationale for granting the vote to freedmen was that it was necessary to protect their other rights. Black people had not used it effectively in the intervening years, even to protect their own interests, Abbott argued. Now they must look to the best Southern white men for protection.[32]

While Abbott and Hillis sparred over Beecher's authority on the franchise, American Missionary Association President Washington Gladden went South to give the baccalaureate sermon at Atlanta University, address its Annual Conference on the Negro, and preach at First Congregational Church. Gladden was impressed by the problems of the South's black people. Conditions in rural areas were more difficult than those facing the freedmen forty years earlier. "Deeper and more dire are their necessities than those of any other class; their poverty is more appalling; the burden that rests upon them is heavier; their path to manhood is thornier; the barriers that stand across their way are more formidable; the influences that tend to their degradation are more powerful," he said. "I think that if the Son of man were here today, his time would be very largely spent among these hopeless people." He was shocked by white Atlanta's refusal to join in the baccalaureate service, despite the acknowledged superiority of the university. "I cannot understand why the tens of thousands of white Christians who dwell in that city should wholly ignore work of this kind," said Gladden. "Contempt of this nature seems to me almost childish; it lacks dignity, to say nothing worse about it."[33]

At the Atlanta University conference, Gladden and Atlanta's Episcopal priest, Carey Breckinridge Wilmer, offered alternatives in racial reform. Wilmer might have been preaching to a gang of field hands sixty years earlier, but his message was compatible with that of the education coalition. Black people should forget politics, rights, and antilynching crusades. "In general, the Negro possesses the primal virtue of loving what is above him," Wilmer allowed. "Inculcate good will toward all men, especially white folks," he urged black pastors. "No cause is rendered easier by hate." Above all, "let the Negro preacher impress on his congregation that salvation [is] the power of righteousness and service of our fellow men." Gladden spoke cautiously, yet with a different tone. Addressing his audience as fellow citizens who sought to contribute to "the welfare of this great commonwealth," Gladden admitted that they were often prevented from performing their civic duty. "I do not wish to make any inflammatory suggestions," he said. "I doubt whether the question of your political rights can be settled by violence." So he counseled patience. But his urging black people to make their exclusion a challenge to greater worthiness won applause from Du Bois, Kelly Miller, and Mary Church Terrell. "People who are thoroughly fitted for good citizenship are not going to be permanently excluded in any part of this country from the responsibilities and duties of citizenship," he said. Leaving Atlanta, Gladden read Du Bois's new book, *The Souls of Black Folk*, on his way home. Its author "is, perhaps, the most thoroughly cultivated man among the American negroes," Gladden thought; "he is a highly organized, sensitive, poetical nature," carefully prepared for scientific investigation of the race problem.[34]

But *The Souls of Black Folk* departed abruptly from the style of Du Bois's earlier work. Now an American classic, it was a heady brew of alien sources: classical mythology, German idealist philosophy, and Afro-American spirituality. No longer the objective historian or sociologist, Du Bois interpreted the experience of his people in fourteen lyrical essays. "The Negro is a sort of seventh son, born with a veil, and gifted with second-sight in this American world,—a world which yields him no true self-consciousness, but only lets him see himself through the revelation of the other world," he wrote. "It is a peculiar sensation, this double-consciousness, this sense of always looking at one's self through the eyes of others, of measuring one's soul by the tape of a world that looks on in amused contempt and pity. One ever feels his twoness,—an American, a Negro; two souls, two thoughts, two unreconciled strivings; two warring ideals in one dark body, whose dogged strength alone keeps it from being torn asunder." Wishing neither to "Africanize America" nor to "bleach his Negro soul in a flood of white Americanism," the black man hoped to be both a Negro and an American, as "a co-worker in the kingdom of culture" to become all that he could be. Already black Americans had a rich folklore and music and an undivided commitment to liberty. "All in all, we black men seem the sole basis of simple faith and reverence in a dusty desert of dollars and smartness," Du Bois said. "Will America be poorer if she replace her brutal and dyspeptic blundering with the light-hearted but determined Negro humility? or her coarse and cruel wit with loving jovial good-humor? or her vulgar music with the soul of the Sorrow Songs?" The survival of the fittest must mean not the victory of greed, impudence, and cruelty, he wrote, but the preservation of all that is "really fine and noble and strong."[35]

Du Bois abandoned scientific methods because their pretense often sheltered malignant influences. "While sociologists gleefully count his bastards and his prostitutes, the very soul of the toiling, sweating black man is darkened by the shadow of a vast despair," he said. Learned men called the shadow "prejudice" and explained it as the natural barrier of the purity, culture, and learning of the "higher race" against the crime, barbarity, and ignorance of the "lower race." So far as it was justified, Du Bois conceded, black people must accept it. "But before that nameless prejudice that leaps beyond all this he stands helpless, dismayed, and well nigh speechless, before that personal disrespect and mockery, the ridicule and systematic humiliation, the distortion of fact and wanton license of fancy, the cynical ignoring of the better and the boisterous welcoming of the worse, the all-pervading desire to inculcate disdain for everything black," he wrote, "before this there arises a sickening despair that would disarm and discourage any nation save that black host to whom 'discouragement' is an unwritten word." For black Americans to become all that they could be, he said, they needed work, culture, and freedom, not singly nor successively, but together. Du Bois's essay, "Of Mr. Booker T. Washington and Others," was his first public criticism of the Tuskegeean. It praised him as "the most distinguished Southerner since Jefferson Davis, and the one with the largest personal following." But Washington's stature and following were won at a price, Du Bois said, for he had

W. E. B. Du Bois, black Christian sociologist and critic of consensus in race relations (Archives, University Library, University of Massachusetts, Amherst)

become the spokesman for a triumphant materialism that compromised black people's rights to civil equality, the vote, and higher education. "So far as Mr. Washington preaches Thrift, Patience, and Industrial Training for the Masses, we must hold up his hands and strive with him, rejoicing in his honors and glorying in the strength of this Joshua called of God and of man to lead the headless host," said Du Bois. "But so far as Mr. Washington apologizes for injustice, does not rightly value the privileges and duty of voting, belittles the emasculating effects of caste distinctions, and opposes the higher training and ambitions of our brighter minds,—so far as he, the South, or the Nation, does this—we must unceasingly and firmly oppose them."[36]

Lyman Abbott's *Outlook* reviewed *The Souls of Black Folk*, comparing it unfavorably with Booker Washington's works. Du Bois is "ashamed of the race," but Washington "is proud of it," ran the journal's litany:

One makes the white man the standard,
   the other seeks the standard in its own race ideals;
one demands social equality,
   the other is too self-respecting to do [so];
one seeks to push the negro into a higher place,
   the other to make him a larger man;
one demands for him the right to ride in the white man's car,
   the other seeks to make the black man's car clean and respectable;
one demands the ballot for ignorant black men because ignorant white
men have the ballot,
   the other asks opportunity to make the black man competent for the
   duties of citizenship, and wishes no man to vote who is not competent;
one would build the educational system for the race on the university,
   the other would build it upon the common school and the industrial
   school;
one wishes first to teach the negro to read the Ten Commandments in
Hebrew,
   the other wishes first to teach him to obey them in English;
to one labor is barely more honorable than idleness,
   to the other industry is the basic virtue.

The *Outlook* caricatured Du Bois's argument while accusing him of doing so to Washington.[37]

Washington Gladden called the *Outlook's* review unfair and urged his congregation to read *The Souls of Black Folk* for a "deeper insight into the real human elements of the race problem than anything that has yet been written." He defended Du Bois from the charge of being hypersensitive, morbid, and ashamed of his race. "Imagine yourself living in a civilization whose overwhelming sentiment puts you into a lower realm of being and means to keep you there," Gladden said; "do you think you could help making that sentiment a pretty large part of your own consciousness? I think that *we* who have surrounded him with a social atmosphere which is somewhat stifling are rather heartless when we exhort him to take deep breaths and not mind it." Disturbed by conditions in the South, Gladden objected to racial disfranchisement. "I do not object to the disfranchisement of ignorance and criminality; I would be quite ready to see the suffrage limited to those who were qualified to exercise it," he said, "but when one law is made for black men and another for white men, the injustice is so glaring that it cannot endure." He was disturbed by the disproportionate emphasis on industrial education for black people. It was important for the black masses, but education for leadership and opportunity for civic responsibility were equally important. "I fear that Mr. Washington is putting too much weight on economic efficiency as the solvent of race prejudice," he said. "All that Booker Washington is doing we may heartily rejoice in, but there are other things that ought not be left undone."[38]

In Chicago, Jenkin Lloyd Jones and a largely white audience heard black community leaders debate *The Souls of Black Folk*. Ferdinand L. Barnett, Ida B. Wells-Barnett, and Charles F. Bentley defended Du Bois's critique of Washington, but Monroe Work and S. Laing and Fannie Barrier Williams sided with Washington. Disturbed by impassioned differences of opinion in the black community, Jones sought common ground: both industrial and classical education were necessary; illiterates, not a race, might be disfranchised. The sense that race relations were deteriorating gave Du Bois's book a melancholic tone, Jones thought, but it was an eloquent reminder that souls came in black as well as "white envelopes." The reactions of Gladden and Jones to *The Souls of Black Folk* were more typical of the social gospel prophets than was the *Outlook*'s. William Hayes Ward's *Independent* thought the book was "a masterly discussion" of black life and destiny. "As an index to the negro's inner life and feeling and as a revelation of the negro's appreciation of his unique situation in American social life," said its reviewer, "*The Souls of Black Folk* will be of incalculable service. It is the best and most logical expression of the clear facts of race hatred yet made by any student of the negro question." Willis Duke Weatherford found the book at times "bitterly pessimistic," but he said it "bears the marks of a keen insight into the thought of the race." *The Souls of Black Folk* persuaded William R. Huntingdon of New York's Grace Episcopal Church that "in the name of God" the Church must demand "full and equal justice be done to all people" and education "in the very best culture" for racial leadership.[39]

As the Supreme Court's decision in *Giles v. Hunter* ended a phase of the disfranchisement debate, *The Souls of Black Folk* brought divisions in the black community to public notice. The strongest center of opposition to Booker T. Washington was in Boston, where William Monroe Trotter was his most aggressive critic. Trotter had studied sociology with Edward Cummings and social ethics with Francis Greenwood Peabody at Harvard. After graduation, he organized the Boston Literary and Historical Association, where the city's black elite gathered for lectures by prominent intellectuals. In 1901, he founded the Boston *Guardian*, a militant advocate of the rights of black people, which voiced bitter, at times petty, attacks on Washington. When Trotter and the radicals tried to win control of the Afro-American Council from the Tuskegeean's conservative allies early in July 1903 at Louisville, Kentucky, the conservatives routed him. There were undignified scenes at the Louisville meeting, but the struggle between Washington's conservative allies and radical critics broke into open warfare when the Tuskegeean appeared in Boston at the end of July. After interrupting T. Thomas Fortune's address to a mass meeting with hoots and catcalls, a radical in the audience tried to force Washington to answer questions intended to expose the weakness of his racial policies. After scuffling between pro- and anti-Washingtonians, the presiding officer ordered the man's arrest and peace was restored. When Washington resumed his talk, Trotter renewed the disruptive questioning. Policemen swarmed into the meeting and arrested him. After a long trial, Trotter was sentenced to thirty days in jail for "inciting to riot." The "Boston riot" drew attention to the struggle between Washington and the radicals. Thereafter, black moderates such as Kelly Miller were critical of both sides but hoped to draw them into a racial united front.[40]

**I**n June 1903, Lyman Abbott's *Outlook* announced that the Secret Service had made arrests for peonage in Alabama. Federal grand juries were preparing indictments against several white people on charges of being parties to "a revolting system of enslaving helpless negro laborers." Since George W. Cable's assault in 1884, the social gospel press had occasionally attacked the South's convict lease system as "A Revival of Slavery in America." But, unlike state leasing of convict labor to private supervisors, peonage as compensation for debt was practiced illegally by local custom. When investigation of the Alabama peonage cases came to Abbott's attention in May, he asked

Booker T. Washington to send him information for the *Outlook's* coverage. If the reports were true, he said, the situation deserved "vigorous condemnation." Since his journal had "spoken the best word we can for the South," said Abbott, it was better positioned to condemn injustice. A week after its initial report, the *Outlook* said "an inhuman form of slave-catching and slave-holding" was practiced in parts of Alabama. *Homiletic Review* called it "slavery as bad or worse than that of ante-bellum days." But as soon as charges of slavery's revival were lodged, the *Outlook* tried to diffuse them. With church and state approval, slavery had bound all black people, without any alleged offense, to involuntary servitude without wages for life, it said. In the alleged peonage cases, against the best judgment of "nearly all elements of Southern life," some black people were forced to work without wages for life in repayment of a debt. Their plight was like that of some immigrants elsewhere in the country. "It is a condition to which the friendless poor of any race may be brought in the absence of a vigilant and humane public sentiment," said the *Outlook*.[41]

Through the summer of 1903, the *Outlook* and the *Independent* kept the nation's attention on peonage. The *Outlook* cited the case of a black woman held involuntarily for nine months in a labor camp near Waycross, Georgia. It was operated by a state legislator who owned 37,000 acres of south Georgia and used both convict laborers and peons. He pleaded guilty to thirteen counts of peonage, but informed Georgians thought it would not threaten his seat in the state legislature or his eligibility to continue leasing convict labor. In July, a United States commissioner who prosecuted peonage cases in north Florida warned readers of the *Independent* that peonage was not a "sporadic and temporary" factor in isolated parts of the South. "It is here in the South to stay permanently," he warned, "unless a strict enforcement of the law is had." Noting its prevalence where black people were disfranchised, the commissioner drew the connection. "It is but a step from the evasion of the Fifteenth Amendment to an actual violation of the Thirteenth Amendment." When the first Alabama case was tried, Judge Thomas Jones's summary to the jury was in effect a directed verdict of guilty, but the jury hung seven to five for conviction. Jones reprimanded the jury for refusing to enforce the law and declared a mistrial. If Southern juries failed to do their duty, warned the *Outlook*, the Constitution empowered Congress to provide means for the redress of grievances. "If public sentiment is weak in Alabama, it must be strengthened by sympathy and help from other parts of the nation," said the *Homiletic Review*. "The demand for the correction of the flagrant abuses is hourly becoming more imperative." After the mistrial, the Alabama defendant pleaded guilty to the peonage charges and was given the lightest fine possible under the law. A second defendant was found guilty by a local jury. The result, said the *Outlook*, confirmed its belief that "the Southern people may be entrusted to enforce the laws for the protection of the negroes."[42]

Yet, as the year's most notorious lynching had already shown, the *Outlook's* claim could not be sustained even thirty miles south of Philadelphia. On 15 June 1903, Helen Bishop left a railroad car to walk home, north of Wilmington, Delaware. Before she got there, the seventeen-year-old was brutally assaulted. She died the next day without regaining consciousness. Local officials arrested George White, a black laborer, on suspicion of murder. The twenty-seven-year-old had served nine years in prison, four for conviction in a similar assault. Committed to the county workhouse, White confessed his guilt to the chief of police on the day after Helen Bishop's death. The grand jury had adjourned and dockets were crowded with civil cases, so the courts resisted pressure for a quick trial. As public agitation mounted, the Reverend Robert A. Ellwood preached a sermon, "Should the Murderer of Helen Bishop be Lynched?" on 21 June in a vacant lot near his Olivet Presbyterian Church. He took his texts from the U.S. Constitution, "In all criminal case prosecutions the accused shall enjoy the right to a speedy and public trial," and 1 Corinthians 5:13, "Therefore put away from among you that wicked person." Ellwood counseled his audience to be calm, but he condemned the court's delay. It was to blame if George White were lynched. Brandishing a fist of bloody leaves gathered from the scene of the crime, the Princeton graduate drew a dramatic picture of Helen Bishop's death. His name might be White, said the preacher, but if he is guilty his was "a heart blacker than darkest midnight and a nature blacker than hell." If his trial was delayed, if he was then found guilty, and if he then escaped a death sentence, the preacher concluded, "the citizens of the state should arise in their might and execute the criminal and thus uphold the majesty of the law."[43]

A coroner's jury found George White responsible for the murder of Helen Bishop on the next day. Despite her father's plea for restraint, a white mob marched on the workhouse to seize the black man that night. Alerted to the danger, thirty Wilmington policemen under Chief George Black went to reinforce the workhouse guards. They found the prison surrounded by a murder-bent mob of five thousand men, women, and children. Rumor had it that the mob had twenty pounds of dynamite to enforce its will. As the police entered the prison's west wing, two thousand men rushed into the building.

Only then did the president of the prison's board of trustees ask the governor for militia to protect workhouse property. Undeterred when warning shots wounded two young men, the crowd attacked the corridor's steel door with cold chisels and sledges. The electric lights were shot out, more fire was exchanged, and the door gave way. Overpowered, the warden directed the mob to the prisoner's cell. Shortly before midnight on 22 June, the Wilmington mob took George White from his cell and carried him to the scene of his attack on Helen Bishop. Begging for mercy and offering to confess, White was tied to a stake and allowed to speak. Admitting that he had promised to release Helen Bishop if she gave him money, the black man said that she had given him sixty cents. But when she said that she would report him, George White had slit her throat.

Excited by the confession, the crowd prepared to burn White at the stake. Split rails were piled about him and a bail of straw was used to ignite the fire. When the cords that bound him burned through, the black man dropped into the fire and leaped to run away. But a member of the mob felled him with a rail. The burning body of George White rolled away from the fire several times and was repeatedly thrown back. When he was dead, more fuel was piled on the burning ashes to consume the corpse. Nearby, Helen Bishop's mother was awakened from a tortured sleep by the noise of the crowd and the light of a human torch. The crowd dispersed as a drizzling rain fell on the funeral pyre. On the next day, some ten thousand people made a pilgrimage to the scene. Fifty of them carried away relics of the night's work, displaying them on the streets of Wilmington. Local ministers met in emergency session to condemn the mob action, but they made no demand that its leaders be brought to trial. The Reverend Robert Ellwood denied regretting anything that he had said and reiterated his prophecy that if a lynching occurred it was the responsibility of the courts. The police could have had the names of a hundred members of the mob, but only one man was arrested. His charge was reduced to homicide and he was never indicted. Leaders of the mob represented the community, local officials reasoned, and had merely executed its will.[44]

The burning of George White renewed public debate on lynching. Dean Richmond Babbitt, rector of Brooklyn's Episcopal Church of the Epiphany, personally investigated Wilmington's mob violence. He found that prior to White's death its newspapers had outlined the mob's plan of action and how it would break into the jail. He condemned public apathy, local authorities who failed to prevent lynching, and mob violence as a "growing menace," a "contagious madness" of American anarchy. Newell Dwight Hillis, the *Outlook*, and the *Independent* condemned the mob's action, the court's delays, and Ellwood's intemperate remarks. "The mob is wrong," said Hillis; "the mob is always wrong." The outrage was "intensely demoralizing, degrading and uncivilizing," said the *Independent*. "The untutored savage satisfies his desire for revenge and his thirst for blood, but even he does not take fragments of bone from the ashes of his enemy and treasure them up for exhibition as mementoes of a notable event." Irrational passion for revenge threatened the foundations of democracy, said the *Outlook*. "The sovereignty of law is to the community what the sovereignty of reason is to the individual—sanity; and the rule of the mob is to the community what the rule of the passions is to the individual—madness."[45]

Cincinnati's Herbert Seeley Bigelow sensed that radical social change was needed to treat the "Causes of Mob Violence." As pastor of Vine Street Congregational Church, he chose to live in the city's worst slums. When a presumably white family in his church was found to be mulatto, some church members demanded the family's dismissal. Bigelow would not allow it. The church was for everyone and those who objected to their presence could leave, said the pastor. Then he reorganized the church democratically as the People's Church and Town Meeting Society. It "ought to be so democratic that no plutocrat will apply for admission," he said. "Had we more Americans of the type of Rev. Herbert S. Bigelow" thought Cincinnati's Wendell P. Dabney, "we would have few racial troubles." Bigelow's text for the sermon on mob violence was Genesis 4:15: "The Lord set a mark upon Cain, lest any finding him should kill him." The punishment of the primeval murderer was banishment from the community. "He was not to be murdered because he was a murderer," Bigelow said. "He was to be protected against the violence of the mob." Banished from society, Cain was to work out his own salvation. The Cincinnati pastor was impatient with the cry to let legal processes carry out the mob's violent intent. "The spirit is the same," he argued. "It is the thirst of blood for blood. If the state may strike back, why not the mob?" Both mob violence and the state's revenge should be abolished. "If there is anything more dastardly than the violence of the mob, it is the cold, calculating, studied, legal murder which the state commits against social offenders," Bigelow said. "For almost without exception those who fill our penitentiaries and die on our scaffolds are among the disinherited of earth, who have been stunted in body and mind by the crimes of the law which presumes to punish them." In place of jails and gallows, he called for democratic penal colonies where social offenders could work out their own salvation.[46]

Two weeks after the burning of George White, there was a race riot at Evansville, Indiana. On 3 July, a policeman tried to arrest Robert Lee, a black man, for threatening to kill another black man. Lee killed the policeman, was taken into custody, and locked in the city jail until a mob of white men tried to remove him. After he was secretly moved from Evansville on 5 July, a mob broke into the jail only to find him gone. With arms stolen from local stores, the mob turned on the city's black community, wrecking houses and driving their inhabitants out of town. A mob gathered at the jail on 6 July, demanding that its sixteen black inmates be released to its custody. The jail was defended by local militia and two hundred deputies, who had bayonetted two rioters by nightfall. At midnight, two thousand people pushed forward, showering bricks, stones, and gunfire on the deputies and militia. The commanding officer gave no order to fire, but they returned the fire in self-defense. As the mob dispersed, it left thirty persons dead or wounded on the pavement. The dead included nine men and a young girl who was watching the excitement with her parents. By 8 July, a Committee of Safety and a military command controlled Evansville. Its local militia was reinforced by seven companies from out of town. Twenty rioters were indicted and as many Negroes were fined for carrying concealed weapons. A local judge ordered Robert Lee's return to Evansville for trial, but the governor countermanded the order, noting that Lee had near fatal wounds and that Evansville was in no mood to give him a fair trial. Many of the city's eight thousand Negroes had fled to sanctuary in nearby Illinois and Kentucky. By 10 July, five companies of militia were withdrawn, and President Theodore Roosevelt congratulated Indiana's governor for restoring order in the city.[47]

Still, the violence continued. In August 1903, Laforest A. Planving, founder of the American Missionary Association's Point Coupee Industrial and High School at Oscar, Louisiana, was shot to death. As AMA president, Washington Gladden asked Louisiana's governor to investigate the murder. No man or woman was safe so long as the "wild beast" of lynching was loose in the land, he wrote. Black people bore a disproportionate burden of the violence because of America's "dark and sinister" race antipathy. "It shows that we are very imperfectly Christianized," said Gladden. "It bids us look well to the beams in our own eyes as a nation, before we proceed to cast the motes out of the eyes of our sister nations. It calls on us to [bear] witness to the truth of the brotherhood of man which Christ came to teach. And it makes us see that the Ethiopian who was compelled to bear the cross of our Lord on his way to his crucifixion is still carrying a burden which we must do what we can to lighten." At an AMA convention two months later, Gladden said the association had gone into the South to prepare the newly enfranchised freedman for a "free, responsible citizenship." But forty years later, "he is not any longer a free and responsible citizen; he is a subject." The AMA would stay in the field until its objective was won. It would not teach its students that they were members of an inferior race or that the United States is a white man's country. "We stand for no unnatural fusion of races, for no impracticable notions of social intercourse," Gladden said; "but we do stand for perfect equality for the Negro before the law, and behind the law; we stand for his rights as a citizen; we stand for his opportunity to be a man among men—not a menial among Lords, not an inferior among superiors, but a self-respecting, self-directing, self-reliant American man." But it was dangerous to teach such ideas in parts of the South. When the AMA school reopened in January 1904, a white man fired on it, nearly hitting the new teacher, Alfred Lawless. A local constable advised him to give up the school. Lawless was a model graduate of Straight University, said an AMA officer; his religion was "well mixed with his ethics" and his preaching reflected the wisdom of a Washington Gladden. "We do not produce such men at order," said a university professor, "and there are many fields quite as needy where they can serve their country and their God." Lawless hoped to move his school to safety, but he was forced to abandon it.[48]

Through July and August 1903, the social gospel press cited and decried additional racial incidents at Albany, Liberty, and White Hall, New York; Red Bank, New Jersey; Indiana and Scranton, Pennsylvania; Shreveport and St. Mary's Parish, Louisiana; Flemingsburg, Kentucky; Lake Butler, Florida; Belleville and Danville, Illinois; Atlanta and Eastman, Georgia; Lorain, Ohio; Dallas, Texas; and Clifton Forge, Virginia. President Roosevelt warned that the epidemic of lynching and mob violence could undermine the foundations of democracy and substitute "violent alternations of anarchy and tyranny."[49] Even when their victim was certain to receive the law's maximum penalty, Benjamin Orange Flower observed, free-born American citizens exercised the mob's illegal determination. While they commonly condemned mob violence, the social gospel prophets had no single answer to it. Herbert Seeley Bigelow decried even legal revenge, but the *Homiletic Review*'s sermon notes on "Punishment for Lynchers" took its text from 1 Kings 18:40: "Let not one of them escape." As 1903's violent summer drew to a close, the *Review* warned of a race war. "Our Christianity is perhaps to be put to the test as never before in our national history," said its editors. "Is it not high time to stop our boasted talk of 'the brotherhood of man' long enough to give the world a practical illustration of that brotherhood?"[50]

In the fall of 1903, John Rogers Commons, Lyman Abbott, and John Spencer Bassett sought common ground on the franchise. In September, the *Chautauquan* published Commons's articles on the "Racial Composition of the American People." "The race problem is coming to be recognized as the fundamental problem of American democracy," its announcement said. Commons was born to a Presbyterian mother from the Western Reserve and a Quaker father whose family fled slavery's influence in North Carolina. "My earliest recollections were thrilling stories of their 'underground railway,' for the escape of Negroes to Canada, across my mother's Western Reserve and my father's Eastern Indiana," he recalled. "Liberty, Equality and defiance of the Fugitive Slave Law were my birthright." While in college at Oberlin, Commons spent a year at Leesburg, Florida, where he remembered "stories of 'crackers' and their bananas, Negro hunts, Negroes brought in dead to our courthouse, or slashing each other at Christmas with razors and filling the gaps with Spanish moss." After graduate study at Johns Hopkins, he began a peripatetic teaching career.[51]

Democracy required both equal opportunity before the law and "equal ability of races and classes to use those opportunities," said Commons. Racial heredity was an intractable determinant of physical, mental, and moral capacity, he believed, more powerful than education or environment in shaping a people's destiny. He saw the increasingly rigid lines drawn against black Americans as an ominous sign, because a nation need not be of one blood, but it must be of one mind. Racial injustice and inferiority prevented mental and moral assimilation, threatening the foundations of democracy. Experience in America had civilized and prepared other immigrants for citizenship, said Commons, but experience as slaves had only "domesticated" black Americans, suppressing the qualities of intelligence and manliness needed for citizenship. Freed and enfranchised in a triumph of partisanship, black people had failed Reconstruction's test of democracy. The Supreme Court's acceptance of black disfranchisement, while allowing white illiterates to vote, nullified the Fifteenth Amendment and meant that black people would not vote in the South for years to come. Already, Southern states were spending less than half as much to educate a black child as they were to educate a white child. Commons believed that most black Americans had not acquired the qualities needed for citizenship, but he acknowledged that many Negroes had them. "To exclude such individuals from the suffrage is to shut the door of hope to all," he argued. "An honest educational test, honestly enforced on both whites and blacks, is the simplest rough-and-ready method for measuring the progress of individuals in these qualities of citizenship." No problem before the American people was more vital to democracy, Commons thought, than that of "keeping the suffrage open to the Negro and at the same time preparing the Negro to profit by the suffrage."[52]

Lyman Abbott and John Spencer Bassett also tried to reconcile the ideals of American democracy with the realities of peonage, disfranchisement, and violence. Northern assumptions of racial equality that led to enfranchising the freedmen had failed to produce responsible government or protect the very people who were enfranchised, said Abbott. Northern cultural imperialism had failed to extend common cultural values throughout the South, which might have made it easier for the two races to cooperate. The nation still had a regional problem: how two races, unequal in wealth, education, and inheritance, could live together in peace. It could only be resolved in terms of Liberty, Equality, and Fraternity, said Abbott. Liberty meant that the Negro must be free to develop to his fullest. "Americans will never consent to see slavery reestablished on this continent and under their flag," even if it is called "peonage," said the *Outlook's* editor. Equality meant that all races must be treated equally before the law. If they were equitably enforced, suffrage restrictions did not violate that principle. If they were inequitably enforced, Fraternity required the North to let Southern believers in the national values point the way. Fraternity meant that the nation owed personal liberty, equality before the law, and education—primary and industrial for the masses, higher education for leaders—to black people. Abbott's appeal to Liberty, Equality, and Fraternity satisfied black conservatives and moderates, from Booker T. Washington to Kelly Miller. But it did not appease Boston's radical, William Monroe Trotter. The *Outlook's* editor was "one of the most dangerous enemies of the Negro because of his intellectual rating and his claim to be a friend of the Negro," said Trotter. Abbott was either "a fool, a knave, or a deliberate falsifier."[53]

John Spencer Bassett was an alumnus of North Carolina's Trinity College, who returned to his alma mater after winning a doctorate in history at Johns

Hopkins. As a historian and Methodist layman, he commended Southern Methodists for their antebellum missions to slaves. But he believed that they had failed to live up to their responsibility since emancipation. "The black man is our brother and will remain so," Bassett said, repeating Atticus Haygood's theme. "To him our church has a duty. Does it perform it by letting him alone?" Privately, he expressed disgust with North Carolina race relations from the Wilmington riot through the white supremacy campaign of 1900. After founding the *South Atlantic Quarterly* two years later, he joined Trinity's president, John C. Kilgo, in condemning lynching. In a review of W. E. B. Du Bois's *The Souls of Black Folk*, which drew attention to the contrasts between Du Bois and Booker T. Washington, Bassett doubted "if another writer can surpass the rhythmical and half-poetical prose in which its chapters are written." He predicted that Du Bois "would make for himself a permanent place among American descriptive writers." William Monroe Trotter was so pleased with Bassett's review that it got front-page coverage in the *Guardian*.[54]

In October 1903, Kilgo's "Our Duty to the Negro" and Bassett's "Stirring Up the Fires of Race Antipathy" in the *South Atlantic Quarterly* pleaded for reason in race relations and argued that church and state had a responsibility to improve the lot of black Americans. Racial agitation could be traced to racial antipathy, signs of progress among Negroes, and race relations' political context, said Bassett. He attacked political exploitation of race hostility and reasserted the value of equal opportunity for black people. "The 'place' of every man in our American life is such as his virtues and capacities may enable him to take," Bassett wrote. "Not even a black skin and a flat nose can justify caste in this country." The Raleigh *News and Observer* led a furious attack on "bASSett" in North Carolina, which fixed on his suggestion that Booker Washington was "a great and good man, a Christian statesman, and the greatest man, save General Lee, born in the South in a hundred years." In Trinity's board of trustees, seven eastern North Carolinians demanded the history professor's ouster. But Kilgo won the professor's retention with the support of eighteen board members from central and western North Carolina. Thus vindicated, Bassett published another article on race six months later. The social gospel press applauded Kilgo's victory for free speech, but within two years the Trinity College professor happily moved to a Northern school. Pointing to Cable, Sledd, and Bassett, Kelly Miller lamented the fate of Southern white liberals in race relations. "If, though still yielding allegiance to the prevailing social dogma, [they] dare lift their voice, even in faintest whisper in protest against the evil perpetuated in its name," said Miller, "they are forthwith lashed into silence by popular fury and scorn. Race hatred is the most malignant poison that can afflict the mind. It chills the higher faculties of the soul."[55]

In November 1903, the National Sociological Society, an organization of black intellectuals, convened the Washington Conference on the Racial Problem in the United States. Led by former Congressman George H. White and Howard University professors Jesse Lawson and Kelly Miller, the Washington conference attracted a significant biracial group of religious reformers. Admitting the gravity of the problem in his opening remarks, Washington's Episcopal bishop, Henry Yates Satterlee, said that the more experience he had with it the less certain he was of its solution. Pessimistic about the two races living together in peace, Bishop Lucius H. Holsey of the Colored Methodist Episcopal Church advocated segregation of black Americans in their own state of the union. The conferees were more sympathetic with Amory Dwight Mayo's call for white America to regard black people as children of God and aid them in attaining complete American citizenship.[56]

The conference was deeply moved by four heirs to abolitionism: Dean Richmond Babbitt, Jesse Macy, Francis J. Grimké, and Algernon Sydney Crapsey. The nephew of abolitionist editor, Gamaliel Bailey, Babbitt said race prejudice was a perverted modern form of a universal instinct to preserve racial integrity. It took on a life of its own in the mind of the mob, where it was more than "the aggregate of the mental acts of its individual members." Recent events convinced him that "the old feudalism of the South, based on race, is not dead"; that the white South was determined to disfranchise the Negro; and that his rights to life, liberty, and the pursuit of happiness were unsafe. Babbitt called for national aid to education, equal enforcement of the law for both races, moral improvement in the black community, black migration throughout the country, and applying humane Christian values to counter antiblack propaganda. Finally, he urged black people to organize to defend their interests. The son of antislavery Quakers who left North Carolina, Iowa's Jesse Macy was associated with George D. Herron and George A. Gates in the Kingdom Movement at Grinnell. Much would be gained by emphasizing the duty of each race to make its own contribution to the common good, he argued. Francis J. Grimké, the mulatto nephew of Angelina and Sarah Grimké, replied that "it is our duty to emphasize our rights and stand up for them. I believe we ought to contend for our rights until every right under the Constitution is accorded." Macy admitted the duty of defending rights but said that there would be less opposition "if you seek to attain those rights through the faithful performance of duty in the exercise of the rights you already have."[57]

Algernon Crapsey, the Episcopal priest from Rochester and grandson of Ohio's antislavery Senator Thomas Morris, recalled preaching to a black congregation at Washington's St. Luke's Church two years earlier. "One of the fundamental principles of life [is] that every man should maintain the integrity of his personality," Crapsey had told them. "He should assert his right to think and his right to act and to speak within the law of reason." Those who gave up their rights under threat of violence betrayed themselves and humanity. Recommending the passive resistance of Christian martyrs, he told the black congregation that it was their duty, "not to kill, but if necessary to be killed in the maintenance of their liberties." The following Sunday he addressed a crowd of three thousand black people at Washington's Metropolitan AME Church, telling them that "in the Kingdom of God, there is neither white nor black, bond nor free, but all are one in Christ Jesus." The duty of every black citizen was to vote in every election, Crapsey insisted. "If in doing so he were to lose his life, his life would be well lost." If a million Negroes were willing to sacrifice themselves, the issue of their political equality would be settled. Later, Crapsey recalled, Bishop Satterlee had rebuked him for preaching such sermons in his diocese. "Any man, no matter how high he may be placed in the church, though he be a mitered bishop on his throne, who tries to square the circle of God's eternal righteousness and to draw around it the lines of race prejudice and class distinction," said Crapsey, "is false to the gospel of Christ and disloyal to the Kingdom of God." If his words were dangerous then, he wished that they could be more dangerous, "for truth is always dangerous to the stability of a society based upon injustice," he said. "I wish my words could kindle a fire that could not be quenched until that spirit of inequality and intolerance which now disturbs the peace of the American people were burnt and purged away."[58]

Now, Crapsey told the conferees, the issue was the humanity of the Negro. "You are animals, as we all are, but you are also of that divine dust into which the Creator has breathed a living soul," said the priest. "You are made in the image of God, and woe unto him who wantonly degrades or defaces that image. And if men, then you have the rights of a man." Lynching and segregation violated those rights. "In the sight of the law the life of the poorest black baby is as precious as the life of the President of the United States. To kill the one is murder no less than the killing of the other, and murder must be punished and checked if society is to survive,". Crapsey said. As for segregation, "a man must defy unholy prejudice and scorn unrighteous laws. We should never rest until every law that draws the color line is taken off the statute books, and every man, black and white, is equal before the law." As a citizen, Crapsey argued, the Negro was entitled to share in the making, execution, and protection of the law. "The day is coming when the men who apologize for the present injustice to the Negro race will lament the stand they have taken," he said, citing Lyman Abbott; "they will see that it is not in conformity with the righteousness of God and dangerous to the American Commonwealth." If Booker Washington and others advised black people not to demand their rights, Crapsey argued that such advice was fatal. "The Negro must make his choice, and make it now between citizenship and servitude," he argued. "Let present forces work unmolested for another generation and servitude will be his fixed condition; citizenship to be recovered only at the expense of another civil war." Crapsey seconded Babbitt's call for national aid to education. "Let us cease to build battleships and begin to build school-houses," he argued. "We are in far more danger from the foes within our borders, race hatred, ignorance and lawlessness, than we are from any foreign enemy." He hoped that the South would make conditions for the franchise equal for both races and he urged black people to organize to defend their rights. "You are men and you are citizens, and it is your duty to live up to your manhood and your citizenship," said the priest. "God has preserved you and us for His great purposes. May He help us to uplift all the sons of men and hasten the coming of the Kingdom of Righteousness."[59]

Booker T. Washington appeared briefly at the conference. It was attempting what no other organization was doing, he said; "no one organization, no one institution, no one individual, can represent all the interests of the race." At its conclusion, the Washington conference's resolutions praised the education revival in the South and asked the federal government to support it. They affirmed the rights of citizens to equal protection, condemned mob violence and segregation, called on Congress to create a commission of inquiry into the condition of black Americans, and appealed to black and white people to support civil rights. But the appeal of the National Sociological Society fell on deaf ears. The *Outlook* noted that the new organization with a "pretentious name" was composed mostly of black people, who cheered the addresses by Babbitt and Crapsey. But the *Outlook*'s Ernest Hamlin Abbott dismissed Crapsey as a "Napoleonic" poseur. Other white conferees, said the journal, directed the "obscure discussions" and "incoherent debate" of "ineffectual but vociferant negro demagogues" toward resolutions emphasizing education, industry, and investigation as alternatives to the suffrage.[60] At the end of 1903, after a decade of crisis in race relations, the Washington Conference on Race Relations produced no palpable result. But it was a harbinger of a time when black and white reformers in race relations would organize to challenge the flood tide of racism.

**E**ven at "the nadir" of postemancipation race relations, one does not find "the racism of Josiah Strong, the faithlessness of Lyman Abbott, and the complicity in silence of Washington Gladden, Walter Rauschenbusch, and the others." But, just as black leaders were polarized on the race issue, a polarization that obscured a spectrum of attitudes, white social gospel prophets were also spread across a spectrum. It ranged from Thomas Dixon, Jr., Alexander McKelway, and Charles H. Parkhurst, in some of his incarnations, who voiced the most racist tendencies of the age, to Herbert Seeley Bigelow, Algernon Sidney Crapsey, Newell Dwight Hillis, and Charles B. Spahr, who militantly defended the rights of black Americans. Moderates of varied hues ranged between the extremes: Lyman Abbott, John R. Commons, Percy Stickney Grant, William DeWitt Hyde, Jesse Macy, Edgar Gardner Murphy, Francis Greenwood Peabody, Henry Yates Satterlee, Anna Howard Shaw, Andrew Sledd, and Carey Breckinridge Wilmer to the right; Dean Richmond Babbitt, Joseph Cook, Quincey Ewing, Benjamin Orange Flower, William Channing Gannett, Washington Gladden, George D. Herron, Jenkin Lloyd Jones, Henry Demarest Lloyd, William Mackintire Salter, and William Hayes Ward to the left. The education coalition's Northern and Southern white reformers in race relations, many influenced by theological personalism, dominated the center right of that spectrum. Northern white evangelical neoabolitionists, many of them leaders of the American Missionary Association and also influenced by theological personalism, dominated the center left of the social gospel's attitude in race relations. But the *via media* was treacherous ground and the mere passage of time would not diminish the sense of crisis.

# 9

# A Prophetic Minority from the Nadir to the NAACP

As racial reformers stirred from complacency, they might repeat Atticus Haygood's appeal to education and time. But they invoked it in different moods. "This is one of the problems which defy complete solution and can only be rendered less troublesome," said Republican politician Carl Schurz. "The slow process of propitiating public sentiment promises after all the most durable results." Race had become a stock subject for "timely" editorials, replied the *Homiletic Review*. "Hardly a day passes that does not ring an alarm-bell in the ears of the nation." It "touches every sphere of activity," keeps religious denominations divided, dominates Southern politics, maintains "bitter animosities" in the nation, inflames anarchy and barbarism in cities and countryside, "and does it so frequently that only once in a hundred times do we do anything more than shrug our shoulders as we read, and pass on to the next news item." If the problem was "timelessly timely," said the *Review*, "then the hope of the nation for a remedy must rest in the vast resources of Father Time. What is he doing for us?" But the appeal was not complacent: "And what are we doing to help him?"[1]

Missionary agencies had spent forty years helping Father Time by educating black Americans. Black people were in the childhood of their race, John R. Rogers told the American Missionary Association in 1903, and time was a factor in their development. "Even the Almighty cannot create character out of mind, at one stroke," he said. "We can make a machine in a few days, but only God *and time* can make a man." If Rogers appealed for time to allow black people to mature, the *American Missionary* saw divisions among black leaders as differing attitudes toward time. Booker T. Washington's conservatives emphasized economic development, which would eventually win recognition. "Time softens asperities," they said. "Wait upon time." Economic development was useful, replied Du Bois's radicals, "but we should not trust to time." Sympathetic to the radical party, *American Missionary* editors held that acquiescence in injustice allowed it to become entrenched. "We cannot trust to time to remedy wrongs, which, by time, are continually growing stronger," they wrote. "If we consent now to the postponement of justice we consent to a more difficult and more nearly hopeless future. Time hardens and does not soften evils." The AMA journal quoted John Dickinson's *Letters from a Farmer in Pennsylvania:* "They make a sad mistake who trust to time to strengthen a right cause," the colonial patriot had said. "Time entrenches usurpations and renders them irresistible."[2]

In January 1904, thirty black leaders of various viewpoints met privately at New York's Carnegie Hall to seek a consensus and present a united racial front to the nation. Eight white men—Andrew Carnegie, who secretly financed the meeting, Lyman Abbott, William H. Baldwin, Robert C. Ogden, George Foster Peabody, Carl Schurz, Oswald Garrison Villard, and William Hayes Ward—spoke to their opening session. Then, after three days of private debate, the black leaders had a consensus. Kelly Miller, a moderate, said that "radical and conservative Negroes agree as to the end in view, but differ as to the most effective means of attaining it. The difference is not essentially one of principle or purpose, but point of view." The Carnegie Hall platform seemed to verify his judgment. It held that the black masses should remain in the South; that it was "of paramount importance" for black men North and South to exercise a "full, free, and equal suffrage"; that unequal transportation and public accommodations should be challenged in court; that common and industrial schooling should be available to all black people and higher education was essential for racial leadership; and that plans for resolving the race problem should be made in concert between progressive black and white people North and South. Finally, the conferees formed a coordinating Committee of Twelve. Washington, Du Bois, and Hugh M. Browne, president of Cheyney Institute, Cheyney, Pennsylvania, were named to it and authorized to select nine other members. But both parties had gone into and left the conference too deeply suspicious of each other. Despite the support of important black and white leaders, the Carnegie Hall Conference and its

Committee of Twelve were no more able to present a united racial front than was the Afro-American Council or was the National Sociological Society to mount a biracial initiative for social justice.[3]

Within months of the Carnegie Hall Conference, Shailer Mathews's *World To-Day* reopened the divisions among black leaders with a symposium, "The Negro Problem from the Negro Point of View." Kelly Miller's argument against rural Southern blacks moving to the city and Jesse Lawson's plea for "fair play" in race relations voiced the conferees' consensus. But Booker Washington's call for success models in rural black communities denigrated the usefulness of traditional higher education. Du Bois outlined his differences with an unnamed leader of the race on education, the franchise, civil rights, and the race's future; and Ida B. Wells-Barnett passionately attacked Washington for currying favor with white racists, undermining higher education, and appearing to condone disfranchisement and narrowed educational opportunity for the race. Startled by the *World To-Day* symposium, Miller asked Du Bois: "Is the Conference truce off for good?" and "What is the use of meeting, if battle still rages along the same old lines?" Du Bois resigned from the Committee of Twelve when Washington organized it in his absence and it adopted a more conservative platform than was agreed to at Carnegie Hall. "I refuse to wear Mr. Washington's livery or to put on his collar," he explained. "At present I propose to fight the battle to the last ditch if I fight it stark alone."[4]

As black leaders struggled, the social gospel press addressed the three major racial issues of the decade: lynching, involuntary servitude, and disfranchisement. Many white social gospel prophets worked with black leaders to score points on the first two issues, but internal divisions allowed disfranchisement to advance. As lynching declined in the South, some social gospel prophets took comfort in the growing number of legal executions as a sign of support for law and order. But there were more murders in Jefferson County, Alabama, in one year than in all of Great Britain, said Quincey Ewing, and Jefferson County did not punish the murderers. Given "the large number of negroes who are yearly hurled into eternity, unshriven by priest and untried by law," said Mary Church Terrell, "as a nation we have fallen upon grave times, indeed. Surely, it is time for the ministers in their pulpits and the Christians in their pews to fall upon their knees and pray for deliverance from this rising tide of barbarism which threatens to deluge the whole land."[5]

Statesboro, Georgia, had an answer for Mary Church Terrell. The south Georgia town was a center of the turpentine industry, with many unskilled black laborers in its work camps. On 28 July 1904, a successful white farmer,

Henry Hodges, and his wife were beaten to death; their three children died in a fire apparently set to cover the crime. Circumstantial evidence pointed to two workers in a nearby camp, Paul Reed and Will Cato. Reed's wife said that they had twice gone to the Hodge's place to search for money. The two black men murdered the Hodges when they were discovered the second time. After dragging their bodies into the house, said Mrs. Reed, they searched it for money and found nine-year-old Kitty Hodges in hiding. She offered them a nickel to spare her life, but her skull was crushed by a lamp base and two younger children died in the fire set by Cato and Reed. Rumors that Kitty Hodges and her mother were victims of a "nameless offense" and threats of a lynching spread through Statesboro. Cato and Reed were arrested and moved to safety in Savannah. There, Paul Reed gave conflicting accounts of the murders, suggesting that they were planned by a secret society of black men, the "Before Day Club." Like rumors of servile insurrection years earlier, reports of conspiracy in Statesboro led fearful white people from Alabama to Virginia to find "Before Day Clubs" in their areas. As they acted on their fears, a black pastor in south Georgia said that his people were living through a "reign of terror."[6]

Two weeks after the murders, Will Cato and Paul Reed went on trial. On Monday, 15 August, Cato was tried and, after Mrs. Reed's testimony, found guilty. Reed was convicted the next day and the two men were sentenced to hang. Reacting to reports of an impending lynching, the state had sent two militia companies to preserve order in Statesboro. But the railroad had put on extra coaches, which brought thousands of armed strangers to town. As court officers congratulated each other at the trial's conclusion, a mob led by the bailiff rushed past the militia, whose guns were not loaded. Reverend Harmon Hodges, who was in Statesboro from Texas after the deaths of his brother's family, asked the crowd to let the law take its course. "We don't want religion," shouted a member of the mob, "we want blood!" Thinking resistance was useless, the sheriff unlocked the courtroom and pointed out the two defendants. The mob marched its captives a mile out of town, chained them to a pine stump, and gave them time to confess and pray. Wagon loads of wood were piled around their feet and twenty gallons of oil were poured over their bodies. Leaders of the mob stood away from their work for a photographer to capture the scene. When the torch was put to the pyre, Paul Reed endured the torture for three minutes, cried "God have mercy!" and lost consciousness. Will Cato writhed in agony as a crown of fire danced in his oil-soaked hair and the hemp rope flamed around his neck. Begging to be shot, he was the target of lightwood knots thrown from the crowd. When a man in the mob bashed his head with a club, Will Cato fell unconscious. At last assured that Cato and Reed were dead, the crowd drifted away. But some of them scrambled in the ashes for links of chain, bits of charred wood, or pieces of bone for souvenirs. Reverend Whitely Langston of Statesboro's Methodist Church published the names of members of his congregation who took part in the lynching. When two of them refused to repent, he expelled them from the church. But twenty-five other church members left to protest his action. The captain of the militia was dismissed and two of his lieutenants were reprimanded, but the sheriff was reelected without opposition. No one in the mob was ever indicted.[7]

The burning of Will Cato and Paul Reed provoked loud protests against the mob's "evil" and "barbarism," which embarrassed the United States before the world. "Tell it not in St. Petersburg; publish it not in the courts of Stambul," cried the *Independent*, "lest Sultan and Czar shall send deputations to Washington to protest against the barbarities of the Republic of the West." After visiting the sites of several atrocities, Ray Stannard Baker found little difference between communities where lynchings occurred and other American towns. "They were all American towns, just like yours and mine. I saw no barbarians," he wrote. Similar brutalities would occur again, "perhaps in your town or mine," he said, because lynching was not a barbarian or a sectional crime, "it is an American crime." The Statesboro mob was no single entity, moved by a single compelling purpose. With "no center, no fixed purpose, no real plan of action," said Baker, it was a headless herd, "torn with dissensions and compunctions, swayed by conflicting emotions." His individualistic interpretation of mob action held that an authoritative individual firmly committed to duty could have stopped it. "Our system too often fails when mob stress is laid upon it," unless a strong man "assumes responsibility and becomes a momentary despot." Baker's analysis was too individualistic, said Dean Richmond Babbitt. "A mob has a mind of its own, which is not the aggregate of the mental acts of its individual members," he argued, "but is a new mental entity, a new mind, a different mind, both in kind and degree, from the particular minds of the members of the mob." A group of individuals is merely a crowd until primal, unconscious instincts seize control of the self, destroy the individualizing influences of other levels of consciousness, and merge with the primal instincts of others to create the mind of the mob, said Babbitt. Thereafter, "one idea, one thought, one passion, one purpose" drives the mob to illegal violence, which conscious individual selves would shun. Baker's appeal to the heroic individual, standing as a bulwark of sanity against mob action was inadequate, Babbitt thought. In a democratic society, collective counteraction was the appropriate response to collective crime.[8]

But should one look to local, state, or federal authority for leadership? Would effective remedies be found in executive, judicial, or legislative channels? Legislation passed in twelve states from 1895 to 1904 increased the power and liability of local authorities for protecting persons in their custody from mobs, but it had not demonstrably reduced lynching. Local and state courts repeatedly failed to convict members of lynch mobs. Federal courts had limited, if any, jurisdiction in such cases. Southern representatives prevented passage of congressional legislation or a constitutional amendment to make lynching a federal offense. The social gospel press tended to side with Ray Stannard Baker, looking to strong state-executive action to prevent lynching and prosecute persons responsible for it. "Time will be required for the effective application of a remedy for lynching," replied James Elbert Cutler. Legislative, executive, or judicial action could not abolish lynching, he thought. The one collective influence against it was a strong public commitment to law and order. "The creation of a public sentiment on any subject is a slow process," Cutler said. Because of racial hatred, antilynching statutes were only palliatives in a larger struggle for public opinion.[9]

Benjamin Orange Flower's *Arena*, Lyman Abbott's *Outlook*, and the *South Atlantic Quarterly* sought to shape public opinion with symposia on the suppression of lynching. Smith College social ethicist Alfred Pearce Dennis, Baltimore's James Cardinal Gibbons, Boston Christian socialist W. D. P. Bliss, and sociologist Wilbur Fisk Crafts tried to build antilynching sentiment. The occurrence of lynching in "communities which build court houses and jails, support Christian churches and contribute liberally to the evangelization of the heathen sitting in darkness," said Dennis, is "a curious commentary upon our civilization." Outlining an idealist's argument that true freedom lay in fulfilling civic potential in obedience to law, he argued that the mob's claim to be the vehicle of social order was specious and for laws holding local communities liable for damages in a lynching. "To give to every man's life a valuation in point of law is to give to human life a distinct valuation in point of morals," Dennis said. "Impose upon local communities a legal assertion of the equal value of human life in terms of cash compensation and any prevailing notion that a life may be accounted cheap because it is vile will pass away in the reestablishment of the ordinary processes of justice under a constitutional government."[10]

Citing the biblical and constitutional grant of restricted authority to take human life to civil rulers, Cardinal Gibbons condemned lynching as "a blot on American civilization. It lowers our civic and moral standard in the estimation of foreign nations," said Baltimore's archbishop; "it is a standing insult and menace to the majesty of the law of the land; it usurps the sword of authority from the constituted powers, and places it in the hands of a reckless and irresponsible mob." Accelerated legal processes would control the mob's excess, he believed, but more would be achieved by removing its cause, race hatred. "This blessed result can be accomplished only by submission to the teachings of the Gospel, which proclaims the equality of all men before God," Gibbons said. The *AME Church Review* praised his "uncompromising condemnation" of lynching and W. D. P. Bliss published it in his *Encyclopedia of Social Reform.* Citing the decline in lynching as a "hopeful fact," Bliss thought the growing number of homicides per public execution, lynching for trivial offenses, and its increasingly exclusive use against black men were "startling" and "alarming" facts that demanded the church's attention. He failed to note another alarming fact: there were proportionately more homicides in the United States than in any other "civilized" country. Lynching was "one of the offenses of which Americans have almost a monopoly," said Wilbur Fisk Crafts. "In no other nation of the world does 'Judge Lynch' execute more than all the civilized courts." Like treason, he said, lynching was an assault on the American idea of popular government.[11]

Yet, the violence persisted. When the black heavyweight boxing champion, John Arthur "Jack" Johnson, defeated a white contender on 4 July 1910, racial violence broke out in thirty American cities. Race problems led to a reign of terror at Slocum, Texas, where a mob of several hundred white men cut telephone lines, moved from cabin to cabin, and systematically killed twenty black inhabitants. Members of the Texas mob should be fined, imprisoned, and disfranchised, said the *Outlook.* A year later, Zachariah Walker, a black man suspected of killing a white industrial guard, was wounded, arrested, and hospitalized at Coatesville, Pennsylvania. On Sunday evening, 13 August 1911, a mob broke into the hospital and, finding him chained to his cot, dragged it a half-mile out of town. There, four thousand people gathered around the bed and a roaring bonfire. After drenching it in oil, the crowd threw the bed on the fire, pulling it down three times until it was sure that the fire had disposed of Walker. Five men were brought to trial for their part in his death, but a grand jury charged that a conspiracy of silence obstructed justice and the men were acquitted. Coatesville was no worse than most American towns, said

William T. Ellis of Chicago's Presbyterian weekly, the *Continent*, but the burning of Zachariah Walker reflected poorly on its eight Christian churches. "The mob's rage, its vengeance-cry, is what makes it the invariable agent of hell," Ellis wrote. "And hell echoes wherever the vengeance-cry is heard tolerantly." In New York, John Lovejoy Elliott, John Haynes Holmes, and Rabbi Stephen S. Wise led a protest meeting of four hundred people at the Ethical Culture Society hall. The Coatesville burning destroyed the myth that race was a Southern problem, said Holmes. Racial injustice had spread like a plague through the land. He called for a new abolitionist crusade to assert the full humanity of black people and challenge injustice everywhere. Later, Holmes received a postcard from Alabama which pictured a lynching party with its victim and promised monthly repetitions of the scene. Meeting in Chicago, the new National Association for the Advancement of Colored People asked the city's pastors to preach against lynching. Endorsing an antilynching crusade, Josiah Strong admitted that mob violence as "merciless and ferocious" as that of "wild beasts" had stamped "the mark of Cain" on the brow of "our country."[12]

The social gospel prophets also attacked involuntary servitude, praising the work of Presbyterian Alexander J. McKelway and Baptist John E. White to abolish the chain gang and convict lease systems in Georgia. Disturbed more by peonage than by segregation or disfranchisement, Booker Washington and the *Outlook* took up the case of Alonzo Bailey, a black agricultural worker charged with violating Alabama's contract labor law. Washington secretly coordinated the efforts of local white sympathizers and important Northern white financial supporters to see the case through two appeals to the Supreme Court. At its second hearing of the case, the Court found Alabama's contract labor law violated the peonage statute passed under the Thirteenth Amendment. The *Independent* published an unsigned editorial written at Tuskegee. "As far as can be learned," it said, "no negro or Northern man took a hand in the fight." If the *Independent* carried a deception, it was to depict peonage as victimizing both oppressed black people and white oppressors, credit conscientious white Southerners with its abolition, and encourage them to move against other forms of injustice. Ray Stannard Baker and the *Outlook* compared Alonzo Bailey with Dred Scott as obscure people who symbolized the continuing battle against slavery in America. It "received a death-blow in the great struggle between North and South, typified by the experience of Dred Scott," said the *Outlook*, "and has now, in its attenuated but far more ignoble form, become outlawed through the experiences of Alonzo

Bailey." Baker was more cautious. So long as white people could exploit black people's ignorance and poverty, forms of slavery would persist, he warned; "but another bar has been placed in the way of the strong white man who would take advantage of the weak colored man. A little less slavery is possible in this world."[13]

Social Christianity's appeal for state supervision of black tenantry was not always made from a liberal viewpoint. In his later years, Richard T. Ely became a biological determinist. He no longer praised the abolitionists or celebrated Southern white apostles and prophets who broke bread with their black brethren. Because of ignorance, laziness, and weakness, he said, Southern black tenant farmers were as advanced on the social scale as could be expected. "Many of the tenants of the South and Southwest are not poor, inefficient, and thriftless because they are tenants, but are tenants because they have these qualities," Ely argued. The Negro's "wisest friends would say that in the vast majority of cases good tenancy is the best thing for him at the present time." Condemned by heredity to a dependent role in life, he needed state protection from exploitation.[14]

Social gospel prophets continued to debate disfranchisement after the Supreme Court accepted it. Rejecting the extremes of Southern white radicals in demanding the exclusion of black men from politics, still Lyman Abbott, Samuel Zane Batten, Richard T. Ely, William DeWitt Hyde, and Shailer Mathews's *World To-Day* endorsed suffrage restriction as legitimate political reform in the South. It should have "not our grudging acquiescence," said Abbott, "but our cordial and hearty cooperation." Batten thought neither literacy nor a general education prepared some people for citizenship. A true democracy accepts "the natural inequalities of men and accords to worth its natural leadership in the State," he wrote. "False democracy with its equal voting is in principle wrong and it has dangers which cannot be minimized. There is grave danger to the state when government is exposed to the caprice and contagion of the least intelligent but most numerous portion of the community. There is a serious menace to real democracy when the people most subject to the sway of the mob mind exist in great number." Batten disapproved of racial disfranchisement, but rule by the black and white *demos* was mob rule and he preferred to see large numbers of the unprepared masses disfranchised.[15]

Many other social gospel prophets—Felix Adler, Ray Stannard Baker, John Bascom, Charles Fletcher Dole, William Channing Gannett, Washington Gladden, Edward Everett Hale, Thomas Cuming Hall, John Haynes Holmes, Jesse

Macy, Frederick A. Noble, William Hayes Ward, and Charles Zueblin—were critical of suffrage restriction. Universal suffrage was not anticipated by the Founding Fathers, Hale admitted, but it grew from the logic of the American Revolution and was at the heart of the nation's genius. Depriving black men of the vote, said Noble, nullified the Constitution, discredited the logic of Emancipation, and held the idea of popular government in contempt. It would undermine the foundations of American citizenship and spread antidemocratic tendencies like a cancer through the body politic, Adler said. Massachusetts's Charles Fletcher Dole accepted a literacy test for voting, but he insisted that it should be framed to encourage those temporarily denied the vote to qualify for it. "No sound democrat," he warned, "could consistently draw any line which would admit ignorant whites and exclude the same class of black or brown or yellow men." William Hayes Ward's *Independent* thought that the franchise might be the privilege of the few in a society where the masses were densely ignorant. But in the United States, where education and culture were commonly acquired, it was properly understood as a right. To forbid a competent man from exercising that right was criminally unjust. "He should demand it, and, if necessary, fight for it."[16]

The United States was imperiled by something worse than a degenerate democracy, said Washington Gladden. Governments ruled in the South by repudiation of the first principles of democracy. Some apologists held that this was a temporary condition and that black people had equality before the law. But he argued that democracy required that all competent people have the opportunity to participate in making the law *and* equal treatment before the law. The anomaly of a racially defined democracy posed a crisis potentially more grave than that of the pre–Civil War period, Gladden said, for the Constitution had been ambivalent about slavery. Given its Reconstruction amendments, disfranchisement publicly flaunted the Constitution. But he had no political remedy. "It must lie in a more just, humane, and Christian feeling in the hearts of the people," Gladden said. Southern white Christians "have got to learn the meaning of the law of Christ" and "apply it to their humblest and neediest neighbors." That would "subdue the senseless antipathies of race," prevent black people from being degraded, and "teach men to respect one another's rights and to dwell together in peace and amity."[17]

As Northern social gospel prophets debated disfranchisement, it swept the South. Intimidation, a poll tax, and a "white primary" had largely nullified black political influence in Georgia by 1900, but nearly 30 percent of the registered voters were black as late as 1904. But a constitutional amendment approved in 1907 required all voters to pay a poll tax and permitted them to register under one of four conditions: a "grandfather clause"; ownership of forty acres of land or of five hundred dollars' worth of taxable property; a literacy test interpreting a paragraph of the United States Constitution to the registrar's satisfaction; or "good character" in the registrar's judgment. The *Outlook* was disturbed by the chance for corruption in the last two provisions. As the *Independent* noted, Atlanta's movement for interracial cooperation did nothing to counter the disfranchisement of black Georgians. Its Southern apologists, such as Alexander McKelway and Lovick P. Winter, said that Georgia's approval of disfranchisement and prohibition could be traced to the Atlanta riot. Alcohol led to both the crimes of passion that preceded the riot and the riot's excesses. "The very worst traits of human nature, and of negro nature especially, are brought out by whiskey," said Winter. Whiskey made the Negro "a criminal, a pauper, a vagrant and a menace." His attraction to cities by the sale of whiskey damaged both rural agriculture and the quality of urban life. "Every real friend of the negro," he argued, "is glad of the enactment of prohibition in Georgia." Were it not for black voters, McKelway and Winter held, it would have been adopted even earlier. McKelway said disfranchisement was rightly seen as a Southern variant of progressive reform.[18]

Disfranchisement did advance through the South with the adoption of progressive reforms. Maryland Democrats proposed a constitutional amendment in 1904, including a literacy test, a grandfather clause, and wide discretionary authority to election registrars. Lyman Abbott's *Outlook* and Baltimore's James Cardinal Gibbons condemned it as discriminatory. Defeated in 1904, the Democrats renewed the effort in 1909 and 1910. Again, Cardinal Gibbons was a powerful influence against it. Similarly, when Oklahoma Democrats sought to disfranchise black voters, the *Independent* and the *Outlook* were outspoken critics of the effort. The struggle against disfranchisement continued for years. The Northern social gospel prophets generally accepted a literacy requirement for the franchise, so long as it was equitably enforced. But they rejected measures such as the "white primary" and the grandfather clause that were obviously intended to restrict suffrage along racial lines.[19]

**B**y 1904, close observers of American race relations believed they were witnessing a reprise of the antebellum crisis. In peonage, the chain gang, convict leasing, sharecropping and tenant farming, segregation, and disfranchisement, the white South was patching together a new system of racial bondage. Rumors of "Before Day Clubs" reflected recurrent white fears of servile insurrection; and lynch law and urban riots marked a determination to meet black aggression with extralegal force if necessary. At the same time, neoabolitionist forces divided along lines similar to those of the antebellum period.

National political effort had repeatedly failed, but black political activists recalled the presidential campaign of 1840 with a National Liberty party in 1904. In March, a leader of Memphis, Tennessee's, black Civic and Political Liberty League, Stanley P. Mitchell, organized the party to draw attention to black disfranchisement by challenging the two national parties in the year's presidential campaign. In early July, delegates from thirty-six states convened at St. Louis. Their platform confronted the nation with demands for restoring civil rights and the vote to black Americans, pensions for Civil War veterans and former slaves, abolition of polygamy and trusts, unsubsidized commercial and industrial competition, and a National Arbitration Board to adjudicate industrial disputes. The party's nominee for president, W. T. Scott of Belleville, Illinois, had to step down two weeks later, when he was convicted of "keeping a disorderly house" and sentenced to twenty days in the Belleville jail. In his place, the Liberty party named George Edwin Taylor of Ottumwa, Iowa, who had been a justice of the peace, newspaper editor, and chairman of the National Negro Democratic League's advisory board. Taylor won attention with articles in the *Independent* and the *Voice of the Negro*, but his candidacy was not taken seriously. "The spectacle of the National Liberty Party 'confronting' the people of the United States is one that no voter with a twinkle in his eye could wish to miss," said the *Independent*. But the year's election returns confirmed a serious trend. Public participation in general elections in the South was far below levels of participation elsewhere. One-fourth to one-sixth of the population voted in Northern and Western states, but only one-ninth to one-twenty-seventh of the population voted in the South. Voter turnout there was so low that black disfranchisement accounted for only part of the disparity. After disfranchisement, most of the South was so solidly Democratic that general elections were uncontested formalities.[20]

Among apolitical neoabolitionists, Ernest Howard Crosby espoused Garrisonian nonviolence. The son of a conservative New York Presbyterian divine, he was converted to the philosophy of nonresistance in 1894 when he read Tolstoy's *My Life*. The discovery of Tolstoy gave Crosby a critical perspective on the American experience, from the hypocrisy of white patriots who fought for their own independence while keeping black people in bondage to current threats of immigration restriction and imperialism to the American dream. Arguing that immigrants made positive contributions to American society, he challenged assumptions of Anglo-Saxon superiority and fought "Americanizing" efforts to strip immigrants of their ethnic heritage. His best known poem was a parody of Rudyard Kipling's "The White Man's Burden":

Take up the White Man's burden.
　Send forth your sturdy kin,
And load them down with Bibles
　And cannon-balls and gin.
Throw in a few diseases
　To spread the tropic climes,
For there the healthy niggers
　Are quite behind the times.

Lynching, rape, and warfare were outrageous acts of violence which should be unheard of among civilized people, said Crosby.[21]

With Tolstoy, Crosby rediscovered Garrisonian nonviolence. He thought new forms of racial bondage and violence in the South vindicated Garrison's argument that, if the South had been allowed to secede from the Union, slavery would have died a natural death. Garrison's nonviolent approach in race relations had a continuing relevance. "Then the question was how to free the negroes from the violence of the slave owners," Tolstoy said; "now the question is how to save the blacks from the violence of all the whites, and the whites from the violence of all the blacks." Tolstoy recalled a discussion with William Jennings Bryan in which Bryan challenged the Russian pacifist's absolute nonviolence with the example of a brigand who violated and killed a child. He had never encountered such a person, said Tolstoy, but he knew of many brigands who exercised legal violence against working people, old people, and children all over the world. The solution of the race problem did not lie in lynching Negroes or in the "artificial and liberal measures of American politicians," but in applying Garrison's nonresistance principle. "Natural relations between intelligent beings should consist, not in violence," Tolstoy argued, "but in rational persuasion and all who wish to serve the good of mankind should aspire to replace violence by the persuasion of reason."[22]

Even among neoabolitionists, Garrison was still controversial in the centennial of his birth and nonviolent protest was only a distant threat. Black radicals such as W. E. B. Du Bois and Reverdy Ransom called black Americans to an unrelenting struggle for freedom in the spirit of Garrison. Evangelical neo-abolitionists such as Amory H. Bradford and Washington Gladden praised Garrison's passion for justice, but Gladden doubted the practicality of his methods and said he was at times "unnecessarily bitter and violent." Non-resistance would never have achieved the abolition of slavery, said the *Independent*. As purist "come-outers" who sought no influence on public policy and fought slavery's friends and foes alike, said the journal, Garrisonians may have done more harm than good. Even Garrison's grandson, Oswald Garrison Villard, saw nonviolent protest as a distant threat. "The negroes have not yet learned the value of unions, of organization, of lawful agitation. The words general strike or boycott mean little to them as yet," said his New York *Evening Post*. "How will it be fifty or a hundred years hence? He who thinks that the negro will submit forever reckons without a knowledge of human nature."[23]

Key evangelical neoabolitionist spokesmen, such as Washington Gladden, Amory Bradford, Charles Cuthbert Hall, and Henry Churchill King, were leaders of the American Missionary Association and appealed to theological personalism for values in race relations.[24] When Gladden and Atlanta's Henry Hugh Proctor became moderator and assistant moderator of the National Council of Congregational Churches in 1904, A. J. Lyman urged Gladden to remain as president of the AMA. "You are a recognized authority outside of Congregational circles upon the Sociological aspects of that 'Southern Question'—'Negro Question'—which is perhaps the most critical—the most menacing of all questions now before the nation," he said. But Gladden stepped down as AMA president. At his last convention as its president, he introduced W. E. B. Du Bois to the delegates and urged them to read *The Souls of Black Folk*. Northern aid to Southern black education was still needed, Gladden said in his address. Fear, ignorance, passion, and prejudice had many voices in the South, but their defeat was sure. "Can anyone conceive that the Creator and Father of all can have any other thought" of black Americans, he asked, "than to lift them up, and fill them with his light, and crown them with his lovingkindness, and put the panoply of his might upon them and make a praise and an honor in the land wherein they dwell?" Gladden observed that Christians who seemed to share the assumption that the Fatherhood of God and the brotherhood of man were the only secure foundation for democracy espoused diametrically opposed policies in race relations. He thought it was "an infinite pity, nothing less than a national calamity" that disfranchisement and segregation should create "such a great gulf . . . in this nation between those who have the greatest power to give and those who are in the deepest need; but such is the decree of the white people of the South and there appears to be nothing that the rest of us can do to change it." The need to educate future black leaders in self-reliant manhood grew more imperative as segregation became more complete.[25]

After the Atlanta riot, Gladden saw two movements struggling to control black Americans' fate. The first, led by men like Edgar Gardner Murphy of the education coalition, would prepare them for full civil rights. It appeared to be losing to the other movement whose leaders, such as Thomas Dixon, Jr., would reduce them to permanent serfdom. Gladden predicted a bitter struggle if the white South continued in that direction. Compelled by its belief in the Fatherhood of God and the brotherhood of man, he thought that the power of Christian civilization would shift the tide of battle against the radical racists and force the white South to grant black people "full opportunity to live a complete human life." Black Americans and white neoabolitionists appreciated Gladden's message. But most responses were "bitter and violent, sadly lacking in logic," he said, convincing him that "the Negroes of the South have never, since the proclamation of emancipation, been exposed to more serious perils than those which now environ them." Finally, Gladden synthesized his thinking about race relations with a personalist's argument against radical white racists. "We shall get it hammered into our heads one of these days that this is a moral universe and that no injustice fails to get its due recompense, now and here." Citing Immanuel Kant's dictum that "Thou shalt treat humanity ever as an end, never as a means to thine own selfish end," Gladden said it applied to races and individuals. "The stronger race that tries to treat the weaker not as an end, but as a means to its own selfish ends, plucks swift judgment from the skies upon its own head," he argued. "On such a race there will surely fall the mildew of moral decay, the pestilence of social corruption, the blight of its civilization."[26]

As he left the AMA presidency to be the Congregationalists' moderator, Gladden traded places with Amory H. Bradford of Montclair, New Jersey. He was "one of the greatest, wisest, and most courageous friends my people ever had," said Henry Hugh Proctor. In *My Brother*, one of the social gospel's more important critiques of racism, Bradford developed the racial implications of the Fatherhood of God and the brotherhood of man. "We believe in the brotherhood of man, because we believe in the Fatherhood of God," he said. His critique was based on theological personalism. Discrimination against color, nationality, race, or social class was a wicked reflection on God and inimical to Christianity because mankind was made in His image. "All men, as

Washington Gladden, the most prominent of social Christianity's evangelical neo-abolitionists (Ohio Historical Society)

men, are sacred," said Bradford. People would increasingly see that "because all human beings have the same parentage, all have by nature the same rights, and should have equal opportunities." In an address to the AMA, he decried segregation as "the most insidiously pernicious and unpatriotic" trend in American life. It implied that allegiance to one's race took priority over loyalty to the nation. "Shame, shame, shame!" on Atlanta, he cried, for segregating black people in public accommodations. Assimilating diverse minorities into the national fabric required free association in public schools, churches, transportation, and recreation facilities. In a world of diverse peoples thrown together in close proximity, Bradford appealed to the power of the Cross to overcome barriers of prejudice. "The hope of the world is in the realization of Brotherhood," he argued. "In every race he who keeps close to the Cross finds his brother. The Cross obliterates divisions, binds nations, unbinds slaves, and reveals men to one another by revealing to them their common ancestry."[27]

Bradford's creed for the AMA summarized his thinking about race relations. First, he said, "We believe in the universal brotherhood." He urged the church and society in his "compromising generation" to live up to traditions of Pilgrim ancestors and abolitionist parents. "Those who are great enough for God to have created ought never to be counted fit only for man's abuse and neglect," Bradford said. "The tendency to call one race inferior to another, and to teach that any should be satisfied with less than the rights which belong to all, is unworthy of those who bear the Christian name." Second, he affirmed, we believe that "the best culture and opportunity is none too good for the poorest in humanity." The AMA took educational opportunity to deprived youth in Southern rice swamps, sugar plantations, cotton fields, and mountain homes because it believed in their great potential. Third, he claimed, we believe that "the worst may sometimes be made the best." All races had their barbaric periods and depraved individuals, but in black graduates of Atlanta, Fisk, Hampton, Howard, Talladega, and Tuskegee Bradford saw examples of what black people could be. Finally, he said, we believe in "America for all its people and all its people for America." The best interests of the nation would be served by equal justice for its black minority. Discrimination based on character was legitimate, but it could not be justified on the basis of color.[28]

Charles Cuthbert Hall, president of Union Theological Seminary, and Henry Churchill King, president of Oberlin College, gave personalism's critique of racism a more sophisticated theological voice. Hall was an important spokesman for black higher education, a member of Atlanta University's board of trustees from 1890 to 1908, and an advocate of Atlanta's radical vision despite efforts to convert him to Tuskegee's more conservative approach. In lectures at Vanderbilt University in 1905, he criticized the provincialism of the "Anglo-Saxon spirit." Efficient and often courageous, Hall said, it was also "a haughty race spirit," aggressive, intolerant, and self-satisfied. Attacking segregation, caste barriers, racial hatred, and sectarian animosity, he appealed for natural interaction among people of different backgrounds. "As culture grows people cannot be kept apart by imaginary barriers," Hall argued; "they attain substantial oneness without plan or intention; they awake, from dreams of prejudice, to see eye to eye beneath the impartial light of reality." His appeal to the Southern white audience was based on the incarnation. "When we broaden our conception of the Incarnation of the Son of God sufficiently in its world-wide significance, with eyes purged of racial prejudice and hearts from which all arrogance is put away," he said, "then we shall be prepared for the larger Church of Christ in which East and West are co-equal and reciprocal."[29]

A year later, the issues raised at Vanderbilt were central to Hall's lectures at Ohio Wesleyan University. He asked university men to break with "the bonds of race prejudice, ignore traditional Anglo-Saxon notions of superiority, and face the world of today in the spirit of the all-encompassing humanism of the heart of Jesus Christ." Hall said three personalist ideas directed Jesus' attitude to other peoples: the Father's impartial interest in humanity, the unqualified value of human life, and the essential unity of the human race. Jesus condemned race hatred and prejudice as contrary to God's abiding interest in all humanity. "The ignorant, the helpless, the idol-worshipping foreigners, the sinner, the harlot, the red-handed soldiers fulfilling their awful duty at His Cross," said Hall, "He comprehended, forgave, loved them all; seeing them all, and the innumerable multitude of whom they were types, in their relation to the impartial interest in the heart of God." The Father's impartial interest in all humanity underscored the value of all human life, he said. "If adorned with wealth, office, religious prestige, it was not thereby more to him. If scarred with poverty, ignorance, sin, and the stain of the pariah, it was not thereby less to Him," Hall argued. "It was all life, human life; and on the face of life Christ saw the likeness of a child to the Father." Those two points led to the third: the unity of the race. "Christ saw humanity as one homogeneous body of life. He regarded His Incarnation as an incorporation of Himself in the common flesh of this undifferentiated race. He was the Son of Man giving Himself for the life of the world," said Hall. "Race divisions, color lines, linguistic barriers,

types of civilization, advancement, retrogression, forms of government, systems of religion, are accidents of variation on the surface of an organism
unified in fact by its 'essential affinity with the nature of God.' " Ignorance,
unfamiliarity, prejudice, and national egotism created instinctive aversions to
the practical implications of the human unity, he admitted. But Hall urged his
audience to buttress their conviction of human unity by an experiential
witness to it.[30]

Henry Churchill King studied, taught, and was president at Oberlin College
from 1877 to 1925. After graduate work at the University of Berlin with
Wilhelm Dilthey, heir to and interpreter of the great German personalist,
Hermann Lotze, King returned to Oberlin to become one of America's leading personalists. All reality, human and divine, he said, must be interpreted in
personal terms. According to human religious experience, God was "at least
personal" and human beings know and experience God by reason of their
being persons. King accepted evolutionary theory, but he rejected its social
analogy. "We are spirits, not organisms," he argued, "and society is a society of
persons, not an organism." The social significance of personalism lay in "the
deepening sense of the value and sacredness of the person," he said.[31]

King discussed race relations in this personalist context. "Only one principle can guide us in the difficulties of the relations of race to race—reverence
for the person as such, absolutely unaffected by color or race connection," he
said. An ontological distinction between races, written into the very nature of
things, setting one race over against, above or below, another underlay the
racism of his day. Arguing against that assumption, King insisted on the
"essential likeness" of races. We should not "drug our conscience with the
deadly sedative that the other race is quite a different being from ourselves,"
he said. "The most horrible cruelties of history have flowed spontaneously
from this lying denial of the likeness of men." A personalist ethic accepted no
racial boundaries. "The essentially friendly life," said King, "must be a life of
universal good will that draws no lines of race prejudice." But when he
became the president of Oberlin in 1901, he found racial discrimination in
college athletics, boarding houses, choirs, literary societies, and even Bible
classes. King addressed it in a series of chapel talks. Reverence for personality
in race relations, he said, involved self-respect, respect for the liberty of
others, and reverence for the inner personality of others. Black Americans
would win the respect of others with self-respect, he argued. Self-respecting
persons would demand justice, but not insist on social acceptance where
they were not wanted. Out of respect for themselves, white people would

eradicate race prejudice and give black people full justice and equal opportunity. Finally, King condemned racial oppression and violence as contrary to the principle of reverence for the liberty and inner personality of others.[32]

As a student of Leo Tolstoy and adopted son of evangelical neoabolitionism, Edward Alfred Steiner synthesized Garrisonian and evangelical traditions in neoabolitionism. Born to Jewish parents in Hungary, he studied in Austria and Bohemia. As a boy, Steiner met a Union army veteran whose reading of *Uncle Tom's Cabin* and stories of the emancipation of American slaves inspired him to dream of liberating Hungarian peasants. But after studying at the University of Heidelberg, Steiner emigrated to the United States. He worked in New York's garment district, Pennsylvania coal mines, and on a Mississippi River boat, where he first met black Americans. "Whatever aversion to the Negro I have ever felt, has not come from association with him," said Steiner, but from the influence of white men. "To me they were a very pleasant variation from the rather monotonous human type which one meets in America, and which, no matter how dissimilar in the beginning, has been shaped into a common likeness by the new and uniform environment."[33]

After his conversion, Steiner studied theology at Oberlin, where Henry Churchill King's personalism and the intelligence of black classmates impressed him. Ordained a Congregational minister in 1891, he served churches in Minnesota and Ohio. At Springfield, Ohio, where a sixth of the city's 42,000 people were black, his study overlooked a colorful shantytown of back alleys. Steiner saw its black people "sunning themselves on the sloping roofs of their shanties or lolling about in most leisurely fashion, wherever they found a prop" to lean against. "The old mammies with their wooly heads tied in gorgeous bandannas, were there doing the 'white folks' washings; while numerous little pickaninnies, all unconscious of the fact that they were born into an unwelcoming world, played in the gutters." To maintain respectable appearances on its street fronts, Steiner learned that white Springfield kept its dance halls, gambling dens, and prostitution in the city's crowded black alleys. He knew his black neighbors first "as loafers, thieves and prostitutes, a horrible outer fringe of the city's life; but I also learned to know them and respect them in their homes, their churches and their lodges." Springfield's black people asked him to give their Emancipation Day Address. His Jewish background and struggle to overcome prejudice enabled him to identify with them. "Parson," Steiner recalled a black man saying, "the only way to get fellowship is to be the fellow in the same ship, and I reckon that's what you are." He invited black people to his church, but the few who came were

Edward A. Steiner, Congregational minister who synthesized Garrisonian and evangelical neoabolitionism (Edward A. Steiner, *From Alien to Citizen: The Story of My Life in America* [New York: Fleming H. Revell Co., 1914], frontispiece)

seated in a pew that was "as safe from invasion as if they had smallpox." Much of the interracial contact in Springfield was steeped in corruption. Bribery and flattery at elections kept a "brazenly immoral" judge in office to preside at trials of the black community's misdemeanors; and a trail of vice from a "purchaseable" police department led to the city's centers of power.[34]

Steiner was not surprised when a race riot broke out in Springfield five years after he left. On 6 March 1904, as a white policeman tried to settle a dispute between Richard Dixon and the woman he lived with, the black man shot them both. The policeman died the next day and Dixon was arrested for murder. A mob gathered at the jail that afternoon. The sheriff asked the crowd to disperse. The chief of police sent eighteen men to reinforce the sheriff's men, but he never appeared on the scene; the mayor hesitated to disperse the crowd with fire hoses; and the local militia was called to its barracks but its commander did not move against the mob. Finally, fifteen hundred enraged white people broke into the jail to seize Richard Dixon. He was dragged through the city's business district, hung on a telegraph pole, and riddled with bullets. Despite the pleas of a Catholic priest, the mob gathered the following evening and burned twenty buildings in shantytown, including the Levee, a strip of black saloons and houses of prostitution.[35]

In Columbus, Washington Gladden protested the "horrible events of the past week in our sister city of Springfield." Shocked by the authorities' failure to defend their charge, the *Independent* cried: "What Are Sheriffs For?" Better that a hundred men should die at the hands of a sheriff, said the journal, than that his prisoner should be lynched. "The Lord give us sheriffs that can shoot!" prayed the *Independent*. Ray Stannard Baker saw the problem in terms of civic lassitude. "If ever there was an example of good citizenship lying flat on its back with political corruption squatting on its neck, that example may be found in Springfield, Ohio," said Baker. "And the worst feature of all is that good citizenship there is apparently well satisfied and comfortable where it lies." Steiner agreed with Baker. "Had I been there when it happened, I fear that I should have been in the thick of it and have pleaded the cause of the black man," he wrote. "If the mob had listened to me, I would have pointed out the real criminals among them, the guilty white men who deserved the terrible end of their victim." He probably could not have swayed the mob and might have been injured, but Steiner hoped he would have had the courage to act. "If the animosity between the races had not been so great," he said, the city would have set "a day of fasting and prayer; for at the bottom of the black man's wickedness lay the white man's vices of lust and greed."[36]

In 1899, Steiner had left Springfield for Sandusky, Ohio, and four stormy years in a difficult parish. Despite good relations with its few black members, Steiner's Jewish background and his work with immigrants and industrial laborers during the week offended his congregation. In 1902, Washington Gladden and Henry Churchill King advised him to prepare for a teaching career. A year later, the *Outlook* commissioned him to write a biography of Tolstoy. While Steiner was doing research at Yasnaya Polyana, he was invited to succeed George D. Herron in the chair of applied Christianity at Grinnell College. Refusing to pay homage to race, class, or religious prejudice, Steiner made human brotherhood and unity the central theme of his teaching and writing. "I teach one religious doctrine with a scientific dogmatism and one scientific doctrine with a religious zeal: that underneath all the differences in races and classes, humanity is essentially one." His immigration studies challenged those who believed that the new ethnic groups would lead to a degenerate mongrelization and those who speculated that it would produce an American superrace. Children born to a variety of racial mixes were more or less normal children, he said. Each immigrant group brought its own experience and made its unique contribution to the American "melting pot," Steiner thought, but few racial characteristics were fixed and the nation's benign conditioning influences would transform immigrant peoples with the American spirit. "I came here with the same blood as theirs and the same heritage of good or ill, bequeathed by my race," Steiner said; "yet I feel myself completely at one with all which this country possesses that is worth living for and dying for." If the American church reclaimed its ancient vitality, it would transform immigrants into Americans.[37]

But race prejudice was pervasive and resilient in America, "where a tint is equivalent to a taint, a crooked nose to a crooked character," and "a peculiar slant of the eyes" suggests that "the race so marked cannot see straight," said Steiner. He made a personalist's argument against the "primitive" and "contagious" prejudice and devoted his life to its defeat. "We need to have created in us the spirit of reverence for the human soul, no matter how encased in crude flesh," said Steiner. A person may be "crude, illiterate, ill-kept and unkempt; yet he is a brother man struggling upward. Whoever, whatever he is, he deserves our respect, if only for the spark of the divine flame within him." Leo Tolstoy won his enduring admiration for transcending racial and national barriers "to meet all human beings upon a high and common level." The Russian novelist taught him a very difficult lesson, said Steiner: "Give everything and ask nothing in return." While not demanding to be treated as a brother, he sought to treat others as such. "When one has finally yielded himself to all men of all races and classes, when one can be unconscious of hampering barriers between, when one does not feel anything but pity for the tainted, a desire to include the halt and the halting rather than to exclude them," said Steiner, "then one has reached the highest point of spiritual experience." Tolstoy pointed to that end. "Young man, you can't make this world right, unless *you* are right," he said as they parted. "The Kingdom of God must be within *you*, if you want to hasten its coming into the world."[38]

**A**s Edward A. Steiner theoretically reconciled Garrisonian and evangelical neoabolitionism, divisions among black leaders were growing. After the Carnegie Hall Conference failed to establish a united racial front, Du Bois began to organize black radicals for the civil rights struggle. In July 1905, he and twenty-eight others met at Fort Erie, on the Canadian side of the Niagara River, to form the Niagara Movement. Its Declaration of Principles called for the suffrage, civil liberties, and equal economic and educational opportunity for black Americans. Protesting racism and segregation in church and society, Du Bois saw Niagara's task as interpreting the real Christ to white "Christians." American Christendom was strangely deformed, largely ignoring "the Golden Rule, the Sermon on the Mount, the divinely beautiful lesson of the Good Samaritan, and the more vital and central truth of the teaching of Jesus himself—the fatherhood of God and the brotherhood of man," said another conferee, William A. Sinclair. "Christ's saying, 'All ye are brothers,' is not interpreted with sufficient breadth to include the negro." The Niagara Movement was little noted in the nation's press, black or white. The *Outlook* rejected its plea for universal suffrage, attack on segregation, and "petulant" tone, saying that Washington's National Negro Business League set a better example for black America. But as the Niagara Movement was being organized, the *American Missionary* urged black Americans to "fight to the last ditch" and "exhaust every legitimate means" to vindicate their civil rights. The Niagara declaration had a "bilious" lack of appreciation for missionary education among black Americans, but otherwise its claims were incontrovertible and its tone justified. "To silently and quietly await the ameliorating influence of time for what others may become good enough to bestow," said the *American Missionary*, "indicates more of the philosophy of Mr. Micawber than it does of the philosophy of history."[39]

The Niagara Movement never aspired to be a mass organization. It appealed to educated black urban professionals and had only several hundred members at its greatest strength. In August 1906, forty-five delegates gathered at Harpers Ferry, West Virginia, to hear Boston's Reverdy Ransom praise the spirit of John Brown. They heard reports of membership growth, pamphlets distributed, petitions submitted, and cooperative efforts with like-minded groups. At Harpers Ferry, Niagara conferees demanded "every single right that belongs to a freeborn American; and until we get these rights we will never cease to protest and assail the ears of America." Black response to the Harpers Ferry Manifesto was mixed. The New York *Age* condemned Du Bois and his allies as an "aggregation of soreheads" and their manifesto as "too bitter and lugubrious." Even the moderate Kelly Miller found it "scarcely distinguishable from a wild and frantic shriek." Booker T. Washington criticized Lyman Abbott's *Outlook* for even noticing the Niagara Movement, but Du Bois recalled that it "pilloried me with scathing articles." The *Outlook* acknowledged the Harpers Ferry Manifesto with an alternative platform, which denied that the suffrage was a natural right, favored segregation in schools, churches, and public accommodations, and insisted that education should prepare people for the kind of work they were most likely to do in the community. "On the whole, we think the Niagara Movement would be more useful if it demanded more of the negro race and put less emphasis on its demands for the negro race," said the *Outlook*. Wishing that Du Bois and Washington would pursue a common program, yet the *Independent* agreed "with every word" of the Harpers Ferry Manifesto.[40]

Shortly after Niagara's radicals met at Harpers Ferry, reaction to a ten-minute shooting spree around the cafés and dance halls near Fort Brown in Brownsville, Texas, showed the need for their plea. Soldiers from three companies of the black Twenty-fifth Regiment roamed through town, randomly shooting into buildings, said local whites. A civilian was killed, a police officer was injured, and racial passions threatened further violence. When the black soldiers maintained their innocence and implicated no one else, President Theodore Roosevelt dismissed the battalion without honor and disqualified its members from civil or military service for the United States. The severity of his action led to an enormous outcry in the black community, embarrassed Booker Washington, who was unwilling to criticize the president in public, and led to a congressional investigation. Months later, the president rescinded his order barring the soldiers from civil service. The congressional committee upheld his actions, but heard testimony that raised serious doubt about the soldiers' guilt. "I have yet to find one officer who was connected with that regiment who expresses the belief that our men were guilty," said the regimental chaplain. If white social gospel prophets betrayed an astigmatism in race relations, it was in the Brownsville affair. The *Outlook* consistently supported Roosevelt. Despite the plea of the respected black Presbyterian, Francis J. Grimké, that none of the soldiers had been proved guilty and although it hoped that they would be proved innocent, the *Independent* reluctantly supported their dismissal. Niagara Movement clergymen threatened to punish the Republicans in the election of 1908, but the *Independent* and the *Outlook* urged black voters not to abandon the Republican party. The Niagara Movement included "some of the ablest and best" black people in the country, said the *Independent*, but their advice to boycott the Republicans was like cutting off a leg to cure a corn.[41]

Reports of lynching, peonage, and disfranchisement, coinciding with the Atlanta and Brownsville riots in August and September 1906 threatened Booker T. Washington's powerful hold on black allies and his influence with white racial liberals. Brownsville strained his close alliance with AME Bishop Abraham Grant and destroyed his friendship with T. Thomas Fortune. Washington lost control of the Afro-American Council in 1907, but black radicals were unable to capitalize on his weakened position. Both the Afro-American Council and the Niagara Movement were largely moribund after 1907. There was no comparable revolt among white racial activists, but the events raised doubt about Washington's wisdom in race relations. Robert C. Ogden remained his loyal ally, but the thrust of his education coalition was blunted by 1906 and he confessed to grave doubts about the future in race relations. "I sometimes almost feel as though our boasted democracy was only a synonym for demagoguery," he wrote. "The South is not yet through with the effort to re-enslave the Negro." New York's Episcopal bishop, Henry Codman Potter, condemned current "bondage to the spirit of caste" as even worse than earlier American prejudice. At the Protestant Episcopal convention in Richmond, Virginia, Potter offended the prejudice of many fellow churchmen by inviting a black bishop to sit at his table during the meeting.[42]

In 1906, Booker Washington and Oswald Garrison Villard asked Ray Stannard Baker to investigate the Atlanta riot. He shared an evangelical Protestantism with many social gospel prophets that elevated morality over fine points of theology and sought expression in social service. Except his articles on lynching in *McClure's*, Baker had little experience in race relations. "In the North we are mildly concerned in many things," he said; "the South is overwhelmingly concerned in this one thing." When his editors encouraged Baker to expand the scope of his reports to a national survey of race relations, he spent two years in wide-ranging interviews and reflection. They appeared in *American Magazine* and were published together as *Following the Colour Line*, the most important account of American race relations before World War I. Baker's reports were episodic, but at its best *Following the Colour Line* attempted significant social analysis. He expected to contrast the radical white racism of Thomas Dixon, Jr., with the black conservatism of Booker Washington. But, as research expanded his perspective, he saw a white "party of duty" in the Southern education movement struggling with a white "party of rights" in the radical racists and a black "party of duty" in Washington's followers struggling with a black "party of rights" in the black radicals. This improved Baker's original conception, forcing his readers to listen to both white conservatives and black radicals. Within this framework, his thinking about race relations worked in sets of unresolved tension: between a collectivist, class analysis and an individualistic approach; between a sense of the immutability and the malleability of the problem; and between visions of white and of black responsibility for resolving it.[43]

Baker's sentiment drifted between Du Bois and Washington for years, but his framework made it possible to side ultimately with the "parties of duty" as more responsible. "Time and patience," he counseled, but time redeemed by discipline, forbearance, education, service, democracy, and practical Christianity. "For good comes to men as they work together with that sympathy and understanding which is the only true Democracy," he said. "The Great Teacher never preached the flat equality of men, social or otherwise. He gave mankind a working principle by means of which mankind could live together in harmony and develop itself to the utmost possibility." The principle was the Golden Rule, "the least sentimental, the most profoundly practical teaching known to man." Baker later felt he had fallen back on "the stock moralities" of his youth in *Following the Colour Line*. But in his diary, he wrote that "the more I think of human ills and remedies, the more I see that the teaching of Jesus Christ is the only solution." *Following the Colour Line* was hailed across a wide spectrum of American racial thought. Alexander McKelway, a Southern white radical, thought it "eminently fair"; and Oswald Garrison Villard said it was "very successful indeed." Washington and Du Bois complimented Baker on his articles, but Du Bois had doubts about the author's implacable optimism.[44]

At the University of Wisconsin, John R. Commons, Richard H. Edwards, and Edward A. Ross began to question popular racial assumptions. In 1906, Edwards organized Sunday evening groups to study social issues in light of the Christian faith and social science. As they grew under the guidance of Commons and Ross, Edwards published study guides for civic organizations on liquor control, poverty, immigration, business ethics, labor, and the Negro. With advice from Du Bois and Alfred Holt Stone, a white Mississippi planter, Edwards struggled for balance on "the Negro problem." Enfranchisement of the freedmen was based on "superficial and incorrect" reasoning, he said, but disfranchisement seemed "unjust and unAmerican." He was impressed with the economic gains of black Americans since emancipation and saw the need of higher education for black students, but he was disturbed by the appearance of immorality in black America. No serious student of American race relations had a panacea to offer, Edwards thought. "The most fruitful emphasis does not seem to be upon political rights and agitation for social equality, on the one hand, or upon white rule as such and imputations of Negro inferiority on the other," he said. The emphases must be on our common humanity, equal justice, magnanimous toleration, mutual interdependence, the necessity of self control, and the "right of every respectable man to be respected for his manhood." Ross had once referred to the belief in racial equality as "monumental folly" and written of "the causes of race superiority." But by 1908 he was skeptical of race as a key to understanding society. " 'Race' is the cheap explanation tyros offer for any collective trait that they are too stupid or too lazy to trace to its origin in the physical environment, the social environment, or historical conditions," he wrote.[45]

Elsewhere, new institutions in racial reform, like the Sagamore Sociological Conference, grew from earlier racial missions to study the problem. Returning from a celebration of the twenty-fifth anniversary of Atlanta's Spelman College, James A. Francis of Boston's Clarendon Street Baptist Church and George W. Coleman, publisher of the *Christian Endeavor World*, decided to organize an annual conference on Christianity and social problems. When Coleman convened the first Sagamore Sociological Conference in June 1907, a visitor described it as "Lake Mohonk on the seashore." There, Edwin Doak Mead urged his audience to solve the race problem "in no other way than Christ's way." An heir to New England abolitionism, Mead arraigned Northern public opinion for its "carelessness and indifference concerning the almost universal disregard of the political rights of the colored people in the South." He called for greater philanthropic support of black education and of settlement houses in black communities. "To the man who has the least advantages our obligations are greatest, to these struggling men we owe the most," Mead told the Sagamore conferees. "We should not tread them down simply because they are trodden down; we should reach the helping hand with the greater alacrity and the greater constancy." The Sagamore Conference's first platform called for finding "common interests between people of different racial elements and forms of faith." Two years later, Ray Stannard Baker spoke of a crisis of the democratic spirit in race relations and appealed for its renewal by education and "passionate preaching of the religion of service." Baker's even-handed presentation was "stinging with truth," an observer said, and his conclusions were "Truth's conclusions." In their responses, Leighton Williams, J. G. Phelps-Stokes, and Walter Rauschenbusch emphasized the need for an economic basis for racial equality.[46]

Other vehicles for the social gospel, like the National Association for the Advancement of Colored People, grew out of the new sense of racial crisis and fixed exclusively on race relations. In 1906, the *Independent's* Hamilton Holt, Mary White Ovington, and Oswald Garrison Villard of the New York *Evening Post*, the city's three leading neoabolitionists, organized the Cosmopolitan Society of Greater New York. It sought to allay race prejudice and hatred in the city by discussions in its interracial membership. On 27 April 1908, the "Cosmopolitan Club" drew a hundred people to dinner at a New York restaurant. A photographer was barred from taking pictures of the diners and a speaker excused himself at the last minute. Otherwise, it was an uneventful gathering. Among several speakers who offered remarks on ways the race problem might be solved, Holt said interracial marriage was unlikely. The next morning's newspapers carried routine accounts of the gathering. But evening papers ran lurid tales of an "Equality Feast" at which Holt advocated interracial marriage, Ovington behaved like a radical advocate of social equality, and burly black men rubbed knees with naive or immoral white women. The *New York Times* condemned the "odious exhibition" by "forces of evil" which sought "by revolution, if necessary, to destroy society, the home and religion." Across the country, the press ran colorful accounts of the gathering. Leaders of the Cosmopolitan Club received such abuse that Mary White Ovington fled from her apartment and her male relatives censored her mail for six weeks. She never knew that Booker T. Washington had arranged the journalists' accounts of the Cosmopolitan Club dinner to discredit the emerging alliance of Northern black radicals and white reformers, which threatened his leadership in race relations.[47]

Three months later, racial tension in Springfield, Illinois, broke into one of the worst riots of the decade. On 14 August, a crowd of four thousand people gathered at the county jail, where two black men, one charged with murder and the other with rape, awaited trial. In the late afternoon, the sheriff diverted the crowd's attention and sent the black men to the Bloomington state prison. Learning that the prisoners were moved in the automobile of a local restaurant owner, the crowd looted his business and burned his vehicle. Despite public officials' pleas, a mob of perhaps four hundred rioters and, now, ten thousand onlookers turned on any black person in sight. One sought refuge on the speaker's platform of the Prohibition party's presidential candidate, Eugene Chaflin, who threatened to shoot anyone who attacked the black refugee. Chaflin was badly bruised by rocks thrown at him from the crowd. The mob concentrated its destruction on the "Bad Lands," a black neighborhood, two blocks from the state capitol and four blocks from Abraham Lincoln's home. It looted stores and saloons, set eighteen fires to burn over four square blocks, and murdered two elderly black men. Nine people died, a hundred were seriously wounded, and property damage amounted to $150,000. Many black men and women lost their jobs; grocers refused to sell them food; and several thousand of them fled the city. Along the routes of their exodus, white villagers posted signs warning them to keep moving. The authorities arrested 150 suspected mob leaders; and the grand jury returned 117 indictments. On his own confession, one man received a prison sentence for burglary, arson, and rioting; and a woman, protesting her innocence, committed suicide. All other charges were dropped, as was the charge of rape against the black prisoner, when his accuser admitted that her assailant was white.[48]

Shailer Mathews's *World To-Day* condemned Springfield's "disgraceful" riot. Graham Taylor found "bitter ironies" in events there. "It is a sorry comment upon American civilization," he said, "that no better use has been made of our resources of law, education and religion" than to have let Springfield's black people become "so depraved" that "the new race of white barbarians . . . trust no means of protecting themselves from them except the blood and fire of extermination." The race prejudice isolating black Americans was bound to produce "a crucifixion of its justice, humanity and religion" like the nation suffered at Springfield. Whatever reparations or punishment were meted out, said Taylor, "the blood of the innocent cries from the ground less for vengeance than for the justice" to "prevent the recurrence of such barbarities by such cooperation of law, education and religion, as will at least civilize our barbarians, both white and black." The *Independent* said "mean racial malice" caused the Springfield riot. The rioters vented "their hatred on other people who were not criminals, but who were black. It was not crime they hated, for they were criminals themselves." Springfield's black women and children might flee, but the men should get police and legal protection, if possible. "If that is not possible," said the journal, "defend, resist to the utmost of human power. That is good law and good morals." But to prevent such extremities, law-abiding people should "invade their own slums with all the possible appliances of persuasion and enforcement" in order "to reform, to civilize and to Christianize the pagans in their own midst." The Independent also published William English Walling's account of "The Race War in the North." The wealthy son of slaveholders, who had become a socialist, emphasized the extremes to which race hatred had gone. In a great Northern capital, the home of Abraham Lincoln, where black people were less than 10 percent of the population, the community approved of racial violence. Its ministers recommended swift "justice" against black people "rather than recommending true Christianity, democracy, and brotherhood." Walling summoned a rebirth of abolition's spirit, lest race warfare spread across the nation, destroying minority groups, public education, and popular democracy.[49]

In January 1909, Walling, Ovington, Villard, Bishop Alexander Walters, and Independent editors Hamilton Holt and William Hayes Ward discussed a national biracial organization to defend black Americans' civil rights. By February, Villard drafted a Call for a National Conference on the Negro to meet in New York on 31 May and 1 June. It outlined black Americans' grievances and called "believers in democracy" to a "discussion of present evils, the voicing of protests, and the renewal of the struggle for civil and political liberty." The one common denominator among sixty people who signed the call for publication on the centennial of Lincoln's birth was their concern for race relations. Jane Addams, Ray Stannard Baker, John Dewey, W. E. B. Du Bois, William Dean Howells, Lincoln Steffins, and Villard were the most prominent among them. Largely a group of white, Protestant, New York professional men, they included black and white men and women, Catholics and Jews, Northerners and Southerners, political radicals and conservatives. Nearly half of them, including Addams, Baker, Du Bois, Holt, Howells, Ovington, Walters, and Ward, were influenced by the social gospel. They included Northern missionaries in the South, Horace M. Bumstead and James

G. Merrill, former presidents of Atlanta and Fisk Universities; black clergymen, Francis J. Grimké and J. Milton Waldron; black churchwomen, Mary Church Terrell and Ida Wells-Barnett; rabbis Emil G. Hirsch and Stephen S. Wise; and white settlement workers, Florence Kelley and Lillian D. Wald.[50]

Ten New York clergymen signed the Call to the National Negro Conference, including Walter Laidlaw, executive secretary of New York's Federation of Churches and Christian Workers, Charles H. Parkhurst, the erratic Presbyterian, and Thomas Cuming Hall, Union Theological Seminary's social ethicist. Hall thought that no promised glory of another world could replace the necessity of righteousness and social justice on earth, "where his children have suffered so long." The longing of black people for another land to work out their destiny could only be "a momentary impulse," he said. "Mr. Booker T. Washington feels more justly and nobly when he teaches his race that here they have been enslaved and suffered, but [here] they are to work out their own highest freedom. God's triumph would not be complete were it only beyond the veil, nor would it be complete were it confined to any one social group." Hall advocated a wide extension of the franchise to educate the uninformed, give self-protection to those who might otherwise be exploited, and offer a legal means to express dissent. "It is enormously important that a politically untrained race of over ten millions of colored blood be compelled to think politically and to think in terms of the whole nation," he argued. "The Southern States that exclude the negro from the ballot are . . . shutting themselves off from knowledge of what the negro wants, and . . . leading him to a dumb and possibly bitter and unreasoning discontent with the order about him." John Lovejoy Elliott, William Mackintire Salter, Anna Garlin Spencer, and Charles Zueblin, the Ethical Culture Society's lecturers in New York, Chicago, and Boston, signed the call. Zueblin was a founder of the Northwestern University Settlement and the University of Chicago's sociology department, who wrote provocatively of "the over-estimated Anglo-Saxon." He was grateful for the democratic legacy of Anglo-Saxon traditions to the United States. But they were the product of a favorable history and geography, he thought, not a racial heritage. Here, they were administered and reinvigorated by people of diverse ethnic and racial backgrounds, whose experience together would undermine race prejudice and require the widest participation in democratic processes.[51]

After publishing the call, Villard found ninety more sponsors, including the white presidents of Howard and Atlanta Universities, Wilbur P. Thirkield and Edward T. Ware, Chicago's Charles R. Henderson and Graham Taylor, California's David Starr Jordan, Wisconsin's John R. Commons, Union Theological Seminary's Arthur Cushman McGiffert, Rochester's Unitarian pastor William Channing Gannett, and Oberlin's Henry Churchill King. When King was unable to address the conference, President Charles F. Thwing of Western Reserve University became the most prominent of the theological personalists at the National Negro Conference. As Villard expanded support for it, he hoped to avoid Booker Washington's active opposition by denying that it was allied with either faction in the black community. "It is not to be a Washington movement, or a Du Bois movement," he said. There was to be "an annual conference similar to the Indian conference at Lake Mohonk, for the discussion by men of both races of the conditions of the colored people" and a permanent organization for work in education, legislation, politics, litigation, and the press. But Washington saw it as a threat to his influence. Its black members unanimously opposed any role for him in the organization and Washington was openly hostile to the NAACP by 1911.[52]

The New York planning committee for the National Negro Conference grew by mid-March to include Ray Stannard Baker, William Henry Brooks, John Haynes Holmes, Alexander Irvine, Anna Garlin Spencer, and Rabbi Stephen S. Wise. A Christian socialist who admired Booker Washington, Irvine had gone South disguised as a laborer to work in and report on the region's turpentine fields, coal mines, and convict labor camps in 1906–7. A few weeks among Alabama's black laborers left him with no desire even to visit Tuskegee. Irvine was convinced that W. E. B. Du Bois was right. Holmes, pastor of New York's Unitarian Church of the Messiah, and Wise, rabbi of the Free Synagogue of New York, were at the outset of four decades as allies in the ministry of reform. Holmes was the son of abolitionists, became America's foremost disciple of Mahatma Gandhi, organized the nation's first "stand-in," and served the NAACP as a national vice president for over fifty years.[53]

John Spencer Bassett, now teaching in New England, and Quincey Ewing, apparently secure as rector of his family's small Episcopal parish in Napoleonville, Louisiana, were among Southern white sponsors of the conference. Ewing's early articles scandalized his fellow Sewanee alumni. "He is so objectionable that I cannot mention him with any patience—such a blatherskite!" one wrote. In "The Criminality of the Negro," Ewing argued that black crime rates were lower than those of white Americans, that false statistics to the contrary were contrived by white racists to justify keeping black people subordinate, and that the courts consistently denied them equal justice. In 1908, he praised graduates of Atlanta University for refuting "the old superstition that the Lord God created one race of people with just enough intellect to [serve] other people, to whom were vouchsafed all the rare treasures of knowledge and wisdom alone." Their achievement proved that there was "but *one human mind*, but *one human heart*, but *one human race*." Unable to attend the National Negro Conference, Ewing published "The Heart of the Race Problem" as the neoabolitionists gathered in March 1909. The heart of the problem is not the black man's deficiencies, he said, but the white man's conviction that the black man is his inferior and thus not entitled to exercise fully human rights. "The problem is the white man's determination to make good this conviction, coupled with constant anxiety lest he should fail to make it good," said Ewing. So long as black people made no claim to human rights, there was no race problem, he argued. It arose because white people were determined to maintain the conditions of slavery long after it was officially destroyed and, then, only when black people expressed qualities supposedly reserved for white people. AMA Secretary Harlan Paul Douglass praised the "courageous candor" of Ewing, "a Southerner of Southerners." Washington, D.C.'s, black Baptist pastor, J. Milton Waldron, paid tribute to him as "one of the few noble and heroic souls" among Southern white men "who believe that the Negro ought to be treated as a man and given all the rights and privileges accorded to any other man."[54]

Three hundred people at the National Negro Conference's first meeting at New York's Charity Organization Hall heard the *Independent*'s William Hayes Ward give the keynote address. Long an AMA officer and the conference's leading evangelical neoabolitionist, Ward urged the conferees "to emphasize that equal justice should be done to man as man, and particularly to the Negro, without regard to race, color or previous condition of servitude." Fifteen hundred people at a Cooper Union mass meeting heard Chicago's Unitarian preacher, Jenkin Lloyd Jones, take up Ward's theme in a "fiery jeremiad." In many quarters, he said, "a painful reaction has silenced the voice of religion, confused the problems of the ballot, and intimidated the one-time champions of the despised race." Jones and Ward drew parallels between the Old South's proslavery argument and justifications of the South's new peculiar institutions and between Old and New South objections to Northern interference. They called on the National Negro Conference to raise abolition's banner of racial justice anew. The final closed session of the National Negro Conference ran late into the night as William Monroe Trotter and J. Milton Waldron argued with the language of every resolution in rancorous debate. As adopted, the resolutions demanded federal enforcement of Reconstruction's constitutional amendments and denounced disfranchisement, lynching, mob violence, peonage, and discrimination in schools and the marketplace. The nominating committee's list for a Committee of Forty on permanent organization "took a middle course," Mary White Ovington recalled, but it "suited nobody." Washington was omitted, as were the black radicals, Trotter, Waldron, and Wells-Barnett. Du Bois, Ovington, Jane Addams, William Henry Brooks, John Haynes Holmes, Charles F. Thwing, Alexander Walters, Stephen S. Wise, and Richard Robert Wright, Jr., were named to the committee. Four additional black people, Kelly Miller, William A. Sinclair, Waldron, and Wells-Barnett, were added to it after the stormy meeting adjourned.[55]

Reaction to the National Negro Conference fixed largely on the opposition of an old abolitionist, Thomas Wentworth Higginson. "In 1868 and ever since," he wrote, "I have regarded the indiscriminate extension of the suffrage to an entire class as a class, whether negroes or others, to be politically inexpedient; that is, not conducive to the general interest, which . . . is more important than the interest of the individual." White people would never submit to the supremacy of any people of color, who should concentrate on education and industrial development instead of political agitation, said Higginson. The *Outlook* agreed that agitation would do more harm than good, but the *Independent* objected. "We do not believe in any indiscriminate restriction of the suffrage," said the journal; "we do believe in the indiscriminate, undiscriminating extension of the suffrage, without regard to race, color, sex or education. We believe that absolute democracy is safe; not only safe, but far safer than any doctrine of oligarchy or aristocracy." The *AME Church Review*, the *Chautauquan*, and the *Independent* welcomed the new national biracial organization devoted to civil rights for black Americans.[56]

The Committee of Forty was managed by Oswald Garrison Villard and Mary White Ovington in New York. It had supporters in Atlanta, Boston, Chicago, Cleveland, New York, Philadelphia, and Washington, D.C., and support from the National Federation of Religious Liberals. But it had no employees until February 1910 and was not yet organized for effective work. At a second conference in May 1910, it became the National Association for the Advancement of Colored People, with a national committee of one hundred members, thirty of whom served as an executive committee. Du Bois recommended that the second conference focus on the franchise and John Haynes Holmes asked New York clergymen to address the issue on Sundays before or after the conference. In public meetings at Cooper Union, Baker, Du Bois,

Holmes, Charles W. Chesnutt, Clarence Darrow, Percy Stickney Grant, Kelly Miller, and Reverdy Ransom debated it. "The spirit of democracy is not of Teutonic origin or Anglo-Saxon birth," Ransom said. "It belongs to no race, no age, no country, and no clime." Ten million American citizens were being denied their rights, Holmes told the conferees; "any man who is silent in the face of this oppression is himself a partner to the crime which is being committed." Disfranchisement "prostitutes the State to the shameful work of mocking and paralyzing the religion that I preach." To do "the work of God," he argued, "we must lift up our voices and spare not!"[57]

But leaders of the NAACP argued about the franchise among themselves. "Let us for the time being accept the laws as they are," Ray Stannard Baker advised, concentrating on those who meet legal requirements but were still denied the right to vote. After his speech, Baker noted that the radicals disagreed with him. "The more I see of this whole matter," he told Washington, "the more I feel sure that you are on the right track." Percy Stickney Grant, who chaired the Cooper Union meeting, was more conservative than Baker in race relations. In his youth, Grant had taught a Sunday school class for black students at his father's Baptist church in Boston. Later, he was a trustee of Berea College and Manassas Colored Industrial School. But Grant was no racial egalitarian. In spite of outstanding individuals, black people were biologically and culturally inferior, he thought. The North had acted on an abstract theory of racial equality since emancipation, but the laissez-faire educational and political theory behind the grant of citizenship to newly emancipated slaves and the offer of "purely intellectual training" to untutored freedmen had failed. The concurrence of that failure with the elaboration of a Darwinian social theory that admitted inequality made a new beginning in race relations mandatory. "When Southerners swear they will not be governed by negroes, are they not obeying [a] true racial instinct of historical superiority?," Grant asked. "When the Southerner denies social equality to the negro, he does [so] because it would be a step toward marriage and race amalgamation." Accepting racial inequality, he sought to replace laissez-faire with a paternalistic policy of federal intervention to educate and elevate the inferior race. "A democracy of *inequality* and *education* is more humane," he argued, "than a democracy of *equality* and *laissez-faire.*"[58]

The NAACP was founded when the second conference confirmed the Committee of Forty's recommendations. John Hope, Henry Churchill King, Kelly Miller, Anna Garlin Spencer, Charles F. Thwing, William Monroe Trotter, Alexander Walters, and Stephen S. Wise served on its national committee.

The executive committee included Jane Addams, William Henry Brooks, John Haynes Holmes, Mary White Ovington, Rabbi Joseph Silverman, and J. Milton Waldron. Du Bois became director of publicity and research and editor of its journal, the Crisis. As the organization took shape, other Northern white spokesmen for the social gospel such as Felix Adler, Isabel Eaton, Edwin Doak Mead, and Frank Mason North rallied to its cause. In 1910, it held local meetings in Cleveland, hosted by Thwing, and Chicago, where Jane Addams, Rabbi Emil Hirsch, and Jenkin Lloyd Jones spoke in its behalf. By 1912, the NAACP was a fledgling national organization, with local branches in Baltimore, Boston, Chicago, Cleveland, New York, Philadelphia, and Washington, D.C.[59]

American race relations reached their nadir in 1903. In the next decade, black and white neoabolitionists built a network of institutions, including the NAACP and the National Urban League, that would roll back the racist tide in a long twentieth-century struggle. These organizations confronted the issue legally, politically, and socially, but spokesmen for American social Christianity had a theological issue to settle among themselves.

# 10

## Theologies of Race Relations

White social gospel prophets were less indifferent to race relations than the historians suggest, but their attitudes spanned broad spectra. The spectrum at the end of chapter 8 suggests its range if the problem is defined politically. But if it is defined culturally, as home missionaries defined it, the spectrum ranged from Josiah Strong's radical assimilationism to Josiah Royce's conservative assimilationism and from Edgar Gardner Murphy's conservative separatism to Thomas Dixon, Jr.'s, radical separatism. These men were "theologians of race relations" because their racial thought was integral to their theology. Whether they were racists hinges on a definition of the term. If racism is a pattern of thought that relates mind to matter by making culture a function of physiology, then only the separatists, Murphy and Dixon, can be understood as racists.[1] The cultural assimilationism of Royce and Strong is a different attitude, based on different, if no more satisfactory, assumptions about race and reality. Another social gospel prophet, Harlan Paul Douglass, saw the strengths and flaws of both assimilationist and separatist postures. Like Murphy and Royce, he saw black people as persons, persons who should enter the American mainstream to be sure, but persons who made their own contribution to it and thus transformed the model of the good and true American. The "racial transformationism" of H. Paul Douglass made him a leading spokesman for evangelical neoabolitionism.

Among the social gospel prophets, Josiah Strong is most commonly seen as a racist. His radical assimilationism celebrated the superiority of Anglo-Saxon culture, but it was at odds with the assumptions of contemporary racism.[2] Strong was nurtured in abolitionism at Hudson, Ohio, where John Brown had vowed to work for slavery's extinction. Later, Brown visited the Strongs there. "I remember distinctly sitting by his knee, when I was a little fellow, and looking up into his face as he told of his struggles with the Border Ruffians," Strong later recalled. He was impressed when Brown pulled from his boot a bowie knife he had taken in a fight with proslavery settlers in Kansas. Later, as the "brave old man" faced execution, Strong's older sister, Mary, wrote that it would leave "a stain" on the character of his judge. She hoped that John Brown's body would be buried in Hudson, with Henry Ward Beecher preaching the funeral sermon. Harriet Beecher Stowe's *Uncle Tom's Cabin* was young Josiah's favorite book; his first artistic effort was a pencil sketch of Eliza and her child in flight from slavery. Yet, little Josiah had no future as an artist; he was literally colorblind. His brothers served in the Union army during the Civil War. Too young to serve, Josiah later recalled that his only regret had been that the war ended before he had killed a rebel. Young Strong once asked his grandfather, an evangelical abolitionist supporter of the American Missionary Association's work among the freedmen, "What is a Democrat?" The old man said: "A Democrat is a man who does not say his prayers."[3]

Josiah Strong won national prominence in Congregational home missions. He graduated from Western Reserve University and Lane Theological Seminary, was ordained, and became a Congregational missionary in Cheyenne, Wyoming. After serving as chaplain and instructor in natural theology at Western Reserve, he went to a Congregational mission in Sandusky, Ohio. In 1881, Strong became regional secretary of the Congregational Home Missionary Society. In that capacity, he visited the denomination's biracial college at Berea, Kentucky. At Chattanooga, he spoke to white Presbyterians in the morning and black Baptists in the evening. In Nashville, he addressed Fisk University students on "Conditions of Success in Life." During these missionary labors, Josiah Strong wrote *Our Country: Its Possible Future and Its Present Crisis*.[4]

A sense of crisis pervades *Our Country*. Heir to all that was great in Western civilization, the religion of Israel, the culture of Greece, and the polity of Rome, Strong wrote, America was destined by Providence to dominate world civilization. Its own future would be settled in two uncivilized areas, the unsettled West and the urban East, which were imperiled by immigration, Roman Catholicism, Mormonism, intemperance, socialism, and concentrated wealth. America could fulfill its destiny only by concerted home missions to civilize the West and the city. The country's salvation "may be certain in the counsels of God," Strong said; "but it is not necessary. I believe it to be conditioned on the church's rising to a higher spirit of sacrifice." This was of world historic importance because America was peculiarly the heir to Anglo-Saxon traditions of civil liberty and spiritual Christianity, the most powerful agents of human progress. "It follows then that the Anglo-Saxon, as the great representative of these two ideas, is divinely commissioned to be, in a peculiar sense, his brother's keeper," said Strong. In the rapid growth and expansion of English-speaking people across the globe, he saw a divine determination to shape the future of civilization. "Does it not look as if God were not only preparing in our Anglo-Saxon civilization the die with which to stamp the peoples of the earth," he asked, "but as if he were massing behind that die the mighty power with which to press it?"[5]

Quickened by the drumbeat of his Anglo-Saxon triumphalism, Josiah Strong upped the rhetorical ante. Powered by their money-making capacity, colonizing genius, and intense energy, he argued, Anglo-Saxons held the world in their sway. "These tendencies infold the future; they are the mighty alphabet with which God writes his prophecies," he wrote. "It seems to me that God, with infinite wisdom and skill, is training the Anglo-Saxon race for an hour sure to come in the world's future." Once America's frontier was closed, Anglo-Saxon power would be loosed on the world. "Then will the world enter upon a new stage of its history—*the final competition of races for which the Anglo-Saxon is being schooled*," Strong trumpeted. "Then this race of unequaled energy will spread itself over the earth. If I read not amiss, this powerful race will move down upon Mexico, down upon Central and South America, out upon the islands of the sea, over upon Africa and beyond. And can anyone doubt that the result of this competition of races will be the 'survival of the fittest'?" In the process, Anglo-Saxons would reshape humanity in their own image. "Is there room for reasonable doubt," he asked, "that this race is destined to dispossess many weaker races, assimilate others, and mold the remainder, until in a very true and important sense it has Anglo-Saxonized mankind?"[6]

Offensive as Josiah Strong's vision of an Anglo-Saxon eschaton may be, it is not rightly understood as racist. He was not always consistent, but "Anglo-Saxon" was not really a racial category for Strong. Anglo-Saxons were English-speaking people who were the vehicles of God's redemptive purposes because of their cultural, not racial, purity. Their superiority derived from a genetic heterogeneity and was strengthened by foreign admixtures in America. It might be "devitalized by alcohol and tobacco" and would "decay but for

Josiah Strong, radical cultural assimilationist (Harlan Paul Douglass, *The New Home Missions* [New York: Missionary Education Movement of the United States and Canada, 1914], opposite p. 132)

the salt of Christianity." The religious life of the Anglo-Saxon was "more vigorous, more spiritual, more Christian than that of any other," he wrote. "Not that Anglo-Saxons are righteous over-much. They will have to answer for many sins against weaker races and against the weaker of their own race. They produce as worldly, as gross, as selfish and beastly men and women as do any other people, but for all that they exemplify a purer Christianity and are today a mightier power for righteousness on the earth than any other race." To convert, to "Anglo-Saxonize," to "Americanize," and to "Christianize" were essentially interchangeable terms for Strong. The church should serve as an "alembic" in which this transformation of other peoples would take place.[7]

In 1886, soon after Our Country was published, the American Missionary Association nominated Josiah Strong to be president of Atlanta University. He declined the offer, leaving Ohio instead to become general secretary of the Evangelical Alliance. It may have been an error to nominate so radical an assimilationist as president of Atlanta University; it was a shocking error if he is rightly regarded as a racist. Strong did plead for immigration restriction to protect Anglo-Saxon stock from the injection of "inferior blood." But in the same breath he said: "I do not imagine that an Anglo-Saxon is any dearer to God than a Mongolian or an African." In The New Era he wrote: "The meeting of many races here as nowhere in the world, with equal rights before the law, with like educational, social, political, and industrial opportunities open to them, is peculiarly favorable to the eradication of race prejudice and the cultivation of a broad sympathy which must precede the coming brotherhood of man." If his nomination as president of Atlanta University was an error, it went unnoticed. His sister, Mary, joined the faculty of the AMA's Talladega College in 1893; later, he served on its board of trustees.[8]

There was considerable praise and criticism of Josiah Strong's Our Country among black intellectuals. The African Methodists' I. D. Barnett commended his "admirable book," the Methodists' J. W. E. Bowen praised it as an "excellent monogram," and the Episcopalians' Alexander Crummell called it an "able, startling, striking Tractate." Crummell objected to the assimilationism, not racism, of Josiah Strong's argument. "Dr. Strong evidently forgets that the principle of race is one of the most persistent of all things in the constitution of man," he said. "It is one of those structural facts in our nature which abide with a fixed, vital, and reproductive power. Races, like families, are the organisms and the ordinance of God; and race feeling, like the family feeling, is of divine origin." The irony of Alexander Crummell's criticism is that he fatally confused two different things: cultural assimilation and racial amalgamation. Something of an ethnocentric himself, he was bitterly opposed to miscegenation, deeply suspicious of light-skinned mulattoes, and feared that Strong was opening the door to racial amalgamation. But Crummell had spent his whole life in mission, spreading Anglo-Saxon cultural values among Africans and black Americans. In Josiah Strong's terms, Alexander Crummell was the foremost black Anglo-Saxon of the age.[9]

An African Methodist Episcopal pastor, Theophilus Gould Steward, challenged Josiah Strong more directly by striking at the myth of Anglo-Saxon civilization that Strong celebrated and Crummell served. Strong was a writer of great "theoretical power" and ability as "a collator of the signs of the times," said Steward, but he suffered from "a singular obtuseness in reading them." His "frantic floundering" on a "sea of speculation" was undirected by "a word from revelation" or "a principle of sound philosophy." The idea of civil liberty and pure spiritual Christianity was embodied "nowhere but in the dreams and fancies of self-applauding men," said Steward. The Anglo-Saxon idea is *clan.* "The civil liberty is always for *us*; subjugation, slavery and death have always been for the rest of mankind," he said. "Clan, first, last, and always! Only the clan idea has broadened to the extent of a nation in Europe, and to the extent of a *color* in America. To this idea all others, whether of liberty, justice or religion, are subordinate." The Anglo-Saxons' "pure spiritual Christianity" apparently meant that "the contemned, despised, hated, darker races will have been civilized off the face of the earth, and the whole world will be white." If one believed Strong, said Steward, God was on the Anglo-Saxon payroll and other races were created to serve it. Even Anglo-Saxon vices would serve their purposes by clearing the obstructing races from their path. "Surely this God is very good to the Saxon, although so very cruel to the Indian, Negro, Chinaman and the rest of mankind," he concluded. "Pray tell us what is this new-fangled doctrine but the old pro-slavery doctrine revamped?"[10]

Twenty years later, an anonymous black intellectual, possibly J. W. E. Bowen, praised Strong as "a brilliant writer on present-day social questions." But he asked the relevant critical question: "Shall we Anglo-Saxonize or Christianize?" Strong's gracious assurance that Anglo-Saxons were no nearer to God than Mongolians or Africans was patronizing, he said. His superficial social Darwinism was "the quintessence of barbarism," the antithesis of biblical ethics, "diametrically opposed to the teachings of the Master of human hearts." The great commandment was not to "Anglo-Saxonize" all nations but to make disciples of them. "The scriptures teach not competition, but co-operation," he said. "It is not the business of civilization to crush out any species of God's humanity. It should help every people to come to the fulness of its manhood as God has endowed them. The attempt to destroy racial idiosyncrasies is contrary to the inherent purpose of the Maker of these different types of the one *genus homo*."[11]

In 1898, Josiah Strong left the Evangelical Alliance to found the American Institute for Social Service, a social reform lecture bureau and publishing agency supported by the conservative Northern philanthropists and Southern educators of the Southern education movement. He sought advice in race relations from Edgar Gardner Murphy and Booker T. Washington. He praised Robert C. Ogden's role in "the educational revival which is taking place in the South," which was "helping to remove some of the old prejudices between the North and South and making these two sections one sympathetically as they are one politically."[12] By 1900, Lyman Abbott, Murphy, and Washington were arguing against imposing Anglo-Saxon culture on black people. Even higher education ought to grow out of one's past experience; otherwise it would alienate talented black people from their own history and the black masses. "The missionary makes a mistake who tries to convert the negro into an Anglo-Saxon," said Abbott. "Let us not be guilty of thinking that the white man and the Anglo-Saxon are the mold to which men must conform themselves." Like Crummell, Andover Theological Seminary's George Harris attacked the assumptions of Strong's cultural assimilationism. "The races themselves are radically unlike," he argued. "The apostle of equality must be zealous indeed if he expects to fuse all racial characteristics in the alembic of equality. He may hope for fraternity, but only in dreams can expect homogeneity." To be Anglo-Saxon, Chinese, Latin, or Negro, said Harris, "is to have certain characteristics which are part of one's constitution and which one cannot change any easier than the leopard can change his spots, or the Chinaman or negro his coloring."[13]

After 1900, even Josiah Strong abandoned the idea that the Anglo-Saxon cultural mold must be stamped on other peoples of the earth. Instead, he saw persistent differences of culture and race as part of a divine economy. In 1905, he endorsed a council of friends of Africa to protect "the undeveloped races of the world from the vices of civilization" and praised the work of an American-educated African prince, Momolu Massaquoi, in Sierra Leone. The prince was "not attempting to make Caucasians out of Africans," Strong wrote, "but in his own words 'to develop an African civilization independent of any, yet, like others, on a solid Christian foundation.'" By 1913, Strong argued that "the race problem is not to reduce all races to a single type, thus silencing the discords which have made so much of the past hideous, but rather to perfect each note and tune them all for heaven's harmony of brotherhood on earth."[14]

Inherited racial antipathy remained a problem in America, Strong believed. "How shall such a heterogeneous multitude be transformed into Christian Americans—made one in loyalty to Christ and country?" he asked. Churches and social settlements could develop a common sense of brotherhood, positive views of others, and racial toleration by teaching the brotherhood of man, the responsibility of brother for brother, and "Biblical evolutionary ethics." He allowed no color line in the brotherhood of man, but Strong held that evolutionary ethics should acknowledge current realities in race relations and differences of development in white and black races. Thus, the church should support separate institutions in black communities, condemn racial violence, and insist on equality before the law regardless of race. Strong also admitted the historic failure of cultural Christianity in race relations. "It was a 'Christian' people or prince who perpetuated the horrors of the Congo," he noted. "It was 'Christian' nations who for generations carried on the African slave trade; and by the irony which had more than poetic fitness, the name of the first slave ship was 'The Jesus.'" Yet, he believed that social Christianity embodied in the law of Christian service could lay the basis for universal spiritual unity, end exploitation of one race by another, and eliminate the conceit of racial superiority.[15]

Josiah Royce's conservative assimilationism was rooted in his social ethic of "loyalty" and looked to salvation in the "beloved community." His English-born parents immigrated to the United States as children, grew up in rural New York, and sought their fortune in California's gold rush of 1849. Young Royce was born in the five-year-old mining town of Grass Valley in 1855 and tutored, largely in the Bible, by his mother until he was eleven years old. This background might have offered the ingredients for a rootless individualism, but Josiah Royce found it otherwise. He recalled being surprised when his mother said that the town had "the characteristics of a new community." But "why do they call all this new?" he mused. "To my mind, the town seemed quite as if it had always been there. The old people taught me the old ways, just as the people in any land teach a child." Life in the frontier mining town fostered cooperation among people of diverse backgrounds. "All about me there were foreigners, French, Spanish, German, Irish, English in their origins," said Royce. "Even in a community composed of the most various nationalities, there was present the same tendency to an assimilation from the outset. The foreigners determined no important part of our life. We in turn were molding to our own ways their life." Royce's attitude toward other peoples was genial, but there was no anguished meditation on what was lost in the process of assimilation. "In the end their systems of ideas must yield to ours,—and did so. We who were Americans early learned the necessity of tolerating that we might assimilate, while the foreigners from the first tended to accept the situation and to become assimilated." All the elements of Royce's conservative assimilationism are in these mature reflections on a community of loyalty in a ten-year-old frontier town.[16]

In 1866, Royce's family moved to San Francisco, where he attended public schools. He entered the University of California five years later to study literature and philosophy. In his senior year, Royce noted that "national pride, prejudice of race, or jealous care of ancestral dignity" often prevent people from being "truly philosophical." Impressed by the young man's potential when he graduated in 1875, local businessmen agreed to pay for a year of study in Europe. In Germany, Royce read Fichte, Hegel, Schelling, and Schopenhauer; he attended lectures on anthropology, history of philosophy, and logic at the University of Leipzig. Given the opportunity to study with Europe's leading metaphysician, he moved to Goettingen to attend Hermann Lotze's lectures on metaphysics and practical philosophy. Leaving Germany under the influence of Lotze's personalism, Royce returned to the United States, completed his doctorate at Johns Hopkins in 1878, and taught literature for four years at the University of California.[17]

In 1882, Josiah Royce joined the philosophy department at Harvard, inaugurating the "golden age" of American philosophy. Its collegial debate between William James, the great American pragmatist, and Royce, the last great American idealist, turned largely on epistemology and definitions of the self, issues removed from social and political philosophy. Royce admitted that "a familiar charge against idealism is that it is an essentially unpractical doctrine." One of his critics called Royce an academic snob who remained aloof from social and political issues. A close student of James and Royce claims that neither of them were "social and political thinkers of any stature." Their work in these areas was "slight," says Bruce Kuklick; "their analyses lacked intellec-

Josiah Royce, conservative cultural assimilationist (Harvard University Archives)

tual substance, and their applications were conventional and often trivial."[18] Yet, from his long effort to ground the human religious sensibility in an absolute idealism through his major essay on race relations to his vision of salvation for the "beloved community," Royce was a thoughtful advocate of a humane approach to race relations in his generation and he bequeathed a legacy of ideas capable of moving masses of people long after his death.

Royce believed that a viciously competitive individualism and the rise of anomic masses threatened to destroy the American sense of community. He drew on his historical studies and religious idealism to develop a social ethic adequate to the challenge. Against both threats, Royce asserted the importance of "loyalty" as the supreme ethical value. The self could become authentically itself only in community, he thought. Loyalty is "the heart of all the virtues, the central duty amongst all duties," and "the fulfillment of the whole moral law." All other virtues—justice, charity, industry, wisdom, spirituality—were definable in terms of enlightened loyalty. By loyalty, Royce meant "*the willing and practical and thoroughgoing devotion of a person to a cause*" that united him or her to other persons. He knew that "loyalty" was an insufficient guide to decisions among competing loyalties, but Royce suggested that you "choose your cause, and so serve it, that thereby you show forth your loyalty to loyalty, so that because of your choice and service to your cause, there is a maximum of increase of loyalty among your fellow men." Even if one made choices with the intent of maximizing loyalty among others, it was possible to be mistaken. "We are fallible," he admitted, "but we can be decisive and faithful; and this is loyalty." Enlightened loyalty excluded false centers of loyalty, according to Royce. It is "at war only with disloyalty, and its warfare is only a spiritual warfare. It does not foster class hatreds; it knows nothing reasonable about race prejudices, and it regards all races of men as one in their need of loyalty."[19]

In a paper related to the development of his ethical theory, Royce addressed Chicago's Ethical Culture Society in 1905 on "Race Questions and Prejudices." It suggested some principles to those who would look at "race questions fairly and humanely." Increasing interracial contact and conflict in the twentieth century would keep questions of the equality, superiority, or inferiority of races before us. "Are they by their presence and their rivalry essentially perilous to one another's interests?" he asked. If so, "what one amongst them is there whose spread, or whose increase in power or in number, is most perilous to the true cause of civilization?" Is humanity's future threatened by a "yellow peril," a "black peril," or, even, a "white peril"?

If social science could answer such questions, he would accept its verdict, Royce said. "When I observe, however, that the *Rassentheoretiker* frequently uses his science to support most of his personal prejudices, I begin to wonder whether a science which mainly devotes itself to proving that we ourselves are the salt of the earth is after all so exact as it aims to be," he said. "When men marshall all the resources of their science to prove that their own race prejudices are infallible, I can feel no confidence in what they imagine to be the result of science."[20]

Royce pointed to the examples of Japan and Jamaica. Western perceptions of Japan had changed several times in his own lifetime. "The true lesson which Japan teaches us today," he said, "is that it is somewhat hard to find out by looking at the features of a man's face, or even at the color of his skin, or even at the reports of travellers who visit his land, what it is of which his race is really capable." Even if black Southerners were innately inferior, Royce asked if they must be kept in their place by methods that agitated both races. In Jamaica, slavery had been severer, the economy less rewarding, and, at 40 to 1, the ratio of black to white population far higher than anywhere in the South. "Despite all these disadvantages," said Royce, "our own present Southern race-problem simply does not exist. There is no public controversy about social race equality or superiority." With a property qualification for voting, he said, relatively few black Jamaicans voted, but a majority of its legislative council was black. There was a rich social differentiation among the black islanders, including a professional class, civil servants, landed proprietors, poor peasants, urban beggars, and criminals. But the black Jamaican was "on the whole, neither painfully obtrusive in his public manners, nor in need of being sharply kept in his place," said Royce. Rather, he was peaceful, law-abiding, loyal, aspiring, advancing in education, and "wholesomely self-conscious." White Jamaicans controlled the island's destiny without the constant agitation characteristic of Southern race relations. The key to Jamaica's amicable race relations, Royce argued, was English administration and reticence. After emancipation, England reorganized Jamaica's government to draw qualified black islanders into it and drew support from the black masses by an evenhanded administration of justice and services. Proper administration inculcated loyalty, order, self-governance, and self-respect without the South's cry of "negro domination." In contrast to strident Southern assertions of "white supremacy," Royce recommended English reticence. "Be my superior, quietly, simply showing your superiority in your deeds, and very likely I shall love you for the very fact of your superiority," he said. "But tell me that I am your inferior, and then I may throw stones. Superiority is best shown by good deeds and by few boasts."[21]

Based on the Japanese and Jamaican examples, Royce held that we too often confuse accidental, external features with essential, internal qualities in assessing other races. Using external features, anthropologists disagreed hopelessly about classifying races. As a philosophical idealist, Royce was more interested in their moral character, mind, and spirit. "We know too little about the natural history of the human mind," he observed, "to give any precise information as to the way in which the inherited aspects of the minds of men really vary with their complexions or with their hair." Anthropology had demonstrated that "primitive races" of all ages were "brothers in error and in ignorance," remarkably similar in morals, mind, and spirit. When we recall that our ancestors were primitive people, he said, the common features do not flatter our vanity. Untutored by the cultural relativism of later anthropologists, Royce dismissed primitive mores as "the common enemy" against which "civilized man has still constantly to fight." For the Harvard idealist, it was the mind and spirit of a people, not biologically determined hair texture and skin color, that were real.[22]

Some races might have a larger "capacity for civilization" than others, Royce allowed, but tests of it rarely occurred in a vacuum. Had Rome tried to civilize the Germanic tribes with rum, guns, infectious diseases, and "such gentle arts as we now often use," he said, German barbarians might have proved their natural inferiority. "For man, whatever his race, is an animal that you unquestionably can debase to whatever level you please," Royce wrote, "if you only have power, and if you begin early enough, and devote yourself persistently enough to the noble and civilized task of proving him to be debased." Descendants of German barbarians should not boast until they had given other races an "equal opportunity to show of what sort of manhood they are capable." Civilization had its origin in no single race. It arose, not because of racial qualities, but because of environmental conditions that favored certain forms of social organization. The ancient Chinese and Indians of Central America had shown that non-Caucasians had given rise to high civilizations. Science knew nothing of a fixed, inherited mental character peculiar to any race, said Royce. If such knowledge could be had, it would only be revealed by a science of the future or at Judgment Day. From a scientific point of view, then, America's race problem was caused by nothing inherent in the races themselves but by race antipathy. It was elemental, instinctive, and widespread, capricious and highly suggestible. It could be cultivated, made sophisticated, and given status as sacred truth. But Royce argued that race antipathies were a "childish phenomena, on a level with a dread of snakes, or of mice; phenomena that we share with the cats and with the dogs, not noble phenomena, but caprices of our complex nature." With proper social conditioning, he said, one might even react with similar antipathy to one's own brother.[23]

Royce's essay on race relations was incomplete. It said little about justice, but his challenge to religious and scientific sanctions for race antipathy was a deeply humane statement. "I am a member of the human race," a race that was "considerably lower than the angels, so that the whole of it badly needs race-elevation," Royce concluded. "In this need of my race I personally and very deeply share. And it is in this spirit only that I am able to approach our problem." Thus, Josiah Royce identified with a universal human condition: fallen, divided by false centers of loyalty, in need of reconciliation and redemption. This universal human community was, nonetheless, beloved of God; and His love and loyalty were made known to us in Jesus Christ. In this way, Royce reinterpreted St. Paul's understanding of the church as the Body of Christ and extended Paul's metaphor to include all humanity as the "Beloved Community." It was, he said, "an ideal community of all the faithful, which was to become the community of all mankind, and which was to become some day the possessor of all the earth, the exponent of true charity, at once the spirit and the ruler of the humanity of the future."[24]

Northern white liberals and black conservatives and radicals praised Royce's essay. "The views of Prof. Royce are calculated to help forward most satisfactorily the question of the relation of the races," said Booker T. Washington, "not only in America, but throughout the world." Mary White Ovington agreed that race, class, and religious antipathies were not sacred and told W. E. B. Du Bois that Royce's essay "is the best word yet." Noting his teacher's death in 1916, Du Bois said black Americans had lost "a fine fibered friend. His book, 'Race Questions and Other American Problems,' should be in every black man's library." By contrast, even Southern white moderates Willis Duke Weatherford and Edgar Gardner Murphy were extremely critical. Royce's book could "hardly be called unbiased or scholarly," said Weatherford; "few Southern men will accept Professor Royce's statement that race antipathies are on a 'level with a dread of snakes and of mice.'" Royce's tendency to ignore the stubborn realities of racial inequality led to "a spurious 'catholicity of race,'" Murphy argued. It subtly told "the weaker group that it has nothing peculiar to itself, which it must sacredly conserve in the interest of all," he said; and subtly made it difficult for "the stronger group" to preserve its individuality as "a thing too sacred, too indispensable to the service of the world, to be delivered up on the one hand to the dragging pressure of lower groups, or to be surrendered, upon the other hand, to those self-corrupting antipathies, to which it is forever tempted." If the state acted on Royce's false egalitarian "racial cosmopolitanism," he argued, it could do untold damage to the weaker black race, the stronger white race, and the whole society.[25]

**N**one of the theologians of race relations was more widely respected than Edgar Gardner Murphy. Lyman Abbott, Washington Gladden, Thomas Wentworth Higginson, Francis Greenwood Peabody, and Josiah Strong praised his "brave" and "statesman-like" work in race relations. Black conservatives Robert Russa Moton and Booker T. Washington, Southern white moderate Willis Duke Weatherford, and Northern white liberal Mary White Ovington all paid him tribute. He has been called a conservative, a liberal, and a progressive, but the humane terms of Murphy's conservative separatism made him the era's foremost spokesman for a genteel American racism.[26] He was a postbellum heir, by adoption, to the traditions of the Old South's plantation elite. Born at Fort Smith, Arkansas, Murphy was raised by his mother in San Antonio, Texas, after his father abandoned the family. Guided by his rector, young Murphy chose to become an Episcopal priest and entered the University of the South at Sewanee, Tennessee, in 1885. There, he was influenced by William Porcher DuBose, who embodied the university's lingering commitment to the values of the Old South and represented the denomination's most sophisticated theological rapprochement with modern thought. To Hermann Lotze's *Last Lectures in Practical Philosophy and Religion*, recalled another student, DuBose "wisely sentenced us for life." After graduating from Sewanee and study at New York's General Theological Seminary, Murphy returned to Texas parishes in San Antonio and Laredo. In 1893, when a black man accused of raping and killing a young white girl was burned to death at Paris, Texas, he called a protest meeting, which approved his resolutions condemning the atrocity. Thereafter, in parishes at Chillicothe, Ohio, and Kingston, New York, Murphy developed a broad churchly theology for his conservative social gospel.[27]

Murphy saw history as the course of development of the divine in human

Edgar Gardner Murphy, conservative racial separatist (courtesy Dr. Lois Murphy, Washington, D.C.)

experience and understood freedom as the fulfillment or perfection of a naturally given potential. He learned from DuBose that an informing principle works to shape the destiny of all things. His explication of Judges 9:8–15 is a revealing example of this attitude. "The trees went forth on a time to anoint a king over them, and they said unto the olive-tree, Reign over us. But the olive-tree said unto them, Should I leave my fatness, wherewith by me they honor God and man, and go to be promoted over the trees? And the trees said to the fig-tree, Come thou, and rule over us. But the fig-tree said unto them, Should I forsake my sweetness, and my good fruit, and go to be promoted over the trees? etc." The fig tree knew that its fulfillment lay not in being king of the trees, said Murphy, but in the sweetness of its fruit. "For the fig-tree to leave its own real task," he noted, "would be to mark it out as a failure of the saddest sort—a failure to be and to do the only thing in all the universe that it was meant to be and do." The olive tree would be perfected as an olive tree, the fig tree as a fig tree, each in appropriate relation to the other. What was true of the trees was true of every generic creature in the universe. "The real measure of the success or failure of each life," Murphy wrote, "is the measure of its self-fulfillment."[28]

Murphy's social and political thought challenged liberal individualism with an anti-individualistic organicism. He traced a wide range of social problems—child labor, the decline of religious authority, and overconfidence in a democratic franchise—to the acids of modern individualism. To be fully human, he said, was to be in community, a community kept stable by ties of habit and enriched by mutual service. It found normal expression in institutions: church, family, corporation, and voluntary societies, a complex of interrelating interests that bound individuals to each other and groups to society as a whole. In them, said the latter-day Burkean, was "the fabric of every institution which time holds dear." As a conservative, Murphy believed that order must take priority over freedom in society because without the former the latter is impossible. But coercion employed to preserve order could lead to society's subsequent corruption. Thus, the rule of law was absolutely necessary in society, he believed. But law must be an organic expression of historical experience, for "our own experience is, somehow, the final authority against arbitrary methods." Even as he was drawn to the social problems of his day, Murphy was impressed by their tenacity. "The great problems of life are never solved in any mathematical or final sense," he said. "They are solved only in the sense that their elements find a working adjustment to one another, an adjustment consistent, in larger and larger measure, with wisdom, right, happiness; but always coincident with the possibility of misconception and with recurrent periods of acute antagonism." But Murphy was cautiously optimistic about society's ability to resolve great social problems in the direction of righteousness because of his strong sense of history's constraining influence upon the present.[29]

In November 1898, Murphy was called to St. John's Episcopal Church in Montgomery, Alabama. He addressed the social crises of the New South from its pulpit: child labor, public education, and race relations. Three years later he resigned from his parish and in 1903 he left the priesthood to concentrate on these issues. In 1901, he organized the Alabama Child Labor Committee and led a campaign to limit and regulate child labor in the state. Felix Adler called Murphy the "founder and father" of the National Child Labor Committee, which was organized in 1904. But the Alabama reformer saw its task as restricted to coordinating the work of state and local committees. States rights logic forced him to oppose national legislation against child labor. When he resigned from his Montgomery parish, Murphy became executive secretary of the Southern Education Board and directed its campaigns for increased state and local support of public education in the South. Education was the safe reform, he said, binding the irresponsible into the responsible, the chaotic into the coherent, and directing unrealized potential toward its ordained fulfillment.[30]

Murphy assumed that race antipathy was a positive force, natural in human society. He shared that assumption with Thomas Dixon; it distinguished their attitudes from those of the racial assimilationists. But, unlike Dixon, Murphy drew a distinction between race hatred and race antipathy. "The former is a curse, the latter is a blessing to the white man, to the Negro, and to the land," he argued. Race antipathy "is a force, conservative of racial integrity, of social purity, and the public good." Wise social policy would not try to eradicate it but to acknowledge its primordial character and "educate it into finer forms." Murphy did not assert multiple origins of the races, but he inherited an intellectual tradition sympathetic to theories of racial polygenesis. He traced racial differences back to history's horizon and projected them into the distant future. "To prove that all men, ages ago, were much alike and that we may not declare dogmatically against the ultimate parity of racial groups," he argued, "does not abolish the obvious stubborn realities of a world in which races are not upon a par and in which the respective families of men are no longer alike." For Murphy, one's race was the foremost source of identity. "The deepest thing about any man—next to his humanity itself—is his race," he said. It was the form of one's humanity, given in nature and struggling through history to its fulfillment. "The negro is no exception," Murphy said. "The force and distinctness of his racial heritage is peculiarly, conspicuously strong. This persisting and persuasive individuality of race is the ground and basis of his essential culture."[31]

If both black and white races were to realize their cultural potential in a biracial society, Murphy believed, they must dwell separately from each other, each developing out of distinctive cultural roots. Because of his race, the Negro was bound to develop a culture with African roots. "In the deeper sense," he wrote, "no negro can escape, or ought to escape the Africa of his past." The claim may sound enlightened in an age that values America's plural heritage, but Murphy undercut its appeal by distinguishing between races that had produced culture and those that had not, insisting that one searched in vain for clues to black identity in African cultural achievement. "Africa itself, in any of the intelligible terms of social experience or institutional achievement, has never spoken," he said. "The race is undiscovered and its soul unfound." Here lay the fundamental perversity of Josiah Strong's radical cultural assimilationism, Murphy thought. "No language of other races, no acceptance of the formulas and the institutions of other human groups, will quite avail," he argued. "For that which race would ask of race is not the culture of *another*, even though that other be itself; but a culture of its own, its own as the instrument of its self-revealing." So the black man's salvation lay not in assimilation, but in separation. "The hope of that race—a race full of distinctive capacities and possessing the genius for an individual destiny—lies in the development of race pride, of generic confidence, of social individuality," said Murphy. "It is just because I profoundly believe in the Negro's destiny that I beg him to follow, not those who would turn him into a white man, but those who would turn him into the worthier and finer possibilities of his own nature."[32]

Edgar Gardner Murphy was his era's most sophisticated intellectual apologist for racial segregation, the institutional form of his cultural separatism. Black people had little cultural achievement to offer, so white Americans could mingle with them only in "terms of tragic loss." It would be "an encroachment of lower standards, of cruder instincts, of weaker will,—not a reciprocal jointure through which the culture of one human family strikes hands with the culture of another," he argued, "but an alliance without an ally; a jointure in which the social achievement of one side stands comparatively at zero." Daily interaction with black people threatened a white person not so much with "Africanization," Murphy argued, but with the danger that he would not "in the freer and higher forms of his social heritage become adequately himself." Murphy's apology for racial segregation was based on a fear of racial amalgamation. He appealed to that fear in his arguments with both radical racial separatists and racial assimilationists. "Build high your walls if you will," he told radical separatists, "but give to this race also a garden of noble spaces." Repression was bad social policy because it was self-destructive. "You can force [a race's life] back and lay it prostrate," he warned, "but when you have driven it even underground it will reappear. Its living roots . . . will find their way below the foundations of your wall, will come up on the outer side—intertwined with your own growth, blended with your stock, and terrible in their confusions and in their fruitage." But if racial repression risked racial amalgamation, the danger of assimilation was more obvious. "Rather than anything which might look directly or indirectly toward the assimilation or amalgamation of these races," he insisted, "I would prefer to see an utter end to both. Better a noble extinction than an ignoble perpetuation." Better dead than light brown. Education and opportunity for black people were important to the white South, Murphy argued, because he understood society in organic, synergistic terms. A race in declension would pull the other into "the descending processes of its ruin" and one growing in efficiency would draw the other into "the ascending processes of its rise." Education and opportunity would reinforce racial identity and solidarity. The properly educated Negro, he said, would "become increasingly and more confidently a deliberate inheritor of [his] destiny, a negro."[33]

Slavery had been a poor school for democracy, Murphy believed. The freedman was suddenly thrust into an alien framework of Anglo-Saxon custom, law, and tradition. His newfound freedom was not truly his own; it was "freedom as expressed and organized through the experience and institutions of another race." Liberty is no abstraction, he insisted; it has no meaning "except under its institutional expressions." Because he understood freedom in terms of human perfection, Murphy did not believe that it could be *given* to anyone. A people can "bestow its institutions; they can give to others the conditions in which they . . . have expressed their consciousness of what a free society is to *them*," he allowed; "they can give to others those forms of self-constraint and of self-development through which their own genius has conceived its destiny. . . . But they can, in a fundamental sense, give freedom to no other race." Although it was burdened with racist assumptions, Murphy's point anticipated the important distinction between the nineteenth century's "emancipation" and the twentieth century's "liberation." Would-be emancipators might strike off the slave's formal shackles. "But the more intimate process of emancipation they cannot bestow," for those must be "self-chosen and self-accomplished." Enfranchisement of the freedmen in Reconstruction had failed, Murphy thought, because it rested on a false understanding of and produced a degenerate caricature of democracy. The suffrage might be the last of the rights black men might acquire in America. For the moment, Murphy preferred literacy or property requirements to disfranchise large numbers of poor whites and most black people. Yet, he argued, all Americans were the beneficiaries of an "invisible inheritance" of education, the rule of law, civil liberties, and religious freedom. Because they were won for him, not by him, said Murphy, the Negro might not fully appreciate these rights, but white people could not deny them to him without denying the genius of their own social order. "In a fundamental sense," he said, "we can no more make a bi-racial division of our civilization than we can make a bi-racial division of the sunshine, the rain, the returning seasons."[34]

The South was being drawn inexorably into the modern world, Murphy believed, by all the processes of social change and should seize the opportunity for an alliance with it. It might even seize leadership in the modern world because it had long grappled with the two great problems of modernity: imperialism and democracy. "For the stronger race so to dwell with the weaker as to upbuild a common state upon the basis of the common welfare and expressive of the common happiness," he wrote, "may be called the distinctive task of a democratic imperialism or of an imperial democracy; yet it is the supreme problem just now challenging the political capacity of modern peoples." This was the opportunity for Southern ascendancy, said Murphy. "The task which day by day engages our Southern States is but the characteristic problem of the modern world," he wrote. "To face this problem is to meet not only the necessity of our welfare but that special task through which we may best serve our country and our age."[35]

Edgar Gardner Murphy developed a conservative racist's critique of the New South's radical racists, such as Thomas Dixon. In them, he said, a healthy, conservative racial antipathy had soured into radical race hatred. Radicals proceeded "by easy stages from an undiscriminating attack upon the negro's ballot to a like attack upon his schools, his labor, his life," he charged, "from the contention that no negro shall vote, to the contentions that no negro shall learn, that no negro shall labor, and (by implication) that no negro shall live." Society's fundamental law could not be arbitrarily revised for temporary circumstances or differentially applied to various classes in the society. "In any society, human life in general tends to become as cheap as the life of its humblest representatives," he wrote. "The law which does not protect the weak, will not—and in the end cannot—protect the strong." Murphy's analysis reflected a profound understanding of radical racism's animus. "Its spirit is that of an all-absorbing autocracy of race," he said, "an animus of aggrandizement which makes an absolute identification of the stronger race with the very being of the state and would thus create a homogeneous society upon the basis of a homogeneity of race." Behind the vicious demands of the radicals lay a yearning for Adamic innocence, Murphy warned. "It is the old effort to begin where the land began, but to ignore its history and to forget its sins," he said, "to erase its tragedies by legislative resolution; to attain the ends of our great adventure by force of doctrine rather than through the stern realities of experience; to repeal, indeed, the very force and arbitrament of nature." The fulfillment of such yearnings was not within the legitimate options of mankind, Murphy concluded.[36]

**T**homas Dixon, Jr., falls at one end of the spectrum of white social gospel thought about race relations, but his books outsold those of Strong, Royce, Murphy, and Douglass combined. When *The Clansman* became the basis for D. W. Griffith's *The Birth of a Nation*, his racial attitudes won a more massive popular audience. The foremost apostle of radical white racism, Dixon spoke for a movement that swept the South and achieved wide influence elsewhere in the nation.[37] He was born during the Civil War on a farm near Shelby, North Carolina. Reduced to poverty by the loss of property in slaves at the end of the war, his father held the family together by farming, small-town merchandising, and preaching in Baptist churches. During Reconstruction, young Dixon recalled, his uncle organized hundreds of white men and boys when rumors said that five thousand armed Negroes were about to invade the county. He remembered fifteen hundred armed Klansmen thundering past the family home one night to seize a Negro accused of raping a white girl and lynch him in Shelby's town square. Dixon sired a mythology from such memories.[38]

Thomas Dixon entered Wake Forest College at fifteen and graduated with top honors four years later. Restless ambition drove him from graduate study at Johns Hopkins to acting on the New York stage. He returned to North

Thomas Dixon, Jr., radical racial separatist (North Carolina Collection, Wilson Library, University of North Carolina at Chapel Hill)

Carolina and was elected to the state legislature at twenty. Defeated in a bid to become Speaker of the House in his first term, Dixon was disgusted by the venality of his colleagues and vowed to abandon politics. Turning to the law, he began a successful practice and became disillusioned with it. After rejecting graduate study, theater, politics, and law within three years of graduation from Wake Forest, Thomas Dixon felt called to the Baptist ministry in 1886. He studied briefly and moved from Baptist pulpits in Goldsboro and Raleigh, North Carolina, to Boston, Massachusetts. On the way to Boston's Dudley Street Baptist Church in 1887, Dixon was astonished by the refusal of a hotel manager to allow the family's black nurse to stay with them as she had elsewhere on the northern journey. "In the name of William Lloyd Garrison and Wendell Phillips I gave him a piece of my mind," he said. "I shook the dust of the place from my feet and moved that night to a small hotel out in Roxbury." In Boston, Dixon attended a lecture on "the Southern problem" at Tremont Temple. The white speaker, who had been on a six-week tour of the region, said that the North must be prepared to face another revolutionary threat from the South. Dixon leaped to his feet in protest, denounced the speaker as a fool and a liar, nearly caused a riot, and risked his own arrest. Thereafter, he studied the Civil War and Reconstruction in order to tell the white South's story to the nation.[39]

Thinking the North was misinformed by bloody-shirt Republican politicians, partisan newspapers, and cranks who took brief tours of the region, Dixon began addressing Northern audiences on "the Southern Question." He espoused a conservative white Southerner's racial attitudes through the 1890s. Race prejudice existed in the South as elsewhere, he said, but black people were bound by ties of affection to the families of former masters and could find productive employment there. The corruption of Reconstruction regimes justified Southern white determination to rule, said Dixon, and it was increasingly expressed by legal means. African colonization was impossible, so he recommended industrial education of black people for responsible citizenship. In the interim, he recommended adopting the secret ballot and a literacy test for the franchise to eliminate two-thirds of the black and one-third of the white electorate. Lyman Abbott's *Christian Union* commended Dixon's thoughts on race relations as those of an "earnest Christian man."[40]

When he moved to New York's Twenty-third Street Baptist Church in August 1889, Thomas Dixon became an impassioned advocate of the social gospel. Jesus "taught the human race—all nations, all races, all kindred, all tribes, all classes—to look up into the heavens and say 'Our Father,'" he wrote. "When He taught the world this lesson He threw around the race the golden chord of a universal human brotherhood. He proclaimed the equality of man; equality in fraternity." But when Dixon spoke of black Americans, his sense of human brotherhood was highly paternalistic. "The South lifted the African from the bondage of savagery into the light and strength of Christian civilization," he wrote. It "lifted him at a bound across the chasm of centuries." Yet, Dixon's paternalism insisted on black Americans' essential humanity. He recalled a Southern white minister who told a black prisoner serving a life term of Jesus' enduring love. When the minister saw the prisoner again fourteen years later, his life had been changed. "Through all the outer surface of this broken life, through the black skin, the wounded body, this preacher had looked and seen in the heart of this man its divine secret," said Dixon. "At a single word of sympathy, laying hold of that divine secret, the life had been transformed, the convict redeemed."[41]

Dixon was a remarkably successful, if controversial, preacher in New York. His audiences exceeded the capacity of the church's sanctuary and worship services were moved to a large YMCA auditorium. When Dixon confessed his hope of building a massive people's temple in mid-Manhattan to John D. Rockefeller, the wealthy oilman offered to contribute half of the $1 million he needed to build it. But Dixon failed to raise the additional funds, was frustrated by the narrow denominationalism of his congregation, and resigned as its pastor in 1895 to found a "People's Church," which met at the Academy of Music. There, he continued his controversial preaching, once being arrested as a result of his attacks on Tammany Hall.[42]

Years later, when Dixon left the ministry to write fiction, the best-selling first novel of his antisocialist trilogy, *The One Woman*, illustrated the sources of his fiction. It drew in part on his experience with John D. Rockefeller and the "People's Church." Its hero is a tall, eloquent preacher, the Reverend Frank Gordon of New York's Pilgrim Congregational Church, to whom women are "instinctively" attracted. He is "the impulsive champion of the people, the friend of the weak," and "the patriot prophet of a larger democracy." Restless with his congregation's narrow vision, he preaches socialism and dreams of building "a great temple of marble, a flaming centre of Christian Democracy." Against the advice of a capitalist friend, Mark Overman, who emphasizes the ties of private property and family values, Gordon abandons his congregation and his Virginia-born wife, Ruth, for a Kentucky-born temptress, Kate Ransom, who pledges a million dollars to build a Temple of Humanity. Gordon renounces the monopolistic constraints of traditional marriage, as he and

Kate take each other as husband and wife. But when Kate refuses to sign the deed to the Temple over to Frank and announces her love for Mark Overman, Gordon kills him and is sentenced to death. He is finally pardoned by Ruth's old beau, who has become the governor of New York, and is reconciled with his former wife. Commentators who know only Dixon's life see *The One Woman* as an elaboration of his own experience. Aware that Dixon's dedication of his *The Failure of Protestantism in New York and Its Causes* (1896) to "George D. Herron, A Modern Prophet of the Kingdom of God" was followed by the scandal of Herron's divorce and subsequent marriage to Carrie Rand, others see *The One Woman* as a vicious attack on Herron.[43] Undoubtedly, Dixon saw both himself and George Herron in Frank Gordon.

Even in the late 1890s, as pastor of the People's Church, Thomas Dixon was a racial conservative. The Spanish-American War stirred him to grand visions of twentieth-century America as "a mighty Republic of three hundred millions of people—Anglo-Saxon people, with Anglo-Saxon government and Anglo-Saxon rulers." Its destiny required a mighty naval force to fulfill a divine command to occupy the tropics as a solemn trust for civilization and progress. After Wilmington, North Carolina's, race riot and a protest meeting at New York's Cooper Union, Dixon issued "a friendly warning to the Negro." He dismissed both the racial radicalism of "Pitchfork" Ben Tillman as "an abnormality, even in South Carolina," and the charges of a Cooper Union speaker that "the white women of the South are tainted by negro blood" as "the baldest ravings of a diseased mind." Dixon saw two classes of black leaders in the South: agitators, demagogues, and low-class politicians "who fatten on the Negro vote"; and noble souls like Booker T. Washington who encouraged property ownership, industry, education, thrift, and the development of character. "I venture the assertion" that Washington "has not an enemy in the white race on this continent," Dixon said. But he agreed with the Tuskegeean's suggestion that black people should "get out of politics and go into business," since it was not for Africans to govern Anglo-Saxons.[44]

Assertions of black inferiority were so common by 1900 that some black people absorbed the assumption. The most notorious of them was William Hannibal Thomas. The son of free people of color in Ohio, he served in the Union army, taught school in South Carolina, was licensed to practice law, and served in the state legislature. Leaving the South for Boston in 1885, he began to write on race issues. Joseph Cook's *Our Day* compared one of his early pamphlets with one by Philip A. Bruce: "Each is thoughtful and shrewd. The vigor of mind of the colored man is quite equal to that of the white."[45] Within a decade, more than any other black writer, William Hannibal Thomas absorbed and expressed the anti-Negro sentiment of his age.

Reverdy Ransom later recalled that Thomas's *The American Negro* was so "nauseating," so "vile and lurid," that Mrs. Thomas wept as she typed his manuscript. It praised slavery for making "rational men out of savage animals, and industrious serfs out of wanton idlers." But thirty-five years after slavery, "the negro is in every respect wholly unlike other races of men," Thomas wrote. He "is immoral. . . . He is lazy. . . . He is a coward. . . . His conscience is dead; his intellect is dense. . . . In speech, [Negroes] are silly and vaunting; in their homes, untidy and negligent; in their associations, coarse and vulgar. Their demeanor toward inferiors is pompous and arrogant, while their conduct toward superiors is always servile and craven. Moreover, as they are improvident and idle, their undertakings often begin in folly and shame, and end in sin and crime." Thomas's delineation of Negro character was a calendar of crime and vice. "So bestial are negro men," he said, "that we have known them to lead wives, mothers, sisters, and daughters to the sensuous embraces of white men." Thomas entered a demurral in his preface that might have exempted him from charges of racial slander. "Any man, of whatever hue, who exhibits the characteristic traits which I shall hereafter describe is a negro," he wrote. "Otherwise, he is not." He might have written a diatribe against an abstraction of evil: anyone who exhibits the qualities of sin and vice is a "negro." Otherwise, he is not. But, fatally, Thomas followed the missionaries' caricature to trace his catalog of evil to African origins. "Strip off negro mannerisms and you find an African savage," he concluded. Had he said "Strip off civil mannerisms and you find a savage," all his readers might have recognized themselves.[46]

*The American Negro* "dropped like a bomb in the camp of the more intelligent colored people of the country," said Reverdy Ransom. "Every one felt humiliated by it." Bishop Alexander Walters of the Afro-American Council said the book was "a wholesale and unwarranted slander of the negro race." Richard R. Wright, Jr., called it the "thoroughly sensational" product of a "distorted and immoral imagination." Such "sweeping," "false," "slanderous," and "malicious charges," said Charles T. Walker, entitled Thomas "to pass alongside Judas Iscariot, Benedict Arnold, and Aaron Burr, the trinity of traitors." The black journalist John Edward Bruce charged that Thomas was "a man who consorts with courtesans, jumps bail for debt, dishonors his notes, and lives on the earnings of women to whom he is not married." He was, in short, "the

worst onion that ever came out of the loins of the black race," Bruce concluded.[47]

Among white social gospel prophets, John R. Commons praised Thomas
for "candidly and in an entertaining literary style" discussing "the moral and
intellectual qualities of his fellows." His "strong but morbid" book "paints in
the blackest colors the mental and moral shortcomings of his own race," said
Lyman Abbott's *Outlook*. But Chicago's Jenkin Lloyd Jones called *The American
Negro* "slovenly and unscrupulous." Thomas was a "renegade" who wrote "as
nasty a book as can be found about his race," said Mary White Ovington. The
author of this "ill-considered and extravagant" book "fouls his own nest," said
the *Independent*. He "shamelessly, scandalously libels multitudes of his own
people" and does his best to hold them "in helpless inferiority and to justify
the brutes who use just his language to defend his oppression and lynchings."
Edgar Gardner Murphy challenged a favorable review in the *New York Times*. In
Thomas's book, "candor seems to have become vindictive and frankness has
passed into ferocity," he argued. Its publication was a "calamity" and its
widespread acceptance would be "little short of catastrophe." Radical white
racists happily circulated *The American Negro*. Thomas Nelson Page, Alexander
Harvey Shannon, and Robert Wilson Shufeldt adopted its anti-Negro rhetoric
in their own polemics and South Carolina's "Pitchfork" Ben Tillman distributed a hundred copies to his constituents. Black students at Harvard
complained that it was used there as a textbook in 1904. Learning of its
increased sales, Robert C. Ogden told Booker T. Washington that he would
ask the Macmillan Company to suppress it. In 1913, Reverdy Ransom noted
the death of his "old friend and sometime neighbor," William Hannibal
Thomas. He was "not a man you could become enthusiastic over at first sight,
and he failed to improve in this wise with time and proximity," said Ransom.
"Running on a small percentage of friendship at the start, he reached in the
end the point where no one felt so poor as to do him honor."[48]

But it was Thomas Dixon, Jr., who gave dramatic expression to and cashed
in on the racial tenor of his time. Dixon abandoned his "People's Church" in
1899 for lecturing and moved his family to Elmington Manor, a grand Virginia
mansion of thirty-five rooms on five hundred acres along the Chesapeake Bay.
At a dramatization of Harriet Beecher Stowe's *Uncle Tom's Cabin* in 1901, he was
incensed by its libel of his Southland. Barely restraining himself from denouncing the play from his place in the audience, Dixon resolved to write a
novel telling the South's "true story." As he toured the lecture circuits, Dixon

gathered a thousand pages of notes collected over fourteen years. In sixty days, he wrote *The Leopard's Spots* and sent the manuscript to his friend, Walter Hines Page of Doubleday, Page and Company. Page began reading late one evening, read through the night, and hurried to his office the next morning. He was so distracted that he stepped off a curb into the path of a streetcar. Page was cut and bruised by the collision, but he picked up the bloody manuscript and rushed off to send a telegram offering Thomas Dixon a contract. *The Leopard's Spots* sold a hundred thousand copies within months. Eventually, it sold more than a million copies. When *The Clansman* appeared three years later, it surpassed the record of its predecessor, ranking fourth in American book sales in 1905.[49]

*The Leopard's Spots* and *The Clansman* are in the tradition of the American race novel. In them, Dixon self-consciously reacted to Harriet Beecher Stowe's images of Southern race relations. *Uncle Tom's Cabin*'s Simon Legree returns as a Scalawag leader of Reconstruction in *The Leopard's Spots*. Stowe's well-educated mulatto, George Harris, reappears to fall in love with the daughter of a prominent Northern politician who suddenly sees the error of radical Recon-struction when Harris asks to marry his daughter. But Dixon was also reacting to Albion Tourgée's race novels, *A Fool's Errand* and *Bricks without Straw*, which were set in Reconstruction. The two men were at opposite poles in race relations, but they developed a grudging respect for each other after meeting in the early 1880s. The wooden plots and stereotypical heroes and villains of Dixon's novels are largely inversions of Albion Tourgée's, fired to life by Dixon's own experience.[50] Edgar Gardner Murphy's claim that the conserva-tive racial "antipathy" of the New York pulpiteer had soured into the radical race hatred of the Virginia novelist is surely correct. But Dixon also distin-guished between two kinds of race prejudice. The first, a mean kind, he said, reacted to the "superior powers or abilities" of another race, such as the Jews, millions of whom might be absorbed by the "Germanic" American race without changing its complexion. The other kind of race prejudice, against the Negro, was an instinct of racial self-preservation. "You can't swallow a single nigger without changing your complexion," he told a New York au-dience. Undoubtedly, Dixon's venom focused singularly on black Ameri-cans.[51]

When he wrote his most important novels, Thomas Dixon was still the Baptist preacher, steeped in biblical mythology. *The Clansman*'s Phil Stone-man/Thomas Dixon spoke for him when he said: "I love these green hills and mountains, these rivers musical . . . , these solemn forests; but for the Black

Curse, the South would be today the garden of the world!" In *The Leopard's Spots*, Dixon hoped to tell how the Civil War and Reconstruction had turned the Negro from "a chattel to be bought and sold into a possible beast to be feared and guarded," a "menace throwing the blight of its shadow over future generations, a veritable Black Death for the land and its people." If Yankee troops threatened to reduce the Southern Garden to a desert, black freedmen were the Beast who would turn it into a jungle.[52]

Thomas Dixon's black characters were not uniformly beastly. *The Clansman's* Jake rightly described himself as an "ole-fashun all-wool-en-er-yard-wide nigger dat stan's by his ole marster 'cause he's his bes' frien', stays at home, en tends ter his own business." But Dixon's "good niggers" are few, comic, and servile. For the rest, he searched his zoological lexicon for the most apt feral description: ape, baboon, beast, brute, donkey, gorilla, leopard, monkey, mule, serpent, snake, and tiger. For those of unmixed African descent, Dixon preferred analogies with the lower primates. They included *The Clansman's* Aleck, a spellbinding black politician, whose small eyes and dancing eyebrows signaled his "eager desires" with an "animal vivacity." "His head was small and seemed mashed on the sides until it bulged into a double lobe behind. Even his ears," Dixon wrote, "seemed to have been crushed flat to the side of his head. His kinked hair was wrapped in little hard rolls close to the skull and bound tightly with dirty thread. His receding forehead was high, indicating a cunning intelligence. His nose was broad and crushed flat against his face. His jaws were strong and angular, mouth wide, and lips thick, curling back from rows of solid teeth set obliquely in their blue gums." Aleck's bare, flat feet and thin, bow-legged shanks held an "oblong, protruding stomach, resembling an elderly monkey's, which seemed so heavy it swayed his back to carry it." Gus, *The Clansman's* uniformed freedman, was more representative of the "black spawn of the African jungle," Dixon thought. Gus had "the short, heavy-set neck of the lower order of animals," he wrote. "His skin was coalblack, his lips so thick they curled both ways up and down with crooked blood-marks across them. His nose was flat and its enormous nostrils seemed in perpetual dilation. His sinister bead eyes, with brown splotches in their whites, were set wide-apart and gleamed ape-like under his scant brows. His enormous cheek-bones and jaws seemed to protrude beyond the ears and almost hide them. With an ugly leer, his flat nose dilated, his sinister bead-eyes wide apart gleaming ape-like," Gus assaulted the delicate, white heroine, Marion Lenoir. "A single tiger-spring, and the black claws of the beast sank into the soft white throat and she was still."[53]

But Dixon usually reserved the feline analogy for mulattoes. Lydia Brown, the mulatto mistress of *The Clansman's* Austin Stoneman/Thaddeus Stevens, is a "strange brown woman of sinister animal beauty," with a "she-devil temper" and the "restless eyes of a leopardess." Her mulatto lover, Silas Lynch, is a man of "charming features for a mulatto, who had evidently inherited the full physical characteristics of the Aryan race, while his dark yellowish eyes beneath his heavy brows flowed with the brightness of the African jungle." On his muscular body and broad shoulders sat a massive head from which tumbled a mass of curly hair in "disheveled profusion," a veritable lion of a man. As George Fredrickson says, Thomas Dixon's novels exploited all the literary possibilities of current ideas of black animality and sexual degeneracy. The attempt to impose "African barbarism" and the rule of "black apes" on the ruins of Southern society, Dixon said, was "a conspiracy against human progress, the blackest crime of the nineteenth century." But even in Thomas Dixon's early race novels, his interpretation of "the Beast" is more complex. When a search party finds that Flora Camp was brutalized by a black assailant, the white community is instantly transformed into the "thousand-legged beast" of a lynching party.[54] The unvarnished black beast's brutal act stripped the veneer of civilization from white men. The Southern garden became a jungle where beast called to beast.

The point was made differently in Dixon's later work. In 1905, he wrote a play, also titled *The Clansman*, based on his first two race novels. A touring company took it from Richmond to New Orleans and Columbus to Topeka before opening in larger cities from Baltimore and New York to Chicago in 1906. In Dixon's hometown, Shelby, North Carolina, it was cheered enthusiastically. But one person, Thomas Dixon, Sr., was critical. "My only criticism is, Son," said the eighty-four-year-old Baptist preacher, "I felt once or twice you bore down a little too hard on the Negro. He wasn't to blame for the Reconstruction. Low vicious white men corrupted and misled him." Young Dixon replied that he tried to make that clear, but the father said: "I wish you had made it a little plainer. You couldn't make it too strong." Perhaps because of his father's criticism, the third of Dixon's racial trilogy, *The Traitor*, was more restrained on race relations than were *The Leopard's Spots* and *The Clansman*. Two years later, eighty-seven-year-old Thomas Dixon, Sr., died. In a eulogy before seven thousand people in the churchyard near Shelby, the Reverend A. C. Irvin recalled that the elder Dixon had founded twenty congregations, built as many churches, and baptized over six thousand converts. But circumstantial evidence suggests that the old Baptist pastor was active elsewhere. Freed now by the death of his father to write a play that "he had long contemplated," Thomas Dixon, Jr., wrote a different eulogy.[55]

Dixon returned to his racial radicalism in The Sins of the Father, which he wrote as a play in 1909 and published as his third important race novel in 1912. An outspoken white supremacist in it, Dan Norton, is drawn to an octoroon seductress, Cleo, a "half-savage young leopardess" from "an African jungle" in the form of "a lithe and graceful" Southern woman. The paradox of Norton's political attitude to black people and his personal attraction to her, says Dixon, was inevitable because "long association with the individual negro in the intimacy of home life had broken down the barriers of personal race repugnance." Helpless before "the silent and deadly purpose in the soul of this sleek, sensuous young animal," Norton hires her as a housemaid who sleeps next to his bedroom. "And through every hour of the long night, maddened by the consciousness of her physical nearness," Dixon tells us, "he lay awake and fought the Beast for the mastery of life." In the Southern garden, the unvarnished octoroon strips the veneer of civilization from the white man and beast calls to beast in a Southern jungle. Cleo conceives a child by Norton and he bans her from the house. Years later, she arranges a meeting between her lovely daughter, Helen, and Tom, Norton's son by his white wife. They fall in love and secretly marry. When Norton learns of the marriage, he tells Tom of his relationship with Cleo. Believing he has married his half-sister, Tom and his father agree to a suicide pact. Norton kills himself, but young Tom recovers from his wound to learn that his wife was not his sister after all. The child of Norton and Cleo had died in infancy. The cunning octoroon had adopted a white child and pretended that it was her child by Dan Norton. Tom and Helen live happily ever after, but Tom becomes a radical advocate of white racial purity and never allows a Negro to cross the threshold of his house again. "The white man's instinct of racial purity is not prejudice," he said, "but God's first law of life—the law of self-preservation."[56]

Several years after The Sins of the Father was published, a black journalist, John Edward Bruce, recalled a telling incident in Thomas Dixon's life. "A 'colored man' arrested in New York City some years ago told the reporter of the [New York] World that he was a half-brother of Thomas Dixon," Bruce wrote. "The statement was communicated to this distinguished lover of the colored race, and his reply was: 'Yes, I know that darky. He is always getting himself into trouble and I have helped him a number of times. His mother was a cook in our family in N.C.' " Dixon did not deny kinship with the arrested man, Bruce noted. *The Leopard's Spots*, *The Clansman*, and *The Birth of a Nation* undoubtedly grew out of an intimate knowledge of interracial sexual exploitation. Given the autobiographical character of Thomas Dixon's novels, the appearance of *The Sins of the Father* shortly after his father's death, and Dixon's failure to deny kinship with the arrested "darky," it seems very likely that Thomas Dixon, Jr., had a mulatto half-brother.[57]

Shortly after publishing *The Clansman*, Thomas Dixon pursued his radical racist logic in an attack on Booker T. Washington and the education of black Americans. Washington was inappropriately familiar with the families of Northern white philanthropists and his school was training black students for economic competition with white workers, which would lead to a race war and black extermination. Washington did not respond to the attacks, but Dixon pursued a campaign of self-promotion through racial vituperation. He delivered packages of his racial tracts late one Saturday night to the homes of many of New York's black clergy, offered $10,000 to Tuskegee if Washington could prove that he did not desire social equality or racial amalgamation, and challenged him to a debate in New York's largest auditorium. Dixon's logic suggested that the only alternative to race war and black extermination was to send all black Americans back to Africa. More directly, he told a Baltimore congregation: "My deliberate opinion of the negro is that he is not worth hell-room. If I were the devil I would not let him in hell." AME Bishop Henry McNeal Turner replied by denouncing the "irreligious, ungodly, hypocritical, blasphemous, and sacrilegious prattle of Dixon and his kind." Turner only regretted that "there will be a host of Negroes that will have to spend eternity in hell with Tom Dixon."[58]

Other social gospel prophets, black and white, lacked Turner's capacity to match Thomas Dixon's vituperation. New York's erratic Presbyterian, Charles H. Parkhurst, endorsed D. W. Griffith's *The Birth of a Nation* when it premiered in New York and Boston. But Federal Council of Churches executive Charles S. McFarland joined the NAACP to protest its distortions.[59] Dixon's novels were "untruthful," "unwholesome," and "immoral," said Jenkin Lloyd Jones. Thomas Wentworth Higginson condemned their "demagogic glorification of the Ku Klux Klan." Dixon's "gospel of hate," said Ernest Howard Crosby, treated delicate issues "in the spirit of the tiger rather than that of a Christian minister." Algernon Sydney Crapsey warned that with a "devilish malignity" Dixon's "infamous" works taught "contempt and hatred" of the Negro "as one who is not and never can be a human being in the same sense that the white man is human." When popular preachers teach a "doctrine of black degradation," he said, "we are face to face with the crucial question of the essential manhood of the human race."[60]

Black spokesmen were equally critical. Dixon's "moral obliquity," "want of charity," and "absence of dignity," said William A. Sinclair, put him "seriously beneath the standards of thousands of educated colored men." Kelly Miller issued a conservative's attack on Dixon as the "chief priest" of race hatred. "Your teachings subvert the foundations of law and established order. You are the high priest of lawlessness, the prophet of anarchy," urging people to violate human and divine law, he charged. "You preside at every crossroad lynching of a helpless victim," Miller wrote; "wherever the midnight murderer rides with rope and torch in quest of the blood of his black brother, you ride by his side; wherever the cries of the crucified victim go up to God from the crackling flame, behold, you are there; when women and children, drunk with ghoulish glee, dance around the funeral pyre and mock the death groans of their fellow-man and fight for ghastly souvenirs, you have your part in the inspiration of it all." T. S. Inborden, principal of the AMA's industrial school at Bricks, North Carolina, answered Thomas Dixon more subtly. A white neighbor stopped at the school with some farm produce before Christmas in 1912. In conversation with Inborden, the farmer spoke favorably of Dixon's books. Declining to debate their merit with a person whom he respected, Inborden offered to lend him two books that expressed his own thinking in race relations. On Christmas Day, he stopped at the neighbor's farm with Henry Churchill King's book on friendship and Amory H. Bradford's *My Brother*. "I have not heard any more about Tom Dixon," Inborden told King.[61]

Inborden might have added the work of Harlan Paul Douglass to his neighbor's reading list. Douglass was among the first to use the term, "the social gospel," but his name does not appear in studies of it. He was the most thoughtful theologian of race relations, but he is largely ignored by the historians.[62] As an evangelical neoabolitionist influenced by theological personalism, he avoided assimilationist and separatist pitfalls by espousing an attitude of racial transformation. Descended from antislavery, Scotch-Irish Presbyterians who became Congregationalists when they left Tennessee for Illinois early in the nineteenth century, Douglass was born in an Osage, Iowa, parsonage. When his father became secretary of the state's Congregational Home Missionary Society, the family moved to Grinnell. There, the Bible,

John Bunyon's *Pilgrim's Progress*, and church periodicals were staples of the family's devotional life. Old Stone Congregational Church was the center for public worship. Wendell Phillips endowed a pew there, provided that it always be free to Negroes. Frederick Douglass and Booker T. Washington spoke from its pulpit. In Sunday school, the little Congregationalists learned to sing:

> If you cannot cross the ocean,
> And the heathen lands explore,
> You can find the heathen nearer,
> You can help them at your door.
>
> If you cannot heal like Peter,
> If you cannot preach like Paul,
> You can tell the love of Jesus,
> You can say he died for all.

Missions had to do with foreign countries, they learned, but also with Negroes, Indians, and Oriental people in America. When a black woman took communion at Old Stone Church, Paul Douglass's younger sister, Grace, asked their mother if she did not dislike drinking from the common cup after the black communicant. "I do not remember her immediate reply," Grace recalled, "but I am reasonably sure that the Sunday afternoon lesson had something in it about equality in the eyes of God."[63]

Douglass entered Grinnell College in 1887 and came under the influence of its new president, George Augustus Gates, who had studied with Hermann Lotze at the University of Goettingen and become a spokesman for theological personalism. After graduating from Grinnell in 1891, Douglass studied theology at Chicago and Andover theological seminaries and took courses in the philosophy and psychology of education with William James and Josiah Royce at Harvard. He returned to Iowa in 1894 to serve Congregational churches and to graduate study at Grinnell with the radical Christian socialist, George D. Herron. He was an able interpreter of Herron's controversial theology and received a Master of Arts degree in 1896. After four years at Ames, Iowa, H. Paul Douglass moved to First Congregational Church at Springfield, Missouri, where he learned of local officials' exploitation of vice in the black community. If the police knew how much money a black woman earned, they would arrest her male loved one as often as she could pay the

Harlan Paul Douglass, racial transformationist (Amistad Research Center, Tulane University)

fine, he said. The black men were vulnerable, of course, but vulnerable white men were not systematically arrested and the policy was not intended primarily to protect the community. Under the fee system, the policeman and every official related to the case got a "rake-off." The graft, said Douglass, was "as regular as washday, as legal as the statute-books, and as damnable as any highway robbery." When a disreputable white woman tried to blackmail his congregation's black janitor, William McArthur, with a threat to charge him with assaulting a child, McArthur sought advice from church officers. They had confidence in him as a property owner of good reputation, but the laymen put McArthur on a midnight train to California where he stayed for six months, until it was safe to return. "This community is likely to lynch first and investigate afterwards," they explained.[64]

On Saturday, 14 April 1906, a Springfield mob sought three black men, two of whom were accused of assaulting a white woman. Their white employer vowed that they were working elsewhere at the time of the alleged assault and the victim failed to identify them, but the mob of several thousand people broke into and ransacked the county jail. Incidentally releasing fourteen prisoners, they seized the two suspects and hung them from an electric light tower, which was surmounted by a replica of the Statue of Liberty. Their bodies were cut down and burned at the foot of the tower. Later, the mob seized a third black man, said to have been guilty of murder, and treated him to the same fate. Bayonets eventually saved the black section of Springfield from the torch, but Douglass charged that "we might as well have had a jelly fish for a sheriff and a set of rag dolls for police." On Sunday morning, as they made their way to Easter celebrations, the city's white Christians stepped around the charred remains of the three black men. A grand jury concluded that the white woman had not been assaulted and that the mob had released from jail the man who was probably guilty of the murder. But all charges against the mob leaders were finally dropped. Shortly after the riot, William McArthur asked Paul Douglass "where under the stars and stripes" a black citizen could sit "in the ordinary security of Christian civilization" under "his own vine and fig-tree." The janitor was no social rebel, Douglass said, but his son had been jailed on criminal charges. The black boy was responsible for his actions, but Douglass thought that he was not given "a square deal." He had seen his father, "a fugitive at midnight," held hostage by a blackmailer. He had heard decent men confess their inability to protect a trusted man who longed to live in peace. He "had smelled the burning flesh of innocent men of his own race" and "his own weakness had been trafficked in by a venal police power." Such tragedies set one's whole attitude against the social order that tolerated them, said Douglass.[65]

Despairing of his ability to improve Springfield's race relations, Harlan Paul Douglass left Missouri for New York to become superintendent of education in the South for the American Missionary Association. "Of course I've got to live with colored brethren a good deal, but I guess I can stand it," he wrote in a candid, patronizing moment to his parents. "My years at Springfield have only made me feel more deeply the debt of white to black and while I have few illusions I am not pessimistic. As a student I do not believe that there is any such thing as essential race inferiority but only race diversity. The Negro's best is not ours, but the world needs it and he must find it." As superintendent of education, Douglass supervised the AMA's work in seventy-five schools. He was initially regarded as "a dangerous radical" by the AMA old guard, said Lura Beam. Despite fears that it would break up the home, he employed married women as teachers. Against strong opposition, he urged hiring black faculty members, turning primary and secondary schools over to local authorities, and placing Southern black and white men on black college boards of trustees. Asked for an analysis of the AMA's work, Douglass published *Christian Reconstruction in the South* in 1909, a year before he became corresponding secretary of the AMA.[66] Invoking memories of evangelical abolitionism's heritage and visions of the social gospel's hope for an age to come, it offered a thoughtful study of Southern race relations and a theological critique of racism.

Like Strong and Royce, Harlan Paul Douglass saw the South's race problem as part of a larger national problem of assimilating diverse minorities—Indians, new immigrants, poor whites, and natives of America's new territories—into the national mainstream. The task was complicated by their concentration in "our weakest spots," in cities and regions of "little assimilative vigor," he said. By assimilation, Strong, Royce, and Douglass meant conformation to the national prototype, absorption into the American mainstream, and acceptance of shared national values. But unlike Strong and Royce, Douglass believed that minorities made a distinctive contribution, thus transforming the model, contributing to the mainstream, and enriching the national values in the course of their assimilation. There were degrees of resistance to and capacities for assimilation, Douglass said, but the greater obstacle to it was the "spirit of caste" that treated minorities as incapable of assimilation under democratic conditions. He rejected the idea that natural equality was necessary for democracy. "Democracy has existed, equality never; therefore democracy does not depend upon equality," he wrote. "Its success has not been based on the natural equipment of its members, but rather on their domination by common ideals. It is the vigor and health of spiritual forces of social control that make democracy possible. 'By one spirit are we all baptized into one body.' "[67]

The Negro was the crucial "dark and massive problem" beside which "every other problem of assimilation dwindles into insignificance," said Douglass. It was the "crux of democracy," the true test of America's assimilative vigor. The temptation was to treat black people undemocratically, reject the aggressive "New Negro," and exalt the Aunt Jemimas and Uncle Bens of the old order as the highest fulfillment of the Negro's place in America. "Yet, the most perfect slave is lower than the most imperfect freeman," he argued. "However admirable the choice fruit of the old order, 'he that is least in the new kingdom is greater than he.' " The South was economically ill-equipped to bring black people into the national mainstream, said Douglass, and when its half-loaf was divided by racial bigotry black people were doubly handicapped. Southern white churches had done little to "Americanize" the region and the states had only belatedly emphasized public education, but black people had made a remarkable effort to educate themselves. The Southern education movement pointed the region in better directions, but Douglass did not embrace it uncritically. He wrote of Robert C. Ogden's education excursions: "One cannot easily be at the same time both guest and philosopher." As an officer of a Northern missionary agency, Douglass praised its more prophetic, Christ-like service. "The prophet has a strange and moving role in human history," he said. He looks down on the human struggle from a distance and grasps the situation better than immediate participants. "The strange outcome is that, 'whom he curses is cursed and whom he blesses is blest,' " said Douglass. "He thinks that his judgment of the tendencies of his day is based upon insight into the purposes of God."[68]

Douglass saw merit in both classical and industrial education, rightly conceived, for black Americans. Classical education had "justified itself both psychologically as fixing the negro's favorable status in the mind of Christendom, and practically, as the most effective strategy of race development," he said. As taught at Hampton and Tuskegee, industrial education could lead to a richer life for black people, Douglass thought; but as commonly conceived it failed to provide broad foundations for adjusting to new conditions, equip students for leadership, or deal with the psychology of underachievement. Beyond the issue of classical or industrial education, Douglass said that black people did not have adequate quality nor quantity of any education. A democratic education for black Americans, he argued, would aim at equalizing opportunity, fulfilling an individual's talents, and assimilating the black minority into the national mainstream.[69]

The South adhered to its racial creed of segregation and white supremacy, said Douglass, with great variation across the region: less severely in the border states and the Southwest than in the lower and older South; less rigorously by Southern aristocrats and businessmen than by the poor whites and their political spokesmen. It was likely to be strictly enforced in collective relationships, but was often suspended in personal ones. Interracial contact between persons of the same sex was often accepted, but contact with members of the opposite sex was highly volatile. A few white Southerners could discuss race relations rationally, but it reduced most of them to passionate tempers, which denied the relevance of common sense, fair play, or Christian ethics to the issue. But for all its variation and occasional suspension, said Douglass, the racial creed had immense subjective and objective impact on black people. Subjectively, it was an "insidious attack" on the manhood of black men and the virtue of black women. Objectively, it necessarily meant inequitable treatment by the state.[70]

Great diversity in the black community also called most generalizations into question. But New South industrialization seemed to be causing black migration to the lower South's black belt and to Southern and Northern cities; social dislocation leading to higher crime and death rates; social differentiation into a mature class structure in the black community; decreased interracial contact delaying the assimilation process; and the emergence of a "Talented Tenth," born in freedom and determined to reap its benefits. Responding to evidence that black Americans lacked physical stamina, economic ability, and moral restraint, Douglass charged the largest part of it to social conditioning and called on white Christians to help change the conditions. "At the core of the negro problem thus lies the problem of the Anglo-Saxon; a difficulty not of the blood of Africa, but of the spirit of America," he said. "Let the nation do justice to the negro in those matters in which his deficiencies are remediable and then turn over to God and posterity their share of the business." Given their degree of exclusion from the nation's common heritage, he said, the Negroes' progress was largely due to their own effort. He saw considerable progress in their growing population, occupational achievement, property ownership, institutional development, and debate between conservative and radical black leaders. Douglass observed evidence of "African survivals" among black people on Georgia's coast and even wondered if they were returning to the customs of a primitive past. If so, he argued, this was only another sign of the thin veneer of civilization that covers all humanity. "We were all digged from this same pit and under the cruder emotions our boasted veneer of civilization dissolves into the primitive," he wrote. "If the Georgia coast negro puts rice into the grave for ghosts to eat, we put flowers there—for ghosts to smell!"[71]

Douglass was not optimistic about the immediate future of race relations in the South. Increasing racial segregation would further estrange the races, but it would also draw out indigenous leadership in the black community. Economic competition would alienate black workers from white employers and white workers, but Douglass thought that common economic interests would ultimately overcome race prejudice, leading black and white laborers to join hands in the struggle against white capitalists. He believed that efforts to emasculate the black community politically had reached high tide, but that social reform might in the long run call it back into the political equation. Finally, he believed that the emergence of a group of black Americans equal to any test of merit was forcing white Americans to choose whether they would serve the God of all humanity or the idol of racial idolatry.[72]

Thus, for Harlan Paul Douglass, America's race problem was ultimately a theological issue. In the modern world, the church could not try to convert alien peoples in domestic and foreign missions and continue to shut the door of fellowship in their faces. America's race problem was the test of humanity's capacity to overcome racial bigotry, he argued. The support given to prejudice by science complicated the problem. A racist social Darwinism that argued that natural competitive processes should eliminate unfit races in the name of an improved humanity identified those processes with the intentions of God. "Does the purpose of God thwart the spirit of Christ?" Douglass asked. This was no mere academic question. "So subtle are the infections of race-feeling that thousands of men of Christian instinct" wonder if "God himself is not against missionary endeavor for the most backward races," he said. They wonder "whether the full Christian hope, especially for the negro, is not mistaken; whether the participation of his race with ours, in the Christian civilization of America, is not impossible, because of the natural racial inequality which God intended." Popular racist suggestions that Negroes were a feral race of low mental capacity, standing on a level between man and animal were without anthropological justification, said Douglass. New evidence suggested that social instincts setting one race apart from another were conditioned by environment rather than heredity. Thus, Douglass was unwilling to grant that science supported the inferiority and nonassimilability of the Negro. But what if it did? What natural processes bound black people to an inferior position or ultimate extinction? "Does the purpose of God thwart the spirit of Christ?"[73]

Douglass's answer drew on the thought of his teachers, George A. Gates and George D. Herron. The spirit of Christ stands in judgment over such an interpretation of God; God is to be interpreted only as revealed in Christ. Douglass held that two Christian considerations challenged popular prejudice and scientific racism. First, there was the personalist argument that "personalities are the ultimate stuff of the universe, and in their mutual interactions the world is a-making." In the meeting of persons regarding each others' dignity, prejudice and racism are transcended and the "race problem" is solved. Whoever structures an unjust relationship with another person violates the sacred nature of human personality. Second, said Douglass, the moral dilemma of the race question is one whose final solution is not an explanation but a choice. "Some of us believe that the order of nature is for us and for human hope," he wrote, "but if not we would go on doing just as we are doing." As the choice of faith, the Christian must follow the impulse of brotherhood even if the processes of nature ran counter to the hopes of black people, Douglass argued. "Is there any other ground of hope for anybody?" he asked. "Is Anglo-Saxon salvation based on the shape of the skull? Was science crucified for you or were you baptized into the name of anthropology? As a mortal man, is the white less transient and futile than the black? Has he any special revelation, a peculiar demonstrable clue to the mystery of life?" Even if one knew that full participation of black people in American society would mean "a lowered physical stamina, a decreasing mental capacity, an increasing moral tragedy for all," said Douglass, "we would still carry out the program of the gospel at any cost."[74]

Douglass illustrated his point with an exercise in "life-boat ethics." Mankind, a huddle of black, brown, white, red, and yellow, sailed by faith in a frail boat on an uncharted sea. There was no guarantee, least of all in science, that they would survive or reach land and salvation. Some would hoard the food supply to themselves or toss alien races from the ship in hope of reaching an Anglo-Saxon heaven. "In the splendor of morning," Douglass wrote, "the superman stands in blonde glory on a fairer shore than ever man trod. He builds his new life as far above ours as ours above the brutes. Intellect is ennobled, beauty perfected, gentleness enthroned. Women are more glorious than any dream, and all men walk in kingly freedom." Yet, the blonde splendor was deceptive. "They look into each other's faces, white and glowing, and are happy," said Douglass, "—until they go out to meet the silent and unwearied contempt of the Stars, to hear all the sounding voices of the seas cry, 'Where is thy brother?' The finest breed of humanity may inhabit a moral hell. Better be lost on the pitiless waters, starving with a huddle of colored folks, delirious but not despicable, agonizing but not ashamed. For not idly is it written, 'It is better for thee to enter into life maimed, than having two hands to go into hell.' And what shall it profit the Anglo-Saxon if he gain the whole world and lost his own soul?" In faith and hope, Harlan Paul Douglass would walk the way of the cross with his black brothers and sisters.[75]

**S**trong, Royce, Murphy, and Dixon differed in the intensity of its assertion and certainty of its permanence, but they agreed on the superiority of Anglo-Saxon culture. For the assimilationists, non–Anglo-Saxon peoples could—indeed, must—participate in Anglo-Saxon culture if they were to survive. For the separatists, black people *could not* truly participate in Anglo-Saxon culture. Attempts at cultural assimilation, they thought, would end in cultural annihilation. It was a rare, even a "prophetic," individual, black or white, who raised fundamental questions about the superiority of Anglo-Saxon culture.

The two radicals, Strong and Dixon, were more widely read than were Royce, Douglass, and Murphy. Strong's radical cultural assimilationism was one of several attitudes in nineteenth-century American home and foreign missions, including post–Civil War Northern missions in the South and American missions to sub-Saharan Africa. Under fire from white separatists and black critics, even Strong abandoned cultural imperialism's radical form by 1900. But in making his peace with cultural pluralism, Strong slipped into a separatist posture. Thomas Dixon moved from his conservative to his radical separatist attitude at the same time. His radically racist novels were overwhelmingly popular, so the public debate among these men shifted dramatically toward the separatists in the first decade of the twentieth century.

Finally, all three men at the "center" of this spectrum—Royce, Douglass, and Murphy—wrote under the influence of Germany's Hermann Lotze and his American students of theological personalism. Whatever the disagreements among them, and they were substantial, they agreed that black people were persons created in the image of the transcendent Person. To radical separatists, they said: "These are persons, not Beasts; they are not to be treated with contempt." To radical assimilationists, they said: "These are persons whose potential for cultural contributions of their own is not to be treated with contempt."

# 11

# Conclusion

Black intellectuals thought that applying the Gospel to race relations seemed certain to have a redeeming effect. The problem's solution depended on "the simple recognition of the Fatherhood of God and the brotherhood of man, and the application of the Golden Rule to the affairs of life," said Kelly Miller. "Let the Negro lay stress of emphasis upon the Ten Commandments and the white man upon the Golden Rule, and all will be well." More critically, W. E. B. Du Bois wrote that "the one great moral issue of America upon which the Church of Christ comes nearest to being dumb is the question as to the application of the golden rule between White and Black Folk." White denominations had grown largely silent, but few of the social gospel prophets, black or white, would have denied the relevance of the Fatherhood of God, the Brotherhood of Man, and the Golden Rule to race relations. As Washington Gladden and Reverdy Ransom noted, the problem was not silence but a babel of voices about their implications for the problem. Still, they called for applying the ethics of Jesus and the spirit of the Declaration of Independence in race relations. "When men confront each other and recognize in their opposite a brother," said Ransom, "barriers are broken down, the confusion is silenced, and in brotherly co-operation they . . . are animated by a common purpose that is the peace, happiness and the common good of all."[1]

Ransom thought he saw barriers breaking down at London's First Universal Races Congress. Felix Adler, founder of the Ethical Culture Society, suggested the idea at the Eisenach Conference of the International Union of Ethical Societies in July 1906. It was promoted by Gustav Spiller, lecturer to London's Ethical Culture Society, at London's Moral Education Congress in 1908 and won support from John E. Milholland, an American philanthropist who belonged to the society. The Universal Races Congress met in the sweltering heat of London's Fishmonger's Hall at the end of July 1911 to discuss relations and encourage closer cooperation "between the peoples of the West and those of the East, between so-called white and so-called coloured peoples." The congress was promoted and financed by the Ethical Culture Society and endorsed by two dozen leaders of American social Christianity. Because Milholland was allied with W. E. B. Du Bois, Booker T. Washington was not involved in planning for it. His allies, Robert Russa Moton and Charles T. Walker, attended the congress, but Washington wrote contemptuously of it and tried to divert attention to an "International Conference on the Negro" which he planned at Tuskegee in early 1912. As the Universal Races Congress convened in London, Du Bois noted that a Mohonk Conference on "dependent people" was meeting at "Mr. Smiley's hotel, where the above mentioned people are not expected to stop." The secretary of a large American delegation in London, Du Bois saw more hope in the Races Congress, where African, Latin American, Middle Eastern, and Oriental delegates could speak for themselves. But there was a great distance between them and white delegates from north Atlantic nations, who dominated the proceedings. William A. Sinclair, a black American delegate, told Mary White Ovington that he was "almost embarrassed" at the attention he got from white delegates anxious for him to know that they had no color prejudice.[2]

At an opening session of the congress, Gustav Spiller's outline of its assumptions did repudiate most popular racist attitudes. Two days later, Felix Adler defended cultural pluralism and the benefits of cultural cross-fertilization. Later, W. E. B. Du Bois presented a report on the deprivation of black people's civil rights in the American South. On the final day of the congress, Louis P. Lochner of the University of Wisconsin cited America's Cosmopolitan Clubs as evidence of the human capacity to form friendships across lines of class, race, religion, or nationality. Discussing organizations for interracial justice in England and the United States, Boston's Edwin Doak Mead proposed to establish a national society for interracial justice in each country, an international bureau of racial justice, and triennial meetings of Universal Races Congresses "until the day of interracial justice and fraternity dawns." The Universal Races Congress was widely criticized. It was composed of "long-haired men" and "short-haired women," "soppy sentimentalists" and long-winded protagonists of every imaginable radical cause, said London's press. Yet it was an important international forum for scientific evidence of racial equality and, even if its British hosts were hostile to open discussion of imperialism, Du Bois was enthusiastic about the opportunity for elite members of races from around the world to meet and exchange views. The congress resolved to reconvene at least quadrennially, but plans for a Second Universal Races Congress at Honolulu in 1913 failed because of inadequate funding. World War I ended hopes for a meeting at Paris in 1915.[3]

In the long run, the Federal Council of Churches was more important than London's Universal Races Congress to American race relations. It gave little attention to the subject in its early years, but the membership of black denominations in the Federal Council from the beginning was important. At meetings preparatory to its organization, African Methodist Episcopal Bishop William B. Derrick spoke on "The Work of Evangelization among the Negroes" and the white Southern Methodist Bishop Charles B. Galloway spoke on "American Christianity and the Colored People." The gathering's voluntary national character limited its stance in race relations to Galloway's appeal for an end to lynching through the rule of law. When the council was organized in Philadelphia in December 1908, it included several predominately Southern white and four large black denominations. "Denominational lines, doctrinal lines, and color lines were all brushed aside by the greater thought of human salvation and the best way to bring it about through the churches," said AME Bishop Levi J. Coppin. Its "Social Creed of the Churches" called on member denominations to stand "for equal rights and complete justice for all men in all stations of life," but it made no specific mention of race relations.[4]

The Federal Council of Churches moved slowly in race relations. In 1912, at its Second Quadrennial Session in Chicago, AME Zion Bishop Alexander Walters joined the council's Commission on the Church and Social Service, the Reverend W. A. Blackwell spoke for the black denominations on "The Uplifting of a Race," and the council passed a resolution congratulating black churches for the work they were doing. In 1914, the Colored Methodist Episcopal Church sought the appointment of a commission on the problems of black Americans. After preliminary planning, a Committee on Special Interests of the Colored Denominations was organized in 1916. Chaired by Methodist Episcopal Bishop Wilbur P. Thirkield, a former president of Howard University, the committee prepared a report for the council's 1916 quadrennial meeting at St. Louis. But its forthright declarations on human unity, black education, lynching, and the application of the Social Creed aroused such opposition that the future of the committee itself was threatened. The Council session adjourned to allow Christian tempers to cool and, when quiet diplomacy prevailed, both the committee and its report had survived.[5]

Like the Federal Council of Churches, the most important institution of the

American social gospel, its greatest theologian, Walter Rauschenbusch, hesitated to address race relations and did so publicly only in the second decade of the century. "For years, the problem of the two races in the South has seemed to me so tragic, so insoluble," he wrote, "that I have never yet ventured to discuss it in public." His experience was far removed from the problem. Born to German immigrant parents at Rochester, New York, in 1861, Rauschenbusch studied in American and German schools, graduating at the Gymnasium of Gutersloh, Westphalia, in 1878. Among the memories of his transatlantic childhood was having seen "a big Negro at night turning a great wheel and casting off ropes" on a ferryboat in New York City. After receiving a bachelor's degree at the University of Rochester in 1884, Rauschenbusch served two summers as the pastor of a German Baptist congregation in Louisville, Kentucky. He graduated from Rochester Theological Seminary in 1886, was ordained, the seventh in a direct line of German pastors, and served a German-speaking Baptist congregation on the edge of Manhattan's "Hell's Kitchen." There, Rauschenbusch supported Henry George's campaign for mayor of New York in 1886 and read widely in Scripture and contemporary social criticism. He was left severely deaf by an illness contracted during pastoral visits to New York tenements in the blizzards of 1888. But Rauschenbusch still heard the cry of New York's poor. His "theology for the social gospel" was born in Hell's Kitchen. Rejecting an exclusively individual gospel, he cited the failure of individual religious conversions to undermine slavery in the antebellum South, and he rejected immigration restriction to affirm the contributions of immigrant peoples.[6]

In the early 1890s, Rauschenbusch prepared a manuscript, *The Righteousness of the Kingdom*, which asserted the universal obligation of Christian love, unimpeded by barriers of class, race, religion, or national origin. "The tendency to draw such limits is as strong as ever," he said. "The history of the Negro, the Indian, and the Chinese can tell how differences of color and race can warp the sense of justice and dull the fine perception of love." He cited the example of a white Baptist in Boston who asked William Lloyd Garrison about the religion of a black fugitive who had been returned to the South. Noting the man's shock at learning that the reenslaved man was a Baptist preacher, Rauschenbusch noted that "the fate of the Negro had left him indifferent," but "the fate of the Baptist touched him." Writing under the influence of Leo Tolstoy and Ernest Howard Crosby, the New York pastor outlined his justification of passive resistance to immoral civil laws and called for a nonviolent crusade for social justice that was more disciplined and militant than brute

Walter Rauschenbusch, theologian of the social gospel (American Baptist Historical Society, Rochester, N.Y.)

force required. Rauschenbusch left New York City to teach at Rochester Theological Seminary in 1897. Only 600 of Rochester's 162,000 residents, less than 0.5 percent of the city's population, were black. But thinking that the heavenly and the earthly cities were intertwined in time, Rauschenbusch taught church history as a history of the Kingdom of God, which moved toward a racially inclusive end. Often, when he spoke of "race," Rauschenbusch meant the human race, in which superiority and inferiority referred to the superiority of democratic institutions over less democratic institutions.[7]

In *Christianity and the Social Crisis*, published in 1907, Rauschenbusch pondered the role of a prophet like Ezekiel, who proclaimed God's judgment on a disobedient people. "How would we feel if a preacher should use a public gathering on Decoration Day or Thanksgiving Day to predict that our country for its mammonism and oppression was cast off by God and was to be parcelled out to the Mexicans, the Chinese and the negroes?" he asked. "The conditions against which the moral sensibility of the prophets revolted could be equalled in any modern industrial centre. And the same sins ought to seem blacker nineteen centuries after Christ than eight centuries before Christ." Rauschenbusch and Ray Stannard Baker appeared together at the Third Sagamore Sociological Conference in 1909. There, he responded to Baker's address by observing that American society was divided by differences of race, religion, and economic class. Since black Americans shared a common religion with most of their fellow citizens, he thought that it was important to reduce economic conflict between them. "A solution of the labor question so thorough that it would be possible to hand over entire industries to the black race without evoking industrial hostility," he said, "would offer a solid hope to the negro." In the winter of 1910–11, Rauschenbusch went to Nashville to speak to a Southern Methodist Bible conference and black students at Fisk University. There, said his biographer, he also visited the city's "black bottom" and saw "Negro life at its worst."[8]

A year later, Rauschenbusch's colleague at Rochester Theological Seminary, Conrad Moehlman, wrote to him from Southern Pines, North Carolina. He had recently attended several worship services in "Jimtown," the black section of the community. "The South believes in segregation and this certainly helps to solve some of their horrendous problems," Moehlman observed.

The worship on this Sabbath was under the auspices of the Ch. of God and saints of Christ—an Adventist branch, Lot #91 of this particular division of the "mighty army." I had imagined that the poor blacks wd. be spared the quarrel over the 7th day, but the "elder" preached a fair legalistic sermon after the pattern of many I've had to listen to in the North. *God said!* And God has never taken it back. They wore brown clothes and white gloves; saluted each other with the holy kiss; jogged, marched around, swung long beribboned sticks, and were to wash feet and have a basket picnic—just like at Corinth.

Having noted the very biblical character of the black Sabbatarians' worship, however, Moehlman offered a characteristic white religious liberal's observation about black folk religion. Many white social gospel prophets thought its ethical dimension was weak, but Moehlman found it "unprogressive." "They began at 10 a.m. and remain in continuous session until 5 p.m.," he said. "I left at 12 n. & walked home rather sad, for it seemed a more urgent problem just why progress especially in religion shd. be so extremely slow." On the next day, however, Moehlman attended Baptist services in Jimtown and was pleased with the orderly worship. When the black Baptists insisted on an address from the visiting white clergyman, Moehlman offered words of advice on religious progress.[9]

In *Christianizing the Social Order*, his second major book, Walter Rauschenbusch discussed the broad human sympathy of Jesus. Jesus "went out of his way to set a Samaritan up as a model of human kindness above the priest and the Levite. That was sand in the mouth of his countrymen," said the Rochester theologian, "just as if an American orator should tell an Illinois crowd of the superior virtues of the 'Dago' and the 'Hunk,' or an Alabama crowd of the brotherhood of a negro. In Jesus we encounter the spirit that smites race pride and prejudice in the face in the name of humanity; and that refuses to accept even from religion any obligation to hold ourselves apart from our fellows. That determined breadth of brotherhood is [a] permanent landmark of the Kingdom ideal as Jesus expressed it." Rauschenbusch reasserted the point two years later in a book entitled *Dare We Be Christians?* "Christianity stands for the doctrine that we must love one another—all men, without distinction of 'religion, race, color or previous condition of servitude,'" he said. "It does not advise eliminating the unfit, but seeks to make them fit. It stands for the solidarity of the race in its weakness and strength, its defects and conquests, its sin and salvation."[10]

Compare Rauschenbusch's use of the Parable of the Good Samaritan with Lyman Abbott's interpretation. A person has little, if any, right to bring a guest into the home who is unwanted by others in the family, he said. It was a "moral blunder" to admit a Negro, a Jew, or a Roman Catholic to a white or a Christian or a Protestant school because the school was merely a larger home. "This is not the way to promote the spirit of human brotherhood," Abbott argued. "It is not recorded that the Good Samaritan took the wounded traveler into his own home. He took him to an inn." By extension, he concluded with a defense of immigration restrictions and of racial segregation in Southern schools. Noting Abbott's "entirely original exposition" of the Parable of the Good Samaritan, W. E. B. Du Bois asked: "Who says there is nothing new under the sun? Surely we are behind the times if we think this parable was meant to teach the lesson of charity at all. Let us, with Dr. Abbott, learn to consider it merely the prototype of American expediency." Two years later, Du Bois dismissed Abbott's exegesis of the parable as another example of his "singular gift in sensing the popular side of any great social question and discovering deep and esoteric reasons for supporting that side." A friend of the freedman in Reconstruction, Abbott slowly "transferred allegiance and became the most subtle and dangerous enemy of the Negro in America," Du Bois said. "He joined the slander of mulattoes, misrepresented and helped disfranchisement, and used every art of his remarkable gift of casuistry to put the religion of Jesus Christ into the service of color caste." Abbott did this, said Du Bois, with "so straight a face and such an assumption of high motives and impeccable respectability that thousands of well-meaning Americans followed his lead."[11]

By contrast, Rauschenbusch's fullest statement on race relations, "The Belated Races and the Social Problems," was published by the American Missionary Association and reprinted by the Southern Methodists' quarterly review and, in part, by the *American Missionary* and the *Crisis*. Rauschenbusch joked that he was familiar only with seminary students as a "belated race," but he took a special interest in work among the "belated races." In near personalist terms, he noted that "the purity of our Christian impulses may be gauged by the value we set on human life *as such*, by our response to purely human needs, by the intensity of our redemptive instinct going out to our lost and backward brothers." He called on the church to implant the motivating power of a progressive religion and develop an unexploitative leadership among the "belated peoples." A progressive religion would offer spiritual values to protect them from the material ravages of modernity and prepare them for cooperative economies. Calling attention to their need of continued access to land ownership, Rauschenbusch warned that "we are only a step or two away from coerced labor." Still committed to Henry George's analysis of land economics, he called for the creation of a system of land ownership in which "*the unearned values*, created by the community, will go to the community which creates them."[12]

Rauschenbusch said a truly Christian religion would instill a deep respect for the dignity of other human life and personality, "however unlovely and broken," and "stiffen the backbone of men and teach them to respect themselves." There was some justification for Nietzsche's charge that Christianity had taught the virtue of a servile patience and submission, he allowed. "I believe in gentleness and meekness, but not in servility," said Rauschenbusch. "I have no faith in force methods, and even believe in non-resistance, but not in a non-resistance of cowardice and silence. There was nothing cringing in Jesus. He did not strike back, but neither did he flinch. He was 'the terrible meek.' I am thinking of the Negro race in saying this." No resolution of race relations by Southern white men that failed to instill hope and self-respect in black men and women or pride and ambition in black communities was acceptable to the nation's Christian conscience. White Southerners who would deny black people's humanity or condemn them to a permanently servile caste might be a minority, Rauschenbusch warned, but small, determined oligarchies with inherited prejudice and economic interest had imperiled national unity and progress in the past. "We owe it to our brethren in the South," he argued, "to say that the solution of the problem does not lie that way and never will. The spirit of Pharaoh never works the will of God." White men and women, North and South, must work together with black men and women, he concluded, "in the spirit of Him who brought the evangel of freedom and human worth to the poor and backward, and through them worked miracles."[13]

Limited by distance from deep involvement in race relations, Rauschenbusch was yet mindful of American race relations in his most mature work, *A Theology for the Social Gospel*, in 1917. He cited lynching as evidence that sin was a pervasive element of human nature not by biological but by social heredity. "When negroes are hunted from a Northern city like beasts, or when a Southern city degrades the whole nation by turning the savage inhumanity of a mob into a public festivity," he argued, "we are continuing to sin because our fathers created the conditions of sin by the African slave trade and by the unearned wealth they gathered from slave labour for generations." Rauschenbusch's theology for the social gospel was an effort to make the doctrine of the Kingdom of God central to theology and organize all other doctrines around it. Short of that, he said, "the idea of redeeming the social order will be but an annex to the orthodox conception of the scheme of salvation. It will live like a negro servant family in a detached cabin back of the white man's house in the South." In his doctrines of God and eschatology, for example, Rauschenbusch criticized white Southern writers who tried to show that black people were descended from "African jungle beasts" rather than from Adam. "The very orthodox authors were willing to accept the heretical philosophy of evolution for black people," he wryly observed, "though of course they claimed biblical creation for the white. The purpose of this religious manoeuvre is to cut the bond of human obligation and solidarity established by religion, and put the negroes outside the protection of the moral law." By contrast, the social gospel would emphasize that "God is the bond of racial unity." If Christianity had a doctrine of reincarnation, he suggested, it would be appropriate to suggest that "a man who has helped to lynch a negro, might be born in a black skin and be lynched by his own grandsons." But a more traditional social eschatology would hold that "the recognition of a single God of all mankind" lays the basis for "an ethical union of all mankind in the future."[14]

When anti-German sentiment swept the United States toward World War I, it cast dark shadows over the last years of Walter Rauschenbusch's life and he identified with the experience of black Americans. When the Louisville *Courier-Journal's* editor, Colonel Henry Watterson, wrote of German-Americans as if they were "niggers," Rauschenbusch saw it as a sign of increasing intolerance of ethnic Americans in the United States. "It has been a milder form of the political disfranchisement inflicted upon the negro race in the South," he wrote. "I think that we must seize once more with conscious determination the political convictions which we have held heretofore by inheritance, and earn our heritage."[15]

Three decades after the death of Walter Rauschenbusch, the first important anthology of his work was edited by Morehouse College President Benjamin E. Mays. His student, Martin Luther King, Jr., was at the time experiencing an intellectual awakening in which Rauschenbusch played a significant role. It would make him the foremost prophet of American social Christianity within a decade. There were many influences at work in the mind of Martin Luther King, Jr., but two are especially important. He was, first of all, nurtured in the struggle of Southern black people. "It is a struggle, for though the black man fights passively, he nevertheless fights," James Weldon Johnson wrote early in the century; "and his passive resistance is more effective at present than active resistance could possibly be. He bears the fury of the storm as does the willow tree. It is a struggle; for though the white men of the South may be too proud to admit it, he is, nevertheless, using in the contest his best energies; he is devoting to it the greater part of his thought and much of his endeavour. The South today stands panting and almost breathless from its exertions." Nurtured in the struggle and the faith of the Southern black church, Martin Luther King, Jr., was bound to proclaim his message in its cadences.[16]

But King's intellectual debt to other dimensions of American social Christianity was significant. He was, in the first place, a "Morehouse man," a graduate of the Northern Baptists' missionary college in Atlanta. There, Benjamin Mays, George D. Kelsey, Samuel Williams, and others were models of the black intellectual as Christian social critic. At Morehouse, he read about nonviolent resistance to injustice in Henry David Thoreau's *Essay on Civil Disobedience*. Later, he was influenced by the teachings of India's Mahatma Gandhi, the twentieth century's most famous advocate of nonviolent civil disobedience. But King did not become thoroughly committed to nonviolence until his conversations with representatives of the Fellowship of Reconciliation shortly after the beginning of the Montgomery Bus Boycott in 1955. Thus, his nonviolence was rooted in an American tradition of nonviolent protest traced back through the Fellowship of Reconciliation, founded in 1915 by John Haynes Holmes and others, to the American followers of Leo Tolstoy, Jane Addams, Ernest Howard Crosby, Edward A. Steiner, and Walter Rauschenbusch, and the antebellum witness of Thoreau and William Lloyd Garrison.[17]

Graduating at nineteen from Morehouse, King went to Crozer Theological Seminary at Chester, Pennsylvania, in 1948. There, he was deeply influenced by the liberal evangelical theology of his major professor, George W. Davis. Reading the classical texts of liberal Protestant theology under Davis's direction, King shared their self-conscious adaptation of religious ideas to modern culture, their belief that God was immanent in and revealed through human cultural achievement, and their conviction that human society was moving toward realization of the Kingdom of God. At Crozer, said King, his reading of Walter Rauschenbusch's *Christianity and the Social Crisis* "left an indelible impression on my mind." He was critical of the Rochester theologian's "optimistic" view of human nature and his tendency to identify the Kingdom of God with a socialist economic order. But King was in debt to Rauschenbusch's critique of industrial capitalism and to his insistence that the gospel applies to the whole self, not alone to a disembodied spirit, and to the community, not alone to an isolated self.[18]

King's decision to do graduate work in religion at Boston University determined the personalist form of his evangelical liberal theology. He was probably unaware of its influence in liberal Protestant circles at the turn of the century or its importance to evangelical neoabolitionists, such as Amory H. Bradford, Harlan Paul Douglass, George A. Gates, Washington Gladden, Charles Cuthbert Hall, Henry Churchill King, Edward A. Steiner, and Charles F. Thwing, and to Southern white moderates such as Edgar Gardner Murphy and Willis Duke Weatherford in their critique of radical white racism. In the intervening years, American academic philosophy had grown indifferent to philosophical idealisms in all forms. At Boston, King studied at the last remaining citadel of philosophical and theological personalism in America and with its leading contemporary advocates, Edgar S. Brightman, L. Harold De-Wolf, Walter G. Muelder, and Peter Bertocci. "This personal idealism remains today my basic philosophical position," he later wrote. "Personalism's insistence that only personality—finite and infinite—is ultimately real strengthened me in two convictions: it gave me metaphysical and philosophical grounding for the idea of a personal God, and it gave me a metaphysical basis for the dignity and worth of all human personality."[19]

Martin Luther King, Jr., was thus deeply indebted both to the black church and to American social Christianity, generally, for the spirit of struggle and the ideas from which his dream was composed. Beyond that, many of the institutions that rallied to move the society closer to his dream—the Fellowship of Reconciliation, the Methodist Federation for Social Service, the National Association for the Advancement of Colored People, the National Council of Churches, the National Urban League, the Southern Regional Council, and others—were founded early in the century by coalitions in which the black and white prophets of American social Christianity played a significant role. The debt of King and the civil rights movement to an earlier American social gospel was clear even in the new organization that he founded. Students of King's thought have noted that the vision of the "beloved community" was its "capstone," the "organizing principle" of all his thought and action. The goal of his Southern Christian Leadership Conference, said King, was "to foster and create the 'beloved community' in America where brotherhood is a reality." It has been commonly noted that for King the "beloved community" was the functional equivalent of the biblical doctrine of the Kingdom of God. It represented his hope for the universal renewal, freedom, and reconciliation of all humanity. But his debt to Josiah Royce for that modern adaptation of a traditional religious idea has rarely been noted. "Since you cannot find the universal and beloved community," Royce had said, "create it."[20]

# Notes

## Chapter 1

1. "Negroes Lynched in Missouri," *Independent* 60 (19 April 1906): 892; "Editorial Notes," *Independent* 60 (7 June 1906): 1390; Harlan Paul Douglass, *Christian Reconstruction in the South* (Boston: Pilgrim Press, 1909), pp. 204–5; Katherine Lederer, "And Then They Sang a Sabbath Song," *Springfield!* 2 (April–May 1981): 26–28, 33–36, and 3 (June 1981): 24–26; Robert T. Handy, "George D. Herron and the Kingdom Movement," *Church History* 19 (June 1950): 110; and James M. McPherson, *The Abolitionist Legacy: From Reconstruction to the NAACP* (Princeton: Princeton University Press, 1975), pp. 346–48.

2. James Dombrowski, *The Early Days of Christian Socialism in America* (New York: Columbia University Press, 1936), pp. 132–70; Ralph Albertson, "The Christian Commonwealth in Georgia," *Georgia Historical Quarterly* 29 (September 1945): 125–42; and John O. Fish, "The Christian Commonwealth: A Georgia Experiment, 1896–1900," *Georgia Historical Quarterly* 57 (Summer 1972): 213–26.

3. Aaron I. Abell, *The Urban Impact on American Protestantism: 1865–1900* (Cambridge: Harvard University Press, 1943); Dombrowski, *Early Days of Christian Socialism*; Donald K. Gorrell, *The Age of Social Responsibility: The Social Gospel in the Progressive Era, 1900–1920* (Macon, Ga.: Mercer University Press, 1988); Charles Howard Hopkins, *The Rise of the Social Gospel in American Protestantism: 1865–1915* (New Haven: Yale University Press, 1940); Henry F. May, *Protestant Churches and Industrial America* (New York: Harper and Brothers, 1949); and Ronald C. White and Charles Howard Hopkins, *The Social Gospel: Religion and Reform in Changing America* (Philadelphia: Temple University Press, 1976).

4. Rayford W. Logan, *The Betrayal of the Negro: From Rutherford B. Hayes to Woodrow Wilson* (New York: Collier, 1965), pp. 11, 171–73, 183, 273–75. Logan borrowed the term from Purvis M. Carter, "The Astigmatism of the Social Gospel: 1877–1901" (M.A. thesis, Howard University, 1950). Many scholars endorse this interpretation: Sydney E. Ahlstrom, *A Religious History of the American People* (New Haven: Yale University Press, 1972), pp. 691, 923; Ahlstrom, "Introduction," in *Theology in America: The Major Protestant Voices from Puritanism to Neo-Orthodoxy* (Indianapolis: Bobbs-Merrill, 1967), p. 75; Glenn R. Bucher, "Social Gospel Christianity and Racism," *Union Seminary Quarterly Review* 28 (Winter 1973): 146–73; Alan Davies, *Infected Christianity: A Study of Modern Racism* (Montreal: McGill–Queen's University Press, 1988), pp. 81–84; Jacob Henry Dorn, *Washington*

*Gladden: Prophet of the Social Gospel* (Columbus: Ohio State University Press, 1966), pp. 291–94; Peter J. Frederick, *Knights of the Golden Rule: The Intellectual as Christian Social Reformer in the 1890s* (Lexington: University Press of Kentucky, 1976), p. 24; George Fredrickson, *The Black Image in the White Mind: The Debate on Afro-American Character and Destiny, 1817–1914* (New York: Harper and Row, 1971), pp. 302–4; Thomas F. Gossett, *Race: The History of an Idea in America* (New York: Schocken, 1963), pp. 172–79, 186–97, 293–94, 316–17; Florette Henri, *Black Migration: Movement North, 1900–1920* (Garden City, N.Y.: Anchor Press/Doubleday, 1976), pp. 222–23; Hopkins, "Foreword to the 1967 Edition," in *Rise of the Social Gospel*, p. vii; Martin E. Marty, *Modern American Religion: The Irony of It All, 1893–1919* (Chicago: University of Chicago Press, 1986), p. 294; Marty, *Righteous Empire: The Protestant Experience in America* (New York: Harper and Row, 1970), p. 206; May, "Introduction to the Torchbook Edition," in *Protestant Churches and Industrial America*, p. ix; Robert Moats Miller, *American Protestantism and Social Issues, 1919–1939* (Chapel Hill: University of North Carolina Press, 1958), pp. 9–10; David Gordon Nielson, *Black Ethos: Northern Urban Life and Thought, 1890–1930* (Westport, Conn.: Greenwood Press, 1977), pp. 22–23; David M. Reimers, *White Protestantism and the Negro* (New York: Oxford University Press, 1963), pp. vii, 53–54, 79–80; Jean Russell, *God's Lost Cause: A Study of the Church and the Racial Problem* (London: SCM Press, 1968), pp. 70–94; Seth M. Scheiner, "The Negro Church and the Northern City, 1890–1930," in *Seven on Black: Reflections on the Negro Experience in America*, ed. William G. Shade and Roy C. Herrenkohl (Philadelphia: J. B. Lippincott Co., 1969), p. 108; David W. Southern, *The Malignant Heritage: Yankee Progressives and the Negro Question, 1901–1914* (Chicago: Loyola University Press, 1968); Leonard I. Sweet, *Black Images of White America* (New York: W. W. Norton and Co., 1976), p. 177; Preston N. Williams, "The Social Gospel and Race Relations: A Case Study of a Social Movement," in *Toward a Discipline of Social Ethics: Essays in Honor of Walter George Muelder*, ed. Paul Deats, Jr. (Boston: Boston University Press, 1972), pp. 232–55; and Forrest G. Wood, *The Arrogance of Faith: Christianity and Race in America from the Colonial Era to the Twentieth Century* (New York: Alfred A. Knopf, 1990), pp. 365–80. The fullest treatment from this perspective is Curtis Robert Grant, "The Social Gospel and Race" (Ph.D. dissertation, Stanford University, 1968).

5. Lyman Abbott, "Remarks on 'How Can Northern and Southern Christians Best Co-operate for the Moral and Spiritual Elevation of the Negroes?," in *Second Mohonk Conference on the Negro Question: Held at Lake Mohonk, Ulster County, New York, June 3, 4, 5, 1891*, ed. Isabel C. Barrows (Boston: George H. Ellis, 1891), pp. 69–70.

6. William A. Clebsch, *From Sacred to Profane America: The Role of Religion in American History* (New York: Harper and Row, 1968), pp. 23–24. See also Jerald C. Brauer, *Protestantism in America: A Narrative History* (Philadelphia: Westminster Press, 1955), p. 252; Robert T. Handy, ed., *The Social Gospel in America: 1870–1920* (New York: Oxford University Press, 1966), pp. 29–30; Handy, "Negro Christianity and American Church Historiography," in *Reinterpretation in American Church History*, ed. Jerald C. Brauer (Chicago: University of Chicago Press, 1968), p. 105; Handy, *A Christian America: Protestant Hopes and Historical Realities* (New York: Oxford University Press, 1971), pp. 179–81; William A. Hutchinson, "Cultural Strain and Protestant Liberalism," *American Historical Review* 76 (April 1971): 411; McPherson, *Abolitionist Legacy*, pp. 346–48; and White and Hopkins, *Social Gospel*, pp. 73–

113. The fullest treatment from this perspective, Ronald C. White, "Social Christianity and the Negro in the Progressive Era, 1890–1920" (Ph.D. dissertation, Princeton University, 1972), was revised for publication as *Liberty and Justice for All: Racial Reform and the Social Gospel (1877–1925)* (San Francisco: Harper and Row, 1990).

7. Arthur Meier Schlesinger, "A Critical Period in American Religion, 1875–1900," Massachusetts Historical Society, *Proceedings* 64 (1932): 523–47. See also Abell, *Urban Impact on American Protestantism*; Dombrowski, *Early Days of Christian Socialism*; Hopkins, *Rise of the Social Gospel*; Arthur Mann, *Yankee Reformers in the Urban Age: Social Reform in Boston, 1880–1900* (Cambridge: Harvard University Press, 1954); and May, *Protestant Churches and Industrial America*.

8. Robert T. Handy and Sidney E. Mead, review of *Protestant Churches and Industrial America*, by Henry F. May, *Journal of Religion* 30 (January 1950): 67–69; Handy, "The Protestant Quest for a Christian America, 1830–1930," *Church History* 22 (March 1953): 8–20; Timothy L. Smith, *Revivalism and Social Reform in Mid-Nineteenth Century America* (Nashville: Abingdon, 1957), pp. 148–62; and Ralph E. Morrow, *Northern Methodism and Reconstruction* (East Lansing: Michigan State University Press, 1956), pp. 246–48. See also White and Hopkins, *Social Gospel*, pp. xiii–xix.

9. Some leads on the social gospel in black churches may be found in Grace Roane Gwaltney, "The Negro Church and the Social Gospel from 1877 to 1914" (M.A. thesis, Howard University, 1949); and S. P. Fullinwider, *The Mind and Mood of Black America: 20th Century Thought* (Homewood, Ill.: Dorsey Press, 1969), pp. 26–46. On the social gospel in the white South, see Robert Moats Miller, "Fourteen Points on the Social Gospel in the South," *Southern Humanities Review* 1 (Summer 1967): 126–40; John Lee Eighmy, "Religious Liberalism in the South During the Progressive Era," *Church History* 38 (September 1969): 359–72; J. Wayne Flynt, "Dissent in Zion: Alabama Baptists and Social Issues, 1900–1914," *Journal of Southern History* 35 (November 1969): 523–42; White and Hopkins, *Social Gospel*, pp. 80–113; John Patrick Dowell, *The Social Gospel in the South: The Woman's Home Mission Movement in the Methodist Episcopal Church, South, 1886–1939* (Baton Rouge: Louisiana State University Press, 1982); J. Wayne Flynt, "'Feeding the Hungry and Ministering to the Broken Hearted': The Presbyterian Church in the United States and the Social Gospel, 1900–1920," in *Religion in the South*, ed. Charles Reagan Wilson (Jackson: University Press of Mississippi, 1985), pp. 83–137; and J. Wayne Flynt, "Southern Protestantism and Reform, 1890–1920," in *Varieties of Southern Religious Experience*, ed. Samuel S. Hill (Baton Rouge: Louisiana State University Press, 1988), pp. 135–57.

10. Hopkins, "Foreword," p. vii; and May, "Introduction," p. ix.

11. Sidney E. Mead, *The Lively Experiment: The Shaping of Christianity in America* (New York: Harper and Row, 1963), p. 63. See also Perry Miller, "From the Covenant to the Revival," in *The Shaping of American Religion: Religion in American Life*, ed. James Ward Smith and A. Leland Jamison (Princeton: Princeton University Press, 1961), p. 354.

12. Clifford S. Griffin, "Religious Benevolence as Social Control, 1815–1860," *Mississippi Valley Historical Review* 44 (December 1957): 423–44; Griffin, *Their Brothers' Keepers: Moral Stewardship in the United States, 1800–1865* (New Brunswick, N.J.: Rutgers University Press, 1960), pp. 177–97; and Charles I. Foster, *An Errand of Mercy: The Evangelical United Front, 1790–1837* (Chapel Hill: University of North Carolina Press, 1960), pp. 223–74.

These studies of the voluntary associations focused on them as organs of social control, but they had no single reform program for slavery and race relations. Some promoted missions to slaves, others supported colonization, and still others pushed antislavery reform. Correctly locating the roots of antislavery reform in earlier voluntary benevolence, Lois W. Banner challenged the social control interpretation in "Religious Benevolence as Social Control: A Critique of an Interpretation," *Journal of American History* 60 (June 1973): 23–41. In questioning the social control motive, Banner went too far, because social reform and social control are functions of each other, except when perfectionism drives the reformer to radical withdrawal from union with social sin. See Ralph E. Luker, "Religion and Social Control in the Nineteenth Century American City," *Journal of Urban History* 2 (May 1976): 363–68.

13. John L. Thomas, "Romantic Reform in America, 1815–1865," *American Quarterly* 17 (Winter 1965): 656–81; and George M. Fredrickson, *The Inner Civil War: Northern Intellectuals and the Crisis of the Union* (New York: Harper and Row, 1965).

14. Richard Lyle Power, "A Crusade to Extend Yankee Culture, 1820–1865," *New England Quarterly* 13 (December 1940): 638–53; and James M. McPherson, "What Yankee 'Schoolmarms' Taught Post–Civil War Blacks," *University: A Princeton Quarterly* 57 (Summer 1973): 1–6, 29–33.

15. Many spokesmen for social Christianity thought of themselves as bold advocates of reform, but Henry May is basically correct in identifying a conservative's preoccupation with social order in the early years of the movement. Over the course of time, many of them came to see industrial conflict as a symptom of prior economic dislocation. See May, *Protestant Churches and Industrial America*, pp. 163–69; and Dorn, *Washington Gladden*, pp. 203–35. Here, as elsewhere, I am indebted to the suggestions of Professor David Wills of Amherst College.

16. The division of the social gospel prophets among three traditions in racial reform is itself suggestive evidence that any notion that the social gospel is a single cohesive movement in American Christianity is itself questionable.

## Chapter 2

1. Josiah Strong, "Mary Strong," [pp. 1–3], Josiah Strong Papers, Union Theological Seminary, New York. See also "Miss Mary A. Strong," *American Missionary* 48 (May 1894): 188–89.

2. Charles J. Ryder, "Fifty Years of the American Missionary Association," *New England Magazine* n.s. 15 (October 1896): 231. See also Fletcher M. Green, "Northern Missionary Activities in the South, 1846–1861," *Journal of Southern History* 21 (May 1955): 147–72; and Charles I. Foster, *An Errand of Mercy: The Evangelical United Front, 1790–1837* (Chapel Hill: University of North Carolina Press, 1960), pp. 183, 199–203. Theodore Abel, *Protestant Home Missions to Catholic Immigrants* (New York: Institute of Social and Religious Research, 1933); Colin Brummitt Goodykoontz, *Home Missions on the American Frontier, with Particular Reference to the American Missionary Society* (Caldwell, Idaho: Caxton Printers, 1939); and Walter Brownlow Posey, *Frontier Mission: A History of Religion West of the Southern Appalachians*

to 1861 (Lexington: University of Kentucky Press, 1966), illustrate the variety of nineteenth-century home missions, but there is no outstanding synthesis of a vast literature.

3. James M. McPherson, ed., *Two Black Teachers during the Civil War* (New York: Arno Press and the *New York Times*, 1969); [William Channing Gannett and Edward Everett Hale], "The Freedmen at Port Royal," *North American Review* 101 (July 1865): 1–28; [William Channing Gannett and Edward Everett Hale], "The Education of the Freedmen," *North American Review* 101 (October 1865): 528–49; William H. Pease, "William Channing Gannett: A Social Biography" (Ph.D. dissertation, University of Rochester, 1955), pp. 31–86, 255–56; Jean Holloway, *Edward Everett Hale: A Biography* (Austin: University of Texas Press, 1956), p. 144; and Willie Lee Rose, *Rehearsal for Reconstruction: The Port Royal Experiment* (Indianapolis: Bobbs-Merrill, 1964), pp. 76, 101–2, 363–70.

4. Richard Bryant Drake, "The American Missionary Association and the Southern Negro, 1861–1889" (Ph.D. dissertation, Emory University, 1957), pp. 15–26; Joe M. Richardson, *Christian Reconstruction: The American Missionary Association and Southern Blacks, 1861–1890* (Athens: University of Georgia Press, 1986), pp. 73–82; Ralph E. Morrow, *Northern Methodism and Reconstruction* (East Lansing: Michigan State University Press, 1956), pp. 154–64; and Lyman Abbott, *Reminiscences* (Boston: Houghton Mifflin Co., 1923), pp. 233–77.

5. Abbott, *Reminiscences*, pp. xxx, 98–106; Holloway, *Edward Everett Hale*, pp. 105–9; and Abbott as quoted in Robert C. Morris, *Reading, 'Riting, and Reconstruction: The Education of the Freedmen in the South, 1861–1870* (Chicago: University of Chicago Press, 1981), pp. 46, 298n.

6. Henry Lee Swint, *The Northern Teacher in the South, 1862–1870* (Nashville: Vanderbilt University Press, 1942), pp. 171–74; and Lyman Abbott, "Southern Evangelization," *New Englander* 23 (October 1864): 701. See also Lyman Abbott, *The Results of Emancipation in the United States of America* (New York: American Freedman's Union Commission, 1867).

7. Lyman Abbott, "Equal Rights," *American Freedman* 1 (April 1866): 103, as quoted in Swint, *Northern Teacher*, p. 19; Abbott to Samuel J. May, Jr., 23 February 1866, Samuel J. May Anti-Slavery Collection, Olin Library, Cornell University; and Abbott, *Reminiscences*, p. 270. See also Abbott, *Reminiscences*, pp. 261–70; Ira Vernon Brown, *Lyman Abbott, Christian Evolutionist: A Study in Religious Liberalism* (Cambridge: Harvard University Press, 1953), pp. 46–47; and Morris, *Reading, 'Riting, and Reconstruction*, pp. 41–42, 224–30.

8. Abbott, *Reminiscences*, p. 268; and Drake, "American Missionary Association," pp. 17–26. See also Morris, *Reading, 'Riting, and Reconstruction*, pp. 59–63.

9. Clifton H. Johnson, "The American Missionary Association, 1846–1861: A Study of Christian Abolitionism" (Ph.D. dissertation, University of North Carolina, 1959); Drake, "American Missionary Association"; Richardson, *Christian Reconstruction*; Morrow, *Northern Methodism and Reconstruction*; Henry M. Johnson, "The Methodist Episcopal Church and the Education of Southern Negroes" (Ph.D. dissertation, Yale University, 1939); Frank Kenneth Pool, "The Southern Negro in the Methodist Episcopal Church" (Ph.D. dissertation, Duke University, 1939); Robert Andrew Baker, "The American Baptist Home Mission Society and the South, 1832–1894" (Ph.D. dissertation, Yale University, 1947), pp. 147–227; Sandy Dwayne Martin, "The American Baptist Home Mission

Society and Black Higher Education in the South, 1865–1920," *Foundations* 24 (October–December 1981): 310–27; Andrew E. Murray, *Presbyterians and the Negro: A History* (Philadelphia: Presbyterian Historical Society, 1966), pp. 161–202; Francis Charles Anscombe, "The Contributions of the Quakers to the Reconstruction of the Southern States" (Ph.D. dissertation, University of North Carolina, 1926), pp. 116–269; and H. Peers Brewer, "The Protestant Episcopal Freedmen's Commission, 1865–1878," *Historical Magazine of the Protestant Episcopal Church* 26 (December 1957): 361–81.

10. Drake, "American Missionary Association," pp. 275–76; and Brewer, "Protestant Episcopal Freedmen's Commission," p. 378. These figures do not include large, private philanthropic gifts, such as the Peabody and Slater funds.

11. The figures are made more incomparable by the fact that a large part of the Freedmen's Bureau budget was expended in assisting to establish the home missions schools. Other estimates of the total Northern contribution to Southern relief and education from 1865 to 1890 range as high as $30,000,000 to $35,000,000. See Joseph C. Hartzell, "The Problem of Education in the Southern States," *Methodist Review* 74 (January 1892): 46–67; and Isabel C. Barrows, ed., *Second Mohonk Conference on the Negro Question: Held at Lake Mohonk, Ulster County, New York, June 3, 4, 5, 1891* (Boston: George H. Ellis, 1891), p. 20.

12. Clarence E. Walker, *A Rock in a Weary Land: The African Methodist Episcopal Church during the Civil War and Reconstruction* (Baton Rouge: Louisiana State University Press, 1982), pp. 52–57; James D. Anderson, *The Education of Blacks in the South, 1860–1935* (Chapel Hill: University of North Carolina Press, 1988), pp. 4–32; and G. S. Ellington, "A Short Sketch of the Life and Work of Rev. A. D. Williams D. D.," in *Programme of the Thirtieth Anniversary of the Pastorate of Rev. A. D. Williams, Ebenezer Baptist Church, Atlanta, Ga. Beginning Monday Night, March 3, Closing Sunday Night, March 16, 1924* (Atlanta: n.p., n.d.), [p. 6].

13. They included Lyman Abbott, Edward and Henry Ward Beecher, A. J. F. Behrends, Amory H. Bradford, S. Parkes Cadman, Aaron L. Chapin, Joseph Cook, Harlan Paul Douglass, George A. Gates, Washington Gladden, George A. Gordon, Newell Dwight Hillis, Charles E. Jefferson, Henry Churchill King, Samuel L. Loomis, Albert J. Lyman, Philip Moxom, Frederick A. Noble, Charles M. Sheldon, Edward A. Steiner, Josiah Strong, Graham Taylor, William Jewett Tucker, Francis Amasa Walker, and William Hayes Ward. These names are drawn from Drake, "American Missionary Association," pp. 289–93, the pages of the *American Missionary*, and occasional papers of the AMA.

14. John Bascom, *Things Learned By Living* (New York: G. F. Putnam's Sons, 1913), p. 37; Clarence Bacote, *The Story of Atlanta University: A Century of Service, 1865–1965* (Atlanta: Atlanta University, 1969), p. 113; Amory H. Bradford, "Is There Any Excuse?," *Independent* 44 (23 June 1892): 866; and Harry Fleischman, *Norman Thomas: A Biography* (New York: Norton, 1967), pp. 23–25.

15. Edward Everett Hale to J. W. Hamilton, 5 December 1892, in "Opinions Not Put Off So Easily," *Christian Educator* 4 (January 1893): 46; Bacote, *Atlanta University*, pp. 85, 113, 115–18; Reverdy C. Ransom, *The Pilgrimage of Harriet Ransom's Son* (Nashville: Sunday School Union, 1949), p. 220; Elsie Strong to the author, 27 September 1967; Samuel A. Eliot, "Francis Greenwood Peabody: His Work and Hopes for Hampton," *Southern*

*Workman* 66 (March 1937): 71–79. During the difficult 1890s, Atlanta University's fund drives won the support of Lyman Abbott, E. Benjamin Andrews, Phillips Brooks, Edward Cummings, Charles W. Eliot, George A. Gordon, Edward Everett Hale, Charles Cuthbert Hall, Thomas Wentworth Higginson, William DeWitt Hyde, Francis Greenwood Peabody, and Charles M. Sheldon. See Bacote, *Atlanta University*, pp. 107–21; and "Atlanta University," *Christian Union* 41 (26 June 1890): 911. See also Charles Lewis Slattery, *David Hummell Greer: Eighth Bishop of New York* (New York: Longmans, Green, and Co., 1921), pp. 205–7, 213–17.

16. George A. Gates, "The Relations of the American Missionary Association Work to the Kingdom of God," *American Missionary* 48 (January 1894): 34–35. See also "Address of Professor Graham Taylor," *American Missionary* 48 (January 1894): 35–38; Frederick A. Noble, "Response of President Noble," *American Missionary* 52 (December 1898): 194–96; and Abbott as quoted in Augustus Field Beard, *A Crusade of Brotherhood: A History of the American Missionary Association* (Boston: Pilgrim Press, 1909), p. 266.

17. Washington Gladden, "Moral Reconstruction," in *The Nation Still in Danger; or, Ten Years after the War: A Plea by the American Missionary Association* . . . (n.p.: American Missionary Association, 1875), p. 15; Amory Dwight Mayo, *National Aid to Education: An Address before the American Social Science Association,* . . . (Boston: The Association, 1883), p. 19; and Michael E. Strieby, "The Nation Still in Danger," in *Nation Still in Danger*, p. 4. See also Joseph Cook, *The Three Despised Races in the United States; or, The Chinaman, the Indian, and the Freedman. An Address* . . . (New York: American Missionary Association, 1878), pp. 18–30; Cook, "Enfranchised Ignorance in the South," in *Boston Monday Lectures: Conscience, with Preludes on Current Events* (Boston: Houghton, Osgood and Co., 1879), pp. 117–23; Cook, "Equal Educational Rights for Black and White," in *Boston Monday Lectures: Marriage, with Preludes on Current Events* (Boston: Houghton, Osgood and Co., 1879), pp. 169–79; Gladden, "Moral Reconstruction," pp. 13–16; Gladden, "The Southern Question," *Independent* 28 (7 September 1876): 3; Amory Dwight Mayo, "The South, the North, and the Nation Keeping School," in *Christian Educators in Council: Sixty Addresses by American Educators; with Historical Notes upon the National Educational Assembly, Held at Ocean Grove, N.J., August 9–12, 1883. Also Illiteracy and Education Tables from Census of 1880*, ed. John C. Hartzell (New York: Phillips and Hunt, 1883), p. 160; Drake, "American Missionary Association," p. 190; Johnson, "Methodist Episcopal Church," pp. 191–95; Morrow, *Northern Methodism and Reconstruction*, pp. 33, 127, 203–33; and Swint, *Northern Teachers in the South*, pp. 86–87.

18. Lemuel Moss, "Results of Home Mission Work," in *Baptist Home Missions in North America: Including a Full Report of the Proceedings and Addresses of the Jubilee Meeting, and a Historical Sketch of the American Baptist Home Mission Society, Historical Tables, Etc., 1832–1882* (New York: Baptist Home Mission Rooms, 1883), p. 205; and "Assimilation in America," *American Missionary* 44 (April 1890): 238. See also Lyman Abbott, "Salvation by Growth," in *Signs of Promise: Sermons Preached in Plymouth Pulpit, Brooklyn, 1887–1889* (New York: Fords, Howard and Hulbert, 1889), p. 195; Washington Gladden, "Congregationalism and the Poor," *American Missionary* 45 (December 1891): 466–69; and "Dr. Griffis' Address," *American Missionary* 51 (December 1897): 303.

19. Northern Protestant missions in the South were suffused with the notion that they were the legitimate heir to Christian traditions. See, for instance, George M. Gray,

"Our Mission in the South," *Christian Educator* 3 (January 1890): 322; J. W. Hamilton, "The Negro and His Assimilation in America," in Hartzell, *Christian Educators in Council*, p. 59; Swint, *Northern Teacher in the South*, pp. 56–59; Chester Forrester Dunham, *The Attitude of the Northern Clergy toward the South, 1860–1865* (Toledo, Ohio: Gray Co., 1942), pp. 81–109, 204–37; and Morrow, *Northern Methodism and Reconstruction*. On Christianization as the social strategy advocated by the social gospel prophets, see Washington Gladden, *Tools and the Man: Property and Industry under the Christian Law* (Boston: Houghton, Mifflin and Co., 1893), p. 1; Samuel Zane Batten, *The Task of Christianity: A Summons to the New Crusade* (New York: Fleming H. Revell Co., 1911), pp. 78–79; and Walter Rauschenbusch, *Christianizing the Social Order* (New York: Macmillan, 1912).

20. James M. McPherson, *The Struggle for Equality: Abolitionists and the Negro in the Civil War and Reconstruction* (Princeton: Princeton University Press, 1964), p. 393; and Johnson, "Methodist Episcopal Church," pp. 296, 300–301. See also Morris, *Reading, 'Riting, and Reconstruction*, pp. 186–87; Morrow, *Northern Methodism and Reconstruction*, pp. 20–21; and Swint, *Northern Teacher in the South*, p. 58.

21. For a defense of this multifunction mission, see "Address of Rev. A. J. Lyman," *American Missionary* 44 (December 1890): 403–4.

22. Swint, *Northern Teacher in the South*, pp. 85–86. Swint's older portrait of the "Yankee school marm" as a stiff-necked, intrusive do-gooder is inverted by two studies largely motivated by Marxist and feminist concerns in which the missionary teachers are the exploited instruments of ineffectual liberal reform. See Ronald E. Butchart, *Northern Schools, Southern Blacks, and Reconstruction: Freedmen's Education, 1862–1875* (Westport, Conn.: Greenwood Press, 1980); and Jacqueline Jones, *Soldiers of Light and Love: Northern Teachers and Georgia Blacks, 1865–1873* (Chapel Hill: University of North Carolina Press, 1980). James M. McPherson, *The Abolitionist Legacy: From Reconstruction to the NAACP* (Princeton: Princeton University Press, 1975), pp. 161–202; Morris, *Reading, 'Riting, and Reconstruction*; and Richardson, *Christian Reconstruction*, pp. 161–86, are critical, but more balanced treatments.

23. Lura Beam, *He Called Them by the Lightening: A Teacher's Odyssey in the Negro South, 1908–1919* (Indianapolis: Bobbs-Merrill, 1967), p. 10; "Augusta, Ga.," *Lend-A-Hand* 3 (August 1888): 466–67; "Hampton, Va.," *Lend-A-Hand* 3 (June 1888): 353; "Atlanta, Ga.," *Lend-A-Hand* 3 (June 1888): 354; and Bradford, "Is There Any Excuse?," pp. 866–67. See also Beam, *He Called Them by the Lightening*, p. 100; "Mobile, Ala.," *Lend-A-Hand* 4 (March 1889): 227; Holloway, *Edward Everett Hale*, pp. 213–15; McPherson, *Abolitionist Legacy*, pp. 172–74; and Jones, *Soldiers of Light and Love*, pp. 167–90.

24. "An Appeal from Alabama," *Lend-A-Hand* 4 (September 1889): 691–92; "Atlanta, Ga.," *Lend-A-Hand* 4 (September 1889): 681; "Mobile, Ala.," *Lend-A-Hand* 4 (March 1889): 227; and "Lexington, Ky.," *Lend-A-Hand* 4 (February 1889): 157. See also Pitt Dillingham, "Calhoun Colored School," *Lend-A-Hand* 15 (September 1895): 210–11.

25. Gladden, "Congregationalism and the Poor," p. 472. See also "Virginia," *Spirit of Missions* 54 (July 1890): 279–80; Ryder, "Fifty Years of the American Missionary Association," p. 242; William Edward Burghardt Du Bois, *The Souls of Black Folk* (Chicago: A. C. McClurg and Co., 1903), p. 100; Harriet E. Emerson, *Annals of a Harvester: Reviewing Forty*

*Years of Home Missionary Work in the Southern States* (East Andover, N.H.: Arthur W. Emerson, Sons and Co., [ca. 1915]), pp. 51–96; Laura S. Haviland, *A Woman's Life-Work: Labor and Experiences* (Cincinnati, Ohio: Walden and Stowe, 1882), pp. 360–520; Joanna P. Moore, *"In Christ's Stead": Autobiographical Sketches* (Chicago: Women's Baptist Home Mission Society, 1902), pp. 55–57, 73–82; 138–41, 143–53, 177–81; and Richard R. Wright, Jr., *87 Years behind the Black Curtain: An Autobiography* (Philadelphia: Rare Book Co., 1965), p. 149.

26. "Address of the Reverend Frank T. Bayley," *American Missionary* 47 (December 1893): 437–38; and A. J. F. Behrends, in "Forty-Eighth Annual Report of the Executive Committee," *American Missionary* 48 (November 1894): 390. See also George W. Gray, "National Perpetuity," *Twenty-First Annual Report of the Freedmen's Aid and Southern Education Society of the Methodist Episcopal Church for the Year Ending July 1, 1888*, p. 56; J. W. E. Bowen, "Why?," *Christian Educator* 4 (October 1892): 3; Bowen, in "The Negro in Art and Literature," *Christian Educator* 4 (April 1893): 126; Morehouse, "Opening Remarks," in Hartzell, *Christian Educators in Council*, pp. 72–73; and Jabez Pitt Campbell, "Assimilation, Not Separation," in Hartzell, *Christian Educators in Council*, pp. 65–67.

27. W. E. C. Wright, "The New Negro," *American Missionary* 47 (January 1894): 10; Will Jackson, "The Future and the Negro," *Christian Educator* 3 (October 1891): 295; and "Missionary Intelligence," *Spirit of Missions* 54 (August 1889): 310.

28. Beam, *He Called Them by the Lightening*, p. 108; Miss Hatch, "Some Features of the Work among Freedmen," *Missionary Review of the World* 17 (June 1894): 441; and "Tuskegee, La. [sic]," *Lend-A-Hand* 2 (October 1887): 606. The themes of self-help and racial solidarity in the black community in this period are explored in August Meier, *Negro Thought in America, 1880–1915: Racial Ideologies in the Age of Booker T. Washington* (Ann Arbor: University of Michigan Press, 1963).

29. Samuel June Barrows, "What the Southern Negro Is Doing for Himself," *Atlantic Monthly* 67 (June 1891): 815. See also the debate over Barrows's strictures on the tenantry system: "The Financial Bondage of the Southern Negro," *Homiletic Review* 22 (July 1891): 96–97; C. W. Humphreys, "The Southern Negro Problem," *Homiletic Review* 22 (August 1891): 192–93; and G. W. Gardner, "Financial Bondage of the Southern Negro," *Homiletic Review* 22 (December 1891): 569–70.

30. Atticus G. Haygood, *Our Brother in Black: His Freedom and His Future* (New York: Phillips and Hunt, 1881), pp. 29, 181, 246; and Harold W. Mann, *Atticus Greene Haygood: Methodist Bishop, Editor and Educator* (Athens: University of Georgia Press, 1965), pp. 27–42. See also Oscar P. Fitzgerald, "A Good Book, but Obsolete," *Methodist Quarterly Review* n.s. 13 (October 1892): 62–64; and Mann, *Atticus Greene Haygood*, p. 183.

31. Louis D. Rubin, ed., *Teach the Freeman: The Correspondence of Rutherford B. Hayes and the Slater Fund for Negro Education, 1881–1893*, 2 vols. (Baton Rouge: Louisiana State University Press, 1959), 1:xx; and Charles Richard Williams, ed., *Diary and Letters of Rutherford B. Hayes*, 5 vols. (n.p.: Ohio State Archaeological and Historical Society, 1925), 4:88. More in the spirit of the American Freedmen's Union Commission than of the denominational agencies, Bacon explained to Hayes that "Christian education" was intended by Slater in the same sense that "the common-school teaching of Massachusetts and Connecticut was 'Christian Education'—that is, it is leavened with a predominant & salutary

Christian influence. . . . It may often & easily happen that the more definitely denominational a school is, the less really Christian." Bacon to Hayes, 21 July 1882, in ibid., 1:52–53. See also J. L. M. Curry to Hayes, 8 July 1882; and Hayes to Curry, 15 July 1882; in Rubin, *Teach the Freeman,* 1:47–48, 50–51; and Williams, *Diary and Letters of Rutherford B. Hayes,* 4:76.

32. For examples, see Haygood, *Our Brother in Black,* pp. 172–73; and "Courses of Study for Schools of the Methodist Episcopal Church in the Southern States," in *To the General Committee of the Freedmen's Aid and Southern Education Society to Convene at Harrisburg, Pa., November 7 & 8, 1892,* pp. 25–32. For the reaction of a prominent graduate, see James Weldon Johnson, *Along This Way: The Autobiography of James Weldon Johnson* (New York: Viking Press, 1968), p. 122; and Eugene Levy, *James Weldon Johnson: Black Leader/Black Voice* (Chicago: University of Chicago Press, 1973), p. 26.

33. Henry Allen Bullock, *A History of Negro Education: From 1619 to 1915* (Cambridge: Harvard University Press, 1967), pp. 60–88; Donald Spivey, *Schooling for the New Slavery: Black Industrial Education, 1868–1915* (Westport, Conn.: Greenwood Press, 1978); and Anderson, *Education of Blacks in the South,* pp. 33–78.

34. Drake, "American Missionary Association," pp. 205–8; Benjamin Brawley, "Early Effort for Industrial Education." Occasional Papers of the John F. Slater Fund, no. 22 (n.p.: n.p., 1923); Timothy Thomas Fortune, *Black and White: Land, Labor and Politics in the South* (New York: Fords and Co., 1884), pp. 38–54; Williams, *Diary and Letters,* 4:615, 635–36; 5:2, 15–16; Mann, *Atticus Greene Haygood,* pp. 177–79; Caro Lloyd, *Henry Demarest Lloyd, 1849–1903: A Biography,* 2 vols. (New York: G. P. Putnam's Sons, 1912), 2:173–76; and Chester McArthur Destler, *Henry Demarest Lloyd and the Empire of Reform* (Philadelphia: University of Pennsylvania Press, 1963), p. 549n. For reports on manual-training schools at Tulane and Washington University in St. Louis, see Amory Dwight Mayo, "Industrial Education in the South," (Washington, D.C.: U.S. Government Printing Office, 1888), pp. 60–86.

35. Haygood to Bacon, 25 January 1882; Haygood to Hayes, 6 December 1882; Haygood to Hayes, 3 January 1883; Haygood to Hayes, 12 January 1885; Haygood to Hayes, 12 June 1885; and Haygood to Hayes, 9 August 1887; in Rubin, *Teach the Freeman,* 1:70, 77–78, 83–84, 150–52, 191, 208.

36. Thomas Underwood Dudley, "How Shall We Help the Negro?," *Century* 30 (June 1885): 278; see also 275–76, 279. On Dudley's career in racial reform, see Charles E. Wynes, "Bishop Thomas U. Dudley and the Uplift of the Negro," *Register of the Kentucky Historical Society* 65 (July 1967): 230–38; and L. Moody Sims, "Thomas Underwood Dudley: A Forgotten Voice of Dissent," *Mississippi Quarterly* 20 (Fall 1967): 217–23.

37. Dudley, "How Shall We Help the Negro?," pp. 273–80; and Sims, "Thomas Underwood Dudley," p. 222. See also Atticus G. Haygood, *Pleas for Progress* (Nashville: Publishing House of the ME Church, South, 1889), pp. 5–8.

38. "Our Reviews," *AME Church Review* 2 (July 1885): 100.

39. George Washington Cable, "National Aid to Southern Schools," in *The Negro Question: A Selection of Writings on Civil Rights in the South by George W. Cable,* ed. Arlin Turner (Garden City, N.Y.: Doubleday, 1958), pp. 191–96; Thomas U. Dudley, "Shall the Federal Government Give Aid to Popular Education?," *Century* 31 (April 1886): 959–61; and

Atticus G. Haygood, "A Nation's Work and Duty: If Universal Suffrage, Then Universal Education," in *Pleas for Progress*, pp. 55–82.

40. Hartzell, *Christian Educators in Council*; and Gordon Canfield Lee, *The Struggle for Federal Aid for the Common Schools, 1870–1890* (New York: Teachers College Bureau of Publications, 1949), pp. 108, 115, 118–23, 158–62. See also Joseph Cook, "Federal Aid to Education," in *Boston Monday Lectures: Orient, with Preludes on Current Events* (Boston: Houghton, Mifflin and Co., 1886), pp. 3–15; Cook, "National Perils from Illiteracy," in *Boston Monday Lectures: Current Religious Perils with Preludes and Other Addresses on Leading Reforms and a Symposium on Vital and Progressive Orthodoxy* (Boston: Houghton, Mifflin and Co., 1888), pp. 83–91; Cook, "Race Riots in the South," *Our Day* 5 (May 1890): 413–14; Richard T. Ely, *Social Aspects of Christianity and Other Essays* (New York: Thomas Y. Crowell and Co., 1889), p. 33; Ely, *The Social Law of Service* (New York: Eaton and Mains, 1896), pp. 47, 185, 197–98, 239, 243; John C. Hartzell, "Problem of Education in the Southern States," pp. 45–46; Amory Dwight Mayo, "National Aid to Education"; George R. Stetson, *The Problem of Negro Education* (Boston: Cupples, Upham and Co., 1884), p. 21; Albion W. Tourgée, *An Appeal to Caesar* (New York: Fords, Howard and Hulbert, 1884); "Editorial Notes," *Independent* 42 (27 February 1890): 285; "What Shall Be Done for the Negro?," *Chautauquan* 11 (August 1890): 634; and Brown, *Lyman Abbott*, p. 82. Tourgée finally opposed the Blair Bill for federal aid to education as offering disproportionately little help to Negro schools in the South. Otto Olsen, *Carpetbagger's Crusade: The Life of Albion Winegar Tourgée* (Baltimore: Johns Hopkins University Press, 1965), pp. 218–19, 242–51, 300–305.

41. Williams, *Diary and Letters*, 5:8; Larry E. Burgess, "We'll Discuss It at Mohonk," *Quaker History* 60 (Spring 1971): 21–24; and "Editorial," *Christian Union* 41 (5 June 1890): 795.

42. George W. Cable to Albert K. Smiley, 21 March 1890; George W. Cable to W. S. Scarborough, 24 March 1890; W. S. Scarborough Papers, Wilberforce University, Wilberforce, Ohio; "Vital Points of Expert Opinion," *Our Day* 6 (July 1890): 63; W. S. Scarborough, "The Race Problem," *Arena* 2 (October 1890): 562; William Hayes Ward, "The Mohonk Conference," *Independent* 42 (12 June 1890): 814–15; Booker T. Washington to George W. Cable, 7 April 1890; George W. Cable to Booker T. Washington, 21 March 1890; W. S. Scarborough to Booker T. Washington, 17 April 1890; and Timothy Thomas Fortune to Booker T. Washington, 23 July 1890, in *The Booker T. Washington Papers*, 14 vols., ed. Louis R. Harlan et al. (Urbana: University of Illinois Press, 1972–89), 3:40–46, 69–70.

43. Isabel C. Barrows, ed., *First Mohonk Conference on the Negro Question: Held at Lake Mohonk, Ulster County, New York, June 4, 5, 6, 1890* (Boston: George H. Ellis, 1890), pp. 12–19, 72–81, 86–93, 131–32, 140–43. The failure of its platform to endorse federal aid to education was probably because a federal aid bill was defeated in the U.S. Senate only days before the first Mohonk Conference convened. Rutherford B. Hayes, Andrew D. White, John Glenn, John Jay, and William T. Harris expressed regret over its defeat. Only Albion Tourgée applauded the defeat of the bill. See Allen J. Going, "The South and the Blair Education Bill," *Mississippi Valley Historical Review* 44 (September 1957): 267–90; and Barrows, *First Mohonk Conference*, pp. 11–12, 72–77, 81, 119, 122. The conference resolved in favor of federal aid to education the next year.

44. Albion W. Tourgée to William B. Anderson, n.d. [1890], no. 5147, Albion W. Tourgée Papers, Southern Historical Collection, University of North Carolina, Chapel Hill.

45. Albion W. Tourgée, "The Negro's View of the Race Problem," in Barrows, *First Mohonk Conference*, pp. 104–5, 106–7, 109, 111.

46. Ibid., pp. 107–8. The conference sparked hope in the social gospel press that it was pointing the way to the amelioration of the race question. See Ednah D. Cheyney, "The Mohonk Conference and the Education of the Negroes," *Open Court* 4 (3 July 1890): 2370–71; "The Mohonk Conference on the Negro Question," *American Missionary* 44 (July 1890): 206–7; "What Shall Be Done for the Negro?," pp. 634–35; Amory Dwight Mayo, "The Progress of the Negro," *Forum* 10 (November 1890): 335–45; "What the Mohonk Conference Asks for the Negro," *Independent* 43 (11 June 1891): 870–71; and "Mohonk Conference," *American Missionary* 45 (July 1891): 249–50.

47. Isabel C. Barrows, ed., *Second Mohonk Conference on the Negro Question: Held at Lake Mohonk, Ulster County, New York, June 3, 4, 5, 1891* (Boston: George H. Ellis, 1891), pp. 82, 108, 119–22; Benjamin F. Trueblood, "Mohonk and Its Conferences," *New England Magazine* 16 (June 1897): 461–62; "Editorial," *Independent* 52 (15 February 1900): 451; and Burgess, "We'll Discuss It at Mohonk," p. 24.

48. Barrows, "Situation of the Negro," in Barrows, *Second Mohonk Conference*, p. 13.

49. Mayo, "Progress of the Negro," pp. 337, 344. See also Olive Ruth Jefferson, "The Negro Woman of the South," *Chautauquan* 17 (July 1893): 405.

## Chapter 3

1. Hugh Douglass to William Coppinger, 27 May 1889, I-A, no. 274. American Colonization Society Papers, Manuscript Division, Library of Congress.

2. From 1816 to 1847, the Colonization Society received an average of $24,144.65 in annual contributions and sent an average of 150 freedmen per year to Africa. Its receipts averaged $64,724.51 and it returned an average of 361 freedmen to Africa from 1848 to 1873. From 1874 to 1899, its receipts averaged $12,736.40 and it returned an average of 52 freedmen per year to Africa. P. J. Staudenraus, *The African Colonization Movement: 1816–1865* (New York: Columbia University Press, 1961), p. 251.

3. Staudenraus, *African Colonization*, pp. 196, 204, 240. See also Leonard Woolsey Bacon, "The Services of Leonard Bacon to African Colonization," *Liberia* 15 (November 1899): 1–21, and 16 (February 1900): 40–55; Stephen Colwell, *New Themes for Protestant Clergy: Creeds without Charity, Theology without Humanity and Protestantism without Christianity, with Notes on the Nature of Charity, Population, Pauperism, Political Economy and Protestantism* (Philadelphia: Lippincott, Grambo and Co., 1851), pp. 65–67, 250–51; Colwell, "The South: A Letter from a Friend in the North. With Special Reference to the Effects of Disunion upon Slavery" (Philadelphia: C. Sherman and Co., 1856); Colwell, *The Five Cotton States and New York; or, Remarks upon the Social and Political Aspects of the Southern Political Crisis* (n.p.: n.p., 1861); D. Stuart Dodge, ed., *Memorials of William E. Dodge* (New York: Anson D. F. Randolph and Co., 1887), pp. 196–99, 343–45; J. Johns, *A Memoir of the Life of the Right Rev. William Meade,*

D. D., *Bishop of the Protestant Episcopal Church in the Diocese of Virginia* (Baltimore: Innes and Co., 1867), pp. 76–77, 117–25, 473–77; Alvin W. Skardon, *Church Leader in the Cities: William Augustus Muhlenberg* (Philadelphia: University of Pennsylvania Press, 1971), pp. 238–45; and [Ephraim Peabody], *Slavery in the United States: Its Evils, Alleviations and Remedies* (Boston: Charles C. Little and James Brown, 1851).

4. William Channing Gannett, *Ezra Stiles Gannett: Unitarian Minister in Boston, 1824–1871* (Boston: Roberts Brothers, 1875), p. 304; and Willis D. Boyd, "Negro Colonization in the Reconstruction Era, 1865–1870," *Georgia Historical Quarterly* 40 (December 1956): 366–67. See also Boyd, "Negro Colonization in the National Crisis" (Ph.D. dissertation, University of California at Los Angeles, 1953); and Eli Seifman, "Education or Emigration: The Schism within the African Colonization Movement, 1865–1895," *History of Education Quarterly* 3 (Spring 1967): 36–57.

5. Boyd, "Negro Colonization," p. 376; E. L. Quade, "Our Africa," *Catholic World* 62 (March 1896): 830; and Edward W. Gilliam, "The African in the United States," *Popular Science Monthly* 22 (February 1883): 436–37, 441, 443–45. See also George M. Fredrickson, *The Black Image in the White Mind: The Debate on Afro-American Character and Destiny, 1817–1914* (New York: Harper and Row, 1971), pp. 239–40, 245–46.

6. "The Future of the Negro," *North American Review* 332 (July 1884): 78–99; W. W. W. Wilson, "Our Church in Her Relation to the Negro," *Methodist Review* 76 (September 1894): 720–21; Richard Lowitt, *A Merchant Prince of the Nineteenth Century: William E. Dodge* (New York: Columbia University Press, 1954), pp. 343–44; and Samuel A. Eliot, "Francis Greenwood Peabody: His Work and Hopes for Hampton," *Southern Workman* 66 (March 1937): 71–79.

7. Amory Dwight Mayo, "The Progress of the Negro," *Forum* 10 (November 1890): 386; Thomas H. Pearne, "The Race Problem—The Situation," *Methodist Review* 72 (September 1890): 703; John Boyle O'Reilly, quoted in John R. Betts, "The Negro and the New England Conscience in the Days of John Boyle O'Reilly," *Journal of Negro History* 51 (October 1966): 258; Boyd, "Negro Colonization," p. 374; Thomas Jefferson Morgan, *The Negro in America and the Ideal American Republic* (Philadelphia: American Baptist Publication Society, 1898), p. 84; and "Address of Rev. A. H. Bradford," *American Missionary* 44 (December 1890): 432.

8. C. H. Richards, "The Future of the Negro in Our Country," *American Missionary* 44 (March 1890): 88–89; Pearne, "The Race Problem," p. 703; Mayo, "Progress of the Negro," p. 386; Thomas Dixon, Jr., "When Will the Negro Be Free?," *Christian Union* 41 (22 May 1890): 730; Samuel J. Barrows, "The Evolution of the Afric-American," in *Man and the State: Studies in Applied Sociology*, by the Brooklyn Ethical Association (New York: D. Appleton and Co., 1892), p. 318; Frederic Perry Noble, "Christendom's Rum-Trade with Africa: A Modern Devil's Mission," *Missionary Review of the World* 18 (June 1894): 418; Morgan, *Negro in America*, p. 50; Robert E. Speer, *Presbyterian Foreign Missions: An Account of the Foreign Missions of the Presbyterian Church in the U.S.A.* (Philadelphia: Presbyterian Board of Publication and Sabbath School Work, 1902), pp. 21–23; Speer, *Missions and Modern History: A Study of the Missionary Aspects of Some Great Movements of the Nineteenth Century*, 2 vols. (New York: Fleming H. Revell Co., 1904), 1:284–85; and Henry Demarest Lloyd, *Man, the Social Creator* (New York: Doubleday, Page and Co., 1906), p. 52.

9. "Negro Colonization," *Independent* 40 (16 February 1888): 203; and Albion W. Tourgée, "Shall We Re-Barbarize the Negro?," *Congregationalist* 41 (4 December 1889): 115. See also "Editorial Notes," *Independent* 43 (27 August 1891): 1277; and Tourgée to C. H. Loomis, 4 February 1892, Tourgée Papers, Southern Historical Collection, University of North Carolina, Chapel Hill. Mississippi's white Baptist populist, Charles H. Otkin, was an exception. See Otkin, *The Ills of the South; or, Related Causes Hostile to the General Prosperity of the Southern People* (New York: G. P. Putnam's Sons, 1894), pp. 8, 201–62.

10. Michael E. Strieby, "The Destiny of the African Races," *American Missionary* 44 (December 1890): 374–75; and Richard Salter Storrs, *Our Nation's Work for the Colored People: A Discourse Delivered in the Church of the Pilgrims, Brooklyn, N.Y., in Behalf of the American Missionary Association* (New York: Holt Brothers, 1890), pp. 19–20. See also Strieby, "The Training of American Freedmen as Factors in African Civilization," in *Report of the Centenary Conference on the Protestant Missions of the World, Held in Exeter Hall (June 9th–19th), London, 1888*, 2 vols., ed. James Johnston (New York: Fleming H. Revell Co., n.d.), 2:390–93; Joseph Cook, "Nullification and Murder in the Southern States," *Our Day* 3 (May 1889): 459–60; J. R. Slattery, "The African Slave Trade," *Catholic World* 50 (February 1890): 676–77; Henry S. Sanford, "American Interests in the African Slave-Trade of 1890," *Our Day* 7 (February 1891): 101–2; Frederic Perry Noble, "An African Devil's Business and Its Arab Agents; or, The Slave Trade of the Present Day: Who Carries It On, Where Are the Slaves Used, and What Can be Done to Stop the Business," *Missionary Review of the World* 14 (June 1891): 435; Charles J. Ryder, "The Theology of the Plantation Songs," *American Missionary* 46 (January 1892): 16; William Brenton Greene, Jr., "Africa," *Missionary Review of the World* 15 (June 1892): 470; Cook, "The Divine Program on the Dark Continent," *Our Day* 12 (September 1893): 193, 201; Josiah Strong, *The New Era; or, The Coming Kingdom* (New York: Baker and Taylor Co., 1893), pp. 355–56; "Address of Rev. Dr. Josiah Strong," *American Missionary* 49 (December 1895): 423–24; Morgan, *Negro in America*, pp. 47–49, 84–85, 95; Noble, "Evangelical Christianity and Africa," *Missionary Review of the World* 21 (June 1898): 426; Joseph C. Hartzell, "The Outlook for Africa," *Liberia* 13 (November 1898): 5; Noble, *The Redemption of Africa: A Story of Civilization*, 2 vols. (New York: Young People's Missionary Movement, 1899), 1:xviii–xix; 2:479, 511–12; Strong, *Expansion under New World Conditions* (New York: Baker and Taylor Co., 1900), pp. 296–99; "Colored Missionaries in Africa," *American Missionary* 56 (July 1902): 322; and Hartzell, "The Open Door in Africa," in *The Open Door: A Challenge to Missionary Advance. Addresses Delivered before the First General Missionary Convention of the Methodist Episcopal Church, Held in Cleveland, Ohio, October 21 to 24, 1902*, by Charles H. Fahs et al. (New York: Eaton and Mains, 1903), pp. 169–70.

11. Atticus G. Haygood, *Pleas for Progress* (Nashville: Publishing House of the ME Church, South, 1889), p. 136; Sallie Stewart to William Coppinger, [ca. 22 December 1889], I-A, no. 275; Byron C. Roach to William Coppinger, 11 March and 19 April 1890, I-A, no. 276; Charles B. Galloway to William Coppinger, 10 August 1891, I-A, no. 280; Samuel Chiles Mitchell to William Coppinger, 11 July 1885, I-A, no. 280, ACS Papers; Dixon, "When Will the Negro Be Free?," p. 730; D. C. Rankin to William Coppinger, 14 January 1890, I-A, no. 276, ACS Papers; and Robert Dabney Bedinger, *Triumphs of the Gospel in the Belgian Congo. Being Some Account of the Missionary Work that has been Carried on in the*

Belgian Congo, Africa, Since 1890 by the Presbyterian Church in the United States (Richmond: Presbyterian Committee of Publication, [ca. 1920]).

12. See Michael McCarthy, Dark Continent: Africa as Seen by Americans (Westport, Conn.: Greenwood Press, 1983); and Clifford Haley Scott, "American Images of Africa, 1900–1939" (Ph.D. dissertation, University of Iowa, 1968).

13. Robert Hastings Nichols, "James Shepard Dennis," in Dictionary of American Biography, ed. Allen Johnson et al. (New York: Charles Scribner's Sons, 1928–88), 6:238–39; "Robert Elliott Speer," in The National Cyclopedia of American Biography (New York: James T. White and Co., 1950), 36:267–68; and W. Reginald Wheeler, A Man Sent from God: A Biography of Robert E. Speer (n.p.: Fleming H. Revell Co., 1956). See also James Shepard Dennis, Foreign Missions after a Century: Students' Lectures on Missions, Princeton Theological Seminary, 1893 (New York: Fleming H. Revell Co., 1893); and Dennis, Christian Missions and Social Progress: A Sociological Study of Foreign Missions, 3 vols. (New York: Fleming H. Revell Co., 1897–1906).

14. Delavan Leonard Pierson, Arthur T. Pierson: A Biography (London: James Nisbet and Co., 1912); and Harris Elwood Starr, "Arthur Tappan Pierson," in Dictionary of American Biography, 14:589–90. See also Arthur T. Pierson, The Crisis of Missions; or, The Voice Out of the Cloud (New York: Robert Carter and Brothers, 1886); Pierson, The Divine Enterprise of Missions (New York: Baker and Taylor Co., 1891); Pierson, The Miracles of Missions, 4 vols. (New York: Funk and Wagnalls, 1891–1901); Pierson, Seven Years in Sierra Leone: The Story of the Work of William A. B. Johnson (New York: Fleming H. Revell Co., 1897); and George M. Marsden, Fundamentalism and American Culture: The Shaping of Twentieth Century Evangelicalism, 1870–1925 (New York: Oxford University Press, 1980), pp. 80–93.

15. "Joseph Crane Hartzell," in The National Cyclopedia of American Biography (New York: James T. White and Co., 1906), 13:128; Noble, Redemption of Africa, 1:307–16; Ferdinand Cowle Iglehart, "Bishop Hartzell and His Work in Africa," Review of Reviews 39 (March 1909): 326–29; "Frederic Perry Noble," in The National Cyclopedia of American Biography (New York: James T. White and Co., 1949), 35:161; and "Frederick Alphonso Noble," in The National Cyclopedia of American Biography (New York: James T. White and Co., 1904), 12:48.

16. Noble, Redemption of Africa, 1:187; Robert Needham Cust, Africa Rediviva. Or, The Occupation of Africa by Christian Missionaries of Europe and North America (London: Elliott Stock, 1891), p. 1; and Pierson, Crisis of Missions, p. 131. See also Noble, Redemption of Africa, 1:187ff.; J. S. Mills, Africa and Mission Work in Sierra Leone, West Africa (Dayton, Ohio: United Brethren Publishing House, 1898), p. 19; Arthur T. Pierson, "Africa: A Wonderful Chapter in Modern History," Missionary Review of the World 11 (June 1888): 435; [Pierson], "The Dark Continent," Missionary Review of the World 11 (June 1888): 469; "Progress of Missions: Monthly Bulletin," Missionary Review of the World 13 (March 1890): 240; Josiah Tyler, "Signs of the Times in South Africa," Missionary Review of the World 16 (January 1893): 48–49; William E. Blackstone, "A Geographical Survey of Africa," in The Student Missionary Enterprise: Addresses and Discussions of the Second International Convention of the Student Volunteer Movement for Foreign Missions, Held at Detroit, Michigan, February 28 and March 1, 2, 3, and 4, 1894, ed. Max Wood Moorhead (Boston: T. O. Metcalfe and Co., n.d.), p. 285; J. C. Hartzell,

"The Open Door in Africa," in Hartzell, The Open Door, pp. 166, 168–69; and James McPherson, The Abolitionist Legacy: From Reconstruction to the NAACP (Princeton: Princeton University Press, 1975), pp. 324–32.

17. W. A. Stanton, "The People of Africa," Missionary Review of the World 14 (June 1891): 450–51; William Stephen Rainsford, The Story of a Varied Life: An Autobiography (Garden City, N.Y.: Doubleday, Page and Co., 1922), p. 121; and Newell Dwight Hillis, The Influence of Christ in Modern Life: Being a Study of the New Problems of the Church in American Society (New York: Macmillan, 1900), p. 98. See also Rainsford, Story of a Varied Life, p. 142; Rainsford, "Can Africa Be Civilized?," Outlook 93 (16 October 1909): 344–46; and Rainsford, The Land of the Lion (New York: Doubleday, Page and Co., 1909), pp. 366–416.

18. Mills, Africa and Mission Work in Sierra Leone, pp. 30–31; "Africa," Missionary Review of the World 31 (July 1898): 560; Speer, Presbyterian Foreign Missions, p. 38; Dennis, Christian Missions and Social Progress, 1:193–94; and Ellen C. Parsons, Christus Liberator: An Outline Study of Africa (New York: Young People's Missionary Movement, [ca. 1906]), pp. 1–2. See also J. M. Sherwood, "Shall Islam Rule Africa?," Missionary Review of the World 13 (July 1890): 552–54; Lemuel C. Garnes, "Shall Islam Rule Africa?," Missionary Review of the World 14 (July 1891): 528–31; Dennis, Christian Missions and Social Progress, 1:194–201; Dennis, Foreign Missions after a Century, pp. 110–11, 117–18; Noble, Redemption of Africa, 1:37–39, 174–77; 2:522–23; Wilson S. Naylor, Daybreak in the Dark Continent (New York: Eaton and Mains, 1905), p. 108; Parsons, Christus Liberator, pp. 64–67; and McCarthy, Dark Continent, pp. 104–7.

19. James S. Dennis, Social Evils of the Non-Christian World (New York: Student Volunteer Movement for Foreign Missions, 1899), pp. 34, 37, 45, 64; and Dennis, Christian Missions and Social Progress, 1:91–92, 128, 237. See also Dennis, Christian Missions and Social Progress, 2:160; Dennis, Social Evils of the Non-Christian World, pp. 45, 64; Mills, Africa and Mission Work in Sierra Leone, p. 32; Noble, Redemption of Africa, 2:582–84; Parsons, Christus Liberator, pp. 67–72; and Speer, Presbyterian Foreign Missions, p. 28.

20. Dennis, Christian Missions and Social Progress, 1:152–55, 160–61, 173–75, 178–79, 181, 324; 2:342–44; and Dennis, Social Evils of the Non-Christian World, pp. 39, 85–88, 91–92, 98–99, 102–3. See also Cook, "Divine Program on the Dark Continent," pp. 197–99; Dennis, Social Evils of the Non-Christian World, p. 107; Noble, "Christendom's Rum-Trade with Africa," pp. 418–19; Pierson, "Africa: A Wonderful Chapter," p. 411; Speer, Presbyterian Foreign Missions, p. 28; and McCarthy, Dark Continent, pp. 107–11.

21. Noble, "Christendom's Rum-Trade with Africa," pp. 412, 416. See also "Africa and Rum," Missionary Review of the World 11 (June 1888): 455–56; "The Two Great Curses of Africa," Independent 42 (2 January 1890): 11; Charles R. Henderson, "Individual Effort at Reform Not Sufficient," in The World's Parliament of Religions: An Illustrated and Popular Story of the World's First Parliament of Religions, Held in Chicago in Connection with the Columbian Exposition of 1893, 2 vols., ed. John Henry Barrows (Chicago: Parliament Publishing Co., 1893), 2:1064; Cook, "Divine Program on the Dark Continent," p. 197; Noble, "Evangelical Christianity and Africa," p. 426; Noble, Redemption of Africa, 1:182–83; Mills, Africa and Mission Work in Sierra Leone, p. 32; Dr. and Mrs. Wilbur F. Crafts and Misses Mary and Margaret W. Leitch, Protection of Native Races against Intoxicants and Opium (New York: Fleming H. Revell Co., 1900), pp. 32–51; Josiah Strong, "Introduction," in "Africa's

Appeal to Christendom," by Momolu Massaquoi, *Century* 69 (April 1905): 927–28; and Parsons, *Christus Liberator*, pp. 75–78.

22. James F. Claflin, "The Dark Problem of the Dark Continent," *The Dial* 11 (September 1890): 118.

23. Noble, "African Slave Trade of 1890," pp. 81, 86, 93–97; and Noble, "An African Devil's Business," pp. 433–35. See also "Africa," *Missionary Review of the World* 8 (July 1885): 321–23; Dennis, *Christian Missions and Social Progress*, 1:136–38; Dennis, *Social Evils of the Non-Christian World*, pp. 73–78; Mills, *Africa and Mission Work in Sierra Leone*, p. 34; Speer, *Presbyterian Foreign Missions*, p. 29; and Parsons, *Christus Liberator*, pp. 78–85.

24. Dennis, *Christian Missions and Social Progress*, 1:137–38; 2:295–96; Dennis, *Social Evils of the Non-Christian World*, p. 73; J. W. E. Bowen, ed., *Africa and the American Negro: Addresses and Proceedings of the Congress on Africa Held under the Auspices of the Stewart Missionary Foundation for Africa of Gammon Theological Seminary in Connection with the Cotton States and International Exposition, December 13–15, 1895* (Atlanta: Gammon Theological Seminary, 1896), pp. 103–12; Heli Chatelain to Booker T. Washington, 5 October 1896, in *The Booker T. Washington Papers*, 14 vols., ed. Louis R. Harlan et al. (Urbana: University of Illinois Press, 1972–89), 4:223–25; Heli Chatelain, *"The Open Sore of the World": Africa's Internal Slave-Trade and a Practical Plan for Its Extinction*, with an introduction by Josiah Strong (New York: n.p., 1896); and Heli Chatelain, "The Open Sore of the World and Its Healing," *Missionary Review of the World* 10 (June 1897): 417–22.

25. Arthur T. Pierson, "The Field is the World," in Johnston, *Report of the Centenary Conference on the Protestant Missions of the World*, 1:184; Samuel S. Sevier, "Mission Work in Africa," *Missionary Review of the World* 9 (November 1886): 532; and Dennis, *Christian Missions and Social Progress*, 1: opposite p. 152. See also "A Christian Colony in Africa," *Missionary Review of the World* 16 (May 1893): 370–71; Wilbur Fisk Crafts, *Lectures on Social Progress: With Outline of the Topic a Month Course of Reform Studies* (Washington, D.C.: Reform Bureau, 1897), p. 70; Rainsford, "Can Africa Be Civilized?," pp. 346–51; Rainsford, "How Can Africa Be Civilized?," *Outlook* 93 (30 October 1909): 501–9; and McCarthy, *Dark Continent*, pp. 111–14.

26. Noble, *Redemption of Africa*, 2:565–69. See also Dennis, *Christian Missions and Social Progress*, 1:450–51; Rainsford, "How Can Africa Be Civilized?," pp. 505–6; and Robert H. W. Shepherd, *Lovedale South Africa: The Story of a Century, 1841–1941* (Lovedale, C.P., South Africa: Lovedale Press, n.d.), pp. 152–72, 244–45, 257.

27. Francis Amasa Walker, "The Colored Race in the United States," *Forum* 11 (July 1891): 501–9; Frederick L. Hoffman, *Race Traits and Tendencies of the American Negro* (New York: Macmillan, 1896); and Washington Gladden, "Black Americans," Sermon 1462 (n.d. [ca. 1897]), Washington Gladden Papers, Ohio Historical Society. See also Fredrickson, *Black Image in the White Mind*, pp. 228–82.

28. Edwin S. Redkey, *Black Exodus: Black Nationalist and Back-to-Africa Movements, 1890–1910* (New Haven: Yale University Press, 1969), pp. 24–26; Robert A. Massey to William Coppinger, 2 August 1886, I-A, no. 264; Sherman G. Grisham to William Coppinger, 30 May 1887, I-A, no. 267; James DuBose to William Coppinger, 4 September 1890, I-A, no. 277; and J. S. Mattison to William Coppinger, 10 July 1890, I-A, no. 277, ACS Papers.

29. H. J. Jones to William Coppinger, 12 October 1885, I-A, no. 261; and Calvin L. Suggs to William Coppinger, 22 June 1886, I-A, no. 263, ACS Papers.

30. D. R. Carroll to William Coppinger, 5 January 1887, I-A, no. 266; William H. King to William Coppinger, 8 October 1888, I-A, no. 273; J. N. O. Young to William Coppinger, 14 May 1892, I-A, no. 283; and C. W. Wofford to William Coppinger, 13 September 1890, I-A, no. 278, ACS Papers. I have put these lines in verse form; otherwise, they appear as Young and Wofford penned them.

31. George W. Smith to William Coppinger, 19 July 1890, I-A, no. 227; Charley Lewis to William Coppinger, 14 November 1890, I-A, no. 278; and John Rose to William Coppinger, 4 November 1888, I-A, no. 273, ACS Papers.

32. B. R. Smith to William Coppinger, 2 August 1887, I-A, no. 268; G. Bailey to William Coppinger, 29 May 1886, I-A, no. 263; and James DuBose to William Coppinger, 15 September 1889, I-A, no. 275, ACS Papers.

33. R. E. Lee to Henry T. Beull, 3 April 1892, I-A, no. 284; and R. L. Davis to William Coppinger, 31 August 1891, I-A, no. 281, ACS Papers.

34. B. T. Willis to William Coppinger, 14 October 1890, I-A, no. 278; Edward W. Leonard to William Coppinger, 27 January 1888, I-A, no. 270; James Thompson to William Coppinger, 1 May 1889, I-A, no. 274; Philander Cooper to William Coppinger, 24 April 1890, I-A, no. 276; W. H. King to William Coppinger, 8 May 1891, I-A, no. 280; and Ann Logan to William Coppinger, 2 October 1891, I-A, no. 281, ACS Papers.

35. M. G. W. Hammond to William Coppinger, 16 January 1888, I-A, no. 270; and L. W. Wyatt to William Coppinger, 10 October 1890, I-A, no. 278, ACS Papers.

36. Lee Anderson et al. to William Coppinger, 20 May 1888, I-A, no. 271; George Byres to William Coppinger, 6 June 1886, I-A, no. 263; Daniel Futrell to William Coppinger, 11 January 1891, I-A, no. 279; and B. W. Whitaker to William Coppinger, 16 August 1885, I-A, no. 260, ACS Papers.

37. John Wright et al. to "James G. Blain," 27 January 1891, I-A, no. 279; D. S. Ford to William Coppinger, 29 March 1890, I-A, no. 276; and R. B. Wynn to William Coppinger, 18 March 1890, I-A, no. 276, ACS Papers.

38. J. Aspinwall Hodge, "America and Africa," *African Repository* 64 (July 1888): 75–85; R. M. Luther, "Reasons for Existence," *African Repository* 65 (July 1889): 65–76; and Redkey, *Black Exodus*, pp. 46, 73–126.

39. George Hodges, *Henry Codman Potter: Seventh Bishop of New York* (New York: Macmillan, 1915), pp. 32–36; James Sheerin, *Henry Codman Potter: An American Metropolitan* (New York: Fleming H. Revell Co., 1933), p. 30; Henry Codman Potter to William Coppinger, 10 December 1885, I-A, no. 260; Potter to Coppinger, 25 January 1886, I-A, no. 262; Potter to Coppinger, 3 April 1886, I-A, no. 263; Potter to Coppinger, 12 December 1887, I-A, no. 269; Thomas G. Addison to Potter, 1 May 1888, I-A, no. 271; Potter to Addison, 7 May 1888, I-A, no. 271; Potter to Coppinger, 8 December 1888, I-A, no. 273; G. W. Sampson to Coppinger, 29 October 1889, I-A, no. 275; Potter to Coppinger, 11 December 1890, I-A, no. 278, ACS Papers; and Henry Codman Potter, "Sermon Commemorative of John David Wolfe," *Waymarks, 1870–1891: Being Discourses, with Some Account of Their Occasions* (New York: E. P. Dutton and Co., 1893), p. 79.

40. Redkey, *Black Exodus*, pp. 117–34; Hodges, *Henry Codman Potter*, p. 262; Sheerin, *Henry Codman Potter*, p. 158; and "Future Work of the American Colonization Society," *Liberia* 1 (November 1892): 5–6.

41. Henry Codman Potter to U.S.A. News Co., n.d., cited in Charles S. Keyser, *Minden Armais: The Man of the New Race, with a Preface and Postface on the Establishment of the Marital Relation between the White and Black Races in the Former Slave States* (Philadelphia: American Printing House, 1892), p. 105; and Henry Codman Potter, "The Two Africas," *Liberia* 4 (February 1894): 12.

42. Potter, "Two Africas," p. 12; and Henry Codman Potter, *Man, Men and Their Master* (New York: Edwin S. Gorham, 1902), pp. 74–75.

43. Potter, "Two Africas," pp. 11–13; and "Address of President Potter," *Liberia* 2 (February 1893): 17–18. Potter's racial thought was influenced by Benjamin Kidd and George Roachford Stetson. On Kidd, see Benjamin Kidd, *Social Evolution* (London: Macmillan, 1894), pp. 51–53, 56, 62, 85, 326–41, 348–53; Kidd, "The Future of the Lower Races," *Liberia* 5 (November 1894): 49–63; Kidd, "The Elevation of Tropical Races," *Independent* 57 (8 September 1904): 545–50; and Henry Codman Potter to J. Ormand Wilson, 22 October 1894, I-A, no. 286, ACS Papers. The enthusiasm of Potter and other social gospel prophets for Kidd's anti-Lamarckian position casts doubt on Curtis R. Grant's argument that the social gospel prophets, including Potter, neglected race relations and the Negro because of their Lamarckian anthropology. Curtis R. Grant, "The Social Gospel and Race" (Ph.D. dissertation, Stanford University, 1968), pp. 156, 158, 167. On Stetson, see Stetson, "The Problem of Negro Education" (Boston: Cupples, Upham and Co., 1884); Stetson, "Commercial Africa," *Liberia* 3 (November 1893): 62; Stetson, "The Developmental Status of the American Negro," *Missionary Review of the World* 18 (June 1895): 437; Stetson, "The Developmental Status of the African Negro . . . ," *Liberia* 7 (November 1895): 23; Stetson, "Cannibals and Cannibalism," *Liberia* 11 (November 1897): 33–39; and H. T. Buell to J. Ormand Wilson, 10 February 1894, I-A, no. 285, ACS Papers.

44. Wendell Phillips Garrison to Robert Wilson Shufeldt, 18 January 1893, in Shufeldt's *The Negro: A Menace to American Civilization* (Boston: Richard G. Gadger, 1907), pp. 159–60; Redkey, *Black Exodus*, pp. 143–44; J. C. Braman to J. Ormand Wilson, 7 February 1894, I-A, no. 285; H. T. Buell to J. Ormand Wilson, 8 February 1894, I-A, no. 285; and Charles Hull Adams to J. Ormand Wilson, 14 February 1894, I-A, no. 285, ACS Papers.

45. Thomas U. Dudley to J. Ormand Wilson, 26 January 1894, I-A, no. 283, ACS Papers; J. E. Rankin, "Negro Emigration to Liberia," *Our Day* 13 (May–June 1894): 228; Joseph Cook, "The Fiendishness of Caste—Bishop Potter on Liberia," *Our Day* 13 (July–August 1894): 334–35; Charles Hull Adams to J. Ormand Wilson, 16 June 1894, I-A, no. 285; and H. T. Buell to J. Ormand Wilson, 16 June 1894, I-A, no. 285, ACS Papers.

46. Elliott M. Rudwick and August Meier, "Black Man in the 'White City': Negroes and the Columbian Exposition, 1893," *Phylon* 26 (1965): 354–61.

47. Joseph E. Roy, "The World's Congress on Africa," *American Missionary* 46 (August 1892): 254–55; "The African Congress," *American Missionary* 47 (October 1893): 306–8; Noble, *Redemption of Africa*, 2:491; Frederic Perry Noble, "Africa at the Columbian Exposi-

tion," *Our Day* 9 (November 1892): 782–88; Albion W. Tourgée to M. B. Castle, 7 July 1893, no. 7110, Tourgée Papers; Noble, "The Chicago Congress on Africa," p. 281; and J. T. Gracey, "The Congress on Africa at the Columbian Exposition," *Missionary Review of the World* 16 (November 1893): 840.

48. Frederic P. Noble, "The Chicago Congress on Africa," *Our Day* 12 (October 1893): 279–300; Frederick A. Noble, "Constitutional Rights of Colored Citizens," *Our Day* 12 (December 1893): 459–72; and "The Negro Congress at Chicago," *Independent* 45 (24 August 1893): 1146–47. Some of the papers were published in the *Methodist Quarterly Review*, the *Missionary Review of the World*, and *Our Day*. Noble used his file of the papers in writing his two-volume study, *The Redemption of Africa*.

49. Noble, "Chicago Congress on Africa," pp. 285–86, 291, 293; and [Benjamin F. Lee, "Editorial,"] *Christian Recorder* 29 (23 July 1891): 4.

50. James B. Simmons to Charles H. Corey, 12 March 1877, in Corey's *A History of the Richmond Theological Seminary, with Reminiscences of Thirty Years Work among the Colored People of the South* (Richmond: J. W. Randolph Co., 1895), p. 106. See also ibid., pp. 127, 129, 143–49, 158–59; L. L. Berry, *A Century of Missions of the African Methodist Episcopal Church* (Philadelphia: Missionary Department of the AME Church, 1942); Wilbur Christian Harr, "The Negro as an American Protestant Missionary in Africa" (Ph.D. dissertation, University of Chicago, 1948); Josephus R. Coan, "The Expansion of Missions of the African Methodist Episcopal Church in South Africa, 1896–1908" (Ph.D. dissertation, Hartford Seminary Foundation, 1961); William Seraile, "Black American Missionaries in Africa, 1821–1925," *Social Studies* 63 (October 1972): 198–202; Sandy Dwayne Martin, "Growth of Christian Missionary Interest in West Africa among Southeastern Baptists, 1880–1915" (Ph.D. dissertation, Columbia University, 1981); Walter L. Williams, *Black Americans in the Evangelization of Africa: 1877–1900* (Madison: University of Wisconsin Press, 1982); and Sylvia M. Jacobs, ed., *Black Americans and the Missionary Movement in Africa* (Westport, Conn.: Greenwood Press, 1982).

51. J. R. Bridges, "The Negro as Missionary," *Missionary Review of the World* 18 (May 1895): 327–31; William H. Sheppard, "Experiences of a Pioneer Missionary on the Congo," in *Students and the Modern Missionary Crusade: Addresses before the Fifth International Convention of the Student Volunteer Movement for Foreign Missions, Nashville, Tennessee, February 28–March 4, 1906* (New York: Student Volunteer Movement for Foreign Missions, 1906), pp. 291–96; Walter L. Williams, "William Henry Sheppard, Afro-American Missionary in the Congo, 1890–1910," in Jacobs, *Black Americans and the Missionary Movement*, pp. 135–53; and Lura Beam, *He Called Them by the Lightening: A Teacher's Odyssey in the Negro South, 1908–1919* (Indianapolis: Bobbs-Merrill, 1967), p. 147. See also Dennis, *Christian Missions and Social Progress*, 3:102–4.

52. R. W. Keeler to William Coppinger, 19 January 1889; enclosed handbill, "A New Departure: A Training School for Africa in Connection with Central Tennessee College, Nashville, Tenn.," I-A, no. 274; Arthur L. Shumway to William Coppinger, 24 November 1888, I-A, no. 274; Ezekiel E. Smith to William Coppinger, 28 April 1891, I-A, no. 280, ACS Papers; "Minute-Book of the Gammon Literary Society, 1885–1895," Special Collections Division, Woodruff Library, Atlanta University Center, Atlanta, Georgia; "A

New and Growing Interest in Liberia and Africa," *Liberia* 6 (February 1895): 67–71; and J. Ormand Wilson, "Stewart Missionary Foundation for Africa in Gammon Theological Seminary," *Liberia* 20 (November 1901): 6–12.

53. Richard S. Rust, "The Needs of African Men"; Frederic Perry Noble, "The Outlook for African Missions in the Twentieth Century"; and J. C. Hartzell, "The Division of the Dark Continent," in Bowen, *Africa and the American Negro*, pp. 211, 61–67, 56–57, respectively.

54. Alexander Crummell, "Civilization as a Collateral and Indispensable Instrumentality in Planting the Christian Church in Africa"; Crummell, "The Absolute Need of an Indigenous Missionary Agency for the Evangelization of Africa"; and Henry M. Turner, "The American Negro and the Fatherland," in Bowen, *Africa and the American Negro*, pp. 119–24, 137–42, 195–96, respectively.

55. T. Thomas Fortune, "The Nationalization of Africa," and John H. Smyth, "The African in Africa and the African in America," in Bowen, *Africa and the American Negro*, pp. 199–204, 73. See also ibid., pp. 75, 82–83.

56. Wilbur P. Thirkield, "Opening Remarks," and Thomas G. Addison, "The Policy of the American Colonization Society," in Bowen, *Africa and the American Negro*, pp. 14, 85–86.

57. Henry M. Turner to "Sir," 29 December 1892, I-A, no. 283, ACS Papers; Redkey, *Black Exodus*, pp. 176–83; and Edwin S. Redkey, ed., *Respect Black: The Writings and Speeches of Henry McNeal Turner* (New York: Arno Press, 1971), p. 146. See also Turner to Byron Sunderland, 29 December 1892, I-A, no. 283, ACS Papers.

58. Redkey, *Black Exodus*, pp. 186–276.

59. Booker T. Washington, *Up from Slavery: An Autobiography* (New York: A. L. Burt Co., 1900), p. 219; Edward W. Blyden, "The African Problem," *North American Review* 161 (September 1895): 338–39; Alexander Crummell to John Edward Bruce, 26 November 1895, John Edward Bruce Papers, Schomberg Collection, New York Public Library; and "Editorial," *Independent* 50 (1 December 1898): 1606. See also Wesley J. Gaines, *The Negro and the White Man* (Philadelphia: AME Publishing House, 1897), pp. 203–12; Redkey, *Respect Black*, pp. 161–63; "A Negro's Opinion of Negroes," *Independent* 52 (7 June 1900): 1378–79; and Hollis R. Lynch, *Edward Wilmot Blyden: Pan-Negro Patriot, 1832–1912* (London: Oxford University Press, 1967), p. 135.

60. *Atlanta Constitution*, 25 September–1 October 1895; and James Melvin Washington, *Frustrated Fellowship: Black Baptist Quest for Social Power* (Macon, Ga.: Mercer University Press, 1986).

61. Howard Potter to C. C. Nott, 6 January 1895, I-A, no. 287; C. C. Nott to Howard Potter, 21 January 1895, I-A, no. 287, ACS Papers; and Redkey, *Black Exodus*, pp. 146–48.

62. William H. Heard, *The Bright Side of African Life* (n.p.: AME Publishing House, 1898), pp. 31, 96. Potter was succeeded by the Reverend Julius E. Grammer, another alumnus of Virginia Theological Seminary who was ordained by Bishop Meade. Orator Cook later joined the U.S. Department of Agriculture where his research helped to combat the boll weevil in the cotton belt. "Orator Fuller Cook," in *The National Cyclopedia of American Biography* (New York: James T. White and Co., 1953), 38:369.

Chapter 4

1. James M. McPherson, *The Struggle for Equality: Abolitionists and the Negro in the Civil War and Reconstruction* (Princeton: Princeton University Press, 1964), pp. 287–307; John L. Thomas, *The Liberator: William Lloyd Garrison, A Biography* (Boston: Little, Brown and Co., 1963), pp. 415–35, 448–49; Irving H. Bartlett, *Wendell Phillips: Brahmin Radical* (Boston: Beacon Press, 1961), pp. 276–385; Tilden G. Edelstein, *Strange Enthusiasm: A Life of Thomas Wentworth Higginson* (New Haven: Yale University Press, 1968), pp. 290–319; and Oscar Sherwin, "Philosopher of Agitation," *Phylon* 6 (1945): 235–39.

2. Jesse Henry Jones, *The Kingdom of God: What It Is; Where It Is; and the Duty of American Christians concerning It* (Boston: The Author, 1871), pp. 204–5, 222–25, 273; Charles Howard Hopkins, *The Rise of the Social Gospel in American Protestantism, 1865–1915* (New Haven: Yale University Press, 1940), pp. 43–49; Henry F. May, *Protestant Churches and Industrial America* (New York: Harper and Brothers, 1949), pp. 74–79; Arthur Mann, *Yankee Reformers in the Urban Age: Social Reform in Boston, 1880–1900* (Cambridge: Harvard University Press, 1954), pp. 86–90, 178–84; and George Fredrickson, *The Inner Civil War: Northern Intellectuals and the Crisis of the Union* (New York: Harper and Row, 1968), pp. 196–98.

3. Bartlett, *Wendell Phillips*, pp. 327–28; and Jesse H. Jones, *His Last Battle and One of His Greatest Victories; Being the Speech of Wendell Phillips in Faneuil Hall on the Louisiana Difficulties, January 15, 1875* (Boston: Wendell Phillips Memorial Association, 1897). James McPherson found that 71 percent of former abolitionists agreed with Phillips's support of Grant's action. McPherson, *The Abolitionist Legacy: From Reconstruction to the NAACP* (Princeton: Princeton University Press, 1975), pp. 46–50.

4. William H. Cook to Joseph Cook, 16 November 1856, in Frederick G. Bascom, ed., *Letters of a Ticonderoga Farmer: Selections from the Correspondence of William H. Cook and His Wife with Their Son, Joseph Cook, 1851–1885* (Ithaca: Cornell University Press, 1946), p. 46; Joseph Cook, *The Three Despised Races in the United States; or, The Chinaman, the Indian, and the Freedman* (New York: American Missionary Association, 1878), pp. 18–19; and Cook, "Enfranchised Ignorance in the South," in *Boston Monday Lectures: Conscience, with Preludes on Current Events* (Boston: Houghton, Osgood and Co., 1879), p. 122. See also Hopkins, *Rise of the Social Gospel*, pp. 39–42; and May, *Protestant Churches*, pp. 164–66.

5. James Jeffrey Roche, *Life of John Boyle O'Reilly, Together with His Complete Poems and Speeches* (New York: Mershon Co., 1891), pp. 142–43, 288–89, 739; Bartlett, *Wendell Phillips*, pp. 381–82; and John R. Betts, "The Negro and the New England Conscience in the Days of John Boyle O'Reilly," *Journal of Negro History* 51 (October 1966): 248, 251–52.

6. John Boyle O'Reilly, "Crispus Attucks," in *A Memorial to Crispus Attucks, Samuel Maverick, James Caldwell, Samuel Gray and Patrick Carr* (Miami: Mnemosyne Publishing, 1969), pp. iv, 1–8; Betts, "Negro and New England Conscience," pp. 252–53, 258; Roche, *John Boyle O'Reilly*, pp. 326, 341, 349, 740–41; and William G. Schofield, *Seek for a Hero: The Story of John Boyle O'Reilly* (New York: P. J. Kennedy and Sons, 1956), p. 272.

7. John Boyle O'Reilly, "Wendell Phillips," in *In Bohemia* (Boston: Pilot Publishing Co., 1886), pp. iv, ix, 1–6; and Roche, *John Boyle O'Reilly*, p. 369. See also the funeral oration by the black Roman Catholic Bishop of Maine, James Augustine Healy, in Roche, *John Boyle O'Reilly*, pp. 372–73.

8. Edmund Wilson, *Patriotic Gore: Studies in the Literature of the American Civil War* (New York: Oxford University Press, 1956), pp. 537, 559–62.

9. Otto H. Olsen, *Carpetbagger's Crusade: The Life of Albion Winegar Tourgée* (Baltimore: Johns Hopkins University Press, 1965), pp. 12–222; and Theodore L. Gross, *Albion W. Tourgée* (New York: Twayne Publishers, 1963), p. 21.

10. George Washington Cable, "My Politics," in *The Negro Question: A Selection of Writings on Civil Rights in the South by George W. Cable,* ed. Arlin Turner (Garden City, N.Y.: Doubleday and Co., 1958), pp. 2–4.

11. Ibid., pp. 6, 8–9; Arlin Turner, "George W. Cable's Beginnings as a Reformer," *Journal of Southern History* 17 (May 1951): 136–51; and Cable, "Segregation in the Schools," in Turner, *The Negro Question,* pp. 26–33. See also Turner, *George W. Cable: A Biography* (Durham, N.C.: Duke University Press, 1956), pp. 75–78; Louis R. Harlan, "Desegregation in New Orleans Public Schools during Reconstruction," *American Historical Review* 67 (April 1962): 663–75; John W. Blassingame, *Black New Orleans, 1860–1880* (Chicago: University of Chicago Press, 1973), pp. 112–22; and Roger A. Fischer, *The Segregation Struggle in Louisiana, 1862–1877* (Urbana: University of Illinois Press, 1974), pp. 119–34.

12. [Anna Julia Cooper], *A Voice from the South, by a Black Woman of the South* (Xenia, Ohio: Aldine Printing House, 1892), pp. 188–89.

13. [Tourgée], *A Fool's Errand by One of the Fools* (New York: J. B. Ford, 1879), pp. 341, 3. This interpretation differs with that of Gross, *Albion Tourgée,* pp. 82–83. For the biblical usage, compare 1 Corinthians 4 and Hebrews 11 with [Tourgée], *A Fool's Errand,* pp. 3–4, 340–41. Tourgée apparently took the title of the novel from a conservative attack on his radical program and gave it the ironic meaning suggested in the text. See Olsen, *Carpetbagger's Crusade,* p. 95.

14. Tourgée, *Bricks without Straw* (New York: Fords, Howard and Hulbert, 1880), pp. 272, 400. See also ibid., [pp. 1–3].

15. Tourgée, *An Appeal to Caesar* (New York: Fords, Howard and Hulbert, 1884), p. 357; Olsen, *Carpetbagger's Crusade,* pp. 218–19, 242–51, 259–60, 286, 300–308; and Daniel W. Crofts, "The Black Response to the Blair Education Bill," *Journal of Southern History* 37 (February 1971): 41–65.

16. Cable, "My Politics," pp. 14–15, 18–19; Cable, "The Good Samaritan," and Cable, "The Freedmen's Case in Equity," in Turner, *The Negro Question,* pp. 36, 68. See also Joel Williamson, *The Crucible of Race: Black-White Relations in the American South since Emancipation* (New York: Oxford University Press, 1984), pp. 97–99.

17. Cable, "Freedmen's Case in Equity," pp. 53, 60, 61.

18. Ibid., p. 63; Cable, "The Silent South," in Turner, *The Negro Question,* pp. 84–85, 113–14; [Tanner], "Our Monthlies," *AME Church Review* 1 (April 1885): 408; and [Tanner], "Our Review," *AME Church Review* 2 (January 1886): 246–47. See also Henry W. Grady, "In Plain Black and White," *Century* 29 (April 1885): 909–17; and Turner, *George W. Cable,* pp. 197–217.

19. Turner, *George W. Cable,* pp. 242–48; and Cable, "What Shall the Negro Do?," in Turner, *The Negro Question,* pp. 154–55. See also *AME Church Review* 5 (October 1888): 159–64.

20. Cable, "The Negro Question," in Turner, *The Negro Question*, pp. 119–52; and Turner, *George W. Cable*, pp. 248–52.

21. Cable was more influential among Northern social gospel prophets on race relations than any other white Southerner except Atticus Haygood before 1900. See Joseph Cook, "Nullification and Murder in the Southern States," *Our Day* 3 (May 1889): 458–59; Richard T. Ely, *Social Aspects of Christianity and Other Essays* (New York: Thomas Y. Crowell and Co., 1889), pp. 58–59; Frederick A. Noble, "Constitutional Rights of Colored Citizens," *Our Day* 12 (December 1893): 466–68; "Recent Fiction," *Independent* 42 (24 April 1890): 561; Cable, "The Negro Question," in *My Brother and I*, ed. William Ingraham Haven (New York: Hunt and Eaton, 1895), pp. 75–124; and John Bascom, *Social Theory: A Grouping of Social Facts and Principles* (New York: Thomas Y. Crowell, 1895), pp. 74–76.

22. Turner, *The Negro Question*, pp. 179–82; Turner, *George W. Cable*, pp. 264–65; and J. B. Eustis, "Race Antagonism in the South," *Forum* 6 (October 1888): 144–54.

23. Atticus G. Haygood, "Senator Eustis on the Negro Problem," *Independent* 40 (8 November 1888): 1426–27; William M. Baskervill et al., "Shall the Negro be Educated or Suppressed: Dr. Haygood's Reply to Senator Eustis, A Symposia," *Independent* 41 (21 February 1889): 225–27; Turner, *The Negro Question*, pp. 169, 177–80; and Turner, *George W. Cable*, pp. 265–66.

24. Turner, *George W. Cable*, pp. 262–72; and Ely, *Social Aspects of Christianity*, pp. 58–59.

25. Emma Lou Thornbrough, "The National Afro-American League, 1887–1908," *Journal of Negro History* 37 (November 1961): 494–512; August Meier, *Negro Thought in America, 1880–1915: Racial Ideologies in the Age of Booker T. Washington* (Ann Arbor: University of Michigan Press, 1963); Robert L. Factor, *The Black Response to America: Men, Ideals and Organization from Frederick Douglass to the NAACP* (Reading, Mass.: Addison-Wesley, 1970), pp. 119–28; and "The Proposed Negro League," *Independent* 41 (November 1889): 1463.

26. Cleveland *Plaindealer*, 12 October 1889, Tourgée Papers, no. 4062. Microfilm, Southern Historical Collection, University of North Carolina, Chapel Hill; and Tourgée to W. S. Scarborough, 27 November 1889. W. S. Scarborough Papers, Wilberforce University. The letter explains in detail how the league might be modeled along the lines of the Klan. I am in debt to Professor Will Gravely of the University of Denver for bringing this letter to my attention.

27. Price's admirers among the social gospel prophets included Lyman Abbott, Henry Ward Beecher, A. J. F. Behrends, Amory Bradford, Phillips Brooks, J. M. Buckley, S. Parkes Cadman, Joseph Cook, William E. Dodge, Atticus Haygood, Archbishop John Ireland, Anson Phelps Stokes, and William Hayes Ward. See W. F. Fonvielle, *Reminiscences of College Days* (n.p.: Edwards and Broughton, 1904), pp. 85–87; and William Jacob Walls, *Joseph Charles Price: Educator and Race Leader* (Boston: Christopher Publishing House, 1943).

28. Price reiterated this theme in Joseph C. Price, "The Negro in the Last Decade of the Century: What He Can Do for Himself," *Independent* 43 (1 January 1891): 5.

29. James H. Moynihan, *The Life of Archbishop John Ireland* (New York: Harper and Brothers, 1953), pp. 6–7, 228; Betts, "Negro and New England Conscience," pp. 253, 253n; "Editorial Notes," *Independent* 42 (15 May 1890): 662–64; and Charles S. Keyser,

*Minden Armais: The Man of the New Race. With a Preface and Postface on the Establishment of the Marital Relation between the White and Black Races in the Former Slave States* (Philadelphia: American Printing House, 1892), pp. 106–7. See also Moynihan, *Archbishop John Ireland*, p. 229; and John Murphy, *An Analysis of the Attitudes of American Catholics toward the Immigrant and the Negro, 1825–1925* (Washington, D.C.: Catholic University of America Press, 1940), pp. 118–40.

30. Meier, *Negro Thought in America*, p. 70; and Joseph C. Price, "Does the Negro Seek Social Equality," *Forum* 10 (January 1891): 564. See also L. M. H. Hagood, "The Southern Problem," *Methodist Review* 73 (May 1891): 434; W. S. Scarborough, "The Negro Question," *Arena* 4 (July 1891): 220; and Tourgée's letters to Price and William H. Anderson lamenting the moderation of the league's course: Tourgée to Price, n.d., no. 11043; Tourgée memo, n.d., no. 4408; Price to Tourgée, 18 March 1890, no. 4568; Tourgée to Price, 3 April 1890, no. 4603; Tourgée to Anderson, n.d., no. 5143; and Anderson to Tourgée, 18 April 1890, no. 4644, Tourgée Papers.

31. Atticus G. Haygood, "A Nation's Work and Duty: If Universal Suffrage, Then Universal Education," in *Pleas for Progress* (Nashville: Publishing House of the ME Church, South, 1889), pp. 55–82.

32. William Channing Gannett, "The Suffrage," p. 12; Gannett, "The Sea Islands and their Disaster," p. 3. Sermons 22 and 509, Gannett Manuscript Sermon File, Colgate-Rochester Divinity School; and Lyman Abbott, "The Powers of the Keys," in *Signs of Promise: Sermons Preached in Plymouth Pulpit, Brooklyn, 1887–1889* (New York: Fords, Howard and Hulbert, 1889), pp. 182–83. See also "Address of President Eaton," *American Missionary* 44 (January 1890): 7; "The Political Rights of Negroes," *Andover Review* 13 (March 1890): 306; Bordon Parker Bowne, *The Principles of Ethics* (New York: American Book Co., 1892), pp. 284–86; Richard T. Ely, *An Introduction to Political Economy* (New York: Chautauqua Press, 1889), pp. 262–63; George W. Gray, "National Perpetuity," in *Twenty-First Annual Report of the Freedmen's Aid and Southern Education Society of the Methodist Episcopal Church for Year Ending July 1, 1888* (n.p., n.d.), p. 57; and John Ireland, *The Church and Modern Society: Lectures and Addresses*, 2 vols. (New York: D. H. McBride and Co., [1896]), 1:166, 176, 179; 2:105–6.

33. Gannett, "The Suffrage," p. 9; Washington Gladden, "Safeguards of the Suffrage," *Century* 37 (February 1889): 620–22; and Wilbur Fisk Crafts, *Practical Christian Sociology: A Series of Special Lectures before Princeton Seminary and Marietta College* (New York: Funk and Wagnalls, 1895), p. 81. See also Bowne, *Principles of Ethics*, pp. 284–86; Charles Fletcher Dole, *The American Citizen* (Boston: D. C. Heath and Co., 1892), p. 148; Gladden, "Relations of Young People to Church and State," pp. 5–6; and Gladden, "Social Movements in Europe," pp. 14–18, Sermons 378 (17 March 1889) and 575 (23 September 1894), Washington Gladden Papers, Ohio Historical Society. On widespread doubt about universal suffrage in the period, see J. Morgan Kousser, *The Shaping of Southern Politics: Suffrage Restriction and the Establishment of the One-Party South, 1880–1910* (New Haven: Yale University Press, 1974), pp. 57, 250–57.

34. Gladden, "Safeguards of the Suffrage," p. 621; and Noble, "Constitutional Rights of Colored Citizens," pp. 465–66. See also Gladden, "Moral Reconstruction," in *The Nation Still in Danger; or, Ten Years after the War: A Plea by the American Missionary Association* (n.p.:

American Missionary Association, 1875), pp. 13–16; and Lyman Abbott, "Salvation by Growth," in *Signs of Promise*, p. 195.

35. "Passage of the Lodge Election Bill," *Independent* 42 (10 July 1890): 959; A. J. F. Behrends, *The Christ of Nineteen Centuries* (Brooklyn: T. B. Ventries, 1909), p. 110; and Cable as quoted in Lawrence J. Friedman, *The White Savage: Racial Fantasies in the Postbellum South* (Englewood Cliffs, N.J.: Prentice-Hall, 1970), p. 105. See also the *Independent's* almost weekly editorials in favor of the Lodge Bill from "Southern Congressional Elections," *Independent* 41 (12 September 1889): 1178–79, through "Fifty-first Congress," *Independent* 43 (12 March 1891): 378.

36. Joseph Cook, "Nullification and Murder in the Southern States," *Our Day* 3 (May 1889): 453, 455–58. See also Cook, "New Duties of the New North," *Our Day* 3 (June 1889): 562–69; and Cook, "Race Riots in the South," *Our Day* 5 (May 1890): 406–18.

37. Albion W. Tourgée, "Shall White Minorities Rule?," *Forum* 7 (April 1889): 144, 150, 155; and Olsen, *Carpetbagger's Crusade*, pp. 303–4. For other arguments for federal intervention in the South, see "Editorial Notes," *Our Day* 2 (July 1888): 78–80; "The Race Question," *Methodist Review* 72 (January 1890): 115–20; Tourgée, "The Right to Vote," *Forum* 9 (March 1890): 78–92; "Vital Points of Expert Opinion," *Our Day* 5 (May 1890): 435–38; W. S. Scarborough, "The Political Necessity of a Federal Election Law," *Our Day* 6 (July 1890): 25–33; Wayland Hoyt, "The Negro a Part of the Country," *Independent* 42 (3 July 1890): 909; F. H. Hitchcock, "The Lodge Bill," *Christian Union* 42 (28 August 1890): 280; and Russell Hall, "Southern Republicans and the Lodge Bill," *Christian Union* 42 (25 December 1890): 894.

38. McPherson, *Abolitionist Legacy*, pp. 134–37; Louis R. Harlan, *Booker T. Washington: The Making of a Black Leader, 1856–1900* (New York: Oxford University Press, 1972), p. 164; Meier, *Negro Thought in America*, pp. 70–71; and Factor, *Black Response to America*, pp. 125–28. On the Lodge Bill, see Richard E. Welch, Jr., "The Federal Elections Bill of 1890: Postscripts and Prelude," *Journal of American History* 52 (December 1965): 511–26; and Kousser, *Shaping of Southern Politics*, pp. 20–22, 29–33.

39. Roche, *John Boyle O'Reilly*, p. 342; Michael E. Strieby, "What the Decade Should Do for the Negro," *Independent* 43 (1 January 1891): 9; "The Political Rights of Negroes," *Andover Review* 13 (March 1890): 308; and "The Outlook," *Christian Union* 42 (10 July 1890): 36. See the *Christian Union's* almost weekly editorials against the Lodge Bill from "Editorial," *Christian Union* 41 (1 January 1890): 1, to "With Charity toward All," *Christian Union* 43 (5 February 1891): 166.

40. Joseph Cook favored both a literacy test for voting and federal supervision of federal elections. See Cook, "Fraudulent Elections, South and North: Possible Future of Political Corruption," *Our Day* 6 (August 1890): 124–37; Cook, "Unsolved Southern Problems," *Our Day* 8 (July 1891): 30–41; Cook, "Fraud at the Ballot Box," *Our Day* 10 (November 1892): 814–24; and Cook, "New Black Codes at the South," *Our Day* 12 (July 1893): 47, 53.

41. "Questions to Specialists," *Our Day* 11 (March 1892): 225; Gladden, "Safeguards of the Suffrage," p. 621; Edward Everett Hale, "Suffrage," *Cosmopolitan* 14 (February 1893): 478; and "Political Rights of Negroes," p. 308. See also Crafts, *Practical Christian Sociology*, pp. 216–17; Thomas Dixon, Jr., *Living Problems in Religion and Social Science*, 2d ed. (New

York: Funk and Wagnalls, 1892), p. 253; "Editorial," *Christian Union* 41 (1 January 1890): 1; "Editorial," *Christian Union* 41 (5 June 1890): 795; "The Outlook," *Christian Union* 42 (4 September 1890): 291; and Lyman Abbott, *The Spirit of Democracy* (Boston: Houghton Mifflin Co., 1910), p. 183.

42. The constitution also contained an "understanding clause" that allowed some illiterates to be registered. Vernon Lane Wharton, *The Negro in Mississippi: 1865–1900* (New York: Harper and Row, 1965), pp. 206–15; Kousser, *Shaping of Southern Politics*, pp. 138–45; and Tourgée to J. Gray Lucas, 28 February 1891, no. 5374, Tourgée Papers.

43. "The Outlook," *Christian Union* 42 (24 September 1890): 291; "The Spectacle of Mississippi," *Independent* 42 (28 August 1890): 1198; and "Editorial Notes," *Independent* 42 (25 September 1890): 1340. See also "The Mississippi Plan of Disfranchisement," *Independent* 42 (4 September 1890): 1236; "Address of Prof. F. G. Woodworth," *American Missionary* 44 (December 1890): 426; and William Channing Gannett, "The Sea Islands and Their Disaster," p. 3, Gannett Manuscript Sermon File.

44. "Editorial Notes," *Independent* 43 (18 June 1891): 911; and "The Mississippi Plan," *Independent* 44 (11 August 1892): 1212.

45. Tourgée to D. Augustus Straker, 27 February 1890, no. 4514; and Tourgée to J. Gray Lucas, 28 February 1891, no. 5374, Tourgée Papers. See also William Lloyd Garrison to Tourgée, 18 April 1894, no. 7638, Tourgée Papers.

46. Tourgée to Anna J. Cooper, n.d. [ca. 1 June 1891], no. 5690, Tourgée Papers.

47. Tourgée to W. S. Scarborough, 29 November 1889, Scarborough Papers; Tourgée to "My Dear Sir," n.d., no. 5145; Tourgée to Joseph C. Price, 3 April 1890, no. 4603; and Tourgée to Anna J. Cooper, n.d. [ca. 1 June 1891], no. 5690, Tourgée Papers.

48. C. Vann Woodward, "The Birth of Jim Crow," *American Heritage* 15 (April 1964): 53; Olsen, *Carpetbagger's Crusade*, pp. 309–10; Sidney Kaplan, "Albion W. Tourgée: Attorney for the Segregated," *Journal of Negro History* 49 (April 1964): 128–33; L. A. Martinet to Tourgée, 5 October 1891, no. 5760; Tourgée to L. A. Martinet, n.d. [ca. 8 October 1891], no. 5813; and Martinet to Tourgée, 11 October 1891, no. 5763, Tourgée Papers. Tourgée and Martinet also hoped to challenge the Mississippi literacy requirement for voting. Martinet to Tourgée, 25 October 1891, no. 5763, Tourgée Papers.

49. Frederick Reed to Albion Tourgée, 29 April 1890, no. 4671; Martha Schofield to Tourgée, 1 September 1890, no. 4912; C. H. Crawford to Tourgée, 7 November 1891, no. 7614; Minnie M. Curtis to Tourgée, 22 December 1891, no. 5667; W. E. C. Wright to Tourgée, n.d. [1893], no. 7614; Clara E. Noble to Tourgée, 13 October 1893; A. J. Steele to Tourgée, 15 September 1894, no. 8033; and David Gregg to Tourgée, 30 April 1890, no. 4670, Tourgée Papers. See also Henry C. McCook to Mrs. Albion Tourgée, 28 May 1890, no. 4761; Francis H. Rowley to Tourgée, 9 September 1893, no. 7321; Tourgée to Rowley, n.d. [ca. 14 September 1893], no. 7370; Rowley to Tourgée, 19 September 1893, no. 7345; Rowley to Tourgée, 2 November 1893, no. 7453; J. C. Hartzell to Tourgée, 29 November 1893, no. 7547; and Rowley to Tourgée, 27 June 1894, no. 7837, Tourgée Papers.

50. Tourgée to George W. Cable, n.d. [November 1891], no. 5899; Cable to Tourgée, 3 December 1891, no. 5818; and Cable to Tourgée, 19 December 1891, no. 5862; Catherine Impey to Tourgée, 16 June 1890, no. 4785, Tourgée Papers; "A True Friend to Visit

America," *AME Church Review* 9 (July 1892): 84–85; and Catherine Impey, "Extracts from the Editor's Diary of a Visit to 'Cedar Hill,'" *Anti-Caste* 7 (April–May 1895): 14–16. After the failure of his Open Letter Club, Cable seems to have had more hope in the meliorating effects of education than in political solutions to civil inequity. See "Address of Geo. W. Cable, Esq.," *American Missionary* 45 (January 1891): 8–13; Cable, "Does the Negro Pay for His Education," *Forum* 13 (July 1892): 640–49; Cable, "Education for the Common People in the South," *Cosmopolitan* 14 (November 1892): 63–68; and Louis D. Rubin, Jr., *George W. Cable: The Life and Times of a Southern Heretic* (New York: Pegasus, 1969), pp. 242–44.

51. Samuel Batty to Tourgée, 19 December 1891, no. 7614; and Horace Baker to Tourgée, 10 June 1892, no. 6317, Tourgée Papers. See also John W. Still[man?] to Tourgée, December 1890, no. 4931; S. P. Lervis to Tourgée, 6 February 1891, no. 5294; Augustus Hammond to Tourgée, 8 February 1891, no. 5300; W. P. Roberts to Tourgée, 14 February 1891, no. 5307; L. Frost to Tourgée, 8 April 1892, no. 6174; and Tourgée to L. L. Frost, n.d. [ca. 25 April 1892], no. 6209, Tourgée Papers.

52. Olsen, *Carpetbagger's Crusade*, p. 313; and John Barnard, *From Evangelicalism to Progressivism at Oberlin College, 1866–1917* (Columbus: Ohio State University Press, 1969), pp. 61–62, 85–105, 114–26. A poll of Oberlin students in 1891 found 72 percent favored a literacy test for voting; see Wilbur Fisk Crafts, "An Oberlin Ballot on Current Reforms," *Our Day* 7 (February 1891): 117–18.

53. Jesse Macy, *The Bible as a Book of Reform: An Address before the Christian Association of Iowa College, Sunday, October 9, 1881* (Grinnell, Iowa: The Association, 1881); George Davis Herron, *The Call of the Cross: Four College Sermons*, introd. George A. Gates (New York: Fleming H. Revell Co., 1892), pp. 53–57; Herron, *The Christian Society* (New York: Fleming H. Revell Co., 1894), pp. 22–23; Herron, *The Christian State: A Political Vision of Christ* (New York: Thomas Y. Crowell and Co., 1895), p. 23; Herron, *Social Meanings of Religious Experiences* (New York: Thomas Y. Crowell and Co., 1896), p. 120; Herron, *Between Caesar and Jesus* (New York: Thomas Y. Crowell and Co., 1899), pp. 268–69; Charles L. Fitch to Tourgée, 24 February 1892, no. 6053; Tourgée to Fitch, n.d. [ca. 28 February 1892], no. 6065; Fitch to Tourgée, 3 March 1892, no. 6079; Fitch and Charles D. Seaton to Tourgée, 17 May 1892, no. 7614, Tourgée Papers. Later, Tourgée was a featured speaker at Grinnell. George A. Gates to Tourgée, 17 April 1897, no. 9298; Gates to Tourgée, 8 May 1897, no. 9347; and Gates to Tourgée, 1 June 1897, no. 9473, Tourgée Papers. The best treatment of the social gospel at Grinnell is Robert T. Handy, "George D. Herron and the Kingdom Movement," *Church History* 19 (June 1950): 97–115.

54. Nathan F. Mossell to Tourgée, 18 November 1891, no. 7514; Tourgée to Mossell, 2 December 1891, no. 5814; Florence A. Lewis to Tourgée, 2 December 1891, no. 5816; Henry O. Tanner to Tourgée, 3 July 1893, no. 7614; Tanner to Tourgée, 3 August 1893, no. 7614; Tanner et al. to Tourgée, 1 October 1893, no. 7614; Tourgée to Tanner et al., n.d. [ca. 5 October 1893], no. 7614; Tanner to Tourgée, 2 March 1894, no. 7623; and Matthew Anderson to Tourgée, 4 March 1895, no. 8360, Tourgée Papers.

55. Charlotte F. Grimké to Tourgée, 18 May 1892, no. 6240, Tourgée Papers. See also George W. Jackson to Tourgée, 3 March 1891, no. 5391; John R. Lynch, P. B. S. Pinchback, Blanche K. Bruce, Frederick Douglass, Jesse Lawson et al. to Tourgée, 9 May 1892,

no. 6225; Tourgée to Grimké, n.d. [ca. 24 May 1892], no. 6297; Grimké to Tourgée, 27 May 1892, no. 7614; Jesse Lawson to Tourgée, 4 June 1892, no. 7614; and Grimké to Tourgée, 7 June 1892, no. 7614, Tourgée Papers.

56. J. H. Jenkins to Tourgée, n.d. [ca. 3 January 1892], no. 5916, Tourgée Papers. See also S. Laing Williams to Tourgée, 31 October 1891, no. 5775; Ida B. Wells to Tourgée, 2 July 1892, no. 6374; J. T. Jennifer to Tourgée, 10 February 1892, no. 7614; Williams to Tourgée, 13 September 1892, no. 7614; Wells to Emma K. Tourgée, 3 November 1892, no. 7614; Wells to Tourgée, 22 February 1893, no. 6645; Wells to Emma K. Tourgée, 19 May 1895, no. 8530; and Wells-Barnett to Emma K. Tourgée, 26 August 1895, no. 8801, Tourgée Papers. For letters of support from black Baltimore and Cleveland, see W. Ashbie Hawkins to Tourgée, 20 November 1893, no. 7508; Charles W. Chesnutt to Tourgée, 18 April 1893, no. 6776; and George W. Prioleau to Tourgée, 7 January 1892, no. 5933, Tourgée Papers. But there were important centers of black opposition to Tourgée, especially in the Northern black press; see Olsen, *Carpetbagger's Crusade*, pp. 318–19.

57. A. M. Middlebrooks to Tourgée, 5 April 1891, no. 5494; Mrs. E. A. S. Mixon to Tourgée, 2 May 1893, no. 6923; G. L. Thornton to Tourgée, 5 October 1892, no. 7614; Alfred O. Coffin to Tourgée, 4 January 1891, no. 5207; and Mrs. H. Davis to Tourgée, 26 March 1892, no. 6142, Tourgée Papers. See also A. P. Hood to Tourgée, 1 December 1895, no. 8846; James William McCray to Tourgée, 13 February [1895 or 1896?], no. 9194; Sylvannus Henry to Tourgée, 18 November 1890, no. 5042, Tourgée Papers; and Otto Olsen, ed., "Albion W. Tourgée and Negro Militants of the 1890s: A Documentary Selection," *Science and Society* 28 (Spring 1964): 183–204.

58. Olsen, *Carpetbagger's Crusade*, pp. 317–18; and Tourgée to "Sir," 10 October 1893, no. 7408, Tourgée Papers. Tourgée's NCRA membership figures are almost certainly inflated, but the sheer bulk of his correspondence with its members is impressive.

59. Olsen, *Carpetbagger's Crusade*, pp. 298, 320–21, 325–26; Francis H. Rowley to Tourgée, 27 June 1894, no. 7663; and Fredrick L. McGhee to Tourgée, 26 September 1894, no. 8050, Tourgée Papers.

60. Tourgée to J. C. Hartzell, n.d. [ca. December 1893], no. 7553; and Julius A. Wayland to Tourgée, 3 July 1893, no. 7117, Tourgée Papers. On Wayland, see Elliott Shore, *Talkin' Socialism: J. A. Wayland and the Role of the Press in American Radicalism, 1890–1912* (Lawrence: University Press of Kansas, 1988).

61. Olsen, *Carpetbagger's Crusade*, pp. 322–34; Joseph Cook to Tourgée, 5 June 1890, no. 4775; Cook to Tourgée, 22 October 1890, no. 5010; Tourgée to T. Thomas Fortune, n.d. [February 1893], no. 6703; Fortune to Tourgée, 6 February 1893, no. 6564; Fortune to Tourgée, 4 March 1893, no. 6708, Tourgée Papers; Tourgée to Cook, 23 August 1893, Joseph Cook Papers, Manuscript Division, Duke University Library; Joseph Cook to Tourgée, 1 September 1893, no. 7294; Fortune to Tourgée, 16 November 1893; and Cook to Tourgée, 20 November 1893, no. 7614, Tourgée Papers. Had Tourgée been able to merge the two periodicals, he might have had a viable journal. Subscribers to Cook's Boston monthly were familiar with its strong civil rights record and would have given Tourgée a readership in New England. The black audience of Fortune's *Age* would have put him in touch with a black elite in eastern cities. The combined audience might

have provided a subscription base that the *Basis* never achieved. But the odds were heavily against any new periodical in 1893 and 1894.

62. Henry H. Handler to Tourgée, 3 November 1891, no. 5778, Tourgée Papers; Woodward, "Birth of Jim Crow," pp. 54–55, 100–101; and Olsen, *Carpetbagger's Crusade,* pp. 326–28. See also Thomas R. Griffin to Tourgée, 15 May 1890, no. 4726; Alexander S. Jackson to Tourgée, 13 November 1891, no. 5788; and F. J. Davidson to Tourgée, 29 March 1892, no. 7414, Tourgée Papers.

63. Woodward, "Birth of Jim Crow," pp. 101–2; and Olsen, *Carpetbagger's Crusade,* pp. 329–30. Otto Olsen's survey shows that editorial opposition to the Court's decision was largely in the religious press. The dissenters included Congregationalism's *Advance, Congregationalist,* and *Independent;* Northern Methodism's Boston *Zion's Herald, California Christian Advocate, Northwestern Christian Advocate,* and *Western Christian Advocate;* African Methodism's *AME Church Review* and *Voice of Missions;* and the journal of Northern Methodism's black members, the *Southwestern Christian Advocate.* The Unitarian *Christian Register,* the *Catholic Globe,* Pittsburgh's *United Presbyterian,* Boston's *Free Baptist Morning Star* and an assembly of Boston clergymen opposed the Court's decision. Dismayed by the lack of protest in the radical, free-thought, and labor press, Olsen concedes that even Southern Methodism's Nashville *Christian Advocate* criticized segregation as late as May 1896. See Otto Olsen, "Introduction," in *The Thin Disguise: Turning Point in Negro History, Plessy v. Ferguson: A Documentary History* (1864–1896), ed. Otto Olsen (New York: Humanities Press, 1967), pp. 25–27, 30n.

64. For evidence that inequities in the distribution of school funds to black schools grew rapidly only after 1890, see Crofts, "Black Response to the Blair Education Bill," pp. 46–47.


Chapter 5


1. Paul H. Buck, *The Road to Reunion: 1865–1900* (Boston: Little, Brown and Co., 1937), pp. 137–244; Stanley F. Hirshon, *Farewell to the Bloody Shirt: Northern Republicans and the Southern Negro, 1877–1893* (Bloomington: Indiana University Press, 1962); and James Elbert Cutler, *Lynch-Law: An Inquiry into the History of Lynchings in the United States* (New York: Longmans, Green, and Co., 1905), pp. 227–28; and chart IV, opp. p. 171. See also *Thirty Years of Lynching in the United States, 1889–1918* (New York: National Association for the Advancement of Colored People, 1919); Walter F. White, *Rope and Faggot: A Biography of Judge Lynch* (New York: Alfred A. Knopf, 1929); Arthur Draper, *The Tragedy of Lynching* (Chapel Hill: University of North Carolina Press, 1933); and Frank Shay, *Judge Lynch, His First Hundred Years* (New York: I. Washburn, 1938).

2. "The Outlook," *Christian Union* 43 (19 March 1891): 363. See also "The Lesson from New Orleans," *Christian Union* 43 (26 March 1891): 398.

3. "Editorial Notes," *Independent* 44 (3 March 1892): 309; Nashville *Christian Advocate* 53 (3 March 1892): 1; and "Editorial Notes," *Independent* 44 (14 April 1892): 517. See also "Editorial Notes," *Independent* 44 (14 February 1892): 236; and Charles Fletcher Dole, *The American Citizen* (Boston: D. C. Heath and Co., 1892), pp. 270–71.

4. Benjamin Tucker Tanner, " 'That's a Race Question with Us,' " *Independent* 44 (14 April 1892): 505–6; *Journal of the General Conference of the Methodist Episcopal Church Held in Omaha, Nebraska, May 2–26, 1892* (New York: Hunt and Eaton, 1892), p. 270; "Barbarism," *Independent* 44 (26 May 1892): 726; "Editorial Notes," *Independent* 44 (26 May 1892): 729; "Editorial Notes," *Our Day* 9 (June 1892): 459–60; *Minutes of the National Council of the Congregational Churches of the United States, 1892* (Boston: Congregational Publishing Society, 1892), p. 39; *Minutes of the General Assembly of the Presbyterian Church in the United States of America* (Philadelphia: Presbyterian Board of Publication, 1892), p. 217; and Otto H. Olsen, *Carpetbagger's Crusade: The Life of Albion Winegar Tourgée* (Baltimore: Johns Hopkins University Press, 1965), p. 321. See also "Editorial Notes," *Independent* 44 (28 April 1892): 588.

5. "Bishop Fitzgerald on Lynching," *Independent* 44 (2 June 1892): 765; "Bishop Fitzgerald on Lynching," *Independent* 44 (23 June 1892): 874; and Frederick Douglass, "Lynch Law in the South," *North American Review* 155 (July 1892): 18, 20, 23–24.

6. Alfreda M. Duster, ed., *Crusade for Justice: The Autobiography of Ida B. Wells* (Chicago: University of Chicago Press, 1970), pp. xiii–xviii, 7–34.

7. Ibid., pp. 35–52, 61–72; David M. Tucker, "Miss Ida Wells and Memphis Lynching," *Phylon* 32 (Summer 1971): 112–17; [Albert Shaw], "The Position of the Negro," *Review of Reviews* 5 (June 1892): 525–26; "Editorial Notes," *Independent* 44 (14 July 1892): 984; Ida B. Wells, "Bishop Tanner's 'Ray of Light,' " *Independent* 44 (28 July 1892): 1045–46; and Frederick Douglass to Ida B. Wells, 25 October 1892, in Wells, *On Lynchings* (New York: Arno Press, 1969), p. 3.

8. Duster, *Crusade for Justice*, pp. 78–82; and Ida B. Wells, "Southern Horrors," in Wells, *On Lynchings*, pp. 5, 6, 11, 14.

9. Duster, *Crusade for Justice*, pp. 81–86; and Wells, "Lynch Law in All Its Phases," *Our Day* 11 (May 1893): 341–47.

10. Atticus Greene Haygood, "The Black Shadow in the South," *Forum* 16 (October 1893): 167–75; Wells, "Lynch Law," pp. 342–43; and P. Thomas Stanford, *The Tragedy of the Negro in America* (Boston: Charles A. Wasta, 1897), pp. 155–59. See also Benjamin Orange Flower, "The Burning of Negroes in the South: A Protest and a Warning," *Arena* 7 (April 1893): 634–35; Joseph Cook, "New Black Codes at the South," *Our Day* 12 (July 1893): 141; Ida B. Wells, "A Red Record," in Wells, *On Lynchings*, pp. 25–32; Duster, *Crusade for Justice*, pp. 84–85; and Robert Wilson Shufeldt, *The Negro: A Menace to American Civilization* (Boston: Richard G. Badger, 1907), pp. 137–38.

11. Edgar Gardner Murphy to Booker T. Washington, 1 January 1900, Booker T. Washington Papers, Library of Congress; and an undated clipping from the *Laredo News* [ca. 1893], in Edgar Gardner Murphy Scrapbook. Edgar Gardner Murphy Papers, Southern Historical Collection, University of North Carolina, Chapel Hill. See also Hugh C. Bailey, *Edgar Gardner Murphy: Gentle Progressive* (Coral Gables, Fla.: University of Miami Press, 1968), pp. 9–10.

12. "Worse Than Lynch Law, Lynching, and Lynchers," *Christian Educator* 4 (July 1893): 137; and "Thugs and Fiends," *Richmond Christian Advocate* (23 February 1893), quoted in "Worse Than Lynch Law," p. 140.

13. Flower, "Burning of Negroes," pp. 636–39. See also "Editorial Notes," *Independent*

45 (9 February 1893): 184; Cook, "New Black Codes," pp. 42–43; Felix L. Oswald, "Autos-da-Fe," *Open Court* 7 (23 February 1893): 3568–69; and "Lynch Law in the South," *Review of Reviews* 7 (May 1893): 471–72.

14. Duster, *Crusade for Justice*, pp. 83–102.

15. Ibid., p. 104; Albion W. Tourgée to T. Thomas Fortune, [ca. 12 July 1893], no. 7179; and Fortune to Tourgée, 9 July 1893, no. 7112. Tourgée Papers, Southern Historical Collection, University of North Carolina, Chapel Hill.

16. "Editorial Notes," *Independent* 45 (13 July 1893): 951. See also "Editorial Notes," *Our Day* 12 (July 1893): 104–5.

17. Francis J. Grimké, "The Anglo-American Pulpit and Southern Outrages," *Independent* 45 (22 June 1893): 844–45. See also "Editorial Notes," *Independent* 45 (4 May 1893): 609; "Editorial Notes," *Independent* 45 (11 May 1893): 644; "Editorial Notes," *Independent* 45 (18 May 1893): 676; and "Editorial Notes," *Independent* 45 (25 May 1893): 711.

18. E. E. Hoss, "Lynch Law and the Southern Press," *Independent* 46 (1 February 1894): 129. See also Edgar Garner Murphy, "Self-Fulfillment," *Homiletic Review* 26 (October 1893): 329.

19. Amory Dwight Mayo, "Is the South Growing Better?," *Independent* 45 (5 October 1893): 1332; "Are We a Nation of Barbarians," *Independent* 45 (28 September 1893): 1306; and Albion W. Tourgée to "Gagg," n.d. [ca. October 1893], no. 7440, Tourgée Papers. See also Charles Richmond Henderson, *An Introduction to the Study of the Dependent, Defective and Delinquent Classes* (Boston: D. C. Heath and Co., 1893), p. 106; Tourgée, "Christian Murders in America," *Our Day* 12 (August 1893): 167–72; "Editor's Notes," *Independent* 45 (3 August 1893): 1050; "The National Crime," *Independent* 46 (1 February 1894): 138; and "A Voice of Warning," *Independent* 46 (8 February 1894): 171.

20. John Higham, *Strangers in the Land: Patterns of American Nativism, 1860–1925* (New York: Atheneum Press, 1963), pp. 68–105; Henry F. May, *Protestant Churches and Industrial America* (New York: Harper and Row, 1949), pp. 91–111; and Atticus Greene Haygood, "Governor Altgeld's Crime," *Independent* 45 (20 July 1893): 969–70.

21. Haygood, "Black Shadow in the South," pp. 167, 174–75.

22. Walter Hines Page, "The Last Hold of the Southern Bully," *Forum* 16 (November 1893): 309; and J. R. Slattery, "The South in the Saddle," *Independent* 45 (16 November 1893): 1537. See also [Levi J. Coppin], "Conditions in the South," *AME Church Review* 10 (January 1894): 440–47.

23. *Independent* 46 (1 February 1894): 129–32; "Questions to Specialists," *Our Day* 13 (May–June 1894): 273; and "Address of General Morgan," *Our Day* 13 (May–June 1894): 274–75. See also "The National Crime," *Independent* 46 (1 February 1894): 138; and "Editorial Notes," *Independent* 46 (22 February 1894): 236.

24. Duster, *Crusade for Justice*, pp. 124–31, 141, 146, 148–76, 190–97. See also Ida B. Wells, "Liverpool Slave Traditions and Present Practices," *Independent* 46 (17 May 1894): 617; and Charles F. Aked, "The Race Problem in America," *Contemporary Review* 45 (January–June 1894): 818–27.

25. Duster, *Crusade for Justice*, pp. 111–13, 131, 136, 164–65. See also James F. Findlay, Jr., *Dwight L. Moody: American Evangelist, 1837–1899* (Chicago: University of Chicago Press, 1969), pp. 278–81.

26. Wells, "A Red Record," p. 84; and Duster, *Crusade for Justice*, pp. 202–3.

27. Duster, *Crusade for Justice*, pp. 204–9.

28. Ibid., pp. 171–87, 215–17; and "Editorial Notes," *Independent* 46 (3 May 1894): 560. See also "Editorial Notes," *Independent* 46 (21 June 1894): 796.

29. Amory H. Bradford, "Our Nation's Shame," *Outlook* 49 (23 June 1894): 1143–44. Bradford refers to Northern Methodist Bishop Randolph S. Foster and his *Union of Episcopal Methodisms* (New York: Hunt and Eaton, 1892); and to Episcopal Bishop William Bell White Howe of South Carolina. See George Brown Tindall, *South Carolina Negroes: 1877–1900* (Baton Rouge: Louisiana State University Press, 1966), pp. 194–200.

30. Joseph Cook, "The Fiendishness of Caste—Bishop Potter on Liberia," *Our Day* 13 (July–August 1894): 320–24; and Frederick Douglass, "Lynching Black People Because They Are Black," *Our Day* 13 (July–August 1894): 298–306.

31. Lewis Harvie Blair, *The Prosperity of the South Dependent upon the Elevation of the Negro* (Richmond: Everett Waddey, 1889), edited with an introduction by C. Vann Woodward as *A Southern Prophecy* (Boston: Little, Brown and Co., 1964); Blair, "The Southern Problem and Its Solution," *Our Day* 12 (November 1893): 361–76; and Charles E. Wynes, "Lewis Harvie Blair, Virginia Reformer: The Uplift of the Negro and Southern Prosperity," *Virginia Magazine of History and Biography* 72 (January 1964): 3–18.

32. Lewis Harvie Blair, "Lynching as a Fine Art," *Our Day* 13 (July–August 1894): 307–14.

33. "Editorial Notes," *Outlook* 51 (19 January 1895): 87; Duster, *Crusade for Justice*, p. 217; Atticus G. Haygood, "Lynching by Wholesale," *Independent* 46 (28 June 1894): 817; and "Editorial Notes," *Independent* 46 (28 June 1894): 828. See also Haygood, "Voters Yet Slaves," *Independent* 46 (9 August 1894): 1015; "Editorial Notes," *Outlook* 51 (12 January 1895): 47–48; Cook, "New Black Codes at the South," p. 36; and Thomas C. Hall, *John Hall, Pastor and Preacher* (New York: Fleming H. Revell Co., 1901).

34. Duster, *Crusade for Justice*, pp. 219–20, 233–34.

35. Ibid., pp. 234–39. See also Dewey D. Wallace, Jr., "Charles Oliver Brown at Dubuque: A Study in the Ideals of Midwestern Congregationalists in the Late Nineteenth Century," *Church History* 53 (March 1984): 46–60.

36. Duster, *Crusade for Justice*, pp. 218–23; "Editorial Notes," *Independent* 46 (12 July 1894): 897; "Editorial Notes," *Independent* 46 (19 July 1894): 925; and "Editorial Notes," *Independent* 46 (6 September 1894): 1152. See also Jerome R. Riley, *The Philosophy of Negro Suffrage* (Washington, D.C.: n.p., 1897), pp. 46–48.

37. Duster, *Crusade for Justice*, pp. 227–31; and Ida Husted Harper, *The Life and Work of Susan B. Anthony*, 3 vols. (Indianapolis: Brown Merrill Co., 1898–1908), 2:815–16.

38. Wells, "A Red Record," pp. 80–81, 86–90; Ida B. Wells to Albion W. Tourgée, 27 November 1894, no. 8202; and Frances E. Willard to Albion W. Tourgée, 21 December 1894, no. 8217, Tourgée Papers. See also Mary Earhart, *Frances Willard: From Prayers to Politics* (Chicago: University of Chicago Press, 1944), p. 360.

39. Earhart, *Frances Willard*, p. 361. See also Ruth Bordin, *Frances Willard: A Biography* (Chapel Hill: University of North Carolina Press, 1986), pp. 216–22.

40. "Anti-Lynching Movement," *Chautauquan* 20 (November 1894): 230; Cutler, *Lynch-Law*, pp. 229–30; and Duster, *Crusade for Justice*, pp. 234–39. See also "Editorial Notes,"

*Independent* 46 (2 August 1894): 991; "Editorial Notes," *Our Day* 13 (September–October 1894): 492–93; and "England's Concern about Southern Lynchings," *North Carolina Christian Advocate* 39 (19 September 1894): 1.

41. See, for instance: "A Bad Week for the Lynchers," *Independent* 46 (13 September 1894): 1187; "Editorial Notes," *Independent* 46 (20 September 1894): 1216; "Straight from the Shoulder and the Heart," *Independent* 46 (4 October 1894): 1280–81; "Editorial Notes," *Independent* 46 (25 October 1894): 1376; "Editorial Notes," *Outlook* 50 (29 December 1894): 1118; "Editorial Notes," *Outlook* 51 (12 January 1895): 47; "Editorial Notes," *Outlook* 51 (19 January 1895): 87; "A Mob and a Lynching," *Independent* 46 (21 March 1895): 374–75; "The Crimes of a Week," *Independent* 46 (7 November 1895): 1503; and Hunter Dickinson Farish, *The Circuit Rider Dismounts: A Social History of Southern Methodism, 1865–1900* (Richmond: Dietz Press, 1938), pp. 227–29.

42. Andrew Wiseby, Jr., *Soldiers without Swords: A History of the Salvation Army in the United States* (New York: Macmillan, 1955), p. 91; and Edward H. McKinley, *Marching to Glory: The History of the Salvation Army in the United States of America* (San Francisco: Harper and Row, 1980), pp. 52–53.

43. "An Encouraging Movement," *American Missionary* 48 (September 1894): 314–15; "Editorial Notes," *Outlook* 50 (15 September 1894): 416; "A Bad Week for Lynchers," *Independent* 46 (13 September 1894): 1187; S. Reece Murray, "Lynch Law and Its Outcome," *Treasury* 14 (1896): 366–72; and Cutler, *Lynch-Law*, pp. 230–44.

44. Wilbur Fisk Crafts, *Lectures on Social Progress: With Outline of the Topic a Month Course of Reform Studies* (Washington, D.C.: Reform Bureau, 1897), pp. 123–24, 126; and Crafts, *Practical Christian Sociology: A Series of Special Lectures before Princeton Theological Seminary and Marietta College*, introd. Joseph Cook (New York: Funk and Wagnalls, 1895), p. 208.

45. J. A. C. McQuiston, "Lynching," *Homiletic Review* 28 (September 1894): 220–24.

46. "Forty-Ninth Annual Meeting of the American Missionary Association," *American Missionary* 49 (December 1895): 387–88; [Washington Gladden], "Address on Lynching," *American Missionary* 49 (December 1895): 406–8; and Jacob Henry Dorn, *Washington Gladden: Prophet of the Social Gospel* (n.p.: Ohio State University Press, 1966), p. 297. See also "Lynching," *American Missionary* 49 (December 1895): 378–79; and "The Urbana Lynching," *American Missionary* 51 (June 1897): 180.

47. Cutler, *Lynch-Law*, pp. 235–45.

48. On the new benevolent empire and the Federal Council of Churches, see chapters 6 and 11; and Hopkins, *Rise of the Social Gospel in American Protestantism*, pp. 177–97.

49. Richard T. Greener, "The White Problem," *Lend-A-Hand* 12 (May 1894): 365–67; Charles W. Chesnutt, "A Multitude of Counselors," *Independent* 42 (2 April 1891): 480–81; and D. Augustus Straker, *The New South Investigated* (Detroit: Ferguson Printing Co., 1888), pp. vi, 40.

50. Henry Codman Potter to J. Ormand Wilson, 1 December 1894, I-A, no. 286, American Colonization Society Papers, Library of Congress; the financial reports in the *American Missionary* from 1893 to 1896, especially: "Our Financial Outlook," *American Missionary* 49 (April 1895): 121; and "Our Present Condition. Help!," *American Missionary* 49 (August 1895): 249; "Annual Report of the Board of Managers to the General Committee," *Christian Educator* 5 (January 1894): 69; "Report of the Board of Managers to

the General Committee," *Christian Educator* 6 (October–November 1895): 114; "Debts of Missionary Societies," *Methodist Review* 58 (November 1896): 981–82; and "Abstract of Proceedings of the Board of Managers," *Spirit of Missions* 60 (July 1895): 279–80. See also H. T. Buell to J. Ormand Wilson, 17 December 1894, ACS Papers.

51. "Report of the Board of Managers to the General Committee," *Christian Educator* 6 (October 1894): 186; "Report of the Board of Managers to the General Committee," *Christian Educator* 8 (December 1896–January 1897): 10–11; "Report of the Board of Managers to the General Committee," *Christian Educator* 9 (December 1897–January 1898): 36; and "What Now?," *American Missionary* 50 (March 1896): 82. See also "Voices from the Mission Field," *American Missionary* 49 (September 1895): 282–86.

52. "Fifty-Second Annual Report of the Executive Committee of the American Missionary Association," *American Missionary* 52 (December 1898): 175; Frederick Leslie Brownlee, *New Day Ascending* (Boston: Pilgrim Press, [1946]), pp. 271–72; "Fifty-Second Annual Report of the Executive Committee of the American Missionary Association," *American Missionary* 52 (December 1898): 175; and "Financial," *American Missionary* 54 (October 1900): 145. See also "A Few Words of Acknowledgement," *American Missionary* 51 (April 1897): 113–14.

53. "At Frederick Douglass Funeral . . . An Address by W. C. Gannett," 26 February 1895, manuscript sermon, in the William Channing Gannett Papers, Rush Rhees Library, University of Rochester; and Joseph Cook, "Frederick Douglass," *Our Day— Altruistic Review* 15 (November 1895): 237. See also J. E. Rankin, "Frederick Douglass' Character and Career," *Our Day—Altruistic Review* 14 (April 1895): 171–75.

54. Jenkin Lloyd Jones, "Frederick Douglass—A Representative of the Ransomed Race," *Treasury* 13 (July 1895): 187–88.

55. "Editorial Notes," *Independent* 42 (30 January 1890): 148; Thomas H. Pearne, "The Race Problem—The Situation," *Methodist Review* 72 (September 1890): 705; "Address of Rev. A. H. Bradford," *American Missionary* 44 (December 1890): 435; "Editorial Notes," *Independent* 42 (2 January 1890): 12; "A Quiet Election," *Independent* 42 (16 January 1890): 75; and "What the Mohonk Conference Asks for the Negro," *Independent* 43 (11 June 1891): 871. See also Arthur A. Smith, "Time as a Factor in Christian Missions," *Missionary Review of the World* 17 (August 1894): 570–73, and 17 (September 1894): 672; and H., "The Negro in the South," *Methodist Quarterly Review* 33 (July 1891): 312.

56. Atticus G. Haygood, "The Negro Problem: God Takes Time—Man Must," *Methodist Quarterly Review* 42 (September–October 1895): 41–43, 45, 50, 53. See also B. J. Ramage, "Mr. Bryce on Southern Politics," *Sewanee Review* 3 (August 1895): 445; and "The Negro Problem," *Review of Reviews* 12 (November 1895): 585.

57. Theodore Thornton Munger, *On the Threshold* (Boston: Houghton, Mifflin and Co., 1892), pp. 106–8; and Josiah Strong, *Our Country: Its Possible Future and Its Present Crisis* (New York: Baker and Taylor Co., 1885), pp. 159–61.

58. F. H. Wines, "Lessons of the Eleventh Census concerning Children in Almshouses," in *Proceedings of the National Conference of Charities and Correction at the Twenty-first Annual Session Held in Nashville, Tenn., May 23–29, 1894*, ed. Isabel C. Barrows (Boston: George H. Ellis, 1894), p. 325; Charles Richmond Henderson, *Social Elements: Institutions, Character, Progress* (New York: Charles Scribner's Sons, 1898), pp. 30, 361; Albion W. Small

and George E. Vincent, *An Introduction to the Study of Sociology* (New York: American Book Co., 1894), p. 179; and Amory H. Bradford, *Heredity and Christian Problems* (New York: Macmillan, 1895), p. 83. See also Bradford, "Does the World Need Christianity," *Independent* 50 (15 December 1898): 1757–60.

59. Lyman Abbott, *Christianity and Social Problems* (Boston: Houghton, Mifflin and Co., 1896), p. 359; and Charles M. Sheldon, quoted in "The Kingdom," *Missionary Review of the World* 19 (June 1896): 470–71. See also Small and Vincent, *Introduction to the Study of Society*, p. 179.

60. George Batchelor, "The Mimicry of Heredity," *New World* 3 (November 1895): 747; Jones, "Frederick Douglass," p. 188; Maurice Bloomfield, "Race Prejudice," *New World* 4 (March 1895): 32–33; and Washington Gladden, *Ruling Ideas of the Present Age* (Boston: Houghton, Mifflin and Co., 1895), p. 124. See also Nicholas Paine Gilman, "The Laws of Daily Conduct," in *Conduct as a Fine Art* (Boston: Houghton, Mifflin and Co., 1891), pp. 138–39; "Race Prejudice—Is It Waning?," *American Missionary* 49 (July 1895): 220–21; "Race Prejudice," *American Missionary* 50 (July 1896): 210–11; and Washington Gladden, *Social Facts and Forces* (New York: G. P. Putnam's Sons, 1897), pp. 75–76, 203–5, 219–20.

61. Martin Luther King, Jr., "Letter from Birmingham City Jail," in *A Testament of Hope: The Essential Writings of Martin Luther King, Jr.*, ed. James M. Washington (San Francisco: Harper and Row, 1986), p. 296; and C. J. Ryder, "Notes from New England," *American Missionary* 44 (June 1890): 175. See also George Washington Cable, "The Negro Question," in *The Negro Question*, ed. Arlin Turner (Garden City, N.Y.: Doubleday and Co., 1958), pp. 146–47.

### Chapter 6

1. Edith Armstrong Talbot, *Samuel Chapman Armstrong: A Biographical Study* (New York: Doubleday, Page and Co., 1904); Suzanne Carson Lowitt, "Samuel Chapman Armstrong: Missionary to the South" (Ph.D. dissertation, Johns Hopkins University, 1952); Philip Whitwell Wilson, *An Unofficial Statesman—Robert C. Ogden* (New York: Doubleday, Page and Co., 1924); and William Bristol Shaw, "Robert Curtis Ogden," in *Dictionary of American Biography*, ed. Allen Johnson et al. (New York: Charles Scribner's Sons, 1928–88), 7:641–42.

2. "Remarks by Samuel B. Capen," *Southern Workman* 22 (May 1893): extra pages; August Meier, *Negro Thought in America: Racial Ideologies in the Age of Booker T. Washington* (Ann Arbor: University of Michigan Press, 1963), pp. 85–99; and Louis R. Harlan, *Booker T. Washington*, 2 vols. (New York: Oxford University Press, 1972–83), 1:60–66.

3. Samuel Chapman Armstrong to Robert C. Ogden, 31 May 1892; Armstrong to Ogden, 6 July 1892, box no. 6, Robert C. Ogden Papers, Library of Congress; Richard Heber Newton, in Timothy Thomas Fortune, *Black and White: Land, Labor and Politics in the South* (New York: Fords, Howard and Hulbert, 1884), p. 303; "Hampton Institute," *Lend-A-Hand* 10 (May 1893): 357; and Lyman Abbott, *Signs of Promise: Sermons Preached in Plymouth Pulpit, Brooklyn, 1887–1889* (New York: Fords, Howard and Hulbert, 1889), pp. 293–94. See also Armstrong to Ogden, 30 April 1892, box no. 6, Ogden Papers; Mrs. H. C. Jenks,

"Hampton, 1889," *Unitarian* 5 (March 1890): 117–19; and Charles Fletcher Dole, *My Eighty Years* (New York: E. P. Dutton and Co., 1927), pp. 329–33.

4. *Southern Workman* 21 (January 1892): 4–6; "Address by Rev. Dr. Parkhurst," *Southern Workman* 23 (June 1894): 90; "General Armstrong," *Christian Union* 47 (20 May 1893): 960; "General Armstrong," *Lend-A-Hand* 11 (July 1893): 9; and "In Memory of General Armstrong," *Christian Union* 47 (10 June 1893): 1130. See also [Benjamin F. Lee], "Editorial," *Christian Recorder* 29 (4 June 1891): 4; [Levi J. Coppin], "The Late Phillips Brooks," *AME Church Review* 9 (April 1893): 412–13; "The Boston Town Meeting," *Southern Workman* 22 (May 1893): extra pages; "Our Founder's Day," *Southern Workman* 22 (February 1894): 22; Lyman Abbott, *The Life That Really Is* (New York: Wilber B. Ketcham, 1899), pp. 210–11; Abbott, *The Temple* (New York: Macmillan, 1909), p. 170; and Abbott, *The Ethical Teachings of Jesus* (Philadelphia: University of Pennsylvania Press, 1910), p. 72

5. "Our Founder's Day," *Southern Workman* 22 (February 1894): 19, 21; and "Address by Rev. Dr. Parkhurst," p. 90. See also "Address by Mr. Edwin Mead," *Southern Workman* 23 (June 1894): 114–15.

6. "Hampton's New Principal," *Outlook* 48 (23 December 1893): 1181–82; Robert C. Ogden to Hollis B. Frissell, 17 May and 23 June 1894, box no. 6, Ogden to Charles W. Stone, 16 April 1896, box no. 13, Ogden Papers; Frissell, "Negro Education," *New World* 9 (December 1900): 630; and Joseph Houldsworth Oldham, "Hollis B. Frissell and Hampton," *Constructive Quarterly* 6 (1918): 569–76.

7. Louise Ware, *George Foster Peabody: Banker, Philanthropist, Publicist* (Athens: University of Georgia Press, 1951); and Samuel A. Eliot, "Francis Greenwood Peabody: His Work and Hopes for Hampton," *Southern Workman* 66 (March 1937): 71–79. See also Sydney E. Ahlstrom, "Francis Greenwood Peabody," in *Dictionary of American Biography*, 22:518–19; and Jurgen Herbst, "Francis Greenwood Peabody: Harvard's Theologian of the Social Gospel," *Harvard Theological Review* 54 (January 1961): 45–69.

8. Eliot, "Francis Greenwood Peabody," p. 73; Peabody, "If Lincoln Came to Hampton," *Southern Workman* 51 (April 1922): 162; [Ephraim Peabody], "Slavery in the United States: Its Evils, Alleviations and Remedies," *North American Review* 73 (October 1851): 347–85; and [Robert Peabody and Francis Greenwood Peabody], *A New England Romance: The Story of Ephraim and Mary Jane Peabody* (Boston: Houghton Mifflin Co., 1920), pp. 126–28.

9. Francis Greenwood Peabody, *The Approach to the Social Question: An Introduction to the Study of Social Ethics* (New York: Macmillan, 1909), p. 197; Peabody, *The Christian Life in the Modern World* (New York: Macmillan, 1916), pp. 82, 103–4, 176–84; Peabody, "The Message of Christ to Human Society," in *The Message of Christ to Manhood*, by Alexander V. G. Allen et al. (Boston: Houghton, Mifflin and Co., 1899), pp. 57–58; and Peabody, *Jesus Christ and the Social Question: An Examination of the Teaching of Jesus in Its Relation to Some of the Problems of Modern Social Life* (New York: Grosset and Dunlap, 1900), pp. 77–78, 123.

10. Peabody, *Education for Life: The Story of Hampton Institute* (Garden City, N.Y.: Doubleday, Page and Co., 1919), pp. 23–24, 274; and Peabody, *Sunday Evenings in the College Chapel* (Boston: Houghton Mifflin Co., 1911), pp. 190–91.

11. Peabody, "Remarks," *Southern Workman* 37 (June 1908): 363–64; Peabody, *Education for Life*, pp. 312–14; and Peabody, *Founder's Day at Hampton: An Address in Memory of Samuel*

*Chapman Armstrong* (Boston: Houghton, Mifflin and Co., 1898), pp. 19–20. See also Peabody, *Education for Life*, pp. 324–25; and Peabody, "Knowledge and Service," *Southern Education* 1 (7 May 1903): 104.

12. Peabody, "Hampton and the New Education," *Southern Workman* 39 (January 1910): 48; Peabody, *Founder's Day at Hampton*, pp. 3, 10–13, 24; Peabody, "Address," *Southern Workman* 35 (June 1906): 357–59; Peabody, "Following the Founder," *Southern Workman* 39 (February 1910): 73–74; Peabody, *Education for Life*, pp. xiv–xv, xviii, 196–99, 210, 240, 271, 300, 324; Peabody, *The Rhythm of Life* (Boston: Houghton Mifflin Co., 1932), pp. 10–11; Peabody, *Reminiscences of Present Day Saints* (Boston: Houghton Mifflin Co., 1927), pp. 183–84, 200; Peabody, "Robert Curtis Ogden," *Southern Workman* 42 (December 1913): 692; and Peabody, "Robert Curtis Ogden," in *A Life Well Lived: In Memory of Robert Curtis Ogden*, by Francis Greenwood Peabody et al. (Hampton, Va.: Hampton Institute Press, 1914), p. 10. Armstrong's concept of education was not so original, but historians credit it as an early form of progressive education. See Merle Curti, *The Social Ideas of American Educators* (Totowa, N.J.: Littlefield, Adams and Co., 1959), p. 293; Lawrence Cremin, *The Transformation of the School: Progressivism in American Education, 1876–1957* (New York: Alfred A. Knopf, 1961), pp. 116–19; James M. McPherson, *The Abolitionist Legacy: From Reconstruction to the NAACP* (Princeton: Princeton University Press, 1975), p. 208; and Talbot, *Samuel Chapman Armstrong*, pp. 170–71, 253–54.

13. Charles Fletcher Dole, *The Coming People* (New York: Thomas Y. Crowell and Co., 1897), pp. 123–25; Charles F. Thwing, "Significant Ignorance about the Bible as Shown among College Students of Both Sexes," *Century* 60 (May 1900): 123–38; and Theodore Thornton Munger, "Significant Knowledge of the Bible," *Century* 61 (December 1900): 273–76.

14. Booker T. Washington, *Up from Slavery* (New York: A. L. Burt Co., 1901), p. 55; and Harlan, *Booker T. Washington*, 1:58.

15. Meier, *Negro Thought in America*, pp. 85–86; Harlan, *Booker T. Washington*, 1:63–64, 67–68, 96–101; and Washington, *Up from Slavery*, p. 87.

16. Booker T. Washington, "Diary," 5 May 1882; Washington to James Fowle Baldwin Marshall, 9 May 1882; Washington, "A Speech before the Alabama State Teachers' Association," 11 April 1888; Washington to Caleb Davis Bradlee, 12 March 1889, in *The Booker T. Washington Papers*, 14 vols., ed. Louis R. Harlan et al. (Urbana: University of Illinois Press, 1972–89), 2:199, 205, 430–31, 516; Washington, "The Tuskegee Normal Institute," *Unity* 24 (16 November 1889): 83; and Harlan, *Booker T. Washington*, 1:151–75. See also Dole, *My Eighty Years*, pp. 335–36; Harlan, *Booker T. Washington*, 1:154; and Jenkin Lloyd Jones to Katherine M. Marvin, 18 March 1896, in Joel Williamson, *The Crucible of Race: Black-White Relations in the American South since Emancipation* (New York: Oxford University Press, 1984), p. 328.

17. Washington, "The Colored Ministry: Its Defects and Needs," *Christian Union* 42 (14 August 1890): 199–200; Francis J. Grimké to Washington, 28 November 1891; Washington to R. C. Bedford, 18 August 1892; "Announcement of the Opening of Phelps Hall Bible School," November 1892, in Harlan, *Washington Papers*, 2:271–72; 3:196–97, 257–58; "The Bible School at Tuskegee," *Outlook* 47 (18 March 1893): 505; and "Work among the Colored People," *Spirit of Missions* 60 (December 1895): 520–22. Washington

traced the article to Lyman Abbott's request for a letter on the subject, but Harlan notes that Washington had already addressed the issue at Fisk University. See Washington, *Up from Slavery*, p. 230; and Harlan, *Booker T. Washington*, 1:194–97.

18. R. C. Bedford, "Twelfth Year of Tuskegee's Work," *Lend-A-Hand* 10 (March 1893): 221; Elizabeth E. Lane, "Tuskegee School: A Practical Solution of the Negro Problem," *Lend-A-Hand* 13 (July 1894): 17–21; Mrs. Booker T. Washington, "The New Negro Woman," *Lend-A-Hand* 15 (October 1895): 254–60; and Edward Alsworth Ross, *Social Control: A Survey of the Foundations of Order* (New York: Macmillan, 1901), p. 336.

19. Nathan B. Young, "A Negro Chautauqua," *Independent* 45 (3 August 1893): 1182; "Tuskegee Summer Assembly" and "The Declaration of the First Tuskegee Negro Conference," in Harlan, *Washington Papers*, 3:456–58, 217–19; R. C. Bedford, "Tuskegee Negro Conference," *Lend-A-Hand* 10 (April 1893): 251–56; Bedford, "Tuskegee Negro Conference," *Lend-A-Hand* 14 (April 1895): 247–51; and Harlan, *Booker T. Washington*, 1:198–201. See also Herbert W. Collingwood, "The Negro as a Farmer: What the Tuskegee Conference Shows," *Outlook* 55 (20 March 1897): 783–86; Max B. Thrasher, "The Tuskegee Conference," *Outlook* 58 (12 March 1898): 674–75; and Thrasher, "The Tuskegee Negro Conference," *Outlook* 67 (2 March 1901): 483–87.

20. Pitt Dillingham, "Calhoun Colored School," *Lend-A-Hand* 15 (November 1895): 372; and "Elevating the Race," *Chicago Inter-Ocean*, 26 January 1895, in Harlan, *Washington Papers*, 3:373–74, 502–6. See also Washington to Nathalia Lord, 30 September 1887, and Lord to Washington, 10 October 1887, in Harlan, *Washington Papers*, 2:390–91; William J. Edwards, *Twenty-Five Years in the Black Belt* (Boston: Cornhill Co., 1918), pp. 18–76; R. C. Bedford, "Mt. Meig's Institute, Alabama, Tuskegee's Child and Hampton's Grandchild," *Southern Workman* 23 (April 1894): 64–65; Charlotte R. Thorne and Mabel W. Dillingham, "Calhoun Colored School," *Lend-A-Hand* 13 (July 1894): 52–55; Amory H. Bradford, "Among Colored Institutions," *Outlook* 56 (19 June 1897): 454–57; Augustus Field Beard, "Samples and Examples," *American Missionary* 52 (June 1898): 61–69; Oswald Garrison Villard, "An American Negro School," *Review of Reviews* 26 (December 1902): 711–14; Dole, *My Eighty Years*, pp. 331, 337, 339; and Rose Herlong Ellis, "The Calhoun School, Miss Charlotte Thorn's 'Lighthouse on the Hill' in Lowndes County, Alabama," *Alabama Review* 35 (July 1984): 183–201.

21. Washington, *Up from Slavery*, pp. 218–25. See also Harlan, *Booker T. Washington*, 1:204–20.

22. John Wesley Edward Bowen to Washington, 12 November 1895; William Edward Burghardt Du Bois to Washington, 24 September 1895; Edward Elder Cooper to Washington, 2 November 1895, in Harlan, *Washington Papers*, 4:78–79, 26n, 69–70; "Editorial Notes," *Independent* 47 (26 September 1895): 1297; and Washington, "Who Is Permanently Hurt?," *Our Day* 16 (June 1896): 311. See also "Editorial Notes," *Independent* 47 (3 October 1895): 1328; Harlan, *Booker T. Washington*, 1:221–27; and McPherson, *Abolitionist Legacy*, pp. 359–61.

23. Dole, *My Eighty Years*, pp. 337–41; Samuel June Barrows to Washington, 12 September 1896, and Isabel C. Barrows to Washington, 26 May 1900, Booker T. Washington Papers, Library of Congress; Washington to William Channing Gannett, 15 January 1898 through 23 May 1914, William Channing Gannett Papers, University of Rochester;

Washington Gladden, "Bond Servants of Sin," 15 February 1898, Sermon 698, Washington Gladden Papers, Ohio Historical Society; Chester McArthur Destler, *Henry Demarest Lloyd and the Empire of Reform* (Philadelphia: University of Pennsylvania Press, 1963), p. 514; Anne Scott, "Introduction," in *Democracy and Social Ethics*, by Jane Addams (Cambridge: Harvard University Press, 1964), p. xlii; and Shailer Mathews to Washington, 16 March 1899, and 20 April 1899, folder 4, box 5, Shailer Mathews Papers, Divinity School Correspondence, University of Chicago Archives. See also Charles Richmond Henderson, *The Social Spirit in America* (Meadville, Pa.: Flood and Vincent, 1898), pp. 327–28.

24. John Langdon Heaton, "Cleveland to Preside," [ca. 1896], box 28, Thomas DeWitt Talmadge Papers, Manuscript Division, Library of Congress; Arthur T. Pierson, *The Miracles of Missions: Modern Marvels in the History of Missionary Enterprise* (New York: Funk and Wagnalls, 1899), pp. 215–47; Thomas J. Calloway, "Booker T. Washington and the Tuskegee Institute," *New England Magazine* 17 (October 1897): 136, 140; and Talmadge, "Booker T. Washington's Good Humor," [ca. 1896–1900]; Talmadge, "Booker Washington as a Leader," [ca. 1896–1900]; and Talmadge, "The Way We Account for Booker Washington," [ca. 1896–1900], box 26, Talmadge Papers. See also E. P. S., "Boston Letter," *Social Gospel* 36 (February 1901): 23–24; and Washington, "A Sunday Evening Talk: The Kingdom of God," in Harlan, *Washington Papers*, 9:87–90. On the creation of Washington's image, see Emma Lou Thornbrough, "Booker T. Washington as Seen by His White Contemporaries," *Journal of Negro History* 53 (April 1968): 160–82; and Harlan, *Booker T. Washington*, 1:229–53. On the Christ-like image in twentieth-century black literature, see S. P. Fullinwider, *The Mind and Mood of Black America: 20th Century Thought* (Homewood, Ill.: Dorsey Press, 1969), pp. 26–46.

25. Washington Gladden, "Some Impressions Gained during a Visit to the Southern United States," 31 May 1903, Sermon 969, Gladden Papers; Washington, *Up from Slavery*, p. 223; Thomas DeWitt Talmadge, "The Bane of the Colored Man," [ca. 1896–1900]; and Talmadge, "The Phenomenon of Booker Washington," [ca. 1896–1900], box no. 26, Talmadge Papers; Pierson, *Miracles of Missions*, pp. 219, 223; and Francis Greenwood Peabody, *Jesus Christ and the Christian Character* (New York: Macmillan, 1905), p. 184. See also Thomas Jefferson Morgan, *The Negro in America and the Ideal American Republic* (Philadelphia: American Baptist Publication Society, 1898), pp. 120–21; and "Booker T. Washington on the Negro's Weakness and Strength," *Review of Reviews* 16 (September 1897): 333–34.

26. Washington to Francis J. Grimké, 8 May 1898, in *The Works of Francis J. Grimké*, 4 vols., ed. Carter G. Woodson (Washington, D.C.: Associated Publishers, 1942), 4:51; and "The Worship of Booker T. Washington," *Independent* 50 (8 December 1898): 1708–9. See also "Editorial," *Independent* 51 (28 September 1899): 2638–39.

27. Abbott, "The Basis of Anglo-Saxon Understanding," *North American Review* 166 (May 1898): 513–21; Abbott, *Life That Really Is*, p. 100; and Abbott, *The Rights of Man: A Study in Twentieth Century Problems* (Boston: Houghton, Mifflin and Co., 1901), p. 263. W. E. B. Du Bois, Rayford W. Logan, and David W. Southern insist on a radical transformation in Abbott's racial attitudes between 1867 and 1900. As much a barometer as a shaper of public opinion, Abbott was always a "moderate." It was conditions and alternatives that changed. See my discussion in chapter 11; Logan, *The Betrayal of the Negro: From*

Rutherford B. Hayes to Woodrow Wilson (New York: Collier, 1965), pp. 180–83, 274–75; and Southern, *The Malignant Heritage: Yankee Progressives and the Negro Question, 1901–1914* (Chicago: Loyola University Press, 1968), pp. 34–36.

28. Abbott, *Life That Really Is*, p. 154; Abbott, *Rights of Man*, pp. 223–26, 228, 272; Sarah Truslow Dickinson, ed., *Problems of Life: Selections from the Writings of Rev. Lyman Abbott* (New York: Dodd, Mead and Co., 1900), p. 92; Abbott, *Henry Ward Beecher* (Boston: Houghton, Mifflin and Co., 1903), p. 276; and Lyman Abbott, "Baccalaureate Sermon," 5 June 1900, Trinity College Papers, Duke University. See also "Booker T. Washington on Our Racial Problem," *Outlook* 64 (6 January 1900): 14–17.

29. Abbott to Washington, 9 December 1899; Abbott to Washington, 9 March 1900, in Harlan, *Washington Papers*, 5:288–89, 453; Abbott to Washington, 1 October 1900, in Harlan, *Booker T. Washington*, 1:247; *Outlook* 66 (3 November 1900) through 67 (23 February 1901); Ernest Howard Crosby, *Garrison the Non-Resistant* (Chicago: Public Publishing Co., 1905), p. 109; George A. Gordon, *Through Man to God* (Boston: Houghton, Mifflin and Co., 1906), pp. 145–46; and Washington Gladden, "Types of American Manhood: Booker T. Washington," 17 November 1901, Sermon 898, Gladden Papers. See also Hamilton Wright Mabie, in Harlan, *Booker T. Washington*, 1:248–49; and Creighton Lacy, *Frank Mason North: His Social and Ecumenical Mission* (Nashville: Abingdon Press, 1967), p. 104.

30. William A. Sinclair, *The Aftermath of Slavery: A Study of the Condition and Environment of the American Negro* (Boston: Small, Maynard and Co., 1905), pp. 200–202; Harlan, *Booker T. Washington*, 1:304–5; and William Lawrence, *Memories of a Happy Life* (Boston: Houghton Mifflin Co., 1926), pp. 181–82.

31. Amory H. Bradford, *My Brother* (Boston: Pilgrim Press, 1910), p. 89; *Atlanta Journal*, 23 May 1903, p. 6; and *Atlanta News*, 23 May 1903, p. 6.

32. Robert E. Speer to Booker T. Washington, 19 September 1902, in Harlan, *Washington Papers*, 6:524–25. See also Harlan, *Booker T. Washington*, 1:252.

33. "Editorial," *Social Gospel* 11 (December 1898): 12; S. E. F., "Equality and Likeness," *Social Gospel* 10 (November 1898): 21–22; "Current Topics," *Social Gospel* 7 (August 1898): 19; "Current Topics," *Social Gospel* 12 (January 1899): 18–19; and "Current Topics," *Social Gospel* 14 (March 1899): 21. See also James Dombrowski, *The Early Days of Christian Socialism in America* (New York: Columbia University Press, 1936), pp. 132–70; Ralph Albertson, "The Christian Commonwealth in Georgia," *Georgia Historical Quarterly* 29 (September 1945): 125–42; and John O. Fish, "The Christian Commonwealth: A Georgia Experiment, 1896–1900," *Georgia Historical Quarterly* 67 (Summer 1972): 213–26.

34. Jane Addams, *Twenty Years at Hull House, with Autobiographical Notes* (New York: Macmillan, 1910), pp. 277–79; and "April at Commonwealth," *Social Gospel* 28 (May 1900): 30. See also "Thirty Days," *Social Gospel* 26 (March 1900): 21.

35. "Colony Notes," *Social Gospel* 2 (March 1898): 21–22; and Samuel Huntington Comings, "Some Educational Plans," *Social Gospel* 3 (April 1898): 10. See also "Colony Notes," *Social Gospel* 3 (April 1898): 25; "Notes of Progress," *Social Gospel* 15 (April 1899): 26; and Comings, *Pagan vs. Christian Civilizations; National Life and Permanence Dependent upon Reform in Education. A Plea for Free Universal Industrial Training on a Self-Supporting Basis* (Chicago: C. H. Kerr and Co., [1905]).

36. Edward Abbott to A. B. Hunter, 12 January 1898, Southern Education Board Papers, Southern Historical Collection, University of North Carolina, Chapel Hill; *Proceedings of the First Capon Springs Conference for Christian Education in the South*, 1898 (Washington, D.C.: n.p., n.d.); "Christian Education in the South," *Independent* 50 (14 July 1898): 128–29; "Capon Springs Conference, West Virginia," *American Missionary* 51 (December 1898): 109–10; Robert C. Ogden to A. C. Kaufman, 18 April 1903, Letterbook, box no. 13, Ogden Papers; J. E. Davis, "Early Days of the 'Ogden Movement,'" *Southern Workman* 44 (November 1915): 615; and Charles William Dabney, *Universal Education in the South*, 2 vols. (Chapel Hill: University of North Carolina Press, 1936), 2:3–5.

37. Ogden to George Foster Peabody, 11 June 1896, Letterbook, box no. 13, Ogden Papers; *Proceedings of the Second Capon Springs Conference for Education in the South*, 1899 (Raleigh, N.C.: Edwards and Broughton, 1899), pp. 7–8; "Rev. Geo. S. Dickerman," *American Missionary* 47 (November 1893): 339; "Fifty-Second Annual Meeting of the American Missionary Association," *American Missionary* 52 (December 1898): 155–59; "Editorial," *Independent* 51 (6 July 1899): 1838–39; George S. Dickerman to Washington Gladden, 1 October 1903, box 5, no. 262; James W. Cooper to Gladden, 6 November 1903, box 5, no. 393, Gladden Papers; and Gladden to Dickerman, 12 October 1903, Dickerman File, Southern Education Papers. See also Ogden to F. C. Briggs, 27 May 1896, Letterbook, box no. 13, Ogden Papers; and "The Conference at Capon Springs," *Review of Reviews* 20 (August 1899): 131–37.

38. Harlan, *Booker T. Washington*, 1:292–93; Wilson, *An Unofficial Statesman*, p. 201; Hugh C. Bailey, *Edgar Gardner Murphy: Gentle Progressive* (Coral Gables, Fla.: University of Miami Press, 1968), pp. 31–36; Edgar Gardner Murphy to Washington, 13 January, 28 March, and 3 May 1900, in Harlan, *Washington Papers*, 5:412–14, 475–78, 493–95; "A Notable Conference," *Outlook* 64 (3 February 1900): 247–48; and "Editorial," *Independent* 52 (15 February 1900): 451.

39. *Race Problems of the South. Report of the Proceedings of the First Annual Conference Held under the Auspices of the Southern Society for the Promotion of the Study of Race Conditions and Problems in the South . . . at . . . Montgomery, Alabama, May 8, 9, 10, A.D. 1900* (Richmond: B. F. Johnson Publishing Co., 1900); "The Eternal Negro," *Independent* 52 (17 May 1900): 1207–8; Bruce Grit, in *"The Negro Problem" as Seen by Southern White Men in Conference at Montgomery, Alabama . . .*, ed. George Allen Mebane (New York: Alliance Publishing Co., 1900), p. 35; Bailey, *Edgar Gardner Murphy*, pp. 48–52; and Booker T. Washington, "The Montgomery Race Conference," *Century* 60 (August 1900): 630–32. See also "The Montgomery Conference," *Outlook* 65 (19 May 1900): 153–55; Isabel C. Barrows, "The Montgomery Conference," *Independent* 52 (24 May 1900): 1257–59; "The Montgomery Conference," *Review of Reviews* 21 (June 1900): 655–56; "The Montgomery Convention," *AME Church Review* 17 (July 1900): 88–90; and Neal C. Anderson, "The Montgomery Conference on Race Problems at the South," *Presbyterian Quarterly* 14 (October 1900): 565.

40. Louis R. Harlan, *Separate and Unequal: Public School Campaigns and Racism in the Southern Seaboard States, 1901–1915* (Chapel Hill: University of North Carolina Press, 1958), pp. 82–83; "The Ogden Party," *Independent* 53 (9 May 1901): 1095; and Ogden to Curry, 6 June 1902, in Harlan, *Separate and Unequal*, p. 82. See also Ogden to Alex Purvis, Esq., 6 March 1900, box no. 6, Ogden Papers; "The Conference on Southern Education," *Review of*

*Reviews* 23 (June 1901): 644–45; Wilson, *An Unofficial Statesman*, pp. 205–6; and Ogden to George W. Boyd, 27 February 1904, Letterbook, box no. 13, Ogden Papers.

41. *New York World*, 28 April 1901, in Comer Vann Woodward, *Origins of the New South*, 1877–1913 (Baton Rouge: Louisiana State University Press, 1951), p. 396; Charles H. Parkhurst to Charles F. Meserve, 23 March 1901, Dickerman File, Southern Education Papers; Wilson, *An Unofficial Statesman*, pp. 206, 216; and Harlan, *Separate and Unequal*, p. 98. See also Wilson, *An Unofficial Statesman*, pp. 229–30.

42. *Proceedings of the Fourth Annual Conference for Education in the South Held at Winston-Salem, North Carolina, April 18, 19, and 20, 1901* (Winston-Salem: The Committee, 1901), pp. 113, 12; and "Editorial," *Independent* 53 (9 May 1901): 1095–96. See also "A Voice from the Past," *Outlook* 74 (2 May 1903): 13–14; "An Account of a Speech in Atlanta," 21 April 1901, and Francis Jackson Garrison to Oswald Garrison Villard, 12 May 1902, in Harlan, *Washington Papers*, 6:92–93, 457–61; and Harlan, *Separate and Unequal*, p. 216.

43. Harlan, *Separate and Unequal*, pp. 80–81; "Mr. Ogden's Party," *Independent* 53 (2 May 1901): 1036–37; Lyman Abbott, "Some Southern Impressions," *Outlook* 67 (27 April 1901): 948; "Shall the Negro Be Educated," *Outlook* 68 (4 May 1901): 13–15; "Education North & South," *Outlook* 68 (11 May 1901): 103–5; and James G. Merrill, "Letter," *Outlook* 68 (11 May 1901): 135–36. See also "Too Much Education" and "Negro Education," *Independent* 53 (16 May 1901): 1147–48, 1153; Charles H. Williams, "The Race Problem," *Colored American Magazine* 3 (September 1901): 353–57; Lyman Abbott to Edgar Gardner Murphy, 31 December 1906, Edgar Gardner Murphy Papers, Southern Historical Collection, University of North Carolina, Chapel Hill; and Abbott to Donald Sage, 2 January 1907, Trinity College Papers.

44. "A Southern Educational Board," *Independent* 53 (21 November 1901): 2795–96; "Fresh Zeal for Southern Education," *Review of Reviews* 24 (December 1901): 650–51; Dabney, *Universal Education in the South*, 2:3–73; Harlan, *Separate and Unequal*, pp. 9–13; and Bailey, *Edgar Gardner Murphy*, p. 138.

45. Harlan, *Separate and Unequal*, pp. 85–87. See also "Educational Conditions in the Southern States," *Educational Review* 23 (May 1902): 479–82.

46. Hugh C. Bailey, *Edgar Gardner Murphy*; Luker, *Southern Tradition in Theology and Social Criticism*, pp. 287–377; Anson Phelps Stokes, "James Hardy Dillard," in *Dictionary of American Biography*, supplement 2, 150–51; "Report of Meetings of C. A. I. L. and of C. S. U.," *Dawn* 6 (June 1894): 85–87; and Benjamin Brawley, *Doctor Dillard of the Jeanes Fund* (New York: Fleming H. Revell Co., 1930).

47. Jerome Davis Greene, "Wallace Buttrick," and Harris Elwood Starr, "Frederick Taylor Gates," in *Dictionary of American Biography*, 2:377–78, and 4:182–83; "Minutes of the Brotherhood of the Kingdom," 19 December 1892, August 1893; and Brotherhood of the Kingdom Conference Visitors Book, 9–11 August 1893, American Baptist Historical Society Library; Charles L. White, *A Century of Faith* (Philadelphia: Judson Press, 1952), pp. 107, 119, 236, 285, 298; and Buttrick to Robert Ogden, 24 December 1907, box no. 10, Ogden Papers.

48. Harlan, *Separate and Unequal*, p. 78n; George S. Dickerman to Edwin A. Alderman, 27 March 1902; Edgar Gardner Murphy to Mrs. B. B. Valentine, 12 March 1903, Edgar Gardner Murphy Letterbook, Southern Education Papers; and "The Southern Educa-

tion Board," *Independent* 54 (24 April 1902): 1008. The bracketed words were inserted by the *Independent*. Ogden replied: "I appreciate very deeply the condescending kindness of judgment upon the ignorance and the 'muddledness' of the 'good men,' whose action, in the judgment of 'The Independent,' has a tendency to deceive Northern men. I am entirely unconcerned as to the opinion 'The Independent' may be pleased to hold regarding the intelligence of the Board or its actions." Robert C. Ogden to Clarence W. Bowen, Esq., 3 May 1902, box no. 6, Ogden Papers. See also "The Southern Education Board," *Independent* 54 (8 May 1902): 1145–46; Wallace C. Buttrick to Ogden, 7 May 1902, box no. 6, Ogden Papers; and, for a sample of the Southern education propaganda, "Need of Education in the South," *Homiletic Review* 44 (July 1902): 82–83.

49. "Pocket Information for the Use of the Hampton-Athens-Knoxville Party, April–May, 1902," George S. Dickerman File, Southern Education Papers; and Felix Adler, "Democracy, the American Ideal," in *Proceedings of the Fifth Conference for Education in the South held in Athens, Georgia, April 24, 25, and 26, 1902* (Knoxville, Tenn.: Southern Education Board, 1902), pp. 77–79. See also Oswald Garrison Villard, *Fighting Years: Memoirs of a Liberal Editor* (New York: Harcourt, Brace and Co., 1939), pp. 172–76.

50. Robert C. Ogden to Colonel A. C. Kaufman, 17 April 1903, Letterbook, box no. 13, Ogden Papers; "The Race Problem," *Outlook* 73 (14 March 1903): 607–10; "Nearing a Solution," *Outlook* 90 (19 December 1908): 859–60; and Abbott, in Augustus Field Beard, *A Crusade for Brotherhood: A History of the American Missionary Association* (Boston: Pilgrim Press, 1909), p. 265.

51. James W. Cooper to Washington Gladden, 6 November 1903, box 5, no. 393, Gladden Papers. See also George S. Dickerman to Gladden, 1 October 1903, box 5, no. 262, Gladden Papers; and Gladden to Dickerman, 12 October 1903, Dickerman File, Southern Education Papers.

52. Edgar Gardner Murphy to D. Clay Lilly, 30 March 1903, Edgar Gardner Murphy Letterbook, Southern Education Papers; and Edward T. Ware to Dickerman, 9 May 1902, Dickerman File, Southern Education Papers. See also D. Clay Lilly, "The Attitude of the South to the Colored People," *Union Seminary Magazine* 16 (February–March 1905): 270–87.

53. Abbott, "The Three Rights of the Less Favored Races," *Southern Educator* 1 (21 December 1903): 416–17; and Francis Greenwood Peabody, "Knowledge and Service," in *Proceedings of the Conference for Education in the South: The Sixth Session. Richmond, Va., April 22d to 24th, and at the University of Virginia, April 25th* (Richmond: n.p., 1903), pp. 224–27. See also "A National Problem," *Outlook* 73 (25 April 1903): 950–52; "The Educational Revival," *Outlook* 73 (9 May 1903): 106–9; and my discussion in chapter 8.

54. Robert W. DeForest, "The South and the North Each Best Fitted to Solve Its Own Problems," in *Proceedings of the National Conference on Charities and Corrections at the Thirteenth Annual Session Held in the City of Atlanta, May 6–12, 1903*, ed. Isabel C. Barrows (n.p.: Fred J. Heer, 1903), pp. 1–3; and Percy Stickney Grant, *New York Times*, 20 April 1903, and "The Negro Question in the United States," *Liberia* 23 (November 1903): 92–93.

55. Washington to Baldwin, 22 January 1904, in Harlan, *Washington Papers*, 7:409–11; Ogden to S. G. Atkins, 21 December 1903; Ogden to Baldwin, 26 February 1904, Letterbook, box no. 13, Ogden Papers; and Lyman Abbott, "Negro Disfranchisement,"

*Social Service* 9 (April 1904): 69. See also Baldwin to Washington, 17 May 1904; and Washington to Baldwin, 31 May 1904, Washington Papers.

56. Thomas Wentworth Higginson to ——, 21 April 1904, in Mary Thacher Higginson, ed., *Letters and Journals of Thomas Wentworth Higginson, 1846–1906* (Boston: Houghton Mifflin Co., 1921), pp. 345–46; and William Lawrence, *Memories of a Happy Life* (Boston: Houghton Mifflin Co., 1926), pp. 179–80.

57. Charles B. Galloway, *The South and the Negro: An Address Delivered at the Seventh Annual Conference for Education in the South, Birmingham, Ala., April 26th, 1904* (New York: Southern Education Board, 1904); Ogden to A. C. Kaufman, 9 May 1904; Ogden to Galloway, 10 May 1904; Galloway to Ogden, 15 May 1904; Higginson to "Mr. Watkins," 23 May 1904; Higginson to Ogden, 23 May 1904; Ogden to Higginson, 24 May 1904; and Galloway to Ogden, 2 June 1904, boxes no. 7 and no. 14, Ogden Papers; Charles Alexander to Booker T. Washington, 13 June 1904, Washington Papers; Ogden to Higginson, 23 June 1904, Letterbook, box no. 14, Ogden Papers; Higginson, "Part of a Man's Life: 'Intensely Human,'" *Atlantic Monthly* 93 (May 1904): 596; and Tilden G. Edelstein, *Strange Enthusiasm: A Life of Thomas Wentworth Higginson* (New Haven: Yale University Press, 1968), pp. 373, 378–79, 387–91.

58. William DeWitt Hyde, "A National Platform on the Race Question," *Outlook* 77 (21 May 1904): 109–10; and "President Hyde's Platform," *Independent* 56 (26 May 1904): 1216.

59. "The Southern Educational Conference," *Independent* 58 (4 May 1905): 1022; "The Conference for Education in the South," "The Addresses," and "The Railway Accident," *Outlook* 80 (13 May 1905): 101–3; Harlan, *Separate and Unequal*, pp. 186–87; Wilson, *An Unofficial Statesman*, p. 208; W. E. Gonzales to Ogden, 31 May 1905, box no. 9, Ogden Papers; Ogden to Washington, 1 June 1905, Washington Papers; Ogden to George S. Dickerman, 1 June 1905, Dickerman File, Southern Education Papers; Washington to Ogden, 5 June 1905, Washington Papers; Julius D. Dreher to Ogden, 10 June and 12 June 1905; and Charles D. McIver to Ogden, 13 June 1905, Ogden Papers. See also Dixon's attack on the "mongrelizing aims" of the Southern Education Movement and on Ogden as the spokesman for the "New Order of Carpetbag" in Dixon, *The Sins of the Father* (New York: D. Appleton and Co., 1912), pp. 200–210.

60. Ogden to Washington, 14 June 1905, Washington Papers; Matthew Anderson to Ogden, 14 June 1905; T. Thomas Fortune to Ogden, 26 June 1905, Ogden Papers; Washington to B. J. Saunders, 18 September 1905, Washington Papers; Washington to J. C. Asbury, 2 October 1905, in Harlan, *Washington Papers*, 8:387–88; and Josiah Strong to Ogden, 24 April 1906, box no. 9, Ogden Papers.

61. Harlan, *Separate and Unequal*, pp. 248–54.

62. Washington to Ogden, 18 July 1906, Washington Papers; and Murphy to Buttrick, 14 November 1907, Murphy Letterbook, Southern Education Papers. See also James Hardy Dillard to Ogden, 31 May 1909, box no. 10, Ogden Papers; and Booker T. Washington to R. R. Moton, 15 September 1909, Washington Papers.

63. Mary White Ovington, *Half a Man: The Status of the Negro in New York* (New York: Longmans, Green, and Co., 1911), p. 267n.

64. Harlan, *Separate and Unequal*, pp. 254–55, 268–69.

Chapter 7

1. John Hope Franklin, *From Slavery to Freedom: A History of American Negroes*, 4th ed. (New York: Alfred A. Knopf, 1974), p. 319; Allen Spear, "The Origins of the Urban Ghetto, 1870–1915," in *Key Issues in Afro-American History*, 2 vols., ed. Nathan I. Huggins, Martin Kilson, and David M. Fox (New York: Harcourt, Brace, Jovanovich, 1971), 2:161–62; James Clark Ridpath, "The Mixed Populations of Chicago," *Chautauquan* 12 (January 1891): 486; and Ray Stannard Baker, *Following the Color Line: American Negro Citizenship in the Progressive Era* (New York: Harper and Row, 1964), p. 109.

2. Richard B. Sherman, ed., *The Negro and the City* (Englewood Cliffs, N.J.: Prentice-Hall, 1970), p. 5; and Franklin, *From Slavery to Freedom*, p. 319. See also Zane L. Miller, "Urban Blacks in the New South, 1865–1920: The Richmond, Savannah, New Orleans, Louisville, and Birmingham Experience," in *The New Urban History: Quantitative Explorations by American Historians*, ed. Leo F. Schnore (Princeton: Princeton University Press, 1975), pp. 184–204.

3. Josiah Strong, *Our Country: Its Possible Future and Its Present Crisis* (New York: Baker and Taylor Co., 1885), pp. 128–44; Frank Mason North, "The City and the Kingdom," in *Social Ministry: An Introduction to the Study and Practice of Social Service*, ed. Harry F. Ward (New York: Eaton and Mains, 1910), pp. 311–12; Thomas N. Chase, ed., *Mortality among Negroes in Cities* (Atlanta: Atlanta University Press, 1896); James P. Kelley, "Information Wanted," *Social Gospel* 8 (September 1898): 9–10; William Edward Burghardt Du Bois, *The Philadelphia Negro* (Philadelphia: University of Pennsylvania Press, 1899), pp. 54–57, 64–65, 238–40, 295–97, 344–48, 449–51; Baker, *Following the Color Line*, pp. 114–17; Willis Duke Weatherford, *Negro Life in the South: Present Conditions and Needs* (New York: Association Press, 1911), pp. 61–83; Richard R. Wright, Jr., *The Negro in Pennsylvania: A Study in Economic History* (Philadelphia: AME Press, 1912), pp. 140–65; Asa E. Martin, *Our Negro Population: A Sociological Study of the Negroes of Kansas City, Missouri* (n.p.: Franklin Hudson Publishing Co., 1913), pp. 114–15; Wendell P. Dabney, *Cincinnati's Colored Citizens: Historical, Sociological and Biographical* (Cincinnati: Dabney Publishing Co., 1926), pp. 378–90; and Peabody, quoted in "The Second Hampton Conference of Graduates and Ex-Students," *Southern Workman* 22 (July 1894): 127.

4. Benjamin Orange Flower, *Civilization's Inferno; or, Studies in the Social Cellar* (Boston: Arena Publishing Co., 1893), pp. 103–4. See also Josiah Strong, *The Challenge of the City* (New York: American Baptist Home Mission Society, 1907), pp. 103–4.

5. Helen Campbell, Thomas W. Knox, and Thomas Byrnes, *Darkness and Daylight; or, Lights and Shadows of New York Life* (Hartford: Hartford Publishing Co., 1896), pp. 237–45, 471–74. See also Jacob A. Riis, *How the Other Half Lives: Studies among the Tenements of New York* (New York: Charles Scribner's Sons, 1890), pp. 117–18; William Thomas Stead, *If Christ Came to Chicago: A Plea for the Union of All Who Love in the Service of All Who Suffer* (London: Review of Reviews, 1894), p. 237; and Mary White Ovington, *Half a Man: The Status of the Negro in New York* (New York: Longmans, Green, and Co., 1911), p. 156.

6. Herbert Gutman, *The Black Family in Slavery and Freedom, 1750–1925* (New York: Pantheon Books, 1976), pp. 447–60; Edward T. Devine, "Housing Conditions in the

Principle Cities of New York," *Charities* 7 (7 December 1901): 496–500; Behrends, Crafts, and Riis, quoted in Wilbur Fisk Crafts, *Practical Christian Sociology: A Series of Special Lectures before Princeton Theological Seminary and Marietta College* (New York: Funk and Wagnalls, 1895), pp. 76–77; Tutwiler, in *Proceedings of the National Conference of Charities and Corrections at the Twenty-Ninth Annual Session Held in the City of Detroit, May 28–June 3, 1902*, ed. Isabel C. Barrows (Boston: George H. Ellis, 1902), pp. 474–75; Tolman, quoted in "Second Summer Conference, July 20–22," *Southern Workman* 27 (September 1898): 172; and Strong, *Our Country*, pp. 128–44. See also W. E. B. Du Bois, *The Souls of Black Folk* (Chicago: A. C. McClurg and Co., 1903), pp. 139–40; Baker, *Following the Color Line*, pp. 112–14; Martin, *Our Negro Population*, pp. 90–94; and Allan H. Spear, *Black Chicago: The Making of a Negro Ghetto, 1890–1920* (Chicago: University of Chicago Press, 1967), pp. 23–24.

7. Jesse Edward Moorland, "The Young Men's Christian Association among Negroes," *Journal of Negro History* 9 (January 1924): 127–34; and Charles Howard Hopkins, *History of the Y.M.C.A. in North America* (New York: Association Press, 1951), pp. 115, 156, 211–16, 275.

8. Charles M. Sheldon, "Practical Christian Sociological Studies," *Andover Review* 14 (October 1890): 371; Sheldon, *His Life Story* (New York: George H. Doran Co., 1925), pp. 88–92; and "Editorial Notes," *Unitarian* 5 (December 1890): 594.

9. Reverdy C. Ransom, "The Y.M.C.A.," *Christian Recorder* 29 (12 March 1891): 3; and Du Bois, *Philadelphia Negro*, pp. 232, 195.

10. Seth M. Scheiner, *Negro Mecca: A History of the Negro in New York City, 1865–1920* (New York: New York University Press, 1965), pp. 145–46; Spear, *Black Chicago*, pp. 52, 62; Hopkins, *History of the Y.M.C.A.*, pp. 217–20, 454, 472–73; William A. Hunton, "Colored Men's Department of the Young Men's Christian Association," *Voice of the Negro* 2 (June 1905): 388–96; Moorland, "Young Men's Christian Association," pp. 134–35; Addie W. Hunton, *William Alphaeus Hunton: A Pioneer Prophet of Young Men* (New York: Association Press, 1938), pp. 1–47: and "President to Negro," *Liberia* 33 (November 1908): 41. See also W. E. B. Du Bois, ed., *Efforts for Social Betterment among Negro Americans* (Atlanta: Atlanta University Press, 1909), pp. 96–99.

11. Gladys Gelke Calkins, "The Negro in the Young Women's Christian Association: A Study of the Development of the YWCA's Interracial Policies and Practices in their Historical Setting, 1865–1946" (M.A. thesis, George Washington University, 1960); Jane Olcott Walters, comp., "History of Colored Work: Chronological Excerpts from Reports of Secretaries and Workers and from Minutes Showing Development of the Work among Colored Women, 1907–1920," typescript copy, YWCA Archives, New York; and Cynthia Neverdon-Morton, *Afro-American Women of the South and the Advancement of the Race, 1895–1925* (Knoxville: University of Tennessee Press, 1989), pp. 207–22. See also Reverdy Ransom, *The Pilgrimage of Harriet Ransom's Son* (Nashville: Sunday School Union, 1949), pp. 202–5; Gilbert Osofsky, *Harlem: The Making of a Ghetto. Negro New York, 1890–1930* (New York: Oxford University Press, 1968), pp. 31, 120, 151; and Spear, *Black Chicago*, pp. 46–47, 100, 102, 174.

12. Graham Taylor, "Washington's Day for Citizenship," *The Survey* 25 (25 February 1911): 380–81; Hopkins, *History of the Y.M.C.A.*, pp. 458, 472; Moorland, "Young Men's

Christian Association," pp. 135–36; Osofsky, *Harlem: The Making of a Ghetto*, pp. 14–15, 41; David A. Gerber, *Black Ohio and the Color Line, 1860–1915* (Urbana: University of Illinois Press, 1976), pp. 455–57; and Du Bois, *Efforts for Social Betterment*, pp. 95–96.

13. Booker T. Washington to Nathalia Lord, 30 September 1887, and Lord to Washington, 10 October 1887, in *The Booker T. Washington Papers*, 14 vols., ed. Louis R. Harlan et al. (Urbana: University of Illinois Press, 1972–89), 2:390–91; Oswald Garrison Villard, "An American Negro School," *Review of Reviews* 31 (December 1902): 711–14; R. C. Bedford, "Mt. Meig's Institute, Alabama, Tuskegee's Child and Hampton's Grandchild," *Southern Workman* 23 (April 1894): 64–65; and Charlotte R. Thorne and Mabel W. Dillingham, "Calhoun Colored School," *Lend-A-Hand* 13 (July 1894): 52–55.

14. "Announcement of the Opening of Phelps Hall Bible School," November 1892, in Harlan, *Washington Papers*, 3:257–58; "The Bible School at Tuskegee," *Outlook* 47 (18 March 1893): 505; R. C. Bedford, "Twelfth Year of Tuskegee's Work," *Lend-A-Hand* 10 (March 1893): 221; Elizabeth E. Lane, "Tuskegee School: A Practical Solution to the Negro Problem," *Lend-A-Hand* 13 (July 1894): 17–21; and Mrs. Booker T. Washington, "The New Negro Woman," *Lend-A-Hand* 15 (October 1895): 254–60.

15. Robert A. Woods and Albert J. Kennedy, eds., *Handbook of Settlements* (New York: Charities Publication Committee, 1911), pp. 6–8, 298; and Florence L. Lattimore, "The Palace of Delights at Hampton," *Survey* 33 (6 March 1915): 625–28. See also "The Settlement Idea in the Cotton Belt," *Outlook* 70 (12 April 1902): 92; Pitt Dillingham, "The Black Belt Settlement Work," *Southern Workman* 31 (July 1902): 383–88, and (August 1902): 437–44; John W. Lemon, "The Calhoun School," *Voice of the Negro* 3 (April 1906): 266–70; Mary White Ovington, *The Walls Came Tumbling Down* (New York: Harcourt, Brace and Co., 1947), pp. 67–74; and Rose Herlong Ellis, "The Calhoun School, Miss Charlotte Thorn's 'Lighthouse on the Hill' in Lowndes County, Alabama," *Alabama Review* 36 (July 1984): 183–201.

16. Lewis W. Jones, "Social Centers in the Rural South," *Phylon* 12 (Third Quarter 1951): 279–84; Allen F. Davis, *Spearheads for Reform: The Social Settlement and the Progressive Movement, 1890–1914* (New York: Oxford University Press, 1967); Dewey W. Grantham, *Southern Progressivism: The Reconciliation of Progress and Tradition* (Knoxville: University of Tennessee Press, 1983), pp. 222ff.; Jane Addams, *Twenty Years at Hull House* (New York: Macmillan, 1910), pp. 49–50; Du Bois, *Souls of Black Folk*, p. 100; and Washington Gladden, "Congregationalism and the Poor," *American Missionary* 45 (December 1891): 466–69.

17. Harriet E. Emerson, *Annals of a Harvester: Reviewing Forty Years of Home Missionary Work in the Southern States* (East Andover, N.H.: Arthur W. Emerson, Sons and Co., [ca. 1915]), pp. 51–96; Laura S. Haviland, *A Woman's Life-Work: Labor and Experiences* (Cincinnati, Ohio: Walden and Stowe, 1882), pp. 360–520; Joanna P. Moore, "*In Christ's Stead*": *Autobiographical Sketches* (Chicago: Women's Baptist Home Mission Society, 1902), pp. 55–57, 73–82, 138–41, 143–53, 177–81; and Richard R. Wright, Jr., *87 Years behind the Black Curtain: An Autobiography* (Philadelphia: Rare Book Co., 1965), p. 149.

18. Davis, *Spearheads for Reform*, pp. 15–22, exaggerates the difference between the two.

19. Scheiner, *Negro Mecca*, pp. 142–44; and Osofsky, *Harlem: The Making of a Ghetto*, pp. 55, 151.

20. Woods and Kennedy, *Handbook of Settlements*, pp. 267–69, 271–75; Vida Dutton Scudder, *On Journey* (New York: E. P. Dutton and Co., 1937), p. 141; Anna Davis, "A Glance at the Philadelphia Settlements," *Commons* 10 (May 1905): 299; Du Bois, *Efforts for Social Betterment*, pp. 123–24; and Wright, *87 Years behind the Black Curtain*, pp. 47–48, 115, 149–53. See also Allen Davis and John F. Sutherland, "Reform and Uplift among Philadelphia Negroes: The Diary of Helen Parrish, 1888," *Pennsylvania Magazine of History and Biography* 94 (October 1970): 496–517.

21. Francis L. Broderick, *W. E. B. Du Bois: Negro Leadership in a Time of Crisis* (Stanford, Calif.: Stanford University Press, 1959), pp. 7–41; Elliott M. Rudwick, *W. E. B. Du Bois: Propagandist of the Negro Protest* (New York: Atheneum Press, 1969), pp. 19–36; and "The Negro's Handicap in the North," *Homiletic Review* 39 (April 1900): 383–84.

22. Charles M. Sheldon, "A Local Negro Problem," *Kingdom* 8 (10 April 1896): 828; Sheldon, *The Redemption of Freetown* (Boston: United Society of Christian Endeavor, 1898); Sheldon, *His Own Story*, pp. 92–95; Thomas C. Cox, *Blacks in Topeka, Kansas, 1865–1915: A Social History* (Baton Rouge: Louisiana State University Press, 1982), pp. 46–82, 144–49; Timothy Miller, "Charles M. Sheldon and the Uplift of Tennesseetown," *Kansas History* 9 (Autumn 1986): 125–37; and Miller, *Following in His Steps: A Biography of Charles M. Sheldon* (Knoxville: University of Tennessee Press, 1987), pp. 46–65.

23. "A Negro Mission in Kentucky," *Outlook* 80 (19 August 1905): 949–50; John Little, "The Presbyterian Colored Mission," in *An Era of Progress and Promise, 1863–1910; The Religious, Moral, and Educational Development of the American Negro since His Emancipation*, ed. William Newton Hartshorn (Boston: Priscilla Publishing Co., 1910), pp. 233–47; Lucien V. Rule, *The Light Bearers: Home Mission Heroes of Presbyterian History* (Louisville: Brandt-Conners and Fowler, 1926), pp. 173–83; and Miriam Gaines, "The John Little Mission, Louisville, Ky.," *Southern Workman* 62 (April 1933): 161–70. For a more critical perspective, see George C. Wright, *Life behind a Veil: Blacks in Louisville, Kentucky, 1865–1930* (Baton Rouge: Louisiana State University Press, 1985), pp. 145–51.

24. Ruth Hutchinson Crocker, "Sympathy and Science: The Settlement Movement in Gary and Indianapolis, to 1930" (Ph.D. dissertation, Purdue University, 1982), pp. 167–233; and Genevieve C. Weeks, *Oscar Carleton McCulloch, 1843–1891: Preacher and Practitioner of Applied Christianity* (Indianapolis: Indiana Historical Society, 1976), pp. 129–30.

25. Charles R. Henderson, *Social Settlements* (New York: Lentilhon and Co., 1899), p. 83. See also ibid., pp. 83–97, 173–78; and Jacob A. Riis, "What Settlements Stand For," *Outlook* 89 (9 May 1908): 69–72.

26. Woods and Kennedy, eds., *Handbook of Settlements*, pp. 31–32, 39–40, 47, 50–51, 97–98, 107, 124, 171, 287, 300; Gerber, *Black Ohio and the Color Line*, pp. 282, 457–58; Caroline B. Chapin, "Settlement Work among Colored People," *Annals of the American Academy of Political and Social Science* 21 (March 1903): 184–85; Jeffrey A. Hess, "Black Settlement House, East Greenwich, 1902–1914," *Rhode Island History* 29 (August–November 1970): 113–27; and Nimmons, "Social Reform and Moral Uplift in the Black Community," pp. 83–129. See also Thomas Lee Philpott, *The Slum and the Ghetto: Neighborhood Deterioration and Middle-Class Reform, Chicago, 1880–1930* (New York: Oxford University Press, 1978), pp. 314–42.

27. S. Timothy Tice, "The Benefits of Social Settlements and Institutional Church

Work in the Cities," in *The United Negro: His Problems and His Progress. Containing the Addresses and Proceedings. The Negro Young People's Christian and Educational Congress, Held August* 6–11, 1902, ed. I. Garland Penn and John Wesley Edward Bowen (Atlanta: Board of Directors of the Congress, 1902), pp. 215–16. Aaron Ignatius Abell, *The Urban Impact on American Protestantism, 1865–1900* (Cambridge: Harvard University Press, 1943), pp. 137–93, is a traditional interpretation of institutional churches which ignores the black experience.

28. Abell, *Urban Impact on American Protestantism*, pp. 28, 157–58; Du Bois, *Philadelphia Negro*, pp. 349–50; Conwell, as quoted in James M. McPherson, *The Abolitionist Legacy: From Reconstruction to the NAACP* (Princeton: Princeton University Press, 1975), p. 340; and William Stephen Rainsford, *The Story of a Varied Life: An Autobiography* (Garden City, N.Y.: Doubleday, Page and Co., 1922), pp. 259, 267.

29. John B. Devins, "The Church and the City Problem," in *Christ and the Church: Essays concerning the Church and the Unification of Christendom* (New York: Fleming H. Revell Co., 1895), p. 194; Alexander Crummell, *Charitable Institutions in Colored Churches* (Washington, D.C.: R. L. Pendleton, 1893); George W. Moore, "Lincoln Memorial Church, Washington, D.C.," *Independent* 44 (7 April 1892): 471; and Moore, "Bondage and Freedom— The Story of a Life," *American Missionary* 56 (February 1907): 109–16.

30. Algernon Sidney Crapsey, *The Last of the Heretics* (New York: Alfred A. Knopf, 1924), p. 165.

31. "Colored Church Work in New York," *Outlook* 54 (22 August 1896): 328; "Religion" and Hutchens C. Bishop, "How to Hold the Young People in the Churches," *Southern Workman* 27 (September 1898): 178–80; "The Color Line: Two Cases," *Homiletic Review* 62 (September 1911): 175; Ovington, *Half a Man*, p. 120; George Freeman Bragg, *History of the Afro-American Group of the Episcopal Church* (Baltimore: Church Advocate Press, 1922), pp. 81–89; Shelton H. Bishop, "A History of St. Phillips Church, New York City," *Historical Magazine of the Protestant Episcopal Church* 15 (December 1946): 298–311; and Osofsky, *Harlem: The Making of a Ghetto*, pp. 41, 106–8, 116–17.

32. Henry L. Phillips, "General Booth's Darkest England and the Way Out of It," *AME Church Review* 7 (April 1891): 405–8; Phillips, "The Social Condition of the Negro," *Charities* 9 (February 1900): 575–78; Du Bois, *Philadelphia Negro*, p. 219; and Bragg, *History of the Afro-American Group*, pp. 111–16.

33. Matthew Anderson, *Presbyterianism: Its Relation to the Negro Illustrated by the Berean Presbyterian Church, Philadelphia, with Sketch of the Church and Autobiography of the Author* (Philadelphia: John McGill White and Co., 1897), pp. 13–46, 135–88, 222, 241–52; Du Bois, *Philadelphia Negro*, pp. 216–17, 226; Archibald Grimké, "Berean Manual Training and Industrial School," *Alexander's Magazine* 4 (15 October 1907): 312–25; Richard R. Wright, Jr., "The Social Work and Influence of the Negro Church," *Annals of the American Academy of Political and Social Science* 30 (November 1907): 89–90; Anderson, "The Berean School of Philadelphia," *Annals of the American Academy of Political and Social Science* 33 (January 1909): 111–18; and Henry Churchill King to Matthew Anderson, 14 April and 28 April 1909, Henry Churchill King Papers, Oberlin College. See also C. James Trotman, "Matthew Anderson: Black Pastor, Churchman, and Social Reformer," *American Presbyterian* 66 (Spring 1988): 11–21.

34. Reverdy Cassius Ransom, *The Pilgrimage of Harriet Ransom's Son* (Nashville: Sunday

School Union, 1949), pp. 15–17, 33–34, 38; and Ransom, *School Days at Wilberforce* (Springfield, Ohio: New Era Co., 1892). See also Calvin Sylvester Morris, "Reverdy C. Ransom: A Pioneer Black Social Gospeler" (Ph.D. dissertation, Boston University, 1982), pp. 14–126; David Wills, "Reverdy C. Ransom: The Making of an A.M.E. Bishop," in Burkett and Newman, *Black Apostles*, pp. 181–212; and W. E. Bigglestone, "Oberlin College and the Negro Student, 1865–1910," *Journal of Negro History* 55 (July 1971): 199–201.

35. Ransom, *Pilgrimage of Harriet Ransom's Son*, pp. 49, 82–88, 91–92, 103–5; Morris, "Reverdy C. Ransom," pp. 127–61; Wright, *87 Years behind the Black Curtain*, pp. 94–96; Wills, "Reverdy C. Ransom," pp. 181–212; Nimmons, "Social Reform and Moral Uplift in the Black Community, 1890–1910," pp. 99–103; Alfreda M. Duster, ed., *Crusade for Justice: The Autobiography of Ida B. Wells* (Chicago: University of Chicago Press, 1970), pp. 249–50; and Spear, *Black Chicago*, pp. 63–64, 95–96.

36. Wright, *87 Years behind the Black Curtain*, p. 148. See also Morris, "Reverdy C. Ransom," pp. 139–43.

37. Linda O. McMurray, *Recorder of the Black Experience: A Biography of Monroe N. Work* (Baton Rouge: Louisiana State University Press, 1985), pp. 18–27, 37–46; Linda O. Hines and Allen W. Jones, "A Voice of Black Protest: The Savannah Men's Sunday Club, 1905–1911," *Phylon* 35 (June 1974): 193–202; and Wright, *87 Years behind the Black Curtain*, pp. 43, 47–49, 100–116, 148–53. See also Wright, "Social Work and Influence of the Negro Church," pp. 509–21; and Monroe N. Work, "The Negro Church in the Negro Community," *Southern Workman* 38 (August 1908): 428–32.

38. Ransom, *Pilgrimage of Harriet Ransom's Son*, pp. 228–34; Ransom, "The Editor's Vision and Task in New York's Black 'Tenderloin,'" *AME Church Review* 30 (October 1913): 149–51; Maude K. Griffin, "Negro Church and Its Social Work—St. Marks," *Charities* 15 (7 October 1905): 75–76; G. L. Collin, "The City within the City," *Outlook* 84 (29 September 1906): 274–77; Du Bois, *Efforts for Social Betterment*, pp. 121–25; Ovington, *Half a Man*, pp. 39–41, 120–21; Woods and Kennedy, *Handbook of Settlements*, p. 243; Adam Clayton Powell, Sr., *Against the Tide: An Autobiography* (New York: Richard B. Smith, 1938), pp. 19–20, 49–50, 67–84; Grace Roane Gwaltney, "The Negro Church and the Social Gospel from 1877 to 1914" (M.A. thesis, Howard University, 1949), pp. 56, 74; and Osofsky, *Harlem: The Making of a Ghetto*, pp. 15, 50–51, 84, 98.

39. Du Bois, *Souls of Black Folk*, pp. 193–94; Martin, *Our Negro Population*, pp. 185–86; Christian Golder, *History of the Deaconess Movement in the Christian Church* (New York: Eaton and Mains, 1903), pp. 409–13; Gerber, *Black Ohio and the Color Line*, pp. 156–58, 438–40; David N. Katzman, *Before the Ghetto: Black Detroit in the Nineteenth Century* (Urbana: University of Illinois Press, 1973), p. 141; and Lily Hardy Hammond, *In the Vanguard of the Race* (New York: Council of Women for Home Missions and the Missionary Education Movement, 1922), pp. 73–77. See also M. L. Latta, *The History of My Life and Work* (Raleigh, N.C.: M. L. Latta, [ca. 1920]), pp. 39–41.

40. Ernest H. Hall, "A Negro Institutional Church," *Southern Workman* 50 (March 1921): 113–18. On other black institutional churches in the South, see Isabel Dangaiz Allen, "Negro Enterprise: An Institutional Church," *Outlook* 78 (September 1904): 179–84; Work, "Negro Church in the Negro Community," pp. 430–32; Hines and Jones, "A

Voice of Black Protest," pp. 193–202; McMurray, *Recorder of the Black Experience*, pp. 37–47; Nimmons, "Social Reform and Moral Uplift in the Black Community," pp. 140–41; Latta, *History of My Life and Work*, pp. 45–47; and Weatherford, *Negro Life in the South*, pp. 50–51.

41. Charles Emerson Boddie, *God's Bad Boys* (Valley Forge, Pa.: Judson Press, 1972), pp. 17–29, 117–25; Randall K. Burkett, *Black Redemption: Black Churchmen Speak for the Garvey Movement* (Philadelphia: Temple University Press, 1978), pp. 113–20; Powell, *Against the Tide*; and John William Kinney, "Adam Clayton Powell, Sr. and Adam Clayton Powell, Jr.: A Historical Exposition and Theological Analysis" (Ph.D. dissertation, Columbia University, 1979).

42. Federation of Churches and Christian Workers in New York City, *Second Sociological Canvass* (New York: The Federation, 1897). See also *New York Times*, 23 March and 4 April 1900; "The Fourth Annual Report," *Federation* 1 (June 1900): 3–4; "The Distribution of the Population in Terms of General Nativity and Color," *Federation* 2 (June 1902): 33–34; "Seven Years of Sociological Exploration," *Federation* 3 (June 1903): 12–17; "Eighth Annual Report of the Federation of Churches and Christian Organizations in New York City," *Federation* 3 (January 1904): 16–17; "One Month's Federation's Work, 1905," *Federation* 4 (October 1905): 13; "Historic Sketch: The Federation of Churches and Christian Organizations in New York City," *Federation* 4 (November 1905): 10–11; Walter Laidlaw, "The Redemption of the City: Church Federation and Evangelistic Work in Cities," *Federation* 4 (April 1906): 84–85; and Abell, *Urban Impact on American Protestantism*, p. 189.

43. Jean Blackwell Hutson, "Victoria Earle Matthews," in *Notable American Women, 1607–1950*, 4 vols., ed. Edward T. James et al. (Cambridge: Harvard University Press, 1971), 2:510–11. See also Victoria Earle Matthews, "Dangers Confronting Southern Girls in the North," *Southern Workman* 27 (September 1898): 173–74; "White Rose Mission," *Charities* 3 (28 October 1899): 6–7; Matthews, "The Redemption of the City," *Federation* 2 (July 1902): 57–58; Scheiner, *Negro Mecca*, pp. 151–52; Osofsky, *Harlem: The Making of a Ghetto*, pp. 55–57; Robert L. Factor, *The Black Response to America: Men, Ideals and Organization from Frederick Douglass to the NAACP* (Reading, Mass.: Addison Wesley, 1970), pp. 111–15; and Gerda Lerner, "Early Community Work of Black Club Women," *Journal of Negro History* 59 (April 1974): 158–62.

44. "An Astonishing Situation," *Federation* 1 (September 1900): 7–10; "Negroes Attacked in New York," *Independent* 52 (23 August 1900): 2007–8; "Editorial," *Independent* 52 (13 September 1900): 2234; Osofsky, *Harlem: The Making of a Ghetto*, pp. 46–50; and Scheiner, *Negro Mecca*, pp. 121–23.

45. A. H. W., "New York Letter," *Social Gospel* 32 (October 1900): 22; "The New York Riot," *Independent* 52 (23 August 1900): 2056–57; "The Race Riots in New York," *Outlook* 65 (25 August 1900): 946; Charles H. Parkhurst, *Our Fight with Tammany Hall* (New York: Charles Scribner and Sons, 1895); Mary Church Terrell, *A Colored Woman in a White World* (Washington, D.C.: National Association of Colored Women's Clubs, 1968), p. 182; *Story of a Riot* (New York: Citizens' Protective League, 1900); Creighton Lacy, *Frank Mason North: His Social and Ecumenical Mission* (Nashville: Abingdon Press, 1965), p. 104; Osofsky, *Harlem: The Making of a Ghetto*, pp. 50–52; and Scheiner, *Negro Mecca*, pp. 123–27.

46. Silas Xavier Floyd, *Life of Charles T. Walker, D.D.* (Nashville: National Baptist Publishing Board, 1902), pp. 104, 108–9; "A Colored Young Men's Christian Association," *Outlook* 79 (15 April 1905): 964; Elizabeth Tyler, "A New York Settlement for Negroes," *Charities and the Commons* 18 (22 June 1907): 328; Du Bois, *Efforts for Social Betterment*, p. 124; Woods and Kennedy, *Handbook of Settlements*, pp. 178–79, 198–203, 205–11; Ransom, *Pilgrimage of Harriet Ransom's Son*, pp. 202–5; and Osofsky, *Harlem: The Making of a Ghetto*, pp. 15, 54, 60, 62, 67.

47. Frances A. Kellor, "The Criminal Negro: A Sociological Study," *Arena* 25 (January–May 1901): 59–68, 190–97, 308–16, 419–28, 510–20; and 26 (June–November 1901): 56–66, 304–10, 521–27; Kellor, "Agencies for the Prevention of Crime," *Southern Workman* 32 (April 1903): 203–7; Kellor, *Out of Work. A Study of Employment Agencies: Their Treatment of the Unemployed and Their Influence upon Homes and Businesses* (New York: G. P. Putnam's Sons, 1904); Kellor, "Southern Colored Girls in the North," *Charities* 13 (18 March 1905): 584–85; "Associations for the Protection of Negro Women," *Charities* 14 (10 June 1905): 825–26; Kellor, "Opportunities for Southern Negro Women in Northern Cities," *Voice of the Negro* 2 (July 1905): 470–73; Kellor, "Assisted Emigration from the South," *Charities* 15 (7 October 1905): 11–14; and "To Protect Negro Women from the South," *Charities and the Commons* 15 (3 March 1906): 746. See also Charles Richmond Henderson, *Introduction to the Study of the Dependent, Defective, and Delinquent Classes and Their Social Treatment* (Boston: D. C. Heath and Co., 1893), p. 247; Osofsky, *Harlem: The Making of a Ghetto*, pp. 57–58; Guichard Parris and Lester Brooks, *Blacks in the City: A History of the National Urban League* (Boston: Little, Brown and Co., 1971), pp. 3–10; and Nancy J. Weiss, *The National Urban League, 1910–1940* (New York: Oxford University Press, 1974), pp. 15–20.

48. Mary White Ovington, "Reminiscences," *Baltimore Afro-American*, 24 September 1932. See also Ovington, *Walls Came Tumbling Down*, pp. 3–11; and Daniel W. Cryer, "Mary White Ovington," in James et al., *Notable American Women*, 4:517–19.

49. Ovington to W. E. B. Du Bois, 10 June 1904, and 20 May 1906, in *The Correspondence of W. E. B. Du Bois*, 3 vols., ed. Herbert Aptheker (Amherst: University of Massachusetts Press, 1973), 1:76–77, 118–21; Ovington, "The Color Line in Social Work," *Charities* 14 (8 April 1905): 645; Ovington, "The Negro and the New York Tenement," *Voice of the Negro* 2 (February 1906): 101–7; "A 'Square Deal' for New York Negroes," *Outlook* 83 (23 June 1906): 398–99; "For the Negroes in New York," *Charities and the Commons* 17 (October 1906): 109; "First Meeting of Persons Interested in the Welfare of the Negroes of New York City," in *Against Racism: Unpublished Essays, Papers, Addresses, 1887–1961*, by W. E. B. Du Bois, ed. Herbert Aptheker (Amherst: University of Massachusetts Press, 1985), pp. 72–74; Ovington, *Half a Man*, p. ix; Ovington, "Reminiscences," *Baltimore Afro-American*, 17 September 1932; Ovington, *Walls Came Tumbling Down*, pp. 11–52; Osofsky, *Harlem: The Making of a Ghetto*, pp. 62–66; Parris and Brooks, *Blacks in the City*, pp. 10–20; Jesse Thomas Moore, Jr., *A Search for Equality: The National Urban League, 1910–1961* (University Park: Pennsylvania State University Press, 1981), pp. 41–43; and Weiss, *National Urban League*, pp. 20–28.

50. Daniel Perlman, "Stirring the White Conscience: The Life of George Edmund Haynes" (Ph.D. dissertation, New York University, 1972), pp. 1–71; and George Edmund Haynes, *The Negro at Work in New York City: A Study in Economic Progress* (New York:

Columbia University Press, 1912), p. 148. See also Samuel K. Roberts, "George Edmund Haynes: Advocate for Interracial Cooperation," in Burkett and Newman, *Black Apostles*, pp. 97–127; Haynes, "The Movement of Negroes from the Country to the City," *Southern Workman* 42 (April 1913): 236; and Haynes, "Conditions among Negroes in the Cities," *Annals of the American Academy of Political and Social Science* 49 (September 1913): 105–12.

51. "Minutes of the First Meeting of the Committee on Urban Conditions among Negroes Held at the School of Philanthropy, September 29, 1910," Urban League Papers, series 11, no. 1, Library of Congress; *Bulletin of the National League on Urban Conditions among Negroes* 1 (October 1911); "Consolidation of Negro Agencies," *Survey* 27 (28 October 1911): 1080–81; and "Minutes of [the First] Annual Meeting of the National League on Urban Conditions among Negroes," Urban League Papers, series 11, no. 1. See also Moore, *Search for Equality*, pp. 42–47; Parris and Brooks, *Blacks in the City*, pp. 26–40; Perlman, "Stirring the White Conscience," pp. 50–82; and Weiss, *National Urban League*, pp. 40–46.

52. Haynes, "Co-operation with Colleges in Securing and Training Negro Social Workers for Urban Centers," *Proceedings of the National Conference of Charities and Correction at the Thirty-Eighth Annual Session, Held in Boston, Mass., June 7–14, 1911* (Fort Wayne, Ind.: Fort Wayne Printing Co., 1911), pp. 384–87; "Interchurch College for Social Service," *Survey* 26 (26 August 1911): 749; "American Interchurch College," *American Missionary* 66 (January 1912): 588; Haynes, "Department of Social Service," *AME Church Review* 29 (July 1912): 70–74; James E. McCulloch to Henry Churchill King, 17 August 1911, and McCulloch to King, 17 December 1912, King Papers; Perlman, "Stirring the White Conscience," pp. 83–108; "President George A. Gates, LL.D.," *American Missionary* 67 (January 1913): 592–96; Isabel Smith Gates, *The Life of George Augustus Gates* (New York: Pilgrim Press, 1915), pp. 46–64; Joe M. Richardson, *A History of Fisk University: 1865–1946* (University: University of Alabama Press, 1980), p. 64; Noreen Dunn Tatum, *A Crown of Service: A Story of Woman's Work in the Methodist Episcopal Church, South, from 1878–1940* (Nashville: Parthenon Press, 1960), pp. 32–33, 245–77, 355–62; and John Patrick McDowell, *The Social Gospel in the South: The Woman's Home Mission Movement in the Methodist Episcopal Church, South, 1886–1939* (Baton Rouge: Louisiana State University Press, 1982), pp. 84–87.

53. Edwin A. Alderman, "Northern Aid to Southern Education," *Independent* 53 (10 October 1901): 2412; Abell, *Urban Impact on American Protestantism*, pp. 240–42; John Lee Eighmy, *Churches in Cultural Captivity: A History of the Social Attitudes of Southern Baptists* (Knoxville: University of Tennessee Press, 1972), pp. 298–99; and W. E. B. Du Bois, "The Atlanta University Conferences," *Charities* 10 (2 May 1903): 435. See also Jerome R. Dowd, "Deficient Charity Work in the South," *Outlook* 54 (26 December 1898): 1185; Dowd, "Paths of Hope for the Negro: Practical Suggestions of a Southerner," *Century* 61 (December 1900): 278–81; Dowd, *Negro Races: A Sociological Study* (New York: Macmillan, 1907); and Dowd, *The Negro in American Life* (New York: Century Co., 1926).

54. Broderick, *W. E. B. Du Bois*, pp. 41–43, 56–58; Rudwick, *W. E. B. Du Bois*, pp. 39–53; and Clarence A. Bacote, *The Story of Atlanta University: A Century of Service, 1865–1965* (Atlanta: Atlanta University Press, 1969), pp. 132–39.

55. Proctor, *Between Black and White: Autobiographical Sketches* (Boston: Pilgrim Press,

1925), pp. 3–46, 91–95; Washington Gladden, "Some Impressions Gained during a Visit to the Southern United States," 31 May 1903, Sermon 969, box 65, Washington Gladden Papers, Ohio Historical Society; Lura Beam, *He Called Them by the Lightening: A Teacher's Odyssey in the South, 1908–1919* (Indianapolis: Bobbs-Merrill, 1967), p. 87; Henry Hugh Proctor, "Self-Supporting Church," *American Missionary* 52 (March 1898): 33–35; and Ernest Hamlin Abbott, *Religious Life in America: A Record of Personal Observation* (New York: Outlook Co., 1902), pp. 102–4. See also David A. Russell, Jr., "The Institutional Church in Transition: A Study of the First Congregational Church of Atlanta" (M.A. thesis, Atlanta University, 1971); and Homer C. McEwen, Sr., "First Congregational Church, Atlanta," *Atlanta Historical Society Bulletin* 21 (Spring 1977): 129–42.

56. Proctor, "From Cabin to Pulpit—Life Sketch," *American Missionary* 56 (June 1902): 291–95; Proctor, "An Example of Congregationalism Southward," *American Missionary* 59 (May 1905): 151–53; Gladden, "Some Impressions Gained during a Visit"; and Proctor, *Between Black and White*, p. 97.

57. Baker, *Following the Color Line*, p. 10; Charles Crowe, "Racial Violence and Social Reform—Origins of the Atlanta Riot of 1906," *Journal of Negro History* 53 (July 1968): 234–56; Crowe, "Racial Massacre in Atlanta, September 22, 1906," *Journal of Negro History* 54 (April 1969): 150–68; and John Dittmer, *Black Georgia in the Progressive Era, 1900–1920* (Urbana: University of Illinois Press, 1977), pp. 123–26.

58. Walter White, *A Man Called White* (New York: Viking Press, 1948), p. 10; Crowe, "Racial Massacre," pp. 166–69; Dittmer, *Black Georgia*, pp. 126–31; and Baker, *Following the Color Line*, pp. 11–14.

59. "An American Kishinev," *Outlook* 74 (29 September 1906): 241–42; and "The Wind and the Whirlwind," *Independent* 61 (27 September 1906): 760. See also "The Butchery in Atlanta," *Western Christian Advocate* 72 (26 September 1906): 6–7; and Reverdy Cassius Ransom, "The Atlanta Riot," in *The Spirit of Freedom and Justice: Orations and Speeches* (Nashville: AME Sunday School Union, 1926), pp. 117–21.

60. Alexander J. McKelway, "The Atlanta Riots: A Southern White Point of View," *Outlook* 84 (3 November 1906): 557–62. See also Alexander Harvey Shannon, *Racial Integrity and Other Features of the Negro Problem* (Nashville: Press of the ME Church, South, 1907), pp. 126–33; and a feminist's rejoinder to McKelway: Mary White Ovington, "The Atlanta Riots," *Outlook* 84 (17 November 1906): 684–85.

61. H. D. Hamill, "The Southern Labor Problem," *Methodist Quarterly Review* 56 (April 1906): 309. See also "Atlanta," *Charities and the Commons* 18 (October 1906): 4; "The Atlanta Massacre," *Independent* 61 (4 October 1906): 799–800; "Law Re-established," *Outlook* 84 (6 October 1906): 296–97; "Racial Self-Restraint," *Outlook* 84 (6 October 1906): 308–10; W. E. B. Du Bois, "A Litany of Atlanta," *Independent* 61 (11 October 1906): 856–58; "Closing Atlanta Saloons," *Independent* 61 (18 October 1906): 893; "Racial Self-Restraint," *Outlook* 84 (3 November 1906): 551–53; and Edward T. Ware, "The Atlanta Riots: From the Point of View of a Missionary College," *Outlook* 84 (3 November 1906): 564–66.

62. Baker, *Following the Color Line*, pp. 18–20; and Proctor, *Between Black and White*, pp. 96–97.

63. Du Bois, quoted in Dittmer, *Black Georgia*, p. 172; Robert E. Park to Emmett J. Scott,

n.d. [1906]; Booker T. Washington to Edgar Gardner Murphy, 2 December 1906; and Park to Washington, 7 December 1906, Booker T. Washington Papers, Library of Congress. See also Dittmer, *Black Georgia*, p. 208; and William Toll, *The Resurgence of Race: Black Social Theory from Reconstruction to the Pan-African Conferences* (Philadelphia: Temple University Press, 1979), pp. 129–30.

64. Annie S. Beard, "Solving the Race Problem in Atlanta," *World To-Day* 12 (February 1907): 215. See also Booker T. Washington, "The Golden Rule in Atlanta," *Outlook* 84 (15 December 1906): 913–16; "Results in Atlanta," *Independent* 62 (3 January 1907): 51–52; "For Law and Order," *Independent* 63 (11 July 1907): 106–7; and Baker, *Following the Color Line*, pp. 20–22.

65. Washington, "Golden Rule in Atlanta," pp. 913–16; Beard, "Solving the Race Problem," pp. 214–15; Hamill, "Southern Labor Problem," pp. 307–8; John E. White, "The True and the False in Southern Life," *South Atlantic Quarterly* 5 (April 1906): 97–113; "'Soldiers of the Common Good,'" *Outlook* 84 (29 December 1906): 1039–40; "The Black and White Problem," *American Missionary* 61 (March 1907): 77–80; White, "The Need of a Southern Program on the Negro Problem," *South Atlantic Quarterly* 6 (April 1907): 177–88; "Ex-Governor Northen's Work in Georgia," *Independent* 72 (13 June 1907): 1423–25; William J. Northen, "The Negro Situation—One Way Out," *World To-Day* 12 (September 1907): 893–96; "To Solve the Race Problem," *Independent* 63 (26 December 1907): 1582–83; Baker, *Following the Color Line*, pp. 24–25; "Broader Sentiment in the South," *Independent* 69 (10 November 1910): 1054; Northen, "Saving the Negro," *American Missionary* 65 (April 1911): 856–58; and Henry Hugh Proctor, "A Southerner of the New School: William J. Northen," *Southern Workman* 42 (July 1913): 403–6.

66. Willis Duke Weatherford, *Fundamental Religious Principles in Browning's Poetry* (Nashville: Publishing House of the ME Church, South, 1907); Wilma Dykeman, *Prophet of Plenty: The First Ninety Years of W. D. Weatherford* (Knoxville: University of Tennessee Press, 1966), pp. 1–41, 63–71; George Peter Antone, Jr., "Willis Duke Weatherford: An Interpretation of His Work in Race Relations" (Ph.D. dissertation, Vanderbilt University, 1969), pp. 15–19, 25–53; and Weatherford, *Negro Life in the South*, pp. v–vi, 176. For the impact of Weatherford's work, see Katharine Dupre Lumpkin, *The Making of a Southerner* (New York: Alfred A. Knopf, 1946), pp. 178–80, 189–93, 197–239; and Francis Pickens Miller, *Man from the Valley: Memoirs of a 20th Century Virginian* (Chapel Hill: University of North Carolina Press, 1971), pp. 18–27.

67. W. T. B. Williams, "Community Work of the Negro School," *Southern Workman* 38 (November 1909): 613; Louie Davis Shivery, "The Neighborhood Union: A Survey of the Beginnings of Social Welfare Movements among Negroes in Atlanta," *Phylon* 3 (Second Quarter 1942): 149–62; Gerda Lerner, "Early Community Work of Black Club Women," pp. 162–65; Ridgely Torrence, *The Story of John Hope* (New York: Macmillan, 1948), pp. 138–40; Dittmer, *Black Georgia*, pp. 64–65, 84–87; and Jacqueline Anne Rouse, *Lugenia Burns Hope: A Black Southern Reformer* (Athens: University of Georgia Press, 1988).

68. Proctor, *Between Black and White*, pp. 99–101, 105–14, 117–29; H. H. Proctor to Washington Gladden, 28 June, 15 August, 29 August 1907, box 10, nos. 189, 212, 217, and 1 January 1909, box 1, no. 1, Gladden Papers; and "The First Congregational Church at Atlanta, Ga.," *American Missionary* 62 (March 1908): 69–71.

Chapter 8

1. Radical and conservative factions struggled to control the Afro-American Council after 1898, but it took a moderate public course. Washington's conservatives held the upper hand from 1902 to 1907, when a radical victory killed the council's effort to present a united racial front. Alexander Walters, *My Life and Work* (New York: Fleming H. Revell Co., 1917), pp. 98–107; Alfreda M. Duster, ed., *Crusade for Justice: The Autobiography of Ida B. Wells* (Chicago: University of Chicago Press, 1970), pp. 254–58; Emma Lou Thornbrough, "The National Afro-American League, 1887–1898," *Journal of Southern History* 27 (November 1961): 494–512; August Meier, *Negro Thought in America, 1880–1915: Racial Ideologies in the Age of Booker T. Washington* (Ann Arbor: University of Michigan Press, 1963), pp. 172–81; and Robert L. Factor, *The Black Response to America: Men, Ideals, and Organization from Frederick Douglass to the NAACP* (Reading, Mass.: Addison-Wesley, 1970), pp. 128–30, 315–21.

2. William T. Stead, *The Americanization of the World; or, The Trend of the Twentieth Century* (New York: Horace Markey, 1901), p. 156; "The Epidemic of Lynching," *Homiletic Review* 37 (June 1899): 569–70; "Editorial," *Independent* 51 (14 December 1899): 3380; "Fanatics and Fools," *Independent* 51 (3 August 1898): 2103–4; Lyman E. Davies, "The Color-Line at Alexandria," *Independent* 51 (31 August 1899): 2355–57; and Edward Leigh Pell, "The Prevention of Lynch Law Epidemics," *Review of Reviews* 17 (March 1898): 321–25. See also Minot Judson Savage, *Our Unitarian Gospel* (Boston: George H. Ellis, 1898), p. 186; "The Lynching of a Postmaster," *Independent* 50 (3 March 1898): 282–83; John Henry Barrows, "The Greatness of a Nation," *Homiletic Review* 35 (May 1898): 432; "Lynching in the United States," *Homiletic Review* 35 (June 1898): 554; "This Week," *Outlook* 61 (29 April 1899): 946; "Worse Than Lynching," *Outlook* 62 (6 May 1899): 8; "Barbarianism in the South," *Missionary Review of the World* 22 (June 1899): 460–61; "Governor Candler Once More," *Independent* 51 (10 August 1899): 2171–72; "Editorial," *Independent* 51 (2 November 1899): 2976; "The Mob Epidemic," *Bibliotheca Sacra* 57 (October 1900): 769–70; "Reign of Lynch Law," *Homiletic Review* 41 (February, 1901): 188–89; "The Lynching Habit," *Independent* 53 (7 March 1901): 575; and "Lynch Law a National Evil," *Chautauquan* 34 (October 1901): 4–5.

3. Ida B. Wells-Barnett, "Lynch Law in America," *Arena* 22 (January 1900): 15–24; "A Double Lynching in Virginia," *Independent* 52 (27 March 1900): 783–84; Wells-Barnett, "The Negro's Case in Equity," *Independent* 52 (26 April 1900): 1010–11; and Duster, *Crusade for Justice*, pp. 262–63.

4. Jane Addams, "Respect for Law," *Independent* 53 (3 January 1901): 18–20; and Wells-Barnett, "Lynching and the Excuse for It," *Independent* 53 (16 May 1901): 1133–36.

5. Quincey Ewing, "The Beginning of the End," *Colored American Magazine* 3 (October 1901): 471–77; New York Sun, 25 August 1901; "The Rev. Quincey Ewing on Lynching," *Independent* 53 (29 August 1901): 2059–61; "The Epidemic of Savagery," *Outlook* 69 (7 September 1901): 9–11; Ewing, "How Can Lynching Be Checked in the South?," *Outlook* 69 (12 October 1901): 359–61; "Sketch of Quincey Ewing," attached to Ewing to Moorfield Storey, 6 April 1919, series C, no. 333, National Association for the Advancement of Colored People Papers, Library of Congress; Ewing to W. E. B. Du Bois, 6

March 1929, in *The Correspondence of W. E. B. Du Bois,* 3 vols., ed. Herbert Aptheker (Amherst: University of Massachusetts Press, 1973), 1:400; and Charles E. Wynes, "The Reverend Quincey Ewing: Southern Racial Heretic in the 'Cajun' Country," *Louisiana History* 7 (Summer 1966): 221–27. For antilynching protests of other Southern white clergymen, see J. B. Cranfill, "The Story of a Mob," *Independent* 53 (24 January 1901): 213–14; William Hayne Levell, "On Lynching in the South," *Outlook* 69 (16 November 1901): 731–33; and John Carlisle Kilgo, "An Inquiry concerning Lynchings," *South Atlantic Quarterly* 1 (January 1902): 4–13.

6. Benjamin Orange Flower, "The Race Problem: A Symposium," *Arena* 21 (April 1899): 421; Thomas J. Morgan, *The Negro in America and the Ideal American Republic* (Philadelphia: American Baptist Publication Society, 1898), p. 155; "An Appeal to the Louisiana Convention," *Independent* 50 (17 February 1898): 217–18; "This Week," *Outlook* 58 (26 February 1898): 509–10; "The Louisiana Convention," *Independent* 50 (31 March 1898): 412–13; and "This Week," *Outlook* 60 (17 December 1898): 992–93. See also Charles Fletcher Dole, *The Coming People* (New York: Thomas Y. Crowell and Co., 1897), pp. 130–31; and Augustus Field Beard, "Concerning Human Rights," *American Missionary* 52 (December 1898): 202–3.

7. "This Week," *Outlook* 64 (10 February 1899): 330–31; "Shame on Shame," *Independent* 51 (23 February 1899): 567–68; Helen G. Edmonds, *The Negro and Fusion Politics in North Carolina, 1894–1901* (Chapel Hill: University of North Carolina Press, 1951), pp. 158–97; Frederick A. Bode, *Protestantism and the New South: North Carolina Baptists and Methodists in Political Crisis, 1894–1903* (Charlottesville: University Press of Virginia, 1975), pp. 129–31; Joel Williamson, *The Crucible of Race: Black-White Relations in the American South since Emancipation* (New York: Oxford University Press, 1984), pp. 195–201; and H. Leon Prather, *We Have Taken a City: Wilmington Racial Massacre and Coup of 1898* (Cranbury, N.J.: Associated University Presses, 1984).

8. Edmonds, *Negro and Fusion Politics,* p. 172; "Race War in North Carolina," *Independent* 50 (17 November 1898): 1372; "A Crime against the Ballot," *Independent* 50 (17 November 1898): 1433–34; "The Race Riots," *Independent* 50 (24 November 1898): 1458–59; "Editorial," *Independent* 50 (24 November 1898): 1519–20; "Negroes Cry Out against Riots," *Georgia Baptist* 18 (1 December 1898): 2; and "The North Carolina Race Conflict," *Outlook* 60 (19 November 1898): 707–9. See also "The North Carolina Race Conflict," *Outlook* 60 (12 November 1898): 646; "The President's Duty," *Outlook* 60 (19 November 1898): 698–99; Augustus Field Beard, "Concerning Human Rights," *American Missionary* 52 (December 1898): 202–3; and Tilden G. Edelstein, *Strange Enthusiasm: A Life of Thomas Wentworth Higginson* (New Haven: Yale University Press, 1968), pp. 388–89.

9. Elijah Embree Hoss, "Why the Difference?," *Nashville Christian Advocate* 59 (1 December 1898): 2; Alexander J. McKelway, "The Cause of Race Troubles in North Carolina," *Independent* 50 (24 November 1898): 1488–92; and McKelway, "The Race Problem in the South: The North Carolina Revolution Justified," *Outlook* 60 (31 December 1898): 1057–59. See also "Is It Negro Rule?," *Independent* 50 (24 November 1898): 1514–17; "The North Carolina Troubles," *Independent* 50 (15 December 1898): 1794–97; Thomas Dixon, Jr., *Dixon's Sermons* (New York: F. L. Bussey and Co., 1899), pp. 112–18; Bode, *Protestantism and the New South,* pp. 122–26; Ralph E. Luker, "In Slavery's Shadow:

North Carolina Methodism and Race Relations, 1885–1920," in *Methodism Alive in North Carolina*, ed. O. Kelly Ingram (Durham, N.C.: Duke University, 1976), pp. 79–80; Herbert J. Doherty, Jr., "Alexander J. McKelway: Preacher to Progressive," *Journal of Southern History* 24 (May 1958): 177–90; and Betty Jane Brandon, "Alexander Jeffrey McKelway: Statesman of the New Order" (Ph.D. dissertation, University of North Carolina, Chapel Hill, 1969).

10. John Bakeless, "Charles Barzillai Spahr," in *Dictionary of American Biography*, ed. Allen Johnson et al. (New York: Charles Scribner's Sons, 1928–88), 9:418–19; Spahr, "The Negro as a Citizen," *Outlook* 62 (1 July 1899): 490–99; and Spahr, *America's Working People* (New York: Longmans, Green, and Co., 1900).

11. McKelway, "The North Carolina Suffrage Amendment," *Independent* 52 (16 August 1900): 1955–57; "Government by Terrorism," *Independent* 52 (16 August 1900): 1997–98; and "Reaping the Whirlwind," *Independent* 52 (11 October 1900): 2469–70.

12. W. E. B. Du Bois, "The Suffrage Fight in Georgia," *Independent* 51 (30 November 1899): 3226–28; "Disfranchisement in Georgia," *Independent* 51 (7 December 1899): 3306–7; "Editorial," *Independent* 51 (14 December 1899): 3382; John Dittmer, *Black Georgia in the Progressive Era, 1900–1920* (Urbana: University of Illinois Press, 1977), pp. 96–97; "North Carolina's Red Shirt Campaign," *Independent* 52 (2 August 1900): 1875–76; "The Election in North Carolina," *Independent* 52 (9 August 1900): 1885; "North Carolina Politics," *Outlook* 65 (11 August 1900): 843; "This Week," *Outlook* 65 (18 August 1900): 896–97; Edmonds, *Negro and Fusion Politics*, pp. 198–217; Bode, *Protestantism and the New South*, pp. 136–40; Joseph Cook, "Educate, Evangelize, Enfranchise," 25 October 1900, Flavius Josephus Cook Papers, Manuscript Division, Duke University Library; and "Fifty-fourth Annual Meeting," *American Missionary* 55 (January 1901): 18.

13. "The Southern Negro," *Homiletic Review* 40 (October 1900): 371; John Bascom, "The Alleged Failure of Democracy," *Yale Review* 9 (November 1900): 258; "The Citizen," *Social Gospel* 38 (April 1901): 24; "Disfranchisement in Several States," *Review of Reviews* 22 (June 1901): 643–44; "The Alabama and Virginia Conventions," *Outlook* 68 (22 June 1901): 420–21; John Smith, "Is the South Dealing Wisely with the Negro Question?," *Homiletic Review* 42 (September 1901): 268; "Negro Disfranchisement," *Chautauquan* 34 (November 1901): 126–27; "Alabama's New Constitution," *Chautauquan* 34 (January 1902): 361–62; "The Virginia Constitution versus Democracy," *Chautauquan* 35 (August 1902): 434–35; and "Democracy in America," *Independent* 54 (18 September 1902): 2260–62. See also J. Morgan Kousser, *The Shaping of Southern Politics: Suffrage Restriction and the Establishment of a One-Party South, 1888–1910* (New Haven: Yale University Press, 1974).

14. Meier, *Negro Thought in America*, pp. 46–47; August Meier and Elliott Rudwick, "Attitudes of Negro Leaders toward the American Labor Movement from the Civil War to World War I," in *The Negro and the American Labor Movement*, ed. Julius Jacobson (Garden City, N.Y.: Anchor Books, 1968), pp. 34–37; Henry George, *Social Problems* (Chicago: Belford, 1882), pp. 157–58; George, *Progress and Poverty: An Inquiry into the Cause of Industrial Depressions and of Increase of Want with Increase of Wealth. The Remedy*, 4th ed. (New York: Doubleday and McClure Co., 1898), pp. 488–90; Rayford W. Logan, *The Betrayal of the Negro: From Rutherford B. Hayes to Woodrow Wilson* (New York: Collier Books, 1965), pp. 150–51; and Vida Dutton Scudder, *Father Huntington: Founder of the Order of the Holy Cross* (New

York: E. P. Dutton and Co., 1940), p. 149. The portrait of a racist Henry George in John L. Thomas, *Alternative America: Henry George, Edward Bellamy, Henry Demarest Lloyd and the Adversary Tradition* (Cambridge: Harvard University Press, 1983), pp. 61–63, 372n, ignores an important distinction between racial and cultural categories.

15. Richard T. Ely, *Recent American Socialism* (Baltimore: Johns Hopkins University Press, 1885), p. 58; Alexander Clark, "Socialism," *AME Church Review* 3 (July 1886): 49–54; Philip S. Foner, *American Socialism and Black Americans: From the Age of Jackson to World War II* (Westport, Conn.: Greenwood Press, 1977), pp. 45–56; Herbert G. Gutman, "Peter H. Clark: Pioneer Negro Socialist, 1877," *Journal of Negro History* 39 (Fall 1965): 413–18; Reverdy Ransom, "The Negro and Socialism," *AME Church Review* 13 (October 1896): 192–200; J. T. Jennifer, "The Labor Question: North and South," *AME Church Review* 13 (April 1897): 371–82; and "Two Valuable Articles," *AME Church Review* 13 (April 1897): 442–43. See also Charles Alexander, "The Socialism of the Negro," *Social Gospel* 32 (October 1900): 33–35; Philip S. Foner, "Reverend George Washington Woodbey: Early Twentieth Century California Black Socialist," in *Black Apostles: Afro-American Clergy Confront the Twentieth Century*, ed. Randall K. Burkett and Richard Newman (Boston: G. K. Hall and Co., 1978), pp. 253–76; and Philip S. Foner, ed., *Black Socialist Preacher: The Teachings of Reverend George Washington Woodbey and His Disciple Reverend George W. Slater, Jr.* (San Francisco: Synthesis Publications, 1983).

16. Herbert N. Casson, "Slavery" and "The Negro and Present Social Reform in America," in *The Encyclopedia of Social Reform*, ed. William Dwight Porter Bliss (New York: Funk and Wagnalls, 1897), pp. 1255–59, 927–29. In 1908, Bliss replaced Casson's articles with Booker T. Washington, "The Negro," in *The New Encyclopedia of Social Reform*, 2d ed., ed. William Dwight Porter Bliss (New York: Funk and Wagnalls, 1908), pp. 818–20, and 3d ed. (New York: Funk and Wagnalls, 1910), pp. 818–20. See also W. D. P. Bliss, "The Negro Question," *Homiletic Review* 53 (February 1907): 112. On Bliss and Casson, see Arthur Mann, *Yankee Reformers in the Urban Age: Social Reform in Boston, 1880–1900* (Cambridge: Harvard University Press, 1954), pp. 86–87, 90–99, 180–83, 231–33.

17. "The Case of Professor Herron," *AME Church Review* 16 (January 1900): 389–90. On Herron, see Robert T. Handy, "George D. Herron and the Social Gospel in American Protestantism, 1890–1901" (Ph.D. dissertation, University of Chicago, 1949); and Phyllis Ann Nelson, "George D. Herron and the Socialist Clergy, 1890–1914" (Ph.D. dissertation, State University of Iowa, 1953).

18. Sterling D. Spero and Abram L. Harris, *The Negro and the Labor Movement* (New York: Columbia University Press, 1931), p. 403; Foner, *American Socialism and Black Americans*, pp. 94–98; Howard H. Quint, *The Forging of American Socialism: Origins of the Modern Movement* (Indianapolis: Bobbs-Merrill, 1953), p. 378; R. Laurence Moore, "Flawed Fraternity—American Socialist Response to the Negro, 1901–1912," *Historian* 32 (November 1969): 2–4; and Ray Ginger, *The Bending Cross: A Biography of Eugene V. Debs* (New Brunswick, N.J.: Rutgers University Press, 1948), pp. 260–61. See also Ira Kipnis, *The American Socialist Movement: 1897–1912* (New York: Columbia University Press, 1952), pp. 130–34; David Shannon, *The Socialist Party of America: A History* (New York: Macmillan, 1955), pp. 50–53; and James Weinstein, *The Decline of American Socialism in America, 1912–1915* (New York: Monthly Review Press, 1967), pp. 63–74.

19. Andrew Sledd, "The Negro: Another View," *Atlantic Monthly* 90 (July 1902): 65–73; "Professor Sledd's Error," *Independent* 54 (14 August 1902): 1977–78; Henry Y. Warnock, "Andrew Sledd, Southern Methodists, and the Negro: A Case Study," *Journal of Southern History* 31 (August 1965): 251–71; Williamson, *Crucible of Race*, pp. 259–61; and Ralph E. Reed, "Emory College and the Sledd Affair of 1902: A Case Study in Southern Honor and Racial Attitudes," *Georgia Historical Quarterly* 72 (Fall 1988): 463–92.

20. Jacob Henry Dorn, *Washington Gladden: Prophet of the Social Gospel* (Columbus: Ohio State University Press, 1966), pp. 294–96; Gladden, "The Missionary Motive," 23 October 1902, Sermon 942, box 63, Washington Gladden Papers, Ohio Historical Society. See also Henry Hugh Proctor to Gladden, 3 November 1902, no. 206, box 4, Gladden Papers.

21. James M. McPherson, *The Abolitionist Legacy: From Reconstruction to the NAACP* (Princeton: Princeton University Press, 1975), pp. 368–69. For the growing sense of crisis, see "Political Rights of Southern Negroes," *Independent* 55 (8 January 1903): 60–61; "The Mississippi Troubles," *Independent* 55 (8 January 1903): 109–10; "Free Speech in the South," *Independent* 55 (15 January 1903): 137–39; "Primitive Savagery," *Independent* 55 (15 January 1903): 166; "The Race Question," *Outlook* 73 (17 January 1903): 139; "Negro Office-Holders," *Outlook* 55 (29 January 1903): 277–78; "Reviving the Race Issue," *Independent* 55 (5 February 1903): 337–38; "The President and the South," *Outlook* 73 (7 February 1903): 272–74; and "Feudalism or Slavery," *Independent* 55 (12 April 1903): 805–6.

22. *New York Times*, 2 February 1903, p. 9; Robert C. Ogden to Wallace Buttrick, 2 February 1903, Letterbook, box no. 13, Robert C. Ogden Papers, Library of Congress; *New York Times*, 16 February 1903, p. 9; "Editorial," *American Missionary* 53 (April 1903): 98; and "The Race or Color Question Revived," *Chautauquan* 37 (April 1903): 9–10. See also Ogden to E. C. Branson, 2 February 1903, and Ogden to Edgar Gardner Murphy, 6 June 1903, Letterbook, box no. 13, Ogden Papers; Newell Dwight Hillis, *A Man's Value to Society* (Chicago: Fleming H. Revell Co., 1896), pp. 15–16, 170, 217–27; Hillis, *The Investment of Influence* (Chicago: Fleming H. Revell Co., 1897), pp. 39–40, 56, 81, 167–68, 211–12; and Hillis, *The Influence of Christ in Modern Life* (New York: Macmillan, 1901), pp. 183, 222–23, 230.

23. Henry Demarest Lloyd, *Man: The Social Creator* (New York: Doubleday, Page and Co., 1906), pp. 18, 73, 79, 106–7; Caro Lloyd, *Henry Demarest Lloyd, 1847–1903: A Biography*, 2 vols. (New York: G. P. Putnam's Sons, 1912), 2:268–77; Chester McArthur Destler, *Henry Demarest Lloyd and the Empire of Reform* (Philadelphia: University of Pennsylvania Press, 1963), pp. 513–14, 521; and James D. Corrothers, *In Spite of the Handicap* (New York: George H. Doran Co., 1916), pp. 72–76.

24. William Mackintire Salter, *Ethical Religion* (Boston: Roberts Brothers, 1889); Philip D. Jordan, "William Mackintire Salter," in *Dictionary of American Biography*, 16:315–16; Howard B. Radest, *Toward Common Ground: The Story of the Ethical Culture Societies in the United States* (New York: Frederick Ungar Publishing Co., 1969), pp. 63–66; Salter, *The Negro Problem: Is the Nation Going Backward?* (Philadelphia: S. Burns Weston, 1903), pp. 163–80; and "Professor Wm. M. Salter on the Negro," *Chicago Broad-Ax*, 4 April 1903.

25. Belle Kearney, "The South and Woman Suffrage," in *Up from the Pedestal: Selected*

*Writings in the History of American Feminism*, ed. Aileen Kraditor (Chicago: Quadrangle Books, 1970), pp. 262–65; Anna Howard Shaw, *The Story of a Pioneer* (New York: Harper and Brothers Publishers, 1915), pp. 307–14; and Andrew Sinclair, *The Emancipation of American Women* (New York: Harper and Row, 1966), pp. 296–300.

26. "The Race or Color Question Revived," *Chautauquan* 37 (April 1903): 9–10; "Restricted Suffrage on Trial," *Outlook* 73 (11 April 1903): 847; "The Union League Club," *Independent* 55 (16 April 1903): 932–33; "The Negro Problem," *Independent* 55 (23 April 1903): 937–38; "The Race Question: Points of Agreement," *Outlook* 73 (25 April 1903): 939; Lyman Abbott, "Impressions of the Conference," in *Proceedings of the Conference for Education in the South: The Sixth Session. Richmond, Va., April 22d to 24th, and at the University of Virginia, April 25th* (Richmond: n.p., 1903), pp. 224–27; and Algernon Sydney Crapsey, "The Duty of the White Man of the North to the Black Man of the South," in *How to Solve the Race Problem: The Proceedings of the Washington Conference on the Race Problem in the United States under the Auspices of the National Sociological Society Held at the Lincoln Temple Congregational Church; at the Nineteenth Street Baptist Church and at the Metropolitan A.M.E. Church, Washington, D.C., November 9, 10, 11, and 12, 1903* (Washington, D.C.: R. Beresford, 1904), pp. 238–39. See also Ellen Collins to Booker T. Washington, 15 April 1903, and Washington to Robert C. Ogden, 15 May 1903, in *The Booker T. Washington Papers*, 14 vols., ed. Louis R. Harlan et al. (Urbana: University of Illinois Press, 1972–89), 7:119n, 147n; Matthew Anderson to Francis J. Grimké, 21 June 1903, in *The Works of Francis J. Grimké*, 4 vols., ed. Carter G. Woodson (Washington, D.C.: Associated Publishers, 1942), 4:78–79; Louis R. Harlan, *Separate and Unequal: Public School Campaigns and Racism in the Southern Seaboard States* (Chapel Hill: University of North Carolina Press, 1958), p. 96; Logan, *Betrayal of the Negro*, pp. 102–4; and John Edward Bruce, "The Madison Square Garden Meeting," in *The Selected Writings of John Edward Bruce: Militant Black Journalist*, ed. Peter Gilbert (New York: Arno Press, 1971), p. 91.

27. *Boston Guardian*, 2 May 1903, p. 4; Katharine Coman to Lyman Abbott, 29 April 1903; Charles Barzillai Spahr to Booker T. Washington, 30 April 1903; Lyman Abbott to Katharine Coman, 2 May 1903; Francis Jackson Garrison to Booker T. Washington, 13 July 1903; Charles Waddell Chesnutt to Washington, 2 May 1903; Chesnutt to Washington, 27 June 1903; Chesnutt to Washington, 11 August 1903, Booker T. Washington Papers, Library of Congress; *Rochester Herald*, 29 April 1903; and Mary T. L. Gannett Diary, 28 April 1903, William Channing Gannett Papers, University of Rochester. See also "The Educational Revival," *Outlook* 74 (9 May 1903): 107–8; McPherson, *Abolitionist Legacy*, p. 373; Helen M. Chesnutt, *Charles Waddell Chesnutt: Pioneer of the Color Line* (Chapel Hill: University of North Carolina Press, 1952), pp. 193–96; Elliott M. Rudwick, "Race Leadership Struggle: Background to the Boston Riot of 1903," *Journal of Negro Education* 31 (Winter 1962): 16–24; Factor, *Black Response to America*, pp. 251–85; and Meier, *Negro Thought in America*, pp. 171–76.

28. "The 'Failure' of Negro Suffrage," and "The Fifteenth Amendment and the Negro," *Chautauquan* 37 (June 1903): 230–31; and *Boston Guardian*, 2 May 1903. See also "Negro Suffrage in Alabama," *Independent* 55 (7 May 1903): 1104–5; "The Alabama Case," *Outlook* 74 (9 May 1903): 95–96; "Shall the Fifteenth Amendment Be Repealed?," *Independent* 55 (28 May 1903): 1277–78; "Negro Suffrage in the South," *Outlook* 74 (13 June

1903): 399–403; and "Negro Suffrage Case Dismissed," *Outlook* 76 (12 March 1904): 620–21.

29. "Editorial," *Independent* 55 (9 April 1903): 875–76; "Pro and Con," *AME Church Review* 19 (April 1903): 740–41; "Editorial," *AME Church Review* 19 (April 1903): 755; "Rev. Parkhurst Flayed," Boston *Guardian*, 18 April 1903; "Dr. Parkhurst Explains," Boston *Guardian*, 25 April 1903; Charles H. Parkhurst, "The Betterment of Man," in *Proceedings of the National Conference on Charities and Correction at the Thirteenth Annual Session Held in the City of Atlanta, May 6–12, 1903*, ed. Isabel C. Barrows (n.p.: Fred J. Heer, 1903), pp. 13–24; Parkhurst, quoted in William A. Sinclair, *The Aftermath of Slavery: A Study of the Condition and Environment of the American Negro* (Boston: Small, Maynard and Co., 1905), p. 98; "Parkhurst, Abbott and Hillis," *Independent* 55 (21 May 1903): 1227; and Boston *Guardian*, [ca. 23 May 1903]. Because of Parkhurst's irritating remarks, Robert C. Ogden excluded his pastor from his tours of the South after 1903. A diplomatic note indicated that the train was already too full to include Parkhurst, but Ogden's correspondence in April 1904 shows that the New York merchant knew who he did not want to include on the junket. Ogden to Parkhurst, 14 April 1904, and surrounding correspondence, Letterbook, box no. 14, Ogden Papers.

30. Sinclair, *Aftermath of Slavery*, pp. 98–102; and Hillis, quoted in "Parkhurst, Abbott and Hillis," p. 1227; Chicago *Broad-Ax*, 23 May 1903; Boston *Guardian*, 23 May 1903, p. 1; *New York Times*, 25 May 1903, p. 9; and Sinclair, *Aftermath of Slavery*, p. 121.

31. "A Voice from the Past," *Outlook* 74 (2 May 1903): 13–14; Hillis, quoted in *New York Times*, 25 May 1903, p. 9; Boston *Guardian*, 30 May 1903, p. 1; and Sinclair, *Aftermath of Slavery*, p. 122.

32. "Parkhurst, Abbott and Hillis," p. 1227; Chicago *Broad-Ax*, 23 May 1903; Factor, *Black Response to America*, p. 281; "A Page of History," *Outlook* 74 (30 May 1903): 264–66; and "Mr. Beecher on Reconstruction," *Outlook* 74 (30 May 1903): 280–81. See also Robert C. Ogden to Matthew Anderson, 23 May 1903, Ogden Papers; and Joseph C. Roy, "What Is the Work before Us?," *American Missionary* 58 (January 1904): 11.

33. Washington Gladden, "Some Impressions Gained during a Visit to the Southern United States," 31 May 1903, box 65, Sermon 969, Gladden Papers. See also Horace Bumstead to Washington Gladden, 22 January 1903, box 5, no. 25; W. E. B. Du Bois to Gladden, 24 January 1903, box 5, no. 26; Henry Hugh Proctor to Gladden, 14 April 1903, box 5, no. 50, Gladden Papers; and Dorn, *Washington Gladden*, p. 298.

34. Carey Breckinridge Wilmer and Washington Gladden, in *The Negro Church: Report of a Social Study Made under the Direction of Atlanta University; Together with the Proceedings of the Eighth Conference for the Study of the Negro Problems, Held at Atlanta University, May 26th, 1903*, ed. W. E. B. Du Bois (Atlanta: Atlanta University, 1903), pp. 203–8; and Gladden, "Some Impressions Gained," Gladden Papers. See also *Atlanta Constitution*, 25 May 1903, p. 3.

35. Du Bois, *The Souls of Black Folk* (Chicago: A. C. McClurg and Co., 1903), pp. 3–4, 11–12, 164. See also Williamson, *Crucible of Race*, pp. 399–413, 547–48.

36. Du Bois, *Souls of Black Folk*, pp. 9–10, 43, 53–54.

37. "Two Typical Leaders," *Outlook* 74 (23 May 1903): 214–16.

38. Gladden, "Some Impressions Gained," Gladden Papers.

39. [Jenkin Lloyd Jones], "The Souls of Black Folk," *Unity* 51 (7 May 1903): 148–49; Ida

B. Wells-Barnett to W. E. B. Du Bois, 30 May 1903, in Aptheker, *Correspondence of W. E. B. Du Bois*, 1:55–56; Duster, *Crusade for Justice*, pp. 279–81; "The Souls of Black Folk," *Independent* 55 (28 May 1903): 1273–74; Willis Duke Weatherford, *Negro Life in the South* (New York: Association Press, 1910), p. 178; and "Notes," *American Missionary* 61 (March 1907): 52–53. See also Richard R. Wright, Jr., *87 Years behind the Black Curtain* (Philadelphia: Rare Book Co., 1965), p. 96; and Ray Stannard Baker, *Following the Colour Line: An Account of Negro Citizenship in the American Democracy* (New York: Doubleday, Page and Co., 1908), p. 158.

40. "The Lynching of Negroes," *Independent* 55 (9 July 1903): 1596; "Booker T. Washington Defines His Position," *Outlook* 74 (11 July 1903): 632–33; "Negro Criticism of Booker T. Washington," *Literary Digest* 27 (11 July 1903): 37–38; "The Opposition to Booker T. Washington," *Literary Digest* 27 (10 August 1903): 187–89; Kelly Miller to Washington Gladden, 26 September 1903, box 5, no. 254, Gladden Papers; Factor, *Black Response to America*, pp. 271–89; Stephen R. Fox, *The Guardian of Boston: William Monroe Trotter* (New York: Atheneum, 1970), pp. 17–80; Louis R. Harlan, *Booker T. Washington*, 2 vols. (New York: Oxford University Press, 1983), 2:136–62; and Meier, *Negro Thought in America*, pp. 173–77.

41. "Illegal Forced Labor in Alabama," *Outlook* 74 (18 June 1903): 301; "A Revival of Slavery in America," *Missionary Review of the World* 22 (June 1899): 445–48; John Davis Anderson, "The Southern Prison Lease System," *Independent* 51 (13 July 1899): 1879–81; Pete Daniel, *The Shadow of Slavery: Peonage in the South, 1901–1969* (New York: Oxford University Press, 1973), pp. 24–25; William Cohen, "Negro Involuntary Servitude in the South: A Preliminary Analysis," *Journal of Southern History* 42 (February 1976): 31–60; Lyman Abbott to Booker T. Washington, 28 May 1903, box 248, Washington Papers; "Peonage in the South," *Outlook* 74 (13 June 1903): 391; "Slavery in Alabama," *American Cooperator* 2 (13 June 1903): 17; and "Negro Slavery in Alabama," *Homiletic Review* 46 (September 1903): 232. On peonage among contemporary immigrants, see Gino C. Sperenzo, "Forced Labor in West Virginia," *Outlook* 74 (13 June 1903): 407–10; Mike Trudics, "The Story of a Hungarian Peon," *Independent* 63 (5 September 1907): 557–64; "White Peonage in North Carolina," *Outlook* 87 (19 October 1907): 319–21; and Daniel, *Shadow of Slavery*, pp. 35–41, 82–109.

42. "Servitude for Debt in Georgia," *Outlook* 74 (27 June 1903): 486; "Peonage in Georgia," *Independent* 55 (24 December 1903): 3079–80; [Fred Cubberly], "Peonage in the South," *Independent* 55 (9 July 1903): 1616–18; "Peonage: A Significant Mistrial," *Outlook* 74 (25 July 1903): 732–34; "Negro Slavery in Alabama," p. 232; "Southern Sentiment concerning Peonage" and "The Case of Turner Ended," *Outlook* 74 (1 August 1903): 772–73; A Georgia Negro Peon, "The New Slavery in the South—An Autobiography," *Independent* 56 (25 February 1904): 409–14; and Daniel, *Shadow of Slavery*, pp. 11n, 54–57.

43. "Negroes Lynched and Burned," *Independent* 55 (2 July 1903): 1536–37; New York *American*, in Robert Wilson Shufeldt, *The Negro: A Menace to American Civilization* (Boston: Richard G. Badger, 1907), p. 216; and James H. Lappen, *Presbyterians on Delmarva: The History of the New Castle Presbytery* (n.p.: n.p., 1972), p. 52.

44. New York *American*, in Shufeldt, *The Negro: A Menace*, pp. 210–17; "Anarchy in Delaware," *Outlook* 74 (2 July 1903): 543–45; and Lappen, *Presbyterians on Delmarva*, pp. 52–55.

45. Babbitt, quoted in Boston *Guardian*, 4 July 1903, p. 1; "The Chautauqua Conference on the Mob Spirit," *Outlook* 74 (22 August 1903): 960; "The Mob Spirit," *Chautauquan* 38 (September 1903): 11–13; "The Anti-Lynching Campaign," *Chautauquan* 38 (October 1903): 111–12; Hillis, quoted in Shufeldt, *The Negro: A Menace*, p. 219; "Lynching by Fire in Delaware," *Independent* 55 (2 July 1903): 1506; and "Anarchy in Delaware," p. 545.

46. Herbert Seeley Bigelow, *The Religion of Revolution* (Cincinnati: Daniel Kiefer, 1916), pp. 11, 21, 34–35, 41–56, 69–70; Zane L. Miller, *Boss Cox's Cincinnati: Urban Politics in the Progressive Era* (New York: Oxford University Press, 1959), pp. 143–46; Wendell P. Dabney, *Cincinnati's Colored Citizens: Historical, Sociological and Biographical* (Cincinnati: Dabney Publishing Co., 1926), pp. 98–99; and Bigelow, "Mob Violence," *American Cooperator* 2 (22 August 1903): 16–17.

47. "Nine Rioters Killed at Evansville," *Independent* 55 (16 July 1903): 1649–50; "The Evansville Mob," *Outlook* 74 (18 July 1903): 677; and Darrel E. Bigham, *We Ask Only a Fair Trial: A History of the Black Community of Evansville, Indiana* (Bloomington: Indiana University Press, 1987), pp. 104–7.

48. Charles J. Ryder to "Friend," 3 September 1903, box 5, no. 224; Gladden, "Murder as an Epidemic," 27 September 1903, Sermon 982; Albert J. Lyman to Gladden, 17 November 1903, box 5, no. 297, Gladden Papers; Dorn, *Washington Gladden*, p. 299; Gladden, *The Negro's Southern Neighbors and His Northern Friends* (New York: Congregational Rooms, [1903]); Alfred Lawless, Jr., to James W. Cooper, 30 January 1904, box 5, no. 22; Lawless to Cooper, 1 February 1904, box 5, no. 24; Lawless to Cooper, 3 February 1904, box 5, no. 27; George W. Henderson to Cooper, 4 February 1904, box 5, no. 29; Oscar Atwood to Cooper, 5 February 1904, box 5, no. 30; Cooper to Gladden, 11 February 1904, box 5, no. 40, Gladden Papers; and Frederick L. Brownlee, *Heritage of Freedom: A Centenary Story of Ten Schools Offering Education in Freedom* (Philadelphia: United Church Press, 1963), pp. 76–77.

49. "For Civilization in Evansville," *Independent* 55 (16 July 1903): 1694–95; "Causes and Cure of Mob Law," *Outlook* 74 (18 July 1903): 677; "The Acts of Lynching Mobs," *Independent* 55 (23 July 1903): 1708–9; "Mob Violence, North and South," *Independent* 55 (30 July 1903): 1769–70; "The Prevalence of Lynching," *Review of Reviews* 28 (August 1903): 135–38; "The Lynching of Negroes," *Independent* 55 (6 August 1903): 1834–35; "A Week's Mob Violence," *Outlook* 74 (8 August 1903): 867; "Mr. Roosevelt's Letter on Lynching," *Independent* 55 (13 August 1903): 1892–93; "The Best Defense," *Outlook* 74 (15 August 1903): 927–29; "Comments on the President's Letter," *Outlook* 74 (22 August 1903): 959–60; and "The President on Lynching," *Review of Reviews* 28 (September 1903): 265–66.

50. Benjamin Orange Flower, "The Rise of Anarchy in the United States," *Arena* 30 (September 1903): 305–11; "Punishment for Lynchers," *Homiletic Review* 46 (November 1903): 392–93; and "A Possible Race War," *Homiletic Review* 46 (September 1903): 240. See also D. S. Gregory, "The Present Problem of Lawlessness," *Homiletic Review* 46 (September 1903): 233–37; Robert S. McArthur, "Lynching—How It Is to Be Regarded and Treated," *Homiletic Review* 46 (October 1903): 283–84; and James M. Buckley, "The Present Epidemic of Crime," *Century* 67 (November 1903): 149–54.

51. "Race Problems in America," *Chautauquan* 37 (May 1903): 129; John Rogers Com-

mons, *Myself* (New York: Macmillan, 1934), pp. 7, 33, 74; and Commons, *Social Reform and the Church* (New York: Thomas Y. Crowell and Co., 1894), p. 9.

52. Commons, "Race and Democracy," *Chautauquan* 38 (September 1903): 33–34, 37, 42; and Commons, "The Negro," *Chautauquan* 38 (November 1903): 223–30. See also Commons, *Races and Immigrants in America* (New York: Macmillan, 1907).

53. Lyman Abbott, "The Race Problem in the United States," *Review of Reviews* 28 (September 1903): 321–25; Boston *Guardian*, 27 February 1904, p. 4; "The Way Out," *Outlook* 75 (26 December 1903): 984–86; and Kelly Miller, "Darkest America," *New England Magazine* 30 (March 1904): 15.

54. John Spencer Bassett, quoted in Luker, "In Slavery's Shadow," p. 81; Bassett to Herbert Baxter Adams, 15 November 1898 and 18 February 1899, in William Stull Holt, ed., *Historical Scholarship in the United States, 1876–1901: As Revealed in the Correspondence of Herbert Baxter Adams* (Baltimore: Johns Hopkins University Press, 1938): 257–59, 265; John C. Kilgo, "An Inquiry concerning Lynching," *South Atlantic Quarterly* 1 (January 1902): 4–13; Bassett, "Two Negro Leaders," *South Atlantic Quarterly* 2 (July 1903): 271–72; and Rudwick, *W. E. B. Du Bois*, pp. 70–71.

55. John C. Kilgo, "Our Duty to the Negro," *South Atlantic Quarterly* 2 (October 1903): 369–85; Bassett, "Stirring Up the Fires of Race Hatred," *South Atlantic Quarterly* 2 (October 1903): 271–72; Rudwick, *W. E. B. Du Bois*, pp. 70–71; Bruce L. Clayton, *The Savage Ideal: Intolerance and Intellectual Leadership in the South, 1890–1914* (Baltimore: Johns Hopkins University Press, 1972), pp. 84–101; Bode, *Protestantism and the New South*, pp. 146–56; Williamson, *Crucible of Race*, pp. 261–71; "His Liberty of Dissent," *Independent* 55 (26 November 1903): 2830; "Professor Bassett on the Race Problem," *Outlook* 75 (5 December 1903): 770–72; "A Southern Victory," *Independent* 55 (17 December 1903): 2939–40; [Bassett], "The Negro's Inheritance from Africa," *South Atlantic Quarterly* 3 (April 1904): 99–108; and Kelly Miller, *Race Adjustment: Essays on the Negro in America* (New York: Neale Publishing Co., 1908), pp. 112–13. See also Thomas Dixon's caricature of Bassett ten years later as the flabby, effeminate Professor Alexander Magaw, who wore a lavender cravat and matching silk stockings. Dixon, *The Sins of the Father* (New York: D. Appleton and Co., 1912), pp. 197–210.

56. Lyman Abbott, J. W. E. Bowen, George W. Cable, Bishop Thomas U. Dudley, Washington Gladden, John Mercer Langston, Robert C. Ogden, Francis Greenwood Peabody, Bishop Henry Codman Potter, W. S. Scarborough, Charles F. Thwing, Bishop Henry McNeal Turner, and William Hayes Ward were unable to attend the conference. *How to Solve the Race Problem: The Proceedings of the Washington Conference on the Race Problem under the Auspices of the National Sociological Society Held at the Lincoln Temple Congregational Church; at the Nineteenth Street Baptist Church and at the Metropolitan A. M. E. Church, Washington, D. C., November 9, 10, 11, and 12, 1903* (Washington, D.C.: R. Beresford, 1904), pp. 23, 29, 40–65, 72–97, 100–140, 271–78.

57. *How to Solve the Race Problem*, pp. 154–57, 206–7. On Macy, see Jesse Macy, *Jesse Macy: An Autobiography* (Springfield, Ill.: Charles C. Thomas, 1933).

58. Algernon Sydney Crapsey, *The Last of the Heretics* (New York: Alfred A. Knopf, 1924), pp. 2–4, 43–48, 174–76; and Crapsey, "The Duty of the White Man of the North to the Black Man of the South," in *How to Solve the Race Problem*, pp. 228–30. On Satterlee's racial

attitudes, see "Bishop Satterlee's Remedy," *Independent* 62 (30 May 1907): 1281; "Bishop Satterlee's Convention Address," *Independent* 63 (18 July 1907): 167–68; and Charles H. Brent, *A Master Builder: Being the Life and Letters of Henry Yates Satterlee, First Bishop of Washington* (New York: Longmans, Green, and Co., 1916), pp. 210, 336–41.

59. Crapsey, "Duty of the White Man," pp. 230–43.

60. *How to Solve the Race Problem*, pp. 3–18, 222–26, 252–56; "The Washington Conference on the Race Problem," *Outlook* 85 (21 November 1903): 674; Ernest Hamlin Abbott, "The South and the Negro: The Confusion of Tongues," *Outlook* 77 (28 May 1904): 224; and E. H. Abbott, "The South and the Negro: According to Their Works," *Outlook* 77 (25 June 1904): 457.

## Chapter 9

1. Carl Schurz, "Can the South Solve the Negro Problem?," *McClure's Magazine* 22 (January 1904): 275; and "Editorial Comment," *Homiletic Review* 47 (April 1904): 243.

2. John R. Rogers, *The Importance of Time as a Factor in the Solution of the Negro Problem* (New York: Congregational Rooms, 1904), p. 9; and "Which Is the Correct Theory?," *American Missionary* 58 (March 1904): 69.

3. Kelly Miller, *Race Adjustment: Essays on the Negro in America* (New York: Neale Publishing Co., 1908), pp. 11–12; Du Bois to Miller, 15 February 1903, in *The Correspondence of W. E. B. Du Bois*, 3 vols., ed. Herbert Aptheker (Amherst: University of Massachusetts Press, 1973), 1:53; Du Bois to Francis J. Grimké, 19 November and 28 December 1903, in *The Works of Francis J. Grimké*, 4 vols., ed. Carter G. Woodson (Washington, D.C.: Associated Publishers, 1942), 4:88–90; Herbert Aptheker, "The Washington–Du Bois Conference of 1904," *Science and Society* 13 (Fall 1947): 344–51; Robert L. Factor, *The Black Response to America: Men, Ideals, and Organization from Frederick Douglass to the NAACP* (Reading, Mass.: Addison-Wesley, 1970), pp. 292–300; Stephen R. Fox, *The Guardian of Boston: William Monroe Trotter* (New York: Atheneum, 1970), pp. 82–86; Louis R. Harlan, *Booker T. Washington*, 2 vols. (New York: Oxford University Press, 1972–83), 2:63–72; Elliott M. Rudwick, *W. E. B. Du Bois: Propagandist of the Negro Protest* (New York: Atheneum, 1968), pp. 77–87; and Miller, "Summary of the Proceedings of the Conference at Carnegie Hall," in *The Booker T. Washington Papers*, 14 vols., ed. Louis R. Harlan et al. (Urbana: University of Illinois Press, 1972–89), 7:384–86.

4. Kelly Miller, "Problems of the City Negro," Jesse Lawson, "A Plea for Fair Play," Booker T. Washington, "The Tuskegee Idea," W. E. B. Du Bois, "The Parting of the Ways," and Ida B. Wells-Barnett, "Booker T. Washington and His Critics," *World To-Day* 6 (April 1904): 511–23; Miller to Du Bois, 23 April and 8 July 1904; and Du Bois to Archibald Grimké, 21 March 1905, quoted in Fox, *Guardian of Boston*, pp. 85–86. See also Factor, *Black Response to America*, pp. 305–6; Harlan, *Booker T. Washington*, pp. 72–83; and Rudwick, *W. E. B. Du Bois*, pp. 82–87.

5. George P. Upton, "The Facts about Lynching," *Independent* 57 (29 September 1904): 719–21; "Editorial," *Independent* 58 (19 January 1905): 166; "Homicides and Lynchings," *Independent* 60 (11 January 1906): 122; William H. Glasson, "The Statistics of Lynchings,"

South Atlantic Quarterly 5 (October 1906): 342–48; William Dwight Porter Bliss, "Facts as to Lynchings," Homiletic Review 53 (April 1907): 273–74; Bliss, ed., The New Encyclopedia of Social Reform (New York: Funk and Wagnalls, 1908), p. 334; "Lynchings," Homiletic Review 55 (March 1908): 194; Bliss, ed., The New Encyclopedia of Social Reform, 3d ed. (New York: Funk and Wagnalls, 1910), p. 334; Quincey Ewing, as quoted in "Editorial," Independent 57 (11 August 1904): 348; and Mary Church Terrell, "Lynching from a Negro's Point of View," North American Review 178 (June 1904): 866–67. See also Henry Churchill King to Mary Church Terrell, 27 August 1904, box no. 8, Henry Churchill King Papers, Oberlin College.

6. Charleton Moseley and Frederick Brogdon, "A Lynching at Statesboro: The Story of Paul Reed and Will Cato," Georgia Historical Quarterly 65 (Summer 1981): 108–10; John Dittmer, Black Georgia in the Progressive Era, 1900–1920 (Urbana: University of Illinois Press, 1977), pp. 132–35; "The Prosecution of Lynchers," Independent 57 (29 September 1904): 700; and "In South Georgia," American Missionary 58 (October 1904): 252–54.

7. "Ex-Communication for Christian (?) Murderers and Lynchers," Voice of the Negro 1 (October 1904): 490–91; Ray Stannard Baker, "What Is a Lynching? A Study of Mob Justice, South and North. Lynching in the South," McClure's Magazine 24 (January 1905): 299–309; Dittmer, Black Georgia, pp. 132–35; and Moseley and Brogdon, "A Lynching at Statesboro," pp. 104–18.

8. "Barbarism," Independent 57 (25 August 1904): 460–61; Baker, "What Is a Lynching? . . . Lynching in the South," pp. 299–300, 306; and Dean Richmond Babbitt, "The Psychology of the Lynch Mob," Arena 33 (December 1904): 586–89. See also "Violence," Outlook 78 (3 September 1904): 9–10; "An Appeal to Terror," Outlook 77 (27 August 1904): 971–72; "Lynching and Southern Opinion," Outlook 77 (10 September 1904): 103; and Upton, "Facts about Lynching," p. 720.

9. Baker, "What Is a Lynching? . . . Lynching in the South," pp. 313–14; and James Elbert Cutler, "Proposed Remedies for Lynching," Yale Review 13 (August 1904): 194–209. See also "Damages for Mob Violence," Outlook 76 (2 January 1904): 5–6; "Law Instead of Lynching," Outlook 76 (27 February 1904): 487–88; "A Lynching," Independent 56 (10 March 1904): 524–25; "Protests against Mob Savagery," Outlook 76 (12 March 1904): 620; "Prosecution of Lynchers in the South," Independent 57 (29 September 1904): 699–700; "A New Way to Prevent Lynching," Independent 57 (29 September 1904): 747–48; "Lynchers and the Race Problem," Independent 57 (6 October 1904): 759; "Lynchings in the South," Independent 57 (27 October 1904): 939–40; "Lynching and Federal Law," Chautauquan 40 (January 1905): 408–9; "Killed at a Texas Mass Meeting," Independent 58 (4 May 1905): 976–77; "The Lynching in Chattanooga," Independent 60 (29 March 1906): 702–3; "An Insult to the Nation," Outlook 82 (31 March 1906): 721; "Lynching and Criminal Procedure," Outlook 83 (9 June 1906): 301; and "Lynching," Outlook 93 (27 November 1909): 637.

10. Benjamin Orange Flower, "Notes and Comments," Arena 36 (September 1906): 335; "Race Riots and Lynch Law: The Cause and the Cure," Outlook 87 (2 February 1907): 259–68; "Some Thoughts on Lynching," South Atlantic Quarterly 5 (October 1906): 349–54; and Alfred Pearce Dennis, "The Political and Ethical Aspects of Lynching," International Journal of Ethics 15 (January 1905): 149–61.

11. James Cardinal Gibbons, "Lynch Law: Its Causes and Remedy," *North American Review* 171 (October 1905): 502–9; "Cardinal Gibbons on the Catholic Church and the Negro," *AME Church Review* 22 (January 1906): 257; "Lynching," in Bliss, *New Encyclopedia of Social Reform*, 2d ed., pp. 737–38, and 3d ed., pp. 737–38; Bliss, "Facts as to Lynching," pp. 273–74; and Wilbur Fisk Crafts, *National Perils and Hopes: A Study Based on Current Statistics and the Observations of a Cheerful Reformer* (Cleveland: F. M. Barton Co., 1910), pp. 24–25, 83–84. See also John Tracy Ellis, *The Life of James Cardinal Gibbons: Archbishop of Baltimore, 1834–1921,* 2 vols. (Milwaukee: Bruce Publishing Co., 1952), 2:396–404; and Christopher L. Weber, "William Dwight Porter Bliss: Priest and Socialist," *Historical Magazine of the Protestant Episcopal Church* 27 (March 1959): 9–39.

12. "Riots and Murder Follow the Fight," *Independent* 69 (7 July 1910): 3; "Many Negroes Killed in Texas" and "A State Disgraced," *Independent* 69 (4 August 1910): 216–17, 266; "Mob Law," *Outlook* 95 (13 August 1910): 808–9; "Barbarism in America," *Chautauquan* 64 (October 1911): 157–58; John Haynes Holmes, "The Contagion of the South," *Crisis* 2 (October 1911): 251–52; "Christian Responsibility for Lynchings," *Current Literature* 51 (October 1911): 404–5; "Is Burning at the Stake to Continue?," *Outlook* 99 (4 November 1911): 551–52; "Holmes on Lynching," *Crisis* 3 (January 1912): 109–11; "Conference on Colored People," *Survey* 27 (23 March 1912): 1986; Holmes to Mary White Ovington, 29 May 1912, series C, no. 336, National Association for the Advancement of Colored People Papers, Library of Congress; Mary White Ovington, "Reminiscences," *Baltimore Afro-American,* 10 December 1932; Ovington, *The Walls Came Tumbling Down* (New York: Harcourt, Brace and Co., 1947), pp. 113–15; Robert L. Zangrando, *The NAACP Crusade against Lynching: 1909–1950* (Philadelphia: Temple University Press, 1980), pp. 26–27; and Josiah Strong, *Our World: The New World-Life* (Garden City, N.Y.: Doubleday, Page and Co., 1913), pp. 203–7. On the later antilynching movement, see Donald L. Grant, *The Anti-Lynching Movement, 1883–1932* (San Francisco: R. and E. Research Associates, 1975); Zangrando, *NAACP Crusade against Lynching*; and Jacquelyn Dowd Hall, *Revolt against Chivalry: Jesse Daniel Ames and the Women's Campaign against Lynching* (New York: Columbia University Press, 1979).

13. "Judge Speer on the Chain Gang," *Outlook* 76 (16 July 1904): 621–22; "A Blow to Convict Camps," *Independent* 57 (28 July 1904): 227; George Herbert Clarke, "Georgia and the Chain Gang," *Outlook* 82 (13 January 1906): 73–79; "Moral Reform in Georgia," *Homiletic Review* 56 (September 1908): 173; Alexander J. McKelway, "The Convict Lease System," *Outlook* 90 (12 September 1908): 67–72; "Forced Labor in America" and "An Oppressive Law," *Outlook* 90 (19 December 1908): 846–48; "The Last Traces of Peonage," *Independent* 70 (26 January 1911): 213–14; "The Case of Alonzo Bailey," *Outlook* 97 (21 January 1911): 101–4; "The Contract Labor Law in Alabama," *American Missionary* 66 (March 1911): 791; Ray Stannard Baker, "A Pawn in the Struggle for Freedom," *American Magazine* 72 (September 1911): 608–10; and Pete Daniel, *The Shadow of Slavery: Peonage in the South, 1901–1969* (New York: Oxford University Press, 1973), pp. 65–81, 195. See also "Convict Hire in Georgia," *Independent* 60 (28 June 1906): 1557; A Camp Physician, "The Alabama Mining Camp," *Independent* 63 (3 October 1907): 790–91; "The Georgia Convict Camps," *Independent* 65 (16 July 1908): 168; "Convict Lease Atrocities," *Outlook* 89 (22 August 1908): 870; "The End of the Convict Lease System in Georgia" and "The New

Law," *Outlook* 90 (3 October 1908): 238–39; and Benjamin M. Blackburn, "The Georgia Convict Lease System," *Outlook* 90 (10 October 1908): 295–97. For the later struggle against involuntary servitude, see Dittmer, *Black Georgia*, pp. 72–89; and Daniel, *Shadow of Slavery*, pp. 82–192.

14. Richard T. Ely, *Ground under Our Feet: An Autobiography* (New York: Macmillan, 1938), p. 279; Benjamin G. Rader, *The Academic Mind and Reform: The Influence of Richard T. Ely in American Life* (Lexington: University of Kentucky Press, 1966), p. 235; Ely, *Property and Contract in Their Relations to the Distribution of Wealth*, 2 vols. (New York: Macmillan, 1914), 2:633, 716–18; Ely, "Progressivism, True and False—An Outline," *Review of Reviews* 51 (February 1915): 211; Ely et al., *The Foundations of National Prosperity: Studies in the Conservation of Permanent National Resources* (New York: Macmillan, 1917), p. 58; and Ely, *The World War and Leadership in a Democracy* (New York: Macmillan, 1918), pp. 70–71, 115.

15. Lyman Abbott, "Negro Suffrage," *Social Service* 9 (April 1904): 69; and Samuel Zane Batten, *The Christian State: The State, Democracy, and Christianity* (Philadelphia: The Griffith and Rowland Press, 1909), p. 208. See also "Suffrage Limitations in the South," *Outlook* 76 (12 March 1904): 632–33; William DeWitt Hyde, "A National Platform on the Race Question," *Outlook* 77 (21 May 1904): 169; "Reduction of Southern Representation in Congress," *Outlook* 79 (7 January 1905): 11–15; " 'To Hell With Such a Law,' " *World To-Day* 12 (January 1907): 3–4; Batten, *Christian State*, p. 187; and Abbott, *The Spirit of Democracy* (New York: Houghton Mifflin Co., 1910), p. 183.

16. Edward Everett Hale, "The American People and Universal Suffrage," *Independent* 61 (25 October 1906): 970–76; "What Do You, Yourself, Think of Disfranchisement" and "Notes," *American Missionary* 58 (January 1904): 20, 85; Charles F. Dole, *The Spirit of Democracy* (New York: Thomas Y. Crowell and Co., 1906), pp. 103–19; Dole, *The Ethics of Progress; or, the Theory and Practice by Which Civilization Proceeds* (New York: Thomas Y. Crowell and Co., 1909), p. 353; and "Is Suffrage a Right or a Privilege?," *Independent* 60 (22 February 1906): 463–65. See also David Gregg, "The Black Forefathers; or, The Negro Race a Factor in American History," *Treasury* 21 (February 1904): 753–54; William Channing Gannett, "The Afro-American Problem in Our Midst," 21 February 1904, Sermon 929, Gannett Sermon File, Colgate-Rochester Divinity School; John Bascom, "The Three Amendments," *Annals of the American Academy of Political and Social Science* 27 (May 1906): 597–609; Charles Zueblin, *The Religion of a Democrat* (New York: B. W. Huebsch, 1908), pp. 140–41; Thomas C. Hall, *Social Solutions in the Light of Christian Ethics* (New York: Eaton and Mains, 1910), pp. 352–53; John Haynes Holmes, *The Disfranchisement of Negroes* (New York: National Association for the Advancement of Colored People, 1910); *New York Age*, 19 May 1910; Ray Stannard Baker, "Negro Suffrage in a Democracy," *Atlantic Monthly* 106 (November 1910): 612–19; and Jesse Macy, quoted in "The White Primary," *Crisis* 1 (March 1911): 20.

17. Washington Gladden, "Where Are We in Democracy?," 25 February 1906, Sermon 1085, Washington Gladden Papers, Ohio Historical Society. See also James M. Harris to Gladden, 7 November 1906, box 10, no. 209, Gladden Papers; and Gladden, "The Negro Crisis: Is the Separation of the Two Races to Become Necessary," *American Magazine* 63 (January 1907): 298.

18. "Disfranchisement in Georgia," *Independent* 60 (29 March 1906): 755–56; "The

Negro in Georgia," Outlook 84 (1 September 1906): 3; "Results in Atlanta," Independent 62 (3 January 1907): 51–52; "Ex-Governor Northern's Work in Georgia," Independent 62 (13 June 1907): 1423–24; "Editorial," Independent 62 (27 June 1907): 1540; "Governor Hoke Smith," Independent 63 (4 July 1907): 53; "Editorial," Independent 63 (25 July 1907): 238; Lovick P. Winter, "Prohibition in Georgia," Independent 63 (22 August 1907): 444; Alexander J. McKelway, "State Prohibition in Georgia and the South," Outlook 86 (31 August 1907): 947–49; "Inviting Corruption," Outlook 87 (14 September 1907): 57–58; McKelway, "The Suffrage in Georgia," Outlook 87 (14 September 1907): 63–66; "Editorial," Independent 63 (19 September 1907): 712; Thomas Jesse Jones, "The Power of the Southern Election Registrar," Outlook 87 (9 November 1907): 529–31; and McKelway, "Hoke Smith: A Progressive Democrat," Outlook 96 (1 October 1910): 267–72. See also Dittmer, Black Georgia in the Progressive Era, pp. 97–103; and J. Morgan Kousser, The Shaping of Southern Politics: Suffrage Restriction and the Establishment of the One-Party South, 1880–1910 (New Haven: Yale University Press, 1974), pp. 209–33.

19. Booker T. Washington to George Freeman Bragg, Jr., 10 March 1904, Booker T. Washington Papers, Library of Congress; "The Maryland Suffrage Proposal" and "Other Symptoms of Race Feeling," Outlook 76 (26 March 1904): 715–16; "The Maryland Campaign," Outlook 76 (15 July 1905): 647; J. A. Graham, "Can the Negro Settle It?," Outlook 84 (13 October 1906): 365–68; L. J. Abbott, "The Race Question in the Forty-Sixth State," Independent 63 (25 July 1907): 206–11; "White Voters Beware!," Outlook 91 (16 January 1909): 89–90; "Disfranchisement in Maryland," Independent 67 (30 September 1909): 1095; "A New Disfranchisement Plan," Independent 68 (30 March 1910): 708–9; "Negro Suffrage in Maryland," Outlook 94 (16 April 1910): 820; "Suffrage in Maryland," Independent 68 (21 April 1910): 872–73; "Disfranchisement of the Negro in Maryland," American Missionary 64 (May 1910): 132–33; "The Grandfather Clause in Maryland," Outlook 95 (May 1910): 666–67; "The Negro in Oklahoma," Outlook 95 (18 June 1910): 328; "Maryland Election Law Unconstitutional," Independent 69 (3 November 1910): 1002; "Editorial," Independent 69 (10 November 1910): 1056; "The Grandfather Clause in Oklahoma," Outlook 96 (26 November 1910): 655–56; "Cardinal Gibbons on Disfranchisement," American Missionary 64 (December 1910): 613; "The Maryland Decision," American Missionary 65 (March 1911): 790; and Ellis, James Cardinal Gibbons, 2:400–401.

20. Ottumwa, Iowa, Evening Democrat, 21 July 1904, p. 1; Ottumwa Daily Courier, 21 July 1904, p. 1; Ottumwa Evening Democrat, 2 August 1904, p. 1; Ottumwa Daily Courier, 8 August 1904, p. 5; Ottumwa Daily Courier, 16 August 1904, p. 2; Ottumwa Daily Courier, 14 September 1904, p. 2; "Sketch of George Edwin Taylor," Voice of the Negro 1 (October 1904): 477–78; George E. Taylor, "The National Liberty Party," Voice of the Negro 1 (October 1904): 479–81; Taylor, "The National Liberty Party's Appeal," Independent 57 (13 October 1904): 844–45; "The Minor Political Parties," Independent 57 (13 October 1904): 870; and "The Southern Voice in National Elections," Outlook 79 (7 January 1905): 1–3. See also Hanes Walton, Jr., Black Political Parties: An Historical and Political Analysis (New York: Free Press, 1972), pp. 50–51; and Kousser, The Shaping of Southern Politics.

21. Peter Frederick, "A Life of Principle: Ernest Howard Crosby and the Frustrations of the Intellectual as Reformer," New York History 54 (October 1973): 396–423; Frederick, Knights of the Golden Rule: The Intellectual as Christian Social Reformer in the 1890s (Lexington:

University Press of Kentucky, 1976), pp. 209–34; Crosby, "Contrasts in Black and White," in *Plain Talk in Psalm and Parable* (Boston: Small, Maynard, 1899), pp. 14–16; and Crosby, "The Real 'White Man's Burden,'" in *Swords and Plowshares* (New York: Funk and Wagnalls, 1902), p. 33. See also James McPherson, *The Abolitionist Legacy: From Reconstruction to the NAACP* (Princeton: Princeton University Press, 1975), pp. 324–32.

22. Crosby, "Count Tolstoy and Non-Resistance," *Outlook* 54 (11 July 1896): 42–53; Crosby, "William Lloyd Garrison," in *Plain Talk in Psalm and Parable*, pp. 140–42; Crosby, *Tolstoy and His Message* (New York: Funk and Wagnalls, 1904), pp. 75–76; Tolstoy, "Garrison and Non-Resistance," *Independent* 56 (21 April 1904): 881–83; "Count Tolstoy on Non-Resistance and the Negro Question," *Review of Reviews* 29 (June 1904): 731–32; and Crosby, *Garrison the Non-Resistant* (Chicago: Public Publishing Co., 1905), pp. 72, 94–95, 106–23. See also Lewis Perry, *Radical Abolitionism: Anarchy and the Government of God in Anti-Slavery Thought* (Ithaca: Cornell University Press, 1973), pp. 1–5, 315–16; and H. T. Kealing, "Tolstoy as a Force in Religion," and "Tolstoy," *AME Church Review* 27 (January 1911): 245–49, 304.

23. W. E. B. Du Bois, "Garrison and the Negro," *Independent* 59 (7 December 1905): 1316–17; Reverdy Cassius Ransom, "William Lloyd Garrison," in *The Spirit of Freedom and Justice: Orations and Speeches* (Nashville: AME Sunday School Union, 1926), pp. 7–14; Amory H. Bradford, "William Lloyd Garrison," *American Missionary* 60 (January 1906): 6–8; Washington Gladden, "Garrison," 10 December 1905, Sermon 1077, Gladden Papers; "Tolstoy, Garrison and Non-Resistance," *Independent* 56 (21 April 1904): 917–18; "The Eulogies of Garrison," *Independent* 59 (28 December 1905): 1550–51; and New York *Evening Post* quoted in "Georgia Justice," *American Missionary* 61 (September 1907): 201–2. Villard was apparently unaware of the black boycotts of segregated streetcars that occurred between 1900 and 1906, but received little national attention. See August Meier and Elliott Rudwick, "The Boycott Movement against Streetcars in the South, 1900–1906," *Journal of American History* 55 (March 1969): 756–75.

24. Harlan Paul Douglass, George A. Gates, Edward A. Steiner, Charles F. Thwing, and William Hays Ward were other leading Northern white evangelical neoabolitionists.

25. A. J. Lyman to Washington Gladden, 22 October 1904, Gladden Papers; Jacob Henry Dorn, *Washington Gladden: Prophet of the Social Gospel* (Columbus: Ohio State University Press, 1966), p. 300; Gladden, "Reflections on a Three Year Term as President of the American Missionary Association," [ca. 20 October 1904], Sermon 1405, Gladden Papers; Gladden, *Christianity and Socialism* (New York: Eaton and Mains, 1905), pp. 20, 65; Gladden, "The Church and Social Problems," *International Quarterly* 11 (April 1905): 139–40; and Gladden, "Vital Religion," [1905?], Sermon 1408, Gladden Papers.

26. Gladden, "The American Missionary Association and the Problems of Emancipation," *American Missionary* 60 (December 1906): 314–15; Gladden, "The Negro Crisis: Is the Separation of the Two Races to Become Necessary?," *American Magazine* 63 (January 1907): 296–301; Gladden, "[Cleveland's Pilgrim Church and the Congregational Convocation of 1907]," 13 February 1907, Sermon 1121, Gladden Papers; Gladden, *Recollections* (Boston: Houghton Mifflin Co., 1909), pp. 371–72. See also Gladden, *The Church and Modern Life* (Boston: Houghton Mifflin Co., 1908), pp. 185–86; C. J. Ryder to Gladden, 28 September 1906, box 10, no. 157; Moultrie Hitt to Gladden, 27 October 1906, box 10,

no. 184; J. L. Phelps to Gladden, 25 June 1907, box 10, no. 188; John Kershaw, Jr., to Gladden, 2 November 1906, box 10, no. 201; John L. F. Tolton to Gladden, 6 November 1906, box 10, no. 212; Charles Cuthbert Hall to Gladden, 2 November 1907, box 10, no. 291; Edward S. Steele to Gladden, 28 December 1907, box 10, no. 337; Gustav Gambetta to Phillips Publishing Co., 3 January 1907, box 10, no. 6; William Boyd Riley to Gladden, 6 January 1907, box 10, no. 8; John Ambrose Price, *The Negro: Past, Present, and Future* (New York: Neale Publishing Co., 1907), pp. 238–43; Samuel Huntington Comings to Gladden, 2 January 1907, box 10, no. 4; and T. S. Inborden to Gladden, 30 November 1909, box 11, no. 245, Gladden Papers.

27. Henry Hugh Proctor, *Between Black and White* (New York: Pilgrim Press, 1925), p. 113; Amory Bradford, *My Brother* (Boston: Pilgrim Press, 1910), pp. 41–42, 46, 51–52, 57, 75–76; "Segregation and Integration," *Independent* 59 (30 November 1905): 1299; and Bradford, *Preludes and Interludes* (New York: Thomas Y. Crowell Co., 1911), pp. 18–20. See also Bradford, "What about Brotherhood?," *American Missionary* 59 (March 1905): 66–68; "Dr. Bradford," *American Missionary* 59 (November 1905): 280–81; A Subscriber, "Race Integrity," *Independent* 60 (18 January 1906): 163; Bradford, "The Kingdom," *American Missionary* 64 (April 1910): 1–2; Bradford, *My Brother*; and "In Memorium," *American Missionary* 65 (May 1911): 84.

28. Bradford, "The Creed of a Philanthropist," *American Missionary* 61 (December 1907): 312–14; and Bradford, *My Brother*, pp. 55–70. See also Bradford, "Our Most Important Missionary Enterprise," *American Missionary* 59 (February 1905): 33–35; Bradford, "Hopeful, Not Hopeless," *American Missionary* 59 (April 1905): 105–8; Bradford, "The Real Negro Problem," *American Missionary* 61 (October 1907): 244–46; and Bradford, *My Brother*, pp. 30–31, 36–37, 230.

29. Basil Douglass Hall, *The Life of Charles Cuthbert Hall: "One among a Thousand"* (New York: Carlton Press, 1965); Robert C. Ogden to Charles Cuthbert Hall, 23 September 1903, Letterbook, box 13, Robert C. Ogden Papers, Library of Congress; and Charles Cuthbert Hall, *The Universal Elements of the Christian Religion: An Attempt to Interpret Contemporary Religious Conditions* (New York: Fleming H. Revell Co., 1905), pp. 129–30, 305–8.

30. Hall, *Christ and the Human Race; or, The Attitude of Jesus Christ toward Foreign Races and Religions* (Boston: Houghton, Mifflin and Co., 1906), pp. xv–xvi, 72–74, 76, 86–87, 92–93, 104, 110–11, 113, 115, 118, 123, 126–27, 180.

31. Donald M. Love, *Henry Churchill King of Oberlin College* (New Haven: Yale University Press, 1956), pp. 2–67; Henry Churchill King, *Reconstruction in Theology* (New York: Macmillan, 1901), pp. vii, 29, 32–33, 93, 169–84; and King, *Theology and Social Consciousness: A Study of the Relation of the Social Consciousness to Theology* (New York: Macmillan, 1902), pp. ix, 9–22, 24–28, 44–45, 49–51.

32. Henry Churchill King, *The Moral and Religious Challenge of Our Times* (New York: Macmillan, 1912), pp. 283–308; King, *The Ethics of Jesus* (New York: Macmillan, 1910), pp. 244, 246–47; King, *Fundamental Questions* (New York: Macmillan, 1917), pp. 128, 157; James M. Whiton to Henry Churchill King, 23 April 1910, [W. F. Bohn or Whiting Williams] to Whiton, 26 April 1910, Mary Church Terrell to King, 4 February 1911, Henry D. King to H. C. King, 22 March 1911, and H. C. King to H. D. King, 23 March 1911, King Papers; H. C. King, "The College and Democracy," *Oberlin College Magazine* 7

(December 1910–January 1911): 126–36; W. E. Bigglestone, "Oberlin College and the Negro Student," *Journal of Negro History* 56 (July 1971): 203–6; and Love, *Henry Churchill King*, pp. 156–57.

33. Edward Alfred Steiner, *From Alien to Citizen: The Story of My Life in America* (New York: Fleming H. Revell Co., 1914), pp. 189–90.

34. Ibid., pp. 292–96; see also pp. 209–77.

35. "Lynch Law and Riot in Ohio," *Independent* 56 (17 March 1904): 580; "The Lynching in Ohio," *Outlook* 76 (19 March 1904): 670–71; and Ray Stannard Baker, "What Is a Lynching? A Study of Mob Justice, North and South: Lynching in the North," *McClure's Magazine* 24 (February 1905): 422–30.

36. Washington Gladden, "Are You Walking in Integrity?," 13 March 1904, Sermon 1006, Gladden Papers; "What Are Sheriffs For?," *Independent* 56 (17 March 1904): 624; Baker, "What Is a Lynching? . . . Lynching in the North," p. 427; and Steiner, *From Alien to Citizen*, pp. 295–96. Springfield, Ohio, had a second race riot in February, 1906. See "Race Riots in an Ohio City," *Independent* 60 (8 March 1906): 535; "The Mob at Springfield, Ohio," *Independent* 60 (8 March 1906): 582–84; "Race Riots in Ohio," *Outlook* 82 (10 March 1906): 536; "Public Responsibility for Mob Violence," *Outlook* 82 (28 April 1906): 920–22; and "Punishment for Lynchers," *Independent* 60 (17 May 1906): 1177.

37. Steiner, *From Alien to Citizen*, pp. 303–21, 326–31; "From the Address of Prof. Steiner," *American Missionary* 59 (November 1905): 274; Steiner, *On the Trail of the Immigrant* (New York: Fleming H. Revell Co., 1906), pp. 296, 300–301, 304, 306–8; Steiner, *The Immigrant Tide: Its Ebb and Flow* (New York: Fleming H. Revell Co., 1909), pp. 54–57, 195–99; Steiner, *Against the Current: Simple Chapters from a Complex Life* (New York: Fleming H. Revell Co., 1910), pp. 211–12, 218, 221–23, 228–29; and Steiner, *The Eternal Hunger: Vivid Moments in Personal Experience* (New York: Fleming H. Revell Co., 1911), pp. 9, 85–86. See also Steiner to Washington Gladden, 13 September and 21 October 1903, box 4, nos. 147 and 190, Gladden Papers; Steiner, "Tolstoy To-Day," "Tolstoy's Marriage and Family Life," "Tolstoy in the Heart of Russia," *Outlook* 75 (5 September, 5 October, and 7 November 1903): 35–42, 267–76, 537–44; Steiner, *Tolstoy the Man* (New York: Outlook Co., 1904); Steiner, *The Broken Wall: Stories of the Mingling Folk* (New York: Fleming H. Revell Co., 1911), pp. 5–6; and Steiner, "What To Do for the Immigrant," in *Conservation of National Ideals*, ed. Mrs. Delphine Bartholomew Wells et al. (New York: Fleming H. Revell Co., 1911), pp. 47–61, 64–65, 69.

38. Steiner, *Broken Wall*, p. 6; and Steiner, "What To Do for the Immigrant," p. 65. See also Steiner, *From Alien to Citizen*, pp. 330–31; Steiner, *Immigrant Tide*, pp. 57, 194–96, 259; Steiner, *Against the Current*, pp. 208, 211, 213, 215; Steiner, *Broken Wall*, pp. 177–87; Steiner, *Eternal Hunger*, pp. 9, 36; and *Boston Globe*, 6 March 1910, in Ford Hall Forum Scrapbooks, vol. 1, American Baptist Historical Society.

39. "The Niagara Movement Declaration of Principles, 1905," in *Afro-American History: Primary Sources*, ed. Thomas R. Frazier (New York: Harcourt, Brace and World, 1970), pp. 231–34; Elliott M. Rudwick, "The Niagara Movement," *Journal of Negro History* 42 (July 1957): 179; William A. Sinclair, *The Aftermath of Slavery: A Study of the Condition and Environment of the American Negro* (New York: Small, Maynard and Co., 1905), p. 4; "A Negro Appeal to the Country," and "Complaint vs. Leadership," *Outlook* 80 (29 July 1905): 795–96;

"Sound Lessons for Any Race," *Outlook* 80 (26 August 1905): 1000–1002; "The Negro's Duty to Himself," *American Missionary* 59 (June 1905): 170–71; and "The Niagara Movement," *American Missionary* 59 (September 1905): 203–4. See also Herbert Aptheker, "The Niagara Movement," in *Afro-American History: The Modern Era* (Secaucus, N.J.: Citadel Press, 1971), pp. 127–58; Factor, *Black Response to America*, pp. 325–39; Fox, *Guardian of Boston*, pp. 86–114; and Harlan, *Washington*, 2:84–106.

40. Fox, *Guardian of Boston*, p. 102; Rudwick, "Niagara Movement," p. 187; Miller, *Race Adjustment*, p. 16; Booker T. Washington to Lyman Abbott, 2 September 1906, in Harlan, *Booker T. Washington Papers*, 9:67; W. E. B. Du Bois, *Dusk of Dawn: An Essay toward an Autobiography of a Race Concept* (New York: Harcourt, Brace and Co., 1940), p. 89; "The Platform of the Niagara Movement" and "The Platform of the Outlook," *Outlook* 84 (1 September 1906): 3–4; "The Negro Problem: Booker Washington's Platform," *Outlook* 84 (8 September 1906): 54–55; and "Editorial," *Independent* 61 (23 August 1906): 472. See also Reverdy Ransom, *The Pilgrimage of Harriet Ransom's Son* (Nashville: Sunday School Union, 1949), pp. 160–67, 196–97; Ransom, *Spirit of Freedom and Justice*, pp. 16–25; Ridgely Torrence, *The Story of John Hope* (New York: Macmillan, 1948), pp. 148–52; "An Appeal from Georgia," *Independent* 60 (1 March 1906): 523–24; "Editorial," *American Missionary* 60 (October 1906): 237; "Which Is Right?," *American Missionary* 61 (April 1907): 99–101; and "Race Separation without Discrimination," *Outlook* 86 (20 July 1907): 576–77.

41. Theophilus Gould Steward, *Fifty Years in the Gospel Ministry* (Philadelphia: AME Book Concern, [ca. 1921]), pp. 361–63; Factor, *Black Response to America*, pp. 330–33; and McPherson, *Abolitionist Legacy*, pp. 370, 384. See also "Those Negro Soldiers," *Independent* 61 (6 December 1906): 1364; "The Affair of Brownsville" and "False Counselors," *Outlook* 84 (29 December 1906): 1038–39; "The Debate on the Brownsville Affray," *Outlook* 87 (26 January 1907): 151–52; "The Brownsville Inquiry," *Independent* 62 (21 February 1907): 455; "Brownsville and the President," *Independent* 63 (11 July 1907): 111; "The Negroes and Secretary Taft," *Independent* 64 (13 February 1908): 374–75; "Professor DuBois's Advice," *Independent* 64 (2 April 1908): 768–69; "'A Friend of the Negro,'" *Outlook* 88 (11 April 1908): 805–6; Mary Church Terrell, "Secretary Taft and the Negro Soldiers," *Independent* 65 (23 July 1908): 189–90; "The Niagara Movement," *Independent* 65 (17 September 1908): 676; "Mr. Taft on Race Discrimination," *Independent* 65 (22 October 1908): 960–62; Horace Bumstead, "The Marvel of Brownsville," *Independent* 68 (12 May 12 1910): 1036; Anne J. Lane, *The Brownsville Affair: National Crisis and Black Reaction* (Port Washington, N.Y.: Kennikat Press, 1971); Emma Lou Thornbrough, "The Brownsville Episode and the Negro Vote," *Mississippi Valley Historical Review* 44 (December 1957): 469–85; and John D. Weaver, *The Brownsville Raid: America's Black Dreyfus Affair* (New York: W. W. Norton and Co., 1970).

42. Harlan, *Washington*, 2:309–37; Lane, *Brownsville Affair*, pp. 76–81; August Meier, *Negro Thought in America, 1880–1915: Racial Ideologies in the Age of Booker T. Washington* (Ann Arbor: University of Michigan Press, 1963), pp. 180–81; Robert C. Ogden to James E. Russell, 27 March 1906, box 9, Ogden Papers; "Caste," *American Missionary* 61 (September 1907): 202; "A Brave Bishop," *Independent* 63 (24 October 1907): 1014; and "Bishop Potter," *Independent* 65 (30 July 1908): 277–78.

43. Booker T. Washington to Oswald Garrison Villard, 20 October 1906; Villard to Washington, 24 October 1906; Washington to Villard, 26 October 1906; Villard to Washington, 4 December 1906, Washington Papers; Harlan, *Washington*, 2:303–8; Robert C. Bannister, *Ray Stannard Baker, The Mind and Thought of a Progressive* (New Haven: Yale University Press, 1966), pp. 4–20, 128; John E. Semonche, *Ray Stannard Baker: A Quest for Democracy in Modern America, 1870–1918* (Chapel Hill: University of North Carolina Press, 1969), pp. 5–16; and Baker, *Following the Colour Line: An Account of Negro Citizenship in the American Democracy* (New York: Doubleday, Page and Co., 1908), pp. 26, 37, 44, 65, 86, 93, 147, 215, 218, 240, 252–64, 269–70. See also Dewey Grantham, "Introduction," to Baker, *Following the Color Line: American Negro Citizenship in the Progressive Era* (New York: Harper and Row, 1964), p. xi; and David Chalmers, "Ray Stannard Baker's Search for Reform," *Journal of the History of Ideas* 14 (June 1958): 428–29.

44. Baker, *Following the Colour Line*, pp. 270–72, 292–93, 301, 307; Chalmers, "Ray Stannard Baker's Search for Reform," pp. 429–30; Grantham, "Introduction," pp. viii–ix; Bannister, *Ray Stannard Baker*, pp. 129–31, 137–40; and Semonche, *Ray Stannard Baker*, pp. 201, 206–7, 215–19, 239. See also "The Atlanta Riot," and "Still At It," *AME Church Review* 24 (July 1908): 78, 92; "The Negro in Africa and America," *Outlook* 92 (29 May 1909): 271; Mary White Ovington, "Two Books on American Race Relations," *Survey* 22 (8 June 1909): 348–52; and Willis Duke Weatherford, *Negro Life in the South: Present Conditions and Needs* (New York: Association Press, 1910), p. 178.

45. Richard Henry Edwards, "The Social Problems Group," *Charities and the Commons* 21 (17 October 1908): 103–7; Edwards to ——, 10 September 1907, and the Edwards–Arthur H. Gleason correspondence, July–October 1908, Richard Henry Edwards Papers, Cornell University Library; Edwards, *The Negro Problem* (Madison, Wis.: n.p., 1908), pp. 12–13; Edward A. Ross, "The Causes of Race Superiority," *Annals of the American Academy of Political and Social Science* 17 (July 1901): 67–89; Ross, *The Foundation of Sociology* (New York: Macmillan, 1905), p. 241; Ross, "Social Darwinism," *American Journal of Sociology* 12 (March 1907): 715–16; Ross, *Social Psychology: An Outline and Source Book* (New York: Macmillan, 1908), p. 3; and Ross, *Seventy Years of It: An Autobiography* (New York: D. Appleton-Century Co., 1936), p. 126.

46. Sagamore Sociological Conference Papers, American Baptist Historical Society; Ronald C. White, Jr., "Social Christianity and the Negro in the Progressive Era, 1890–1920" (Ph.D. dissertation, Princeton University, 1972), pp. 232–40; Edwin Doak Mead, "Present Day Problems," in *First Year of the Sagamore Sociological Conference* (Boston: Arakeyan Press, 1907), p. 29; Mead, "The Frederick Douglass Centre in Chicago," *Boston Transcript*, 29 January 1906, clipping in the Edwin Doak Mead Papers, Peace Collection, Friends Historical Library, Swarthmore, Pa.; Fox, *Guardian of Boston*, pp. 119–20; Arthur Mann, *Yankee Reformers in the Urban Age: Social Reform in Boston, 1880–1900* (Cambridge: Harvard University Press, 1954), pp. 159–63; Ray Stannard Baker, "The Negro in a Democracy," in *Third Year of the Sagamore Sociological Conference* (Boston: Edwin L. Slocum, [1909]), pp. 9–12; Baker, "The Negro in a Democracy," *Independent* 67 (9 September 1909): 584–88; and Amos R. Wells, "Brotherhood at Sagamore," *Christian Endeavor World* 24 (15 July 1909): 863.

47. Addie W. Hunton, "The Cosmopolitan Society of Greater New York," *Voice of the*

*Negro* 4 (May 1907): 185–86; "An Account of the Cosmopolitan Club Dinner in the New York *American*," 28 April 1908, and Hamilton Holt to Booker T. Washington, 1 May 1908, in Harlan, *Booker T. Washington Papers*, 9:515–21, 524; "Cosmopolitan Club File," King Papers; Oswald Garrison Villard, *Fighting Years: Memoirs of a Liberal Editor* (New York: Harcourt, Brace and Co., 1939), pp. 196–98; Mary White Ovington, *Walls Came Tumbling Down*, pp. 43–46; Warren F. Kuehl, *Hamilton Holt: Journalist, Internationalist, Educator* (Gainesville: University of Florida Press, 1960), pp. 47–49; Charles Flint Kellogg, *NAACP: A History of the National Association for the Advancement of Colored People, 1909–1920* (Baltimore: Johns Hopkins University Press, 1967), pp. 71–72; Louis R. Harlan, "The Secret Life of Booker T. Washington," *Journal of Southern History* 37 (August 1971): 413–15; McPherson, *Abolitionist Legacy*, pp. 374–76; and Harlan, *Washington*, 2:376–78.

48. "The Riot at Springfield," *Outlook* 89 (22 August 1908): 869–79; An Eye Witness, "The So-Called Race Riot at Springfield, Illinois," *Charities and the Commons* 20 (19 September 1908): 709–11; James Crouthemal, "The Springfield Race Riot of 1908," *Journal of Negro History* 45 (July 1960): 164–81; and Roberta H. Senechal, "In Lincoln's Shadow: The Springfield, Illinois, Race Riot of 1908" (Ph.D. dissertation, University of Virginia, 1986).

49. "The Springfield Race Riots," *World To-Day* 15 (October 1908): 994; Graham Taylor, "The Race Riot in Lincoln's City," *Charities and the Commons* 20 (29 August 1908): 627–28; "Atlanta Outdone," *Independent* 65 (20 August 1908): 442–43; and William English Walling, "The Race War in the North," *Independent* 65 (3 September 1908): 529–34.

50. Kellogg, *NAACP*, pp. 11–15, 297–99. See also Ovington, *Walls Came Tumbling Down*, pp. 100–103.

51. Thomas Cuming Hall, *Social Solutions in the Light of Christian Ethics* (New York: Eaton and Mains, 1910), pp. 115–16, 352–53; Henry Neuman, *Spokesman for Ethical Religion* (Boston: Beacon Press, 1951); Howard B. Radest, *Toward Common Ground: The Story of the Ethical Culture Societies in the United States* (New York: Frederick Ungar Publishing Co., 1969), pp. 63–66, 109–21, 154–55; "Charles Zueblin," in *The National Cyclopedia of American Biography* (New York: James T. White and Co., 1917), 14:454–55; Zueblin, *The Religion of a Democrat* (New York: B. W. Huebsch, 1908), pp. 54, 82, 140–41, 190–91; Zueblin, *Democracy and the Overman* (New York: B. W. Huebsch, 1910), pp. 37–61; and "The Eternal Problem," *Crisis* 5 (January 1913): 126. See also Upton Sinclair, *The Brass Check: A Study of American Journalism* (Pasadena, Calif.: The Author, 1920), p. 325.

52. Kellogg, *NAACP*, pp. 16–17; Charles F. Thwing, "The Worth of Personality," *Homiletic Review* 32 (August 1896): 122–27; Villard to Washington, 26 May 1909, and Washington to Villard, 28 May 1909, in Harlan, *Booker T. Washington Papers*, 10:116–20. See also William English Walling to John C. [sic] King, 6 February 1909; Henry Churchill King to Walling, 12 February 1909; Walling to King, 5 March 1909; Walling to King, 22 March 1909; King to Walling, 24 March 1909; Walling to Sir, 12 May 1909; King to Walling, 21 May 1909, King Papers; Walling to William Channing Gannett, 5 March 1909, William Channing Gannett Papers, University of Rochester; and Harlan, *Washington*, 2:359–78.

53. Board of Directors Minutes, [?] March and 27 April 1909, box A-8, NAACP Papers, Library of Congress; Mary White Ovington to W. E. B. Du Bois, 13 April 1907, in Aptheker, *Correspondence of W. E. B. Du Bois*, 1:132–33; Alexander Irvine, "From the

Bottom Up," *World's Work* 18–19 (July–December 1909): 11788–98, 12027–37, 12281–85, 12365–77, 12448–55, 12586–88; and Carl Herman Voss, *Rabbi and Minister: The Friendship of Stephen S. Wise and John Haynes Holmes* (New York: Association Press, 1964), pp. 102–3. See also Melvin I. Urofsky, *A Voice That Spoke for Justice: The Life and Times of Stephen S. Wise* (Albany: State University of New York Press, 1982), p. 100; Holmes, *Through Gentile Eyes: A Plea for Tolerance and Goodwill* (New York: Jewish Opinion Publishing Corporation, 1938), pp. 75–76; Holmes, *My Gandhi* (New York: Harper and Row, 1953); and Holmes, *I Speak for Myself* (New York: Harper and Brothers, 1959), pp. 196–201.

54. S. B. Elliott to William T. Manning, 25 September 1904, William Thomas Manning Papers, General Theological Seminary, New York; Harlan, *Washington,* 2:253–55; "One More Southern Opinion," *American Missionary* 62 (September 1908): 212–13; Ewing, "The Heart of the Race Problem," *Atlantic Monthly* 103 (March 1909): 389–97; Harlan Paul Douglass, *Christian Reconstruction in the South* (Boston: Pilgrim Press, 1909), p. vii; and J. Milton Waldron, "The Problem's Solution," in *Proceedings of the National Negro Conference, 1909* (New York: Arno Press and New York Times, 1969), pp. 161–62. See also Ewing, "An Able Appeal for the Southern Industrial Institute, Camp Hill, Ala.," *Alexander's Magazine* 4 (May 1907): 53–60; and "The Higher Education of the Negro," *American Missionary* 64 (April 1910): 40–41.

55. "Address of William Hayes Ward," and Jenkin Lloyd Jones, "The Race Problem," in *Proceedings of the National Negro Conference,* pp. 9–13, 131–35; Du Bois, "National Committee on the Negro," *Survey* 22 (12 June 1909): 399; "Resolutions," *Proceedings of the National Negro Conference,* pp. 222–25; William English Walling to Du Bois, 8 June 1909, in Aptheker, *Correspondence of W. E. B. Du Bois,* 1:147–49; Ovington, *Walls Came Tumbling Down,* pp. 105–7; Duster, *Crusade for Justice,* pp. 321–28; Elliott M. Rudwick, "The National Negro Committee Conference of 1909," *Phylon* 18 (Fourth Quarter 1957): 413–19; and Kellogg, *NAACP,* pp. 21–30. See also George Wharton Jones, "Jenkin Lloyd Jones and His Master-Work, The Abraham Lincoln Center," *Arena* 37 (April 1907): 375–86.

56. Tilden G. Edelstein, *Strange Enthusiasm: A Life of Thomas Wentworth Higginson* (New Haven: Yale University Press, 1968), pp. 373, 377–79, 387–92, 400; "The Hurt of Unwise Friends," *Outlook* 92 (12 June 1909): 342; "The Indiscriminate Extension of the Ballot," *Independent* 66 (17 June 1909): 1352–53; "The Race Conference in New York," *AME Church Review* 26 (July 1909): 87–88; "The Negro: His Past and Future," *Chautauquan* 55 (August 1909): 299–300; and "Liberty, Equality, and Fraternity, Limited," *Independent* 66 (10 June 1909): 1302–3.

57. Henry W. Wilbur and Charles W. Wendte to Anna Garlin Spencer, 11 May 1910, box A-8; Board of Directors Minutes, 14 February, 6 September, and 29 November 1910, box A-8, NAACP Papers; Kellogg, *NAACP,* pp. 31–45; *New York Age,* 29 May 1910; Ransom, *Spirit of Freedom and Justice,* pp. 42–50; and Holmes, *The Disfranchisement of Negroes* (New York: National Association for the Advancement of Colored People, 1910), pp. 4, 5, 16.

58. Board of Directors Minutes, 21 April 1910, box A-8, NAACP Papers; Baker to Washington, 13 May 1910, and Washington to Baker, 24 May 1910, in Harlan, *Booker T. Washington Papers,* 10:333–34; Baker, "Negro Suffrage in a Democracy," *Atlantic Monthly* 106 (November 1910): 612–19; John Haynes Holmes, "Percy Stickney Grant," *Dictionary of*

*American Biography*, ed. Allen Johnson et al. (New York: Charles Scribners' Sons, 1928–88), 7:490–91; Grant, "American Ideals and Race Mixture," *North American Review* 195 (April 1912): 513–25; and Grant, *Socialism and Christianity* (New York: Brentano's, 1910), pp. 123–50.

59. Kellogg, *NAACP*, pp. 31, 42–45, 120–29, 304–5; Rudwick, *W. E. B. Du Bois*, pp. 120–42; Creighton Lacy, *Frank Mason North: His Social and Ecumenical Mission* (Nashville: Abingdon Press, 1965), p. 105; Isabel Eaton to Oswald Garrison Villard, n.d.; John E. Milholland to Isabel Eaton, 19 May 1910; John Haynes Holmes to Mary White Ovington, 4 July 1910, box C-1; and Board of Directors' Minutes, 29 November 1910, box A-8, NAACP Papers.

## Chapter 10

1. Ralph E. Luker, "The Social Gospel and the Failure of Racial Reform, 1877–1898," *Church History* 46 (March 1977): 87. Michael C. Coleman's studies of Indians and Protestant missions corroborate this interpretation. See Coleman, "Not Race, but Grace: Presbyterian Missionaries and American Indians, 1837–1893," *Journal of American History* 67 (June 1980): 58; and Coleman, *Presbyterian Missionary Attitudes toward American Indians, 1837–1893* (Jackson: University Press of Mississippi, 1985).

2. On Strong as a racist, see William H. Berge, "Josiah Strong: An American Paradox" (M.A. thesis, Vanderbilt University, 1959), pp. 71–75; Glenn R. Bucher, "Social Gospel Christianity and Racism," *Union Seminary Quarterly Review* 28 (Winter 1973): 146–73; Henry Steele Commager, *The American Mind: An Interpretation of American Thought and Character since 1815* (New Haven: Yale University Press, 1950), p. 47; Merle Curti, *The Growth of American Thought*, 3d ed. (New York: Harper and Row, 1964), pp. 652–53; Alan Davies, *Infected Christianity: A Study of Modern Racism* (Montreal: McGill–Queen's University Press, 1988), pp. 81–84; Ralph Henry Gabriel, *The Course of American Democratic Thought: The Intellectual History since 1815* (New York: Ronald Press Co., 1940), pp. 341–44; Thomas G. Gossett, *Race: The History of an Idea in America* (New York: Schocken Books, 1965), pp. 185–90; Florette Henri, *Black Migration: Movement North, 1900–1920* (Garden City, N.Y.: Anchor Books/Doubleday, 1976), pp. 222–23; Richard Hofstadter, *Social Darwinism in American Thought*, rev. ed. (Boston: Beacon Press, 1955), pp. 178–79; Rayford Logan, *The Betrayal of the Negro: From Rutherford B. Hayes to Woodrow Wilson* (New York: Collier Books, 1965), pp. 172–73; Martin E. Marty, *Righteous Empire: The Protestant Experience in America* (New York: Harper and Row, 1970), p. 206; Marty, "Ethnicity: The Skeleton of Religion in America," *Church History* 41 (March 1972): 20; Michael McCarthy, *Dark Continent: Africa as Seen by Americans* (Westport, Conn.: Greenwood Press, 1983), p. 103; David Gordon Nielson, *Black Ethos: Northern Urban Life and Thought, 1890–1930* (Westport, Conn.: Greenwood Press, 1977), pp. 22–23; David M. Reimers, *White Protestantism and the Negro* (New York: Oxford University Press, 1965), p. 53; Jean Russell, *God's Lost Cause: A Study of the Church and the Racial Problem* (London: SCM Press, 1968), pp. 80–81; James Sellers, *The South and Christian Ethics* (New York: Association Press, 1962), pp. 72–73; Harvey Wish, *Society and Thought in Modern America: A Social and Intellectual History of the American People from 1865*, 2d ed.

(New York: David McKay Co., 1962), pp. 389–90; and Forrest G. Wood, *The Arrogance of Faith: Christianity and Race in America from the Colonial Era to the Twentieth Century* (New York: Alfred A. Knopf, 1990), pp. 378–79.

William A. Clebsch made exaggerated claims for Strong's racial enlightenment and Dorothea R. Muller offered his most spirited defense in Clebsch, *From Sacred to Profane America: The Role of Religion in American History* (New York: Harper and Row, 1968), pp. 23–24; Muller, "The Social Philosophy of Josiah Strong: Social Christianity and American Progressivism," *Church History* 28 (June 1959): 183–201; Muller, "Josiah Strong and American Nationalism: A Reevaluation," *Journal of American History* 53 (December 1966): 487–503; and Muller, "Josiah Strong and the Social Gospel: A Christian Response to the Challenge of the City," *Journal of Presbyterian History* 39 (September 1961): 150–75.

Robert T. Handy, Jurgen Herbst, Winthrop Hudson, Hans Kohn, and Paul R. Meyer wrote more even-handedly about Strong's cultural assimilationism in Handy, *A Christian America: Protestant Hopes and Historical Realities* (New York: Oxford University Press, 1971), pp. 179–80; Herbst, "Introduction," to Strong, *Our Country: Its Possible Future and Its Present Crisis* (Cambridge: Harvard University Press, 1963), pp. ix–xxvi; Hudson, *Religion in America*, 3d ed. (New York: Charles Scribner's Sons, 1981), pp. 322–23; Kohn, *American Nationalism: An Interpretative Essay* (New York: Macmillan, 1957), pp. 157–60, 251–52; and Meyer, "The Fear of Cultural Decline: Josiah Strong's Thought about Reform and Expansion," *Church History* 43 (September 1973): 396–405.

3. Berge, "Josiah Strong: An American Paradox," p. 5; Elsie Strong and Margary Strong, "Biography of Josiah Strong" (unpublished manuscript), 2:15, 3:1–3, 9–10, 14–16; and Josiah Strong, "The Relation of the Races," Sagamore Sociological Conference, 1910, Josiah Strong Papers, Union Theological Seminary, New York.

4. Josiah Strong to Sixty Nine, 12 November 1869; Strong, "Manuscript Biography," 4:23, 6:7–8, Strong Papers; Berge, "Josiah Strong," pp. 8–9; and Strong, *Our Country: Its Possible Future and Its Present Crisis* (New York: Baker and Taylor Co., 1885).

5. Strong, *Our Country* (1963 edition), pp. xvii, 200–202, 205. See also ibid., pp. 13–186; and Strong, *The New Era; or, The Coming Kingdom* (New York: Baker and Taylor Co., 1893), pp. 54, 69–71, 354.

6. Strong, *Our Country* (1963 edition), pp. 212–17. See also Strong, *New Era*, pp. 79–80. For other white and black social gospel prophets' predictions of racial extinction, see Adolphus Julius Frederick Behrends, *The World for Christ: A Series of Addresses on Missions, Delivered at Syracuse University on the Graves Foundation, 1896* (New York: Eaton and Mains, 1896), pp. 97–98; and Kelly Miller, "The Ultimate Race Problem," *Atlantic Monthly* 103 (April 1909): 539–42.

7. Strong, *Our Country* (1963 edition), pp. 210–11, 215; Strong, *New Era*, pp. 54–55; and Strong, *Religious Movements for Social Betterment* (New York: Baker and Taylor Co., 1900), pp. 54, 90–97.

8. Myron W. Adams, *A History of Atlanta University* (Atlanta: Atlanta University Press, 1930), p. 22; Clarence A. Bacote, *The Story of Atlanta University: A Century of Service, 1865–1965* (Atlanta: Atlanta University, 1969), p. 85; Josiah Strong, "North America and the World's Future," *Our Day* 10 (August 1892): 608; Strong, *New Era*, pp. 77–78, 80; "Miss Mary A. Strong," *American Missionary* 48 (May 1894): 188–89; "Mary A. Strong Memorial," Josiah

Strong to Margary Strong, 2 February 1914, Strong Papers; and Elsie Strong to the author, 29 September 1967. For the combination of Anglo-Saxon triumphalism and a strong assertion of black civil and political equality, see also J. Will Jackson, "The Future and the Negro," *Christian Educator* 3 (October 1891): 294–97.

9. I. D. Barnett [Ida B. Wells-Barnett?], "Emigration," *AME Church Review* 12 (October 1895): 222; J. W. E. Bowen, "Why?," *Christian Educator* 4 (October 1892): 6; and Alexander Crummell, *Africa and America: Addresses and Discourses* (Springfield, Mass.: Willey and Co., 1891), p. 46. In Reverdy Ransom, "The Negro and Socialism," *AME Church Review* 13 (October 1896): 193, it is unclear whether Ransom refers to Josiah Strong or to Benjamin Kidd as "one of the clearest and profoundest writers on social and industrial questions." On Crummell, see Wilson J. Moses, "Civilizing Missionary: A Study of Alexander Crummell," *Journal of Negro History* 60 (April 1975): 229–51; Moses, "Cambridge Platonism in the Republic of Liberia, 1853–1873: Alexander Crummell's Theory of Development and Culture Transfer," *New England Journal of Black Studies* 3 (1983): 2–11; and Moses, *Alexander Crummell: A Study of Civilization and Discontent* (New York: Oxford University Press, 1988).

10. Theophilus Gould Steward, *The End of the World; or, Clearing the Way for the Fullness of the Gentiles* (Philadelphia: AME Book Rooms, 1888), pp. 71–77. Steward had his own eschatological agenda to substitute for Josiah Strong's Anglo-Saxon vision. It suggested that, aided by other ethnic groups, the Anglo-Saxon had reached fruition in the United States; that there would be a clash of nations in which Christianity would be freed of its bondage to the clan principle; and that "new nations, born as it were in a day, will come out of darkness and walk in the light of the one great God, with whom there are no superior races and no inferior races." Ibid., pp. 79–99, 119–27. I am grateful to Professor David Wills of Amherst College for calling my attention to Steward's critique of *Our Country*. See also James Weldon Johnson, *The Autobiography of an Ex-Coloured Man* (Boston: Sherman, French and Co., 1912), pp. 162–63.

11. "Shall We Anglo-Saxonize or Christianize," *Voice of the Negro* 2 (July 1905): 492–93.

12. Josiah Strong, "The American Institute for Social Service," *Social Service* 6 (October 1902): 65–71; and Strong, *Inaugural Address* (New York: American Institute for Social Service, 1903). His supporters in the Southern education coalition included William H. Baldwin, Charles W. Dabney, Charles W. Eliot, Charles D. McIver, Robert C. Ogden, Walter Hines Page, Francis Greenwood Peabody, George Foster Peabody, Albert Shaw, and Booker T. Washington. See Josiah Strong to Booker T. Washington, 15 November 1905, Washington to Strong, 18 November 1905, Booker T. Washington Papers, Library of Congress; Robert C. Ogden to W. H. Tolman, 26 February 1903, Letterbook, box 13, Strong to Ogden, 14 April 1906, box 9, Robert C. Ogden Papers, Library of Congress; Washington, "What Has the Negro Been Doing?," in *Social Progress: A Year Book and Encyclopedia of Economic, Industrial, Social, and Religious Statistics*, 1905, ed. Josiah Strong (New York: Baker and Taylor Co., 1905), pp. 145–47; ibid., 1906, pp. 172–74; and Strong, "The Negro in the United States," *Homiletic Review* 70 (August 1915): 135–36.

13. "Two Typical Leaders," *Outlook* 74 (23 May 1903): 215; Lyman Abbott, "The Race Problem in the United States," *Review of Reviews* 28 (September 1903): 321–25; and George Harris, *Inequality and Progress* (Boston: Houghton, Mifflin, and Co., 1897), p. 18.

See also "Booker T. Washington on Our Racial Problem," *Outlook* 64 (6 January 1900): 15; "Higher Education for Negroes," *Outlook* 64 (13 January 1900): 97–98; "Education North and South," *Outlook* 68 (11 May 1901): 103–5; Abbott, "Higher Education, Too," *Southern Education* 1 (21 December 1903): 416–17; Abbott, "Christianity, First for the Negro," *Southern Workman* 24 (December 1905): 681; Abbott, "The Qualifications of a Leader," *Southern Workman* 26 (February 1906): 73–76; and Abbott, *The Twentieth Century Crusade* (New York: Macmillan, 1918), pp. 67–68.

14. Strong, *Expansion under New World-Conditions* (New York: Baker and Taylor Co., 1900), pp. 34–41; Strong, *The Next Great Awakening* (New York: Baker and Taylor Co., 1902), p. 190; Strong, "Introduction," in "Africa's Appeal to Christendom," by Momolu Massaquoi, *Century* 69 (April 1905): 927–28; McCarthy, *Dark Continent*, pp. 103, 148–49; and Strong, *Our World: The New World-Life* (Garden City, N.Y.: Doubleday, Page and Co., 1913), pp. 168, 174–75. See also Francis J. Grimké, "Fifty Years of Freedom," in *The Works of Francis J. Grimké*, 4 vols., ed. Carter G. Woodson (Washington, D.C.: Associated Publishers, 1942), 1:515; Strong, "After the War, What?," *Gospel of the Kingdom* 7 (January 1915): 13; Strong, "The Race Problem," *Homiletic Review* 70 (August 1915): 133–36; and Strong, "Christian Cosmopolitanism: The Contribution of the Races," *Homiletic Review* 70 (September 1915): 219–25.

15. Strong, "Relation of the Races," p. 49; Strong, *The Challenge of the City* (New York: American Baptist Home Mission Society, 1907), pp. 152, 205–6; Strong, "The Race Question," *Homiletic Review* 58 (August 1909): 128–29; Strong, *The Social Center Movement: Address Delivered to the First National Conference on Civic and Social Center Development, Madison, Wis., Oct. 25, 1911* (Madison: University of Wisconsin, 1911), pp. 6–9; Strong, *Our World: The New World-Religion* (New York: Doubleday, Page and Co., 1915), p. 263; and Strong, "Race Problem," pp. 16–20, unpublished manuscript, apparently cut from the text of *Our World: The New World-Life*, Strong Papers. See also Strong, *Our World: The New World-Life*, pp. 90–91, 159–67; 204–6, 218–20; and Strong, "Race Problem," pp. 130–33, 136–37.

16. Royce, *The Hope of the Great Community* (New York: Macmillan, 1916), pp. 122–23; and Josiah Royce, unpublished manuscript, quoted in Powell, *Josiah Royce* (New York: Twayne Publishers, 1974), pp. 5–6. John Clendenning, *The Life and Thought of Josiah Royce* (Madison: University of Wisconsin Press, 1985), and Bruce Kuklick, *Josiah Royce: An Intellectual Biography* (Indianapolis: Bobbs-Merrill, 1972), are helpful biographies.

17. Powell, *Josiah Royce*, pp. 13–14; Royce, *Hope of the Great Community*, p. 128; and John Clendenning, "Introduction," in *The Letters of Josiah Royce*, ed. John Clendenning (Chicago: University of Chicago Press, 1970), pp. 16–19.

18. Royce, *Race Questions, Provincialism, and Other American Problems* (New York: Macmillan, 1908), p. vii; John Jay Chapman, "Portrait of Josiah Royce, the Philosopher," *Outlook* 120 (2 July 1919): 377; and Bruce Kuklick, *The Rise of American Philosophy: Cambridge, Massachusetts, 1860–1930* (New Haven: Yale University Press, 1977), pp. 306–7.

19. Clendenning, "Introduction," p. 36; Royce to Frank Thilly, 17 November 1908, in Clendenning, *Letters of Josiah Royce*, p. 533, 533n; and Royce, *The Philosophy of Loyalty* (New York: Macmillan, 1908), pp. vii, 15–17, 138, 156, 196, 214. See also Royce, *Philosophy of Loyalty*, pp. 19–20, 51–52, 202–3; Royce, *Race Questions*, pp. 80–108; Royce, *Hope of the Great Community*, p. 45; Michael D. Clark, "Josiah Royce and American Conservatism,"

*Modern Age* 13 (Fall 1969): 342–51; Earl Pomeroy, "Josiah Royce, Historian in Quest of Community," *Pacific Historical Review* 40 (February 1971): 1–20; and John J. McDermott, "Josiah Royce's Philosophy of the Community: Danger of the Detached Individual," in *American Philosophy*, ed. Marcus G. Singer (Cambridge: Cambridge University Press, 1985), pp. 153–76.

20. Josiah Royce, "Race Questions and Prejudice," *International Journal of Ethics* 16 (April 1906): 265–88, as reprinted in Royce, *Race Questions*, pp. 3–53; Royce to George Platt Brett, 14 July 1908, Brett to Royce, 16 July 1908, and Royce to Brett, 21 July 1908, in Clendenning, *Letters of Josiah Royce*, pp. 523–26; and Royce, *Race Questions*, pp. 5–6, 8–9. Studies of Royce and of American racial thought largely ignore this essay. L. Moodey Simms, Jr., "Josiah Royce and the Southern Race Question," *Mississippi Quarterly* 21 (Winter 1969): 71–74, has little to say, but see William T. Fontaine, "Josiah Royce and the American Race Problem," *Philosophy and Phenomenological Research* 29 (December 1968): 282–88; and Werner Sollors, *Beyond Ethnicity: Consent and Descent in American Culture* (New York: Oxford University Press, 1986), pp. 179–95.

21. Royce, *Race Questions*, pp. 14–29. See also Charles M. Bakewell, "Royce as an Interpreter of American Ideals," *International Journal of Ethics* 27 (April 1917): 314–15. For other references to Jamaica as a positive model for race relations, see Julius Mortzen, "Has Jamaica Solved the Color Problem," *Gunton's Magazine* 20 (January 1901): 31–46; "Mr. Washington on the Jamaica Color Problem," *Gunton's Magazine* 20 (May 1901): 464; "The Race Problem Solved in Jamaica," *Review of Reviews* 33 (May 1906): 623–24; Frank Jewett Mather, "An Object Lesson in the Solution of Race Problems," *Arena* 36 (October 1906): 364–69; and James L. Hill, "Not Negro Churches, but Churches," *American Missionary* 66 (January 1912): 579–83.

22. Royce, *Race Questions*, pp. 31–40.

23. Ibid., pp. 40–47.

24. Ibid., p. 53; Josiah Royce to Washington Gladden, 3 November 1913, box 14, no. 288, Gladden Papers, Ohio Historical Society; Royce, *The Problem of Christianity* (Chicago: University of Chicago Press, 1968), pp. 125, 139–40, 196–98, 318–19, 403–4; and Royce, *Hope of the Great Community*, pp. 36–37. For fuller discussions of Royce's understanding of the "Beloved Community," see John E. Smith, "Introduction," in Royce, *Problem of Christianity*, pp. 9–11, 15; Smith, *Royce's Social Infinite: The Community of Interpretation* (New York: Liberal Arts Press, 1950), pp. 126–61; and Peter Fuss, *The Moral Philosophy of Josiah Royce* (Cambridge: Harvard University Press, 1965), pp. 228–57.

25. Booker T. Washington to Oswald Garrison Villard, 20 April 1906, Washington Papers; Mary White Ovington to W. E. B. Du Bois, 20 May 1906, in *The Correspondence of W. E. B. Du Bois*, 3 vols., ed. Herbert Aptheker (Amherst: University of Massachusetts Press, 1973), 1:120–21; Mary White Ovington, "Two Books on American Race Problems," *Survey* 22 (5 June 1909): 352; [W. E. B. Du Bois], "Josiah Royce," *Crisis* 13 (November 1916): 10; Willis Duke Weatherford, *Negro Life in the South: Present Conditions and Needs* (New York: Association Press, 1910), p. 180; and Edgar Gardner Murphy, *The Basis of Ascendancy: A Discussion of Certain Principles of Public Policy Involved in the Development of the Southern States* (New York: Longmans, Green, and Co., 1908), pp. xiii, xvi–xviii. See also John Haynes Holmes, *The Disfranchisement of the Negro* (New York: National Association

for the Advancement of Colored People, 1910), pp. 14–15. Murphy's further reply to Royce, "Are There Lessons in Jamaica?," in his *Issues Southern and National*, was unfinished and the volume unpublished when Murphy died in 1913. See Murphy, *Basis of Ascendancy*, p. xiiin; and Hugh C. Bailey, *Edgar Gardner Murphy: Gentle Progressive* (Coral Gables, Fla.: University of Miami Press, 1968), p. 243n.

26. Francis Greenwood Peabody to Murphy, 20 February 1908, and 16 November 1909, Robert Russa Moton to Murphy, 22 September 1909, and Lyman Abbott to Murphy, 18 April 1912, Edgar Gardner Murphy Papers, Southern Historical Collection, University of North Carolina, Chapel Hill; Washington Gladden, *Recollections* (Boston: Houghton Mifflin Co., 1909), p. 370; Thomas Wentworth Higginson, "Introduction," in *The Aftermath of Slavery: A Study of the Condition and Environment of the American Negro*, by William A. Sinclair (Boston: Small, Maynard and Co., 1905), pp. xi–xiii; Josiah Strong, "The Race Problem," *Homiletic Review* 70 (August 1915): 136; Booker T. Washington, "The Negro and the 'Solid' South," *Independent* 67 (25 November 1909): 1195–99; Weatherford, *Negro Life in the South*, p. 179; and Mary White Ovington, "The Basis of Ascendancy," *Survey* 23 (6 November 1909): 169–70. For a variety of interpretations of Murphy's career, see Virginius Dabney, *Liberalism in the South* (Chapel Hill: University of North Carolina Press, 1932), pp. 240–43; Allen J. Going, "The Reverend Edgar Gardner Murphy: His Ideas and Influence," *Historical Magazine of the Protestant Episcopal Church* 25 (December 1956): 391–402; Daniel Levine, "Reform and the Elite: Edgar Gardner Murphy," in *Varieties of Reform Thought* (Madison: State Historical Society of Wisconsin, 1964), pp. 78–94; Jack Temple Kirby, *Darkness at the Dawning: Race and Reform in the Progressive South* (Philadelphia: J. P. Lippincott Co., 1972), pp. 59–72; Ronald C. White, "Beyond the Sacred: Edgar Gardner Murphy and a Ministry of Social Reform," *Historical Magazine of the Protestant Episcopal Church* 49 (March 1980): 51–69; Joel Williamson, *The Crucible of Race: Black-White Relations in the American Souls since Emancipation* (New York: Oxford University Press, 1984), pp. 415–58; and Ralph E. Luker, *A Southern Tradition in Theology and Social Criticism, 1830–1930: The Religious Liberalism and Social Conservatism of James Warley Miles, William Porcher DuBose, and Edgar Gardner Murphy* (New York: Edwin Mellen Press, 1984), pp. 287–377.

27. Bailey, *Edgar Gardner Murphy*, pp. 1–20; and Luker, *A Southern Tradition*, pp. 185–311, 379–423.

28. Edgar Gardner Murphy, *The Larger Life: Sermons and an Essay* (New York: Longmans, Green, and Co., 1897), pp. 182–86; and Murphy, "Self-Fulfillment," *Homiletic Review* 26 (October 1893): 328. See also Luker, *A Southern Tradition*, pp. 295–301.

29. Murphy, *The Larger Life*, pp. 11–13, 24–25, 45, 49–50, 59–60, 62, 112, 125–27, 129–30, 158–60; Murphy, *Basis of Ascendancy*, p. 31; Murphy, *Problems of the Present South: A Discussion of the Educational, Industrial, and Political Issues in the Southern States* (New York: Macmillan, 1904), pp. ix, 8, 163–64; and Murphy, *The Task of the South: An Address before the Faculty and Students of Washington and Lee University, Lexington, Virginia. December 10th, A.D. 1902* (Montgomery, Ala.: n.p., 1903), pp. 7–8. See also Murphy, *Words for the Church* (New York: James Pott and Co., 1897), pp. 1–2; Murphy, *Problems of the Present South*, pp. 13, 49, 81–82; Murphy to Felix Adler, 27 May 1907, Murphy Papers; and Luker, *A Southern Tradition*, pp. 302–17. For the Burkean influence on Murphy, see Murphy, "The Task of the Leader,"

Sewanee Review 15 (January 1907): 4; Murphy, *Basis of Ascendancy*, p. 57; and Edward N. Sheppard to Murphy, 19 May 1904, Murphy Papers.

30. Bailey, *Edgar Gardner Murphy*, pp. 65–108, 138–85; Luker, *A Southern Tradition*, pp. 328–52; Louis R. Harlan, *Separate and Unequal: Public School Campaigns and Racism in the Southern Seaboard States, 1901–1915* (Chapel Hill: University of North Carolina Press, 1958); and Murphy, *Basis of Ascendancy*, pp. 112–13, 115–16.

31. Murphy, *The White Man and the Negro at the South: An Address Delivered under Invitation of the American Academy of Political and Social Science, the American Society for the Extension of University Teaching, and the Civic Club of Philadelphia in the Church of the Holy Trinity, Philadelphia, on the Evening of March 8th, A.D. 1900* (n.p., n.d.), p. 19; and Murphy, *Basis of Ascendancy*, pp. xii–xiii, xxii, 79. See also Luker, *A Southern Tradition*, pp. 76–81, 278–79, 320–22, 356–58.

32. Murphy, *Basis of Ascendancy*, pp. 77–81; and Murphy, *White Man and the Negro*, pp. 19, 45–46. See also Murphy, *Problems of the Present South*, pp. 34–37, 63–64; and Murphy, "Task of the Leader," pp. 6–7.

33. Murphy, *Basis of Ascendancy*, pp. 40–41, 104, 107, 126–27, 166; and Murphy, *Task of the South*, pp. 9–11. See also Murphy, *Basis of Ascendancy*, pp. 42–43, 53–56, 94, 112–16; and Murphy, *Task of the South*, pp. 5–7.

34. Murphy, *Basis of Ascendancy*, pp. 12, 16, 19–20, 62–64, 130–31. See also ibid., pp. 226–35; Murphy, *White Man and the Negro*, pp. 21, 27–36; Murphy, "Shall the Fourteenth Amendment Be Enforced?," *North American Review* 180 (January 1905): 109–33; and Bailey, *Edgar Gardner Murphy*, pp. 55–63. On the distinction between "emancipation" and "liberation," see Ross Evans Paulson, *Women's Suffrage and Prohibition: A Comparative Study of Equality and Social Control* (Glenview, Ill.: Scott, Foresman and Co., 1973), p. 7.

35. Murphy, *Basis of Ascendancy*, pp. 222–23; see also pp. 57, 195–96, 201–5, 248.

36. Ibid., pp. 26, 29–32, 34. Williamson, *Crucible of Race*, pp. 111–323, is the best study of the era's radical racists, stressing the psychosexual rather than the mythical character of radical racism. Arkansas's Marxist Episcopal Bishop William Montgomery Brown, the Southern Presbyterians' Alexander Jeffrey McKelway, Georgia's Mrs. L. H. Harris, and the Southern Methodists' Alexander Harvey Shannon were other religious radical racists. On Brown, see Brown, *The Crucial Race Question: or, When and How Shall the Color Line Be Drawn* (Little Rock: The Arkansas Churchman's Publishing Co., 1907); Brown, *My Heresy* (New York: John Day Co., 1926); Brown, *The American Race Problem* (Galion, Ohio: The Bradford-Brown Educational Co., 1930); E. Clowes Chorley, "The Church in Arkansas and Its Bishops," *Historical Magazine of the Protestant Episcopal Church* 15 (December 1946): 345–47; and John L. Kyser, "The Deposition of Bishop William Montgomery Brown in New Orleans, 1925," *Louisiana History* 8 (Winter 1967): 35–52. On McKelway, see chapter 8, n. 9. On Mrs. Harris, see Harris, "A Southern Woman's Point of View," *Independent* 51 (18 May 1899): 1354–55; and Harris, "Negro Womanhood," *Independent* 51 (22 June 1899): 1687–89. On Shannon, see Shannon, "The Racial Integrity of the Negro," *Methodist Quarterly Review* 55 (July 1906): 525–38; and Shannon, *Racial Integrity and Other Features of the Negro Problem* (Nashville: Press of the ME Church, South, 1907).

37. A. R. Allen, "Thomas Dixon, Jr. and Political Religion: From Social Reformer to Racist," *Foundations* 14 (April–June 1971): 136–52; Maxwell Bloomfield, "Dixon's *The*

*Leopard's Spots: A Study in Popular Racism*," *American Quarterly* 16 (Fall 1964): 387–401; Everett Carter, "Cultural History Written with Lightning: The Significance of *The Birth of a Nation*," *American Quarterly* 12 (Fall 1960): 347–57; Raymond Allen Cook, *Fire from the Flint: The Amazing Careers of Thomas Dixon* (Winston-Salem, N.C.: John F. Blair, 1968); Cook, *Thomas Dixon* (New York: Twayne Publishers, 1974); F. Garvin Davenport, Jr., "Thomas Dixon's Mythology of Southern History," *Journal of Southern History* 36 (August 1970): 350–67; Max Frank Harris, "The Ideas of Thomas Dixon on Race Relations" (M.A. thesis, University of North Carolina, Chapel Hill, 1948); Williamson, *Crucible of Race*, pp. 140–79; and J. Zebulon Wright, "Thomas Dixon: The Mind of a Southern Apologist" (Ph.D. dissertation, George Peabody College for Teachers, 1966).

38. Cook, *Fire from the Flint*, pp. 3–34; and Cook, *Thomas Dixon*, pp. 19–31.

39. Cook, *Fire from the Flint*, pp. 67–72; and Cook, *Thomas Dixon*, pp. 40–41.

40. Dixon, "The Southern Question: Some Difficulties of the Situation," in *Living Problems in Religion and Social Science*, 2d ed. (New York: Funk and Wagnalls, 1892), pp. 244–53; Dixon, "When Will the Negro Be Free?," *Christian Union* 41 (22 May 1890): 729–30; and "Editorial," *Christian Union* 41 (22 May 1890): 725. See also Yeoman, "The 'Ignorant Negro' and the 'Vagabond Indian,'" *Christian Union* 42 (10 July 1890): 58; and H. Shelton Smith, *In His Image, But . . . : Racism in Southern Religion, 1780–1910* (Durham, N.C.: Duke University Press, 1972), pp. 275–76.

41. Dixon, *The Failure of Protestantism in New York and Its Causes* (New York: Victor O. A. Strauss, 1896), pp. 54, 56; and Dixon, *Dixon on Ingersoll: Ten Discourses Delivered in Association Hall, New York* (New York: John B. Alden, 1892), pp. 148–50. See also Dixon, "Christian Union," *Homiletic Review* 20 (December 1890): 513; and Dixon, *Dixon on Ingersoll*, pp. 141, 183–84.

42. Allen, "Thomas Dixon, Jr. and Political Religion," pp. 136–52; Cook, *Fire from the Flint*, pp. 76–95; and Cook, *Thomas Dixon*, pp. 41–50.

43. Dixon, *The One Woman: A Story of a Modern Utopia* (New York: Doubleday, Page and Co., 1903). Contrast Cook, *Fire from the Flint*, pp. 122–26, and Cook, *Thomas Dixon*, p. 82, with John Spargo, "Views and Reviews," *Comrad* 2 (September 1903): 281–82; Upton Sinclair, *The Brass Check: A Study of American Journalism* (Pasadena, Calif.: The Author, 1920), pp. 114–15; and Phyllis Ann Nelson, "George D. Herron and the Socialist Clergy, 1890–1914" (Ph.D. dissertation, State University of Iowa, 1953), p. 314.

44. Dixon, *Dixon's Sermons* (New York: F. L. Bussey and Co., 1899), pp. 11, 26–37, 86, 112–20.

45. James M. McPherson, *The Abolitionist Legacy: From Reconstruction to the NAACP* (Princeton: Princeton University Press, 1975), pp. 340–41; William Hannibal Thomas, *The American Negro: What He Was, What He Is, and What He May Become: A Critical and Practical Discussion* (New York: Macmillan, 1901), pp. xi–xviii; and "Book Notices," *Our Day* 5 (June 1890): 500–502. See also Thomas, "The Democratic Return to Power," *AME Church Review* 1 (January 1885): 225–27; Thomas, "Shall Negroes Become Landowners," *AME Church Review* 3 (July 1887): 481–91; Thomas, "Some Observations on Southern Industrial Development," *AME Church Review* 4 (January 1888): 259–68; Thomas, "Toil and Trust," *AME Church Review* 4 (April 1888): 367–76; Thomas, "Till Another King Arose,

Which Knew Not Joseph," *AME Church Review* 5 (October 1888): 332–43; Thomas, *Land and Education: A Critical and Practical Discussion of the Mental and Physical Needs of the Negro* (Boston: Wallace Spooner, 1890); and Thomas, "Religious Characteristics of the Negro," *AME Church Review* 9 (April 1893): 388–402.

46. Reverdy Ransom, "Noted Here and There within the Sphere," *AME Church Review* 30 (April 1914): 355; and Thomas, *American Negro*, pp. x, xxiii, 21, 117, 122, 179, 405.

47. Ransom, "Noted Here and There," p. 355; Alexander Walters, "Negro Progress," *Independent* 53 (21 March 1901): 651–52; Richard R. Wright, Jr., review of *American Negro*, by Thomas, *American Journal of Sociology* 6 (May 1901): 849–52; Silas Xavier Floyd, *Life of Charles T. Walker* (New York: National Baptist Publishing Board, 1902), p. 143; and John Edward Bruce to Booker T. Washington, 20 March 1901, in *The Booker T. Washington Papers*, 14 vols., ed. Louis R. Harlan et al. (Urbana: University of Illinois Press, 1972–89), 6:56n. See also "Negro Women," *Independent* 53 (14 March 1901): 633; Kelly Miller, *Race Adjustment: Essays on the Negro in America* (New York: Neale Publishing Co., 1908), p. 96; and Helen M. Chesnutt, *Charles Waddell Chesnutt: Pioneer of the Color Line* (Chapel Hill: University of North Carolina Press, 1952), pp. 159–63.

48. John R. Commons, "The Negro," *Chautauquan* 38 (November 1903): 234; Review of *American Negro*, by Thomas, *Outlook* 67 (26 January 1901): 229; [Jenkin Lloyd Jones], "The Souls of Black Folk," *Unity* 51 (7 May 1903): 148; Ovington, "Reminiscences," *Baltimore Afro-American*, 1 October 1932; "The American Negro," *Independent* 53 (14 February 1901): 393; Edgar Gardner Murphy, "Thomas on Negroes," *New York Times*, 24 February 1901; Shannon, *Racial Integrity*; Robert Wilson Shufeldt, *The Negro: A Menace to American Civilization* (Boston: Richard G. Gadger, 1907), pp. 49–50, 93–96, 139–45, 161; Robert C. Ogden to Booker T. Washington, 21 May 1904, Ogden to Washington, 2 June 1904, Ogden to Thomas Nelson Page, 1 July 1904, and Ogden to Kelly Miller, 24 October 1904, Letterbook, box 14, Ogden Papers, Library of Congress; Robert W. Taylor to Washington, 6 May 1904, Washington to Taylor, 8 May 1904, Taylor to Washington, 10 May 1904, and Ogden to Washington, 27 May 1904, Washington Papers; and Ransom, "Noted Here and There," p. 355. See also William Hayes Ward to Francis J. Grimké, 21 February 1901, in Woodson, *Works of Francis J. Grimké*, 4:69; George R. Stetson, "The Racial Problem," *Liberia* 20 (February 1902): 43–45; "The American Negro," *Outlook* 67 (30 March 1901): 733–36; Murphy to Booker T. Washington, 20 March 1901, in Harlan et al., *Booker T. Washington Papers*, 6:53–54; Bailey, *Edgar Gardner Murphy*, p. 55; Albert Bushnell Hart, *The Southern South* (New York: D. Appleton and Co., 1910), p. 15; and Weatherford, *Negro Life in the South*, p. 180.

49. Dixon, *The Life Worth Living: A Personal Experience* (New York: Doubleday, Page and Co., 1914); Cook, *Fire from the Flint*, pp. 95–112; and Harris, "Ideas of Thomas Dixon on Race Relations," p. 58.

50. Willie Lee Rose, "Race and Region in American Historical Fiction: Four Episodes in Popular Culture," in *Region, Race, and Reconstruction: Essays in Honor of C. Vann Woodward*, ed. J. Morgan Kousser and James M. McPherson (New York: Oxford University Press, 1982), pp. 113–39. See also Thomas Dixon, Jr. to Albion Tourgée, 25 February 1888, no. 3368; E. H. Johnson, " 'The Leopard's Spots' and 'The Fool's Errand,' " [*Baptist Watch-*

man?], 24 April 1902, no. 9689; and Tourgée to E. H. Johnson, 15 May 1902, no. 9691, Albion Tourgée Papers, Southern Historical Collection, University of North Carolina, Chapel Hill.

51. "The Negro a Menace Says Thomas Dixon," *New York Times*, 9 June 1903, p. 2; and Bloomfield, "Dixon's The Leopard's Spots," p. 395. Williamson's brilliant portrait of Dixon's complex character ignores his racial conservatism prior to 1898 and does not explain his transition to racial radicalism by 1901. See Williamson, *Crucible of Race*, pp. 140–76.

52. Dixon, *The Clansman: An Historical Romance of the Ku Klux Klan* (New York: Doubleday, Page and Co., 1905), p. 282; and Dixon, *The Leopard's Spots: A Romance of the White Man's Burden, 1865–1900* (New York: Doubleday, Page and Co., 1902), pp. 5, 33. See also Dixon, *Leopard's Spots*, pp. 95–96, 119, 337. Like the Jewish immigrant, the Yankee intruder, such as Phil Stoneman, could be assimilated, whereas the black freedman could not. See Dixon, *Clansman*, p. 276.

53. Dixon, *Clansman*, pp. 248–50, 290, 216–17, 304. See also ibid., pp. 294, 323; and Dixon, *Leopard's Spots*, pp. 149, 379.

54. Dixon, *Clansman*, pp. 79, 93–94; and Dixon, *Leopard's Spots*, pp. 149, 196, 368–74. See also Dixon, *Clansman*, pp. 145, 156, 162, 208, 273–74; and George M. Fredrickson, *The Black Image in the White Mind: The Debate on Afro-American Character and Destiny, 1817–1914* (New York: Harper and Row, 1971), pp. 280–81.

55. Cook, *Fire from the Flint*, pp. 135–55.

56. Dixon, *The Sins of the Father: A Romance of the South* (New York: D. Appleton and Co., 1912), pp. 25, 34, 36–37, 97, 401.

57. John Edward Bruce, "Color Prejudice among Negroes," in *The Selected Writings of John Edward Bruce: Militant Black Journalist*, ed. Peter Gilbert (New York: Arno Press, 1971), p. 126. This adds a new dimension to Williamson's colorful psychoanalytic portrait of Thomas Dixon. See Williamson, *Crucible of Race*, pp. 158–76.

58. Dixon, "Booker T. Washington and the Negro: Some Dangerous Aspects of the Work at Tuskegee," *Saturday Evening Post* 178 (19 August 1905): 1–2; "A Dixon Pamphlet Stirs Negro Clergy," *New York Times*, 18 December 1905, p. 4; Louis R. Harlan, *Booker T. Washington*, 2 vols. (New York: Oxford University Press, 1972–83), 2:431–32; Dixon, as quoted in Harris, "Ideas of Thomas Dixon on Race Relations," p. 37 and Sinclair, *Aftermath of Slavery*, p. 222; and Turner, as quoted in Edwin S. Redkey, *Black Exodus: Black Nationalist and Back-to-Africa Movements, 1890–1910* (New Haven: Yale University Press, 1969), p. 277. Dixon's later attack on Washington as "a notorious negro of doubtful moral character" is in Dixon, *Sins of the Father*, pp. 197–210.

59. Thomas Dixon, Jr., to Rolfe Cobleigh, 27 March 1915; Rolfe Cobleigh to Mary White Ovington, 30 March 1915; Rolfe Cobleigh to May Childs Nerney, 30 March 1915; May Childs Nerney to Charles H. Parkhurst, 2 April 1915; May Childs Nerney to Butler R. Wilson, [5 April 1915]; "The Birth of a Nation," clipping from *The Congregationalist and Christian World* (22 April 1915): 496; May Childs Nerney to Rolfe Cobleigh, 26 April 1915; and Charles S. McFarland to May Childs Nerney, 29 April 1915, series C, nos. 299–300, NAACP Papers.

60. Jenkin Lloyd Jones, "The Souls of Black Folk," *Unity* 51 (7 May 1903): 148; Thomas

Wentworth Higginson, "Introduction," in Sinclair, *Aftermath of Slavery*, p. xi; Ernest Howard Crosby, *Garrison the Non-Resistant* (Chicago: Public Publishing Co., 1905), pp. 109–15; and Algernon Sydney Crapsey, "The Duty of the White Man of the North to the Black Man of the South," in *How to Solve the Race Problem: The Proceedings of the Washington Conference on the Race Problem in the United States under the Auspices of the National Sociological Society Held at the Lincoln Temple Congregational Church; at the Nineteenth Street Baptist Church and at the Metropolitan A.M.E. Church, Washington, D.C., November 9, 10, 11, and 12, 1903* (Washington, D.C.: R. Beresford, 1904), p. 233. See also "The Leopard's Spots," *Independent* 54 (26 June 1902): 1548–49; Benjamin Orange Flower, "Books of the Day," *Arena* 28 (August 1902): 217–18; "Mr. Dixon Once More," *Independent* 55 (3 September 1903): 2116–18; "The Negro and His Creator," *Outlook* 77 (16 July 1904): 635–36; "The Clansman," *Independent* 58 (9 February 1905): 325–26; H. M. Hamill, "The Southern Labor Problem," *Methodist Review* 56 (April 1907): 309; Hart, *Southern South*, pp. 9–10, 360–61; Charles Edward Stowe, "The Religion of Slavery," *Crisis* 5 (November 1912): 37–38; and "Progressive Protest against Anti-Negro Film," *Survey* 34 (5 June 1915): 209–10.

61. Sinclair, *Aftermath of Slavery*, p. 222; Kelly Miller, "As to the Leopard's Spots," in Miller, *Race Adjustment*, pp. 28–56; and T. S. Inborden to Henry Churchill King, 11 April 1912, Henry Churchill King Papers, Oberlin College. See also Reverdy Cassius Ransom, "Race Problem in Christian State" [sic], in *The Spirit of Freedom and Justice: Orations and Speeches* (Nashville: AME Sunday School Union, 1926), pp. 128–37.

62. But, see Robert T. Handy, "George D. Herron and the Kingdom Movement," *Church History* 19 (June 1950): 110; McPherson, *Abolitionist Legacy*, pp. 346–48; and, on his later career, Edmund deS. Brunner, "Harlan Paul Douglass: Pioneer Researcher in the Sociology of Religion," *Review of Religious Research* 1 (Summer and Fall 1959): 3–16, 63–75; and Frederick A. Shippey, "The Concept of Church in H. Paul Douglass," *Review of Religious Research* 4 (Spring 1963): 155–71.

63. Hale Douglass, "The Life and Labors, the Lamentations and the Longings of a Librarian, as Related by Himself in Ten Minutes," pp. 1–2; Grace Douglass Orr, "Growing Up in Grinnell, Post-Cyclone Years: 1882–1902," pp. 51–63, Harlan Paul Douglass Papers, Amistad Research Center. See also Ralph E. Luker, "The Northern Social Gospel Prophets and the Negro: 1890–1917" (M.A. thesis, University of North Carolina, Chapel Hill, 1969), pp. 161–236.

64. "Rev. H. Paul Douglass, D. D., Educational Superintendent in the Field," *American Missionary* 60 (October 1906): 232; George A. Gates, *Personality: The Ultimate Fact of Philosophy and Life. Baccalaureate Address* (Grinnell: Iowa College, 1889); H. Paul Douglass, "The Kingdom of God—A Resume of the Teachings of Professor George D. Herron. D.D.," *Our Day* 14 (1895): 274–86; and Harlan Paul Douglass, *Christian Reconstruction in the South* (Boston: Pilgrim Press, 1909), pp. 203–4. See also Handy, "Herron and the Kingdom Movement"; and Herbert Romaine Dietrich, Jr., "Radical on the Campus: Professor Herron at Iowa College, 1893–1899," *Annals of Iowa* 37 (Fall 1964): 401–15.

65. "Negroes Lynched in Missouri," *Independent* 60 (19 April 1906): 892; "Editorial Notes," *Independent* 60 (7 June 1906): 1390; Katherine Lederer, "And Then They Sang a Sabbath Song," *Springfield!* 2 (April–May 1981): 26–28, 33–36, and 3 (June 1981): 24–26; and Douglass, *Christian Reconstruction*, pp. 204–5.

66. Harlan Paul Douglass to Truman Orville and Maria Greene Douglass, 21 July 1906, Douglass Papers; Lura Beam, *He Called Them by the Lightening: A Teacher's Odyssey in the Negro South, 1908–1919* (Indianapolis: Bobbs-Merrill, 1967), pp. 123–24; and "Our New Secretary," *American Missionary* 64 (May 1910): 108–9. See also H. P. Douglass to M. G. Douglass, 7 August 1906, Douglass Papers.

67. Douglass, *Christian Reconstruction*, pp. 20–26, 30–34, 130, 378–79. See also ibid., pp. v, 374–75; and Douglass, *The New Home Missions* (New York: Missionary Education Movement of the United States and Canada, 1914), pp. 171–72.

68. Douglass, *Christian Reconstruction*, pp. v, ix, 23, 35, 43, 56–65.

69. Ibid., pp. 117, 240–52, 268–302. See also Harlan Paul Douglass, *Congregational Missionary Work in Porto Rico* (New York: American Missionary Association, [ca. 1910]), pp. 22–24; and Douglass, "Educational Standards of the Negro," *American Missionary* 65 (May 1911): 88–89.

70. Douglass, *Christian Reconstruction*, pp. 99–118. See also Harlan Paul Douglass, *From Survey to Service* (New York: Council of Women for Home Missions and Missionary Education Movement, 1921), pp. 130–32.

71. Douglass, *Christian Reconstruction*, pp. 77–96, 132–302. See also Douglass, "Civilization in the Lower Mississippi Valley," *American Missionary* 65 (June 1911): 145–46; Douglass, "The Negro according to the New Census," *American Missionary* 65 (November 1911): 457–58; and Douglass, *New Home Missions*, pp. 182–83.

72. Douglass, *Christian Reconstruction*, pp. 120–26.

73. Ibid., pp. 367–88. See also "H. Paul Douglass," *American Missionary* 61 (December 1907): 319–20.

74. Douglass, "Kingdom of God," pp. 278–80; and Douglass, *Christian Reconstruction*, pp. 391–94. See also Douglass, *New Home Missions*, pp. 157–60; and "H. Paul Douglass," pp. 320–21.

75. Douglass, *Christian Reconstruction*, p. 397. See also "H. Paul Douglass," pp. 321–22.

## Chapter 11

1. Kelly Miller, *Race Adjustment: Essays on the Negro in America* (New York: Neale Publishing Co., 1908), p. 151; W. E. B. Du Bois, "The Souls of White Folk," *Independent* 69 (18 August 1910): 342; Washington Gladden, *Christianity and Socialism* (New York: Eaton and Mains, 1905), pp. 20, 65; Gladden, "The Church and Social Problems," *International Quarterly* 11 (April 1905): 139–40; and Reverdy Cassius Ransom, *The Spirit of Freedom and Justice: Orations and Speeches* (Nashville: AME Sunday School Union, 1926), pp. 62–70, 84–87. See also Elias Camp Morris, *Sermons, Addresses and Reminiscences and Important Correspondence* (Nashville: National Baptist Publishing Board, 1901), pp. 36–40; and Miller to Gladden, 26 September 1903, box 5, no. 254, Washington Gladden Papers, Ohio Historical Society.

2. Gustav Spiller, ed., *Papers on Inter-Racial Problems Communicated to the First Universal Races Congress Held at the University of London, July 26–29, 1911* (London: P. S. King and Sons, 1911), pp. xiii, xliii–xlvi; Elliott D. Rudwick, "W. E. B. DuBois and the Universal Races Congress of 1911," *Phylon* 20 (Fourth Quarter 1950): 372–74; Herbert Aptheker, ed., *The*

*Correspondence of W. E. B. Du Bois,* 3 vols. (Amherst: University of Massachusetts Press, 1973), 1:172–75; John H. Harris to Booker T. Washington, 1 December 1910; Washington to Harris, 23 January 1911; Harris to W. E. B. Du Bois, 13 March 1911; Robert E. Park to Washington, 12 April 1911; Robert Russa Moton to Emmett J. Scott, 20 May 1911; Washington to Moton, 23 May 1911; Moton to Washington, 23 July 1911; Scott to Park, 3 August 1911; and Scott to Park, 28 August 1911, Booker T. Washington Papers, Library of Congress; "Social Uplift," *Crisis* 3 (December 1911): 51; and Mary White Ovington, "Reminiscences," *Baltimore Afro-American,* 24 December 1932, p. 24. See also Howard B. Radest, *Toward Common Ground: The Story of the Ethical Culture Societies in the United States* (New York: Frederick Ungar Publishing Co., 1969), pp. 93–94; Michael D. Biddiss, "The Universal Races Congress of 1911," *Race* 13 (July 1971): 37–46; and William Toll, *The Resurgence of Race: Black Social Theory from Reconstruction to the NAACP* (Philadelphia: Temple University Press, 1979), pp. 146–48.

3. Spiller, *Papers on Inter-Racial Problems,* pp. 29–39, 261–67, 348–64, 439–52; W. E. B. Du Bois, "The First Universal Races Congress," *Independent* 71 (24 August 1911): 401–3; "The Races Congress," *Crisis* 2 (September 1911): 202–9; Ulysses G. Weatherly, "The First Universal Races Congress," *American Journal of Sociology* 17 (November 1911): 315–28; Felix Adler, "Report of the First Universal Races Congress, Held at London, June 26–29, 1911," in *Report of the Commissioner of Education for the Year Ended June 30, 1911* (Washington, D.C.: U.S. Government Printing Office, 1912), 1:609–17; Ovington, "Reminiscences," p. 24; Rudwick, "DuBois and the Universal Races Congress," pp. 374–78; and Biddis, "Universal Races Congress of 1911," pp. 43–45.

4. Elias B. Sanford, ed., *Church Federation: Inter-Church Conference on Federation, New York, November 15–21, 1905* (New York: Fleming H. Revell Co., 1906), pp. 283–87, 520–24; Sanford, ed., *Federal Council of the Churches of Christ in America: Report of the First Meeting of the Federal Council* (New York: Revell Press, 1909); Levi J. Coppin, "The Federal Council of the Churches of Christ in America," *AME Church Review* 25 (January 1909): 227–30; L.U.X., "The Great Federal Council Meeting in Philadelphia," *AME Church Review* 25 (January 1909): 231–37; Charles S. McFarland, *Christian Unity in the Making: The First Twenty-five Years of the Federal Council of the Churches of Christ in America* (New York: Federal Council of Churches, 1948), pp. 116–19; and Robert T. Handy, "Negro Christianity and American Church Historiography," in *Re-interpretation in American Church History,* ed. Jerald R. Brauer (Chicago: University of Chicago Press, 1968), p. 106.

5. W. A. Blackwell, "The Uplifting of a Race," in *Christian Unity at Work: The Federal Council of Churches of Christ in America in Quadrennial Session at Chicago, Illinois, 1912,* ed. Charles S. McFarland (New York: Federal Council of Churches of Christ in America, 1913), pp. 225–30; *Annual Reports of the Federal Council of the Churches of Christ in America for the Year 1914* (New York: n.p., 1914), p. 229; *Annual Reports of the Federal Council of the Churches of Christ in America for the Year 1915* (New York: n.p., 1915), p. 217; McFarland, *The Progress of Church Federation* (New York: Fleming H. Revell Co., 1917), pp. 117–20; and John Franklin Piper, Jr., "The Social Policy of the Federal Council of the Churches of Christ in America during World War I" (Ph.D. dissertation, Duke University, 1964), pp. 62–66.

6. Walter Rauschenbusch, "The Belated Races and the Social Problems," *Methodist Review* series 3, 40 (April 1914): 258; Dores Robinson Sharpe, *Walter Rauschenbusch* (New

York: Macmillan, 1942), pp. 27, 52–58, 82–83, 92–93, 96–97; Winthrop S. Hudson, ed., *Walter Rauschenbusch: Selected Writings* (New York: Paulist Press, 1984), pp. 49–59; and Max L. Stackhouse, "The Continuing Importance of Walter Rauschenbusch," in *The Righteousness of the Kingdom*, by Walter Rauschenbusch (Nashville: Abingdon Press, 1963), p. 33n.

7. Rauschenbusch, *Righteousness of the Kingdom*, pp. 66–67, 194–95, 244–50; and Rauschenbusch, *Die Politische Verfassung unseres Landes: Ein Handbuch zum Unterrichte für die deutsch-americanische Jugend* (Cleveland: P. Ritter, 1902), pp. 7–9. See also Stackhouse, "Eschatology and Ethical Method: A Structural Analysis of Contemporary Christian Social Ethics in America with Primary Reference to Walter Rauschenbusch and Reinhold Niebuhr" (Ph.D. dissertation, Harvard University, 1964), p. 120n.

8. Rauschenbusch, *Christianity and the Social Crisis* (New York: George H. Doran, 1907), pp. 37–38, 222; Rauschenbusch, *Christianizing the Social Order* (New York: Macmillan, 1912), p. 154; Ray Stannard Baker, *The Spiritual Unrest* (New York: Phillips Publishing Co., 1909), pp. 260–85; Rauschenbusch, "A Sense of Human Equality Comes Slowly," in *Third Year of the Sagamore Sociological Conference. Sagamore Beach, Mass., U.S.A., June 29,–July 1, 1909* (Boston: Edwin L. Slocum, [1909]), p. 12; Sharpe, *Walter Rauschenbusch*, pp. 165–66; "The Midwinter Bible and Missionary Conference at the Methodist Training School, Nashville, Tennessee, December 28, 1910–January 5, 1911"; James E. McCulloch to Walter Rauschenbusch, 17 January 1911; Mary Lambeth to Rauschenbusch, 23 January 1911; Wilbur Fisk Tillett to Rauschenbusch, 28 January 1911; Rauschenbusch to Augustus H. Strong, 25 April 1911, Walter Rauschenbusch Papers, American Baptist Historical Society. See also Rauschenbusch, *A Theology for the Social Gospel* (New York: Macmillan, 1917), p. 185.

9. Conrad Henry Moehlman to Rauschenbusch, 11 March 1912, Rauschenbusch Papers.

10. Rauschenbusch, *Christianizing the Social Order*, p. 60; and Rauschenbusch, *Dare We Be Christians?* (Boston: Pilgrim Press, 1914), pp. 57–58. See also Rauschenbusch, *Dare We Be Christians?*, pp. 31–32, 36, 58–59; and Rauschenbusch, "Justice and Brotherhood," in *The Path of Labor. Theme: Christianity and the World's Workers*, by Mary Katharine Bennett et al. (New York: Council of Women for Home Missions, 1918), p. 167.

11. Lyman Abbott, "Letters to Unknown Friends," *Outlook* 100 (20 January 1912): 115–16; [W. E. B. Du Bois], "What to Read," *Crisis* 3 (April 1912): 261; [Du Bois], "Dr. Abbott and the Good Samaritan," *Crisis* 3 (May 1912): 18–19; and [Du Bois], "An Unswerving Friend," *Crisis* 7 (March 1914): 224. See also [Du Bois], "Hampton," *Crisis* 15 (November 1917): 10–12; [Du Bois], "Advice," *Crisis* 15 (March 1918): 215; and Du Bois, "A Protest," *Crisis* 16 (May 1918): 10–11. For a contrasting view, see "Lyman Abbott, Friend of Hampton Institute," *Southern Workman* 51 (December 1922): 541a–c.

12. Rauschenbusch, "Belated Races and the Social Problems," pp. 252–58. See also Rauschenbusch, *The Belated Races and the Social Problems* (New York: American Missionary Association, 1914); Rauschenbusch, "The Problem of the Black Man," *American Missionary* 68 (March 1914): 732–33; and "The Negro and the Church," *Crisis* 7 (February 1914): 232–33.

13. Rauschenbusch, "Belated Races and the Social Problems," pp. 258–59.

14. Rauschenbusch, *A Theology for the Social Gospel*, pp. 60, 79, 131, 184–85, 185n–86n, 230–31.

15. Walter Rauschenbusch to Lewis S. Gannett, 24 April 1917, Lewis S. Gannett Papers, Houghton Library, Harvard University. See also Sharpe, *Walter Rauschenbusch*, pp. 356–92.

16. Benjamin E. Mays, ed., *A Gospel for the Social Awakening: Selections from the Writings of Walter Rauschenbusch* (New York: Association Press, 1950); Benjamin E. Mays, *Born to Rebel: An Autobiography* (New York: Charles Scribner's Sons, 1971); James Weldon Johnson, *The Autobiography of an Ex-Coloured Man* (Boston: Sherman, French, and Co., 1912), pp. 74–75; and Martin Luther King, Jr., *Stride toward Freedom: The Montgomery Story* (New York: Harper and Row, 1958), p. 90. See also David J. Garrow, *Bearing the Cross: Martin Luther King, Jr., and the Southern Christian Leadership Conference, A Personal Portrait* (New York: William Morrow and Co., 1986), pp. 32–51; and Taylor Branch, *Parting the Waters: America in the King Years, 1954–1963* (New York: Simon and Schuster, 1988), pp. 27–68.

17. King, *Stride toward Freedom*, p. 91; David J. Garrow, "The Intellectual Development of Martin Luther King, Jr.: Influences and Commentaries," *Union Seminary Quarterly Review* 40, no. 4 (1986): 9–11; Carl Herman Voss, *Rabbi and Minister: The Friendship of Stephen S. Wise and John Haynes Holmes* (New York: Association Press, 1964), pp. 140–41; and Lewis Perry, *Radical Abolitionism: Anarchy and the Government of God in Antislavery Thought* (Ithaca: Cornell University Press, 1973), pp. 1–5.

18. Kenneth L. Smith and Ira G. Zepp, Jr., *Search for the Beloved Community: The Thinking of Martin Luther King, Jr.* (Valley Forge, Pa.: Judson Press, 1974), pp. 21–45; Kenneth Cauthen, *The Impact of American Religious Liberalism* (New York: Harper and Row, 1962), pp. 41–143; William R. Hutchison, *The Modernist Impulse in American Protestantism* (Cambridge: Harvard University Press, 1976); King, *Stride toward Freedom*, pp. 91–92; King, *Strength to Love* (New York: Harper and Row, 1963), pp. 137–38; and Drexel Timothy Brunson, "The Quest for Social Justice: A Study of Walter Rauschenbusch and His Influence on Reinhold Niebuhr and Martin Luther King, Jr." (Ph.D. dissertation, Florida State University, 1980).

19. Smith and Zepp, *Search for the Beloved Community*, pp. 99–118; Warren E. Steinkraus, "Martin Luther King's Personalism and Non-Violence," *Journal of the History of Ideas* 34 (January–March 1973): 97–110; and King, *Stride toward Freedom*, p. 100.

20. John J. Ansbro, *Martin Luther King, Jr.: The Making of a Mind* (Maryknoll, N.Y.: Orbis Books, 1982), p. 319n; Adam Fairclough, *To Redeem the Soul of America: The Southern Christian Leadership Conference and Martin Luther King, Jr.* (Athens: University of Georgia Press, 1987); and Thomas R. Peake, *Keeping the Dream Alive: A History of the Southern Christian Leadership Conference from King to the Nineteen-Eighties* (New York: Peter Lang, 1987).

# Bibliographical Essay

In the course of my research, I consulted numerous manuscript collections. Listed here, by repository, are those that I found most helpful.

American Baptist Historical Society, Rochester, New York
   Ford Hall Forum Papers
   Minutes of the Brotherhood of the Kingdom, 1892–1915
   Walter Rauschenbusch Papers
   Sagamore Sociological Conference Scrapbooks, 1907–17

Amistad Research Center, New Orleans, Louisiana
   Harlan Paul Douglass Papers

Atlanta University Center Library, Atlanta, Georgia
   Minute-Book of the Gammon Literary Society, 1885–95

University of Chicago, Chicago, Illinois
   Charles R. Henderson Papers
   Shailer Mathews Papers
   Albion W. Small Papers

Colgate-Rochester Divinity School, Rochester, New York
   William Channing Gannett Manuscript Sermon File

Cornell University, Ithaca, New York
   Richard Henry Edwards Papers
   Samuel J. May Anti-Slavery Collection

Duke University, Durham, North Carolina
   George Washington Cable Papers
   Flavius Josephus [Joseph] Cook Papers
   Trinity College Papers

Emory University, Atlanta, Georgia
   Atticus Greene Haygood Papers

General Theological Seminary, New York, New York
   William Thomas Manning Papers

Harvard University, Cambridge, Massachusetts
  Lewis S. Gannett Papers
  Thomas Wentworth Higginson Papers
  Francis Greenwood Peabody Papers
  Josiah Royce Papers

Library of Congress, Washington, D.C.
  American Colonization Society Papers
  Ray Stannard Baker Papers
  John Haynes Holmes Papers
  National Association for the Advancement of Colored People Papers
  National Urban League Papers
  Robert Curtis Ogden Papers
  Thomas DeWitt Talmadge Papers
  Booker T. Washington Papers

New York Public Library, New York, New York
  John Edward Bruce Papers
  Alexander Crummell Papers
  Richard Heber Newton Papers

University of North Carolina, Chapel Hill, North Carolina
  Edgar Gardner Murphy Papers
  Southern Education Papers
  Albion W. Tourgée Papers (microfilm)

Oberlin College Archives, Oberlin, Ohio
  Henry Churchill King Papers

Ohio Historical Society, Columbus, Ohio
  Washington Gladden Papers

Princeton University, Princeton, New Jersey
  Robert E. Speer Papers

University of Rochester, Rochester, New York
  William Channing Gannett Papers

Swarthmore College, Swarthmore, Pennsylvania
  Jane Addams Papers
  Edwin Doak and Lucia True Ames Mead Papers

Union Theological Seminary, New York, New York
  Robert E. Speer Pamphlet Collection
  Josiah Strong Papers

Wilberforce University, Wilberforce, Ohio
  W. S. Scarborough Papers

Useful editions of papers include Herbert Aptheker, ed., *The Correspondence of W. E. B. Du Bois*, 3 vols. (Amherst: University of Massachusetts Press, 1973–78); Carter G. Woodson, ed., *The Works of Francis J. Grimké*, 4 vols. (Washington, D.C.: Associated Publishers, 1942); Louis D. Rubin, Jr., ed., *Teach the Freeman: The Correspondence of Rutherford B. Hayes and the Slater Fund for Negro Education, 1881–1893*, 2 vols. (Baton Rouge: Louisiana State University Press, 1959); Charles Richard Williams, ed., *Diary and Letters of Rutherford B. Hayes*, 5 vols. (n.p.: Ohio State Archaeological and Historical Society, 1925); Mary Thacher Higginson, ed., *Letters and Journals of Thomas Wentworth Higginson, 1846–1906* (Boston: Houghton Mifflin Co., 1921); John Clendenning, ed., *The Letters of Josiah Royce* (Chicago: University of Chicago Press, 1970); Otto H. Olsen, ed., "Albion W. Tourgée and Negro Militants of the 1890s: A Documentary Selection," *Science and Society* 28 (Spring 1964): 183–208; and Louis R. Harlan et al., eds., *The Booker T. Washington Papers*, 14 vols. (Urbana: University of Illinois Press, 1972–89).

For conference records of black missionary education in the post-Reconstruction South, see *Baptist Home Missions in North America; Including a full Report of the Proceedings and Addresses of the Jubilee Meeting, and a Historical Sketch of the American Baptist Home Mission Society, Historical Tables, Etc., 1832–1882* (New York: Baptist Home Mission Rooms, 1883); and Joseph C. Hartzell, ed., *Christian Educators in Council: Sixty Addresses by American Educators; with Historical Notes upon the National Education Assembly, Held at Ocean Grove, N.J., August 9–12, 1883. Also Illiteracy and Education Tables from Census of 1880* (New York: Phillips and Hunt, 1883). Isabel C. Barrows, ed., *First Mohonk Conference on the Negro Question: Held at Lake Mohonk, Ulster County, New York, June 4, 5, 6, 1890* (Boston: George H. Ellis, 1890), and *Second Mohonk Conference on the Negro Question: Held at Lake Mohonk, Ulster County, New York, June 3, 4, 5, 1891* (Boston: George H. Ellis, 1891), record a failed approach to Southern black education, but conferees on the subject measured their success by its intentions for the next two decades. I made little use of denominational minutes, but early Northern protests against lynching are found in *Journal of the General Conference of the Methodist Episcopal Church held in Omaha, Nebraska, May 2–26, 1892* (New York: Hunt and Eaton, 1892); *Minutes of the National Council of the Congregational Churches of the United States, 1892* (Boston: Congregational Publishing Society, 1892); and *Minutes of the General Assembly of the Presbyterian Church in the United States of America* (Philadelphia: Presbyterian Board of Publication, 1892).

American missionary attitudes toward sub-Saharan Africa are found in James Johnston, ed., *Report of the Centenary Conference on the Protestant Missions of the World, Held in Exeter Hall (June 9th–19th), London, 1888*, 2 vols. (New York: Fleming H. Revell Co., n.d.); John Henry Barrows, ed., *The World's Parliament of Religions: An Illustrated and Popular Story of the World's First Parliament of Religions, Held in Chicago in Connection with the Columbian Exposition of 1893*, 2 vols. (Chicago: Parliament Publishing Co., 1893); Max Wood Moorhead, ed., *The Student Missionary Enterprise. Addresses and Discussions of the Second International Convention of the Student Volunteer Movement for Foreign Missions, Held at Detroit, Michigan, February 28 and March 1, 2, 3, and 4, 1894* (Boston: T. O. Metcalf and Co., n.d.); J. W. E. Bowen, ed., *Africa and the American Negro: Addresses and Proceedings of the Congress on Africa Held under the Auspices of the Stewart Missionary Foundation for Africa of Gammon Theological Seminary in Connection with the Cotton States and International Exposition, December 13–15, 1895* (Atlanta: Gammon Theological Seminary, 1896); Charles H. Fahs et al., eds., *The Open Door, A Challenge to Missionary Advance. Addresses Delivered before the First General Missionary Convention of the Methodist Episcopal Church, Held in Cleveland, Ohio, October 21 to 24, 1902* (New York: Eaton and Mains, 1903); and *Students and the Modern Missionary Crusade: Addresses Before the Fifth International Convention of the Student Volunteer Movement for Foreign Missions, Nashville, Tennessee, February 28–March 4, 1906* (New York: Student Volunteer Movement for Foreign Missions, 1906).

On the Southern education movement, see Conference for Education in the South, *Proceedings*, 1898–1913; and *Race Problems of the South: Report of the Proceedings of the First Annual Conference Held under the Auspices of the Southern Society for the Promotion of the Study of Race Conditions and Problems in the South at . . . Montgomery, Alabama, May 8, 9, 10 A.D. 1900* (Richmond: B. F. Johnson Publishing Co., n.d.). There are important sources on white attitudes and the black experience in National Conference on Charities and Corrections, *Proceedings*, 1890–1917; W. E. B. Du Bois's annual Atlanta University Conferences on the Study of Negro Problems (titles vary), particularly nos. 1, 3, 8, and 14 (Atlanta: Atlanta University Press, 1896–1909); and I. Garland Penn and J. W. E. Bowen, eds., *The United Negro: His Problems and His Progress. Containing the Addresses and Proceedings. The Negro Young People's Christian and Educational Congress, Held August 6–11, 1902* (Atlanta: Board of Directors of the Congress, 1902). Northern initiatives in racial reform are found in *How to Solve the Race Problem: The Proceedings of the Washington Conference on the Race Problem under the Auspices of the National Sociological Society Held at the Lincoln Temple Congregational Church; at the Nineteenth Street Baptist Church; and at the Metropolitan A.M.E. Church, Washington, D.C., November 9, 10, 11 and 12, 1903* (Washington, D.C.: R. Beresford, 1904); the First (1907), Third (1909), and Eighth (1914) Year of the *Sagamore Sociological Conference* (Boston: various publishers); and *Proceedings of the National Negro Conference, 1909* (New York: Arno Press, 1969).

The racial interests of the Federal Council of Churches are found in Elias Sanford, ed., *Church Federation: Inter-Church Conference on Federation, New York, November 15–21, 1905* (New York: Fleming H. Revell Co., 1906); Sanford, ed., *Federal Council of the Churches of Christ in America: Report of the First Meeting of the Federal Council* (New York: Revell Press, 1909); Charles Stedman McFarland, ed., *Christian Unity at Work: The Federal Council of Churches of Christ in America in Quadrennial Session . . . 1912* (New York: Federal Council of Churches of Christ in America, 1913); Samuel McCrea Cavert, ed., *The Churches Allied for Common Tasks: Report of the Third Quadrennium of the Federal Council of the Churches of Christ in America, 1916–1920* (New York: Federal Council of the Churches of Christ in America, 1921); and the council's annual reports. Gustav Spiller, ed., *Papers on Inter-Racial Problems Communicated to the First Universal Races Congress Held at the University of London, July 26–29, 1911, and Record of the Proceedings of the First Universal Races Congress* (London: P. S. King and Sons, 1911), report on international dimensions of the problem.

Beyond selected reading in dozens of other journals and newspapers, I used the following intensively:

*The African Repository*, 1885–92
*Alexander's Magazine*, 1904–8
*The Altruist*, 1893

The AME Church Review, 1884–1920
American Cooperator, 1902–3
American Journal of Sociology, 1895–1920
American Missionary, 1890–1914
Andover Review, 1890–93
Arena, 1890–1909
Atlantic Monthly, 1890–1920
Bibliotheca Sacra, 1890–1901
Bulletin of the National League on Urban Conditions among Negroes, 1911–20
The Catholic World, 1890–1920
The Century Magazine, 1884–1920
Charities (title varies), 1899–1909
The Chautauquan, 1885–1914
The Christian Educator, 1889–1900
The AME Christian Recorder, 1891
The Christian Register, 1902–13
Christian Union, 1885–93
Constructive Quarterly, 1913–20
Crisis, 1910–20
The Dawn, 1889–96
Federation, 1902–6
The Forum, 1886–1920
Georgia Baptist, 1898–1920
The Gospel of the Kingdom, 1909–16
Gunton's Magazine, 1891–1904
The Homiletic Review, 1890–1920
The Independent, 1885–1922
The International Journal of Ethics, 1890–1920
Lend-A-Hand, 1886–97
Liberia, 1892–1909
Southern Methodist Quarterly Review (title varies), 1890–1908
Northern Methodist Review, 1890–1920
The Missionary Review of the World, 1890–1920
The New England Magazine, 1890–1912
The New World, 1892–1900
The Open Court, 1888–1908
Our Day, 1888–95
The Outlook, 1893–1922
Presbyterian Quarterly, 1887–1901
Review of Reviews, 1890–1920
Sewanee Review, 1892–1920
The Social Gospel, 1898–1901
Social Service, 1899–1906
South Atlantic Quarterly, 1902–20

Southern Education, 1903
Southern Workman, 1890–1917
Spirit of Missions, 1889–1920
The Survey, 1909–20
The Union Seminary Magazine, 1889–1920
The Unitarian, 1886–96
The Unitarian Review, 1890–91
The Voice of the Negro, 1904–7
The World To-Day, 1904–11

Many autobiographies are unilluminating, but Washington Gladden's *Recollections* (Boston: Houghton, Mifflin and Co., 1909), is exceptional; and Edward A. Steiner's *Against the Current: Simple Chapters from a Complex Life* (New York: Fleming H. Revell Co., 1910), *The Eternal Hunger: Vivid Moments in Personal Experience* (New York: Fleming H. Revell Co., 1911), and *From Alien to Citizen: The Story of My Life in America* (New York: Fleming H. Revell Co., 1914) are too neglected. Beyond Booker T. Washington's *Up from Slavery* (New York: A. L. Burt, 1900), black social gospel prophets' autobiographies worthy of mention include: Matthew Anderson, *Presbyterianism: Its Relation to the Negro Illustrated by the Berean Presbyterian Church, Philadelphia, with Sketch of the Church and Autobiography of the Author* (Philadelphia: John McGill White and Co., 1897); James David Corrothers, *In Spite of the Handicap* (New York: George H. Doran Co., 1916); Adam Clayton Powell, *Against the Tide: An Autobiography* (New York: Richard R. Smith, 1938); Hugh Henry Proctor, *Between Black and White: Autobiographical Sketches* (Boston: Pilgrim Press, 1925); Reverdy Ransom, *The Pilgrimage of Harriet Ransom's Son* (Nashville: Sunday School Union, 1949); Theophilus Gould Steward, *Fifty Years in the Gospel Ministry* (Philadelphia: AME Book Concern, [ca. 1921]); Alexander Walters, *My Life and Work* (New York: Fleming H. Revell Co., 1917); and Richard Robert Wright, Jr., *87 Years behind the Black Curtain: An Autobiography* (Philadelphia: Rare Book Co., 1965). The recollections of white female missionaries such as Lura Beam's *He Called Them by the Lightening: A Teacher's Odyssey in the South, 1908–1919* (Indianapolis: Bobbs-Merrill, 1967), Harriet E. Emerson's *Annals of a Harvester: Reviewing Forty Years of Home Missionary Work in the Southern States* (East Andover, N.H.: Arthur W. Emerson, Sons and Co., [ca. 1915]), and Joanna P. Moore's *"In Christ's Stead": Autobiographical Sketches* (Chicago: Women's Baptist Home Mission Society, 1902), are wonderful sources. Mary White Ovington's "Reminiscences," *Baltimore Afro-American*, 1932–33, are more illuminating than her *The Walls Came Tumbling Down* (New York: Harcourt Brace and Co., 1947); and Alfreda M. Duster, ed., *Crusade for Justice: The Autobiography of Ida B. Wells* (Chicago: University of Chicago Press, 1970), is indispensable for the antilynching crusade of the 1890s.

Many prophets of American social Christianity wrote no books about race relations. Their perspectives are scattered in books, periodicals, and elsewhere. *Our Nation Still in Danger; or, Ten Years after the War . . .* (New York: American Missionary Association, 1875), is a rare pamphlet with contributions by Frederick Douglass, Washington Gladden, and others on conditions in the South at the end of Reconstruction. The works of four late nineteenth-century crusaders are in Arlin Turner, ed., *The Negro Question: A Selection of*

*Writings on Civil Rights in the South* by George W. Cable (Garden City, N.Y.: Doubleday and Co., 1958); Joseph Cook's *The Three Despised Races in the United States; or, The Chinaman, the Indian, and the Freedman. An Address* (New York: American Missionary Association, 1878) and his *Boston Monday Lectures* . . . (Boston: Houghton, Osgood and Co. and Houghton Mifflin and Co., 1879–88); Atticus Greene Haygood, *Our Brother in Black: His Freedom and His Future* (New York: Phillips and Hunt, 1881), and *Pleas for Progress* (Nashville: Publishing House of the ME Church, South, 1889); and Albion Winegar Tourgée's *A Fool's Errand* (New York: Fords, Howard and Hulbert, 1879), *Bricks without Straw* (New York: Fords, Howard and Hulbert, 1880), and *An Appeal to Caesar* (New York: Fords, Howard and Hulbert, 1884), as well as his only novel recognized by historians of the social gospel, *Murvale Eastman: Christian Socialist* (New York: Fords, Howard and Hulbert, 1884).

On white American social Christianity's attitude toward sub-Saharan Africa, see James S. Dennis, *Christian Missions and Social Progress: A Sociological Study of Foreign Missions*, 3 vols. (New York: Fleming H. Revell Co., 1897); Dennis, *Social Evils of the Non-Christian World* (New York: Student Volunteer Movement for Foreign Missions, 1899); J. S. Mills, *Africa and Mission Work in Sierra Leone, West Africa* (Dayton, Ohio: United Brethren Publishing House, 1898); Wilson S. Naylor, *Daybreak in the Dark Continent* (New York: Eaton and Mains, 1905); Frederic Perry Noble, *The Redemption of Africa: A Story of Civilization*, 2 vols. (New York: Young People's Missionary Movement, 1899); Ellen C. Parsons, *Christus Liberator: An Outline Study of Africa* (New York: Young People's Missionary Movement, [ca. 1906]); William S. Rainsford, *The Land of the Lion* (New York: Doubleday, Page and Co., 1909); Robert E. Speer, *Missions and Modern History: A Study of the Missionary Aspects of Some Great Movements of the Nineteenth Century*, 2 vols. (New York: Fleming H. Revell Co., 1904); and Speer, *Presbyterian Foreign Missions: An Account of the Foreign Missions of the Presbyterian Church in the U.S.A.* (Philadelphia: Presbyterian Board of Publication and Sabbath-School Work, 1902).

My assessment of white racial attitudes is informed by major black voices. In the late nineteenth century, they include Anna Julia Cooper, *A Voice from the South, by a Black Woman of the South* (Xenia, Ohio: Aldine Printing House, 1892); T. Thomas Fortune, *Black and White* (New York: Fords and Co., 1884); Wesley J. Gaines, *The Negro and the White Man* (Philadelphia: AME Publishing House, 1897); T. G. Steward, *The End of the World; or, Clearing the Way for the Fullness of the Gentiles* (Philadelphia: AME Church Book Rooms, 1888); and D. Augustus Straker, *The New South Investigated* (Detroit: Ferguson Printing Co., 1888). Alexander Crummell, *Africa and America: Addresses and Discourses* (Springfield, Mass.: Willey and Co., 1891); and Edwin S. Redkey, ed., *Respect Black: The Writings and Speeches of Henry McNeal Turner* (New York: Arno Press, 1971), offer two important black nationalist perspectives. William Hannibal Thomas, *The American Negro: What He Was, What He Is, and What He May Become: A Critical and Practical Discussion* (New York: Macmillan, 1901) is the epitome of black accommodation to white racism. For important later statements of black social Christianity, see Ida B. Wells, *On Lynchings* (New York: Arno Press, 1969); Elias Camp Morris, *Sermons, Addresses and Reminiscences* (Nashville: National Baptist Publishing Board, 1901); W. E. B. Du Bois, *The Souls of Black Folk* (Chicago: A. C. McClurg and Co., 1903); William A. Sinclair, *The Aftermath of Slavery: A Study of the Condition and Environment of the American Negro* (Boston: Small, Maynard and Co., 1905); Kelly Miller, *Race Adjustment:*

*Essays on the Negro in America* (New York: Neale Publishing Co., 1908); and Reverdy C. Ransom, *The Spirit of Freedom and Justice: Orations and Speeches* (Nashville: AME Sunday School Union, 1926).

Early studies of the black urban experience still worth consulting include Federation of Churches and Christian Workers in New York City, *Second Sociological Canvass* (New York: The Federation, 1897); W. E. B. Du Bois, *The Philadelphia Negro* (Philadelphia: University of Pennsylvania, 1899); Mary White Ovington, *Half a Man: The Status of the Negro in New York* (New York: Longmans, Green, and Co., 1911); George Edmund Haynes, *The Negro at Work in New York City: A Study in Economic Progress* (New York: Columbia University Press, 1912); R. R. Wright, Jr., *The Negro in Pennsylvania: A Study in Economic History* (Philadelphia: AME Press, 1912); Asa E. Martin, *Our Negro Population: A Sociological Study of the Negroes of Kansas City, Missouri* (n.p.: Franklin Hudson Publishing Co., 1913); John Daniels, *In Freedom's Birthplace: A Study of the Boston Negroes* (Boston: Houghton Mifflin Co., 1914); and Wendell P. Dabney, *Cincinnati's Colored Citizens: Historical, Sociological and Biographical* (Cincinnati: Dabney Publishing Co., 1926). W. D. P. Bliss, ed., *The Encyclopedia of Social Reform* (New York: Funk and Wagnalls, 1897); R. R. Wright, Jr., "Social Work and Influence of the Negro Church," *Annals of the American Academy of Political and Social Science* 30 (November 1907): 509–21; and Robert A. Woods and Albert J. Kennedy, eds., *Handbook of Settlements* (New York: Charities Publication Committee, 1911), are valuable sources.

Northern white social gospel prophets' unrest with conditions in the South is found in such works as Charles B. Spahr, *America's Working People* (New York: Longmans, Green, and Co., 1900); William Mackintire Salter, *The Negro Problem: Is the Nation Going Backward?* (Philadelphia: S. Burns Weston, 1903); Edward A. Steiner, *Tolstoy the Man* (New York: Outlook Co., 1904); Ernest Howard Crosby, *Tolstoy and His Message* (New York: Funk and Wagnalls, 1904); Crosby, *Garrison the Non-Resistant* (Chicago: Public Publishing Co., 1905); Charles F. Dole, *The Spirit of Democracy* (New York: Thomas Y. Crowell and Co., 1906); John R. Commons, *Races and Immigrants in America* (New York: Macmillan, 1907); Ray Stannard Baker, *Following the Colour Line: An Account of Negro Citizenship in the American Democracy* (New York: Doubleday, Page and Co., 1908); Richard Henry Edwards, *The Negro Problem* (Madison, Wis.: n.p., 1908); Charles Zueblin, *The Religion of a Democrat* (New York: B. W. Huebsch, 1908); Zueblin, *Democracy and the Overman* (New York: B. W. Huebsch, 1910); Thomas Cuming Hall, *Social Solutions in the Light of Christian Ethics* (New York: Eaton and Mains, 1910); and John Haynes Holmes, *The Disfranchisement of Negroes* (New York: National Association for the Advancement of Colored People, 1910).

The social gospel prophets' theologies of race relations are found in their books. Josiah Strong's radical cultural imperialism is most evident in *Our Country: Its Possible Future and Its Present Crisis* (New York: Baker and Taylor, 1885) and *The New Era; or, The Coming Kingdom* (New York: Baker and Taylor, 1893). His later attitude is most accessible in *Our World: The New World-Life* (Garden City, N.Y.: Doubleday, Page and Co., 1913) and *Our World: The New World-Religion* (Garden City, N.Y.: Doubleday, Page and Co., 1915). Thomas Dixon's claim to be regarded as a social gospel prophet is founded in his early work, *Living Problems in Religion and Social Science*, 2d ed. (New York: Funk and Wagnalls, 1892); *The Failure of Protestantism in New York and Its Causes* (New York: Victor O. A. Strauss,

1896); and *Dixon's Sermons* (New York: F. L. Bussey and Company, 1899), when he espoused a racial conservatism. Dixon did not see his radical racial separatism as a repudiation of social Christianity. It appeared in his later fiction, but that no more rules him out of the company of the prophets than it does Charles Sheldon or Albion Tourgée. Among his later works, I drew heavily on *The One Woman: A Story of a Modern Utopia* (New York: Doubleday, Page and Co., 1903); *The Leopard's Spots: A Romance of the White Man's Burden, 1865–1900* (New York: Doubleday, Page and Co., 1903); *The Clansman: An Historical Romance of the Ku Klux Klan* (New York: Doubleday, Page and Co., 1905); "Booker T. Washington and the Negro," *Saturday Evening Post* 178 (19 August 1905): 1–2; and *The Sins of the Father: A Romance of the South* (New York: D. Appleton and Co., 1912).

Theological personalism was ubiquitous among the social gospel prophets who rejected both radical cultural imperialism and radical racial separatism; all of the following shared it to some degree. Josiah Royce's conservative assimilationism is found in *Race Questions, Provincialism, and Other American Problems* (New York: Macmillan, 1908), which should be supplemented by his *The Philosophy of Loyalty* (New York: Macmillan, 1908) and *The Hope of the Great Community* (New York: Macmillan, 1916). Edgar Gardner Murphy's conservative separatism is found in his *The Larger Life: Sermons and an Essay* (New York: Longmans, Green, and Co., 1897); *Problems of the Present South: A Discussion of the Educational, Industrial, and Political Issues in the Southern States* (New York: Macmillan, 1904); and *The Basis of Ascendancy: A Discussion of Certain Principles of Public Policy Involved in the Development of the Southern States* (New York: Longmans, Green, and Co., 1909). His theological personalism and conservative separatism are shared by another Southerner, Willis Duke Weatherford, in his *Fundamental Religious Principles in Browning's Poetry* (Nashville: Publishing House of the ME Church, South, 1907) and *Negro Life in the South: Present Conditions and Needs* (New York: Association Press, 1911); and by the Yankee social ethicist Francis Greenwood Peabody in his *Jesus Christ and the Social Question: An Examination of the Teaching of Jesus in Its Relation to Some of the Problems of Modern Social Life* (New York: Grosset and Dunlap, 1900) and *Education for Life: The Story of Hampton Institute* (New York: Doubleday, Page and Co., 1919).

The sources that shaped my understanding of personalism and evangelical neoabolitionism include George Augustus Gates, *Personality: The Ultimate Fact of Philosophy and Life* (Grinnell: Iowa College, 1889); Harlan Paul Douglass, "The Kingdom of God—A Resume of the Teachings of Professor George D. Herron. D.D.," *Our Day* 45 (1895): 274–86; Charles F. Thwing, "The Worth of Personality," *Homiletic Review* 32 (August 1896): 122–27; Washington Gladden, *The Negro's Southern Neighbors and His Northern Friends* (New York: Congregational Rooms, [1903]); Gladden, "The Negro Crisis: Is the Separation of the Two Races to Become Necessary?" *American Magazine* 63 (January 1907): 296–301; Charles Cuthbert Hall, *The Universal Elements of the Christian Religion: An Attempt to Interpret Contemporary Religious Conditions* (New York: Fleming H. Revell Co., 1905); Hall, *Christ and the Human Race; or, The Attitude of Jesus Christ toward Foreign Races and Religions* (Boston: Houghton, Mifflin and Co., 1906); Edward A. Steiner, *On the Trail of the Immigrant* (New York: Fleming H. Revell Co., 1906); Steiner, *The Immigrant Tide: Its Ebb and Flow* (New York: Fleming H. Revell Co., 1909); Harlan Paul Douglass, *Christian Reconstruction in the South* (Boston: Pilgrim Press, 1909); Amory H. Bradford, *My Brother* (Boston: Pilgrim Press,

1910); Henry Churchill King, "The College and Democracy," *Oberlin Alumni Magazine* 7 (December 1910–January 1911): 87–102, 126–36; and Walter Rauschenbusch, *The Belated Race and the Social Problems* (New York: American Missionary Association, 1914).

My work is informed by that of previous historians even where I disagree with them. Our understanding of the social gospel is largely shaped by Arthur M. Schlesinger, Sr.'s, "A Critical Period in American Religion, 1875–1900," Massachusetts Historical Society, *Proceedings* 64 (June 1932): 523–47. In the next three decades, historians working within Schlesinger's framework included James Dombrowski, *The Early Days of Christian Socialism in America* (New York: Columbia University Press, 1936); Charles Howard Hopkins, *The Rise of the Social Gospel in American Protestantism: 1865–1915* (New Haven: Yale University Press, 1940); Aaron I. Abell, *The Urban Impact on American Protestantism: 1865–1900* (Cambridge: Harvard University Press, 1943); Abell, *American Catholicism and Social Action* (Garden City, N.Y.: Doubleday and Co., 1960); Henry F. May, *Protestant Churches and Industrial America* (New York: Harper and Row, 1949); and Arthur Mann, *Yankee Reformers in the Urban Age* (Cambridge: Harvard University Press, 1954). Donald K. Gorrell's *The Age of Social Responsibility: The Social Gospel in the Progressive Era, 1900–1920* (Macon, Ga.: Mercer University Press, 1988), follows a well-beaten path. Robert T. Handy and Sidney E. Mead questioned Schlesinger's interpretation in a review of May's book in the *Journal of Religion* 30 (January 1950): 67–69. To his credit, an extended challenge to Schlesinger's work came from his own student: Timothy Smith, *Revivalism and Social Reform: American Protestantism on the Eve of the Civil War* (Nashville: Abingdon Press, 1957). Handy and Mead developed their interpretations in Sidney E. Mead, *The Lively Experiment: The Shaping of Christianity in America* (New York: Harper and Row, 1963); Robert T. Handy, "The Protestant Quest for a Christian America, 1830–1930," *Church History* 22 (March 1953): 8–20; Handy, ed., *The Social Gospel in America: 1870–1920* (New York: Oxford University Press, 1966); and Handy, *A Christian America: Protestant Hopes and Historical Realities* (New York: Oxford University Press, 1971). In a variety of ways, Handy, Mead, and Smith suggested that there were larger degrees of continuity in nineteenth-century reform than Schlesinger's and May's framework allowed and called attention to the need to consider the theology or theologies implicit in the social gospel. They bear no responsibility for my work, but it responds to both of these points.

Rayford Logan's students at Howard University did not challenge Schlesinger's framework, but they reacted both to the racial blinders in white social Christianity and to the "whiteness" of the literature about it in Purvis M. Carter, "The Astigmatism of the Social Gospel: 1877–1901" (M.A. thesis, Howard University, 1950); and Grace Roane Gwaltney, "The Negro Church and the Social Gospel from 1877 to 1914" (M.A. thesis, Howard University, 1949). Logan gave insufficient attention to the import of Gwaltney's work, but made effective use of Carter's in *The Negro in American Life and Thought: The Nadir, 1877–1901* (New York: Dial Press, 1954), extended and reissued as *The Betrayal of the Negro: From Rutherford B. Hayes to Woodrow Wilson* (New York: Collier Books, 1965). By then, the issue of the indifference or "racism" of the social gospel was raised by Thomas F. Gossett, *Race: The History of an Idea in America* (New York: Schocken Books, 1963); and David M. Reimers, *White Protestantism and the Negro* (New York: Oxford University Press, 1965), who were soon joined by two dozen other historians (see chapter 1, nn. 3 and

10, and chapter 10, n. 2). Their position informed Curtis Robert Grant's "The Social Gospel and Race" (Ph.D. dissertation, Stanford University, 1968). Accumulating doubts about their generalizations, however, were expressed by Ronald C. White's "Social Christianity and the Negro in the Progressive Era, 1890–1920" (Ph.D. dissertation, Princeton University, 1972) and my own "The Social Gospel and the Failure of Racial Reform, 1885–1898" (Ph.D. dissertation, University of North Carolina, 1973), which was summarized in Church History 46 (March 1977): 80–99. Ronald C. White and Charles Howard Hopkins, eds., The Social Gospel: Religion and Reform in Changing America (Philadelphia: Temple University Press, 1976), is a useful sourcebook; White's revised dissertation appeared as White, Liberty and Justice for All: Racial Reform and the Social Gospel (1877–1925) (San Francisco: Harper and Row, 1990).

Three works on Protestant social Christianity, three on race relations, and one on both helped to reshape my thinking. Kenneth Cauthen, The Impact of American Religious Liberalism (New York: Harper and Row, 1962), offered a typology of liberal Protestant thought that helped me to understand its complex relationship to historic evangelical Protestantism. William R. Hutchison, The Modernist Impulse in American Protestantism (Cambridge: Harvard University Press, 1976), rejected the typologies but reasserted the vitality of Protestant liberalism for a doubting generation. Janet Forsythe Fishburn, The Fatherhood of God and the Victorian Family: The Social Gospel in America (Philadelphia: Fortress Press, 1981), probed the sexist limits in the language of the social gospel's transcendent vision. George M. Fredrickson, The Black Image in the White Mind: The Debate on Afro-American Character and Destiny, 1817–1914 (New York: Harper and Row, 1971), studied the meaning of racism in a "herrenvolk democracy" from the Age to Jackson to the Progressive Era; James M. McPherson, The Abolitionist Legacy: From Reconstruction to the NAACP (Princeton: Princeton University Press, 1975), argued that there was a persistent abolitionist tradition from emancipation to the founding of the NAACP; and Joel Williamson, The Crucible of Race: Black-White Relations in the American South since Emancipation (New York: Oxford University Press, 1984), found the roots of both a frail Southern white racial liberalism and a powerful Southern white radical racism in a pervasive Southern racial conservatism. H. Shelton Smith, In His Image, But: Racism in Southern Religion, 1780–1910 (Durham, N.C.: Duke University Press, 1972), focused on the same issues in Southern religion. Jack Abramowitz, "Accommodation and Militancy in Negro Life: 1876–1916" (Ph.D. dissertation, Columbia University, 1950); August Meier, Negro Thought in America, 1880–1915: Racial Ideologies in the Age of Booker T. Washington (Ann Arbor: University of Michigan Press, 1963); Robert L. Factor, The Black Response to America: Men, Ideals and Organization from Frederick Douglass to the NAACP (Reading, Mass.: Addison-Wesley, 1970); Leonard I. Sweet, Black Images of America, 1784–1870 (New York: W. W. Norton and Co., 1976); and William Toll, The Resurgence of Race: Black Social Theory from Reconstruction to the Pan-African Conferences (Philadelphia: Temple University Press, 1979), helped me to understand black social Christianity.

Older denominational studies of Northern missionary education in the South, mostly unpublished dissertations (chapter 2, n. 9), have been supplemented by newer studies, which often ask more provocative questions. Among the latter, I find Robert C. Morris, Reading, 'Riting, and Reconstruction: The Education of the Freedmen in the South, 1861–1870

(Chicago: University of Chicago Press, 1981); and Joe M. Richardson, *Christian Reconstruction: The American Missionary Association and Southern Blacks, 1861–1890* (Athens: University of Georgia Press, 1986), most helpful. Edwin S. Redkey's *Black Exodus: Black Nationalist and Back-to-Africa Movements, 1890–1910* (New Haven: Yale University Press, 1969), is essential for understanding late nineteenth-century black nationalism and African emigration movements. The black American missionary effort is surveyed in Walter Williams, *Black Americans in the Evangelization of Africa: 1877–1900* (Madison: University of Wisconsin Press, 1982); and Sylvia M. Jacobs, ed., *Black Americans and the Missionary Movement in Africa* (Westport, Conn.: Greenwood Press, 1982). White American attitudes toward sub-Saharan Africa are explored in Clifford Haley Scott, "American Images of Africa, 1900–1939" (Ph.D. dissertation, University of Iowa, 1968); and Michael McCarthy, *Dark Continent: Africa as Seen by Americans* (Westport, Conn.: Greenwood Press, 1983).

Edmund Wilson's brilliant *Patriotic Gore: Studies in the Literature of the American Civil War* (New York: Oxford University Press, 1956), drew me to the work of Cable and Tourgée in the late nineteenth century. Their failure is traced in the work of C. Vann Woodward and his students: Woodward, *The Strange Career of Jim Crow* (New York: Oxford University Press, 1974); J. Morgan Kousser, *The Shaping of Southern Politics: Suffrage Restriction and the Establishment of the One-Party South, 1880–1910* (New Haven: Yale University Press, 1974); and Louis R. Harlan, *Separate and Unequal: Public School Campaigns and Racism in the Southern Seaboard States, 1901–1915* (Chapel Hill: University of North Carolina Press, 1958). There is no first-rate history of lynching and the antilynching movement before 1910, but local studies such as Charlton Moseley and Frederick Brogden's "A Lynching at Statesboro: The Story of Paul Reed and Will Cato," *Georgia Historical Quarterly* 65 (Summer 1981): 104–18; and Katherine Lederer, "And Then They Sang a Sabbath Song," *Springfield!* 2 (April–May 1981): 26–28, 33–36, and 3 (June 1981): 24–26, are helpful. Local studies of urban violence are also more helpful than the survey literature. See, for example, Charles Crowe, "Racial Violence and Social Reform—Origins of the Atlanta Riot of 1906," *Journal of Negro History* 53 (July 1968): 234–56; Crowe, "Racial Massacre in Atlanta, September 22, 1906," *Journal of Negro History* 53 (July 1969): 234–56; and James Crouthemal, "The Springfield Race Riot of 1908," *Journal of Negro History* 45 (July 1960): 164–81. Pete Daniel's *The Shadow of Slavery: Peonage in the South, 1901–1969* (New York: Oxford University Press, 1973); and William Cohen's "Negro Involuntary Servitude in the South: A Preliminary Analysis," *Journal of Southern History* 42 (February 1976): 31–60, suggest the need for additional and comparative studies of the subject.

The black urban experience is surveyed in Allan Spear, "The Origins of the Urban Ghetto, 1870–1915," in *Key Issues in Afro-American History*, 2 vols., ed. Nathan I. Huggins, Martin Kilson, and Daniel M. Fox (New York: Harcourt, Brace, Jovanovich, 1971), 2:153–66; and Zane L. Miller, "Urban Blacks in the South, 1865–1920: The Richmond, Savannah, New Orleans, Louisville, and Birmingham Experience," in *The New Urban History: Quantitative Explorations by American Historians*, ed. Leo F. Schnore (Princeton: Princeton University Press, 1975), pp. 184–204. My own "Missions, Institutional Churches, and Settlement Houses: The Black Experience, 1885–1910," *Journal of Negro History* 69 (Summer–Fall 1984): 101–13, interprets a large body of information on the institutions of redemption in the urban ghetto. Norris Magnuson, *Salvation in the Slums: Evangelical*

Social Work, 1865–1920 (Metuchen, N.J.: Scarecrow Press, 1977), has a chapter on evangelical social missions in black America. Charles Howard Hopkins, History of the Y.M.C.A. in North America (New York: Association Press, 1951), treats the black experience with the "Y" adequately. The Urban League is generously covered by Guichard Parris and Lester Brooks's Blacks in the City: A History of the National Urban League (Boston: Little Brown and Co., 1971); Nancy J. Weiss, The National Urban League, 1910–1940 (New York: Oxford University Press, 1974); Jesse Thomas Moore, Jr., A Search for Equality: The National Urban League, 1910–1961 (University Park: Pennsylvania State University Press, 1981); and Arvah E. Strickland, History of the Chicago Urban League (Urbana: University of Illinois Press, 1966). But Charles Kellogg's NAACP (Baltimore: Johns Hopkins University Press, 1967), needs replacing, and the Fellowship of Reconciliation still seeks a historian.

Much of the best work is found in state and local studies: David A. Gerber, Black Ohio and the Color Line, 1860–1915 (Urbana: University of Illinois Press, 1976); John Dittmer, Black Georgia in the Progressive Era, 1900–1920 (Urbana: University of Illinois Press, 1977); Seth M. Scheiner, Negro Mecca: A History of the Negro in New York City, 1865–1920 (New York: New York Univerity Press, 1965); Allan Spear, Black Chicago: The Making of a Negro Ghetto, 1890–1920 (Chicago: University of Chicago Press, 1967); Constance McLaughlin Green, The Secret City: A History of Race Relations in the Nation's Capital (Princeton: Princeton University Press, 1967); Gilbert Osofsky, Harlem: The Making of a Ghetto. Negro New York, 1890–1920 (New York: Harper and Row, 1968); David M. Katzman, Before the Ghetto: Black Detroit in the Nineteenth Century (Urbana: University of Illinois Press, 1973); Kenneth L. Kusmer, A Ghetto Takes Shape: Black Cleveland, 1870–1930 (Urbana: University of Illinois Press, 1976); Thomas Philpott, The Slum and the Ghetto: Neighborhood Deterioration and Middle-Class Reform, Chicago, 1880–1930 (New York: Oxford University Press, 1978); Thomas C. Cox, Blacks in Topeka, Kansas, 1865–1915: A Social History (Baton Rouge: Louisiana State University Press, 1982); George C. Wright, Life behind a Veil: Blacks in Louisville, Kentucky, 1865–1930 (Baton Rouge: Louisiana State University Press, 1985); and Darrel E. Bigham, We Ask Only a Fair Trial: A History of the Black Community of Evansville, Indiana (Bloomington: Indiana University Press, 1987).

The most helpful biographies include Ira Vernon Brown, Lyman Abbott, Christian Evolutionist: A Study in Religious Liberalism (Cambridge: Harvard University Press, 1953); Arlin Turner, George W. Cable: A Biography (Durham, N.C.: Duke University Press, 1956); A. R. Allen, "Thomas Dixon, Jr., and Political Religion: From Social Reformer to Racist," Foundations 14 (April–June 1971): 136–52; Raymond Allen Cook, Fire from the Flint: The Amazing Careers of Thomas Dixon (Winston-Salem, N.C.: John F. Blair, 1968); Jacob Henry Dorn, Washington Gladden: Prophet of the Social Gospel (Columbus: Ohio State University Press, 1966); Daniel Perlman, "Stirring the White Conscience: The Life of George Edmund Haynes" (Ph.D. dissertation, New York University, 1972); Robert T. Handy, "George D. Herron and the Kingdom Movement," Church History 19 (June 1950): 97–115; Betty Jane Brandon, "Alexander Jeffrey McKelway: Statesman of the New Order" (Ph.D. dissertation, University of North Carolina, 1969); John R. Betts, "The Negro and the New England Conscience in the Days of John Boyle O'Reilly," Journal of Negro History 51 (October 1966): 246–61; Samuel A. Eliot, "Francis Greenwood Peabody: His Work and Hopes for Hampton," Southern Workman 66 (March 1937): 71–79; Jurgen Herbst,